D1484109

GOOD GUY
BAD GUY

Also by Yves Lavigne:

Hell's Angels®,
Taking Care of Business

GOOD GUY BAD GUY

DRUGS AND THE CHANGING FACE OF ORGANIZED CRIME

YVES LAVIGNE

RANDOM HOUSE
TORONTO

Published in Canada in 1991 by Random House of Canada Limited, Toronto.

Canadian Cataloguing in Publication Data

Lavigne, Yves, 1953-
Good guy, bad guy : drugs and the changing
face of organized crime

ISBN 0-394-22172-9

1. Drug traffic.   2. Narcotics and crime.
3. Organized crime.   I. Title.

HV5801.L38 1991   364.1'77   C91-093994-2

Printed and bound in the United States

Major portions of Chapter 12: Hell's Angels: Taking Care of Business have been
reprinted from *Hell's Angel's: Taking Care of Business* by Yves Lavigne (Ballantine
Books, 1989).

10 9 8 7 6 5 4 3 2 1

To my mother and father, for believing

"Drugs are to organized crime what gasoline is to the automobile." — Sterling Johnson, Jr., special narcotics prosecutor for New York City.

"The curse of drug addiction, which hovers like a dark cloud over entire nations, is surely one of the most serious menaces to freedom in our time." — Pope John Paul II on October 3, 1989.

"Coca has been transformed into a revolutionary weapon for the struggle against American imperialism. The Archilles heel of imperialism are the *estimulantes* of Columbia . . . the Third World's atomic bomb." — Carlos Lehder, a leader of the Medellin drug cartel, describes cocaine.

"We follow Fidel's orders to penetrate and addict US youths with drugs to prevent them from thinking, to prevent them from having opinions, to prevent them from speaking, and to keep the population asleep. As Lenin said of religion, that religion is the opium of the people, and so we are giving them real opium." — a lieutenant colonel in the Cuban navy explains why Cuba protects and escorts ships and planes smuggling marijuana and cocaine from Colombia to the United States.

"Unless we take decisive action to fight the crisis that hard-core addicts are causing in this country, our streets and schools will never be safe — and a large part of this generation of Americans will be lost." — Senator Joseph R. Biden, Jr., Chairman, Senate Judiciary Committee, on May 10, 1990.

Contents

CONTENTS

Acknowledgments

I thank the individuals and agencies that helped my investigation of drug gangs. Many helpful persons and organizations on both sides of the law prefer to remain anonymous. I am grateful for their assistance and their trust.

Some of the agencies are the California Bureau of Narcotic Enforcement, the California Department of Corrections, the California Campaign Against Marijuana Planting program, the Compton Police Department, the Los Angeles Police Department, the Sacramento Police Department, the Maryland State Police, the Broward County Sheriff's Office, the Metro Dade Police Department, the US Attorney's office in Miami, the US Drug Enforcement Administration, the US Bureau of Alcohol, Tobacco and Firearms, the US Federal Bureau of Investigation, the US Marshal's Service, the US Customs Service, the California Attorney-General's Office, the New York State Police, the Western States Information Network, the Criminal Intelligence Service of Canada, the Canadian Association of Chiefs of Police, the Ontario Provincial Police, Canada Customs, Revenue Canada, the Royal Canadian Mounted Police, the Metro Toronto Police, individual officers from police forces across North America, staff members of several US Senate committees.

Special thanks to Bert Sousa for his time and effort, to Rich Matranga's keen eye, to Lou Barbaria for his knowledge, to Bill Perry, Larry Karson, and the US Customs interdiction crews at Homestead Air Force Base—the drug war's coolest dudes—for their professionalism and for showing me a good time on the front lines.

ACKNOWLEDGMENTS

To those who stood in my way, thanks for the adversity. That's the rocket fuel that powers my turbines.

In memory of Grandpa Joe, who died at eighty-six on November 17, 1990. He couldn't go hunting that year, though I jokingly offered to release grouse in his back yard. For the first autumn in ages, his red canvas rucksack hung on the basement wall, empty of game. He never told a tall tale — never had to; he knew every fishing hole the backwoods had to offer. For a long lifetime, he carved gold out of hardrock thousands of feet below his beloved forests and beaver dam backwaters. Whatever he took from nature he passed on in kindness. His thick fingers turned trees into boats and toys for his grandchildren in a basement heavy with the biting scent of fresh-cut cedar. He's gone back to the earth off which he lived. I prefer to think he's gone fishing. Bye, Grandpa.

Introduction

The supremacy of white organized crime is over. The era of ethnic gangsters has begun. Organized crime is no longer synonymous with, or dominated by, one group—Italians—whose underworld pre-eminence earned them the law-enforcement moniker, "traditional organized crime." Like North American society, the underworld has become multicultural.

Gangsters of all colors share the underworld today, not as tokens, but as full-fledged hard-core criminals whose organizations will outlive their members. Their fuel is drugs. Their goal is money and power. The drug revolution of the 1960s has put society on the path to destruction with organized crime pushing the cart.

Drug trafficking is a $500-billion-a-year industry worldwide. While interdiction teams fight a high-tech war with drug traffickers along nearly 100,000 miles of US and Canadian coastline and land border to keep drugs out of North America, streets have become war zones as gangsters fight for supremacy in an apparently insatiable drug market.

All ethnic groups are victim to criminals who prey on their own insular communities. For the longest time, those criminals didn't stray from their neighborhoods. Easy drug money and the lure of larger profits have caused these gangsters to spread their wings and ply their trade wherever the market is. North America has opened its arms and pockets to a multitude of criminals from cultures around the world, and they are taking full advantage of the land of opportunity.

The proliferation of black drug-trafficking gangs—the brushfire spread of Jamaican posses and black street gangs across North America in the last decade—seriously threatens society not only because of the spiritually and physically maiming drugs gangs sell, but through the violence they spread and the underground economies they support.

The posses and black street gangs such as the Crips and the Bloods reflect the insidious proliferation of subculture-supported psychopaths who don't care about the norms, values, and laws of the society they prey on. Like all gangsters, they need violence and fear to survive. Black street gangs not only take lives that jeopardize their earnings, but kill for the sheer joy of depriving someone else of the opportunity to breathe.

Chinese triads and street gangs have seriously cut into the mob's heroin business as they move their empires from southeast Asia to North America. Vietnamese street gangs have taken over from Chinese street gangs and terrorize and extort from Chinatown businesses across the continent.

Though ethnic gangsters dominate the underworld in number, white supremacists can rest assured that white trash is well represented by outlaw motorcycle gangs and the Aryan Brotherhood prison gang that deal drugs and death with the best of them.

Drug traffickers threaten the freedom and security of North Americans from within our borders and from abroad. They corrupt and weaken families, communities, and social institutions. The values upon which North American society is founded are being rent. Life is losing its worth. Innocence fades earlier with each new generation. More than 200,000 drug-addicted babies are born in the US every year. And the full repercussions from the disintegration of families and communities have yet to be felt.

Drugs have contributed to an unmanageable increase in crime, especially since the advent of crack cocaine in 1984. There are 2,200,000 hard-core cocaine addicts in the United States—one out of every hundred Americans uses coke weekly. In New York State, one in forty persons is a cocaine addict. One in five people arrested in the US is a hard-core cocaine addict. An entire generation of inner-city children has grown up thinking that guns, drugs, and killing police officers are all there is to life.

Between 50 and 70 percent of all crimes are drug-related. The staggering number of drug cases before the courts has paralyzed the justice system. There aren't enough jail cells to hold convicted drug offenders. There aren't enough courts to handle them.

On October 18, 1990, the Supreme Court of Canada ruled that forcing an accused person to wait more than eight months for trial violates the Charter of Rights and Freedoms. Within eight months, 40,600 charges were thrown out of courts in the province of Ontario alone. Accused rapists, wife beaters, drunk drivers who killed, purse snatchers, thieves, break-in artists, drug dealers, and robbers were set free as victims sat with their mouths agape.

Since 50 to 70 percent of crimes are drug-related—dopers seeking money for drugs—where's the so-called deterrent effect of the justice system in the war on drugs? Criminals know their crimes will go unpunished because an overloaded system can't prosecute them. The Supreme Court of Canada erred and failed its duty terribly with a ruling that undermines the concept of justice and shows no consideration for the welfare of society and the security and comfort of victims.

Government, in all its institutions from police forces to courts, can no longer protect life, liberty, and property. Justice no longer exists in North America. It has regressed to little more than a concept. The will to create and defend a just and free society has died. Pretenders have undermined fundamental rights and liberties by forcing their extension to the criminal underworld, to the detriment of those who abide by laws.

Civil libertarians have created, supported, and defended the right of individuals to commit crimes without police interference. They've made it nearly impossible for law-enforcement officers to eavesdrop on organized crime phone calls; they've curbed the use of hidden tape recorders to gather incriminating evidence on gangsters; they say outlaw bikers have a right to live outside the law. The rights that libertarians pretend to protect verge on extinction as they are extended to criminals.

It is no coincidence that the civil libertarians and the drug generation blossomed side by side in the 1960s. The fight against drugs has many times been the target of civil libertarians who thrive on pitting themselves against the forces of government. Authority is easy to attack. It tempts the rebel in all. But what of the reign of terror gangsters impose on society? What of the fear that keeps people off the streets of their own neighborhoods? What of the teenager's fear of quitting the streets and suffering a bloody gang retaliation? We are no longer free to roam the city. We are no longer free to enjoy our nights outdoors. Many are prisoners in their own houses. People in crack-infested inner cities watch television and eat their meals lying on the floor to avoid stray bullets. Crime is a greater threat to freedom than the forces that combat it. Those who claim to unshackle us from the grip of government and law and order would surrender us to the lawless.

At this writing, gangsters abound on the silver screen: *Miller's Crossing*, *GoodFellas*, *The Godfather, Part III*. And always, Hollywood conveys the message that there is something to admire and worship in a man of power, however evil. While movie-goers gawk at the romantic version of traditional organized crime, the real thing flourishes around them, slinks through their neighborhoods, and weasels into their lives.

Our affection for criminals bodes poorly for the future of our world. If we support the forging of invulnerable drug empires now, to what depths will we descend when those empires expand into other realms of our lives? Organized crime does not stop at drugs. It creeps into every walk of life.

Drug money corrupts. Organized crime buys politicians, judges, and police officers. Gangsters buy political protection for criminal enterprises and immunity from police and the courts. Government, police, and military officials in all countries are loyal to drug-trafficking paymasters. Who safeguards our interests when criminals influence the apparatus of state?

Who is guilty of letting drug trafficking thrive? Drug users, the complacent, and those who would legalize drugs rather than support the fight against them.

The acceptance and forgiveness of Ben Johnson's steroid use by Canadians and Athletics Canada officials exemplifies the attitude that underlies the drug epidemic that threatens North America — even morality has its price. Athletes, fans, and officials believe in winning at all cost, even if it means breaking the rules and lying. Supporting Ben Johnson means tacitly approving all cheats and liars. A man is only as good as his word. If his word means nothing, the man is nothing.

Welcome to the 1990s — have you sold your soul today?

Part I

DUDES ON THE MOVE

1

Bang bang to gang bang:
A history of gangsterism
and drug trafficking
in North America

Drug trafficking has created more gangsters and organized crime groups than any other illicit activity in history. By the time law enforcement finally convinced the courts that La Cosa Nostra exists — a feat that took nearly half a century — other organized crime groups had emerged to take their cut of the action. These include white, black, and Mexican prison gangs, outlaw motorcycle gangs, Chinese triads, Chinese street gangs, Vietnamese street gangs, Colombian drug cartels, black street gangs, and black crime syndicates. They have a common goal: money and power through drug trafficking. The faces may have changed, but the demon beneath the skin remains the same — greed.

Gangsterism was born on January 16, 1920, when the Volstead Act created Prohibition. That fourteen-year dry spell in the United States spurred industrious criminals to import and sell enough booze to finance multinational, self-perpetuating criminal empires whose original liquor-smuggling savvy equipped them well for the drug trafficking that is their mainstay today.

Creators of the Volstead Act knew it would be a tough law to enforce. Dry agents and narcotics agents were each issued a badge, grenades, a machine gun, a .45-caliber pistol with an extra magazine, and 3,000 rounds of ammunition. Cops today should be so lucky. Agents for the Federal Bureau of Narcotics, such as Eliot Ness, sported distinctive plates on their cars: USNB official. There was no mistaking narcs in those days.

The onset of Prohibition saw countless entrepreneurs and organized gangs scramble to meet an unquenchable public thirst for alcohol. Booze smugglers hid kegs under false decks on boats. Michigan smugglers filled a torpedo-like metal cylinder with Canadian booze, sank it five feet beneath the lake's surface, and hauled it across along a steel cable. They were called rumrunners and the methods they used to sneak booze into the United States are used today by dope smugglers. The Sunset Fleet of feeder boats waited along Rum Row—past the twelve-mile US territorial limit—for mother ships to supply them with the booze they would then run to shore past the US Coast Guard.

The bad guys' boats were faster than those of the good guys and they used an arsenal of tricks and evasive tactics—from smoke screens to decoy boats—to foil arrest. A diesel-powered cruiser was equipped with a fake smokestack to make it look like a slow lunker. One speedy sailboat had collapsible masts that allowed it to duck under low bridges where the good guys couldn't follow. One bunch of gangsters bought a submarine and torpedo boat from the US government to run contraband. And although women's lib was an expression forty years in the offing, many smuggling boats were owned by women like Florida's Spanish Marie, who ran around with a pistol on her hip and a knife in her belt.

Three gang wars marred the Roaring Twenties, which could have been named for the bursts of machine-gun fire rather than the bon vivant attitude that permeated the debauched era. The first was among ethnic gangsters, with the Italians winning over the Irish and Jewish gangs. The second war was between Italians: the Mafia, whose members had to be Sicilian, and the Camorra, made up of Neapolitans and Calabrese, or mainland Italians. The result of the bloody, drawn-out shoot-'em-up was a merger of the gangs and the formation of La Cosa Nostra, which required only that a member's father be Italian.

La Cosa Nostra is the traditional organized crime network that exists today in the United States and has been romanticized in movies as the Mafia. The true Mafia exists only in Italy, and some old-time mafiosi will dispute even that. They argue that men of honor no longer exist; organized criminals today are just bums out to make a buck. La Cosa Nostra goes by many names. In Chicago, it is called the Outfit. In other cities, it is called the Arm, the Black Hand, or the mob.

Two years before the end of Prohibition, a power play by Charles (Lucky) Luciano set the mob on the course it follows today. Luciano was fed up with the mustache-Pete attitude of Italian mobsters who got their jollies by shooting each other's heads and kneecaps off. He thought the mob should polish its act and get serious about the business of making money rather than waste time fighting itself. Luciano resorted to old-fashioned bloodshed to implement his money-making scheme.

Luciano had a long association with crime and drugs before the gang wars of the twenties. He was first arrested in New York City in 1915 for possession of heroin, a drug that would become the mainstay of his empire. He served six months of a one-year jail sentence. He became a rumrunner and drug dealer and kept a whorehouse for Giuseppe "Joe the Boss" Masseria after joining his gang in 1920. Luciano was arrested in 1923 for selling heroin, but went free after ratting on his friends. He was arrested in 1928 for the murder of Arnold Rothstein, a dope dealer and gambler. The charge was dismissed after the son and son-in-law of Colonel Levi G. Nutt, deputy commissioner of Prohibition in charge of narcotics, were accused of having "indiscreet" relations with Rothstein.

Luciano belonged to one of two Sicilian groups fighting for control of New York City in 1930. By then he was righthand man to "Joe the Boss" Masseria, whose stable of goons included Vito Genovese, Carlo Gambino, Frank Costello, and Albert Anastasia. Masseria was at war with the gang of Salvatore Maranzano, which included Joe Bonnano, Joe Profaci, Stefano Magaddino, and Thomas Luchese. Maranzano was winning the war in early 1931, thanks to the help of gangsters from other cities. Luciano and Genovese, not wanting to be on the losing side, defected to Maranzano to get in on the ground floor of a healthy criminal empire.

To prove his loyalty, Luciano, with Maranzano's OK, arranged to have lunch with Masseria at a restaurant in Coney Island on April 15, 1931. Luciano went to the washroom during a card game after lunch. While he was gone, several men entered the restaurant and fired twenty shots at Masseria, six in his back. With his opposition in the ground, Maranzano called a mob meeting in the Bronx where he announced he was the *capo di tuti capi* (boss of bosses) of all the mob families. Then he selected five families, which still run New York. The bosses of those families were Lucky Luciano, Joe Profaci, Joe Bonnano, Tom Gagliano, and Vincent and Philip Mangano.

Maranzano didn't get along with Luciano and Genovese. He hired hit man Vincent (Mad Dog) Coll to kill them during a meeting. Luciano figured it was a setup and asked his friend Meyer Lansky for help. On September 10, 1931, the day of the meeting, four men pretending to be detectives walked into Maranzano's office and stabbed him six times before shooting him to death. The next day, forty of Maranzano's allies across the United States were murdered and Luciano began to re-shape organized crime. Instead of having one man run the show, he created a commission to rule democratically. It was made up of twelve members representing twenty-four families in 1957. Today, nine of the twenty-four mob family bosses sit on the commission: the five bosses of the New York families, and the bosses of Buffalo, Detroit, Chicago, and Philadelphia. Because of his success with Meyer Lansky, Luciano encouraged mob families to work with non-Italian criminals. The Lansky connection proved invaluable for Luciano's drug business.

La Cosa Nostra (literally, "this thing of ours") expanded and refined its operations during the next two decades, priming itself into a well-oiled crime machine ready to capitalize on any opportunity to make money.

Luciano turned his booze-smuggling operation into a heroin ring after Prohibition was repealed in 1933. The Shanghai heroin cartel that underwrote General Chiang Kai-shek's rise to power supplied Luciano's heroin. It was in the tormented political machinations of pre-Communist China that the mob, the precursor to the CIA, and drugs first became intertwined to form a deadly triangle that, to this day, continues to shred the fabric of society. (Luciano and Meyer Lansky later worked with agents of the Office of Strategic Services during the Second World War.) The OSS became the CIA. US agents in the Far East helped Chiang Kai-shek fend off the Japanese and the rebel Communist movement led by Mao Zedong. The Flying Tigers, basically American mercenaries recruited from the US Air Force with their government's blessing to bolster China's air defence, fought Japan. Many Flying Tigers later flew OSS supply and insertion missions in China, Burma, and any southeast Asian hell-hole where covert actions were fought.

Heroin money financed the battle to save China from Japan on the outside and from Communists on the inside. The experience created a cadre of US secret agents well versed in the use and benefits of funding political causes with the proceeds of narcotics sales. The knowledge was later put to use in Central America, where the CIA-backed contra rebels shipped drugs to the US in the 1980s to finance their insurgency against Nicaragua's Sandinista government.

Luciano ran his drug empire from a New York prison after he was locked up in the late 1930s. His gang—the 107th Street Gang—smuggled opium into the United States from Mexico and converted it to heroin in a New York City lab. The streets of Washington, New York, San Antonio, Boston, and Chicago were flooded with red heroin pills selling for two cents each in the 1930s. Narcotics agents started investigating Chinese "tongs" after a pill press was found in a Chinese laundry in New York City. They dismembered the Hip Sing Tong, the largest Chinese drug ring in the United States and discovered that tongs got their drugs from Lucky Luciano, not from China.

The Chinese in the United States had a long history of involvement with drugs, beginning with opium, which was unregulated until 1914. Prohibition brought not only a crackdown on alcohol during the 1920s, but also on other drugs, as this article from a San Francisco newspaper indicates:

A combined army of federal narcotic agents, prohibition officers and members of the Chinatown police squad descended yesterday upon the elaborate establishment of Sing Fat and Co., the largest store in San Francisco's Chinatown and one of the largest Chinese importers in the US. They combed it from top to bottom of its several stories in a search for contraband of various sorts.

Following an alleged confession that he was the owner of four five-tael tins of opium seized in the raid on the store, Tong Gee, son of Tong Pong, store manager, was charged with violating the Harrison Narcotic Act and the Narcotic Import and Export Act. When federal agents found a large quantity of choice liquors and wines, Tong Pong and two sons, Tong Poy and Tong Kee, and his wife, Lum Shee, were arrested and charged with violating the Volstead Act. The raid on the Sing Fat Store came after five years of patient labor by federal narcotic agents to prove their suspicions that the famous store was the center of a large dope distributing traffic.

Lucky Luciano was not the only mobster involved in heroin trafficking and he tried to ensure he had a piece of everyone's action. George and Elias Eliopoulos were known as the Drug Barons of Europe. They shipped millions, maybe billions, of dollars of heroin and morphine to the United States. One of their shipments was seized in New York City in 1930 when narcotics and customs agents grabbed twenty-five cases marked "furs" shipped from Istanbul to Brooklyn on the S.S. *Alesia* and found 17,500 cans each containing an ounce of morphine. The Eliopoulos brothers also traveled to China to buy drugs, which they sold to American gangsters such as Dutch Schultz, Legs Diamond, and Louis "Lepke" Buchalter. Like all true criminals, the Greek brothers ratted on their fellows when it suited their purpose. They are credited with inventing the double deal; when successful customers became competitors, they tipped off the cops.

Other international drug traffickers, such as Solomon Gelb, supplied Al Capone's mob with heroin. Lucky Luciano distributed the $10 million in heroin that Louis Lepke's organization smuggled into the United States in the 1930s. Lepke, Jacob Lvovsky, and Jasha Katzenberg came to police attention in 1937 when chemist Pietro Quinto accidentally blew up a heroin-conversion lab in New York City. The Lepke organization then made six round-the-world trips to Shanghai and smuggled 649 kilograms of heroin into the US. Lepke's mob handled 50 and 100 kilogram lots—a lot of dope considering the number of addicts. Lepke was better known as Public Enemy Number One and ran Murder, Inc., the mob's enforcement arm. He was executed in the electric chair at Sing Sing in 1944. He is the only mob leader to have been legally executed in the United States.

Gangsters had a large market for drugs, a market whose origins can be traced back more than 150 years, but more practically, to the American Civil War. One of the great tragedies of the war that pitted brother against brother was the number of morphine addicts it created. Nearly half a million men were wounded during the Civil War. Thousands had limbs amputated. Morphine was administered to them liberally to silence their screams, as it was given to those suffering from incurable cholera, smallpox, typhus, and yellow fever. There were so many drug-dependent soldiers that addiction became known as the soldier's disease.

Morphine was refined from opium in the early nineteenth century. Like cocaine fifty years later, it was praised as a drug that would end addiction. Doctors had no qualms about giving addictive drugs to the sick, the insane, and the neurotic. More than 50,000 cure-alls containing addictive drugs were sold over the counter in 1900. Narcotics were available in drugstores and by mail and were found in everything from teething to cough syrups. A chest cold remedy called Dr. Agnew's Catarrah Powder contained 10 grams of cocaine per ounce. A new and supposedly non-addictive drug called heroin was the base for Adamson's Botanic Cough Balsam. Users of Dr. Brutus Shiloh's Cure for Consumption got stoned on its heroin and chloroform. Similarly, Kohler's One-Night Cough Cure zapped its users with morphine sulphate, chloroform, and marijuana. Germany's Bayer family sold heroin as a cough suppressant until the turn of the century. Morphine base was first transformed into heroin in 1874. By 1890, it was hailed as a cure for morphine addiction.

The United States didn't start regulating narcotics until the Harrison Narcotic Act became law on March 1, 1915. By then, there were enough addicts in the United States to support a lucrative black market for drugs. Failure to recognize and combat the problem of drug addiction then created a nightmare that only gets worse today.

Drugs swept through the world of show business. Billie Holiday had a $40-a-day heroin habit—not a cheap thrill in the 1940s. The world's most beautiful women—dancers with the Ziegfeld Follies—turned to drugs. One dancer was arrested for forging prescriptions in Los Angeles in 1939. Celebrity drug users had their own diamond-encrusted pipes and solid silver syringes with jeweled plungers.

Many of the drug expressions used today originated in the Roaring Twenties. Heroin was sold in one-ounce boxes of White Horse or Red Dragon brands. White Horse first appeared in the 1920s and by the 1930s "horse" became synonymous with heroin. The Great Depression gave rise to numerous rumors. Press reports blamed unrest and racial tension in the American southwest on the "killer drug" marijuana.

Marijuana was sold in Prince Albert tobacco tins, an accepted street measurement for weed. Today that unit is called a lid of grass. Marijuana cigarettes were called mooters or reefers.

Many governments understood the debilitating and enslaving power of drugs and used them to their advantage. The Japanese plied conquered countries with drugs in the 1930s. A booklet issued to Japanese soldiers said, "The use of narcotics is unworthy of a superior race like the Japanese. Only inferior races, races that are decadent like the Chinese, Europeans, and East Indians, are addicted to the use of narcotics. That is why they are destined to become our servants and eventually to disappear." During the Japanese occupation of Seoul, Korea, one factory produced 1,244 kilograms of heroin in 1938.

"Wherever the Japanese army goes, the drug traffic follows," the American government complained to the League of Nations. "In every territory conquered by them, a large part of the people become enslaved with drugs. This is another form of chemical warfare that is as deadly as that of the prohibited gases."

Luciano ran his drug operation from Italy after he was paroled in 1945 and deported. He smuggled Chinese heroin into the United States from Cuba, where the regime of Fulgencio Batista allowed the mob to entrench its gambling and smuggling activities. Meyer Lansky, the financial genius of the underworld, ran Cuban casinos out of Florida during the Second World War through his trusted lieutenant, Santo Trafficante. By the time he died in 1954, Trafficante had trained his son Santo, Jr., to take over the Cuban gambling business and become the mob boss in Florida.

Dark clouds gathered over the southern part of Trafficante's realm as political rumblings shook a debauched Cuba. Communism, which since 1917 had swept through and conquered the two largest countries in Asia—Russia and China—had found its way across the Atlantic Ocean and settled in the driven vision of rebel leader Fidel Castro. Luciano and Trafficante foresaw that their drug network, which suffered a temporary setback when China fell into Communist hands, was about to be dealt another blow. They moved quickly to replace the unstable pipeline of Chinese heroin.

A 1957 mob conference hosted by Vito Genovese in Apalachin, in upper New York state, set the stage for the mob's effective takeover of the drug underworld. In the late 1950s, Corsican gangsters controlled the labs that manufactured all the illicit heroin in Europe. These gangsters wanted to expand into the US market but couldn't because heroin distribution there was controlled by mobsters in Italy. La Cosa Nostra, on the other hand, was looking for a heroin supplier so it could capitalize on a growing market in its back yard and mitigate its losses if the heroin pipeline through Cuba were cut. Both sides met at Apalachin and negotiated a business arrangement that became known as the French Connection. By year's end, the Corsicans and La Cosa Nostra controlled nearly all French and Turkish heroin sold in the United States. A fruitful meeting, to say the least.

Oddly enough, one man's idiosyncracies allowed the mob to flourish in the drug trade and build an unprecedented network that let gangsters reap billions of dollars that they used to bolster their organizations. For the longest time J. Edgar Hoover, the FBI director, refused to acknowledge the existence of organized crime and would not allocate resources to fight it. In doing so, he actually sheltered organized crime from public scrutiny, from the grasp of law enforcement, and from the punishment of the courts. Organized crime flourished under the reign of the US's most powerful lawman and set down roots that will never be eradicated. If organized crime owes anyone a debt, it owes it to J. Edgar Hoover.

While La Cosa Nostra flourished selling heroin in the 1960s, other events conspired to change the face of the world and of drug trafficking, creating opportunities for other groups to reap the benefits of illicit drug sales.

The Cuban revolution was the first of these. Thousands of Cubans fled their country when Castro took power in 1959. They settled in the strongly entrenched Cuban communities of southern Florida where Santo Trafficante ran the *bolita*—a Cuban lottery. Trafficante knew the Cuban community's criminal milieu well. Most of his goons, couriers, and heroin dealers were Cuban refugees who appreciated the opportunities he gave them to earn money. The former OSS agents with whom Trafficante's father collaborated during the Second World War also appreciated the opportunities he could give them. They were now part of the CIA, and the CIA was part of the US's defence against the great Red menace rising ninety miles to the south.

Trafficante participated in three CIA schemes to oust Castro. In 1961, he was part of an aborted scheme to poison the cigar-chomping president. He also provided the CIA with 2,000 Cuban gangsters and exiles willing to invade their former island home. The CIA taught them how to kill, make bombs, and fight guerrilla warfare. These survivors of the botched Bay of Pigs invasion returned to Florida equipped for a war that would eventually be fought in the streets of Miami against Colombian opponents fifteen years later. Trafficante took over Luciano's drug network when the father of the modern mob died in 1962, and he helped the CIA launch an aborted boat raid against Cuba in 1963. By then, however, events elsewhere in the world were causing him more worries, since the seeping Communist tide was once again threatening to hurt his heroin business.

The Vietnam War opened the door for new opportunists to find new underground trade routes to the heroin labs of Laos, Cambodia, and Thailand. These opportunists were black American servicemen who accomplished in a few short years what their entire race had been unable to do under nearly 200 years of white oppression. They broke the bonds that forced them to buy heroin from white importers in the United States—mostly La Cosa Nostra—and started their own smuggling and distribution networks. They controlled it from beginning to end. Blacks imported, often in the caskets of servicemen killed in Vietnam. Blacks distributed. Blacks marketed. Blacks reaped the benefits. Blacks got rich.

The Vietnam War grubstaked black organized crime's first ventures and allowed it to become the public menace it is today. From these exotic roots, black organized crime has spread to all levels of North American society, much as La Cosa Nostra did in its early days, but rather than having a membership of 2,000 as does traditional organized crime, the black mob numbers in the hundreds of thousands. Its ranks include street gangs, the most notorious being the Los Angeles-based Crips and Bloods, and the violent Jamaican posses, which have shown an uncanny ability to walk into drug-free communities and create insatiable markets for marijuana and crack cocaine.

While the Vietnam War helped establish new drug networks, its end severed others. The Americans' pullout of Vietnam in 1975 cut the source of opium that fed heroin laboratories in Marseilles and fueled the French Connection. This compounded the devastating seizure of several hundred pounds of heroin and seven heroin-processing laboratories in France. The French Connection was dealt a double blow from which it never recovered. The Turkish government's ban on growing opium poppies in 1972 also weakened traditional organized crime's grip on the heroin market. The United States agreed on June 30, 1971, to pay Turkey $35 million a year for three years, starting in 1973, to subsidize farmers while substitute crops were found for opium poppies. Other drug-trafficking organizations were quick to fill the gap and muscle in on the market.

Accordingly, Hispanic dealers in the United States developed Mexican sources of heroin and picked up where traditional organized crime left off. Drug smuggling was nothing new to the Mexicans. Ignacia Jasso Gonzales was known as La Nacha, Queen of the Border Dope Traffic, in the 1940s. La Nacha controlled poppy fields and a lab in the mountains of the Guadalajara. Her organization smuggled morphine into the United States in the modified gas tanks of cars.

The Herrara family in Mexico, steeped in a long dope tradition, was quick to fill the American need for heroin caused by the collapse of the French Connection. They didn't supply China White, but a gritty kind of horse called Mexican Brown—that name sounded better than its original label, Mexican Mud. The family paid small farmers in isolated valleys to grown opium poppies from which heroin was refined in Herrara-owned laboratories. By 1977, after a start in Chicago, the Herraras had expanded nationally and supplied 80 percent of the American heroin market.

The Mexican monopoly was shortlived, however, as La Cosa Nostra gradually re-built its smuggling operations to regain 80 percent of the market. Then a series of successful prosecutions in the mid-1980s threw the mob into disarray. This created another vacuum that was quickly filled by newly arrived Asian entrepreneurs with years of experience smuggling southeast Asian heroin.

Immigration policies in Canada and the United States since the 1960s have allowed vast numbers of Chinese into both countries, greatly swelling the Chinatowns in New York, San Francisco, Toronto, and Vancouver. The increase in business and the booming economy that followed in these insular communities provided Chinese youth gangs with easy prey for their extortion rings. The tongs and street gangs laid the groundwork for the triads that followed in the 1970s. Police forces across North America have been slow to recognize—some still don't— the arrival of Asian organized crime groups to our shores. Hong Kong-based triads are centuries-old secret societies that have turned into organized crime gangs with secret oaths much like the Italian Mafia. They arrived in dribs and drabs to prey on the growing Chinese communities with Asian and Vietnamese street gangs. But when Britain decided in 1984 not to renew its lease on Hong Kong in 1997, giving ownership of the Crown colony back to China, triads started moving their empires, to Canada, primarily, and to the United States and Australia. These criminals know that the People's Republic of China will make it difficult for them to do business in Hong Kong. However, since most of their income is derived from activities such as prostitution, gambling, bribery, extortion, and narcotics trafficking committed within the Chinese community, they need the shelter of large Chinese populations. The exodus of thousands of legitimate businessmen from Hong Kong has provided them with a cover to move billions of dollars and many of their 80,000 members to North America.

Traditional organized crime has been the first victim of the triads' expansion in the land of opportunity. Half the US's 500,000 heroin addicts live in the New York City area. La Cosa Nostra's share of heroin imported to feed those hungry veins has dropped dramatically in the last five years as Chinese traffickers hustled to take over 40 percent of the market.

In September 1986, cops raided a Chinese restaurant in New York City and seized 33 pounds of pure heroin worth about $40 million on the streets. Earlier in the year, 50 pounds of China White heroin concealed in picture frames was seized at JFK Airport. That's more than police seized from La Cosa Nostra in all of 1985. The Drug Enforcement Administration seized 1,000 pounds of Chinese-imported heroin in 1985 and 1986. The figure grows every year.

Getting involved in heroin smuggling and trafficking in North America is a big step for triads and other Chinese organized crime groups because it marks the first time they have expanded their criminal empires outside the boundaries of their own community. Where they were once protected by the veil of silence and disdain for police authority in their communities, Chinese criminals are now more vulnerable to detection, arrest, and prosecution. Dealing drugs has given Chinese criminals a higher profile, one that they would prefer not to have. On the other hand, their well-developed and disciplined organizations are cutting deeply into the activities of other North American organized crime groups.

Although heroin is not the drug of choice of most North American dopers—there are 550,000 heroin addicts in the United States and Canada compared to 3 million cocaine addicts (there are many more casual users) and 45 million pot smokers—the networks developed by the gangsters who first imported the drug to North America became the model for smuggling networks to come. Heroin smugglers broke ground for the *contrabandistas* who followed with marijuana, cocaine, and Quaaludes. Auguste Joseph Ricord, a former Gestapo agent sentenced to death in France, was head of a South American gang of *narcotraficantes* who smuggled French heroin into the United States from their base in Paraguay. Ricord was among the first international drug traffickers to set up smuggling routes from South America to North America. The paths have become well worn.

The criminals among Cuban exiles trained for the Bay of Pigs invasion made good use of their skills when the market for marijuana and cocaine started flourishing in the early 1970s. As business boomed, so did their numbers in Florida and New York City as Castro emptied his prisons during the 1980 Mariel boat lift. It was to their great advantage to be at the receiving end of a major smuggling route that has resisted all attempts to close it.

Although Trafficante employed Cubans in his heroin business, there were more criminals available to him than he could use. No gangsters used this Latin connection to greater advantage than did the Colombians, who expanded their businesses from a cottage industry serving dopers in Colombia in the early 1960s to a multinational cocaine and marijuana steamroller that continues to flatten North American brain cells despite the best attempts of men and money.

Colombian drug lords, like all other dope gangsters, had humble beginnings. They began as petty crooks who got into drugs by catering to the local market for marijuana and cocaine. The use of *bazuco*, which is cocaine base, reached epidemic proportions in Colombia in 1982, a full two years before the introduction of rock or crack cocaine in North America. Colombians started out as drug producers, became couriers for other drug networks, started shipping the stuff themselves, then took over the trafficking and distribution end of the operation. It didn't happen overnight, and not without bloodshed.

Several factors combine to give the Colombians the edge over other drug organizations. Besides having an ideal growing climate, remote areas to shelter laboratories, and a poor standard of living amenable to corruption, Colombia sits on the doorstep of the largest drug market in the world. Barranquilla is 1,100 miles from Miami. Colombian criminals are second to none in business savvy and in their willingness and ability to use violence to achieve their ends. But, more importantly, their network includes thousands of Colombians living in Miami, New York, Los Angeles, and more recently Houston, the major centers from which the cartels distribute cocaine.

The Colombian cartels evolved through several stages, much as La Cosa Nostra did in the Roaring Twenties and Dirty Thirties. Until the mid-1960s, Colombians grew marijuana and imported and distributed cocaine for the home market. Colombian traffickers then started selling to Mexicans and Cuban traffickers in the States. They also became middlemen and couriers for Bolivian and Peruvian cocaine traffickers. At the same time, they began producing cocaine with coca paste imported from Bolivia and Peru, the two major producers of coca plants. When the American drug demand grew in the early 1970s, the Colombians started to ship bales of marijuana across the Caribbean Sea and set up cocaine laboratories in the jungles.

By the late 1970s, Colombians were so adept at supplying American traffickers that they decided to increase their profits and expand their business by taking control of cocaine and marijuana distribution in the United States—a move known as forward integration in business terms.

They didn't want Cubans, blacks, the Dixie Mafia, or traditional organized crime groups selling their cocaine and marijuana any more. They wanted to do it themselves. They went to extremes to convince ensconced traffickers to give up their turf. In the process, they became known as the Cocaine Cowboys.

The Colombians learned from dealing with American dealers that there is no honor among thieves. They could not trust the dealers, who would skim 10 kilos off the top of 100-kilo cocaine shipments and rake $200,000 off a $1-million bundle of cash being returned to Colombia. They wanted to replace these thieves with their own people; now, they even replace their own dealers every six to eight months so they don't get any fancy ideas about stuffing their pockets. Colombian distributors and dealers in the States are also less likely to become police informants because the cartel ensures they have family back home to worry about.

The arrival of Colombian middlemen—distributors and dealers—in Florida was signaled by an exponential growth in gruesome murders reminiscent of the gang wars in Chicago and New York in the 1920s and 1930s. Traffickers shot each other over turf, new alliances, revenge, power struggles, and ripoffs, as well as to eliminate witnesses. While the Colombians went after the Cuban traffickers to take over their distribution businesses, American traffickers who wanted a direct connection to the suppliers knocked off Cubans who acted as middlemen between the Colombians and Americans.

Miami police labeled the decade the Roaring Seventies. Drug-related murders in Miami rose from 6 in 1975 to 35 in 1979 to 101 in 1981. The Colombian disregard for life scared their enemies into submission and sent witnesses into hiding.

Here are some examples. On September 13, 1978, a Cadillac pulled up beside Calixto Izquierdo's car and forced it to the curb. The driver got out and shot Izquierdo with a handgun. The passenger pumped him full of lead with a shotgun. Izquierdo was suspected of having engineered a 2,000-pound marijuana ripoff.

On March 17, 1979, Emilio and Aristides Diaz met with their boss in a Miami disco on Biscayne Bay to discuss their drug import business. The Diaz brothers were heavy dealers in Puerto Rico, Miami, and New York. Aristides was also a hit man. The meeting ended at 3 a.m. The brothers hopped into their day-old Cadillac Seville and drove away. Within two blocks, another car pulled alongside the Cadillac. A MAC-10 submachine gun was thrust out the window and riddled the brothers with bullets.

On April 23, 1979, gunmen in a Pontiac exchanged fire with four Latin men in an Audi they were chasing on an expressway south of Miami. A police cruiser joined the pursuit and was shot at by gunmen

from both cars. The Pontiac got away. The Audi stopped and two men
ran off. Police arrested the two others. They found 60 pounds of milk
sugar in the car and the tied and strangled body of an illegal Colombian in
the trunk. The dead man, Jaime Suescum, died the same way he had
killed a Colombian woman a week earlier.

In mid-afternoon on May 29, 1979, a car pulled up beside Jésus
Hernandez's red Mustang and the driver fired off fifteen .45-caliber
machine-gun rounds through Hernandez, who slammed into several
parked cars in a nearby mall.

On July 11, 1979, German Jimenez Pannesso, a Colombian drug
kingpin, walked into a liquor store south of Miami with a henchman.
Seconds later, a large white van disguised as a party supply company
vehicle pulled up and two men jumped out. They walked into the store
and fired more than 100 shots from their MAC-10 submachine guns.
The two dopers were killed and two other people were wounded. The
gunmen sprayed the parking lot with their machine guns as they ran from
the store to keep witnesses away. The hit men abandoned the van. It
contained eleven automatic weapons and was reinforced with bulletproof steel plates and bulletproof vests hung across the back doors as if
on a clothesline. The van even had portholes for guns. The vehicle had
fewer than 100 miles on the odometer.

On October 18, 1979, three cars stopped Juan Delgado's car. Several
men jumped out and fired fifty to sixty shots with rifles, handguns, and
shotguns at Delgado and his girlfriend. Delgado lost an eye. His
girlfriend wasn't hit.

Witnesses are always difficult to find for shootings between drug
traffickers. On December 26, 1979, Angel Luis Colon was shot to death
in Oscar's Lounge, a Colombian hangout in Miami. Investigators found
only the body in the deserted building. Even the bartender was gone. On
October 27, 1979, Osvaldo Morejon was shot to death in the same bar.
The eighteen people there at the time of the shooting had little to tell
police. On October 12, 1979, Ruben Rivera was shot in the head and
chest at the Sportsman's Bar. People on the street saw fifteen to twenty
people run from the bar and drive away. Once again, investigators found
only the body in the bar.

The love generation gave the world its largest-ever consumer market for
drugs. Outlaw motorcycle gangs were one group to seize the opportunity to shed their poverty and set up multinational criminal empires.
The Hell's Angels are the epitome of bad guys gone worse. They tapped
into the California hippy market in the 1960s and got in on the ground
floor of the now awsome clandestine drug-laboratory industry. Biker
labs popped up all over North America in kitchens, bathrooms, mobile

homes, even milk trucks to supply a rapidly expanding market for LSD, speed, PCP, MDA, and other chemical drugs. Outlaw bikers control 75 percent of the North American methamphetamine market.

While many organized crime groups grew out of the drug business, many individual entrepreneurs also made fortunes smuggling and dealing dope in the land of opportunity. College kids were quick to set up rings that smuggled marijuana from Mexico and Colombia. Later, they brought in cocaine. Doctors and lawyers impatient with profits from their time-share condos bankrolled many expeditions to the heartland of ganja country to bring back plane-loads of leaf-green or powder-white brain fodder. Then there are what some people like to believe are basic down-home hippies, but are really cutthroat, murderous farmers growing megatons of marijuana all over the United States.

The battle against drugs in North America started in earnest when President John F. Kennedy convened a White House conference on drug abuse in 1962. Its chairman was Attorney General Robert F. Kennedy. The younger Kennedy quoted Henry David Thoreau when he stated, "There are a thousand hacking at the branches of evil to one who is striking at the root. We have not been striking at the root." The Kennedy attack on drugs has been cited as reason enough for the mob to arrange the assassinations of the two men. Though conspiracy theories abound concerning their deaths, those linking the shootings to the mob are most believable. And when you're talking mob and drugs, you're also talking CIA. Their paths have crossed too often.

Though most narcotics used in the United States and Canada in the 1940s, 1950s, and 1960s were shipped through Europe, foreign governments did little to combat drugs, which they considered a North American problem. Colombian politicians and drug traffickers use the same argument today — 'It's your problem, man. We couldn't sell if you didn't buy.' True, but if they weren't selling, there would be nothing to buy.

President Richard M. Nixon said in a special message to Congress on July 14, 1969, "Within the last decade the abuse of drugs has grown from essentially a local police problem into a serious threat to the personal health and safety of millions of Americans." Nixon described drugs and the increased crime they caused as "this rising sickness in our land."

On June 17, 1971, Nixon declared an "all-out war" against heroin addiction in a speech to Congress. "If we cannot destroy the drug menace in America, then it will surely destroy us.

"I am proposing additional steps to strike at the supply side of the drug equation — to halt the drug traffic by striking at the illegal producers of drugs, the growing of those plants from which drugs are derived, and trafficking in these drugs beyond our borders."

In August 1972, Nixon said, "Drug abuse is one area where we cannot have budget cuts, because we must wage what I have called total war against public enemy No. 1 in the US—the problem of dangerous drugs."

On March 28, 1973, Nixon told Congress, "This administration has declared an all-out global war on the drug menace."

New York State Governor Nelson Rockefeller also called for a war on drugs in 1973, demanding tougher prison sentences, more prison cells, more treatment facilities, more judges, more police, and more money to curb the "reign of terror."

Does all this sound familiar? George Bush, in his first nationally televised speech as president on September 5, 1989, declared a multi-billion-dollar war on drugs, "the gravest domestic threat facing our nation."

Bush wanted stiffer penalties for users, more money for cops, more prisons and treatment programs, more education and prevention.

"In short, drugs are sapping our strength as a nation. . . . Who's responsible? Let me tell you straight out, everyone who uses drugs, everyone who sells drugs and everyone who looks the other way."

What does that tell us about Bush's speech writers, who set up a drug buy in Lafayette Park across the street from the White House to get the crack cocaine that the president held up to the television camera during his twenty-two-minute speech?

The speech was broadcast live in Colombia. Two Medellin banks were bombed within thirty minutes.

Senator Joseph Biden, chairman of the US Senate judiciary committee, wondered if the government was willing to fight a real war on drugs, or whether it was spouting the same macho rhetoric that past administrations had: "What we need is another D-day, not another Vietnam—not a limited war, fought on the cheap, and destined for stalemate and human tragedy."

The drug war also has a history. It is long and punctuated with too few victories. Just as every generation discovers drugs, so does every political administration. It is a never-ending war for which politicians seek a finale. It is a war they try to squeeze into their term in office. They don't ask what they can do for the war, they ask what the war can do for them.

If drug use and abuse were eliminated, the war would be won, but we would then have to live in a constant state of vigilance. There is no sleep in the battle against drugs. Can drug abuse be eliminated? If history is any indication, if an ongoing political will to fight a real war against drugs is not there, the answer is *no*.

2

Taking It to the Streets:
Black kingpins in the white powder trade

"As far as black gangs are concerned, all they lack is running boards on cars. They are real gangsters. They've replaced the Thompson machine gun with AK-47s and MAC-11s."
—SACRAMENTO DETECTIVE CHRIS (BUCKWHEAT) KUNTZ ON THE CRIPS AND BLOODS STREET GANGS.

"They're very proud of their gangster Al Capone-type mystique."
—LOS ANGELES POLICE DEPARTMENT DEPUTY ROLLAND GARCIA.

The evolution of black drug dealers from lone bros hawking their wares on street corners to sophisticated and deadly gangs has brought to life tight-assed white America's worst racist nightmare: rich niggers with an attitude.

Within three decades, black organized crime has expanded from inner-city streets to international narcotics networks. Its success reflects not only an acute, sharp-edged business sense among black criminals of all ages, but a violent streak and blood lust that help them achieve their goals—money and power. Black organized crime has a terrible weakness, however. Black criminals are extremely selfish and self-centered. When the heat is on, their first loyalty is to their own asses. If that means selling out someone else's, they'll do it.

Bad, Bad Leroy Barnes

In the scuzbag, gutter-level world of jive-talkin', moon-walkin', boogalooin', crotch-gropin', swivel-hipped heroin dealers, one man was king of the entire United States from 1970 to 1977. Well, New York City anyway, which contained more than one-half of the 500,000 American heroin addicts in the entire country. He peddled his horse to black junkies in New York City's Harlem district, in small amounts at first, and by himself. But as independent black dealers started making more and more money, he teamed up with six brothers (as in bros) to form a ruthless, murderous Council that oversaw the distribution of multi-millions of dollars of heroin in Harlem, Brooklyn, and the Bronx. The mob-style Council was one of the first well-organized black crime groups and a model for the black drug organizations that followed. The king among kings was a man who didn't need this new organization to make money: Leroy (Nicky) Barnes, Mr. Untouchable, even if he said so himself.

Bad, bad Leroy Barnes started doing heroin at fourteen and stopped at twenty-four. The experience proved useful to Barnes, as it did for five other Council members.

"That is how I learned the narcotics business—through being a user. And that is how, as a Council member, it was my feeling that we could control our neighborhood better—not through violence, but through putting out very good narcotics. Because when I was a user, I always went to the person who had the best narcotics," he told the President's Commission on Organized Crime.

Nicky Barnes walked out of jail in 1970 with a well-defined sense of who he was and what he wanted. Never again would he get busted for dealing heroin and God forbid he would lack money. And for eight years, he lived up to his expectations.

"In 1970, '71, I was quite successful," said Barnes. "I was up and around in a short time. Initially when I came home, I started out with maybe a package, a kilo or two kilos, and as my business began to develop, I graduated to upper levels, like four or five. When I came home, I started out primarily with a retail business. A retail business consisted of what we called quarters. It was about a quarter of an ounce of cut heroin, and I would take the powder, the narcotic, after I had purchased it and it would be diluted to quarter-ounce units. There were times when I dealt as few as 1,000 [quarters], and there were times when I dealt as many as 10, 15,000 of them."

Nicky Barnes was ranked among the top five heroin dealers in the United States by 1973, running a $1-million-a-month business. That was when other Harlem dealers asked him to band together with them.

"At that time, I was supplying some of the brothers from East Harlem and among them one of my principal customers was a person named Frank James. Frank James and a group of other guys from East Harlem had decided they wanted to form a group of black narcotics dealers. It eventually evolved into what we identified as the Council. At that point, I saw no need for me to become involved with the Council because I didn't see any advantages that would accrue through being involved. But as time passed, I later changed my mind. . . .

"We had planned to pool our money together to be able to purchase narcotics at a cheaper price. We would pool our resources to make sure that we had materials to cut with. As a Council member, we had formed a corporation so we would have rolling stock, automobiles for our women, for our friends, and to carry on our business, and we would be able to . . . better able to monitor the drug scene as a group than we would be able to as individuals."

However, the Council, like all the black organized crime groups that have followed it, had one tragic flaw: under any external pressure, members suddenly forgot any previous loyalty they owed to the Council. Unlike the *omerta* of the Mafia and other traditional organized crime groups in Italy, and La Cosa Nostra in the United States, the black criminal's word to his colleagues isn't worth the spit on which it is uttered.

"The oath of brotherhood [taken by Council members] was primarily centered on the degree of loyalty which was supposed to exist between us," said Barnes. "But there was no loyalty. That never developed. And we thought it would kind of bind us together as a unit."

As the Council got its act together, members tried to get better deals on its dope, linked up with new suppliers, stocked up on mannitol and quinine to cut their heroin and maximize profits, and found underworld craftsmen to supply them with false identification, cars, and muscle.

The Council's principal, most reliable, and consistent supplier, until his arrest for smuggling in 1975, was Matty Madonna. His disappearance from the heroin scene hurt the Council because very few suppliers were as honest as Madonna. Despite the added control that smuggling their own heroin would have given the Council, members preferred to deal with suppliers. "I think we were satisfied with the amount of money we were making," said Barnes. "And I think we were also satisfied to let someone else take the responsibility of having it shipped into the United States, that we were sufficiently under enough surveillance distributing, as it were, and I don't think we wanted further surveillances." This tack put them at the mercy of suppliers.

"We had problems with a supplier known as Mike Pugliese," said Barnes. "Mikey had begun doing business with us through one of the other Council members and, at one point during the time that he was supplying us, we got a supply of powder which we classified as synthetic. We gave it the name 'synthetic' because after it was mixed with the dilutant, the quinine or whatever we decided to cut it with, after it was mixed, the reaction of cut with the powder caused the quality to sharply drop. And we had always classified that as synthetic heroin.

"He didn't tell us it was synthetic. As a matter of fact, I think that he didn't know at the time because I believe he valued our business too highly to have lost it through something that was inferior." The synthetic heroin was bad for business because junkies didn't want it. They sought out other suppliers.

"It would disrupt the flow of money from the streets to myself and from myself or whatever Council member was responsible at that particular time for supplying the narcotic."

Mike Pugliese survived selling the Council synthetic heroin, but couldn't escape a vicious tongue.

"At one point, information had come to us that Mikey Pugliese was an informant," said Barnes. "Well, after we had received the information and we funneled it through our source to determine whether or not it was valid, we had a Council meeting about the problem of Mikey Pugliese and we reached a unanimous Council agreement that Mike Pugliese would have to be eliminated."

A Council member and several associates rubbed out the supplier, the first of at least a dozen victims murdered on the group's orders. Robert Atkinson and Ronald Bell were killed for trying to rob Council members. Lawrence Billings, accused of the same offence, survived the attempted hit. A Council member had his brother-in-law stabbed with an ice pick. One killer dissected his victim with a chainsaw. An ambitious hit man auditioning for a Council job killed an innocent passerby. But killings were brief bursts of adrenaline that punctuated a steady routine of cranking out heroin from mills where the drug was cut and re-packaged for street dealing.

"There were times when I had as few as four workers and as many as ten or twelve [in a heroin mill]," said Barnes. "That would be dependent upon the amount of merchandise that I had to make available for the street at any particular time. And it would depend upon the rhythm of the business at any time. There wasn't any exact format as to how that would be operated. That would depend on whatever my instincts would dictate to me would be the safest way to conduct the operation at any time. I would pass my instructions along to my lieutenant and he would see that they were carried out."

In 1976, Barnes began to feel police heat. He was under surveillance. To cool off, he merged his street operation with that of Guy Fisher, another Council member.

"Within the Council, we pinpointed certain areas in Harlem which we classified as profitable areas, street areas within which narcotics would be sold," said Barnes. "We had agreed among ourselves that no Council member would infringe upon the area of another Council member. But as I said, within the Council we also formed independent alliances. So Guy Fisher was located in the Bronx but, through mutual agreement among Council members, we would agree to have other workers work our neighborhoods.

"It doesn't mean that we had the neighborhood exclusively to ourselves, because we concluded that if we were the same person that was selling narcotics in a particular area, and that area became the object of any law enforcement, then, naturally, the people that were being surveilled would be our people. But if we sold our narcotics in an area that was widely used by other sellers, then we wouldn't be the sole object of any surveillance. So we didn't own any area by virtue of strength or through violence or whatever the case may be. We would prefer being in an area where there would be some shade on our activity.

"We competed by having the best powder because drug addicts don't buy names, they buy the quality. So, because we had an abundant supply, we usually tried to make sure that we had the best narcotic, so when the buyers came on the scene, they would go to our workers, and if our workers were unavailable, then they would buy the other, the second best."

As with any successful criminal enterprise that takes in thousands of small bills daily, the Council had to ensure the money was quickly laundered.

"Usually we had among us Council members who had access to banks or people who worked in banks, because there were times when suppliers that we were dealing with would accept only hundred-dollar bills. Or if we needed to stash money, it would be very difficult to stash $100,000 in five-dollar bills. So we would have the money changed over in banks, for the most part.

"We would usually have an arrangement made with some bank person and the particular bank person would determine how the transaction should be conducted and we would abide by that determination," said Barnes. "We usually paid one point [1 percent of the total] for the changeover."

Although law-enforcement agencies are often criticized for busting street-level pushers and not going after Mr. Big, Barnes said he was hurt most by arrests of his dealers.

"I think that the greatest damage was done to our operation when your middle level and street dealers were arrested, because when the powder comes through, I usually get mine on consignment. And I think most of the big dealers usually get it on consignment. And when reliable street people get knocked off, like they say—I might have a guy that is giving me anywhere from forty to eighty thousand dollars over a ten-day period—when a couple of these guys get pinched, or whenever the neighborhood gets too hot, and I can't do anything, my supplier gets on my back and he tells me that his supplier is on his back."

Barnes figures he made several million dollars during his stint with the Council. Was it worth it?

"I think that becoming a member of the Council was probably the worst mistake I ever made. Because not only did I become the object of a lot of surveillance by various law-enforcement agencies, but the principal reason why we were together—I wouldn't say the principal reason—one of the primary reasons why we were together was that we agreed to watch the back of one another if any of us had gotten into any trouble, and after I got arrested and after I got sentenced, they forgot about me. So the Council was good as long as I was there and I was able to contribute. But when I needed them to look out for me, they didn't do it. No, I think it was a bad mistake."

Barnes was sentenced to life imprisonment without parole in 1978.

"As a Council member, I was a number one among the numbers one. After I went away and I was unable to contribute, the guys just forgot about me and they never came to see me, never took care of lawyers for me, never did anything for me after I started serving time. But there were times when they asked me to do things for them, like try to introduce them to different guys who were inside and who had access to amounts of powder, and they wanted to go through me to try to reach out to the guys in the Council."

Forty-eight years old and four years behind bars, Barnes started to pick up bad vibes in 1981. Council members had taken over his business and one was fucking his favorite woman. Barnes began dealing information—he ratted on his former buddies. "I have no way to reach to get to 'em, and I want to get back at 'em," he said. So far, he's helped indict forty-four major traffickers and convict sixteen. He even put the woman who bore two of his four children behind bars. In return, Mr. Untouchable's former buddies have put a $1-million contract on his head.

There's no honor among black criminals. There never was.

Just months after Nicky Barnes started doing time, another heroin organization geared up to mainline powder into Harlem. According to testimony before the President's Commission on Organized Crime, Papa D's Family spent most of 1979 buying a hotel, two candy stores, a three-story brownstone building at 119 West 130th Street—buildings from which they could run their operation—and a limousine service. Bodyguards kept their handguns there as well as shotguns and scoped rifles for hits. While Pop Washington took care of the real estate, his second-in-command, Clarence Wynn, recruited a team of enforcers, distributors, and lieutenants to oversee the business. Pop Washington boasted to his employees that an attorney called Mother Superior would handle the Family's financial matters and take care of members when things got hot. The organization was in full swing by the summer of 1980, when it ordered its first hit.

"There was an individual that owed money to the Family, and he failed to pay, and he was on the run, and he ran to California, and they ran him down there, and they did, you know, the job to him, and his body was sent back to New York to be buried," said a former member of Papa D's Family to the Commission. Because the organization can have him killed, we'll call him Sugar Lips.

"To make up his payments for the loss, there was heroin stuffed into the coffin and sent back," Sugar Lips said. "This was synthetic heroin made, I guess, in the United States." Mother Superior had arranged for it to be stuffed into the casket. Although there were no problems with transportation, the stuff didn't do well on the street. Synthetic heroin can't be cut with the same amounts of quinine or bonita used to dilute organic heroin. It must be mixed in a 1:2 or ½:2 ratio. Something was wrong with the casket batch.

"It wasn't selling the way a normal shipment would be selling and we were losing customers at that time," Sugar Lips said. "And it caused a controversy between one of Pop's sons and the people in other organizations [Guy Fisher and Freddy Myers] that were also sharing rooms in the hotel. [Addicts] were complaining they were getting headaches, they weren't getting the same high. It wasn't lasting long enough, and also, the lieutenants and workers were complaining about it as well.

"It had an effect to the point where the money for buying our next shipment was running short and we couldn't, you know, put the money together because we lost most of our customers."

Pop swallowed pride and called a sit-down with Guy Fisher and Freddy Myers at a hotel on 116th Avenue and, later, at the Bunch of Grapes bar to discuss pooling their resources to buy a shipment. He offered his two competitors such a good return for their investment that Harlem's first heroin cartel was created. Pop knew how to turn tough luck into hard cash.

"It was Pop's philosophy [that the organization] should be run as a business. Take no chances," said Sugar Lips. "If people you know paid their money, you should always be courteous and thank them. And if they didn't and wanted to cause trouble, rub them out. Get rid of them." Although Pop called the shots, he made sure he was distanced enough from the daily operation to insulate himself from busts. The daily routine of getting the powder to the streets was left to touters, lieutenants, mules, and enforcers.

"The lieutenant's job was to distribute to the workers," said Sugar Lips. "He would come to the various locations, pick up his supply, and distribute them to the workers, and the workers would feed the touters in the morning, who, in turn, for their feeding would run out and get customers that, you know, customers would come to them, say a customer came from Staten Island, Long Island, or Jersey, and he wanted to buy, he would have faith in them because they knew, you know, that these guys use the stuff every day. So, therefore, he would bring them to the workers who in turn would sell them the stuff.

"That is their position—to manage and make sure that, you know, nobody, none of our workers get ripped off, and, you know, all the money is accountable for." Lieutenants were not allowed to use heroin for fear it would impair their ability to make money and protect the Family. Touters, on the other hand, were kept in line by being deprived of heroin at night.

"These are drug addicts who, in the morning, they need their fix in the morning," said Sugar Lips. "They are ill in the morning, so we would get them well. They would get them well in the morning and their job was to go out and get customers. You know, they would bring their regular customers."

Unlike Nicky Barnes's Council, Papa D's Family imported its own heroin with specially trained mules to maximize profits.

"We had eight women, eight female women," Sugar Lips said. "They were, you know, executive-looking types, secretary-looking types. They didn't mess with drugs or nothing. . . . They would travel under their true names, but they did have passports under various names. There used to be an individual in the Bronx. He was an insurance man. He would supply all of the passports, sometimes pick up 150, sometimes 50 at a time. . . . The job of the enforcers was to make sure that these eight women reached their destination safely when they came in with their shipments.

"They wouldn't travel in groups, but they would travel over to London [or the Bahamas] and back to the United States, from JFK or LaGuardia airports. Twice a week. They had to, in their two trips, they had to average a pound or two pounds—a pound per trip." They carried the heroin in their vaginas or rectums or strapped under their breasts. "It was the driver's job to make sure they got back to 119 and, you know, they would go upstairs into the house. Then they would, you know, strip and unload their cargo there, you know, whatever they were carrying, and then, you know, Pop would take it downstairs and we would, you know, they would put it in the safe or whatever."

The brownstone at 119 West 130th Street was equipped with video cameras that covered both sides of the street from the first and second floors. It was also protected by armed guards around the clock. While the candy store and limousine service were used as drop-offs for heroin and money, most of the heroin was sold at the Family's hotel. How profitable was business? "An average of $200,000 on a bad day," said Sugar Lips. The money was collected in a mail bag and dropped off in Pop's room. He took it to Mother Superior to pay for shipments and within two days the mules were on the road.

Papa D's Family also imported and trafficked in cocaine. "The thing in New York is supply and demand," said Sugar Lips. "And a lot of people like cocaine just like a lot of people like heroin. And there was money to be made, and there was a demand, and, you know, we were supplying it. Cocaine was picked up in, basically, Miami, Orlando, and Jacksonville, Florida, and we could take most — we would take a car down sometimes, or either Amtrak, and we would stay overnight in the hotel, and they would pick it up, you know, the girls did all the transportation and bring it back to New York. One time, when the connection went dry, we traded — we traded heroin for cocaine. We did most of the trading in New York."

Papa D's Family sold cocaine in rock form, although not the rock or crack found on the streets today. "We couldn't afford to sell it the same way we bought it," said Sugar Lips. "So what we would do is break it down and cut it with lactose, 62[%], 70[%], and then take a compressor, man-made compressor, and compress it back into rock. We take base plates, two street base plates [manhole covers], and we weld one with a fence around it and one with a hook arm. Make one like a cup, and we would put a hydraulic jack underneath it and compress it to the top base plate with the coke inside of it. That's all it did, just change its appearance." And the materials used to dilute the coke? "As a matter of fact, you wind up selling more of that than you would anything else." Papa D's team bought barrels of quinine at a pharmacy on 125th Street. After a few years of business in New York City, Papa D's thirty-five-member Family spread its tentacles and supplied Boston, Detroit, Pennsylvania, Chicago, Washington, and North Carolina.

Young Boys, Inc.

David Milton (Butch) Jones was convicted of manslaughter at seventeen and sentenced to seven to fifteen years behind bars. Unlike his fellow prisoners, he did not kill time. Butch Jones nurtured a dream as he lay on his prison bed from 1975 to 1980. He dreamed he was a rich man surrounded by men he made rich. He dreamed he organized a group of drug traffickers who controlled the mass distribution of heroin throughout his hometown of Detroit, in the housing projects, in Highland Park, in Pontiac, and in Flint. And in his dream he was always untouchable. It's a favorite dream among black criminals.

But Butch Jones devised a way to become untouchable. In his dream, he hired kids as young as twelve to sell coin envelopes of heroin to addicts. These kids were his buffer against arrest. If they were caught, they'd get off because kids can't be sent to jail. And the cops could arrest as many kids as they wanted, because he had a lot of kids who'd work for money given the opportunity. Butch Jones had a name for his dream: Young Boys, Inc.

When Butch Jones got out of jail in the winter of 1980, he returned to the Monterey-Dexter area of Detroit and rounded up a bunch of neighborhood guys in the playground. He told them he was going to make them millionaires selling heroin.

Butch Jones didn't do drugs, didn't drink, and didn't party. He expected his workers to be as cool as he was and told them to get high on money, cars, jewelry, and clothes rather than on the junk they would sell. Indeed, with time, members of the 300-strong Young Boys organized crime gang were taking photographs of each other with piles of money and jewels or in big cars.

Butch Jones and his most trusted cronies bought most of their heroin from Sylvester Seal Murray, a major black importer of heroin and cocaine with connections on the east and west coasts and in the Caribbean. Murray was so successful he'd have up to $700,000 at any given time in garbage bags in any of his stash houses. The Young Boys took the heroin to a hookup house, where it was cut or mixed with lactose, dormin, and quinine and packaged for distribution. Six or more people working at long tables did this every time a shipment of heroin came in. They cut the heroin and spooned it into hundreds of coin envelopes stamped with brand names the Young Boys used to distinguish its product from that of the competition, a practice that began in drug circles in the mid-1970s: Who-IE-Con, Murder One, Rolls Royce, CBS, Whipcracker. Sealed envelopes were put in bundles of ten, each bundle worth $100. Then bundles were placed in paper bags with the place of distribution, the number of bundles, and the money to be returned to the organization written on the outside of each bag in shorthand.

Other members of the gang dropped off the bags at spots in apartment buildings, housing projects, and houses. A top-dog supervised each spot and distributed the heroin to young runners who sold it. Addicts are a finnicky lot and Butch Jones made certain his organization ran like clockwork. All bags had to be dropped off and distributed by runners between 9:00 and 9:30 every morning. When the cops turned up the heat, Young Boys started hooking up between 1 a.m. and 3 a.m. when the narcs were in bed. Butch Jones or his chief lieutenant, Timothy Peoples, supervised the hookup crew, which was made up of the most trusted members of the gang. They wore plastic gloves and surgical masks while hooking up so they wouldn't get hooked on the pure heroin. In fact, Murray would boast that the stuff he delivered to Young Boys was so good it would kill. Indeed, most of it was more than 71 percent pure. By the time the hookup crew was finished cutting it, a coin envelope contained 0.3 grams of 1 percent heroin.

Sunday was payday for Young Boys' employees and they met at a club in a Detroit warehouse that featured gambling and entertainment. Workers were paid salaries according to their responsibilities in the organization. Those who dropped off bags of bundles were paid $50 a day and $20 for gas and expenses. Runners got $300 or more a week and between $1 and $2.50 for each envelope sold. Top dogs got $700 or more a week for running their spots. Butch Jones provided a lawyer if any adult in the organization was arrested and one female gang member using an alias bonded gang members out of jail as soon as they were arrested. Gang members were given fake identifications, which included forged Michigan drivers' permits, birth certificates, and social security cards. Butch Jones rented expensive, posh homes as dormitories for his workers. One even had a pool table with a gold name plate inscribed YBI. Each of these houses was wired with a microphone outside so people inside could hear conversations on the street.

Butch Jones also had a group of enforcers called the wrecking crew, which kept gang members in line, resolved disputes, prevented ripoffs, and protected gang members. Supervisory-level gang members caught using drugs were worked over by the wrecking crew and dumped. The wrecking crew took orders only from Butch Jones or Peoples. Runners between the ages of twelve and seventeen were the only gang members allowed to use drugs. They were expected to stop if promoted to higher positions in the organization.

Drug dealers have many ways of endearing themselves to the neighborhoods they work in. Most of these involve giving people something they can't afford. But while they give, drug dealers always take. They never do something for nothing. In New York City's Harlem district, for example, black drug dealers foot the bill for more than 80 percent of the summer basketball league for teenage boys. They set up tournaments and pay for jerseys, sneakers, and trophies. Good clean fun. But sometimes it gets violent. One referee was beaten to death for making a questionable call.

What do the dealers get out of it? For starters, a good public image; entertainment—they bet thousands of dollars on games; and recruits— their expensive cars and jewelry, plus the fact they are not behind bars, give kids the impression that dealing drugs is the way to get ahead.

Posses

Not many black drug dealers were harder and meaner than Delroy (Uzi) Edwards. Many dealers were a lot smarter, but few were cold-blooded enough to beat and shoot their own employees the way Uzi Edwards did. This violence is a Jamaican trait, a trademark of the Jamaican posses that

infiltrated the United States and Canada in the late 1970s and early
1980s, taking advantage of lenient immigration policies that favored
poor people from the islands. They called themselves posses because
they grew up watching American westerns on television. They liked the
bang, bang, you're dead, black-and-white approach to life that Hollywood offered. They liked the blood. Blood meant you had accomplished something. You had reached deep inside someone and hurt them.
Blood was an offering, a concession, a surrender. Blood on your enemy
set you free. Blood. We are blood.

Uzi Edwards was a product of politics and poverty. He wasn't strong
enough to rise above both. He wasn't weak enough to be crushed by
either. He followed his baser instincts and did what must have come
naturally to primitive man thousands of years ago. He attacked and took,
attacked and took, never looking back, never looking ahead. He carved
out his niche in the present and inched his way through life one second at
a time. He was an angry man, but didn't know why. He lashed out at
those around him, but didn't know why. All he knew was that he had to
do what he had to do. It's a simple philosophy for the simple-minded.

Uzi Edwards was born like another bead of sweat in Kingston,
Jamaica, in 1959, dripping into life on a downward course to nowhere
with not enough time to get there. He was baptized in the steaming
cauldron of Jamaican politics in 1980, during a rematch of the island's
two political heavyweights. And not unlike political turmoil in other
countries, the CIA was lurking in the cool shadows, throwing spitballs
and making kings.

Politicians in Jamaica have always had the backing of the street gangs
in their constituencies. In fact, Jamaicans are born into political parties,
they don't choose. You go with the flow. If your neighborhood votes
Social Democrat (left), you vote Social Democrat. If it votes Labor Party
(right), you vote Labor Party. The loyalty lasts until death. Jamaican
immigrants even settle in American and Canadian neighborhoods with
Jamaicans of the same political bent. So politicians could always count on
the brash support of the gangs and their ganja or cocaine money.

The stage onto which Uzi Edwards walked was first set in 1976, when
his mind was on matters more important than money or politics. Prime
Minister Michael Manley and his Social Democrat party were under
severe attack by unknown forces trying to destabilize his government.
Those forces were led by then-CIA director George Bush, who, like
many Americans, feared any political party that claimed to help people.
Manley's right-wing opponent, Edward Seaga, the leader of the Jamaican Labor Party, was supported by both the CIA and the island's
southeastern-section cocaine gangs. The underbellies of each party went
at each other with submachine guns.

Manley won the 1976 battle and retained his post. During the next four years, Uzi Edwards grew up, the street gangs called posses became more powerful, and the American hunger for drugs accomplished what the CIA couldn't. The 1980 rematch of Manley and Seaga proved to be Uzi Edwards's coming-out party. The island's posses aligned themselves for battle. The Shower posse sided with Seaga. The Spangler posse supported Manley.

The Shower had gained its power not in Jamaica, but in the United States, where it flourished like crotch rash, feeding on America's insatiable lust to numb reality with marijuana and cocaine. The hardscrabble posses found the pickings easy on the paved streets of New York and Miami, from which they built drug networks that criss-crossed the country in a matter of years—networks built with muscle, brains, and street savvy, and always oiled with blood.

The Shower posse, which had humble beginnings in the Tivoli Gardens section of Kingston, started sending cash and hundreds of guns to Jamaica in 1979 to help Seaga's election bid. The gangs supporting the two politicians squared off in a ten-month war that stained the tin shack ghetto sections of Kingston with the blood of a thousand people. Today they have been immortalized in island lore as the sufferers.

This was Uzi Edwards's finest hour. His Renkers posse was appropriately formed during the bloody 1980 election campaign. (Renkers means the smell of piss against a wall.) Uzi Edwards was paid $10 a week to shoot up neighborhoods that supported Manley. He doesn't seem to have kept a body count.

Politics being what they are, Seaga had little use for posse gunslingers once he was in office. He dispatched police eradication squads to wipe out the hit men who had paved his way to parliament with a carpet of blood. Seaga almost literally drove them out of the country. And where do you think the bad guys settled? In the home country of George Bush and the CIA and in Canada. Bush, of course, had moved on to greater things. By the end of 1980, he was vice-president elect of the United States. By the time he took office, the posses were growing in numbers and strength. Members entered the United States and Canada on visitor's permits and stayed illegally, or crossed the borders on band-ooloos—forged passports.

Uzi Edwards, too, arrived in New York in 1980 on a visitor's passport. His father, Lloyd (Pants) Edwards, was a former tailor who left Jamaica to run a grocery store and peddle ganja in the Crown Heights section of Brooklyn. The enterprising poor always seem to have access to something the moneyed folk want. Uzi Edwards followed in his father's footsteps. Someone murdered the elder Edwards in 1982—the finger has been pointed at his son—and Uzi Edwards moved into the apartment above the Rogers Avenue store with his wife, Winsome Lorde.

Uzi Edwards was a gang man and he missed the Renkers. He gradually recruited Jamaicans, letting them sell his marijuana, and rebuilt his gang. By 1985, he had enough seed money to start dealing cocaine.

Crack cocaine had just hit the streets of New York after receiving a one-year standing ovation in Los Angeles. Crack was a dealer's dream. Here was a drug that could be sold in pieces as cheaply as $5, making it affordable to everyone; it offered an instant high because it was smoked; and the high lasted ten to twelve minutes, leaving the smoker craving more. Cocaine was no longer a drug for the privileged rich. It had worked its way down.

During the next two years, Uzi Edwards ran a fifty-member organization that earned $100,000 a week selling crack, powder cocaine, and marijuana. Couriers picked up kilograms of cocaine at $17,000 each in Miami, the Bahamas, and Los Angeles. Uzi Edwards cooked the crack at home and hawked it at eight spots in Brooklyn, luring customers away from the competition by offering two-for-one deals. Some spots were better than others. The spot outside the grocery store on Rogers Avenue reaped $14,000 a day. Another spot on Pacific Street had buyers from a nearby housing project lining up forty deep to buy crack. That spot sometimes earned $30,000 a day.

Uzi Edwards paid his workers $250 to $1,000 a week. In 1986, he teamed up with his uncle, Kenneth (Bud) Manning, and expanded to Washington, Baltimore, and Philadelphia. There was less competition in those cities. Back in Brooklyn, the aggressive Renkers fought over drug spots with the Wild Bunch and the Forties, another Seaga-supporting posse from Rockfort in Kingston. The Renkers were also having trouble with the posse in blue—dirty cops from the 77th Precinct who wanted a cut of the action. Despite the problems he had to put up with, Uzi Edwards had a good time. He bought a $150,000 house in Amityville, Long Island, paying in cash. He dumped the money—in a variety of denominations—out of a duffel bag when he closed the deal. It took the seller nearly four hours to count it. He also bought a $17,490 ride 'em-cowboy Jeep Cherokee—cash. This time it was in a brown paper bag.

Uzi Edwards had a knack for making money, but had no clue how to run a business or treat employees. If he had kept proper books, he would have realized that his uncle and business partner, Bud Manning, was ripping him off for $5,000 a week.

Uzi didn't like rip-offs. He let everyone know it by making examples of those who tried to line their pockets with his money. One of those victims was Norman (Egghead) Allwood. The seventeen-year-old dealer tried to do Uzi for $400. Uzi shot him in the leg in November 1986. Then Egghead ripped off some of Uzi's crack. Uzi arranged for some of his Renkers to lure him into the basement of a crack house in January 1987. Dane Trail pulled a gun on Egghead while Uzi and other Renkers pulled out baseball bats.

"He was crying," said Renker Conroy Green, who had just joined the posse. By the Ides of March, he had taken part in three killings and five assaults. "He was denying stealing any money. . . . He kept saying, 'Help me, Dane.' "

But Dane just kept the gun pointed at Egghead while the Renkers beat him senseless. Bud Manning grabbed a bat from one Renker's hands and jumped in. Manning poured boiling water from the furnace on Egghead's face to revive him.

"His skin started to strip," Green said, "and he started to move around. Bud said, 'Oh, you're not dead.' "

They wrapped Egghead in chains and hung him from the ceiling. The next day, Uzi sent four Renkers to get rid of the body. Victor Francis stepped on Egghead's stomach to make sure he was dead. The nervous Renkers had a hell of a time getting the corpse into garbage bags. "Couldn't stay. Keep springing back out," Renker Milton Cooper said. They dumped the body on Forties' turf.

The killing was typical of Uzi's rule on Rogers Avenue—murders, kidnappings, assaults, robberies—a reign of terror that really wasn't good for business, since violence attracts police. Uzi's wealth gave him the power to order his posse members around. Most of those orders were to kill people. Some victims were competing drug dealers, but most were innocent bystanders. Once Uzi was shot by a member of another posse. He ordered Stanley McCall to go out and shoot anyone who looked Jamaican in the posse's territory.

"I walked up to the store and I seen three guys standing there," McCall said. "The closest guy to me, he had his back to me, so I just pulled out the gun and I shot him in the back." He shot and paralyzed an innocent man. Renkers also knocked on a door and shot through it, killing a woman before she could answer.

Uzi ordered his uncle to kill Devon Steer. Manning sat in the back seat of a car while Steer sat in the passenger seat beside the driver. Manning pulled a .45-caliber pistol.

"I shoot Johnny's cousin in the head," he said. "Back of his head. Once."

The driver opened the passenger door and tried to dump the body, but the foot caught and the body dragged alongside the car. Manning finally shoved the corpse out and ordered the driver and a posse member to burn the car. Then he fell asleep.

Uzi was finally caught—there was too much blood on the streets for the police to ignore him—and after a nine-month investigation, they rounded up the posse in March 1988. Half of the twenty-four posse members indicted testified against Uzi, although doing so wouldn't reduce their sentences, which all exceeded twenty years. Uzi's sentence totalled 501 years for convictions on forty-two charges: six murders, fifteen shootings, one kidnapping, armed robbery, attempted robbery, money laundering, seventeen racketeering charges, plus the drug and weapons offences.

Bud Manning evaded arrest for one month. He paid a voodoo doctor to keep the law at bay with spells and washed himself in goat's blood. When he was caught, he paid $15,000 to put a hex on the judge.

Jamaican posses are the fastest-growing group of organized gangsters in North America. From their humble shantytown beginnings in Kingston, they set up operation bases in the heart of Jamaican enclaves in Miami and New York and within five years spread across the United States and into Canada. There are about thirty posses with 5,000 members selling crack cocaine, powder cocaine, and marijuana in Miami, New York, Philadelphia, Boston, Cleveland, Detroit, Dallas, Houston, Chicago, Los Angeles, San Francisco, Denver, Kansas City, Rochester, Hartford, Washington, Toronto, and Montreal. And those are just the cities where their presence has been noted because of the murders their members have committed.

Regardless of the city in which they operate, most posse members end up working in New York or Miami at one time or another. Both cities are major ports of entry into the United States for Jamaicans. When the posses first set up their US drug networks, 80 to 90 percent of the cocaine and 50 percent of the marijuana entering the United States came through Miami. Interdiction has forced many smugglers to pipe it in through Mexico and southern California in recent years. New York is one of North America's major distribution centers. And most illegal gun purchases in the States are made in Miami. Most Jamaicans who enter Canada do so in Toronto, where the country's largest Jamaican population, 250,000, is responsible for more crimes per capita than any other racial group in the city.

Posses have a higher profit margin on their drug sales than any other organized crime group, up to 1,000 percent more. Few of the importers, such as La Cosa Nostra or the Colombian cartels, sell their drugs at street level. Posses not only manufacture and import, but also wholesale, distribute, and push on the street. They grow their own marijuana in Jamaica, smuggle it into the States and Canada, then break it down into the smallest saleable unit and push it. No member in the network gets paid until the dope hits the street. Though posses started out selling marijuana, they control the crack market in most of the east and southern parts of the United States and in Toronto, where posse members have taught black youths in housing projects how to cook and sell crack for them.

Posse members flash cash, jewelry, big cars, and hot babes to impress the young. Then they get them to do their dirty work. Kids act as lookouts at drug-dealing spots, runners who race back and forth between the spot and the stash, or back and forth between a customer's car and the apartment lobby the dealer works out of.

Members of the Shower, Spangler, and Striker posses have taken over high-rise housing projects that house hardworking Jamaicans in Toronto. They never deal in their own building. They go over to the next complex and set up shop in a building's lobby. Usually it is the building farthest from the main road and with the best view of the surroundings. Customers pull up in their cars in front of a building. Young runners approach them to take the order and the money. A runner takes the cash into the lobby and gives it to the dealer. The dealer hands over the amount of crack or sends a runner to get it from a nearby stash. The flow of customers is endless, many coming back three and four times in one night.

Other dealers prefer to work out of apartments—never their own, though. They entice young, single welfare mothers to let them move in. They turn the apartment into a crack house or stash house, to which buyers are directed to make purchases. Dealers prefer to work this way because if cops raid the place, the dealer splits and the woman gets busted.

Posses, like many other organized crime groups, consider women as animals to be used. Fuck 'em and leave 'em. They give a woman some easy cash and a plane ticket to a warm place and tell her she can have a nice two-week holiday as long as she brings back a parcel a friend will deliver to the hotel room. Many women don't realize that posses consider mules expendable. They either make it across the border, or they don't. As long as *they* do the time in prison and not the posse member.

Robyn Jones was a twelve-year-old Grade 6 student in May 1990. Her friend, Leca Arbuckle, was fifteen. Sometimes she attended her Grade 9 classes, sometimes she didn't. They lived in graffiti-splattered, public-funded apartment buildings in northeast Toronto, an area that rivals northwest Toronto's claim of housing more Jamaican drug dealers than any other housing projects in North America. Despite their age, the girls weren't angels. They ran with street gangs and were known to the police. The gangs they ran with were controlled by members of the Galloway Massive posse. The posse even has a mini version of itself for kids—Galloway Juniors. White kids in the neighborhood are so impressed by the swashbuckling Jamaican drug dealers that they imitate their incomprehensible island patois.

The girls had an older friend, a woman crack addict and drug dealer who took them to the park or to McDonald's. They sometimes babysat for her. One day she told the girls that some guys owed her a favor. She showed them color brochures of Jamaica, told them how beautiful it was, then asked if they'd like to go.

Well, wow. That's like asking them if they'd like to meet the New Kids on the Block. The girls knew about drugs and wondered if they'd have to bring any back. The woman said all they had to do was have a good time. (Shortly after the girls were arrested, however, a friend in Toronto said they had been promised $5,000 each to smuggle the drugs for Jamaican dealers in Toronto. Their mothers also said this was the case.)

The woman called several weeks later and told the girls the trip was on. A man showed up five minutes later to pick them up. The girls told their mothers they were going to a cottage. All mothers let their little girls go away to cottages by themselves, don't they? Leca had ID, but Robyn didn't. She had to borrow a card from a sixteen-year-old friend. The girls spent a few days at a hotel near Lester B. Pearson International Airport in Toronto before flying south.

Two men picked them up at the airport when they arrived in Jamaica. Obviously someone had called to tell them what the girls were wearing. They took the girls to a motel and disappeared. The girls were too scared to go to the beach more than once. They flitted around the pool instead. Five days later, the men returned. They told the girls they had to take drugs back to Toronto. The girls weren't surprised, although they really didn't want to do it. The men wrapped cotton around their stomachs and taped pouches of marijuana totaling thirteen pounds to them.

The girls were so nervous that when a woman in uniform stopped them at Donald Sangster International Airport in Montego Bay on June 8, Leca pulled up her shirt.

They were the youngest smugglers ever arrested at the airport. Ten days later, they were fined a total of $15,000 (Cdn.) and released. Nearly all that fine was paid by sympathetic Canadians donating money to a trust fund for the girls.

While the two little mules were before the courts, nineteen-year-old Lorrie MacLeod was arrested with five pounds of marijuana in the false bottom of the suitcase her newly found Jamaican boyfriend had asked her to carry. MacLeod met the man several weeks earlier at a Jamaican dance club in Hamilton, Ontario, a thirty-minute drive south of Toronto. They flew to Montego Bay for a week's holiday. As they were about to return to Canada, he claimed to have last-minute business to take care of and asked her to take his suitcase, which he said contained sugar cane, mangoes, and other fruit.

Sean Smith was a mule for a Jamaican drug dealer in Toronto. The twenty-year-old was promised $6,000 to $10,000, plus an all-expenses-paid trip, to pick up fifteen pounds of marijuana in Montego Bay in 1990. He got caught, of course, and hasn't heard from the dealer since. Smith spent two weeks in a three-bunk jail cell he shared with ten to fifteen other people. He was fed hard bread, rice, and cane juice. Once a week he was allowed to hose himself down.

Another Toronto woman was paid $2,000 a trip to carry six pounds of marijuana from Montego Bay for a dealer. She stopped only after getting caught and spending nine months in jail. The twenty-two-year-old woman and a girlfriend were given tickets to Jamaica, accommodation at a good hotel, and $500 in fun money. Once in Jamaica, the women handed over their garment bags to a man they met in a restaurant. When they got them back, the linings had been taken out and replaced with custom-fitted linings that held compressed marijuana. One bag held six pounds, the other seven pounds. At the airport the next day, one woman recognized a man who had been her connection on an earlier run. Unfortunately, he also recognized her. He had been burned by the dealer who sent the women to Jamaica. In retaliation, he pointed the mules out to the police.

An official for the Canadian consulate in Montego Bay said Canadians are arrested with drugs on nearly every Toronto flight. Seven Canadians were caught on one flight. Jamaica has a zero-tolerance crackdown program on drugs. You can get busted for a marijuana seed. Mules who think they can fool Jamaican police, whom they believe to be a backwater police force, are kidding themselves. The Jamaicans have not only sniffer dogs but highly sophisticated scanners that probe suitcases, parcels, and people to reveal hidden contraband.

Most mules don't understand how drug dealers work. They often line up as many as ten mules for one flight to spread out the shipment. If the shipment's overseer spots trouble, he may tip off police so one or two mules get busted, but the rest get through. Dealers would rather sacrifice one or two mules than lose an entire shipment. It seems American mules are easier to nab than Canadians. About seventy Canadians are caught with drugs at Jamaican airports every year compared to 1,200 Americans.

Competing drug traffickers also point out to police another

trafficker's mules to curb competition and deflect attention from their own runners.

These are some of the posses identified in the United States and Canada: Shower, Spangler, Striker, Jungle Lites, Waterhouse, Tivoli Gardens, Towerhill, Nanyville, Back Bush, Paneland, Reema, Spanish Town, Montego Bay, Riverton City, Bushmouth, Flethees Land, Marvally, Bibour, Cuban, Samacon, Trinidadian, Banton, Superstar, Super, Tel Aviv, Dog, Dunkirk, Nineties, Southee, Okra Slim, Exodus. Jungle Lites posse members are suspected of having been trained in guerrilla warfare tactics in Cuba.

The Shower posse is the largest, most powerful, and best organized in North America, although its two leaders are fugitives in Jamaica. Lester Coke is wanted for twelve murders in Florida. Vivian Blake was indicted in 1988 for a series of posse-related crimes. Coke went underground after the Supreme Court of Jamaica acquitted him of murder charges. His supporters outside the courthouse gave him a Jamaican salute: they pointed their guns at the sky and fired them. Not only has the Shower posse cornered a large section of the North American crack market, it also smuggles cocaine into Britain, the Netherlands, and West Germany. Much of the cocaine and marijuana smuggled into the United States is now done by posse pilots in posse planes. The posse has become so wealthy it operates like a Colombian cartel. Members launder money through legitimate businesses such as car rental and travel agencies.

Vivian Blake is the mastermind behind the Shower posse's rapid expansion in the drug trade, according to authorities trying to locate him in Jamaica so he can be extradited to the United States to face numerous charges. He allegedly set up the posse's drug network in the United States and traveled to Canada in April 1984, to claim prime drug-selling turf in a country that consumes more drugs per capita than do Americans.

This is how Blake is alleged to have run the posse's drug network: he spent most of his time in Miami, where he bought cocaine and marijuana, some of it flown in from the Bahamas. He packed the marijuana and cocaine into suitcases and arranged for couriers to transport it to cities across North America. Profits from the sales were hand-delivered to Blake or wired through Western Union. Blake also ran a network of people who bought guns for the posse to intimidate and murder people. He is alleged to have participated in murders in Miami on November 6 and November 30, 1984, and in Los Angeles on September 25, 1985. The two most powerful Shower posse members after Blake and Coke were Errol Hussing and Tony Bruce, who operated the posse's drug distribution centers in New York City. Hussing is alleged to have killed one man in the Bronx on July 5, 1984, one month after bribing a witness.

The Lockie Daley Organization (LDO) is a posse that started manufacturing and selling crack cocaine in Philadelphia in the early 1980s. It was well organized and extremely successful. Couriers used cars, trains, and planes to transport cocaine powder from Florida and New York to Philadelphia. Packagers packaged and bagged the cocaine and crack, which was made by the organization. The LDO sold plastic packets of cocaine for $15, $20, and $25. They sold crack in plastic vials or packets for $5 and $10.

Sellers sold cocaine and crack at gatehouses throughout Philadelphia. Gatehouses operated twenty-four hours a day, seven days a week. Workers worked twenty-four-hour shifts for up to one week at a time and sold the drugs through openings in or under the gatehouse door. Delivery persons transported cocaine and crack from stash houses to gatehouses. They also delivered food to gatehouse workers and collected drug money from them.

Bookkeepers kept track of gatehouse sales, cocaine inventories, and arranged for the profits to be shipped from Philadelphia to Florida and Jamaica. The profits were either delivered by a courier or wired through Western Union. Armed guards protected the stash houses, and LDO members used violence to discipline and control workers, to prevent theft of drugs and profits, to prevent workers from co-operating with police, and to deter competition.

A posse that runs fifty crack houses in a large city makes about $9 million a month. For example, a posse buys an ounce of powder cocaine for $700. That gives them 28.2 grams of crack cocaine, which can be broken down into 112 quarter grams sold for $30 apiece. The profit on the original ounce of cocaine is $2,660—$3,360 less the $700 purchase cost. If seventy-five crack houses in a large city such as Dallas sell two ounces of cocaine every day, that gives the posse a daily profit of $399,000. A posse that brought its crack business to Kansas City, Missouri, in 1985 had seventy-five crack houses within two years that brought in $400,000 a day.

You would think that seventy-five crack houses are more than enough to satisfy the needs of Kansas City crack addicts, but they aren't. The Bloods street gang from Los Angeles also peddles its crack in the city.

How do posses set up a drug network so quickly? Sheer balls, enterprise, and hard work. Too bad they don't become legitimate businessmen. Few legitimate businessmen could run a drug network. It takes

more than the ability to sign checks and survive power lunches to wheel
and deal in the underworld. A man seen as a ruthless shark on Wall Street
would be a minnow in the drug world.

Posses reap drug profits in small towns as well as in large cities.
Jamaicans moved into Martinsburg, West Virginia, as migrant apple and
peach pickers in 1984. Within two years, they created a cocaine and
crack market demanding enough to support as many as seventy-five
curbside dealers. High-school kids became runners for the dealers and
started dressing like Los Angeles street gang members—gold chains,
name-brand running shoes and jogging suits. Even a former homecom-
ing queen was bopping one of the Jamaican dealers and posing for dirty
photographs. The murder rate swelled, as did the cases of venereal
disease and the bank accounts of the posse drug dealers.

Little of this money is earned without bloodshed. Simply put, Jamaican
posse members are maniacs. They have no regard for human life and will
murder for no reason, especially a cop. They just like to discharge guns.
Posse members have killed more than 1,500 people in the United States
and Canada since 1984. That's when law enforcement started keeping
tabs on them. Who knows how many were killed in the five previous
years?

In January 1986, two Jamaican posse members—one already wanted
for murder in Pennsylvania—commandeered a car in Virginia and
forced the driver to take them up I-81. A Virginia state trooper stopped
the car for a traffic offence. One of the men shot him. The hostage
jumped out and tried to run away. He was shot in the back. The
Jamaicans abandoned the car and ran away. They broke into a house,
looking for another getaway car. They shot the husband in front of his
children and took the wife hostage. When police closed in, they shot the
wife and committed suicide.

On May 27, 1986, two New York City police officers were wounded
in a gunfight with a Jamaican posse member. His gun was bought in
Texas by a woman crack addict who traded guns for cocaine.

On June 28, 1986, a police officer in New York City was shot in the
head by a posse member who walked up to him while he reloaded his gun.

Three New York-based posses fought for drug turf in predominantly
Jamaican housing projects across the city of Toronto in 1989 and 1990.
The Shower, Spangler, and Striker posses gunned down members of
rival gangs in attempts to intimidate them.

On February 22, 1989, two men kicked open the door of Lyndon
(Machete Man) Gayle's Toronto apartment and shot Gayle and his
twenty-five-year-old girlfriend, Jennifer MacIntosh. They survived.
One man arrested in connection with the shooting was Spangler posse

member Anthony Thompson, a twenty-seven-year-old resident of Brooklyn, New York. Thompson, who also used the name Michael Noble, was on the FBI's most wanted list at the time as a suspect in another shooting. Two other Spanglers were charged in the shooting. Machete Man is either very lucky or unlucky, depending on how you look at it. The twenty-eight-year-old was walking along a west Toronto street at 3 a.m. on Sunday, August 12, 1990, when three black men—two with dollar signs shaved into their heads—pulled up beside him in a car. One man got out and demanded his gold chain. Machete Man refused to hand it over. The man pulled a gun and shot him in the stomach.

Luck ran out for Hugh (Ricky) Price on September 17, 1989. He was out on the streets after paying $20,000 bail on charges of shooting a drug dealer named Barrington Parker, who lived in his apartment building. Price, twenty-three, and his thirty-three-year-old brother Douglas (Edgar) Barr were gunned down by a posse hit man armed with a .45-caliber pistol.

Anthony (The Fox) Aransibia wasn't cunning enough to avoid pissing off members of his own Striker posse who were struggling among themselves over crack cocaine turf in Toronto. Aransibia, a violent drug dealer, was gunned down in the stairwell of an apartment building where he had gone to buy a large amount of crack on January 17, 1990. Someone even stole the wristwatch from his corpse as it lay in the coffin at the Brown Brothers Funeral Home.

Four Metro Toronto Police officers investigating a disturbance outside an apartment building in northwest Toronto on January 4, 1990, ran for cover as gunfire hailed down on them from apartment windows. They weren't hit and the gunmen weren't caught. An argument between members of the same posse ended in a gunfight outside an apartment building on the same street on December 14, 1989. Stray bullets shattered apartment windows.

Seventeen-year-old Mark Yorke was crippled in a car accident in 1987. But that didn't stop the Toronto quadriplegic from having a good time. He was in the front seat of a car leaving a house party at 3:30 Sunday morning on August 26, 1990. A twenty-five-year-old Jamaican called Ninja was in the back seat. Ninja thrust his arm out the window and fired off a Jamaican salute—about twelve shots from a semi-automatic pistol. When Ninja pulled his arm back into the car, the gun discharged, sending a bullet through the back of the front seat, through Yorke's body, and into his leg. Yorke survived—barely.

Guns are a tool of the narcotics trade. You don't deal drugs unarmed, unless you want to get ripped off or killed. Most posse members are illegal aliens or convicted felons. They have to get their guns illegally.

They use false identification and falsify paperwork to buy guns. Sometimes they get someone else to buy the gun for them. What they don't buy they steal. Four gun dealers in Kansas City and Miami were ripped off for 369 guns over two years in the mid-1980s. Thirty-four have been recovered, all in the hands of Jamaican drug dealers. Two Toronto area gun shops were ripped off during nighttime break-ins in 1990. Most of the guns recovered were seized from Jamaicans, many of whom get a kick out of riding ten-speed bicycles through housing projects while wildly discharging .45-caliber pistols. The biggest seizure came after someone reported a black kid selling handguns door to door in an apartment building.

Someone systematically stole fifty guns from a New England gun manufacturer in 1983. An undercover operation nabbed two Jamaicans. Two more Jamaicans, a Dominican, and a Cuban were arrested with six of the guns in 1984.

Two Jamaican posse members from New York were arrested in Tampa, Florida, on July 31, 1987, with sixty-five handguns, two rifles, and eight boxes of ammunition. Between March 6 and July 31 that year, they illegally bought 149 guns from dealers in the Tampa area using fake driver's licenses. They were the guns most favored by posses; mini-TEC 9s, Ingram mini-MACs, Glock pistols, and AR-15 assault rifles.

The Bureau of Alcohol, Tobacco and Firearms started investigating posses in 1984 at the request of Interpol, which asked the organization to trace guns seized in Jamaica. ATF agents found that 50 of 143 guns bought by seventeen posse members in south Florida were seized in drug-related arrests in the United States and Jamaica.

Many murders committed by posses go unsolved because the victims are illegal aliens. Posses—especially the Shower—send members from New York and Miami across the United States and into Canada to oversee narcotics distribution. If they are killed, no one knows who they are. If they kill someone, they split before they can be identified. Like outlaw bikers and members of black street gangs, most posse members are known only by nickname. It's pretty difficult to trace a Sugarbelly or a Dong Man. It's also impossible to infiltrate a posse. The groups are too tightly knit. All members are Yardies—from the same neighborhood in Jamaica—who know that ratting on the posse means death.

Posses have expanded their criminal empires outside the realm of drugs. They are also involved in fraud, assaults, robberies, money laundering, home invasions, kidnapping, murder, and fire-arms trafficking.

Law enforcement has been determined not to let the posses gain a foothold the way La Cosa Nostra did while J. Edgar Hoover refused to recognize its existence for decades. The good guys have wasted no time building cases against posses and shutting down their operations. In

October 1988, law-enforcement agents arrested 200 posse members, many of them from the Shower, in twenty states. A sixty-two-count indictment accused thirty-four Shower posse leaders of drug and weapons offences, nine murders, and five attempted murders.

3

Bad Blood:
Tales from the Crips and the Bloods

Black street gangs: they are ruthless, deadly, and merciless. They out-number La Cosa Nostra, outlaw bikers, Colombian *narco-traficantes*, prison gangs, and Jamaican posses. They are just as efficient as drug dealers, more cold-blooded as hit men, and certainly more enterprising as businessmen.

But they are tragically flawed. The weakness that makes them vulnerable is the ego of the individual member. Among black street gangs, there's no loyalty to the gang. Every swaggering one of them hides behind the gang's strength, seduces on the gang's reputation, and gets wealthy on the gang's enterprise. Time and time again, a member will strut his bravado for the homeboys or take someone out for insulting the gang. But get the same one alone, with his ass on the line and no one aware of it but you and him, and he'll sing, sing, sing. The gang is his strength, his identity, his reason for being. Without it, he is nobody. But the gang also puts him in situations the nobody can't handle. And when the gang isn't around to protect him, he shits his drawers, cries and blubbers, begs for mercy, and offers to sell his buddies' lives in return for his own.

Sometimes gang bangers are more than willing to talk because they consider themselves businessmen and they like to boast of their drug-dealing successes. These entrepreneurs have no qualms about ratting on the competition, even if that competition is a member of their own gang. Less competition means more money for them.

There have always been black street gangs. They haven't always been the violent, headline-grabbing punks they are today, but they've always been there, gang banging, doing their thing—robberies, break-ins, hold-ups—whatever it takes to keep a few bucks and a safe in their pockets. Sometimes rival neighborhood groups had fist fights, but rarely a shoot-out. Matters would have stayed that way if history had not conspired to set the gangs on a different path, one that is taking them to the top of the criminal empire and making them the most formidable threat to society, law enforcement, and the underworld.

Gangs and their violence evolved out of the social upheaval and turmoil generated by the convergence of several changes in the decade paradoxically credited with creating the love generation. By the end of the so-called enlightened 1960s, the Vietnam War was at its height, the Civil Rights movement was actively promoting racial tolerance, and black pride was at its fiercest.

The worst harm done to poor, black inner-city kids by the anti-war demonstrations was cancellation of the military draft. Conscription provided these kids with a place to go and something to look forward to. It took them off the street at a critical age—between eighteen and twenty—and provided them with a structured environment and discipline they would otherwise never know. (The gangs only gave them recognition, status, and support, all for the commission of crimes.) The draft also gave them the chance to learn a trade, something they could bring back to their neighborhood or take elsewhere once they were discharged from service. Most of all, it gave them a chance to achieve and to strive for the kinds of goals that television advertisements flaunted daily before their envious eyes.

The two most notorious black street gangs in the world were born in this political and economic climate. Black pride created the Crips and the Bloods.

1969: Gang Banging Hits Its Stride

Between 1955 and 1965, black street gangs mushroomed in south-central Los Angeles and in Compton, as neighborhood youths banded together to fend off other gangs. These gangs restricted their activities to their neighborhoods, and most fights with other gangs occurred in parks, at parties, and at high-school sporting events. Some of these original gangs included the Farmers, Slausons, Huns, Businessmen, Sir Valiants, D'Tagnions, Gladiators, 135s, Roman 20s, Pueblos, Swamps, Orientals, Treetops, and Valiants.

These gangs began to change from 1965 to 1969 as members became more politicized and aware of their color. The idea that "black is beautiful" sank into their inner-city brains and black pride reared its frizzy head in the ghettos of Los Angeles and Compton. The growing perception among gang members that blacks were one against the system found fertile ground for the idea of amalgamating into a huge brotherhood. Although that dream came close to being realized in one sense, the duality of human nature ensured the brotherhood split in two.

The first Crips gang was formed in 1969 at Washington High School in southwest Los Angeles. Within a year, other Crips gangs were formed across south-central Los Angeles and in Compton. The origin of the name Crips remains uncertain, even to gang members. One tale suggests that it was derived from a Vincent Price horror movie called *Tales of the Crypt*. Some say the name was derived from a street gang called Cribs, an offshoot of the Slauson street gang, the largest black street gang in south-central Los Angeles in the 1960s. Some say an original gang member was crippled — a crip. The first Crips did carry canes to identify themselves. Another story says the gang's name was a bastardization of Kryptonite, the only material that could kill Superman.

The Crips adopted the color blue — one of the colors of Washington High School — to identify themselves. Some of their gangs — called sets — wear other colors, such as black, brown, or purple with the blue to identify their particular set. Members wear blue caps, handkerchiefs, belts, or shoelaces. Crips also call each other cuzz, an old black slang term that signifies the speakers are from the same race.

The first Crips gangs were punks who beat up high-school students and neighborhoods kids, extorting and stealing their money. They quickly became known for their violence. Roving bands of Crips wreaked havoc during a concert at the Hollywood Palladium in 1972, stealing expensive jackets off people's backs.

Their viciousness caused the youths in many neighborhoods to band together for protection. One of these gangs was formed on Piru Street in Compton, an area with a long history of gang rivalries with Los Angeles gangs. The Compton Piru became the first Bloods gang in Los Angeles. In calling themselves Bloods, members applied an old black slang expression denoting that they belong to the same race. They adopted the color red to identify themselves. It is also one of the colors of Centennial High School in Compton where the original gang members went to school. Now gangs control all the inner-city schools in Los Angeles.

The Compton Pirus gained such a fierce reputation for fending off the Crips gangs that other gangs, such as the Brims, Bounty Hunters, Swans, and Family, started calling themselves Bloods. However, Bloods gangs from Compton still call themselves Pirus. The Bloods kept the Crips at bay during the 1970s until their numbers dwindled and the Crips drove out many of the Bloods set from the area. Today, Crips outnumber

Bloods three to one in Los Angeles. There are 214 Crips sets and 67 Bloods sets, with 18,000 known gang members.

As word spread about the battles between the two factions, other gangs in south-central Los Angeles took sides and changed their names to reflect blue or red affiliation. Intense rivalries developed between the gangs.

Being in a street gang is like being on stage—members have to continually project a tough, bad image. They are the ultimate macho men. Most of the violence is directed at other gangs. The Crips, however, are notorious for fighting among themselves, something the Bloods don't do. Bloods come from middle-class neighborhoods and act differently. They're more laid-back, less rambunctious, and just as deadly.

And because the Crips and Bloods are relatively young gangs without tradition, there is little individual loyalty to the colors. The black gang member considers himself number one and the gang and homeboys number two. Hispanics, whose gangs have generations of tradition, see their gang as number one, themselves as number two, and homeboys in third place.

1975: Gang Rivalry – Them Boys Got Lead In Their Pants

"The rivalry began to develop and in 1975, they began shooting each other," said Commander Hourie Taylor of the Compton Police Department. "This violence was a reincarnation of what they saw on television. They imitated the mystique of the Mafia in the 1930s, where gangsters shoot at each other off the running boards of cars. The gangs developed drive-by shootings to imitate this."

Taylor grew up in the streets of Compton and knows what he's talking about. He is one of the most respected and able street gang investigators in the world. His appearance is deceptive. He's a bit plump and laid-back and walks with a limp. But he's sharp as a razor and quicker than a viper. When he calls to a Crip gang member selling drugs on a street corner, "You, boy, come'ere," the dealer does not hesitate to obey. Gang bangers respect people who are tougher than they are.

By 1975, rumbles were a thing of the past for the Crips and Bloods. They took their violence to the extreme. The Compton courthouse is a daily reminder of that violence. Numerous drive-by shootings at judges have prompted officials to paint its windows black to prevent passers-by from seeing into the building.

"The sad thing about the gang violence," Taylor said, "is that it was a minority inner-city problem and the powers that be didn't do anything about it. They allowed it to grow as long as it stayed in the inner city.

Then, on January 28, 1988, in Westwood [near the University of California in Los Angeles], a woman was killed. She was upper-middle-class white and Jewish. Karen Toshima was caught in the crossfire between two rival gangs. Then the media blitzed the world with the story that Los Angeles had a gang problem. No one bothered to point out that this problem has existed since 1969. All of a sudden, money started being allocated for enforcement. Los Angeles County geared up for the war on gang violence. More probation and parole officers were hired."

The nineteen-year head start given the black street gangs made it possible for them to build a power base that guarantees law enforcement cannot conquer them. There were 287 gang-related murders in Los Angeles County in 1986. The motives ranged from a gang member not liking someone to retaliating against another gang or neighborhood for an insult. In 1987, there were 387 such murders; in 1988, 452; in 1989, 572. And that's the year assault rifles were banned. In 1990, the toll was well over 600.

"The media did a disservice by saying the shootings were related to drugs and the crack war," Taylor said. "Most of the violence was related to gang activity, not drugs. Gangs sold cocaine in their own areas. So, if a gang wanted to shoot a rival gang, they went to where they sold cocaine."

This is a fine distinction but an important one. In other words, the killings would continue even if the flow of drugs was stopped. The gangs themselves must be stopped. Drugs have simply allowed the gangs to expand and by now it may be too late to control let alone destroy them.

Gang violence escalated quickly from fists to Uzis. The high death toll reflects the increased sophistication of the weapons used by Crips and Bloods. They no longer use homemade zip guns, Saturday-night specials, or sawed-off shotguns. The prestige of gang members, and the amount of respect they are accorded, is measured by the types of weapons they pack—large caliber handguns and semi-automatic rifles, preferably AK-47 assault rifles with banana clips that allow them to spray thirty to forty .223-caliber bullets within seconds. The odds of missing someone with a gun like that are pretty slim.

Hate is an attitude among gangsters. A gang member will shoot someone just to maintain his tough guy image. There are so many victims of gang shootings in Los Angeles that US Army doctors train twenty-four hours a day in the emergency room of Martin Luther King–Drew Medical Center in Watts, where they treat gunshot wounds usually seen in war zones. The hospital gets more than 100 shooting cases a month beyond knifing, beating, and chain-whipping victims.

Getting caught on rival gang turf can be fatal. A black youth from New York was visiting relatives in Los Angeles in 1976. His car broke down.

He got out. A gang of Bloods walked by and asked him where he was from. He told them the east coast. They killed him thinking he was an East Coast Crip.

A black college student returned to Fairfax High in Los Angeles to visit former teachers in the mid-1980s. He used a phone not knowing it was the Crips' dope phone. They told him to get off and he told them to screw off. The Crips shot him.

A Crip drove to a Blood neighborhood to retaliate for an insult. He pulled a bandanna over his face, pulled up beside a Blood, and misfired three times. The Blood pulled out his own gun and shot the Crip twice in the head.

Patricia Tawana Thomas was all of fourteen and a member of the 118th Street East Coast Crips, the largest Crips gang in California. Her best friend, a thirteen-year-old, was also a Crip. The young teens were having a little tiff over a mutual boyfriend when Thomas quit the Crips and joined the Bloods. The thirteen-year-old wasn't going to take that. She got herself a piece on June 2, 1989, and stood outside Thomas's house, telling passers-by she was "gonna smoke" the girl. She shot her point-blank and later boasted to gang members that she had killed a "Swan"—a Blood.

Dashin Dan—not his real name—followed his brother into the Los Angeles East Coast Crips set when he was twelve. He later joined the Grape Street Watts Crips. When he described his gang history during a long night in July 1990, he was twenty-five years old, six feet one inch tall, and weighed 230 pounds. He had moved away from his neighborhood and didn't gang bang any more, though he would have to if asked. He claimed to have served time for a murder he did not commit.

A check with California and FBI officials showed he was also arrested by the Los Angeles sheriff's office for narcotics possession. The charge was dismissed.

"When you get courted in, you have to fight an OG [original gangster]," Dashin Dan said. "If you get hit and start crying, you don't get in. The gangs started not only in high school but in elementary school.

"They're weak today. Drive-bys, ha. We used to walk up to somebody to take care of them. We went after each other just to see who could be the best, who could be the biggest.

"You're never out, especially if you put in work—you rob, you kill. That's how you move up. Your enemies never forget; your gang members don't either. Even though I've moved away [to southwest Los Angeles], the gang can ask me to do things. Leaving is like going A.W.O.L."

Although police officials say black street gangs have no official hierarchy, gang bangers claim that sets are ruled by a godfather.

"If the godfather says take this person out, you do it," said Dashin
Dan. "If you don't do it, then you get taken out. If the godfather wants
war, you have war. The Inglewood Family [Bloods] was growing fast
and taking over people's territory. We had to put a stop to that. The
godfather called a meeting and declared war. This was in 1978-79. I've
never seen so much blow. The police put an end to it, but the Bloods lost
hold in Compton.

"Coming from the outside, you'd have trouble understanding how and
why people join gangs. Everybody got their reasons. A lot of people
grow up into it. Their brother, sister, were members. Women members
wear colors, too. Some of them will come up to you with a gun and take
your money."

About police efforts to curb gang banging: "They'll never stop cocaine on the streets. They'll never stop gangs. Gangs are not set up like
the mob, but they're organized. Some gang members join the mob. Some
OGs get taken on by the mob as killers. Some people from the gangs get
smart, make money, and take over territories. Even without drugs, gangs
would still be gangs.

"I went to jail for murder. [He said he spent eighteen months in jail.] I
didn't do it. I could have been killed if I didn't take the rap. I got let out
after a detective scared a kid against testifying against the real killer. I had
to do work in jail because I was an OG. When I was let out, I was put in a
halfway house for six to twelve months because they said I had a prison
attitude."

Dashin Dan said Crips and Bloods wore their colors in prison. They
do indeed, and the black street gangs are on the verge of becoming a
major force among prison gangs.

To Be Or Not To Be Cool

The Crips and Bloods have so influenced black street gangs in Los
Angeles that the only distinction between the thousands of black gang
bangers today is blue and red. The Crips and Bloods are broken down
into sets denoting neighborhood factions of the gang. Some are affiliated
in geographical groups, such as the Compton Crips, Hoover Crips, East
Coast Crips, or Rollin' Sets—Rollin' 30s, Rollin' 60s.

Some of the Crips sets are Acacia Crips, Compton Crips, East Coast
Crips, Fronthood Crips, Ghost Town Crips, Harbor City Crips, Main
Street Crips, Payback Crips, Raymond Crips, Rollin' 20s, Rollin' 30s,
Rollin' 60s, Bible Crips, Dodge City Crips, Eight Tray Gangsters, 43
Gangster Crips, Grape Street Watts Crips, Insane Crips, Original
Valley Gangster, Playboy Crips.

Some of the Bloods sets are Athen Park Boys, Bounty Hunters, Black P-Stone, Brim Sets, 89 Family Blood, Inglewood Family Blood, Outlaws, Cedar Block Piru, Leuder Park Piru, Rollin' 30s Piru, Ujima Village Blood, Bishop Sets, Bloodstone Villains, Blood Fives, Denver Lane Sets, Harvard Park, Miller Gangsters, Compton Piru, Cross Atlantic Piru, Lime Hood Piru, Main Street Swans, Van Ness Gangsters.

Black street gangs have little formal structure. They are made up of hardcores, associates, and peripherals. Hardcores are full-fledged gang members who wear the colors and commit crimes with the gang; associates hang out with the gang in the neighborhood but don't participate in gang activities; peripherals use the gang for protection. The latter are mostly women.

There are three or four distinct groups within a gang. Original gangsters (OGs) are older gang members; gangsters are hardcores between the ages of sixteen and twenty-two; baby gangsters are gang members between the ages of nine and twelve; some gangs also have tiny gangsters who are even younger. Although some gang members claim their group is run by a godfather, most are run by the richest or most violent members. They are called the shot callers. Older members always use younger members to sell drugs or kill people. Younger members are more than willing to prove they are worthy of belonging to the gang.

These gang bangers take on nicknames that reflect the way they see themselves, or sometimes how others see them: C-Bone, Gangster, T-Loc, Tone Bone, Fat Melvin, Yell, Rabbit, Q-Ball, Dre-Dog, Killer Wayne, Mikey Ru, Snake, Big Mike, Playboy. Every gang banger wants to be a cool dude like Mr. T, Run-D.M.C., LL Cool J, M.C. Hammer, or Tone Loc. Those who don't brag about their successes with women or drug dealing boast that they are ruthless and deadly: Killer Kev, Crazy Ed, Psycho Paul. They like posing for the camera sporting the latest expensive fashions — Fila, Nike, Gucci — and load themselves down with heavy gold jewelry.

"Clothing manufacturers have started to cash in on this situation," Commander Taylor said. "Fila, who used to make an all-white tennis shoe that had three white stripes on the side of it, or white striping, now make multiple-color running shoes. They make all white, they make a blue and white, and they make a red and white. These kids wear them. Now you can't tell me clothing manufacturers don't know what they're doing.

"These are a pair of tennis shoes. Their brand name is British Knights. But the logo that the manufacturer uses on the side of the shoe is BK — Blood Killer. Kids are getting killed over colors on tennis shoes in Los Angeles!"

Drug dealers set fashion trends. They have the cash to buy clothing that most black kids can only dream of. And they can afford to toss it out as soon as something new comes along. Many drooling kids turn to drug dealing just to be able to dress like their neighborhood heroes. The drug dealers even outfit their runners with the freshest running shoes. One Boston sports clothing store reputedly calls in drug dealers over their beepers to show them the latest in styles as they arrive.

Gang bangers also have a style of dress called saggin' and raggin': pants slung low on the hips so the crack of the ass shows, and a colored bandanna—rag—stuck into a hip pocket. They also like to wear belts with the initials CK (Crip Killer) or BK (Blood Killer) on the buckle.

"The Latinos wear their pants somewhere up around their Adam's apple," said Deputy Rolland Garcia of the Los Angeles Police Department. "The Latinos cover their face with their fly. To blow their nose they have to pull [the] fly down. ... For blacks it's OK to show off half your butt. But it's not OK to show your whole butt covered by the pants. You wear it halfway off your ass. To wear your pants like normal human beings is homosexuality. Normal people don't wear their pants so low unless they want to give it up."

Bloods wear Cincinnati Reds baseball caps and put a slash through the C to show disrespect for Crips, or they add a K after the C. Sometimes they put CM187 on the cap: Crip Murderer—187 is the homicide section of the California penal code. Crips wear blue Seattle Mariners caps.

Crips wear Dallas Cowboy jackets. Bloods wear Washington Redskin jackets. The Lime Hood Piru set likes to wear lime-colored clothing. The Grape Street Watts Crips like the color purple. They also adore Prince because of his song "All My Purple Life." More discreet gangsters will show gang affiliation with a red or blue comb or key chain. Some position their fingers on plastic key chains to demonstrate their gang hand sign.

Gangsters who have been stopped by police for their telltale clothing now understand it may pay to advertise if you're attracting customers or intimidating competitors, but it's not so smart to let the heat in on the secret.

Police must use their judgment when stopping a black person who dresses like a gang member. A person is not a drug dealer because he is black, drives a BMW, and wears gold chains. One cop who didn't use common sense stopped LeVar Burton, who starred in "Roots," and jacked him around because he was driving a BMW and wearing a blue bandanna.

Drug-dealing gang bangers like to be flashy in other ways, too. They like expensive cars with costly tires, wheels, and cellular telephones—all the flamboyant accoutrements they know babes really dig. They come across as real bigtime players. They tattoo their bodies with Playboy bunnies, money signs, or bags of money. And they have names such as Money Mike, Player, or Gold Dog. They'll also tell anyone who'll listen that they are very much in demand with sweeties because they have big dicks. Don't you believe it, baby.

A black female rap group called Bytches with Problems has a song called "Two Minute Brother." A member of the group said in an interview in October 1990 that the song is about black dudes who boast of being great in bed, when all they've got is two inches that lasts no longer than two minutes. Tell it, sister.

Graffiti

Like other street gangs, black street gangs use graffiti to communicate between themselves and with other gangs. Through graffiti, they pass on messages, friendly or hostile, to show respect for the dead, and to mark territory. They spray walls just as dogs piss on fire hydrants. The graffiti is crude and not very artistic, unlike the elaborate scrawls and drawings of Hispanic gangs. The lettering is often backwards, and depending whether the graffiti is Bloods or Crips the letter C or B will have a slash through it to show disrespect for the rival gang.

Graffiti also reflects gang bangers' egocentric attitudes. Crips and Blood graffiti starts with the name of the writer in large letters, followed by the gang's name or initials in smaller letters. They might include the names of one or two homies beneath in even smaller letters.

Hand Signs

Gang bangers throw signs—communicate with hand signals—to identify each other and to challenge rival gangs. Each set has its particular sign.

They don't always know what the signs mean, although they're willing to flash them to impress people. Members of one Chicago gang driving by a bus stop shot and killed a blind man communicating with sign language. They mistook his gestures for the hand signs of a rival gang.

Tattoos

The difference between Hispanic and black gang tattoos, besides the artistry, is that Hispanics will never put enemy names on their bodies the way black do. Hispanics would rather go into an enemy's neighborhood and slash their own names on the enemy's arm. Black tattoos are crude mainly because ornate ones don't show up well on black skin; they have to be large and simple to be seen. Favorite tattoos among black gangsters are dollar signs, money bags, and Playboy bunnies, all of which mean: I'm a player. I'm a high roller. I've got it going on. I've got a lot of freaks [women].

These are some expressions used by black street gang members:

-base head: cocaine smoker
-be down for my friends: willing to gang bang, help fellow gangsters
-bucket: older car
-buckets: shotgun or small-caliber handgun
-bullit: one year in county jail
-bumpin' titties: fighting
-buster: a wannabe gangster
-busting fresh: wearing the latest fashions
-cheese toes: a derogatory term for Crips
-chill out: stop doing something
-chillin': hanging around
-cholo: Hispanic gang banger
-cluck: cocaine smoker
-courted in: the beating given a prospective member to see if he has what it takes to gang bang; also called jumped in
-crab: derogatory term for Crip
-crumbs: tiny pieces of rock cocaine
-cuzz: slang for Crip
-D: drugs
-dime: one-tenth ounce of cocaine
-dog city: working hard for money
-do-rag: the bandanna that shows gang affiliation—blue for Crip, red for Blood
-drive by: shooting someone from a vehicle
-deuce, deuce: .22-caliber gun
-eight-ball: one-eighth ounce of cocaine
-ends: money
-E-Rickets: derogatory term for Bloods
-flashing: decked out in tons of jewelry à la Mr. T
-freak: pretty girl
-fresh: latest style, something new
-gauge: shotgun
-gang banging: fighting, shooting, committing crimes with the gang
-gang warden: cop
-gat: gun
-get jumped: when an initiate stands in a circle of homies and fights a gang member
-get with him/her: either fight or meet someone

-got it good: has lots of drugs
-got it goin' on: engaged in illegal activity
-g-ride: stolen car
-happy stick: marijuana cigarette laced with PCP
-hittin' up: painting graffiti
-homeboys, homies: fellow gang members
-hood: neighborhood
-hoo rah: loud talking
-hubba: rock cocaine
-hubba whore: woman who fucks for rock cocaine
-in the mix: involved in gang activity
-jam: getting frisked by cop for guns
-Jim Jones: marijuana cigarette laced with cocaine and dipped in PCP
-kibbles and bits: tiny pieces of rock cocaine
-kickin' it: taking it easy
-lit up: shoot at somebody
-loc: loco/Crip
-lok: loco/Blood
-love: rock cocaine
-mission: criminal activity, contract hit
-mobile freak: an extremely pretty girl
-911: warning that cops are near
-OG: original gangster
-187: California penal code section for murder (a graffiti favorite)
-one hitter quitter: crack soaked in PCP
-one time: warning that cops are in the area
-ooze: any automatic gun
-played out: over, no longer used
-players: dudes who've got it going on—cash, wheels, and babes
-put 'em in check: discipline someone
-put in some work: do a shooting
-puffer: cocaine smoker
-rag: a colored bandanna showing gang affiliation
-ragging: wearing the rag, usually in back pocket
-ranking: denying gang affiliation
-raspberry: a female who takes anything for sex
-rock: crack cocaine
-rock star: a cocaine prostitute
-roll 'em up: arrested, forced out of scene
-rollers: gangsters who have done well in the drug business
-rollin' good: selling drugs
-saggin': wearing pants low to expose underwear or crack of ass
-set: gang

-sherms: Brown Sherman (cigarette) dipped in embalming fluid
-shotcaller: person in charge
-sidewalk servers: crack dealers who sell to customers in cars
-six-pack: a police line-up
-slingers: street pushers
-slobs: derogatory term for Bloods
-sloops: derogatory term for Crips
-smoker: rock cocaine user
-snaps: money
-space base: PCP, rock cocaine
-speedball: cocaine and heroin
-strawberry: blow job for cocaine
-stuffing: hiding dope, usually during a bust
-sup: what's up, what's going on
-taken out: shot or beaten
-toss up: girl used for sex
-to the curb: broke, no money or drugs
-tray eight: .38-caliber revolver
-tweaker: a cocaine user
-under cover: plain car
-uzi: term for any semi-automatic gun
-victor: stolen car, from police code 1029 Victor

Crips don't say words starting with the letter B, and Bloods don't say words starting with the letter C. Crips will say canana instead of banana. Bloods say bigarette instead of cigarette, Bompton rather than Compton. They even have Bompton put on their driver's licences.

North America's materialistic society measures success not by the amount of good you do, but by the amount of money you make. Inner-city kids looked around and saw that the reality portrayed on television was not their world. They had no money, no big cars, no swimming pools, no hot white blondes crawling over them—and no prospect of ever getting employment that would make those things possible.

Then they saw their drug-dealing buddies down the street flaunting wealth no inner-city kid imagined possible. They had cars, women, and good times. The kids also saw drugs in the White House, drugs in professional sport, drugs on Wall Street. So they started selling drugs. They justified it by giving money to mom. And they know the prison system is so overcrowded they wouldn't get much of a sentence if caught, especially for a first offence.

1982: The White Powder Boom

The Crips and the Bloods, who had been selling marijuana and PCP, started dealing drugs in a big way to cater to the unprecedented hunger for cocaine that started gnawing at the nostrils of North American dopers in 1982. Not since the heady mid-1960s, when the booming market for hallucinogens in San Francisco offered the Hell's Angels the opportunity to fatten their coffers on the way to becoming major players in the criminal underworld, had any group been given such a chance to climb out of its rut.

The Crips and the Bloods started dealing all the cocaine they could get their hands on. Most of it was sold in their neighborhoods. The one thing they didn't do was use it. They may have smoked a little grass themselves, but gang bangers knew cocaine enslaved its users. And becoming a slave is not something that a proud, black gang banger wants to do. These guys see themselves as hustlers, players, people who make their mark in the world. They can't have that kind of image if they do drugs—just if they sell them.

Crips and Bloods have become so successful as drug dealers that they have by-passed the white middlemen and now deal directly with Colombians for their cocaine. The Colombians, who detest whites but have been forced to deal with white middlemen, are more than happy to deal with the blacks. Cutting out the middleman has also cut the price of cocaine on the street. The US Drug Enforcement Administration and local law-enforcement agencies in Florida and California ran a two-year money-laundering sting operation called "Operation Pisces II" in the mid-1980s to identify smugglers and dealers. Cops who operated a fake money-laundering operation videotaped a conversation between two Colombian smugglers talking about a black dealer in Florida.

"That s.o.b., he just ordered and ordered; it was hard to keep him stocked," one Colombian said.

"Those blacks are really the best ones," said his buddy.

PCP is a more profitable drug than cocaine and has become more popular since the Colombians started holding back and warehousing cocaine in 1990 to drive the price up. The price of cocaine in Los Angeles went from $300 to $600 to $900 an ounce during the first six months of 1990. The shortage prompted gang bangers to cut cocaine with procaine, which causes chest pains when smoked.

Ethnic groups in Los Angeles differ in their choice of drugs. Blacks prefer cocaine, heroin, and marijuana. Hispanics use PCP and marijuana. Whites prefer hallucinogens. Blacks won't get into dealing ice, which is smokeable crank, because they aren't big on hallucinogens and because ice and crank keep the customer stoned too long. Black dealers want their customers to come back every ten or fifteen minutes.

The advent of rock cocaine (known as crack in the east) in California in 1984, and the rapid spread of the recipe to make it, proved to be the catalyst that turned the Crips and Bloods into underworld contenders.

Even the slowest gang banger was quick to realize that more money could be made selling rock than robbing banks. And the risk of getting caught or shot was less. Within years, the Crips and Bloods could boast multi-millionaires in their ranks. One gang banger under investigation in 1990 was worth about $20 million.

"I talked to a lawyer," said Commander Taylor of the Compton Police Department. "I asked him about a particular client of his. He said, 'Well, this is privileged communication, so I'll tell you.' I said, 'How much is your client worth?' He said, 'Ten million dollars.' The kid is twenty-seven years old.

"There are a lot of individuals like that. They're paying these lawyers $50-60,000 cash. They're putting them on large retainers — $50-75,000 a year. The money is there. These guys are getting smart and starting to invest their money. They're taking their money and buying property, buying vehicles, and putting it in other people's names. They're learning to hide their money and they're doing it well. We seem to think that they are just a group of dumb kids, but over the last three, four, five years, they've started to become more sophisticated."

A manuscript seized from a Crips set details how the gang should better organize itself to make money. "Power in this society is money, so the sword we must possess is money.... We must adopt a business mentality." If anything, the manuscript indicates that black street gangs are not only an organized crime group but a serious threat to other drug traffickers.

Rock cocaine has been for the black Crips and Bloods in the 1980s what Prohibition alcohol was to Italian gangsters in the 1920s. Like La Cosa Nostra, black criminals from Los Angeles neighborhoods made so much money selling drugs that they spread across the United States and into Canada to expand their market. But there are two notable differences between La Cosa Nostra and the Crips and Bloods: these two black gangs have 18,000 members as opposed to La Cosa Nostra's estimated 2,000; and they are much more violent than the mob.

In fact, black street gangs have accumulated enough money, savvy, and experience that they are operating as an organized crime group that could easily overshadow traditional organized crime within ten years. Drugs have given them the opportunity to escape the ghetto. Now they're ready to take on the world.

1985: On The Road

Two factors forced many Crip and Blood gang bangers to expand their drug operations beyond Los Angeles; by 1985, stiff competition in Los

Angeles had driven down the price of cocaine. The increase in gang shootings made it dangerous for rock dealers to walk up to a car of potential customers; they could be rival gang members luring them into a shooting.

In 1982-83, a gram of cocaine in Los Angeles sold for $125, an ounce for $1,000, and a kilo for $30-40,000. By 1989, a gram sold for $30. A kilo could be had for $11-15,000. Los Angeles was snowed under by a glut of cocaine. This is good for the consumer, bad for the seller. The heat was also becoming intolerable from both cops and ripoff artists who made a living holding up rock dealers.

The more enterprising young dealers decided to pack up and set up shop elsewhere. Los Angeles has no shortage of drug dealers. About 10 to 15 percent of the 18,000 Crips and Bloods sell drugs. That's 1,800 to 2,700 dealers. And that's only the black street gangs. Think about the dealers from other organized crime groups as well as the entrepreneurs. There are 650 street gangs in the Los Angeles area with a membership of 70,000 to 80,000.

Police in the inner city also put the heat on customers to reduce curbside drug sales. Curbs were painted red to prevent parking. Pay phones were removed from street corners. Remaining phones were re-wired to allow outgoing calls only. Dealers could no longer call each other over pay phones.

Setting up a drug operation in another city offered gang bangers several advantages over dealing in Los Angeles. The police in other cities didn't have a clue who they were and how they operated. The police also weren't as aggressive in trying to shut down their operations. The price of cocaine was still high in these cities compared to Los Angeles. Gang bangers were looked up to by kids in other cities who had heard about them through the media. And it was a real thrill for a fifteen-year-old who had never been out of Compton in his life to fly out of state and triple his money with little effort.

The first LA gangsters to hit the road traveled 500 miles north on Interstate 5. They belonged to the Shotgun Crips, Santana Block Crips, 107th Hoover Street Crips, Playboy Style Crips, and the Van Ness Gangsters (Bloods). They looked like any other Los Angeles gang-sters—male blacks fourteen to twenty-four years old; no identification; temporary driver's license; false name; short hair or jeri curls; Fila, British Knights, or Troop tennis shoes; matching jogging suit; 501 Levis or blue, gray, or brown corduroys; Dickies brand cotton work pants; a national sports team jacket and cap; gold neck chains; pager; cellular phone; Louis Vuitton belt, wallet, bags, and hat; snakeskin belt.

Los Angeles gangsters targeted Sacramento, the capital of California, as

the first city into which they would expand in 1985. A gram of cocaine
that sold for $30 in Los Angeles went for $100 in Sacramento. An ounce
of cocaine that cost $300 to $500 in Los Angeles sold for $2,800 only
500 miles north. Crips and Bloods hopped on a Greyhound bus for $28
at 11 p.m., arrived in Sacramento at 6 a.m., sold their dope, and returned
to Los Angeles the same day. Fifteen-year-old kids flew into the city for
$49 on a turnaround flight with $300 of rock cocaine that they sold for
$2,800 and returned home the same day with a $2,451 profit.

The success of US Customs interdiction efforts in southern Florida is
one reason the price of cocaine dropped so drastically in Los Angeles in
1985. Colombians avoided Florida as much as possible and found new
smuggling routes into the country—they were really old heroin and
marijuana routes that led into California. The Colombians put so much
cocaine into the Los Angeles market at cheap prices that they created an
unprecedented demand for the drug, mostly from people who couldn't
afford it at higher prices.

Gang bangers who fled the crazy Los Angeles market used Sacramento as a springboard. They learned how to sell dope in a new town,
how to make money, and how to get along with other gangs. Los Angeles
dealers who infiltrated Sacramento stood side by side with local dealers
selling a rock of crack (hubba on the street) for $20 and undercut them by
doubling up—selling two rocks for the same price.

Sacramento dealers eventually found themselves unemployed. The
LA gang bangers got them strung out on crack, then hired them to sell
their rocks. Then they'd make the Sacramento dealers' old ladies rock
stars; they'd turn tricks in rock houses. Los Angeles gang bangers had it
easy in Sacramento. The local dealers just couldn't compete with the
street-wise LA boys.

Gangsters quickly set up Los Angeles-style rock houses, with
wrought-iron bars barricading the inside of windows and doors so
people on the outside couldn't tell the houses were fortified. They
locked sellers inside so they wouldn't split with the dope and money,
while they returned to the safety of their motel rooms. Gang bangers are
considerate, though. They brought the sellers food and more drugs when
they picked up the money.

The Los Angeles Crips and Bloods drug dealers who moved their
businesses to Sacramento used different techniques to infiltrate the city.
Some took over streets and houses. Others flew their colors to advertise
and intimidate. The more violent went into apartment complexes in
black, low-income areas, painted their graffiti on walls, and sprayed
them with machine guns to let people know they were there to do
business. Residents didn't turn to the police for fear of being shot. Then
the gang bangers hooked up with welfare mothers and made them into

hubba mothers and rock stars, turning tricks and selling rock in their apartments. They also made their thirteen-year-old kids sell crack in the streets.

One dealer, DW, paid one kid $100 a day to sell one ounce of crack while the dealer made $2,800 on the sales. The kid loved the dealer because he had given him a pager—a status symbol. DW controlled five to eight women in each of five housing complexes. It's easy to do. He got the women strung out on rock cocaine and he hooked the kids with money.

Los Angeles gang bangers also got into Sacramento (and later into other cities) by visiting relatives and using their homes as a base for their operations. When the relatives saw the money pour in, they even offered to use their names to rent pagers for the dealers. Dealers wore expensive clothes to show the community they had money and could make money for them. They left business cards with phone numbers and symbols such as dollar signs or Playboy bunnies.

> Have heart have $ – Jughead – Rolling 60
> beeper # ....

Dealers approached elderly people with fixed incomes and offered them $50 to $100 a day to use their houses to sell rock cocaine. Many Los Angeles gang fugitives also used Sacramento as a hideout.

Danny (Big Dog) Torres and Chris (Buckwheat) Kuntz are the two Sacramento narcotics squad detectives who first noticed in 1986 that Los Angeles Crips and Bloods drug dealers were setting up shop in their city.

"We started seeing a pattern and we contacted out-of-state agencies," Kuntz said. "Other states had some problems, but they thought it was isolated incidents. We realized the problem was going to go nationwide. But we had trouble convincing agencies to let us teach them how the problem is growing. We had to teach narcs on our own time at conferences. They gave us half an hour and we ended up speaking for two hours at the California Narcotics Officers Association convention. We told a cop from Hawaii they'll have problems because of the transient black population. He said no way. This was in 1987. Five months later, he called from Hawaii because a narc had been blown away by a Crip."

Torres and Kuntz, along with Commander Taylor and Deputy Garcia, have a traveling road show to teach cops about Crips and Bloods drug dealers.

"As far as black gangs are concerned," said Kuntz, "all they lack is running boards on cars. They are real gangsters. They've replaced the Thompson machine gun with AK-47s and MAC-11s."

There were eighteen drive-by shootings in fifteen days in Sacramento in 1987 involving Los Angeles gangsters and local Crips and Bloods. This brought so much heat down on the gangs that the LA boys decided to leave the gang banging at home and concentrate on making money, which is so much more important than gang affiliation that LA Crips now supply Sacramento Bloods with drugs.

Crips and Bloods are now dealing rock cocaine and PCP in Phoenix, Las Vegas, Seattle, Portland, Denver, Cleveland, Houston, Dallas, Chicago, Vancouver, and Anchorage, and in the states of Louisiana, Maryland, New Mexico, Nevada, Oklahoma, Utah, and Hawaii.

One thirty-year-old Sacramento dealer got probation after being convicted of possessing one pound of rock cocaine in 1990. He was later arrested in Kansas City, Missouri, with four kilos of cocaine and a 9mm pistol. He was sentenced to thirty years, but escaped. Then he was caught with thirty kilos of cocaine.

Crips setting up rock houses in western New York state brought in homeboys from Los Angeles to provide muscle for their operation when local drug dealers balked in the late 1980s. The hitters sprayed lead from Buffalo to Cheektowaga to intimidate opponents of the Crips drug network. By the summer of 1990, the Crips were well entrenched in the western part of upper New York state and had crossed the border into Canada to set up rock houses in Fort Erie, Ontario.

Most gang bangers follow the same procedure when shipping cocaine to Sacramento for their rock houses. They travel in convoys of three cars—two or three persons to a car, with a woman holding the dope—late at night when there are fewer California Highway Patrol and County Sheriff cars on the road. The first car is a "Ma and Pa" car, a nondescript junker that carries the dope. It is followed by a chase car. If a police car pulls up behind the Ma and Pa car, the chase car blows by them and picks up a citation. Not that it matters. Gang bangers have fake TDLs (temporary driver's licenses) that don't require photographs, so they can't be traced. If the cop doesn't go after the chase car, the third car in the convoy—the weapons car—takes him out.

The convoy usually pulls off at one of the first three exits coming into Sacramento: Mack Road, Florin Road, or 47th Avenue. They stay at the nearest motel. Gang bangers are creatures of habit and if something has worked for them once, they keep doing it.

They are also getting smarter at smuggling their dope following some well-publicized seizures. A Barstow, California, cop stopped a car that had not turned on its lights after leaving a gas station. The driver looked like a typical black Los Angeles drug dealer—gold chains, pager, cellular phone—so the police officer asked if he could search the car. The driver told him to go ahead, that he'd be using a rental car if he were smuggling drugs. The cop found seven kilos of cocaine in the back seat.

Police in Fairfield, California, found 3.25 pounds of rock cocaine, an AR-15 assault rifle, $5,000 in cash, and four LA boys in a Suzuki Samurai in a motel parking lot. Once again, habit had tipped their hand. In 1986, dealers preferred BMWs, S10 Blazers, and El Caminos. In 1987, they drove Camaro Iroc Zs, red or blue. In 1988, their vehicles of choice were the Suzuki Samurai, the 5.0-liter Mustang convertible, and the Cavalier Z24.

Many dealers now ship drugs by courier services to avoid having their cars seized. Sometimes, especially when they ship drugs over state lines to cities such as Tacoma or Seattle, dealers put the drugs on a bus, which they follow by car. They pick up the drugs at the depot.

After too many seizures, smugglers started hiding cocaine in false containers: fake Coke cans, fake 12-volt car batteries, phoney heads of lettuce that screwed open, fake rocks, fake cans of Penzoil, hollowed-out flares. They also hid drugs in the cross members of trunk lids, inside tires, inside door panels, in air-conditioning vents, and, since rock cocaine is not water soluble, in the radiator water return container. They carried guns in the engine compartment or in welded boxes under the car.

Detective Danny Torres filed an affidavit for a judge explaining the gang problem in Sacramento. Within one week, it was printed in the local newspaper, describing the profile of a typical Los Angeles gang banger drug dealer: Fila running shoes, colors, gold ropes around the neck (Mr. T starter sets), and pagers. One month later, Torres and his partner, Detective Chris Kuntz, stopped a car pulling out of a motel. The black driver, who didn't have a driver's license, was trying to hide his pager under the front seat.

"Where's your gold ropes?" Kuntz asked.

"They're in my shoes."

"Why are they in your shoes?"

"I heard you cops are looking for gold jewelry around our necks and now we carry them in our shoes when we're moving on the street."

Dealers who make it to a motel are easy to spot. They pay cash, rent several rooms at the back, refuse maid service (so she doesn't see their scales, powder cocaine, and rocks), register a Sacramento address with a Los Angeles zip code, make phone calls to LA, and order Domino's pizza (cops have followed several deliveries to Los Angeles drug dealers). There is much vehicle traffic and foot traffic to the rooms and a lot of phone calls come in as orders are placed for rock cocaine to be sent to rock houses. The dealers sleep in one room, deal out of another, and keep their drugs in a third, separate room.

Dealers who arrive in Sacramento by plane also have peculiar habits. They sit in the middle or back half of the plane and are last to disembark. They always look around to see if they're being followed. They'll stop for a drink of water and look back. Then they deke into a washroom and pull the dope out of their pants because it's damn uncomfortable. One dealer was so nervous when Detective Kuntz stopped him at the Sacramento airport that he dropped his drawers in front of 200 people when asked if he could be searched. Then in the washroom, he handed his coat to Kuntz and said, "That ain't my coat." Kuntz found 2.5 ounces of rock cocaine in the pocket.

"We lie to these guys," Detective Torres said. "When we stop them at the airport, we tell them we work for LAPD. Some of us here have LA County sheriff's hats. And we tell them there's fifty of us assigned to the airport task force only because we know they're coming to Sacramento. Well, the word gets back.... When we do them, we tell them we don't like them. They take your kindness for weakness. And we try not to let them see too much kindness."

Kuntz and Torres don't pull punches when busting rock houses or dealers in motels. They used to turn off water service to the buildings one hour before they raided so dealers couldn't flush the dope down the toilet. Now dealers keep a tap running. When the water stops, they know a raid is going down.

One rock house dealer flushed a plastic bag full of rock cocaine down the toilet before the police got to him. They took the pipes apart and found that the air in the bag had made it float so it got stuck. Kuntz and Torres use the okey-doke technique to prevent dealers in motel rooms from flushing their coke down the toilet. They call the room and tip the dealers off that the cops are coming. The dealers run out and hide the dope under the watchful eyes of the two detectives.

Los Angeles cops don't take any bullshit when they deal with Crips and Bloods. When a cop stops them, these suckers have learned to put their hands and feet on the ceiling of the car. In fact, that's one way Sacramento cops identify LA gangsters—when they pull them over, the feet and hands go up automatically.

There are 15 million people in southern California, 20,000 cops, and 80,000 black, white, Latino, and Asian gangsters in more than 600 gangs. The cops are outnumbered by a group that makes up less than one-tenth of the population, yet it is responsible for a large percentage of crimes.

Arresting gangsters doesn't stop gang banging. It just provides a different kind of victim for the gangs.

"These individuals are extremely predatory," said Deputy Garcia. "They do not stop their activity in custody."

There are 24,000 prisoners in the Los Angeles County jail system's six prisons. Many prisons have 8,000 inmates crammed into a facility built for 5,000. "That type of scenario is the perfect one for these people to prey on other inmates," Garcia said. "Five to six years ago our crime rate was disproportionately high. Gangs made up 17 to 20 percent of inmates, but were responsible for 70 percent of crimes. Inmates were getting raped, robbed, assaulted, and extorted. They threw a guy off a tier. He didn't want to pay one week. Five dollars. They threw him off a tier."

Crips and Bloods sued Los Angeles County for keeping gang bangers apart in prison. They won and the gangs are now kept together in two wings reserved for them in the Los Angeles County Jail where they wear their colors behind bars.

Rules and Regulations for Dealing

Los Angeles Crips who moved their drug operations to Sacramento toned down their gang banging and refined their behavior to keep the heat off their backs. The following three notes were seized from a gang member. The first outlines the structure of the gang and shows precautions taken by the gang bangers to prevent arrest. The note had an organizational diagram illustrating the first point of the note under the title: Game Plan. (The typographical errors are theirs.)

Vic:
(1) Let only Tez & Charles & Dex know where you live.
(2) Give pager # to everyone else and give them a code.
(3) Never keep more than $150-$200 on you unnessissarily.
(4) Give only Charles & Tez & Dexter house #.
(5) Always look to make sure your not followed.
(6) Always turn pager off when being pulled over.

The second note is a dress and behavior code for gang banging drug dealers and the penalties for breaching them.

Dress Codes
1st 1 week suspension
2nd termanation

No hats
No Levis
No sagging pants
Cords only with shirts and shoes only
No hanging earrings studs only
No excessive jewerly
No beepers showing, must be consealed
No tennis with jeans
No cursing in public
No loud thinking in public
Must conduct yourself in proper way at all times
No getting high in public

The third note is a list of rules and regulations for running a rock or crack house, along with the penalties for breaching them.

Rules and Regulations
Rules: Penalty
1. No stealing - termination
2. No puffingpremos or the pipe - termination
3. No playing with fire arms - instant termination
4. No secret documents to be reviled – automatic death
5. No excessive getting high while working – 3 day suspension
6. Respect all co-workers properly –1 day suspension
7. No members can have company – 3 day suspension
8. No sleeping on the job – 3 day suspension
9. Customers must be seated – 1st time warning-2nd time suspension
10. Customers cannot open or close doors – same as #9
11. Doors must be locked at all times – 3 day suspension
12. Members obey ranking officers – 3 day suspension
13. No fighting each other without permission from the board – 3 day suspension
14. No gang-banging – 3 day suspension
15. No loud noise – 3 day suspension-2nd time termination
16. Respect each others girlfriend (friends) – 2 day suspension
17. No fronting other members off – 3 day suspension
18. All work places should be kept clean – 3 day suspension
19. Each member must perform duties at beginning and ending of shifts – 3 day suspension
20. Members while working have first choice on everything – 3 day suspension
21. All books must be correct and accurate – 3 day suspension
22. Members must call officers before leaving any place vacant – 3 day suspension

23. Absence and tardiness only in emergency (must check in) – 3 day suspension (after two)

24. Customers must never outnumber members – 3 day suspension

25. Members must turn down sounds within one block of place –1st time warning-2nd time 3 day suspension

26. No violation of any rule three times –2 week suspension, if done 3 times, 4th time, termination

27. Members must not spend over $25.00 out of pot without permission from chairman –3 day suspension

28. All officers must be present at all meetings – 1 week suspension

29. Reaching peak of 1000.00 must notify officers (until one is reached) – 3 day suspension

30. No members can have company –- 3 day suspension

31. All members must accept any phone call from other members

32. All members must remember all codes

33. No horseplay in spot

34. All members agrees not to talk of arrested

No legitimate corporation has rules this stringent. The only other organizations that have rules like this are outlaw motorcycle gangs, La Cosa Nostra, and Chinese triads.

Crack in the Big Smoke

How dangerous is crack cocaine? Here's what it did to New York City.

Crack cocaine showed up in the Bronx and upper Manhattan in the fall of 1985. By the spring of 1986, it was available everywhere in New York City and the surrounding area. Crack requires no dangerous chemicals or sophisticated lab equipment and is so easy to make that hundreds of independent dealers staked out their turf and started raking in the bucks. The huge profits allowed small trafficking groups to grow into structured organizations that controlled crack sales over large areas. These groups had heads, distributors, cookers, runners, and street dealers. They expanded their market through intimidation and violence to drive smaller dealers out.

Another type of trafficking organization also developed. These were confederations of smaller groups that absorbed independent trafficking groups in the areas they wanted to take over. If the group was willingly absorbed, it handled street distribution for the confederation in the area. If the group didn't want to be part of the confederation, the guns came out and the better shooters won the turf. Crack trafficking is controlled by organizations today. Small dealers can't compete. The large organizations run their crack labs twenty-four hours a day in three shifts.

Crack is sold three ways in New York: wholesale distribution, street distribution, and crack houses. Wholesalers sell packaged or un-packaged crack, sometimes in large uncut chunks weighing several kilos that lower-level crack distributors have to shave and pack in vials. Some wholesalers sell vials and heat-sealed plastic bags in multiples of 100. In 1989, 125 grams of unpackaged crack sold for $1,000 and wholesale amounts of packaged crack (100 or more vials) sold for $5 a vial.

The vials are similar to those used to package perfume samples and semiconductor parts. They are easy to transport and shove up the ass; they are waterproof; they allow buyers to check out the merchandise before paying. Some dealers put the vials in glassine bags (a time-honored heroin tradition) stamped with brand names such as "White Cloud," "Cloud Nine," "Super White," "Serpico," "Conan," "Lido," "Baseball," and "Handball." Dealers in Suffolk County, New York, sell crack in Pyrex tubes that can be used to smoke the drug.

Young punks have ripped off crack users by selling them chunks of plaster, brown soap, or the coconut section of Mounds candy bars. Hey, who are they going to complain to? A ten-year-old boy sold stale bits of pizza crust as crack on Manhattan's Lower East Side in 1989. Someone kicked the shit out of him for it. Many dealers now cut their crack with lidocaine, a local anesthetic, heroin, and methamphetamine. In fact, about one-third of the crack sold on New York streets in 1989 was really crank.

Street distribution in New York has been curbed by heavy police enforcement, which has forced dealers to set up heavily fortified crack houses in apartments and abandoned buildings. Drug sales are made through a slot in a locked door. Apartment-building lobbies and stair-wells are also popular selling spots, with buyers driving through and giving orders to runners who run inside to get the crack from the dealer. Some crack houses are like the opium dens of old, providing the dope and a place to smoke it.

Blacks control the crack market in New York. Dominicans have the best organized and most sophisticated crack-trafficking networks. They have staked out upper Manhattan and the Bronx. Blacks control middle-class and inner-city areas of Brooklyn, Queens, and parts of the Bronx. Jamaicans operate mainly in Brooklyn and have connections across the United States.

One New York Dominican trafficking organization run by brothers in the Dominican Republic started with a few street-corner crack sellers and grew into a 10,000-vials-a-day outfit that marketed its product under the name "BASED BALLS." The leaders of the twenty-six-member gang never left the Dominican Republic. They entrusted the New York end of the multi-million-dollar operation to lieutenants. Many crack sellers have embossed business cards they hand out on the streets: "Crack It Up" or "Buy One, Get One Free."

Crack has had such a violent effect on the streets of New York that the New York City Police Department created a separate crack enforcement unit within its Narcotics Division. The Special Anti-Crack Unit has 300 detectives. Two-thirds of the 90,000 drug arrests in 1990 were for cocaine and more than half of those arrests were for crack.

One of the most disturbing crack trends is the use of children to sell and transport the drug because there is little the courts can do to punish children, who also can't tell police much about the trafficking organization. On January 16, 1989, police arrested a ten-year-old and a twelve-year-old in Wyandanch, Long Island. The youngest held three $20 vials of crack in a bag and they had a total of $226 in their pockets. In late December 1988, police arrested an adult, a fourteen-year-old, and a ten-year-old selling crack in the same spot. The adult was overheard coaching the kid how to sell and told to yell "Five-O" if he saw a police car. The kids made $500 a week at their jobs. On January 31, 1989, an eleven-year-old Bronx boy was arrested at his public school with more than 400 vials of crack.

About 600,000 of New York City's 10 million people are cocaine addicts, most of them crack smokers. The two most important factors in the dramatic rise in crack addiction are smoking and price. Smoking is the most efficient way to take in cocaine. It goes from the lungs to the bloodstream to the brain for a quicker and more intense high than that given by snorting or injecting. The high is short, though, lasting ten to twelve minutes. The rapid crash sends the user scrambling for more crack and addicts often spend $1,000 on crack binges that last days.

Heroin users become addicted after three to five months; powder cocaine users after eighteen months; 75 percent of crack users are hooked after smoking the drug three times or within two weeks. Heroin and cocaine addicts often live with their addiction three to five years before seeking treatment. Crack addicts seek help within six months. They all return to the drug. Crack addiction, so far, is incurable.

At as little as $10 a vial, the cheap price of crack brought a drug associated with a jet-set lifestyle down to street level. Inner-city kids couldn't afford $100 for a gram of powder cocaine. Ten bucks was no big deal. Although blacks control the crack market, users come in all colors and from all walks of life. The saddest and most far-reaching increase has been among inner-city women. When crack hit the New York streets in 1985, the number of women seeking treatment at Phoenix House, which treats more than 1,000 addicts a year, jumped from 20 percent in 1985 to 31 percent in 1986 to 32 percent in 1987.

Women play the central family and social role in the inner city. The US Census Bureau found that the number of black and Hispanic families headed by women more than doubled between 1970 and 1984. In 1980, among the poorest third of black families, 70 percent were headed by women. Crack abuse threatens to undermine the fabric that binds many inner-city families and neighborhoods. This could create nasty situations. Already, child abuse cases involving drug-using parents tripled in New York City from 1986 to 1988, from 2,627 to 8,521. Crack has been blamed for driving up abuse and neglect cases from 41,464 in 1986 to 52,568 in 1988. Three out of four children killed by parental abuse or neglect in 1987 were victims of parental drug abuse. This compares to one in ten in 1985.

The number of babies born with drugs in their urine—mostly cocaine—more than tripled from 1,325 in 1986 to 5,088 in 1988. The director of Pediatrics at Harlem Hospital reported in June 1988 that for the first time, babies were admitted with neurological damage from inhaling crack fumes in homes where mothers smoked the drug. The Brooklyn District Attorney blames crack abuse for an increase in the abuse of elderly people from 85 in 1986 to 305 in 1987. The old people were abused by children and grandchildren who wanted money to buy crack.

A comment made by a character in Samuel Beckett's *Waiting for Godot* could well have been referring to crack mothers when he said, "They give birth astride of a grave." More than 1,000 crack babies are born every week in the United States. More than 200,000 drug-addicted babies are born in the United States every year. The crack babies are born to mothers whose hunger for the drug has deprived them of any vestige of maternal feeling. They smoke crack while pregnant and perform any sexual act demanded of them with as many men who want it to obtain the drug. They give birth and disappear. If they keep the baby, the child receives no love, no caring, and a lot of abuse.

I have yet to see an animal show neglect for its newborn. Animals will suffer incredibly to safeguard their offspring. Drug-using human beings are the only creatures I have seen who abuse life and shun their responsibility to protect it. Drugs and motherhood cannot co-exist. Drugs have created a generation of monster mothers.

Babies born to crack mothers are underdeveloped. They have smaller bones, smaller brains, and weigh less than normal babies. Cocaine can destroy brain tissue in the fetus, causing cerebral palsy or mental retardation. It can constrict a fetus's blood vessels during pregnancy and cut off oxygen to the brain, causing the equivalent of a stroke and brain damage. Some babies are born with tiny heads. Some are missing fingers. All are underweight, some weighing as little as two pounds. Studies show they probably will never be normal.

Before crack hit the streets of New York in 1985, 3 percent of the babies born at Harlem Hospital had addict-mothers. In 1990, 20 percent of the mothers who gave birth there were drug addicts, most of them crack users. One in five babies born at Harlem Hospital of the 3,000 born there every year suffered the effects of drugs before it drew its first breath. Twenty-four percent of those newborns require intensive care. By comparison, the average number of newborns at hospitals across the United States requiring intensive care is 7 percent. A woman who considers using crack should first take a walk through the maternity ward at Harlem Hospital.

Babies born to cocaine-using mothers are prone to respiratory problems, such as apnea, a suspected cause of Sudden Infant Death Syndrome. Studies by the US National Association for Perinatal Addiction Research and Education indicate that babies born with cocaine in their systems show long-term development problems—75 percent in one study could not speak a single word at eighteen months. At three years, 42 percent of the children needed therapy because they had severe trouble speaking or couldn't articulate properly. However, little is known about the long-term effects of crack on babies since the first generation of crack babies is only six years old.

Unless cocaine is found in the baby's system or the mother admits to using crack, there are few ways to tell if a baby has been exposed to the drug. Cocaine disappears from the body in a few days and won't show up in blood and urine tests if the mother stopped doing drugs a few days before birth. Researchers at the Hospital for Sick Children in Toronto have found only one way so far to determine cocaine use by mothers, by analyzing hair samples from mothers and babies. This allows them to properly diagnose and treat sick babies. The analysis must be done within six months, before the baby's hair is replaced.

Babies can be born addicted to cocaine, but theirs is a psychological, rather than a physical, addiction. They're not as obviously impaired as heroin-addicted babies, who need to be treated with drugs to break the addiction. Cocaine-addicted babies are sleepy. They can't be handled— they scream, cry, shriek for five or six days non-stop.

Crack babies are not unique to Harlem Hospital or to black mothers. But because crack is concentrated in black inner cities, its effects are more pronounced among blacks. The infant mortality rate in Washington, D.C., already among the highest in the United States, increased 40 percent in the first six months of 1989 because of a surge of crack babies. The infant mortality rate rose from 23.3 deaths per 1,000 live births to 32.3 deaths per 1,000 live births before the age of one. In six months, 169 babies died. This infant mortality rate is higher than that of China, Chili, Costa Rica, or Jamaica.

In 1988, 18 percent of the babies delivered at D.C. General Hospital were born to drug-addicted mothers. Half of the women who give birth at Howard University Hospital are addicts.

In Washington, as in New York, crack addicts abandon their babies in hospitals, leaving nurses to name them. This has led to a phenomenon known as "boarder babies." Hospitals have become orphanages while overloaded social service systems scramble to find foster homes for the unexpected influx of homeless. These babies live in donated cribs, wear donated clothes, and play with donated toys while their mothers selfishly return to their crack habits. About 75 percent of all abandoned babies are born to drug addicts. There were 45 abandoned crack babies in District of Columbia hospitals in March 1990. The oldest was seven months old. They stay at the hospital until completion of the paperwork required before they can be handed over to social service agencies. If the mother of an abandoned child even tries to contact the baby, the paperwork has to start over. Smart nurses aren't recording phone calls from the inquisitive mothers of abandoned babies. The cost to D.C. General Hospital to keep ten boarder babies for six weeks in 1989 was $500,000.

Medical examiners in Philadelphia started to investigate ten infant deaths from 1987 to 1989. The babies all had cocaine in their blood. Coroner Haresh Mirchandani initiated the investigation after a ten-month-old girl called Tasha died on April 6, 1989. Tests showed some of the cocaine in her blood had been introduced into her system the night before she died. The baby had cocaine residue and active cocaine in her blood. Cocaine usually breaks down in the body in two hours. Dr. Mirchandani said the baby died from inhaling crack smoke from her mother and others who smoked in the house.

The coroner is investigating the deaths of six girls and four boys aged twenty-eight days to ten months who died in Philadelphia. Seven lived in houses where an adult smoked crack. Several slept in small rooms in crowded row houses. Makes you wonder about the passive inhalation of cigarette smoke, doesn't it?

These disturbing facts apply only to the 50,000 crack babies born every year in the United States. But pregnant mothers abuse a wide variety of drugs. Chicago's National Association for Perinatal Addiction Research and Education estimates that 375,000 babies are born in the United States every year with cocaine, PCP, marijuana, or other drugs in their systems.

Crack cocaine is taking its toll on Toronto children too. A confidential three-year study by the Children's Aid Society of Metro Toronto of twenty-five inner-city families and their sixty-eight children between the ages of twenty months and six years whose parents are cocaine and crack addicts found widespread neglect and physical, sexual, and emotional abuse. Mothers turned their apartments into crack houses and sold their bodies and drugs to support their addictions. Two-thirds of the children watched the adults fuck. One-third of the children were fucked by the adults.

During the study, from 1986 to 1989, 16 percent of the parents had no fixed address. Eighty percent of the remaining twenty-one households were used as crack houses or gathering places for stoned, depressed, paranoid, and violent dopers.

"Several times the children were found wandering the streets looking for food [while the mother was stoned or spaced out]," the study said. Mothers slept in and kids missed morning classes. "Their clothes were either sold for drugs or unwashed."

Nine out of ten children had to be taken away from the parents and placed in foster care or with relatives. One five-year-old girl stopped her social worker in a stairwell and asked to be put in a foster home. Most of the parents were single mothers, 75 percent of them younger than twenty-five. Only one mother completed a drug-addiction program and got her child back.

By mid-1990, New York crack babies were being warehoused in foster homes, as modern-day orphanages are called, because no one wants to adopt the child of a drug-abusing mother. On one hand, you can't blame prospective parents. Even the most desperate couple will think twice before adopting a child that may be severely physically, emotionally, and psychologically scarred.

The *Toronto Star* runs a column called "Today's Child" by Elizabeth Marsh. Every day, the column features a child available for adoption. There's always a photo of the little gaffer, and if a kid is retarded this is explained in a humane way. The saddest column I have ever read ran on April 7, 1990, under the photo of a tiny black baby.

"For the first time in the history of this column, we are presenting a baby born to a known cocaine-user mother. It's not a very happy milestone.

"Eva is 5 months old now, a cute and appealing little girl with big dark eyes and long, thick black hair.

"For the first few months of her life, she slept most of the time. Her sleep was so deep that at times some of her automatic reflexes were absent. Eva appeared not to feel pangs of hunger, and had to be wakened for feeding. Such behavior seems to be consistent with infant cocaine withdrawal symptoms.

"But the good news is that Eva now appears to be developing well and meeting her milestones on time. Her foster mother says she is a good and happy baby who loves to be held and rocked, and she has bonded well with other members of the family.

"Adopting parents for Eva should be prepared to accept the uncertainties of her future development. Doctors are not sure what realistic expectations are for cocaine-addicted infants. At present, though, Eva appears to be a normal, delightful baby, and could be a rewarding daughter for some fortunate family."

Crack has also been blamed for a dramatic rise in venereal disease because of the rabid screwing that takes place in crack houses where women trade sex for crack. They will fuck and suck dozens of men during a crack binge. Male addicts commit crimes for money to buy more crack.

It is ironic that crack should lead to an increase in venereal disease. Many dopers turned to smoking drugs after needle use was shown to transmit AIDS. The number of syphilis cases in New York City remained stable from 1959 to 1985, when crack arrived in the city. Then syphilis cases jumped from 2,111 in 1986 to 4,548 in 1987.

Where venereal diseases such as syphilis go, you can bet your life AIDS follows. One reason is that lesions caused by syphilis and other venereal diseases are perfect entries for the AIDS virus into the body. A survey of 500 addicts by the State University Health Science Center in Brooklyn found that 35 to 40 percent of the people going into crack houses had injected drugs, placing them in the AIDS high-risk category. One in three New York City hookers carries the AIDS virus and one in eight New Yorkers has been exposed to AIDS.

Crack is also responsible for an increase in violence. New York has never been a safe city and crack has made it less so. The city's homicide rate jumped from 1,588 in 1986 to 1,691 in 1987 to 1,867 in 1988. In Queens, where crack gangs fight for turf, killings jumped 25 percent from 234 in 1986 to 293 in 1987. Drugs are now involved in 40 percent of New York murders compared to the average 20 percent in the decade before crack arrived on the scene. Crack gangs have taken to torching buildings used by rival gangs, or to get revenge on informants and witnesses.

The most notorious crack murder in New York City was the gangland execution of police officer Edward Byrne on February 26, 1988, while he sat in a marked cruiser guarding the home of a witness in a drug case.

Police believe the hit was ordered by two leaders of a black trafficking gang in southeast Queens.

One crack addict was panhandling on Manhattan's Lower East Side, using his girlfriend's three-year-old daughter in a stroller to elicit sympathy. Someone passing noticed the girl wasn't sleeping; she was dead. The doper, stoned on crack, had beaten her to death the previous night because she was crying.

Another addict's one-month-old daughter wouldn't stop crying one night when he was stoned on crack. So he fucked her. He took her to Bellevue Hospital in mid-town New York the next day with a bleeding vagina.

On November 10, 1987, a crack-crazed Brooklyn man barricaded himself in a woman friend's apartment after several hours of smoking and killed her three-year-old son with a semi-automatic pistol. Police counted twenty-six bullet entry wounds in the boy.

On November 11, 1987, rival crack dealers shot it out in a Staten Island housing project. Three people were killed and three others, including a two-year-old boy, were wounded.

In January 1988, a teenager who had never acted violently went on an eight-day murder and robbery spree in his neighborhood, killing five people and wounding six.

On January 7, 1988, a Bronx mother pleaded guilty to four counts of rape for selling her six-year-old daughter to buy crack at four different places in the fall of 1986. She also admitted to holding her daughter down while several men fucked her.

On March 2, 1988, an eighteen-year-old Manhattan crack addict allegedly tore his one-month-old daughter's guts out when she started crying while he smoked crack.

In June 1988, an alleged crack dealer chopped off a woman's right hand, partially severed her left arm, and cracked her skull with a machete during an argument.

On June 9, 1988, a crack addict was convicted of stabbing a nun to death at a shelter for homeless men when she refused to give him money to buy crack.

On July 7, 1988, a crack-crazed Harlem man killed his grandmother, barricaded himself inside the apartment, then jumped twenty-six stories when the cops broke down the door.

On August 19, 1988, a crack dealer was killed and another person was wounded at a Brooklyn housing project, prompting a revenge attack in which seven bystanders were wounded, including thirteen- and fifteen-year-old girls.

On January 2, 1989, a sixteen-year-old Bronx kid allegedly stabbed his mother to death when she refused to give him $200 he owed a crack dealer. He allegedly stripped her to make police believe she had been raped and murdered by an intruder. Then he went to school.

Crack violence is seldom planned; it is random and explosive. Crack dealers jokingly refer to innocent bystanders at shoot-outs as "mushrooms" because they pop up unexpectedly. More than thirty innocent bystanders were hit by stray bullets during crack-related gunfights over two years — eighteen were killed and fourteen were wounded.

They're Out To Get Us: The White Conspiracy Theory

Many blacks cry out that whites are conspiring to exterminate them by giving them access to drugs so they can destroy themselves. This is called the genocide plot, an age-old bogeyman whose most recent incarnation revolves around drugs. The argument is based on four racist presuppositions: that blacks are too stupid to get drugs on their own; that blacks are predisposed to abuse drugs; that blacks are predisposed to kill other blacks with drugs in order to make money; that black politicians and black law-enforcement officers are in league with whites to kill blacks. None of these is true, but they are crucial to the theory.

The genocide plot is not something that is mumbled about behind closed doors. Prominent black activists hammer it into the heads of their constituents over and over again at public meetings and in the media to incite hatred and distrust of whites. The fomented hatred provides fertile ground for the racist, nihilist seeds activists plant in black minds, seeds of hate and violence destined to grow into the club they need to crush white America

Louis Farrakhan, the black nationalist leader of Nation of Islam, preaches at rallies that "Whites are out to get you." He gives as an example the arrest and conviction of Washington's mayor, Marion Barry, on cocaine charges, for which he received six months in jail out of a possible twenty-six-year sentence. While blacks see Barry's conviction as a flagrant example of white racism, Colombians — both politicians and drug cartel leaders — have mocked the sentence as proof that America is not serious about fighting drugs.

For the record, Farrakhan is against many things, including racial integration and religious tolerance, two of the greatest achievements of the black civil rights movement of the 1950s and 1960s, cornerstones of black society that many courageous people died for — not only Martin Luther King, Jr., but the hundreds of unnamed blacks and whites who disappeared at the hands of racist organizations such as the Ku Klux Klan. Every race has its racists, even blacks.

Black film director Spike Lee also sees life in black and white. Lee believes only blacks should make movies about blacks. (Gremlins about gremlins? ET about ET? Collies and German Shepherds about Lassie and Rin Tin Tin?) Get real, Spike.

The Reverend Al Sharpton stirred up violent racism in New York in 1988 by espousing the cause of Tawana Brawley, who claimed six white men had raped her for four days. The story was proved to be false. Sharpton, like other activists, has little regard for fact. He incites hatred by preaching victimization and the genocide theory.

The National Urban League's state-of-black-America report in 1989 said, "There is at least one concept that must be recognized if one is to see the pervasive and insidious nature of the drug problem for the African-American community. Though difficult to accept, that is the concept of genocide."

Prominent black activists and clergymen point not only to drugs as evidence of the genocide plot, but to AIDS, which they claim the US government tested on homosexuals before using the virus to wipe out blacks. Contrary to their claims that AIDS is a black disorder, twice as many whites as blacks have died of AIDS.

Drug abuse has no racial limits. All races use, abuse, and sell drugs. White trash—generally your friendly neighborhood outlaw biker—makes methamphetamine. White trash is its main abuser. Colombians make and sell cocaine, which they sell to whites, blacks, Cubans, and Hispanics, who in turn sell and abuse the drug. Colombians were major abusers of *bazuco* in the early 1980s. *Bazuco* is cocaine base, known as crack or rock in North America. Pakistanis, Afghans, Burmese, Chinese, Turks, and many other ethnic groups grow opium poppies and make heroin. The Chinese control the greater part of the heroin market in North America. They have also sold opium to their own. Colombians, Mexicans, and Jamaicans grow marijuana for Colombians, Mexicans, Jamaicans, and all North Americans. White and black Americans grow marijuana for all Americans.

Crack cocaine is a black drug because blacks got into the crack business first and have monopolized it through violence, strict adherence to fundamental business stratagems, a strong work ethic countered by an equally strong desire to party and impress peers and, perhaps most importantly for some, a desperate drive to get out of the inner cities.

If anything, the success of blacks in the drug business attests to the entrepreneurial spirit and business acumen, however misguided, that racists have accused blacks of lacking. Most crack dealers do not abuse the drug because they know its harmful effects. But they do sell equally to blacks and whites. It is ironic that dealing crack to whites has given young blacks a chance to break out of the cycle of poverty and escape the ghetto. Drugs have given black youth the opportunity to achieve the

ultimate North American dream—to become financially independent on
their own terms. No college degree could have achieved what the access
to crack cocaine and the ghetto markets have done for a generation of
black youth. It's not an achievement to be proud of, but some of the
richest and most respected white families in the world had less than
pristine beginnings.

Blacks say drugs are destroying families and neighborhoods. They are.
Blacks complain that drugs are taking men away from black families
when they are arrested for drug dealing, creating matriarchal families.
Black families in North America have traditionally been matriarchal.
Black women have always worn the pants and borne the brunt of
carrying their families through hard times.

One of the disturbing facts I encountered while researching this book
is that a large number of black men pride themselves on fathering
numerous children through a variety of women, none of whom they can
support. These women are left to raise the children alone.

Blacks point to statistics that indicate black men are more likely to die
young than white men and are more likely to end up in jail. When you do
the crime, you do the time. It is important to remember that they're not
ending up in jail for nothing. Black street gangs have been waging war
with Uzis, MAC-10s, and AK-47s for more than a decade. When tens of
thousands of black gangsters across North America try to wipe out each
other with assault rifles, statistics are bound to show a higher mortality
rate among young blacks, whose motto, like that of most young gangsters, seems to be: Live fast, die young, and leave a good-looking stiff.

Finally, if the complaint that drugs are a white conspiracy to destroy
blacks were true, then whites have failed miserably. If anything, the drug
trade in North America is part of a documented plot by Colombians and
Cubans to destroy that society. They are using blacks, whites, and
anyone greedy enough for drug money to carry out their plan. Colombian cartel leaders put cocaine and the recipe for making crack into the
hands of black gangsters in southern California. Colombians have done
away with the white middlemen who linked them to blacks. Colombians
now deal with black gangsters directly and supply them with more than
enough cocaine at prices much cheaper than they demanded when they
dealt with whites.

The white conspiracy theory, the genocide plot, removes the need to
accept responsibility for the drug abuse problem and the need to do
something about it. Sit back and blame someone else. It's so easy. Blacks
who espouse the conspiracy theory would be better off emulating blacks
in inner cities across North America who have taken to the street to drive
black drug dealers out of their neighborhoods. Muslims in Philadelphia

march down streets to save young blacks from drugs sold by young blacks. A Detroit woman made the cover of *Time* magazine fighting black crack dealers in her neighborhood. These people aren't sitting back and pointing the finger at whites. They're cleaning the bad apples out of their own barrel. They have the strength to face and handle their problems. And they have no hidden agendas.

Cry Wolf, Cry Racism

Toronto the Good. That's how generations of politicians have flogged the city known to its inhabitants as Hogtown. Much effort and money is spent to portray Toronto as a clean, safe city without the crime, fear, and racial problems of American cities. That public relations effort is designed to attract tourists. Toronto has in fact become just as dangerous as any major American city. Toronto has a problem with gun-toting black and Asian criminals. Toronto has murders, rapes, robberies, and swarmings. Toronto has a massive drug problem and is home to a wide variety of organized crime groups ranging from the Italian mob to Asian triads and street gangs to heavy-duty biker gangs to Jamaican posses.

Toronto is also the home of the largest Jamaican community in Canada, possibly in North America. They are hardworking people scraping together money to carve out their niche in a land populated by immigrants. They are also the victims of the criminals within their own ethnic group. Both have escaped the poverty of the islands.

But something curious is happening within Toronto's black community. Blacks scream "racism" whenever police arrest black criminals. If a black man is shot by police—there have been six in twelve years—blacks cry racism. When police conduct drug sweeps in black housing projects, blacks cry racism.

These allegations are unfounded. And they are not spontaneous expressions of disgust but carefully orchestrated attacks to discredit the police force and drive a wedge between the black and white communities. The same activists pop up all the time, spouting Marxist refrains and making outrageous and unsupported claims while a dutiful liberal, ass-kissing press records it all without question.

Why are these activists using the police force's need to curb black criminals as a springboard to foment hatred and distrust within the Toronto community? While blacks cry racism and discrimination, why do they ban whites from their organizations? Why does the rhetoric of the Black Action Defence Committee sound so similar to that spouted by the Black Panthers in the 1960s? Even the beret has been resurrected by Dudley Laws, its main spokesman.

While the police struggle to control black crime in Toronto, where

Jamaican posses control the crack cocaine market and a large part of the
marijuana market, black activists stir up the black community against
police as they try to do their jobs.

In February 1989, Metro Toronto Police Staff-Inspector Julian Fantino released these figures to a race relations committee: while blacks
make up 6 percent of the population in Toronto's notorious Jane-Finch
corridor, they accounted for 82 percent of the robberies and muggings,
55 percent of the purse snatchings, and 51 percent of the drug offences.
Staff-Inspector Fantino was not implying that blacks are prone to crime.
He was pointing out that black criminals were out of control and preying
upon their own community.

Well, black activists jumped on the white-bashing bandwagon, and
before the week was out Toronto's white liberal politicians cowered and
pressured the police force management to dump all over Staff-Inspector
Fantino. He was forced to publicly apologize for releasing the figures
and the police department promised to never again keep statistics based
on criminals' ethnic background.

Great. How the hell are cops supposed to do their job? There is
nothing discriminatory about keeping statistics on criminals. That is not
labeling a community as prone to crime. It is identifying a community as
crime-plagued.

Metro Toronto Chairman Alan Tonks came out in support of keeping
crime statistics because of their usefulness in pinpointing and combatting problems that create a climate of fear in the city. He was quickly
denounced by black activists and forced by the politicians on Metro
Council to apologize for his comments. Left-wing politicians accused
him of reinforcing the stereotype that blacks are more dangerous than
whites.

Communism may be dead in the Soviet Union, but Canada sure has its
share of the socially degenerate trying to destroy the country. They are
undermining the ability of its institutions to maintain law and order and
make the country a safe place for everyone.

How level-headed are the militant black activists whose protests actually
shelter black criminals?

Dudley Laws, who runs the Black Action Defence Committee with
lawyer Charles Roach, described Toronto's police in May 1990 as the
"most murderous and racist" police force in North America. The chief
of police was denounced as a "white supremacist." Such inflammatory
comments would not be tolerated by politicians or reported by the media
if they had been made about blacks. Yet a few black militants were
allowed to slander an entire police force of nearly 6,000 officers.

After the sixth shooting of a black man in Toronto in twelve years,

black militants distributed hate literature that called for the murder of
police officers. (Three of these cases were before the courts at this
writing. Police in three others were absolved by the courts of any
criminal intent.) If any other group had published this kind of propaganda against anyone else, they would have been arrested. One pamphlet
distributed at an anti-police rally was titled: "What if We All Killed a
Cop?"

"Let's use a new style. Organize ourselves. Get together. Fight the
MAN. So far we've let them get away with it. We've been victims of
violence for too long. It's time for some self-defense. They try to hide in
their uniforms, planning their little sneak attacks on our people ... They
all act the same ... The cops ain't nothing but puppets of the MAN, the
system. Just little blue-and-white puppets shooting off their deadly guns
...In the last year-and-a-half alone the boys and girls in blue have shot
three of our brothers and sisters. What are were going to do about it?
Should we avenge them? Should we arm and protect ourselves? Or do we
call for another task-force? ... Are we target practice for the cops? ...
Why the hell are we being shot at? ... You know why! They know they
can do it ... Let's get it together and stop the violence against us."

Metro Toronto Police Constable David Deviney shot and killed Lester
Donaldson in a rooming house after the black man lunged at his partner
with a knife in August 1988. Black militants called the constable a
murderer and pressed their case. The Black Action Defence Committee,
which identified activist Dudley Laws and activist-lawyer Charles
Roach as members, distributed so-called fact sheets about the shooting.
Roach called for an independent investigation into the shooting because
he didn't trust the homicide squad to conduct a proper investigation into
one of their own. One sheet read: "The police from 13 Division were
well familiar with Donaldson. He had been fighting with them for a five-
year period.... David Deviney is known to be violent, to disregard the
dignity of poor people, and to be a Racist.... We are saying that there is
reason to believe there was a deliberate, intentional taking of Lester's life
by the police." (I report these outrageous allegations with due respect to
David Deviney. His rights were much abused in the wake of the
shooting.)

The press repeated the allegations, extending them into the realm of
libel and seriously affecting the police officer's right to a fair trial.
Constable Deviney was tried for murder and acquitted after the court
ruled he acted in self-defense. Black roomers testified that they lived in
fear of Donaldson, a violent man of questionable mental stability. Immediately after the acquittal, militant black activists held a press conference
where they denounced the verdict and warned that whites were going to

die. Dudley Laws called the trial a "blatant mistrial of justice" and
warned that the black community's anger had reached the boiling point.
Tidy Francis, another member of the Black Action Defence Committee,
warned, "We're not going to be able to fix what is going to develop
without some degree of bloodshed." Committee member Dari Mead
said, "We are heading down a collision course in this city. It's getting
explosive."

Charles Roach has lived in Canada for about twenty-five years. He has
often made outrageous allegations against whites, accusing them of
picking on blacks. In fact, racial harmony existed in Toronto until
activists stirred up trouble. And the white press has been quite happy to
report the allegations of racism for fear of being labeled racist otherwise.
Roach refused to become a Canadian citizen because he won't swear
allegiance to the Queen of England, who is still technically the head of
state in Canada. Where exactly do his loyalties lie?

On May 14, 1990, sixteen-year-old Marlon Neal was shot twice near a
radar trap in Metro Toronto. Constable Brian Rapson, a traffic officer,
was charged with attempted murder, which he denied. The charge was
dropped after a judge ruled it wasn't supported by evidence. Ontario's
attorney-general reinstated the charge in May 1991. On June 12, a
coalition of black groups demanded of provincial politicians that traffic
cops not carry guns. Charles Roach spoke for the coalition, which also
demanded that a civilian board be set up to investigate complaints against
police.

"The more we have room for discretionary actions [by police inves-
tigators], the more we have room for an absence of justice," he said. In
other words, the cops are corrupt and civilians like him aren't.

The Jamaican-Canadian Association asked that police officers have
university educations instead of the current requirement of Grade 12
because university-educated people are more racially tolerant. It's a good
point, but such a policy would effectively rule out the hiring of the
immigrant blacks the community also wants.

The following day, on June 13, police arrested a black man in a
housing project. He was wanted on a warrant for a vicious assault on a
security guard in August 1989. The guard's jaw, gums, and teeth were
shattered to the tune of $15,000 in repairs. As Detective-Constables
John McLean and Mike Healy led the man out of the building, he yelled
to friends for help. He then punched one policeman in the head and
stomach in an attempt to get away. Twenty black youths surrounded the
cops and yelled and taunted them.

"Shoot me. Shoot me," they yelled.

Twelve uniformed police officers had to form a corridor through the gang of youths for the detectives to get through with their prisoner. The following week, two black men stopped in a speed trap taunted the police officer with the same phrase, "Shoot me," before beating him up.

Ten Metro Toronto Police officers executing a search warrant on May 18, 1990, used a sledgehammer to smash down an apartment door secured with five locks. They charged thirty-four-year-old Hansel Alonzo with possession of marijuana for the purpose of trafficking and with possession of cocaine. They took him to the police station at 41 Division. When a police officer noticed a trail of cocaine powder leading from the cruiser to Alonzo, they removed the handcuffs to search him. A video camera recorded everything. Seconds after the cuffs came off, Alonzo stuffed a plastic bag with half a gram of cocaine taken from his hair into his mouth. Police officers grabbed him.

"Spit it out. Out. Out. Open your mouth. He swallowed it. Bet it's cocaine. Sure it was."

Alonzo was not roughed up. He was taken to his cell. The video camera recorded him standing, talking to himself. He sat down. Talked to himself. Stood. A few minutes later, police took him out of the holding cell at 12:08 a.m. He collapsed and went into a coma. Two weeks later, on June 2, he died in hospital.

Police and firefighters stood around the police station talking after Alonzo left in an ambulance.

"Was he breathing?"

"He was twitching just when I left."

"Hansel Alonzo, you know, we worked him three times [arrested and convicted three times on cocaine charges].... I was just saying to someone the other day, I wondered what happened to him."

"Now you know."

Militant black activists started rabble rousing, claiming Alonzo had been beaten by police. They refused to believe that he swallowed a bag of drugs. James Lockyer, the lawyer hired by Alonzo's family, wrote, "Given recent events between the police and the black community, I cannot accept the police version without independent corroboration."

Hansel Alonzo was buried on June 8, 1990, at the Pine Hills Cemetery. About 100 mourners surrounded his casket. Someone pulled a 9mm semi-automatic pistol and fired off six shots—a Jamaican salute in recognition and respect for the dead man, a thrice-convicted drug dealer. Charles Roach and Dudley Laws attended. So did immigration consultant Calvert Lewin. Police questioned mourners, who had surrounded the grave so as to make the gunman invisible from the roadway. No one saw anything.

"It could have been a car backfiring," Laws told reporters.

"They sounded like fireworks," Roach said of the detonations. Four months later Roach said the noises "sounded like crackers." Laws said, "I said at the time I heard no shots and I'm still saying that."

Calvert Lewin said he didn't recall the funeral. Then he said maybe he missed the shots. Then: "I don't know who fired them, in fact. It was an explosion."

On June 10, the Black Action Defence Committee was conducting a protest outside the Royal Ontario Museum against an African exhibit centered on artifacts brought back by missionaries. About 150 blacks marched outside the museum chanting that the exhibit was racist. The crowd stood silent for a moment in memory of Hansel Alonzo. Charles Roach said, "We are holding the cops responsible for the death of Hansel until it is proven otherwise. We want an inquest." Interesting that a lawyer would presume someone guilty until proven innocent.

Roach called the police "racist" and "facist."

"The struggles with the ROM and the Metro Police are welded together," he told the protesters. "Inside the ROM is institutional racism and outside is the brutal reality."

One of the demonstrators was Marjorie Lopez Alonzo, Hansel's mother. She told a reporter his newspaper was "satanic" for covering her son's funeral and reporting the gunshots.

Alonzo's family finally saw the police videotape of the father of seven (an eighth on the way) swallowing the cocaine. No one apologized. Now family lawyers are arguing the police didn't rush Alonzo to hospital quickly enough. But it's difficult to argue with a videotape with digital time imprint.

On September 30, 1990, Kareem O'Brien walked into a townhouse party held to raise rent money for a twenty-three-year-old single mother of three. O'Brien, an outgoing, athletic fifteen-year-old black, didn't do drugs or hang out with gangs. Partyers drank and danced to loud reggae music. Five minutes after O'Brien got there, a man walked up to him in the basement of the house and shot him in the head. Most party-goers split before the cops arrived and those who remained said they saw nothing. O'Brien died in hospital nine hours later. His murder remains unsolved.

A ballistics expert compared the shell casing ejected from the pistol used to murder O'Brien to casings found around Hansel Alonzo's grave at Pine Hills Cemetery nearly four months earlier. They had been ejected by the same gun.

The person who fired the shots at the funeral probably shot Kareem O'Brien. If he had been turned over to police after the funeral, O'Brien would be alive today.

Charles Roach and Dudley Laws are quick to cry murder when police shoot someone in the line of duty. They are also quick to allege that the justice system is white and corrupt when a police officer is acquitted of shooting someone. They have said nothing when black drug dealers have shot police officers. They didn't have much to say when an innocent black teenager got wasted for no reason. They had less to say when told the gun that killed the kid was fired by someone who discharged it near them at Alonzo's funeral. The good die young. Kareem O'Brien's community died long before he did. All that remains is a gaggle of vultures feeding off the corpse.

4

Teeth of the Dragon:
The growing menace of Asian organized crime

"Unfortunately, Asian organized crime is expanding faster than law enforcement's ability to track it. Asian organized crime has worldwide connections and it is impacting the United States and Canada dramatically. Asian organized crime is difficult to penetrate, due to its language, cultures and transient figures."
—FROM AN INVITATION LETTER FOR THE NINTH ANNUAL ASIAN ORGANIZED CRIME CONFERENCE IN LOS ANGELES IN 1986.

"The established, well-financed and -connected Hong Kong triad groups and crime syndicates remain, to our mind, the biggest long-term threat to Canadian law enforcement and society. It is these groups that possess the financial backing, the know-how and the connections to enable them to operate successfully with the minimum of interference from law enforcement. Many have reached that level of O.C. [organized crime] where they are insulated from prosecution but through their connections still finance and control criminal activity. They are sophisticated in their methods of operation and exhibit a high degree of knowledge of how best to frustrate and prevent the gathering of evidence by law enforcement."
—RESTRICTED 1989 REPORT OF THE CRIMINAL INTELLIGENCE SERVICE OF CANADA.

"Whatever Triads might have been in the past and notwithstanding their criminal objectives the Triad Society today is simply a gang of vicious criminals; they deliberately exploit the fear and mysticism generated by the name Triad in order to bind themselves together and by similar means hold in fear a large and susceptible section of the public."
—ROYAL HONG KONG POLICE REPORT.

"Asian and other ethnic criminal groups represent significant challenges to federal, provincial and municipal police agencies. Difficulties normally associated with the investigation of organized crime are compounded by the problems of cultural differences, language barriers and the fear and general attitude of reluctance by the Asian community to co-operate with law enforcement.

"With the dramatic increase in the number of persons immigrating to Canada from Hong Kong, I think many would agree that the Asian organized crime problem in North America is only in its infancy. These increases will likely continue until the end of Britain's lease on Hong Kong in 1997 at which time the Colony will return to Chinese sovereignty. Our main concern, of course, is that the increase in immigrants will result in an increase in the number of Triad members in Hong Kong looking for a haven in Canada.

"The propensity for violence among gang members and the ruthless behaviour of Asian groups instills a fear within the community in which they exist. Consequently, witnesses and victims alike are afraid to co-operate with law enforcement for fear of retaliation by gang members."
—DIRECTOR OF THE CRIMINAL INTELLIGENCE SERVICE OF CANADA IN A RESTRICTED CISC WORKSHOP DOCUMENT IN SEPTEMBER 1989.

Two Vietnamese hit men in their early twenties wearing bright colored clothing walked into the Kim Bo Restaurant on Dundas Street in Toronto's downtown Chinatown at 12:30 on December 27, 1990. They hurried to a table near the northeast wall, far from the restaurant's front door. Seven people sat at the table, one of eleven in the restaurant. The two Vietnamese pulled small-caliber handguns and shot three people before running off with their lookout.

Dan Vi Tran, thirty-one, died in the restaurant. Mau "Au Mah" Luy Quach, nineteen, suffered severe internal injuries. Hoan "Japanese Boy" Thanh Luu, twenty-one, hauled ass, but walked into a nearby hospital an hour later with a bullet in his chest.

Tran was a frequent visitor to Toronto from New York state, where he worked in a hotel. He had confided to friends he was on the run. He had fled Vietnam with his family in the late 1970s and arrived in San Francisco on July 28, 1979. From there he moved to a refugee camp in Louisville, Kentucky, where he was sponsored by Catholic Charities refugee services.

Son Long, twenty-eight, a member of the New York City Vietnamese street gang Born To Kill, was charged with Tran's killing on February 14, 1991. Long was arrested on Canal Street, where the BTK and the Ghost Shadows Chinese gang have been conducting a bloody gang war for several years. Thanh Tat, also twenty-eight, a former Vietnamese gang leader from Winnipeg, Manitoba, was also charged with Tran's murder after being arrested on gun charges in Vancouver, British Columbia, on February 10. Police investigating a noise complaint arrested six men, including Tat, and seized a handgun, a sawed-off shotgun, machetes, knives, and six ski masks.

On January 4, 1991, Do Cu Quan got into a staring match with a gangster sitting at another table in the Quan Saigon Me Kung restaurant on St. Andrew Street in Toronto, several blocks from where Tran was murdered. The hood rose, walked over to the thirty-five-year-old Quan's table, pulled a gun, and fired four shots from a distance of four feet, apparently to scare him. One bullet grazed Quan's temple. Another pierced the ceiling, entered a bedroom above the restaurant, and tore a hole in a mattress.

The restaurant's owner didn't call police. He said he was in the kitchen and didn't hear anything.

Four Asian men walked along Dundas Street near the Kim Bo Restaurant in Toronto at 5:37 p.m. on Sunday, February 3, 1991. One of the men was twenty-nine-year-old Vinh Duc Tat, a Vietnamese refugee who had spent four years in a Thailand refugee camp with his brother Duc Trai Tat before immigrating to the United States in 1987. The brother stayed in New York City when Vinh Duc Tat moved to Toronto a year later and organized a gang of Vietnamese thugs that extorted protection money from Vietnamese-run gaming houses in Chinatown. He was known as Lee Mo on the streets.

Three Asian men in their twenties walked up to Vinh Duc Tat and his three buddies just west of Spadina Avenue. One pulled a handgun and fired at least eight shots. A bullet hit Tat in the left temple and blew out the back of his skull. The gun was so close to his head that the detonation left powder burns on his forehead. Tat also took a hit in the chest.

Quong Vinh Duong, twenty-five, was shot in the leg. My Chong Thich, sixteen, was shot in the back as he ran. He kept running. Phaiboun Souydalai, twenty-seven, a Laotian, was shot in the neck.

Duong, his upper leg bleeding, tried to help Tat to his feet. He looked to the gathering crowd and yelled, "Help! Help! Help! Help!" Tat tried to get up from the sidewalk, but collapsed in a pool of his own blood and died. Souydalai, blood pouring down his own body, ran to a jewelry store and pounded on the door for help. The store was closed.

Thich ran off. He ripped off his shirt as he ran and wrapped it around his torso to stop the bleeding from the bullet hole. He finally decided he needed medical help and flagged down a taxi to take him to Toronto General Hospital.

Tat was buried in a white silk tuxedo. His murder was allegedly ordered by Toronto's Asau Tran, a convicted extortionist and one of the most powerful Vietnamese gangsters in North America.

On February 16, 1991, twenty-nine-year-old Thien Ngo was stabbed to death by another Vietnamese man in a west Toronto café-nightclub owned by Asau Tran. Ngo was stabbed at 11:25 p.m. after an argument in the Chieu Tim Cafe, a storefront social club in the heart of the city's Portuguese district. Phat Van Lee, twenty-six, was arrested in Ottawa on February 18 and charged with Ngo's murder.

Two well-dressed hitmen armed with a TEC submachine gun and a semi-automatic pistol waited outside the Pot of Gold Restaurant in the heart of Toronto's Chinatown in the early hours of August 16, 1991. Their target was Asau Tran, leader of the violent Vietnamese underworld in Toronto. The thirty-eight-year-old Saigon-born ethnic Chinese gangster had come a long way since first making his mark in the criminal underworld by providing muscle for the Kung Lok triad in the early 1980s. His association with a popular Kung Lok leader gave him face and power in the Asian community. His control of violent Vietnamese gangsters eventually allowed him to take over the streets from the Chinese criminals he served, driving the Kung Lok to the suburbs while his hoods extorted and robbed businesses in Toronto's downtown Chinatown.

At 3 a.m., Asau Tran left the Pot of Gold with Tony Pun, his thirty-three-year-old concert business partner and assistant night manager at the restaurant. They were accompanied by twenty-eight-year-old waitress Tin Wah (Amy) Lui.

The gunmen donned balaclavas, riddled the trio with bullets, and professionally dropped their guns before fleeing down a narrow side-street. Tran was hit three times in the head. Pun was shot in the head and neck. Lui was shot in the neck and chest. All died.

It was the second triple murder in Chinatown since March, when teenaged hit men machine-gunned patrons at the A Dong karaoke club. In nine months since December 1990, nine persons were murdered in the streets and restaurants of Toronto's Chinatown.

This gunplay is not a case of American violence spilling across the border into Canada. Asian gangs don't recognize borders. For them, North America is a big playground. Asian gangsters are highly mobile and move from city to city committing crimes. Many Asian gangsters in the US started out in Canada but ran out of large cities with Asian communities in which they could hide from police. Toronto now has the second largest Asian community in North America after San Francisco: 350,000 Asians in a metropolitan area of nearly 3 million; one in nine people is Asian. Of all organized crime groups, Asian gangsters, especially the Vietnamese, are the most ruthless, brutal, and senseless killers. And, like all organized crime groups, Asian gangs have one goal: power and wealth.

Tran's murder capped a year when violence among Asian groups finally broke out in the streets of Toronto for all to see. It had been preceded by years of hushed-up beatings, stabbings, shootings, robberies, and extortions. On December 4, 1990, Bin Van Pham, thirty-seven, was stabbed to death on the sidewalk outside Thuong Hai Vietnamese nightclub by two Vietnamese patrons. As with most crimes involving Asians, no one saw anything although more than 100 people had watched the altercation. Pham, owner of the Hoai Huong Vietnamese Restaurant, had connections in the Vietnamese underworld.

Fifteen gangsters from two gangs—one Vietnamese, the other mainland Chinese—started arguing in a Chinatown bar at 1:30 a.m. on October 13, 1990. They threw glasses, tables, and chairs at each other. The fight spilled out onto Dundas Street West where the gangsters pulled knives and hacked at each other in a running battle. Since most of the stabbing was done on the run, the wounds were in the men's backs. One man was stabbed in the head.

During the summer of 1990, a bullet grazed a man's ankle during a shoot-out between two gangs one block from the Kim Bo restaurant. Earlier in the summer pedestrians had scrambled as two gangs shot it out in a crowded Chinatown intersection.

Toronto has been hiding its filthy laundry from the world. In the meantime Chinatown has become very dangerous.

Toronto's Chinese businessmen were hit heavily in 1990 as armed, masked Asian gangsters burst into homes, gaming houses, restaurants, beauty parlors, and medical offices seeking cash. Eight Toronto restaurants, including hundreds of customers, were robbed. This statistic does not include those robberies not reported to police. Only one in thirteen is reported. Gangsters walked in, fired a shot into the ceiling, then ordered everyone to hand over wallets and jewelry. Restaurant owners felt the pinch by year's end as frightened Chinese patrons changed their eating habits. Some owners, like Peter Tsang, decided to sell their restaurants rather than live in fear. Chinese weddings were protected by off-duty police officers hired to guard large cash gifts.

Few home invasions were reported to police. Asians distrust police. And they fear losing face. So they gave their valuables to the punks who burst into their homes. Gangsters also abducted family members and held them for ransoms that were paid. Now some Chinese businessmen want more Chinese-speaking police officers. But Chinese families consider it a dishonor for a child to become a police officer. They can't have it both ways. Until they change some of their ways, they are inviting gangsters to take advantage of them.

Pickpockets have become such a nuisance in the Toronto area's five Chinatowns—Dundas Street, Spadina Avenue, Broadview-Gerrard, Scarborough, and Mississauga—that police have put up posters in Chinese and Vietnamese to warn shoppers about light-fingered fiends.

All of a sudden, the worst fears of Toronto's money-grubbing politicians have been realized. For years politicians had put pressure on the police force to play down, if not deny, the presence of Asian organized crime gangs in the city. Chinese businessmen had convinced the politicians that the billions of dollars Chinese immigrants took out of Hong Kong would not find their way to Canada's cleanest city if word got out that organized criminals had set up shop there. Toronto is the main port of entry for Chinese immigrants in North America. Thousands of law-abiding Chinese settle in Toronto every year. Many of them are fleeing the gangs of extortionists and robbers that plague businessmen in Hong Kong.

On November 24, 1990, I witnessed something I had long expected but which still surprised me. Toronto's Chinese businessmen held a news conference to publicize the wave of violence and crime that has terrorized the city's Chinatowns.

"The whole Chinese community feels scared and helpless," said Andie Shih, vice-president of the Chinese Herbal Products Association and a director of the East Toronto Chinese Businessmen's Association. In two and one-half years Shih's store had been robbed three times of $100,000 of ginseng and herbs. Other stores lost money selling goods to pickpockets who paid with stolen credit cards.

What is happening to Toronto? What is happening across North America?

Chinese organized crime gangs called triads are moving their international headquarters to Toronto to avoid confronting the Communist Chinese government when the People's Republic of China takes over Hong Kong in 1997. Why? Fear of the Dragon. China has promised to reinstate the death penalty in Hong Kong. A country that executed three moonshiners with a bullet to the back of the head in April 1990, sure as hell won't be sympathetic to the gambling, drug, extortion, prostitution, and murder habits of triad members. In China they execute people for soccer hooliganism.

In 1990, Communist China mounted a sweeping anti-corruption campaign against the six social evils of prostitution, gambling, drug smuggling, pornography, superstition, and the selling of women and children. More than 62,000 people were arrested during the first three months of the year. The country periodically embarks on rectification campaigns to curb "political errors" in publications ranging from newspapers to books by putting them out of business. It is a country whose history and heroes keep changing depending on who is in power.

Triad leaders also believe that Beijing will disrupt the social and financial order when it takes control of the 5.5 million residents of Hong Kong, the third largest financial center in the world after New York and London. Hong Kong's organized crime gangs want to move their operations to safer grounds. Toronto is ripe for the picking because no one gang controls the Oriental community.

When Britain signed the deal in 1984 to terminate its lease agreement and to give Hong Kong back to the Chinese, triads—secret crime societies—started funneling millions of illegally earned dollars into

Toronto real estate and businesses to create a new power base from which to direct their worldwide crime operations. They chose Canada because it does not require immigrants to report the cash they bring into the country, whether in suitcases or through banks. Dirty money is difficult to trace and easy to launder amid the multi-billions of dollars that legitimate Chinese immigrants and investors are pouring into the country. Michel Caron, Canada's associate deputy minister of finance, estimated in May 1990 that Hong Kong investors bring $3 billion to $4 billion a year into Canada. Hong Kong has 1,500 residents worth more than $200 million (US).

The number of Chinese immigrants to Canada has increased dramatically since the 1984 announcement that Hong Kong will revert to the People's Republic of China in 1997: in 1984, 7,696; in 1985, 7,380; in 1986, 5,853; in 1987, 16,170; in 1988, 22,802; 1990, 28,566. More than 87,000 Chinese emigrated from Hong Kong to Canada from 1987 to the end of 1990. A similar influx of Chinese will probably occur when the Portuguese colony of Macau is returned to mainland China in 1999.

Police intelligence shows that for every legal Chinese immigrant to Canada, four more enter the country illegally. Most of these immigrants are clean, as is their money. But their numbers shelter thousands of criminals.

"They're bringing the money over a little at a time so they have assets here when the time comes," a Metro Toronto police officer who monitors organized crime said of the triads. "Everybody wants a piece of the Toronto market. It's the market to have. The gang in power in 1997 will have power for a long time."

Triads earn money worldwide through heroin smuggling, extortion, gambling, prostitution, fraud, and robbery. Toronto is the main North American link in a triad heroin-smuggling network that dwarfs the defunct French Connection.

Triad members are well armed. One gang sold Uzis on the streets of Toronto for $2,000 a piece. Triads and other Asian gangs, such as Chinese street gangs, Chinese youth gangs, and Vietnamese street gangs, are well ingrained in Toronto's Chinatown districts and those of other North American cities. At the November 6, 1986, sentencing of two Vietnamese gang members convicted of extorting money from a Chinatown concert promoter, Constable Kenneth Yates of the Metro Toronto Police Oriental Crime Unit testified that "almost every business" in the Oriental community is paying protection money to gangs.

Law-enforcement and diplomatic corps officials agree that Asian organized crime gangs are becoming a major problem in Canada and the United States as they flood the countries with heroin, clash among themselves, and fight established criminal gangs for underworld supremacy. For some back-asswards and shortsighted reason, the local and federal governments in Canada and the United States aren't providing law enforcement with the money and manpower it needs to properly monitor the influx of Asian criminals, let alone combat them. At best, cops are dealing with daily occurrences and aren't getting the big picture.

Because Asian gangsters have restricted their crimes to their own community, whose members are afraid to complain to police, there has been no pressure on politicians to deal with the issue. Chinese business associations have even lobbied politicians to ensure the triad problem remains low profile for fear of scaring away rich investors and immigrants. Both groups figure Asian criminals will continue to prey on the Asian community, which can hush up its problems, and no one will be the wiser.

The Royal Hong Kong Police have analyzed triad and other Chinese organized crime activity in North America based on their own experience: "Illegal activities would be mostly confined to within the Chinese community which represents a sufficient source of revenue without encroaching into the Caucasian territory."

According to them, Asian criminals are more likely to prey on Asians than whites because the Chinese community is traditionally close-knit. It avoids contact with law-enforcement agencies or government institutions if it can. Restaurant and store operators avoid attracting official attention that could expose tax evasion tactics such as hiring illegal immigrants at low salaries that are paid under the table. There is a strong belief among many Chinese that triads cannot be eliminated and that it is more profitable to pay for peace quietly than to seek an outsider's help to fight criminals.

Ironically, Toronto's police force has an international reputation as the foremost authority on Asian organized crime in North America. A major Vietnamese gang leader arrested by the Metro Toronto police in 1986 revealed he had fled to Los Angeles because pressure by Toronto police had hampered his activities. He said Los Angeles cops had no idea what they were up against and he had committed crimes at will in California. He had returned to Toronto once to attend a family function and was arrested for extortion. He jumped bail and returned to California fast.

The long-standing Chinese mistrust of police officers stems from mass corruption in the Royal Hong Kong Police force, whose officers are often bought off. This mistrust prevents Asians from reporting crimes for fear the police will alert or side with the criminals. Toronto's

Chinese community started to trust police enough to turn in extortionists only in the mid-1980s.

Police officers in Canada and the United States are reluctant to share criminal intelligence with the Royal Hong Kong Police. "We won't deal with them," said a high-ranking Canada Customs official.

Participants at a conference on Asian organized crime held in Los Angeles in November 1986 were told that many of Hong Kong's 30,000 police officers are triad members. "These police have [six] years to work and make money [before 1997]," one official said. "Money is the big thing."

Detective-Superintendent A.T. (Tony) Lee, head of criminal intelligence for the Hong Kong police, complained that his force is "still lacking factual information from other law-enforcement agencies on what is happening overseas." He said his force does not believe the triads will leave Hong Kong. "Money can still be made in Hong Kong. There are criminals involved in illegal activities that will survive under any government." Asked why Hong Kong triad members travel the world so extensively, as documented by North American police, Superintendent Lee replied, "To go traveling, meeting up with old friends who immigrated somewhere else."

Some rival triad leaders on both sides of the ocean have tried to establish a temporary truce to aid their move to North America. "During the early 1980s, the principal leaders of Chinese organized crime in North America, or the representatives of those leaders, met in Hong Kong to discuss a possible detente between major rival groups," the US President's Commission on Organized Crime reported in 1986. Among the leaders was Toronto's Danny Mo, then head of the Kung Lok in Canada. "The meeting resulted in a recognition of territories and an agreement to assist one another when necessary. Then the participants 'burned the yellow paper,' a ritual that symbolizes brotherhood and the start of a new venture."

Toronto's Oriental community, on which Asian gangs have preyed in one form or other since the turn of the century, is growing rapidly. Toronto's population of about 290,000 ethnic Chinese and 60,000 Vietnamese is expected to double and even triple by 1997. Just as Italian crime families moved their operations to North America by following and preying on immigrants in the Little Italys across the continent, triads have gained a foothold in the Chinatowns that exist in every major city. The historical parallels are not lost on law-enforcement officials who document the increase in crime and violence to control lucrative Chinatown turfs. "It's like the Mafia in the thirties," said a Canada Customs official.

Toronto triad leaders, anticipating a vicious struggle for supremacy during the next ten years, are recruiting the most violent and conscienceless criminals to help take over the city's underworld. These criminals, members of Vietnamese street gangs who have ruthlessly fought triads for control of Chinatown since 1983, are seen by the Chinese as unsavory but necessary bedfellows. Anyone who controls the Vietnamese will control the Toronto market.

The US President's Commission on Organized Crime showed in 1984 that Hong Kong triads are exerting more control over Chinese street gangs in the United States. The commission interpreted this as proof that the triads are trying to reorganize or relocate before 1997. US law-enforcement agencies are also aware that Hong Kong triads are interested in Canada. Most American reports on Oriental gangs refer to gang affiliations in Toronto and Vancouver. California Attorney-General John Van De Kamp said in a report to the California Legislature, "The Luen Kung Lok is reportedly laundering money by purchasing property in Canada and Los Angeles."

The History Of Triads

Chinese triads are shrouded in more ritual and mystique than Italian organized crime. They were formed as quasi-military organizations to overthrow the non-Chinese Qing dynasty of the Manchus in the seventeenth century. Today they are powerful criminal organizations. The seventy-two triads based in Hong Kong have an estimated 80,000 members. In comparison, the twenty-four Italian organized crime families in the United States have 2,000 made members with 25,000 to 35,000 associates. Police have no idea how many triad and Asian street gang members there are in North America. Some adhere to centuries-old traditions; some don't.

The Ming emperor in Imperial China was emasculating his country in the seventeenth century. He appointed ass-kissers to his court and they ran the country into the ground. They filled their pockets with money from public coffers, which ran out as the country withered under a prolonged drought. The Chinese people had been pushed to the wall. On the other side of the Great Wall, Manchurian armies waited patiently for the empire to crumble.

A group of honest officials fed up with the corruption in their government formed a secret organization disguised as a money-lender's shop. They planned to build an army of honest people to flush out the Imperial Court and restore honesty and efficiency to the dynasty. Before they could get their act together, the peasants revolted and captured Beijing. The emperor committed suicide.

The Ming general who guarded the Great Wall against the hordes of Manchurians steamed at the thought of peasants on the Dragon Throne. Greedy, he told the Manchurians they could sweep through China with him if they promised to let him take the throne. The Manchurians happily agreed. Both the Ming and Manchu armies slaughtered the peasants. The Ming army took a hell of a beating in the process. By the time they go to Beijing, they were in no shape to fight the Manchu army when it reneged on its promise and seized power. The Manchurians proclaimed the First Emperor of the Qing Dynasty. The Chinese were pissed off—a foreigner on the Dragon Throne.

The group that set up the money-lending shop expanded their secret organization until they had accumulated enough supporters to rebel against the Qing. They took a bad beating. The Manchu continued to control northern China for the next fifty years, but had to stay alert to fight a bloody host of pro-Ming organizations that kept popping up in the rest of the country like groundhogs at a target shoot.

The secret organizations in China at that time were divided into two groups: the religious White Lotus in northern China and the political Hung Society—Tien Ti Hui or Heaven and Earth Society—in south, west, and central China. The triad society was formed from the Hung Society around 1674 by monks in the Shaolin, or Siu Lam, Temple in Fukien Province where the temple's abbot trained 108 monks in the martial arts of Kung Fu (remember grasshopper David Carradine?). The warriors volunteered when the Manchu emperor asked for help to fend off an invading tribe of barbarians. They won and returned to the Siu Lam Monastery after politely refusing rewards from the emperor. Machiavellian at heart, he understood he couldn't afford to have a crew of dangerous monks drop-kicking around the countryside. Accordingly, he had the mountain monastery destroyed and the monks killed. Only eighteen escaped.

Five of these survived dangers described as mythical and founded five lodges in China's five main provinces. They became the Five Ancestors of the Triad—a name derived from the Hung Society's symbol: an equilateral triangle with the sides representing heaven, earth, and man.

The political Triad Society, with its secret codes and hand signs, gave rise to the Chinese proverb, "Officials draw their power from the law, the people from the secret society." Triads flourished during the eighteenth and nineteenth centuries in feudal China and spread as southern Chinese migrated to southeast Asia and the Malay Archipelago. Chinese communities in Hong Kong, Singapore, and Malaya shielded themselves from government corruption behind the triads. Immigrants had to join a lodge to be accepted into a community. The first triads were bred out of a distaste for corruption and a desire for patriotism, chivalry, fraternity, and traditional morality.

The Manchu dynasty ended on February 15, 1912, when Dr. Sun Yat-sen, the first president of the Republic of China and father of Democratic China, deemed the Qing rule over. At that point, the triads transformed themselves from political groups to criminal organizations. In fact, the criminals had controlled them for a long time under the guise of working for the good of the people.

Triads used political figures to protect their criminal empires. Politicians used triads to protect their social empires. General Chiang Kai-shek, who succeeded Sun Yat-sen, financed his battle against Mao Zedong's usurping Communist forces with triad money and support. Triad members did the dirty work the army wouldn't do. When the Communists appeared ready to gobble up the Kuomintang, thousands of nationalists—soldiers, police, civil servants—joined the triads in mass initiation ceremonies. Many of their leaders fled with Chiang to Taiwan, where the link between organized crime and government remains strong to this day. Other triad leaders moved to Hong Kong where they set up the organizations that are moving to North America today to escape the impending Communist takeover of that country. The triads may finally be rid of the *gwai lo* (foreign devils) who took over the the country when Hong Kong became a British Crown colony in 1842, but the devils in red arouse more fear than disgust.

Criminals and governments, however legitimate, have always found a way to work hand in hand. The Japanese used a triad-financed Peace Corps to police Hong Kong during its Second World War occupation. For this assistance, they allowed triads to continue their criminal activities.

The triads got out of hand in 1956 with riots that started on October 10, the double ten anniversary of the 1911 uprising against the Manchu dynasty. When order was finally restored, 59 people were dead, 384 injured, 72 factories were looted, and 400 buildings were burned. The Hong Kong cops belatedly pulled themselves together and formed a unit to investigate the triads. More than 10,000 triad members were arrested from 1956 to 1960; 600 were deported to Taiwan. By 1960, 500,000, or one in six Hong Kong residents, were triad members. The triads gained strength in the 1960s as police focused their energies instead on Communist subversives.

The main reason the Hong Kong police were so ineffective at combatting triads, though, was the number of high-level cops on triad payrolls. There are several reasons this happened: Hong Kong residents had little say in the way the colony was run; the cops were poorly paid and worked long hours; they not only policed crime, but acted as security guards during periods of unrest, which did not ingratiate them with the colony's citizens; Hong Kong was overcrowded and rife with poverty; it lacked social stability in light of the Communist takeover of the colony in 1997; Hong Kong culture epitomizes the Me Generation and puts wealth and self-gratification ahead of the common good, praising the rich and enterprising and despising those on government payrolls, such as cops; police investigation budgets were nil because the government prided itself on running at a profit.

By the early 1970s, corruption on the Royal Hong Kong Police Force could no longer be ignored. A commission investigating corruption exposed high-level officers who raked in millions of dollars on the side. Many of them fled to Taiwan and Canada.

The following description of triad hierarchy and initiation rites was obtained from two classified police documents, one American, one Canadian. It also comes from the only two such triad documents seized in North America, both taken from the home of a Toronto man. New York City triads have put contracts on the lives of the two undercover Federal Bureau of Investigation agents who penetrated their ranks to obtain some of these secrets.

The name triad is an English designation derived from the triangle symbol of the Hung Society, from which all triads derive. The Chinese of Hong Kong refer to the society as the Sam Hop Wui (Three United Associations); Tin Tei Wui (Heaven Earth Association); Hung Mun (Hung Society); or Hak Sh'e Wui (Dark Society Association). The first society was made up of five lodges across China. The second lodge covered the Guangdong/Guangxi area, from which Hong Kong's major triads are descended.

Rank and Numbers

Triad members are ranked with names and numbers given secret-meanings through punning and intonation. Mandarin has four tones; Cantonese has nine. The higher their number, the higher a person's status within the triad.

The head of a triad is called Shan Chu, 489, or First Route Marshal. He is also known as Mountain Lord. He is sometimes unofficially called Dai Lo or elder brother and has final say in all triad matters. It is not uncommon for a triad to have more than one member with the number 489, especially older gangs with several experienced members who have earned the title.

The deputy head of a triad is called Fu Chan Chu, 438, or Second Route Marshal. He is also known as Assistant Mountain Lord. Sometimes he is called Yee Lo or second elder brother. Two other gang members also are called 438: Sin Fung, the Vanguard, who is responsible for recruiting members, and Heung Chu, the Incense Master. Both officiate at ceremonies.

Hung Kwan, 426, or the Red Pole, is the chief fighter and battle strategist—the triad's heavy. He breaks the legs and arms of members who break triad laws and those who don't pay protection dues.

Cho Hai, 432, or the Straw Sandal, is the liaison and messenger. He communicates with gang members and organizes battles and meetings with other triads. He also delivers demand notes for ransom or protection money.

Pak Tsz Sin, 415, or the White Paper Fan, is an advisor responsible for general administration within the triad.

Sze Kau or 49 is an ordinary member. New recruits are given the number 36. Sheung Fa, or Double Flower, is an honorary member.

In the triad's Hong Kong branch, Chu Chi is the chief and Cha So is the treasurer.

The significance of the numbers can be found in the Chinese occult and ancient mythology and rites. The number 4, which precedes all ranks, is said to represent the four seas the Chinese believed surrounded the earth. The number 4 also stands for the universe and contains a punning reference to the Chinese quotation: "We are brothers within the Four Seas."

The leader's number is broken down this way: 4+8+9=21. The Chinese character for 21 echoes the character for Hung, the name of the Hung Society. In 438, the 4 is set aside, leaving 3 and 8, which combine in written Chinese to refer to the character for the Hung Society. The number 426 is analyzed this way: 4×26+4=108, the number of legendary heroes of the Sung Dynasty who fought against imperial tyranny. It is also a common mystical number throughout the Far East—there are 108 mudras in Indian traditional dance, for example. Similarly, with the number 415, 4×15+4=64, the number of hexagrams in the *I Ching*, or *Book of Changes*. The number 432 breaks down into 4×32=128, the number of patriots said to have practiced martial arts in the Siu Lam, or Shaolin, Monastery. The name Straw Sandal refers to the miraculous sandal that turned into a boat and carried some of the monks to safety when they were pursued by enemies. The number 49 breaks down into 4×9=36, the number of vows an initiate must take, another mystical number.

Initiation Ceremonies

Although triad initiation ceremonies differ from gang to gang, three steps must be followed for the rite to be legitimate.

It must be held in a triad lodge decorated with flags, banners, and ancestral titles.

There must be a blood brotherhood ceremony. Blood is drawn from the left index finger of the new member and mixed with wine and water, then drunk by all present to symbolize unwavering loyalty.

Thirty-six oaths are taken calling not only for the member's loyalty but also for that of his family. Treason or the disclosure of oaths, aims, or practices of the society is punishable by death.

A shortened version of the ceremony for the impatient is called "hanging the blue lantern." A recruit swears an oath of loyalty to the triad in the presence of his sponsor, pays a small fee, learns some hand signs to identify himself to others, and learns the thirty-six triad oaths.

Signs

New members are also taught secret finger signs to enable them to identify themselves to fellow member and to indicate their rank.

"A member in distress can then always find shelter and protection from other members even though he is a stranger," one police document says. "All he needs to do to prove his membership is to return the hand challenges or verses directed at him. The penalty for each type of offence being known to every member, there is little risk of one member failing in his obligation toward another."

These are some of the signs that have evolved over the centuries:
—Place a full cup of tea in front of the teapot. It means "I am a brother. Help me." If the other can help, he drinks the tea. If not, he throws it away and pours a fresh cup.
—When a full cup is placed on top of an empty one, a member pours tea from the full one into the empty one until they are equal and then drinks.
—If a brother asks a member to drink a cup of tea or wine, he presents it to him with his middle finger held above the cup. The other should receive it with his middle finger at the bottom.
—When offering cigarettes, three are offered, with the center one protruding more than the other two. That cigarette is called the Five Founders cigarette and can be accepted only by the master of ceremonies or higher ranking officers. Other members have to push back the three cigarettes with the left forefinger and pull out one at the bottom.
—A bowl of rice is presented to a stranger. Chopsticks are placed across

stretched fingers and offered to the stranger. A triad member will push the bowl away.

—A person who has committed a murder cuts off some of his hair and ties it to his left arm. When he asks for refuge, he "shall wipe his left eye and the brotherhood shall provide him with expenses and means of escape."

Code Phrases

A draft of wind—a spy, the police.
Shoot partridges—robbery.
Bridge flanks—double-edged sword.
To make a circuit—to plunder a town or village.
To wash the body—to kill a man.
Hung obeys heaven—vinegar.
To bite clouds—to smoke opium.
To bite ginger—to smoke tobacco.
The gun—the opium pipe.
To walk the thread—to travel.
Green lotus—tea.
To wash the face—cut off the head.
To lure the fair wind—cut off the ears.
The lion's club—a dagger.
Orange board or lion—a sword.
Black dog—pistol.
Son of a leper—non-member.
Family harmony—wine.
To let loose horses—hold a meeting.
To wave the willow—piss.

Drugs

"Heroin is by far the most serious threat from Asian organized crime groups."—Joe D. Whitley, acting associate Attorney General of the United States.

Chinese drug-smuggling organizations in North America today owe much of their power to the racist attitudes among both Chinese and whites that isolated Oriental communities from the cities they existed in more than one hundred years ago. The Chinese banded together out of fear and distaste for the *lo fan* or outsiders, whose way of life they despised. The whites preferred that the Chinese stay in Chinatowns, where they seemed to live quietly and didn't disturb anyone. The isolation of Chinatowns kept white law enforcement and government out of Chinese life. It also allowed for the creation of Chinese organizations—tongs—that ran the community. Although tongs were founded for the good of the Chinese, they soon became power bases for criminals who preyed on the community as well.

The On Leong Tong on Mott Street and the Hip Sing Tong on Pell Street in New York City's Chinatown are the two most powerful tongs in the city. They were formed in the midst of a mostly male Chinatown that was settled in the mid-1800s by Chinese immigrants from the village of Toy Shan in the Guangzhou (Canton) region of China. A racist American Congress feared these people would reproduce like rabbits so they passed Exclusion Acts that cruelly banned Chinese women from the United States for more than sixty years. This left the men in New York City's Chinatown, as well as Chinese railway workers and gold-field miners on the west coast, with little to do but gamble and drink. Gaming houses became big moneymakers, and where there's easy illegal money there's organized crime.

The On Leong Tong's ties with General Chiang Kai-shek's Kuomintang party and China's Nationalist government until the Communist takeover of China in 1949 provided the links that form a formidable international drug-trafficking operation today. Although Chinese traffickers have brought opium and heroin into North America for more than one hundred years, Mao Zedong's takeover of China provided the impetus for the mass entry of Chinese into the drug underworld. Nationalist party officials, including Chiang Kai-shek, had financed their political aspirations through drug smuggling. They were well connected to the poppy patches of the Golden Triangle and continued their drug smuggling after fleeing China. Then, as today, China White heroin from southeast Asia was most easily smuggled into North America using the Commonwealth connection—from Hong Kong to Toronto, sometimes using London as an intermediate stop.

The On Leong Tong provided the connections needed in Toronto and New York to move heroin on the streets. As business prospered and the Italian mob started to feel the sting of law enforcement and collapsing suppliers, the Chinese linked up with the Carlo Gambino family in New York. An On Leong Tong restaurant manager in New York is the all-important link between the Chinese smugglers and the mob.

The massive influx of Hong Kong Chinese into North America since 1965 has changed the face of the continent's Chinatowns. The reliance on and respect for the tongs diminished as generations of Chinese who have had nothing to do with them go about their own lives, be they honest working people or criminals. Street gangs made up of Hong Kong Chinese started running their own little criminal empires—at first with the backing of the tongs, then without them. Punks were always willing to run tong drugs for a buck, picking them up in Toronto and carrying them across the border to New York.

Although triads have had a piece of the North American drug market for decades, they moved into it heavily when they foresaw the end of their Hong Kong empires. Triad members set up versions of their criminal organizations first in Canada, then the United States, using their influential Hong Kong links to piece together international smuggling networks. Other criminals set up copy-cat triads. They had few links to the Hong Kong gangs but knew how to use fear and intimidation to get things done. Whether or not modern North American triads follow the detailed and lengthy rituals of the original triads is irrelevant. Their aims are the same—money and power.

Although many law-enforcement agencies classify the Ghost Shadows as a triad, the gang first saw light as a New York City street gang under the leadership of the legendary Nicky Louie. Louie is a legend because the media made him one. His ability to avoid criminal charges added to his power and "face." Nicky Louie's street gang, which continually struggled for supremacy and face in gunfights with rival gangs, had no name until a *New York Times* reporter fumbling with the nuances of the Chinese language called them the Ghost Shadow in a 1969 story. Louie's original gang was made up of younger members of the Kwon Ying Gang. A rival gang member told the reporter these punks were ghost shadow, which was intended as an insult. In Chinese, the word ghost implies a person is not all there. The Chinese use the word to denigrate whites (*bak guey* or white ghost), and blacks (*hak guey* or black ghost). The reporter called the gang the Ghost Shadows in print and the gangsters liked it.

Chinese street gangs play a major role in importing heroin into North America. While established trafficking groups prefer to hide large shipments in cargo, gangsters smuggle smaller amounts on their bodies. They don't have the money or the contacts to hide heroin in cargo shipments. A gangster can buy a pound of heroin in Bangkok for $4,000 and sell it in the States for $65,000 to $70,000. Mules usually carry three pounds per trip. Gangsters rely on the Hong Kong triads to set up the buys for them, giving them another foothold in North America.

Freelance Chinese smugglers also bring a fair amount of heroin into Canada and the US. They are generally new immigrants who realize they can get ahead more quickly with a few quick deals. Garment or restaurant workers with connections to a Hong Kong supplier and a Toronto or New York buyer pool their money to finance a smuggling operation. Then they use the profits to set up legitimate businesses.

Chinese drug traffickers—triads, tongs, street gangs, and entrepreneurs—control the North American heroin market, half of which is based in New York City. New Yorkers have always had an affinity for heroin.

Jack Kerouac often described his frenzied forays through Times Square looking for his beloved junkie friend Herbert Huncke in the late 1940s and early 1950s. He couldn't drive through the area without keeping his eyes peeled for Huncke, who survived both Kerouac and his manic buddy Neal Cassady and finally published his memoirs in 1991.

It shouldn't surprise anyone that the Chinese filled the vacuum while the Italian mob was having problems with the cops in the early 1980s. They were poised to take over the market anyway. The mob's own weakness, the result of prosecutions, merely prevented a drug war over turf. The cops knew little about the Chinese drug networks and there were few Chinese-speaking police officers who could clue in to what was happening. Things won't change until a white person gets killed.

The Chinese moved quickly over the last decade to flood the market in Toronto and New York with southeast Asian China White heroin of a purity never before seen on the streets. In 1982, 3 percent of the heroin in New York City came from southeast Asia and 96 percent came from Iran, Pakistan, and Afghanistan. By 1986, southeast Asian heroin took up 40 percent of the market and southwest Asian heroin made up the rest.

The Chinese used a clever, but deadly, marketing strategy to hook their addicts. First, they avoided the middleman, who traditionally has been a member of the mob and diluted the heroin before passing it down the ladder to distributors. The Chinese sold directly to distributors. They had so much of the drug that they could afford to let it hit the streets at levels of purity never seen before. It used to be 3 to 15 percent pure at that level.

Today, heroin ranging in purity from 40 to 75 percent is being sold on the streets of New York and Toronto. While this may please the addicts, it also kills them. They aren't used to horse this powerful and they don't dilute it. Southeast Asian True Value brand bought in the Bronx and East Harlem in 1989 was 55.3 percent and 74.9 percent pure. Southeast Asian Red Heat brand heroin bought in New York's Lower East side in 1989 was 52.5 percent pure. Southeast Asian Day & Nite brand heroin bought in the Bronx in 1989 was 68.1 percent pure. One batch of heroin found in Harlem was 90.7 percent pure.

There are several reasons for this: new street-dealing groups such as the Dominicans aren't used to cutting heroin and are diluting it only once or twice, as they would cocaine. Also there's so much heroin on the market that it doesn't have to be cut to supply demand. And dealers are competing with cheap and potent crack cocaine. Pushers are also lowballing—selling at dirt-cheap prices—to attract cocaine users. They encourage those who would like to try heroin but fear needles to "chase the dragon"—smoke brown heroin from southwest Asia.

Pushers don't bother telling addicts their heroin is 90 to 98 percent pure rather than the customary 25 to 30 percent. When addicts start dying and the police figure out why, they take to the streets and warn dopers that the heroin they are using is too potent. New York City police drove through junkie stomping grounds with megaphones warning addicts about a bad batch of heroin in February 1991. Metro Toronto police warned addicts, too, after four junkies died in March 1990 after injecting speedballs—the same mixture of heroin and cocaine that killed John Belushi.

Chinese drug traffickers from Hong Kong, Taiwan, Thailand, China, Malaysia, Singapore, and Macau put aside their differing political backgrounds once in the United States to supply the streets with heroin. Unlike the Italian mob, which deals heroin in quantities of one- to ten-kilogram lots, the Chinese routinely deal ten- to fifty-kilogram shipments and import multi-hundred-pound shipments by sea and air freight. Chinese traffickers have a near monopoly on the southeast Asian heroin market. They have also formed strong links with drug-trafficking organizations in Bolivia, Uruguay, Panama, and Mexico. While the Chinese control the heroin market in Canada and the US, the rest of the market is supplied by Nigerian, Ghanian, Pakistani, and Israeli traffickers.

Triads ship heroin from Thailand to Singapore, then to western Europe and Toronto, where New York gang members pick it up. Twice in 1986, Royal Canadian Mounted Police and Canada Customs officers arrested New York gang members trying to pick up a total of $20 million in heroin that couriers had flown to Toronto from the Orient through Europe. In both cases, the couriers called Hong Kong with a code indicating safe arrival. Hong Kong then got in touch with the New York gang members.

In one case, two members of New York's Tong Lok triad tried to pick up the shipment. In the other, one of the two pickup men was allegedly a member of the New York Tung On street gang, which is connected to the Sung Yee On triad in Hong Kong. This triad has ties with Italian organized crime in the United States.

The Chinese supply Dominican drug distribution networks in New York. Dominican traffickers made contact with Chinese suppliers in prison when many newly arrived Chinese were arrested for robbery and extortion in the 1970s. These Chinese put the Dominican traffickers in touch with their suppliers. Police found China White heroin wrapped in Chinese newspapers during a raid on a Dominican heroin mill in Queens, New York, on July 1, 1987. The uncut drug had gone straight from the Chinese to the Dominicans. A Dominican trafficking ring busted in 1989 distributed more than ten kilos of heroin a week in the Bronx.

The entire eastern seaboard of the United States is supplied with heroin that arrives through Toronto and New York. Southeast Asian heroin from New York was seized in Rhode Island in 1989 already packaged for street sale under brand names such as Hurricane, High Explosion, Hot Stuff, Blue Diamond, and Superfly.

The traffickers deal quickly with any problems that threaten their livelihood. Health officials could learn from the rapidity of their responses. As soon as statistics showed that one-third of AIDS victims were intravenous drug users, traffickers started selling a combined package of a bag of heroin and a hypodermic needle for $25. Some sold extra needles. That's a free-market response.

Washington, D.C., has the inglorious reputation of being Murder City, USA. A task force of Washington, D.C., police and agents from the Bureau of Alcohol, Tobacco and Firearms was formed in 1985 to stem the flow of guns to the streets to reduce the murder rate. It hasn't had much effect. One of their investigations found that many guns seized on the streets had been stolen from gun shops in the area or in adjoining states. They also found that cigarettes stolen during break-and-enters were sold to store owners in the city's Chinatown.

In the curious way by which information arrives on the right desk, a black punk arrested for trying to kill a cop and for break-ins decided to bargain his way to a lighter sentence by informing the task force that Peter Yuen, a Chinese grocery store owner, bought guns with cocaine and sold stolen cigarettes. The FBI sent a Spanish undercover agent to Yuen; the agent managed to buy cocaine from the storekeeper. When Yuen told the narc he could also get heroin, they made a deal to trade cocaine for heroin. The FBI then sent in a Chinese undercover narc and an ATF agent to meet Yuen. The Chinese narc posed as the Hong Kong connection of a crime syndicate. In March 1987, the narcs bought 1.5 pounds of heroin from a Chinese man they met through Yuen.

While the drug setup was going on, guns that had been stolen and sold in Washington showed up in the hands of Chinese gang members in New York City. The agents turned their attention to New York and found that Chinese gangs were buying large shipments of guns in Dallas, Texas. Three New York Chinese gang members sold an undercover ATF agent twenty handguns from Texas. They were also shipping guns to organized crime groups in Taiwan and Japan with the help of employees at JFK Airport. The gangsters were also selling heroin. Members of the gang were always armed with small machine guns and had links to the On Leong Tong and the Flying Dragons gang in New York City, Vietnamese gangs in New York and Texas, and Italian organized crime families.

As if drugs and guns weren't enough, the Chinese syndicate was involved in diamond smuggling; theft; forged passports, green cards, and New York City parking permits; and offering hit men for contract killings. The gang was able to supply 100 pounds of high purity heroin each month. By the time the organization was busted in Washington, New York, San Francisco, Los Angeles, and Texas, the gang had sold undercover cops sixty-three guns. Fifty machine guns were seized during the busts.

Peter Woo looked like any other old Chinese shopkeeper—a pudgy, jolly fellow who sold booze at his Tai Pei Liquors store in Manhattan. The seventy-two-year-old Woo was community-minded and politically inclined. He knew many politicians, was photographed with New York City mayor Ed Koch, and formed the Chinese Democratic Society. He was once known as the godfather of New York's Chinese community. Woo's good friend David Kwong was a younger man who owned a butcher shop near the liquor store. Both men worked hard and were extremely well connected.

Sometime in the 1970s, Woo and Kwong branched out from booze and meat into a more profitable commodity—heroin. They started small, with multi-million-dollar shipments. They set up a drug network from Thailand to Toronto to New York. En route, they dealt with some of the world's most powerful and nefarious men. They bought their heroin from General Khun Sa, the Burmese revolutionary warlord who funds his wars and feeds and arms his 16,000-man army with the taxes he levies on heroin and opium produced in the country's vast poppy fields. Triad couriers smuggled the heroin into Canada and arranged for it to be carried into the United States.

The smuggling network's main man in Canada was Cheung Wai Wong, known on the street as Kenny "Baby Face" Wong, a thirty-year-old Calgary, Alberta, cook who never held a job during the ten years he lived in the prairie city. Wong was the most unlikely international drug-smuggling mastermind. A man who never owned a car and lived with his mother, four brothers, and two sisters in a suburban house set up multi-million-dollar heroin deals halfway around the world and plotted smuggling schemes in Toronto hotels and restaurants.

Despite his apparent lack of sophistication in Cow Town, Kenny Wong was a world traveler. His two passports—one Canadian and one

Hong Kong—show more than twenty trips to Hong Kong, the Philippines, Macau, and Bangkok. He didn't even spend money on taxis to the airport; he bummed rides. Wong was well connected to triads, which organized couriers, smuggling routes, and distribution of the heroin from southeast Asia's Golden Triangle. The heroin usually arrived in Vancouver and was stored in Calgary while triads in Toronto set up sales to American customers. Once a deal was made, heroin was shipped to Toronto and carried across the US border by mules selected from Toronto's large Chinese community.

Hong Kong couriers brought the heroin into Canada instead of directly into the United States because they could enter the country without visas, which meant they weren't subjected to stringent checks by Canada Customs.

Sometime in 1988, Woo and Kwong decided to bag an elephant. They plotted to bring into the United States 800 pounds of 90-percent pure China White heroin worth $1 billion on the street. The shipment was so big that Burmese warlord Khun Sa assigned his lieutenant Chan Hok Pang to plot the shipment's route. Pang dealt with members of the Sun Yee On and 14K triads in Calgary and Toronto make the necessary arrangements. Accordingly, the heroin-filled tires of 264 golf carts made their way from Singapore to Los Angeles. From there they were trucked to two houses in Queens, New York.

Then a law-enforcement project called White Mare, sparked by information from Simon Au Yeung, who infiltrated the smuggling network for the FBI, ended the Woo-Kwong white powder business. Police arrested fifty-four people in Toronto, Buffalo, New York, Los Angeles, San Francisco, Chicago, Vancouver, Singapore, and Hong Kong on February 21, 1989. Narcs had been on Woo's tail for two years, following him to Canada every time he flew to Toronto. Kwong's trips to Toronto to negotiate with Hong Kong couriers were also monitored, as were his discussions at the Scarborough Inn. Woo's telephone chats with Kenny Wong, his Hong Kong connection, were also recorded. Wong split to Hong Kong when the busts went down, but was quickly arrested and extradited to the US.

To put Woo's smuggling network in perspective, it made the French Connection look like a street-corner pushing operation. The case forced law-enforcement agencies to take a second look at the meager funds they had allotted to investigating Asian organized crime. Obviously, they had missed the boat. They considered Asian criminals an oddity more than a threat. Woo's arrest and the seizure of so much heroin made US law enforcement realize what Canadian cops have understood for more than a decade: Asian organized crime is here to stay and before long it will dominate the underworld.

Veng-Tat (Peter) Lau was having problems making ends meet at his Oriental Regency Chinese Restaurant in Brampton, Ontario, just outside Toronto. So he said. Unlike other businessmen, Lau had connections he decided to use to increase his income.

He arranged in 1989 for eighty-seven pounds of China White heroin from southeast Asia's Golden Triangle to be shipped to China where the powder was hidden in five of 300 boxes of umbrellas at a Guangzhou factory. It would be worth $87 million on the street. Peter Lau was a smart cookie. He even used a false name to negotiate the deal—Ah Chu. The man had a sense of humor. Ah Chu remained at arm's length from the initial wheeling and dealing, entrusting the footwork to a middleman through whom he offered a courier $300,000 to get the drugs to Canada.

Ah Chu may have been smart, but he was not lucky. The middleman he chose was a rat. He tipped off the Communists and they notified the Interpol Guangdong Liaison Office, which found the drugs on March 31, 1989 while searching the boxes on a Guangzhou dock. The Chinese enlisted the aid of the US Drug Enforcement Administration office in Hong Kong, the Royal Hong Kong Police, and the Royal Canadian Mounted Police.

Undercover narcs watched the shipment of umbrellas being loaded into a cargo container and hauled aboard a China Ocean Shipping Company freighter on April 26. The heroin was on its way to Vancouver, where Canada Customs agents noticed the waybill was written out for 295 cartons of umbrellas, not 300. The Chinese had not replaced the five boxes of heroin they seized. Customs agents fudged a new waybill so Ah Chu wouldn't get suspicious, and the boxes were loaded into a CP Rail boxcar headed for Toronto. The shipment was then trucked to a discount store in Ajax. Ah Chu met a courier in Toronto and told him to get the heroin to New York. The courier was a DEA agent, who flew the heroin to a private landing strip in New Jersey in a DEA plane on May 5.

The thirty-six-year-old Ah Chu, by then identified as Peter Lau by police, walked down 42nd Street at Broadway on May 6 with a sweetie on his arm. He had made arrangements to sell the heroin in Chinatown. The narcs who surrounded him with drawn guns as he walked out of the Ramada Inn watched the smile drip off his face. Police also arrested another man in Elmhurst, New York, with seven and a half pounds of heroin. He was to arrange for its delivery. A third man who was to deliver it was arrested in Whitestone, New York.

The DEA set up "Operation Sea Horse" in February 1987 to combat the rapid increase of southeast Asian heroin-trafficking groups. The operation seized more than 500 kilos of heroin and $15 million in assets and

dismantled four major southeast Asian heroin-trafficking groups operating in twelve countries and fifteen American cities.

Law-enforcement officers in the People's Republic of China seized
4.5 kilos of southeast Asian heroin stuffed inside live goldfish bound for
San Francisco in March 1988.

A persistent Toronto cop following a hot tip led to the bust of a major
Big Circle Boys smuggling ring that brought 1,200 pounds of near-pure
China White heroin into North America from 1988 to 1990 for a
wholesale profit of $72 million, according to seized gang documents.
Metro Toronto Police Detective-Constable Kenneth Yates was tipped
off about a heroin-smuggling network in March 1990, five months after
more than a pound of 99-percent pure heroin worth $3.1 million was
seized in Scarborough, one of the cities that make up Metro Toronto.

An eleven-month investigation of the Big Circle Boys in Canada, the
United States, and Hong Kong was carried out by Metro Toronto Police
intelligence officers, the Royal Canadian Mounted Police, the US DEA,
the Federal Bureau of Investigation, the Ontario Provincial Police, the
Montreal Urban Police, the Royal Hong Kong Police, and Canadian and
US customs and immigration services.

The investigation ended during the first week of February 1991, when
police arrested six people in Toronto and six in New York City. They
seized twenty-five pounds of heroin worth $77.5 million (Cdn.) during
the course of the investigation and $8.6 million (US) cash in twenty bags
and eight pieces of luggage in two Brooklyn, New York, houses. They
also found a submachine gun, several pistols—one of them equipped
with a silencer—body armor, heroin presses, and cloth cylinders used to
smuggle the heroin from Thailand. The heroin was shipped from
Thailand to eastern Canada. From there it was distributed through
Toronto and Montreal and taken to New York.

"They're a bunch of vicious bastards," said one cop. "They'd shoot us
if we stand in the way."

The Golden Triangle's opium fields produce 40 percent of the world's
heroin; 43 percent of the heroin that enters the United States and 40
percent of the heroin seized in New York City comes from southeast
Asia. It is the best heroin in the world, rarely less than 85 percent pure.
Street-level southeast Asian heroin in New York City averages 65
percent purity. Southeast Asia heroin generates abut $80 billion in
revenues each year, according to the Drug Enforcement Administration.
General Khun Sa figures the more than 2,000 tons of heroin produced in
the Golden Triangle every year brings the area $1.5 trillion dollars. If all

that heroin were sold on North American streets, it could fetch $10 trillion dollars.

Obviously experts have no idea how much heroin is available in the world and what it's worth. That means they don't know how many addicts there really are and how many people traffic in the stuff. So the problem is much, much bigger than anyone suspects.

The opium/heroin market in Myanmar (formerly Burma) is controlled by armies in parts of the country the Rangoon government has never been able to control. Drug traffickers include Burmese warlords and their armies, Burmese Communist rebels, various ethnic independence movements, and even Chinese generals still loyal to the Kuomintang nationalist cause more than forty years after their flight from Communist China. The traffickers buy opium grown by farmers in the hills and convert it to heroin in jungle laboratories before carrying it over the hills to secret trading spots near Thailand where they meet with buyers from all over the world.

General Khun Sa, whose real name is Chang Chi-Fu, collects a 40-percent tax from producers in his 162,000-square-mile Shan state. The fifty-seven-year-old warlord has been nicknamed the Money Tree by his Mong Tai Revolutionary Army soldiers for the amount of cash he draws from the drug trade—an estimated $400 million in 1989. The half-Chinese, half-Shan general has claimed that the DEA and CIA have tried to assassinate him forty-two times. It could be true. Khun Sa first got involved with drugs in 1967 when he started what became known as the opium wars—a struggle between his Mong Tai soldiers and the armies of former Chinese Kuomintang soldiers who fled China in 1949 to live off the drug trade in Burma. Today the various armies who all feed off the poppy fields understand the voracious drug market is big enough for all of them. Khun Sa is the best known drug general, but not the biggest. There are larger trafficking organizations in the Burmese, Laotian, and Thai jungles that even the CIA and DEA know nothing about—or won't talk about.

Khun Sa has a better solution to drug addiction than North America does. Addicts in his domain are given a chance to get off the stuff. Those who can't are shot. He knows how to curb demand for enslaving drugs. He also knows North American authorities don't or won't.

These are some seizures of southeast Asian heroin destined for New York.

On June 23, 1985, 210 pounds of heroin was seized from a commercial shipment of ice buckets at Seattle-Tacoma Airport.

On December 5, 1985, 15 pounds of heroin destined for New York City was seized in Hong Kong. Telephone calls were made from the

U.N. Plaza Hotel to Hong Kong giving directions for delivery. Another 45 pounds of heroin was found hidden in the center of tea tins also destined for New York City.

On January 19, 1986, police seized 50 pounds of heroin from five metal wall plaques that arrived at JFK Airport from Tokyo.

On April 2, 1986, customs officials seized 51 pounds of heroin at Ottawa Airport on a flight arriving from Hong Kong.

On the same day, Steven Tan was arrested in connection with 16 pounds of heroin seized at San Francisco Airport destined for New York City. Tan admitted to supplying Harlem connections.

On June 1, 1986, Charles Wain was arrested in connection with 14 pounds of heroin seized from the bottom of an air conditioner shipped from Thailand to New York via London.

On September 3, 1986, Chiu-Ping Hu was arrested in connection with thirty-three pounds of heroin seized in Thai teakwood furniture delivered to Queens, New York. The shipment arrived in a cargo container in Seattle and was shipped by rail to New Jersey.

On November 8, 1986, police made a seizure of 10.5 kilos of heroin from ginseng tea boxes at Kai Tak Airport in Hong Kong.

A Hong Kong man and his Chinese and Vietnamese associates were arrested in the US in early January 1990, after 143 pounds of heroin worth $64 million on the street were found in 192 cans of lichees in syrup in Los Angeles.

Three leaders of a Hong Kong drug-trafficking ring were arrested in Toronto in the fall of 1988 after the Royal Canadian Mounted Police intercepted $9 million in heroin destined for New York via Hong Kong, Vancouver, and Toronto.

A Hong Kong man and a former native of Hong Kong who had lived in New York for six years were arrested in Toronto after Canada Customs officials noticed a Chinese man wearing oversized high-cut running shoes clomping through Lester B. Pearson International Airport on Saturday, September 27, 1986. The man had flown from Thailand to Singapore to Zurich and Toronto. The RCMP followed him to a nearby hotel where they searched his running shoes and found one kilo of 100-percent pure heroin in the hollowed-out soles. Those are expensive odor eaters.

By 1988, China White heroin from southeast Asia replaced Mexican black tar as the major form of heroin sold in California. China White went from 15 percent of the California market to about 80 percent in a matter of years. About one-half of the heroin in the US enters through California. Law-enforcement officials in California fear that turf wars could develop between Cambodian, Thai, and Vietnamese gangs and black and Hispanic gangs that traditionally control street-level heroin sales. This would give California its version of the Colombian cocaine cowboy wars in Miami in the late 1970s and early 1980s. Two DEA agents were murdered while trying to carry out an undercover heroin buy from Taiwanese and Thai dealers in February 1988.

North America isn't the only continent targeted by triads. The 14k triad out of Hong Kong controls the Australian heroin market. At least nine Chinese gangs based in Melbourne and Sydney are building power bases on that continent by linking up with Italian and Lebanese gangs. Australian cops found out how wealthy their new gangsters were in the autumn of 1988 when they were tipped off that Hong Kong criminals had bought a yacht and planned to sail to a port near Sydney. Police searched the boat and found forty-three kilos of heroin worth $40 million. Then they set a trap. They flew two men from the boat to Australia at the end of October, when the boat was scheduled to dock, and had them pretend they were delivering the heroin. Police arrested fourteen people in Hong Kong and seven in Australia.

Money Laundering

Triads have a variety of ways to launder their ill-gotten gains, most of them through Hong Kong, which has gained notoriety as a collection point for the profits of southeast Asian heroin. Some money is washed through the Chinese underground banking system. Triad members set up a line of credit at any number of businesses such as money exchangers and jewelry shops and receive credit in associated stores in the United States. Millions of narcotics, gambling, and extortion dollars change hands over a handshake and are safely legitimized. Some drug profits are converted into precious metals, gems, or other commodities to avoid cash-reporting requirements in the United States.

A study by the US Treasury Department found that 35 percent of US dollars entering Hong Kong and returning to the States were in denominations of $50 or less—a trusty indicator of drug money. The flow of American money between Hong Kong and the US was more than $100 million in 1982, while it was only $12 million with West Germany and $8.8 million with France.

Many Hong Kong banks help move multi-billions of narco-dollars across the ocean to the United States and Canada, where the money is invested in real estate. Vancouver and Toronto have the two fastest-appreciating real estate markets in North America thanks to Hong Kong dollars—some legit, some not. A major sting by the US Internal Revenue Service in the early 1980s showed banking complicity in laundering drug dollars. The sting was set up to help the IRS figure out how the laundering system between Hong Kong, Europe, and North America worked. No one really expected great results.

Two IRS undercover agents set themselves up as drug dealers who needed to launder big bucks in small bills. They first linked up with a Vancouver wheeler dealer who offered to do the job for 5 percent of the money he laundered and a $10,000 fee. The agents found out he was dealing with Kwong Shing So, vice-president for North America of the Liu Chong Hing Bank in Hong Kong. The family-owned bank had one office outside Hong Kong, in San Francisco's Chinatown. That branch accepted only customers who did business with the bank's Hong Kong branches.

The agents deposited $150,000 in small bills at the bank. They posed as businessmen involved in aviation leasing and consulting in Miami. They also claimed to represent people in Atlantic City, New Jersey. They let it be known they had suitcases of cash to move. They arranged to meet So, the bank's vice-president, in a nightclub. They explained they wanted to move $1 million a month through the bank.

"The type of people that we deal with, they deal in currency," one agent told So. "And very often, because of the nature of their business and where they take the aircraft and what they do with them, sometimes we . . . have had the aircraft seized. . . . Do you care how we make our money?"

"I don't care," said So.

"Do you care whether our money is legal or illegal?"

"I don't care. I will handle your business for 1 percent."

"Well, that's fine with me," the agent said.

"Let's shake on this," said So. "Gentlemen, you just bought yourself a Chinese laundry."

The IRS laundered $1.3 million through So's bank, which helped set up an intricate laundering operation with fake corporations.

Mexican drug-trafficking organizations on the southwest US border launder their money in currency-exchange houses owned and operated by Chinese businessmen. The traffickers want Mexican money and prefer to deal with the exchange houses because Mexican bank officials sometimes ask too many questions. The large amounts of money transferred by exchange houses allow traffickers to hide their laundering from prying eyes.

It is impossible to measure the amount of criminal money that is entering North America from Hong Kong. Kon Yu-Leung, allegedly a major heroin trafficker based in Hong Kong who is also known as Johnny Kon and Ricky Wong, was arrested in New York City by the US Drug

Enforcement Administration on March 14, 1988. He owned $20 million of real estate in the United States—$12 million in two commercial properties in New York City, and $8 million in San Francisco property. He was charged with importing one ton of heroin into the US over three years. Kon, a native of China and resident of Hong Kong, had entered the States with a fraudulent Costa Rican passport issued to Ricky Wong. He had five other false passports and traveled under many aliases. Jonathan Ruotolo, a retired New York City Police sergeant, was charged with being the US distributor for Kon's heroin.

There are more than 400 card clubs in Los Angeles County, gambling casinos that cater to Asian customers. These operate without being controlled and licenced by gaming commissions, as are casinos in Las Vegas and Atlantic City. Instead they are licenced by the cities in which they operate. The city gets a percentage of the club's revenue, so it is in the best interest of the local politicians to keep the clubs open. The Los Angeles County Sheriff's Department estimates that a local club pays about $650,000 a month to that city the licenses it. That's enough to grow love handles on any politician.

The department has shown that some card clubs launder money by reporting gross revenues greatly in excess of their actual income. They don't mind paying the city a percentage of their inflated revenues, since it allows them to launder a lot of money that can then be legitimately spent. Since the cities are getting mounds of money without pinching taxpayers, no one's complaining. The cops have linked clubs to loan-sharking, prostitution, murder, corruption, and robbery.

I followed a money launderer for an hour at a well-known casino in Las Vegas in September 1988. The kid, who couldn't have been older than eighteen, kept buying mounds of chips at different cashiers' wickets with stacks of small bills. He later cashed the chips in for a cashier's check and disappeared, only to return with more small bills for another mound of chips. He never gambled. He just laundered dirty money and no one seemed to care.

The Political Cover-Up Of Asian Organized Crime

The Canadian public has been kept in the dark about Asian organized crime gangs and the extent of their operations for political reasons.

In December 1986, I ended four months of investigations with a two-part, three-story exposé in the *Globe and Mail* on Chinese triads and Vietnamese gangs operating in Toronto's Chinatowns. The stories explained how Chinese-organized crime groups were moving money and operations to Canada. They also detailed the increase in violent crimes in the Chinese community as gangs increased their use of violence to extort money from businessmen. Reaction to the stories was negative, vicious, irrational, and immediate. It also came from unexpected quarters.

The Metro Toronto police inspector responsible for Toronto's downtown Chinatown responded by contradicting years of police evidence and denying that Chinese triads existed in the city. Inspector Ronald Prior's first denial came at a public meeting on December 17, 1986, the day the second part of the series appeared. His comments were made at a Chinatown crime prevention meeting, which turned into an angry session as Inspector Prior, members of the Chinese community, and municipal politicians denounced the stories.

"We know we have some problem with crime in the Chinatown area," Prior told forty-five business people and residents in attendance. "We're dealing with these as a police problem, not as an organized crime problem or a triad problem." He described the news reports as "nothing more than sensationalism. It is taking hold of a report [on organized crime] that was issued in the US and speculating that this could happen here. We have no evidence."

In fact, the three stories were based in part on police documents and interviews with sources in the police department, in the Oriental crime street and intelligence units. Toronto police officers had testified in courts across Ontario for nearly fifteen years to the existence of triads. Three days before the inspector's denial, Constable Kenneth Yates, one of the three members of the 52 Division Oriental Crime Unit, testified in District Court that two Vietnamese men convicted of armed robbery were connected to the Kung Lok triad. He testified in court in the autumn of 1986 that "almost every business" in the Chinese community was paying protection money to gangs.

But Inspector Ronald Prior, of the force's 52 Division in downtown Toronto, asserted in a tape-recorded interview on December 18, 1986, "We haven't found anything in our investigations where we can say there are people under the control of triads."

Prior said the police force's administrative officers were angry at the stories. Sources within the intelligence unit confirmed that intense political pressure had been put on the police force's brass to play down Asian crime in the city. The stories also raised the ire of some Chinese businessmen, who worried that business would suffer and real estate values would drop because of investor fear of organized crime, Y.L. Yates, a reporter for the *Chinese Canadian Daily*, said in an interview at a crime-prevention meeting where Inspector Prior denied the existence of triads.

Metro Toronto police have gained credibility in court testifying about triads. In 1980, Lau Wing Kui was deported from Canada after police said he founded the Kung Lok in Toronto in 1974, shortly after arriving from Hong Kong. In 1985, police described Danny Mo in court as the leader of the Kung Lok triad in Toronto. Mr. Mo was found guilty of stealing $13,000 worth of concert tickets in an effort to disrupt a Chinese concert at the O'Keefe Centre. The conviction and the four-and-a-half-year jail sentence were quashed at a retrial in June 1986 after a crucial witness failed to show.

Sergeant Barry Hill, then with the Oriental crime squad of the Metro Toronto Police intelligence bureau, testified about triads in Toronto before the US President's Commission on Organized Crime in 1984. Using that information, the commission reported in April 1986, "The international scope of the Chinese crime gangs is evident in the Canadian chapter of the Hong Kong-based triad Kung Lok. This group undertakes the standard range of crimes against Chinese Canadians, and is considered active in Toronto, Montreal, Ottawa, Vancouver, Hamilton and other metropolitan areas."

In its annual report released in the summer of 1986, the Criminal Intelligence Service of Canada elevated triads, once considered an exotic curiosity because little was known about them, to the same level as Italian organized crime and outlaw motorcycle gangs. A confidential Metro Toronto police intelligence report, prepared with the Royal Canadian Mounted Police, described the criminal activities and members of two of Toronto's three triads, the Kung Lok and the Ghost Shadow. "All evidence indicates the Kung Lok is the principal threat to law and order in the Chinese community in Toronto," the report said.

Asked about all this evidence, Inspector Prior replied, "I'm going to terminate this discussion," then hung up the telephone. Deputy Chief William Kerr, appointed force spokesman on Oriental crime after the appearance of the *Globe* stories, would not deny the existence of triads when dared to. "Triads probably are here," he said, "but we feel we have a good handle on it." Then he referred all questions to Inspector Prior and refused further comment.

Internal politics within the Metro Toronto police force also led to the rejection in 1987 of a detailed proposal by a senior officer to form a Metro-wide Asian Crime Task Force. At the time, the force's Asian crime intelligence unit was embroiled in a power struggle with the force's street units. The intelligence unit wanted total control of all information, which caused many unfortunate and childish incidents in which the intelligence unit failed to share information with street cops. By 1990, the force was scrambling to keep tabs on crimes committed daily by Asian gangs and the intelligence unit was still withholding information from street units. It took an increase in Asian gang violence and crime to convince the police force that the officer who proposed a task force to combat the problem in 1987 was correct in his assessment of the threat the gangs posed.

On May 7, 1990, a one-year project called Crime Against Persons — Asians was set up. (The name was changed to Asian Investigative Unit on May 1, 1991, to appease politicians who wanted to avoid using the words "crime" and "Asian" together.) The joint forces' operation combined twenty-eight experts from the Metro Toronto Police, the Ontario Provincial Police, and the Royal Canadian Mounted Police. It was a welcome addition to the law-enforcement arsenal against Asian organized crime, but a sad reminder that most police forces are short-sighted and reactive rather than proactive. Instead of acting to prevent crimes, the police are geared to investigating them. That attitude will always keep them one step behind the criminals.

Letter Campaign

Inspector Prior's denial that Asian-organized crime existed in Toronto was followed by a campaign by Chinese activists and businessmen to label the *Globe* stories racist and detrimental to the community. Community members orchestrated a phone-in campaign to protest the stories. Then they started writing letters to the newspaper.

Before publishing them, the *Globe and Mail* had a practice of letting reporters see any letters that are critical of their stories. This allowed for the removal of erroneous and potentially libelous claims by letter writers.

None of these letters was shown to me, from publication of the first one, which appeared in December 1986, through the following months. The newspaper did not once show me the letters before their appearance in print. The letters made unsubstantiated accusations of racism. They quoted segments out of context and made widely disparaging and erroneous remarks about accuracy. They also berrated the reporter. The *Globe* ran letters from the Chinese Canadian National Council and the Toronto Chinese Business Association to appease the portion of the Chinese community that was complaining. No explanation was ever given to me, though I often demanded one, as to why the newspaper's highest editors were allowing these letters to run.

The next step in the campaign against the stories was taken at the political level. The same people who wrote the letters complained to the Toronto mayor's committee on race relations on January 13, 1987. They said the stories were inflammatory and adversely affected the Chinese community. Sidney Poon of the Chinese Canadian National Council asked the committee to condemn the stories and help his organization seek an apology from the *Globe*. Members of the committee agreed with the criticism and offered to join the complainants at a meeting with *Globe* editors. Mayor Arthur Eggleton, echoing the other committee members, said it was unfortunate that, in writing about crime, the newspaper "has cast aspersions on the Chinese community in general." The Chinese community was portrayed as a victim of Chinese triads, Chinese street gangs, and Vietnamese street gangs in the stories. The stories stated that pressure from criminals in Toronto's original Chinatown was forcing businessmen to move out of the downtown area to nearby Scarborough.

Committee member Peter Maloney, a lawyer and activist with a penchant for criticizing police, complained the stories contributed to a "they're taking over" mentality among the public. Soo Ping (Susan) Eng, a tax lawyer, vice-president of the Urban Alliance on Race Relations, and a close friend and protegée of Maloney, attacked the stories as she had attacked any media depiction of the Asian community over the years: she accused them of inciting racism. "The entire tenor of the articles is that the Chinese-Canadian community is rife with crime," she said.

By 1991, Eng was a member of the Metro Police Services Board, the police commission, and still denounced stories or comments about Asian crime as racist. She called for the resignation of fellow board member Norm Gardner in January 1991 after he made a presentation to a federal House of Commons committee that was studying proposed gun-control legislation. Gardner, a competitive handgun shooter and outdoor enthusiast, spoke on behalf of the Ontario Federation of Anglers and Hunters. He repeated police claims that illegal aliens, among other groups including outlaw bikers, are responsible for smuggling guns into Canada. He gave as an example Asian gangs and Jamaican posses.

Eng, ignoring the distinction between legitimate immigrants and illegal aliens, jumped to the defence of illegal aliens by attacking Gardner's comments.

"It feeds into the anti-immigrant sentiments that are unhealthy in our society today," Eng said of Gardner's testimony before the federal committee. "People looking for a way to vent their racist venom do not have to do anything themselves any more. Public officials are doing it for them."

Legal Asian and Jamaican immigrants should be incensed by her support, in the guise of righteous indignation, for those who cheat the system.

In the summer of 1988, the University Settlement House reported the findings of its study of employees in Toronto's Chinatown restaurants. They were working seventy- to eighty-hour weeks without paid breaks or overtime in contravention of Ontario labor laws. Eng, who grew up above her father's downtown Toronto restaurant, condemned the report and its findings as propaganda against restaurant owners.

On Thursday, March 28, 1991, Ontario premier Bob Rae, leader of the province's first socialist government, endorsed Eng as his choice for chairman of the Metro Police Services board. Eng, thirty-eight, got the nod after a week of controversy sparked by speculation that she would be given power to set policies and priorities for Canada's second-largest police force after the RCMP. The board oversees a 6,000-member police force with a $500-million annual budget. The chairman, who is paid $90,963 and gets a limousine and chauffeur, is the only full-time member of the seven-member board.

Politicians of all stripes, including fellow board members, noted that Eng refused to swear the oath of allegiance to the Queen when she became a member of the police commission in 1989. It's the same oath every police officer in Ontario takes. All criminal charges are laid in the name of the Queen. Eng missed twice as many meetings as other board members, left meetings early after television cameras had left, attended only a few of the board's regular meetings with four minority groups, and attended only one of many board meetings with the 550-member Chinese Restaurant Association after the rash of shootings in Chinatown in late 1990 and early 1991.

Her critics argued that she was unfit for the chairman's job for lack of judgment and dedication, and an embarrassingly obvious thirst for media attention. Eng responded to questioning about her qualifications to become police commission chairman by crying racism.

"You know," she said, "what really bothers some people, what really gets up people's noses, is that it's me. These positions are usually not reserved for ethnic minorities."

After their warm welcome at City Hall in 1987, the disgruntled Chinese who objected to my stories took their complaints to the Ontario Human Rights Commission and demanded that the commission help them seek redress from the *Globe*. Provincial race relations consultant Dennis Strong arranged a January 20 meeting at the *Globe* editorial offices with him, senior editors, and members of the Chinese Canadian National Council and the Toronto Chinese Business Association. I was forbidden by the *Globe* to attend. I was not told what was discussed there. (On April 22, 1987, I was told in a memo responding to my query that "the stories did not point out that Chinatown was still considered a relatively safe area for visitors and others.") On February 17, 1987, the *Globe* printed one of the longest letters it has ever had on its Letters page. It was signed by two members of the disgruntled Chinese organizations who had already had letters printed in the previous two months. As with past letters, this one was not shown to me beforehand and it was inaccurate, libelous, and inflammatory.

After the January 20 meeting, I was ordered by *Globe* management to stop investigating and writing stories about Asian criminals and to stay out of Chinatown.

The *Globe* also refused to enter the Chinese organized crime stories in competition for the National Newspaper Awards. Entries had to be made in January. I entered them on my own, which is allowed under NNA rules as long as I pay the entry fee. Then I found out inadvertently that the *Globe*'s city editor told an NNA officer, who mentioned I had entered the stories, to pull them from competition. I called the NNA offices to check this and they confirmed that he had indeed asked them to withdraw the stories. They admitted he had no right to ask them to withdraw the stories without my consent. By this time, it was too late to re-submit the stories. They were sorry. The editor could not provide a satisfactory answer to me other than turning red, which told me all I had to know.

So the complainants from the Chinese community had achieved some measure of success with their campaign.

What did the *Globe* get? Good public relations?

The *Globe* opened an advertising bureau in Hong Kong in April 1987, four months after my stories appeared—three months after I was prohibited from reporting on Chinese criminals.

By 1990, the lid started coming off Chinatown's dirty little secret. Asian gangsters, brazen through years of getting their way, threw aside the subtlety that was once their trademark. Where are the people who four years earlier described my stories as inaccurate and sensational?

The Chinese, like the blacks, have been quick to enlist the racial smoke screen that keeps law enforcement at bay. They scream they are being picked on because of color when the police investigate crime in their communities. They use human rights' laws as shields behind which to hide their community's flaws. Canada is probably the only country in the world where politicians and cops curb investigations into ethnic organized crime groups for fear of being labeled racist. This country prides itself on being multicultural. That should not mean that immigrants have the right to establish criminal empires here to prey on their own people. Investigating ethnic crime groups has nothing to do with racism and everything to do with justice and freedom—justice for immigrants seeking a safe world in which to start new lives, and freedom from the fear that gangs create through their empires of terror.

On Remembrance Day, November 11, 1987, after getting five stories on Asian gang activities into the newspaper—while the city editor and managing editors who didn't want me to write such stories were on holidays—I was forbidden to write any crime stories and ordered not to deal with my police contacts. I was crime reporter at that time. After ten and a half years of reporting, I was relegated to writing three-inch briefs and offered the prospect of an unprecedented full-time assignment on the night shift.

I left the *Globe* on November 23, 1987, and headed for Mexico. There I learned to water-ski in a brackish, crocodile- and jellyfish-infested lagoon and went scuba-diving four times off the Yucatan peninsula before the instructor found out I couldn't swim and kicked me out. I spent the next three and a half years making surreptitious forays into the drug underworld of North, Central, and South America researching this book.

5

A Tradition of Silence:
Saving face in Chinatown

Metro Toronto police are quick to qualify any statement about violence among Asian gangs with the needless and obvious observation that crime does not reflect a violent streak in the Oriental community. They have to say this because of the severe reaction of Chinese Canadians to stories indicating problems involving their own people—they take straight news reports as a serious affront to their reputations and label them racist. They prefer that criminal acts in the Chinese community not be reported.

"Like any other community, 98 percent of the population of Chinese are honest, hard-working people who come from a culture that generates this work ethic," said Staff Sergeant Harry D'Arcy former head of the plain-clothes unit of 52 Division in the heart of Chinatown. Staff Sergeant D'Arcy was responsible for the five-member Oriental Crime Unit (pressure from the Chinese community forced police to change the name to Asian Crime Unit in 1987, then to the nondescript Special Task Force). The traditional silence of the Chinese community in the face of adversity makes them easy prey for the 2 percent of the community that lives through crime.

"They pick on the weak links in the business community—small variety stores, bookstores, cafés, mom-and-pop operations," Staff Sergeant D'Arcy said, emphasizing that gangs seem to prey only on Oriental businessmen, not on tourists, shoppers, or strollers. "The Vietnamese come here and see what the Chinese people have. They want a piece of it. How better than to victimize the Chinese, whom they know are peaceful? So they extort from Chinese business people and the Chinese willingly pay."

The increase in extortion attempts on Chinese businessmen coincides with the influx of Vietnamese immigrants—not the older people, but uneducated boys and men who operate on the fringe of the community. Unlike Chinese gangs, the Vietnamese are not highly organized. Easy pickings in extortion keep them together. Extortionists and their victims usually meet two or three times before a deal is struck. The extortionist may ask for $1,000 at the first meeting. They haggle and settle for $250. The victim thinks he is getting a deal. In Chinatown, as in the Far East, this is a way of life.

There are four Chinatowns within the boundaries of Metro Toronto. The oldest Oriental business section extends east of Spadina Avenue to Bay Street, and south of College Street to Queen Street. The second oldest Chinatown borders Spadina Avenue north of Dundas Street. The third is at Broadview Avenue and Gerrard Street in Riverdale, and the fourth is in Scarborough. A fifth Chinatown has been built in neighboring Mississauga at Dundas Street and Dixie Road.

The police set up the Oriental Crime Unit to inspire public confidence and help combat crime in Chinatown. Members of the unit meet regularly with Chinese businessmen, to whom the chief of police has written in several Chinese dialects asking that they report all crimes. Police try to befriend Chinatown citizens and let them know, through regular patrols by plain-clothes officers who understand their culture, that they can turn to them for help. Gangsters are less likely to extort money from businessmen they know will go to the police.

"There was no trust between the police and the Oriental community," Staff Sergeant D'Arcy said. "We had to gain their trust. It's gradually coming our way. People are reporting crimes."

But many victims still aren't talking to police. Twenty-one-year-old Duong Tat was a regular at the Golden Springs Restaurant in east Toronto and was seated with his friends ahead of two other Vietnamese men waiting for a table on October 28, 1989. The two men complained and started a fight with Tat. The men left, returned with another man, and shot Tat in the stomach in front of a full restaurant. No one reported the incident—not the restaurant owner, staff, the victim, or other patrons. Police found out when hospital officials alerted them that a man had undergone stomach surgery for a bullet wound.

Face

The temporary halt of Kung Lok operations after its leader's conviction for extortion in 1985 reflects an important aspect of Oriental culture: despite circumstances, one must not lose face.

"Face is everything to the Chinese," Staff Sergeant D'Arcy said. "A

Chinese criminal is more embarrassed when he is arrested in public than alone, because he loses face. The Kung Lok thought they were impregnable. When the big man (Danny Mo) went down, they lost a lot of face. They thought they were being targeted. The gang split. Some went to Hong Kong, Montreal, Vancouver, and San Francisco."

Face is the most important concept to grasp when trying to understand Oriental culture. Appearance is everything to Asians. Face consists of status, honor, reputation, prestige, respect, and esteem. It is the esteem in which a person is held by others. Face has nothing to do with being a good, law-abiding person. If face can be gained by theft, corruption, and murder, which impart an aura of wealth and power to the person committing the crimes, then so be it. It's the end result that counts. Face is easily lost through humiliation, a show of weakness, or even a spoken insult. The concept of face depends on the forsaking of individuality. It involves seeing oneself through the eyes of others. It has nothing to do with being a strong individual, but is more akin to an insecure and malleable person willing to do anything to please others. Orientals cannot stomp through life as most North Americans do. Turn down a lunch invitation from an Oriental and he could lose face. Face is a big bluff. When the bluff is called, a person accepts the loss of face or must retaliate to regain esteem.

In the Chinese organized crime underworld, a gangster who loses face loses power. A restaurant owner may not present a powerful criminal with a bill in recognition of his status, his face. A less important gangster may not be presented with a bill, which allows him to appear powerful, although he'll have to settle the tab at the end of the month. A hooker who leaves one gang's employ to work for another could cause her original employer to lose face. The second gang saves it by paying the first gang for her.

Asian gangsters know that the public perception that they are untouchable by authorities adds to their power and mystique. They visibly court politicians and policemen, giving the impression they have them in their pocket, even though they are only photographed shaking hands with them or sitting next to them at public functions.

Three Chinese triads operate in Great Britain. The Wo Shing Wo is the most powerful. Its members are involved in drugs, gambling, burglary, kidnapping, extortion, and video piracy. The 14K triad is involved in the same crimes. The Wo On Lok is made up of Chinese businessmen who hire Vietnamese thugs to do their dirty work. The Wo On Lok triad lost status in 1986 when it was announced the 14K triad was entering two lions in London's Chinese New Year parade. To regain status, the Wo On Lok brought the On Hei Lion dance team from Hong Kong. The imported lion was the best in the parade and the Wo On Lok not only saved face, but added to its membership a number of skilled fighters to collect protection money. Customs officers found $50,000 of watches and jewelry on the dancers when they arrived—items to be sold to pay their expenses.

Chinese street gangs are prone to using violence when they perceive they have lost face. It is common for a gang member to demand compensation from his girlfriend if she leaves him. If the girl and her new boyfriend don't pay a satisfactory amount after negotiations, the gangster and his friends will beat them to save face.

Police officers should be careful when stopping Asians. Some cops like to call people over to them by gesturing with their forefingers. Asians regard this as a gesture to be used with animals or inferiors. They consider it an act of provocation. While being arrested causes an immeasurable loss of face, being handcuffed is insufferable and many Asians will resist it. Asians who lived through the Vietnam War may refuse to put their hands against a wall and spread their legs while being searched. This position was often the last one assumed by people being executed during the war.

The Kung Lok Triad

"All evidence indicates the Kung Lok is the principal threat to law and order in the Chinese community in Toronto."—a confidential police report.

Danny Mo's conviction triggered the Kung Lok's second internal leadership struggle since the deportation of the Toronto founder in 1980. In that power struggle, many Kung Lok members broke away and recruited Vietnamese followers.

The triad in North America was formed by Lau Wing Kui, who was born in Hong Kong on April 19, 1929. The former leader of the Leun Triad Group in Hong Kong had extensive connections with Chinese criminals around the world. When he arrived in Canada in 1974, he saw an opportunity for a good criminal to make a lot of money by exploiting Chinatown's traditional codes of silence and mistrust of police. The Kung Lok quickly spread from coast to coast. From Canada, the triad spread into the United States and the Dominican Republic.

By the end of the 1970s, police had convinced the courts of the danger of triads. The Supreme Court of Ontario ruled in a case in St. Catharines, in the province's Golden Horseshoe, that proof of membership in the Kung Lok was evidence of criminal intent during the commission of an offence.

"The origins in China and the existence in Hong Kong and Toronto [where the accused lives] of an organization known as the Kung Lok, a derivative organization from one known as the Triad, dedicated to violence and whose members are mutually supportive for life, is a most relevant and logically probative consideration as to the accused's possible motive in the alleged offence," the court ruled. By 1979, the Kung Lok had grown rapidly to 150 hard-core members who struck fear into the heart of Chinatown with brutal acts of violence. The triad's first setback came in 1980 when Lau was arrested and deported under section 40 of the Canadian Immigration Act. Several Kung Lok members fought for control of the triad, each claiming to have Lau's blessing. The triad expanded by recruiting impressionable visa students and made pacts with gangs in Boston and New York.

Today Kung Lok leaders are businessmen in their thirties and forties who have fought their way to the top and sit comfortably behind desks, far from the streets where their money is made. They have legitimate business fronts, such as restaurants, through which they launder their illegal gains. Gang leaders spend much of their time traveling around the world, insulating themselves from prosecution by leaving the dirty work to soldiers ranging in age from sixteen to twenty-five.

The US President's Commission on Organized Crime had this to say about Toronto's Kung Lok triad in its final report published in April 1986:

"The international scope of the Chinese crime gangs is evident in the Canadian chapter of the Hong Kong-based triad Kung Lok. This group undertakes the standard range of crimes against Chinese Canadians, and is considered active in Toronto, Montreal, Ottawa, Vancouver, Hamilton and other metropolitan areas. Unlike the hybrid Tong-triad arrangements that prevail in the US, the Kung Lok is a more traditional triad establishment. Its members in Canada undergo the same ritual initiation as those in Hong Kong. There is a constant traffic of Kung Lok members among Canada, the United States, and various Caribbean locations, particularly Santo Domingo.

"In the early 1980s, the Kung Lok established an illegal gambling house on Division Street in New York, through agreement with the Hip Song and the On Leong. Lau Wing Kui, the recently deported leader of the Kung Lok in Canada, owns an interest in at least one casino in Santo Domingo and has interests in several Hong Kong gambling [houses]. It is believed that the Kung Lok members carry large sums of cash out of Canada to be laundered at the Santo Domingo casino before the money is brought into the United States."

The triad today has about 450 members in Canada who import heroin on a large scale and smuggle it into the US, run and protect gaming houses, extort businessmen and individuals, deal in American counterfeit money, deal in weapons, and control the Chinese live-entertainment business and all acts that enter North America for tours and concerts.

Canada is the major North American point of entry for southeast Asian heroin. Couriers use body packs or secret luggage compartments to get the heroin into Canada. These couriers are usually Hong Kong-born Chinese who hold British passports. Since they don't require a visa to get into Canada, they aren't subjected to drug-carrier profile checks as they would be if they flew into the United States. Once in Canada, the courier calls a gang member in the US. The American gangster crosses the border by car to pick up the drugs and smuggles them into the US.

The Kung Lok has ties to Asian gangs in the States and in the Far East. These ties are made through a ceremony called Burning the Yellow Paper, which strengthens the brotherhood bond between the gangsters through an oath of loyalty. The Kung Lok has connections with the Ghost Shadow street gang in New York and has burned the yellow paper with the Ping On in Boston and the Wah Ching in San Francisco and Los Angeles. The gangs hide each other's fugitives and trade services such as hit men and weapons.

The 14K Triad

The 14K triad, which has the largest membership worldwide, has about 160 members in Canada who import heroin and smuggle it into the US, run gaming houses, and extort. Toronto's 14K triad members are mostly former members of the defunct Ghost Shadow gang in Toronto. The 14K runs a rough-and-tumble operation and, more than the other triads, actively recruits Vietnamese refugees. In trying to retain many of its traditions, the 14K triad brings senior triad officials from New York and the Far East to Toronto for initiations.

One alleged leader is the brother of the notorious New York City founder of the Ghost Shadow street gang, on whom a character in the movie *Year of the Dragon* was based. The Toronto brother owns a bakery and restaurant in the heart of Chinatown that police say is a front for criminal activity. The triad has solid ties with Italian organized crime. The Ghost Shadows have strong links to triads in New York and Chicago and to the gang once operated by Paul (Godfather) Lee in Boston. Lee was murdered in 1982.

Many members practice the martial art Sun Da and put themselves into trances to immunize themselves from pain. Then they draw sharp knives across their bodies, eat burning joss sticks, or grind out burning joss sticks on their bodies. Shades of Gordon Liddy.

A classified police document says this about triad membership in Toronto:

"The majority of gang members ... appear to be between the ages of 16 and 25. They are recruited for the most part from high schools and universities. Many are on student visas and some are overstays; a sizable portion do not even attend classes or attend only enough to achieve marginal passes. A disturbing number come from well-to-do families and meet the classical definition of spoiled adolescents—these are easy pickings for gang members who take their money in return for the empty gestures of brotherhood and companionship which the gang seems to offer.

"Other members are landed immigrants who hold lowly jobs such as waiters and kitchen help. For them, the gang is a way to achieve face within their own ethnic community in a simple straightforward way that is easily understood and never challenged."

Vietnamese Street Gangs

"No one will dare challenge us in Chinatown."—wiretap comment of a Toronto Vietnamese gang member.

Vietnamese street gangs are made up of refugees better known to North Americans as the boat people. The Vietnamese gangs and the Big Circle Boys from mainland China have taken over the streets of Toronto's Chinatowns from the triads and rob and extort businesses with far more violence than the Chinese used.

Toronto appears to be the only North American city where Vietnamese street gangs have not adopted names—they believe this would attract more police attention and help police identify gang members. They are eager to become good criminals and acknowledge they are not as organized and patient as the Chinese, whom they observe to learn how to operate. They want to adopt initiation rites to instil discipline and order in their own gangs. Gang members in Canada and the United States use their links to other Vietnamese gangsters made in the Far East and in refugee camps.

Gang members travel extensively across North America to commit crimes. Two Vietnamese jewelry stores in Toronto were robbed in December 1986 by seven Vietnamese later arrested in Lowell, Massachusetts. They were connected to the Ping On in Boston and are believed responsible for similar robberies in Seattle, Chicago, Boston, and Toronto.

Two San Francisco Vietnamese gang members who flew to Toronto in June 1987 were arrested robbing an illegal gaming house five hours later. Such robberies are usually organized by local gang members.

Most street gang members are nineteen or twenty and unemployed.

They hang out in pool halls and nightclubs. They like drinking, expensive cars, and fashionable clothing. Competition among the 150 to 200 hard-core members for easy cash is fierce.

Triads recruit stronger, energetic, and more reckless Vietnamese hoodlums to add muscle to their organizations and to keep the unruly Vietnamese where they can watch them. Though triad membership was once restricted to Hong Kong or China-born Chinese, it has recently been expanded to include Malaysians and Vietnamese in return for money and brute strength. Though Vietnamese street gangs are relative newcomers who started arriving after the fall of Saigon in 1975, they dare to confront the triads on their own ground.

Vietnamese street gangs have wrested control of downtown Toronto streets from triads and face no opposition in Toronto's original Chinatown east of Spadina Avenue. At the November 6, 1986, sentencing of two Vietnamese gang members convicted of extorting money from a Chinatown concert promoter, Constable Kenneth Yates of the Metro Toronto Police Oriental Crime Unit testified that "almost every business" in the Asian community is paying protection money to gangs.

Evidence existed in the early 1980s that Vietnamese refugees were going to cause major problems in North American cities. Yet North American law enforcement, especially Canadian immigration officials, ignored the warnings. Reports from Hong Kong in 1984 indicated that violence and crime had become commonplace in Vietnamese refugee camps. Police seized 972 homemade weapons after one raid. The camps were breeding and recruiting grounds where Vietnamese youths were preparing to link up with existing gangs in Canada. Canadian immigration authorities, pressured by church, political, and activist groups, let large numbers of Vietnamese, Laotian, and Kampuchean refugees into the country in 1986 without checking into their backgrounds or even verifying their identities. In fact, there was little way to check out the refugees, since the countries they came from had little of their former bureaucracy left. So, like the Mariel boat lift from Cuba in 1980, the boat people from southeast Asia harbored in their midst thousands of criminals seeking a new land and new victims.

The viciousness of Vietnamese gangs in Toronto has created an unprecedented crime wave that has forced businessmen to flee the downtown for the relatively safer streets of suburban Scarborough to the east and Mississauga to the west. The Chinese business community has acknowledged to police that it is being victimized by Oriental extortionists and the police chief has promised them in writing that police will deal with complaints quickly. The Chinese Businessmen's Association and Metro Toronto Police periodically hold seminars in Cantonese to give tips on how to prevent robbery and extortion.

Triad members intimidated by vicious Vietnamese gangs are also leaving the downtown Chinatown for newly constructed Chinatowns in the suburbs where the Chinese population has increased dramatically since the mid-1980s, with a corresponding surge in Oriental business. The practical distinction between triads and Vietnamese street gangs is simple: triads are more intellectual; the gangs are physical. Until about 1985, triad members used meat cleavers or knives on the rare occasion when a threat was not enough. Vietnamese gang members liberally use stolen handguns. That difference in philosophy has prompted the Vietnamese to attack the triads openly. In October 1986, members of a Vietnamese gang publicly expressed defiance and lack of respect for the 14K triad. Gang members walked out of a Chinatown restaurant owned by a prominent 14K member without paying a $300 bill. The owner did not complain.

In January 1985, the same owner narrowly escaped being killed by a bumbling Vietnamese hit man in another Dundas Street restaurant. As the eighteen-year-old pulled a .22-caliber revolver from the front of his trousers, the hammer snagged a thread. When his finger yanked the trigger, he fired the gun into the floor, nearly shooting his dick off. The intended victim fled along Dundas Street, where the gunman, who had been hired by the Kung Lok triad, shot him in the chin.

A Vietnamese slapped out a triad member in a Toronto Chinatown restaurant in 1988 after overhearing the man boast to friends how powerful his gang was. The gangster also demanded an apology, which the Chinese hood gave, suffering irreparable loss of face in the process. The incident underlined how much Vietnamese gangs had wrested control of Chinatown's streets from triads, although triads had cut back on street crimes such as extortion and robberies in the late 1980s to focus on international heroin smuggling. The profit margin in heroin smuggling is much larger and the chance of getting caught is minimal compared to extorting in Chinatown, where it's no longer a sure bet that victims will keep their mouths shut.

Toronto's Vietnamese gangs are affiliated with gangs in Calgary and Ottawa. Toronto gang members go to Ottawa to extort for a local gang whose members are too well known. Weapons seized from Toronto gang members underscore their extensive connections. A .38-caliber revolver seized in March 1986 was stolen from a California sheriff's home. A .32-caliber gun taken from a gang member during another arrest the same month was stolen in Montreal.

"We can see more widespread violence coming soon to Chinatown," a police officer who investigates Oriental crime said in December 1986. "The guns there are incredible. If the criminals have guns, the citizens will get them too. Every gang has one or two in its possession. They're all stolen." His prediction came true in December 1990.

Police are so tied up dealing with daily crimes committed by Vietnamese gangs that they have little time to investigate triads. The Oriental Crime Unit in Toronto's downtown 52 Division had three constables in 1986, one of whom was Chinese. A similar unit was set up in 14 Division, just west of the downtown, in October 1986. That unit had one sergeant and two constables. More units had been created by 1990, but by then triads and gangs had become well entrenched. Although the Chinese keep a respectful distance from the cops, the Vietnamese have no qualms about killing them.

Metro Toronto Police Sergeant Wayne King and Constable Frank Yee of the 14 Division Asian Crime Unit walked into a two-day-old Vietnamese nightclub in downtown Toronto after midnight on Sunday, September 20, 1987, to check for illegal liquor.

"We were speaking to the owner inside when Frank Yee stepped out to where they take the tickets," Sergeant King said. "Five men were standing there blocking the stairway. He asked them to clear the stairway. They took exception and pushed him. He got jumped, kicked, and punched. Frank's a sizeable guy. He managed to keep himself from being overwhelmed, but took a fair punishment. One man got over him with a knife and swung at him."

Constable Yee was pinned to the wall by two men while one Vietnamese punk tried to plunge a 10.5-inch serrated knife into his chest. Yee dodged by throwing himself down a long flight of stairs. The attackers followed him, and the man with the knife took another swipe at him before running west along Queen Street and south on Bathurst. Constable Yee pulled his service revolver and chased him. The man was waiting around the corner and slashed at Yee as he turned onto Bathurst Street, but missed. The twenty-seven-year-old man was arrested after a chase down a laneway.

The attack followed two death threats made against members of the Asian Crime Unit in Toronto's 52 Division the previous month. The unit received a letter on August 4, 1987, containing a .25-caliber bullet — the type of ammunition most commonly used by Vietnamese street gangs. The letter said the six officers in the unit would be killed. Tuan Minh Trinh, a nineteen-year-old Vietnamese street gang member linked by police to the Kung Lok triad, threatened to kill two policemen while being arrested on August 15 for breaching probation imposed in 1986. He had been convicted for possessing a restricted firearm. The

.38-caliber handgun, stolen from a California sheriff, was seized from Trinh during the curbside arrest of a Vietnamese gang on its way to confront another gang.

Thirteen Vietnamese gangsters walked into the Wok and Bowl Seafood Restaurant on Dundas Street West in Toronto's downtown Chinatown on Sunday, March 4, 1990. They were armed with baseball bats, meat cleavers, machetes, and a bored-out .22-caliber starter's pistol. They wore hockey pads to protect their arms and one punk had strapped a weightlifting belt over his stomach to protect against knives. They were looking for a rival gang that had swarmed one of its members outside the Spectrum dance club in the city's east end several weeks earlier. Ten of the punks dropped their weapons when police arrived. Constable John Dorey looked out the back door and spotted three gang members waiting to ambush anyone escaping the rumble. He chased them. Two punks threw their cleavers under cars. A fourteen-year-old gangster stopped near City Hall and fired a pistol at the police officer before running off. Police found a functional bomb in the gang's safe house. Gang members tried to extort $5,000 from a Chinatown restaurant owner in April 1990 for a legal fund to defray the cost of gang members before the courts on the shooting charges.

Kien Ahn Lu and four Vietnamese friends shuffled like cool dudes across Dundas Street West in Toronto on April 30, 1989. Two men driving to a religious festival honked at them because they blocked their way. One of the punks threw a knife at the car. The passenger got out. Lu, nineteen, knocked him to the ground and stabbed him in the face and hand. Lu and his friends walked away congratulating themselves.

The Latvian Hall on College Street in Toronto was hopping on Saturday, August 16, 1986. There was a wedding reception in the basement and a Vietnamese dance on the first floor. At 12:30 on Sunday morning, the groom went out to the sidewalk for some fresh air and found six Vietnamese punks leaning on his car. He told them to get off and they told him to fuck off.

The groom returned to the reception to get some help. The Vietnamese got their buddies from the dance. The groom, four male friends, and a woman walked out to find thirty Vietnamese milling around the car. The groom tried to get into the car. Two punks from Kitchener, Ontario, jumped him and knifed him in the chest. He collapsed, but survived. His friends got messed up.

Vinh Vuu, a leader of the Born to Kill Vietnamese gang in Manhattan and head of the gang's Canal Boys faction, was plugged by members of a rival Asian gang during a drive-by shooting at Canal Street and Broadway on Thursday, July 26, 1990. The twenty-one-year-old gangster took four slugs in the chest. The message: Get off our turf.

The Born to Kill gang was formed in 1986 by Vietnamese punks who had worked as hit men for the Ghost Shadow and the Flying Dragon gangs. The Chinese gangs had dumped the Vietnamese for their lack of discipline and refusal to obey authority. The Vietnamese named their new gang after the slogan that American GIs scrawled on their helmets in Vietnam. The new gangsters robbed, assaulted, and murdered, being too impatient and greedy to get involved in long-term criminal schemes. They are the epitome of the Me Generation—dispossessed people wanting everything they see in the new world around them *now*.

A two-day Buddhist service was held for Vuu. Canal Boys walked through the streets of Manhattan's Chinatown carrying signs bearing the gang's name. Gang members approached store owners they regularly extorted from on Canal Street and asked for money to pay funeral costs.

More than 120 Vietnamese mourners arrived at the Rosedale Memorial Park Cemetery in Linden, New Jersey, in nineteen cars. Most were gang members and carried cellular phones and pagers. Vuu's coffin, draped in a red and black flag with "Canal Boys" written on it, was lowered into the grave at 2:30. Four men wearing sunglasses approached the casket with large wreaths. They dropped the wreaths and opened fire with an Uzi submachine gun, a shotgun, and two handguns. The mourners panicked, some jumping into open graves. Five people were shot, one twenty-year-old man four times. Others were injured in the scramble to get away from the action. Born to Kill members pulled their guns and shot back. Tombstones were pockmarked on both sides by bullets. During the police investigation, $23,240 in cash was seized from a mourner's purse.

The cemetery shooting is believed to be the handiwork of the Ghost Shadows. The two gangs have been shooting it out in the streets of Manhattan since 1986. Three BTK gang members were plugged in the head in a New York City parking lot in October 1990 and their bodies were left piled together. The shooting was in retaliation for the murder of a Ghost Shadow gangster. The BTK, whose members sometimes tattoo the gang initials on the web between the thumb and forefinger, are notorious for shooting people. Life means little to criminals who survived the atrocities of Vietnam during and after the war. And North American justice is no deterrent compared to the harsh punishment they would have received in their native country—death.

The Long Posse and the Young Bloods are two Asian youth gangs fighting for turf and face in Toronto's downtown Chinatown. Two gang members, sixteen and nineteen years old, tried to walk out of the Dragon Mall restaurant on Spadina Avenue on June 8, 1990, when six Young Bloods blocked their way. A sixteen-year-old Young Blood pulled a knife and stabbed both rival gang members in the chest and back.

Such attacks occur almost daily between gangs. During one fight, a punk on the losing side tried to escape by jumping a fence. Rival gang members caught him, slit open his pants, and cut two tendons behind his knee. Then they smashed his knee with a baseball bat.

Toronto police started to become aware of these fights only late in the 1980s, although such rumbles had been going on unnoticed for a long time.

I walked out of a Chinatown speak-easy run by a friend in the winter of 1983 and found myself in the middle of an all-out rumble between two Chinese street gangs at 4 a.m. They were jumping all over the place, drop-kicking each other, adopting classical Kung Fu stances, and screaming Chinese obscenities. I picked my way through the melee carefully, hoping they wouldn't pull guns.

The Big Circle Boys

The Big Circle Boys, or Daai Huen Jai, are the most recent Chinese gang to invade North America. Gang members are political refugees from the People's Republic of China and illegal immigrants smuggled into Canada for $20,000 to $60,000 a head. They are believed to have been formed in re-education camps in China during the Cultural Revolution of the 1960s. Gang members in Canada import heroin and smuggle it into the US, extort, commit robbery and fraud, pickpocket, shoplift, run gaming houses, commit break-and-enters, and run whorehouses with Malaysian women they lure to Toronto with advertisements for maids. Unlike other Asian gangs, the Big Circle Boys avoid confrontation with other gangs and plot only to make money rather than to gain face.

The Big Circle Boys first came to police attention in Vancouver on Canada's west coast in 1987 after a series of ten armed robberies between November 1986 and January 1987. They had robbed restaurants, theaters, and video stores to which they had been steered by members of the long-established Lotus Gang. On January 30, 1987, two police officers who were parked one block north of Vancouver's Fisherman's Gambling Club watched several Asian men run from the building. They drove over. A frantic man spoke to them in Cantonese and pointed to the club. Two other Asian men were hauling ass out the front door. One cop nabbed one after a one-block chase. The second cop approached the club entrance. Another man ran out and pointed a

.357-magnum revolver at his chest. The cop lunged for the gun. Six members of the Big Circle Boys gang were arrested in connection with the hold-up. Siu Hung Mok, thirty-two, had been in the country three months. He got seven years in jail.

Many gang members migrated to Toronto after police crackdowns in Vancouver. Gang members broke into a number of Chinese herbal shops to steal $500,000 in herbs and ginseng, which they shipped to Vancouver. Police have been unable to gather enough evidence to arrest the members they suspect of stealing the herbs. They checked the odometer on a truck that they believed a gang member rented to drive the stolen goods to Vancouver. There wasn't enough mileage registered to cover the trip. An officer checked the truck's registration in an off-line search of the national police computer system and learned the same truck had been stopped by Ontario Provincial Police far enough from Toronto to indicate the odometer had been disconnected.

Big Circle Boys also lend their muscle to collect gambling debts. They leaned on one Chinese businessman who owed a gaming house and borrowed his identification papers for one week. They used the papers to obtain credit cards and open bank accounts that they used to commit fraud in cities across Canada.

Big Circle Boys first came to the attention of Toronto police after an unprecedented rash of pickpocketing in the downtown Chinatown and on the crowded public transit system. Stolen credit cards were used to buy luxury items for resale. The gangsters also used stolen Bell Canada credit cards to call hoods in Hong Kong to the tune of $10,000 a month. They bought $400,000 of merchandise from March to May 1989 with credit cards stolen from women shoppers. Teams of two to five middle-aged men stalk women in crowded shopping centers and steal from purses left in grocery carts or slung over shoulders while one thief distracts the victim. They're so smooth the women don't notice the cards are missing until they want to use them.

Three masked Big Circle Boys robbed the Tai Pei Beauty Centre in downtown Toronto of $32,000 in cash, jewelry, and fur coats in February 1990. On April 4, 1990, two armed BCB walked into U-Travel and Tours and forced the owners to open the safe before taking their personal jewelry and cash, a haul of $3,750, which they put into a shopping bag before escaping in a waiting cab. On April 5, 1990, two armed and masked Big Circle Boys robbed the Leader TV and Video Store in east Toronto of its cash.

The Big Circle Boys prefer gold credit cards because of their extended credit ratings—some as high as $100,000. They flatten the numbers and re-emboss the cards with legitimate numbers obtained from bank records by associates and gang members working in banks.

They also electronically alter and re-code the magnetic strip on the back of the cards.

The Big Circle Boys are part of a well-used international organized crime network between Hong Kong, Toronto, and Vancouver. They are so ruthless in their pursuit of money that they will kill their own. In early October 1987, Siu Ming Li, a prominent Big Circle Boys gangster in Hong Kong, arranged with Vancouver gang member King Hung Wong to smuggle diamonds into Canada. The gems were carried by two Hong Kong couriers: Hoi Chau Lin and Chiu Tai Man. Wong got greedy and decided to rip off the diamonds once they got to Vancouver. To do so, he had to kill the couriers.

Wong and another buddy rented a house on Windsor Street in Vancouver on October 9, 1987. He met the couriers Lin and Man at Vancouver International Airport on the twenty-first and took them to the East Hotel in Vancouver's Chinatown. He spent the twenty-sixth with them and convinced them to stay at the Windsor Street house with him. When they got to the house, Wong gave Man a small set of keys and ushered them into the house ahead of him. Wong told Man to unlock a small padlock on the door at the end of the hallway. Man, with Lin looking over his shoulder, had trouble opening the lock. Wong told him to insert the key deeper. Man kept trying. Gunshots exploded in the hallway behind him. Lin took the first .22-caliber bullet. He died as he fell to the floor, his brain stem severed. A bullet hit Man in the left wrist. He fell to the floor and played dead. "Are you done yet?" he heard Wong ask. "Yes, I'm done," the gunman said.

The killers rummaged through the couriers' suitcases and fled in Wong's car. Man ran out and crossed the street. He saw Wong's car coming towards him and hid while it drove past. He ran into a house. Wong, for some reason, had called the cops and reported a shooting in the house next door to where the killing took place. Police finally found the right house and had to enter through an upper deck because the doors on the main floor had been tied together. Wong was caught and convicted of first-degree murder.

The Royal Hong Kong Police arrested Siu Ming Li on March 22, 1988, for the robbery of the Artland Watch Co. in November 1987. They found ten handguns and a hand grenade in his house. More than $1 million (Hong Kong dollars) in jewelry and cash was found in his girlfriend's safe deposit box. Li was sentenced to twenty-two years in jail for armed robbery and firearms offences.

Asian Youth Gangs Terrorizing Schools

The violence that crept through Toronto's Chinatowns in the mid-1980s found its way into schools in the fall of 1987. Asian youth gangs terrorized students at eleven of twenty high schools in the city of Toronto through random violence. A rash of attacks during the last week of October and the first week of November in 1987 prompted the Toronto Board of Education at a closed meeting to call an emergency meeting of the director, superintendents, and principals to discuss ways to deal with the problem and to assuage the fear that was spreading among students.

Eight high school students were attacked or threatened by Chinese and Vietnamese gangs during a ten-day period at Harbord, Riverdale, and Bloor Collegiate Institutes. Knives, a pipe, and a hatchet were used in the attacks. School board officials were reluctant to talk about the problem, but realized it would only get worse if they hushed it up. One of two Chinese attackers had slashed a student at Harbord Collegiate Institute with a hatchet in the school hallway. A teacher frightened the punks off. The attackers were not students at the school. Three Chinese girls beat another Chinese girl at Riverdale Collegiate Institute. According to the reports, the victims were equally divided between Oriental and non-Oriental.

Fifteen Chinese and Vietnamese youths between the ages of fourteen and eighteen were arrested and charged with assaulting students in Toronto's west end. Unlike rumbles that occur periodically between rival factions in high schools, the violence inflicted by Asian youth gangs is arbitrary. Ten of them jumped one kid and beat and kicked him before walking away.

"These gang members are not students," the school board's associate director said. "These gangs cruise the city. They don't seem to be connected to a school. That's what's frightening. The kids don't know when they are going to get jumped. Some people think it's an extortion bid and they're frightening kids. They do it to set up a reign of terror for demands they'll make later. Once in a while, there seems to be a kid pressed into the gang. Part of the terrorizing is to get somebody into the gang. They put an end to a kid's career in school when he joins. Our students are afraid to talk. They're plain scared. They don't want to point the finger. I was at a commencement last Friday and everyone was still shocked by an attack hours earlier. A kid who was jumped and beaten made his way back to school for help."

There are 25,000 Hong Kong students studying in Canada. Asian youth gangs and street gangs consider them a source of money and recruits. A gangster beats a student; then another gang member approaches him and offers protection for a fee. The original attacker may even complain he had to inconvenience himself to beat the student and demand compensation. Then students are forced into joining the gangs. The son of a Malaysian politician, Hang-Hau "Jimmy" Hong, was a nineteen-year-old visa student in Toronto when he disappeared on May 3, 1987. Police believe he was abducted by gang members. Two Asians were photographed by bank video cameras using Hong's bank card three times to withdraw $1,000.

The tall Chinese teenager was a *dai lo*—big brother or leader—of a gang of Asian students at Toronto's Albert Campbell Collegiate high school in 1989. He called the shots for his group, who, like many high school Asian gangs, copy Chinese triads. The *dai lo* is a powerful kid. He must be approached to settle differences between Chinese kids, even if they attend different schools. Many Chinese high school hoods carry guns, the *dai lo* said. One eighteen-year-old was the middleman responsible for getting guns from suppliers to students. Guns are a big thing with Asian kids.

Two men approached the *dai lo* one day. One was a Vietnamese gangster. The other was a member of the Big Circle Boys. They asked him to provide armed muscle to protect their gaming houses. This is a common recruiting technique among Asian gangs. Students work for cheap and will do anything to impress professional criminals. The most vicious are eventually absorbed into the gangs.

The *dai lo*, like many Chinese with wealthy parents, was a spoiled brat. He eventually moved out of his parents' suburban house and into the apartment of a *sifu*—a Kung Fu master—who was also a triad member with connections to the Ghost Shadows and On Long Tong in New York. The *sifu* taught Kung Fu and obedience to initiate teenagers into his gang. Then the kids committed assaults and extortions for the *sifu*, who also squeezed money from their parents.

The *dai lo*'s father had $250,000 in his checking account. The kid forged his father's signature to get $10,000 to run away to Montreal. He had a great time impressing people by spending money, but soon got bored and returned to Toronto where he hooked up with the *sifu* again. A tip from the bank finally got the *dai lo* arrested.

Extortion

Five members of a Vietnamese gang operating a protection racket in Toronto's downtown Chinatown district threatened to kill a Chinese entertainment promoter in January 1986 if he didn't pay them $10,000 during the year to "protect" his concerts. The businessman complained to police. On Monday, March 7, 1986, he met nine people at the corner of Dundas and Huron streets and gave them $500, raising to $1,000 his payments to gang members since they had begun leaning on him in January. Metro Toronto police followed the nine and arrested them at the Kim Moon Bakery restaurant on Dundas Street West and charged three men and a youth with extortion. A fifth man was charged with illegally possessing a .32-caliber Smith & Wesson snub-nosed revolver with the serial numbers filed off.

Before the police set up their Oriental Crime Unit in 1984, they would not have heard about the extortion. The businessman would have paid up and shut up. The Oriental tradition has its roots in the distrust of corrupt civic officials in the Far East.

In February 1985, five Vietnamese gang members mailed shotgun shells or bullets to various people in Toronto, with demands for $2,000. They followed up each letter with a telephone call and arranged a drop-off point for the money. One intended victim complained to police, who arrested the men. They were convicted on three counts of extortion.

Six other Vietnamese gang members were convicted of extortion for their attempt to collect $5,000 from a Toronto businessman who had declared bankruptcy. The men were hired by one of the businessman's creditors and indicated to their victim they were armed. They were caught after the man complained to police.

Kingston, Ontario, is home to the largest collection of incarcerated criminals in Canada. That makes it one of the country's most concentrated drug markets, as there's little to do behind bars but bugger, get buggered, and get stoned. Chinese businessmen there are extorted by powerful triad heroin couriers to smuggle drugs into the area's penitentiaries for jailed triad leaders. The couriers walk into Chinese restaurants and convince owners to visit the leaders in jail with drugs up their ass — or their kids get killed. In many cases, the wife or daughter of the restaurant owner visits a leader on a "conjugal visit" to give him the drugs. Of course the poor restaurant owner's wife or daughter is also fucked in the process.

Five Asian gang members were hired by Hong Kong interests to retrieve money from a bad business deal north of Toronto in January 1990. The armed gangsters forced their way into a Richmond Hill home and held four people captive for three days. They took a couple to two banks and forced them to write certified checks for $380,000. Then the hoods deposited the checks. The following day, they were caught trying to break into another Toronto home.

Two armed Asians kidnapped Michael Vong from the front porch of his Bridle Path home in Toronto at 1 a.m. on August 21, 1989. They drove him around for twenty-five minutes before taking him to a garage where several people told him they needed $200,000 to finance a heroin deal in New York. Vong talked them down to $100,000, which he offered to pay in two installments. The abductors forced him to strip naked and took photographs, which they promised to give him once payment was made. Then they dropped him off and warned they'd kill his family if he called the police. Vong arranged to drop off the first installment in a white bag. The punks picked it up. Then the cops picked them up. No one knows what became of the photos.

David Lam, a Vietnamese, tried persistently to extort $2,000 from a sixteen-year-old Chinese exchange student in Toronto in October and November 1986. Lam accused the student of insulting him and told him he must pay appeasement money. Lam tried to convince two of the student's friends to talk him into giving them the money. Early on November 21, Lam and Vy Dan Tran and two other men went to the student's home armed with two handguns. The student wasn't there so they visited the friends and abducted them at gunpoint instead. They forced the friends, dressed in their underwear, to accompany them in their car. They returned to the student's house and abducted him too. Like the others, he was clad only in his underwear.

Lam and Tran threatened the student at gunpoint and demanded the money. They drove the three near-naked young men to the waterfront and made them stand in the snow as a show of respect for their four abductors. The student promised to pay Lam $1,000 later that day. The two others were so scared that they offered to pay the money if their friend couldn't. They were driven home and immediately packed their bags and moved out. Two of them contacted the police, who arrested one abductor in a pool hall and three others in a café. The third student hasn't been seen since.

Chen Fai Law emigrated from mainland China to Canada with his family when he was eleven years old. At eighteen, he made repeated phone calls to Tit-Kin Chu, saying his daughter had borrowed $2,000 from him. He asked the Toronto man for $5,000, warning that he would otherwise find his children's bodies at Riverdale Collegiate in the city's east end. Chu agreed to pay and met Law, who was wearing a disguise and was armed with two imitation pistols, a knife, and a screwdriver. The cops busted the punk and Hugh Locke, a Toronto District Court judge, one of the most thoughtful and socially aware judges on the Toronto bench, made these comments while sentencing Law to two years in jail on March 29, 1990:

"Extortionists are terrorists because the object is to create fear. [Extortion] is prevalent, especially in the Asian community in Canada and in other groups of our multi-racial society. This Metro area teems with criminals from all over the world. Some feel that if they victimize their own community they will not be punished by those who have always lived here. That notion must be dispelled. Extortion is a very serious crime that will be dealt with seriously by all Canadians regardless of their culture or background."

Two Chinese men—one a member of the Big Circle Boys gang in Vancouver—jumped Frank Yuen in his underground garage in Toronto on October 18, 1990. Yuen fought back and one of the kidnappers shot his buddy in the hand. They finally knocked down the thirty-eight-year-old janitor, tied his hands, and took him to Dr. Norman Bethune Collegiate nearby. They made him kneel. The gunman put his gun to Yuen's head and fired. Incredibly, he missed. The kidnappers put Yuen into his own car and drove to the northeast part of the city. Yuen opened the door and jumped out of the moving car to escape.

Two Asian men armed with replica handguns abducted two Hong Kong students in Toronto while pretending to deliver food on April 12, 1989. They drove them to a house where they were questioned and released without paying money.

The thirty-two-year-old owner of the Cafe Nam Gio in downtown Toronto paid $100 to a Vietnamese extortionist who threatened him in early September 1989. The extortionist returned later in the month and demanded more money. The owner refused to pay. On Thursday, September 28, the extortionist and three other men walked into the restaurant and started a fight with the owner and customers and threatened to kill the owner.

William Chan, an eighteen-year-old high school student from Hong Kong, was leaving his Toronto high school in October 1989 when a man approached him and said he wanted to talk about some problems. He followed the man to a car. Two men forced Chan into the car, taped his eyes, and handcuffed him. They drove him to an apartment where he was kept for three days by men who spoke Cantonese with Vietnamese accents. They asked for $4,000, an amount he said he couldn't afford. Except for a punch in the head, Chan was freed unharmed. His former girlfriend, whom he had dated for six months before breaking up one month before the kidnapping, was also in the apartment.

"She sat beside me and I was surprised she was there," Chan said. "I asked her how she got there."

An Asian gang led by a nineteen-year-old man and made up of six teenage boys and one girl threatened Asian visa students in Toronto with guns, knives, and sawed-off pool cues to force them to pay up to $200 weekly in protection money in the fall of 1989. The victims, between the ages of fourteen and sixteen, lived alone in Canada, had wealthy parents and access to large amounts of money.

An Asian man walked into a downtown Toronto Chinatown business at 5 p.m. on Tuesday, June 30, 1987, and allegedly told the fifty-seven-year-old owner he was collecting a debt on behalf of another businessman. He demanded $100,000. The alleged extortionist said that the businessman would pay with his life if he couldn't pay the debt with money. The businessman called police, who arrested thirty-one-year-old Raven Ip-Shun Tsoi after finding a 12-gauge, pistol-grip shotgun and shells in the trunk of his luxury car.

The same Raven Tsoi was identified as a leader of the Kung Lok triad on Friday, September 11, 1987, at the sentencing of a Vietnamese street gang member convicted of threatening to kill two police officers. Metro Toronto Police Constable Ben Eng (now a sergeant) told the court Tsoi had admitted taking nineteen-year-old Tuan Minh Tinh, a Vietnamese immigrant, under his wing.

Federal tax and police officials teamed up for the first time that day to combat Asian organized crime in Toronto. Investigators with the Department of National Revenue, armed with a photograph of Tsoi, stopped him in the second-floor hallway of the University Avenue courthouse and served him with notices to justify his income for the past three years. Tsoi was in court that day to set a trial date on charges of extortion and carrying a concealed weapon. He was given thirty days to explain his financial affairs for 1984, 1985, and 1986. Tsoi signed the three forms to acknowledge receiving them and told a police officer accompanying the tax officials, "Thank you. Thank you very much."

Revenue Canada officials are bound by the secrecy provision of the Income Tax Act not to discuss any case. A source close to the investigation said Tsoi had come to the attention of Revenue Canada's special investigation section through newspaper accounts of his arrest. Tsoi was acquitted of the extortion and concealed-weapon charges after a co-accused pleaded guilty. He called police in January 1990 to get his shotgun back. It is not illegal to carry a shotgun in the trunk of your car in Canada.

Quay Truong and Dieu Tan Quach approached a Toronto promoter of Chinese concerts in February 1986 and threatened to destroy the man and one of his concerts if he didn't pay protection money. The Chinese man objected to paying the Vietnamese extortionists and went to police. They rigged him with a body pack to record his next conversation with the gangsters, in which they demanded $500. The money was paid in marked bills. The court was told that the men belonged to an Asian gang whose leader couldn't be identified because he was before the courts on extortion charges. The leader gained notoriety in the community after being acquitted of murder. "With the notoriety you get power, and with power you get money," Metro Toronto Police Constable Kenneth Yates of the Asian Crime Unit testified. The concert promoter was so terrified by the attempted extortion that he fled the country even though the police offered him twenty-four-hour protection.

Vietnamese gangsters in Melbourne, Australia, hacked off the fingers of people who refused to pay their extortion demands in 1981. Vietnamese with missing fingers were showing up in hospital emergency wards.

Asian gang violence intimidates its victims into silence. Vancouver police had five unsolved Asian gang murders in 1987 after the Red Eagles Chinese street gang launched a war with the rival Lotus and Jung Ching gangs. On Friday, January 23, 1987, a sixteen-year-old gangster sat behind a fourteen-year-old Asian watching a double feature in a Chinese theater and shot the younger boy in the back of the head with a .38-caliber revolver. The boy survived but lost an eye. The Chinese Benevolent Society screamed for more Chinese police officers. Vancouver police chief Bob Stewart responded that his officers could better control crime in Chinatown if that community cooperated with police he already had instead of saying nothing.

Twenty-nine-year-old Jimmy Ming and his thirty-year-old wife Lily worked eighteen-hour days managing a three-table restaurant in Vancouver's east end to make enough money to help Ming's father buy a bigger restaurant on Robson Street. They dubbed the new business the Yangtze Kitchen Restaurant and hired a staff of Vietnamese boat people. The Mings attended a wedding on January 20, 1985, where a brawl broke out among the 300 mostly Vietnamese guests. When they returned to their Chinatown home, they were abducted by Vietnamese gangsters who had smashed a basement window to get in. The kidnappers sent a $700,000 ransom note to the Ming family.

"You have a good family," the first note said. "You have a good business. We don't have anything. We have a lot of brothers and you won't catch us all. We are even in the United States. You will not be the last. There will be other restaurants."

Ping Chang Ming, the abducted man's father and owner of the Yangtze Kitchen Restaurant, didn't have the money to pay the kidnappers. He called the police. The kidnappers got angry and forced Ming to apologize and plead for the lives of his son and daughter-in-law in advertisements run in a Chinese newspaper.

The first advertisement: "Mr. Ching, last time I was wrong. Please forgive me. We will do according to your wish. You demand too much. I have the heart but not the strength. Hope you will consider." The February 13 and 19 ads were signed "Mr. Yang."

A March 3 advertisement read: "Mr. Wong, your demand is acceptable. I really want to cooperate with you deep down in my heart. You make the plans for what you want me to do. But without a chance to talk to you, it's difficult. Please think. In the newspapers, it's really hard to explain. I am willing to give you the money but understand my hardship. Asking the bank for money, you have to have a good reason. The house is already mortgaged but that's not enough. Please can I personally speak to my son and his wife. Get them individually to write a letter so I can see. Please be kind and think it over."

Ming received one telephone call from the kidnappers, which was traced to Victoria. The kidnappers were not the swiftest people in the world. They arranged only once for a meeting to exchange the hostages for money. Their note was found by Ming the day after the exchange was supposed to take place. Jimmy and Lily Ming were strangled and butchered, their chopped-up bodies stuffed into canvas sacks and rolled down an embankment north of Lions Bay near Vancouver. They had been killed long before the March 12 deadline the kidnappers had imposed.

Robbery

Asian gangs find robbing illegal Chinese gaming houses as profitable as extortion. Toronto police hacked away at their bottom line by closing down the five permanent gaming houses in Chinatown where running games brought owners more than $1 million a year in the mid-1980s. The criminals have resorted to floating gaming houses, which are equally difficult for police and robbers to find, as they usually operate for one night.

Gaming-house holdups are routine for Asian gangs, unless an undercover cop happens to be sitting at one of the tables. Metro Toronto Police Asian Crime Unit officers decided to check out illegal gambling, especially off-track betting, at the Club de Hong Kong on April 14, 1990. Stupid move number one: The police picked an inexperienced cop for the dirty job of going into the club undercover. They borrowed him from another division, although he had been a uniform cop in the same division where he was to work undercover that night. Stupid move number two: They sent the cop into the club with his police badge, identification card, and handcuffs. Stupid move number three: Two experienced plainclothes cops went to dinner with the newly created undercover colleague and left their service revolvers locked in the trunk of the rental car he was driving. The undercover cop took the car keys into the club. While two other armed cops watched the front door of the club, the two unarmed cops watched the back door. The undercover cop came out at one point and went to a doughnut shop with the two unarmed cops. They still hadn't noticed they had left their guns in the trunk of the car, so that's where they stayed.

At 1:30 a.m., four masked and armed Asian gangsters walked into the club where thirty-five people were watching a live satellite broadcast of horse races from Hong Kong. Two scouts—a male and female—were already inside the club. Many patrons recognized the undercover cop from his previous beat in the area, but assumed he was a crooked cop out for a night of gambling. The two armed cops at the front door called the division station for uniform backup. The two unarmed cops at the back of the building didn't dare show their faces at the front without their guns.

Meanwhile, the gangsters lined patrons up against a wall and searched them for money and valuables. They found the cop's badge in his wallet. They beat him viciously. One gangster put his pistol in the cop's mouth and pulled the trigger. It failed to fire. While this was going on, the two unarmed cops kept their distance as uniformed cops roared up and jumped out of their cruisers. One unarmed officer raced to the nearest station for a shotgun. It was a gesture that made sense only to someone who knew they were unarmed. They weren't about to admit it themselves.

The hoods scooped cash from the till and their booty from the patrons and fled the club. The first two gangsters out the door were arrested. The next two realized what was happening, grabbed the two scouts, and pretended they had taken hostages. They walked to their white Honda with guns to their accomplices' heads. The car was ditched after a high-speed chase and the hoods were eventually caught. One of them was fourteen years old.

Police reports of the incident played up the fact that an undercover officer was in the gaming house when the robbery occurred and that all six suspects were arrested. There was no mention of the foul-ups that could have caused the cop's death. The police officer who emptied the cartridges from the revolver that was put in the cop's mouth found one with a dented primer. The firing pin had hit, but without enough force to detonate the primer. Constable Peter Yuen, the undercover cop, was named the force's officer of the year for 1990.

In October 1985, a Vietnamese gang member shot an employee of an illegal Chinese gaming house at Broadview Avenue and Gerrard Street during a robbery. He was convicted of attempted murder.

Three masked Vietnamese men wielding machetes and a handgun burst into Toronto's Young Chinese Recreation Club at 3 a.m. on Sunday, June 22, 1986, and forced fifteen to twenty patrons into a back room where they took money and jewelry worth $2,700. Then they locked their victims in the room and ran off. Only five people hung around long enough to talk with police.

Five masked Asians walked into a west Toronto home on Saturday, April 27, 1990, and held up thirteen men having a friendly game of cards. The robbers forced them to lie on the floor unless they wanted to die while they stole $2,000 in cash and jewelry.

A gangster knocked on the door of a Toronto apartment building penthouse on September 26, 1990. As the doorman opened the door of the floating Chinese gaming house, the Asian man shoved an AK-47 semi-automatic rifle through the opening and sprayed five shots into the room. One .223-caliber bullet pierced two walls and hit a twenty-four-year-old woman in the upper right arm. The doorman slammed the door on the rifle and the hood and his accomplices fled, leaving the gun behind.

One Vietnamese gang went on a spree in January 1990. Four gunmen held up Man Ho, owner of the Man Fat meat market in east Toronto, outside his house as he arrived home from work with $4,000. Three gunmen walked into a Laotian family's apartment in Toronto's west end and made off with $17,000. Two gunmen pistol-whipped a twelve-year-old boy while forcing their way into a west Toronto home where they stole $10,000 and jewelry.

Four Vietnamese men armed with semi-automatic handguns used a steel rod to smash a display case in La Difference Jewellers in downtown Toronto on Monday, April 30, 1990, and made off with twenty-eight Rolex watches worth $155,000.

Police estimate twelve Oriental businesses are robbed for every one that is reported. They won't say how many Asian businessmen are robbed or extorted every year, but extortions are second only to robberies. Police investigated 143 such extortions in 1989. Toronto's world-famous Chinese restaurants are feeling the effects of the robberies. Regular patrons avoid them at night.

Three gangsters walked into the Centura Chinese restaurant in Richmond Hill, north of Toronto on September 5, 1990, and fired semi-automatic pistols over patrons' heads to get their attention. They forced sixty diners to lie on the floor while they stole their money and jewelry. They took $4,000 from one woman and a $5,000 ring from another diner. They ripped telephones from the wall and fled. The robbery was one of three meticulously planned by three Asian men who staked out the restaurants before robbing them. They held up twenty-eight diners in the Eastcourt Restaurant in September and thirteen customers and staff at the King Chai Restaurant in August.

A lone gunman walked into the Chop Suey House restaurant in Toronto and tried to herd patrons into the basement. After one man escaped, he panicked and fled.

Asian gangsters blasted away in a downtown Toronto Chinese restaurant in July 1990, accidentally hitting a man in the knee. He ran out of the restaurant and down the street toward Toronto Western Hospital. A gunman followed him, firing two more shots.

Three Vietnamese gangsters sat at the back of the Viet Huong Restaurant on Toronto's College Street on Friday, May 23, 1986. After half an hour, two of the men walked out. The third approached the bartender, pulled a snub-nosed .38-caliber revolver, and demanded $500. The bartender refused. The gangster fired a shot into the floor. He walked over to the owner and fired into the floor again. The owner, who thought the gun was a fake, also refused to pay and chased the gunman out into the street. The gunman fired several times at the pursuing owner, hitting the getaway car in which his two buddies sat. They took off and abandoned their friend. A police cruiser turned the corner as the car burned rubber to get away and the cops took off after it. The driver of the getaway car lost control and crashed.

Two masked men walked through the kitchen door of the Magic Wok Cantonese Cuisine in Toronto shortly after midnight in mid-August 1986. They leveled semi-automatic pistols at ten lounging workers and herded them to one side of the room. One of the gunmen ran into the dining room and ordered ten waiters and waitresses to set aside their teacups and cigarettes.

"They pushed all of us into the kitchen and made us sit on the floor with our faces to the wall," a waitress said.

One of the men unlocked the restaurant's front door, letting in two accomplices, who were also wearing blue ski masks. They armed themselves with kitchen knives.

"They ordered us not to move," the waitress said. "I was scared. They said they wanted money. After they got it [about $5,000], they said it wasn't enough."

The robbers demanded everyone's jewelry. Thirty-one-year-old Kwok-Cheen Yuen refused. He argued with the robbers, who spoke Cantonese with accents that could have been Vietnamese. One robber grabbed a meat cleaver from the rack and slashed Yuen on the shoulder. No one else objected.

Two Vietnamese men armed with handguns walked into the Hong Kong Delight restaurant in north Toronto at 10:10 p.m. on June 13, 1990, and ordered everyone to lie on the floor while they robbed the till. Two days later, two Asian men armed with a sawed-off shotgun robbed the Hing Ming Trading Co.

Three armed Asian men burst into the closed Wok and Bowl Restaurant in Toronto at 6 a.m. on December 1, 1989, smashing one man in the face with a gun and shooting another through the shoulder. Police couldn't find out from a dozen people in the restaurant what had happened and why they were there so late after closing.

Two armed Vietnamese men robbed six Chinese food stores over two weeks in November 1989, taking money from the till and jewelry and wallets from customers.

A masked Vietnamese man walked into a store on Broadview Avenue in Toronto's east-end Chinatown, pulled a gun, and screamed, "Don't shout or I'll kill you," to a woman and her son who were working after hours. The gangster handcuffed the woman to a rack of videotapes and tied her son to the rack with a belt. He then demanded money. When told there wasn't any, he called to a second hood watching the door to come in and help him search the store. They left emptyhanded.

Home Invasions

The most popular new crime perpetrated by Asian gangs in North America is the home invasion. These and kidnappings have long been a major source of income for the gangs in Hong Kong. Gangsters target a wealthy Asian businessman and stake out his house. Sometimes they break in and wait for the owner to come home. More often, they burst in late at night or early in the morning and tie everyone up at gunpoint. They ransack the house and beat family members to find hidden money or jewelry. American gangsters have shot and killed children to get their parents to cooperate. Often it is one of the businessman's children who sets up the robbery after being courted by gang members with promises of money, sex, and drugs. Many Chinese kids love the attention, regardless of who gives it to them and its price tag.

Ly Ratanawong is a machine operator who immigrated to Canada from Laos in 1981. He kept $10,000 in his apartment safe because he didn't like to have all his savings in the bank. He also had $7,000 in uninsured antique jewelry in the safe. Ratanawong's eighteen-year-old son answered a knock at the door during the evening of January 30, 1990. A Vietnamese youth pointed a gun at him and three gangsters burst into the apartment. They made Ratanawong and his two sons lie on a bedroom floor and bound their hands behind their backs with belts. They forced the mother to unlock the safe and ripped off her wedding rings, chains, and bracelets.

Three masked Oriental men robbed a Toronto couple at gunpoint in their restaurant in late February 1990. Two weeks later, the same men armed with handguns and knives burst into their home at 4:30 a.m., bound and gagged them, and stole $2,500 the couple had brought home from the restaurant, as well as credit cards, furs, and jewelry. The family dog lunged at a thief, who kicked it in the head.

Three armed Vietnamese men aged twenty to twenty-four burst into a Toronto apartment at 12:30 a.m. on July 17, 1990, and demanded money that had been collected by members of the Vietnamese community for their relatives overseas. The three, wearing stocking masks, forced the family onto the seventeenth-floor balcony while they searched for the money. The nineteen-year-old son climbed down to the sixteenth-floor balcony and asked the tenant to call police. The punks fled when they noticed he was missing. One of them ran into a cop and pointed his gun at him. The smooth-talking cop convinced him to surrender it.

Two masked Asian gang members walked into a downtown Toronto medical office on the evening of Friday, August 17, 1990, and terrorized a doctor and four patients with handguns before robbing them of $1,200.

Three masked Vietnamese men brandishing two handguns walked into a Toronto apartment in September 1990, herded the children into a bedroom, banged the Vietnamese father around, and asked for the $9,500 he had from the recent sale of his car. They also grabbed jewelry.

Canadian Immigration – Crime Without Punishment

How is it that thousands of Asian criminals get into Canada when immigration authorities are supposed to screen them? Easy. Immigration officials are often not the smartest or hardest-working civil servants. Canadian immigration procedures are at best lax. At their worst, they're a crime.

Kok Chi-yin, known on the street as Kwok Ka, was a member of the Big Circle Boys who made his way to Hong Kong from China. He was slated for execution in Hong Kong when he escaped from death row. A Hong Kong police report described Ka as a "hardened, professional and ruthless" killer. The man filed immigration papers to get into Canada and swore he had no criminal record. That was good enough for immigration officials. So killer Ka was allowed to escape to Toronto. He was locked up in a New York state jail in 1990 under indictment for conspiracy to traffic $8 million of heroin into New York City through Toronto.

Canada has a holier-than-thou attitude in foreign affairs, not really understanding what is happening in other countries, but passing judgment anyway just to look sophisticated. For example, consider the hard-core criminals from Vietnam who arrived in the country as refugees—the infamous boat people. Most of them were honest people escaping Communist oppression. But many gangsters used them as shields to escape death in a country that does not tolerate criminals. Canada refuses to deport any Vietnamese caught committing crimes against Canadian for fear they will be punished in Vietnam. Instead, they turn them loose on Canadian streets to continue their lives of crime.

Canadians pay taxes for protection and the peace of mind to run businesses and walk the streets without fear. Politicians and bureaucrats give criminals the peace of mind to commit crimes without fear of punishment.

One member of a Vietnamese gang that tried to extort money from a Toronto Chinese concert promoter in early 1986 was a juvenile. He had several laws working in his favor in Canada: one is immigration procedure not to deport Vietnamese refugees; the other is the federal Young Offenders Act, which prohibits publication of the names of criminals under the age of eighteen. The law was drafted under the misguided notion that these impressionable youths have been temporarily misled and have made a terrible error in judgment that they would not have made if older and more mature. Drafters of the law claimed these poor kids should be given anonymity so they would not be forever branded by society and deprived of a chance to rehabilitate. So young criminals are allowed back into the community and no one knows who they are. We can publish the lurid details of their crimes but not their names.

This is where the second protection offered by the Young Offenders Act comes into play. It allows for a maximum sentence of three years for any crime—murder included. After three years, the killer is free and anonymous. A long-haired punk who killed his parents and sister got three years. He's out on the street now and could be dating your daughter. The law is protecting him, not her. What did she do to deserve this risk?

The juvenile Vietnamese extortionist was tried on Thursday, August 7, 1986. Provincial Court Judge Robert Dnieper, one of the more sensitive yet brutal judges on the Ontario bench, called for immediate deportation proceedings against the juvenile, who belonged to a Vietnamese street gang that terrorized Toronto's downtown Chinatown. Judge Dnieper described the juvenile as "a vicious person who is more adult than adult criminals with a long record" and sentenced him to thirty-four months in jail. He reduced the sentence from three years after the defense lawyer noted the youth had two months left to serve on a six-month sentence for assault. Judge Dnieper said the youth would never be rehabilitated and that the "only answer for him is deportation and the suggestion that he try his gang activities in Ho Chi Minh City." Judge Dnieper directed Crown counsel to write to the Minister of State for Immigration and ask that the youth be deported to allow the gang's victims to sleep in peace.

But James Bissett, executive director of immigration, objected. "It's highly unlikely we would send anybody back to Vietnam because of the harshness of what might await him," he said. "I don't think extortion of $500 would be considered as serious enough to send someone back to Vietnam, especially if the family were refugees."

"It is a primary responsibility of any government to permit its citizens to live without fear," Judge Dnieper said while sentencing the extortionist. "It is a primary duty of the system of criminal justice to see that citizens live without fear. If citizens do, in fact, live in fear, then justice has failed. This cannot and will not happen." He called for Vietnamese gangs to be "wiped from society completely.... Our nation is seen by these people as being impotent in dealing with them. More frightening, too, is the perception that we are without the backbone to deal with them.... All means available to our government, through criminal justice or other institutions, must be taken to stamp out this evil cancer," he said, referring to the immigration department's refusal to deport gang members.

Metro Toronto Police Constable Kenneth Yates described the Vietnamese gang to which the youth belonged as one having twenty to thirty members. Its leader, Asau Tran, came to Canada as a refugee from Vietnam in the 1980s. Tran gained notoriety after the 1983 shooting of three men on Bellevue Street in Toronto's Kensington Market during an argument over who was a better dancer. A nineteen-year-old man died of his bullet wounds. Tran and two other men were arrested in the shooting but were later acquitted. Since no one was ever convicted in the shootings, Vietnamese gangsters felt immune to prosecution and stepped up their wave of terror in the Chinese community.

Judge Brian Stevenson in the Court of Queen's Bench in Calgary, Alberta, also won't tolerate Vietnamese gangsters. Alex Zhen Liu and Wei Hua Hung, both of Boston, were part of an eight-man gang that held up the Kim Hoang jewelry store in Calgary's Chinatown on December 28, 1989. Two gunmen held the owners at bay while three youths stole $120,000 in gold jewelry from smashed display cases. Three other gang members waited in two getaway cars. The whole holdup took forty seconds. Judge Stevenson sentenced the two men on April 11, 1990, to fifteen years in prison. An Oakville, Ontario, gang member was sentenced to seven years in jail the previous week.

"Let the word go out the jaws of our federal penitentiaries yawn open for them," Judge Stevenson said in words the Asians are bound to understand. "Most of them entered into Canada with the intent of breaking our laws and breaking them with violence if necessary."

The ignorance, laziness, incompetence, and lack of professionalism of some Canadian immigration officials is best demonstrated by a report prepared by the Immigration Operations Branch. It summarizes highlights from an immigration intelligence report on Asian crime. The way it underlines how far out of touch with reality some immigration officials are is frightening. It also shows the uselessness of their data base. The one-page memorandum dated October 9, 1986, is prefaced by a two-page apology from the director general of immigration for the Ontario region who politely and politically warns readers that the report's conclusions are based on nothing at all.

Chinese Triads and Criminality in the Asian Ethnic Community from January 1, 1978 to January 1, 1986

Attached for your information is a copy of a report prepared by Intelligence Division, Operations Branch, Immigration, NHQ.

The data base for this study was information contained in established Immigration Data Banks. Conclusions have been drawn on the premise that all visitors and permanent residents convicted for a criminal offence are reported pursuant to the Immigration Act. In addition, this study does not concern itself with Canadian citizens of any ethnic origin since it is stated they are beyond the mandate of Immigration.

The validity of these prerequisites for the study, however, is questionable. Concerning the reporting of all visitors and permanent residents, two simple examples illustrate that this prerequisite is not accurate.

A visitor in Canada who is convicted of Possession of a Narcotic under Section 3(1) of the Narcotic Control Act where the Court proceeded summarily is not reportable.

A permanent resident who is convicted of Assault under Section

245 (b) of the Criminal Code and sentenced to a fine or a term of imprisonment of less than six months is not reportable.

The reliance on statistics of criminal convictions exclusively, also substantially reduces the data base for this study. The lack of a conviction being registered for an offence does not negate the fact that a crime has been perpetrated.

Law enforcement agencies will tell you that the Chinese community is a very close-knit and tight-lipped group. Because of these facts, gathering sufficient evidence in order to proceed to Court and obtain a conviction is very difficult.

Concerning Canadian Citizens being outside the mandate of Immigration, it is a fact that Canadians are investigated by the Commission regularly for such offences as alien smuggling, rackets, aiding or abetting, etc.

It is often impossible to know which crimes are gang related. A committed offence may appear only as an isolated occurrence but may be part of a larger pattern of criminal activity. The nature and composition of a gang is never very firm. While leaders have been identified, identifying other members and their exact number has proven more difficult.

Please review this study and provide me with your comments.

D. Conn

The questionable memorandum from National Headquarters:

A report entitled Chinese Triads and Criminality in the Asian Ethnic Community has recently been completed by the Immigration Operations Branch.

This report was commissioned last year to improve the information base upon which judgements about our policy response to Hong Kong 1997 would be made. It is based on an examination of reports made pursuant to the Immigration Act over an 8-year period. Its preparation is quite timely in light of the fact that the Criminal Intelligence Services of Canada are also expected to present a brief with recommendations to control the growth of Asian organized crime.

Highlights of this report are as follows:

1) it concludes that the visitor and permanent resident population of Chinese/orientals is very law abiding;

2) it does not support the widely held view within the enforcement environment, that there is extensive serious crime in the Chinese community in Canada;

3) it does not support the existence of much organized or "gang" crime.

This is not to say that serious criminality committed by Chinese visitors and permanent residents does not exist; it's just that our data revealed little evidence of it.

Not all Canadian immigration officials are incompetent. The National Headquarters' memorandum and the intelligence report it summarized cause a lot of grief for many immigration officers in touch with reality. One of those officers was George Best, district intelligence officer for the immigration department's Toronto District, probably the most multi-racial area in the world. He wrote a confidential thirteen-page memorandum to his superior on September 4, 1986, tearing apart the National Headquarters' memo and report.

This memorandum starts with a reference to an article on Asian gangs I wrote in the Toronto *Globe and Mail* on August 30, 1986, which he included with his submission. Then he mentioned the August 1986 law-enforcement conference to assess Oriental organized crime in Ontario. Some of the agencies represented there were the Criminal Intelligence Service of Ontario, several sections of the Royal Canadian Mounted Police, the Metro Toronto Police, and Ontario Provincial Police units dealing with Asians, police forces from major cities in the province, and the Canadian Security Intelligence Service, which is the Canadian CIA.

"The Conference was a direct result of disagreement with the contents and conclusions of the paper from N.H.Q.," he wrote. "Those attending to whom we spoke, and who had read the N.H.Q. paper, were extremely critical of both its content and conclusions. There was a strong feeling expressed to the effect that Immigration was deliberately ignoring and down playing an existing and potentially greater problem." Heavy words when you consider who the complainants are.

Best continued his tale of bureaucratic ineptitude and his desperate, futile attempts to get his hands on a report prepared by someone in his own department.

1. In early June 1986 the writer was contacted by a Criminal Intelligence Services Ontario (C.I.S.O.) Operating Body member concerning the above report which was described in extremely uncomplimentary terms. At this same time we were asked to make a joint presentation to C.I.S.O. on 25-6-86 along with Sgt. Cowley, the Metropolitan Toronto Police Officer-in-Charge of the Oriental Organized Crime Squad (O.O.C.S.), concerning "Orientals in Ontario." We would be expected to field any questions arising from this subject.

2. We advised C.I.S.O. that we had never seen the report and could they provide us with a copy. They stated they would hesitate to do so in view of the originators having marked the report

"confidential" and not having seen fit to share it with myself—and possibly others.

3. We contacted Ontario Region in order to determine whether they had seen the report. The answer was negative, but an attempt would be made to obtain a copy from N.H.Q. We were later told by the Acting Regional Intelligence Officer that N.H.Q. would forward a copy directly to us. A week went by without receiving the report. We contacted Mr. Houdon at N.H.Q. who advised that the report had not been sent, but that when it would be sent, it would be directed to Region.

4. Subsequently, we were asked by C.I.S.O. to attend a meeting concerning the report at 2:00 P.M. on 20-6-86. Representatives from the O.O.C.S. would also be attending. We again pointed out that we had never seen the report in question and therefore would not comment on its contents. On the day prior to the meeting C.I.S.O. provided us with a copy of the report which we were able to read the night prior to the meeting.

5. The copied report from C.I.S.O. is the only report made available to us.

Best goes on at length to tear apart the report line by line. Here are some quotes from the report followed by his comments.

Report: "Innocuous secret oaths and ceremonies do not cause harm."
Best: "The author does not seem to appreciate the significance, vis-à-vis the joining of a gang, etc. taking oaths, rituals, etc. Should we ignore the 'innocuous' rituals of an outlaw motorcycle gang—beatings, rapes, abductions, intimidations, murder, etc."

Report: "The [Immigration] Commission ought not to concern itself with the issue of criminal gangs claiming or having Triad connections."
Best: "We disagree. Surely in relation to intelligence gathering and decision making, information that an individual was/is a Triad (or any other gang) member cannot and should not be ignored."

Report: "[E]ven though Hong Kong appears in the top five countries whose nationals are convicted of a criminal offence while visiting Canada, visitors from the Asian countries studied ... do not pose a significant threat...."
Best: "Considering that Hong Kong is number three on the list we believe the author's argument could in fact be reversed."

Report: "[M]embers of the known Chinese gangs in Canada ... consist mainly of Canadian citizens.... If ... the threat is from citizens, the role of Immigration in reducing the problem is not entirely clear."

Best: "Only three years after 'Landing' a person can become a Canadian Citizen and if that person has resided permanently in Canada prior to 'Landing' he can become a citizen in less than three years. Once gaining citizenship (unless revoked) there is nothing Immigration can do in the 'enforcement sense' against this particular person. On the other hand Immigration allowed entry in the first place and often this same person will wish to sponsor others. The fact he has become a Canadian Citizen does not remove Immigration's responsibility to be alert to what this person may be doing under certain circumstances."

Report: "Visitors from Hong Kong have been convicted of very few serious crimes .... The majority of crimes relates to stealing e.g. theft, possession of stolen property, fraud, etc."

Best: "We, and no doubt the victims, would consider these serious crimes even if the author does not."

Best:

7. The essence of N.H.Q.'s draft report seems to be that in the opinion of the author there is essentially very little for Canadians to be concerned about in relation to Chinese/ Asian Organized Crime. It is not a threat; nor does it pose a threat. The fact that concerned agencies (not just police) have been meeting on an annual basis for a good number of years in order to try and resolve problems created by Asian Organized Crime appears to have escaped the author's notice. These agencies have included representatives from the U.S., Hong Kong, Australia, West Germany and, of course, Canada. In 1985 well over 200 agencies attended the Houston Conference.

8. In reading this report, we are left with the impression that the author was somewhat less than objective, with pre-conceived—not to say prejudicial—ideas as to what the report should contain. We notice a certain bias where the police are concerned. The general thrust of the report appears directed toward disparaging the police community. Their conclusions are myths. We suspect the author has little in depth background experiences with respect to Asians or Asian crime in particular.

10. We are firmly of the opinion that this report, which may well contribute to future Immigration policy, should not

have set such narrow parameters. Any role played by Canadian Citizens in Asian organized crime should not and cannot be ignored. By the same token nor can criminal involvement prior to coming to Canada be ignored. The author has deliberately decided to do so.

11. The author, in relying so completely on Immigration reports relating to criminal convictions, either is unaware of, or has deliberately ignored, the fact that two major Chinese gang leaders were removed from Canada, not on the basis of any criminal conviction (neither had any), but on the basis of a mass of intelligence information gathered by police forces at the municipal, provincial and federal levels. The vehicle used was A39/40. Action under 40 of the Act had been contemplated against a third Chinese, involved in drugs, but unfortunately, he became a Canadian Citizen.

14. Triads in the classical sense may no longer exist, but Chinese/Asian gangs do; both in Asia and in Canada. Every effort should be made to neutralize these gangs. Immigration has an active role to play. Our interest cannot and should not be confined simply to what happens after a visitor or immigrant arrives in Canada—as has been done by the author of this report. It should not be forgotten that two of Parliament's objectives with respect to the present Immigration Act are: "to maintain and protect the health, safety and good order of Canadian society"; and "to promote international order and justice by denying the use of Canadian territory to persons who are likely to engage in criminal activity."

16. Not too many years ago an Attorney General for Ontario denied the existance [sic] of Italian organized crime in this province. Possibly it was politic to do so at the time. We doubt if any Attorney General would make that statement today.

17. Immigration cannot bury its head in the sand and pretend that a similar situation does not exist in Canada tody with respect to the Asian community—a situation which has the potential for serious consequences as 1997 approaches and Hong Kong enters the 50 year transitional period prior to complete assimilation by China.

Compare the approach to Asian organized crime by Canadian immigration officials to that taken by the US Immigration and Naturalization Service in this 1989 report:

The U.S. Immigration and Naturalization Service (INS) recognizes that Chinese Organized Crime (COC) groups are probably the most significant and prominent of all the emerging ethnic criminal organizations in the United States today, in that these groups now

    –control and dominate heroin trafficking into the United States;

    –maintain a sophisticated and intricate network worldwide that can facilitate any type of criminal endeavor, virtually anywhere;

    –control and dominate the Chinese communities in the United States; and,

    –are no longer limited to the "Chinatowns" of America, but have spread their narcotics networks, prostitution rings, and gang violence to places like Portland, Maine; Keene, New Hampshire; Denver, Colorado; and Tulsa, Oklahoma.

As with all the newly-emerging ethnic crime groups, INS has a crucial role to play in thwarting the activities of Chinese organized criminal groups because of its unique and exclusive jurisdiction, and its daily interface with these ethnic communities. INS agents have tremendous ability and experience in dealing with alien communities, and have particular skill in cultivating informants, using as a lever highly-coveted immigration benefits.

These guys don't sit around pretending that nothing is happening. They have a job to do and they get it done.

Part II

DIRTY DANCING

6

Harvesting the Devil's Dandruff:
Business practices of the rich and heinous

"We are up against an organization stronger than the state."
FORMER COLOMBIAN PRESIDENT BELISARIO BETANCUR ON THE MEDELLIN DRUG
CARTEL.

Max Mermelstein imported fifty-six tons of Colombian cocaine into the United States from 1981 to 1985. In 1985, the year he was arrested for supplying the cocaine in the John DeLorean case, he became the highest ranking member of the Medellin cartel to turn government informant.

"I was arrested in June and when I was arrested, there was a piece of paper in my pocket which had a good deal of personal data about Adler Barry Seal, who was a government witness at that time. Knowing that I had this paper in my pocket, I immediately notified the boys in Colombia to hold the contract. At this time there was a contract on Barry Seal and they had me looking actively for Barry Seal. I told them that I had been arrested and I had this paper on me. It was related to me directly by Fabio Ochoa, Jr., on the telephone, along with Pablo Escobar personally, either kidnap him or kill him. I wasn't asked to do this. I was told to do this.

"What I had in my possession was a piece of paper which was written by Rafael Cardona with personal information about Seal: his home address, registry numbers on a couple of his airplanes, his places of business, some of the cars that he and his family were driving—locator information, if you will.

"And when I told the boys in Colombia that this piece of paper was found on my person when I was arrested, and to hold off on the entire operation, I was told point-blank: No, it is going ahead full steam and they are bringing in a team from Colombia to finish it off. So now I am not only looking at drug charges. I am looking at the possibility of conspiracy to commit murder. And I wasn't particularly interested in killing anybody anyway, so I had my attorney notify the government about the contract on Seal, and the government knew about it in July 1985."

Mermelstein's Colombian friends were not impressed. They've pegged his life at $3 million—the reward offered in an open contract to anyone who kills him.

Max Mermelstein became a member of the Medellin cartel after he witnessed a murder committed by Rafael Cardona, one of its members, and was allowed to live. He described to a United States Senate committee how this led to his involvement in the drug trade.

"From that point on," said Mermelstein, "I was owned by Rafael Cardona and I was to do his bidding. I tried on several occasions [to quit the drug business] and I was told point-blank there are only two ways out: either going to jail or going out in a box." Cardona himself went out in a box after being gunned down in February 1987.

Mermelstein knows the operations of the Medellin cartel inside out. He described its workings as typical of any large corporation. He recalled the most minute details of running a cocaine-smuggling operation because Medellin cartel operatives were required to keep accurate records with the help of a cartel accountant who transferred the information to the organization's main books in Colombia.

"On the operational line, we'd start with the Ochoa brothers. The three brothers, the oldest of which is Juan David Ochoa, the middle brother, Jorge Ochoa, and the youngest brother, Fabio, Jr. Basically the business was started amongst the three brothers by Juan David, who later backed out, and Jorge took over and he has controlled it basically ever since. Past the Ochoa brothers, we've got Pablo Escobar, basically on the same level, probably a little higher right now. We had Pablo Correa involved at that time, in the beginning. Pablo also was cut down in a hail of gunfire. Gonzalo Rodriguez Gacha, better known as El Mexicano, out of Bogotá, also a very high-level member in the cartel. Hiro Mejira, also a very high-level member of the cartel. The upper echelon is six or eight people, basically, who control it worldwide.

"My basic reporting chain of command, if you will, was through Rafael Cardona. But Cardona had a very bad habit—free-basing. So, for the most part, I reported directly to the Ochoa brothers, especially on anything involving flights coming in or out."

Mermelstein first met one of the Ochoa brothers in 1978 during a drug deal.

"I arranged for Cardona to sell a kilo of cocaine, which was to take place at my house in Miami. The arrangements were set and the kilo was delivered by Fabio Ochoa, Jr. In April of 1981, Jorge requested that I fly down to Colombia to meet him and several other members of the cartel, which I did [at L'Hacienda Vera Cruz, Jorge's west coast farm]. And I

again flew down and met with him and several other members through
Panama later on in 1981. I met Escobar on several occasions, the first
time being in 1981 in Panama."

Although Colombians control cocaine smuggling, the process of producing the drug begins in the jungles of Bolivia and Peru where coca leaf
is grown and processed into paste. The coca leaf is also grown in the
Calca Valley of Colombia.

"The Bolivian end of the operation is controlled by Roberto Suarez
and his family, and although Roberto is in jail, I am quite sure that he still
maintains rigid control of his business. [The coca paste] is taken from the
jungles of Bolivia and Peru into the laboratories either in Colombia, or
when Tranquilandia went down, I don't know where the new laboratories are being established, but there was a lot of talk about northern
Brazil. [Cocaine-refining labs were set up on cartel ranches in the
department of Antioquia and in the area where Colombia, Brazil, and
Peru share borders.] It is flown from the jungle processing labs, the
paste, into the labs for crystalization [into cocaine hydrochloride]."

Although there are many ways to smuggle cocaine into the United
States—by commercial or private boats and planes and by body carriers—Mermelstein shipped his fifty-six tons in private planes and small
boats.

"I would say about 40 to 45 percent coming into the country is still
coming in by private plane. A good deal now—and the larger shipments
are coming in on commercial carriers: cargo ships, commercial aircraft—in cargoes, in shipments. That's basically the way the cartel has
been able to exist and flourish. [It] is that they can change faster than the
US government can. The US government is setting up to stop all air
traffic coming into the United States—surveillance planes, radar—so
they are watching that window and will open up another one: we'll bring
it in by boat. If you start watching the water, we'll switch back to the
airplanes. The ability to change fast is basically what has kept them
alive."

Smugglers are also helped by the US bureaucracy, which will deem air
surveillance ineffective and switch to maritime surveillance, cutting
back on air operations. This gives the cartels the flexibility to switch
their operations to the path of least resistance. To be effective, US
surveillance must be maintained on all fronts.

Cardona and Escobar own 1,000-ton cargo ships they use to smuggle
cocaine. Cartel traffickers spend millions on equipment to move drugs.
They send their pilots to American training facilities to learn how to fly
the latest planes. While traffickers in the US kill each other over turf, the
Medellin cartel has no rivals.

"There aren't any competitors, really. Well, now there are because there is so much cocaine [and] the market is limited. But the big problem when I was in it was getting it up fast enough to be distributed. The problem was that there was more demand than there was supply. As far as other cartels, in my opinion, there is only one real organization, and that is out of Medellin. The other groups—the group out of Cali, the group out of Barranquilla—it is a regional operation, but you don't have the close cooperation and the close ties that you have in the Medellin group. And in my own opinion, there would only be one formal cartel, so to speak. There are hundreds of independents in the Medellin area.

"In my estimation, Medellin is shipping approximately 60 percent [of the cocaine smuggled into the United States]. I figure Cali for about 15 percent—and their end of the market is growing little by little. Barranquilla, 5 to 8 per cent. Independents are another 5 percent. And I would not be surprised at this point if growing and processing labs are in existence in Jamaica and Haiti.

"One of the pilots that we utilized on a from-time-to-time basis would fly through Jamaica. . . . Some of the people from Cali were extremely involved with setting up laboratories and trying to grow the coca plant in Jamaica itself. Jamaica produces a fairly fine grade of coffee compatible to the coffee out of Colombia, and where you can grow good coffee, you can grow good coca. . . .

"I know Jamaica was being used as an interim landing point, and Cuba was being used as an interim landing point, and Haiti was established also. But my group had no need for it, basically. In 1981, it was direct flights in. In 1982, 1983, 1984, it was an intermediate in the Bahamas. In 1985, just before I was arrested, I brought in three direct flights again. . . .

"We only had one incident with Cuba. One of our planes was forced down—mechanical trouble, not by the Cuban Air Force—in Cuba. It came in to a military air base and he figured it was over. But the commandant of the base told him no, arrangements could be made: $10,000 any time he wanted to land there, he would be allowed to land under his personal supervision and allowed to take off again. In this case, he let him take off free because the pilot wasn't carrying any money, but the money was sent back. We never ran any further flights through Cuba. It was just a fluke."

During his stint smuggling cocaine into the United States, Mermelstein lost only one plane.

"Knowing where they are in respect to where we are is the key to the entire operation. We knew where their planes and boats were, and we knew what they were doing. We would just avoid those areas. We were monitoring their planes and boats during our entire mission."

And the plane that got caught?

"We were testing a new plane and we broke Air Defense Command. We were too high and too fast. But even though we were intercepted, that plane landed empty. They did not get one gram of cocaine—except the following day, they found it floating in the Gulf of Mexico. But when that plane was forced down, it was empty and clean. The pilots were released that night. It was a few days later that they went back to get them. One they got. The other one was gone."

Mermelstein assesses Pablo Escobar, public enemy number one on the US Drug Enforcement Administration's most wanted list, as a smart, tough operator. "Pablo Escobar is an extremely ambitious individual. Sometime mid- to late-1983, he started experimenting with and growing poppies in Colombia for the production of heroin in Colombia. He brought the poppies, the plants, and the people from the Far East and established his own heroin industry in Colombia. He is shipping heroin into the United States today.

"At one time they were involved with Quaaludes when Quaaludes were a big thing in the United States, but they dropped that end of it completely. They have their own factories in Colombia producing bootleg Quaaludes. They are not afraid to diversify."

Shortly before his arrest, Mermelstein participated in a smuggling technique that US interdiction officials first detected in 1989—five years after Colombian smugglers started using it. Smugglers shipped cocaine base to the US rather than cocaine hydrochloride. The water-proof and virtually indestructible cocaine base was tied to the underside of ships and processed into powder in clandestine American labs.

"It can be brought in in many different methods: under a boat, directly in the water—it wouldn't have any effect on it—dropped off offshore and left underwater for a few days and then picked up by a pleasure boat later on," Mermelstein said. "Water damage is not a problem with the base. One of the last shipments I received in late 1984 had 150 kilos of base, which I was told to ship to New Orleans for processing in a laboratory in New Orleans."

Eight Colombian families whose organizations have 3,000 members control most of the cocaine trafficking into the United States. An estimated 22,000 Colombians work for more than 300 cartel organizations in Central and South America, Mexico, the United States, and Canada as brokers, expediters, smugglers, supervisors, trafficking managers, distributors, money launderers, loaders, couriers, lookouts, and guards. They reap an estimated $5 billion a year. The cartels don't get involved in street-level trafficking. They don't have the networks, which are controlled by neighborhood dealers. They also shun police attention, which street level dealers get a lot of.

Mermelstein estimates that Escobar, El Mexicano, Hiro Mejira, and the Ochoas have become billionaires selling cocaine. How wealthy are Colombian drug traffickers? They often don't count their money, they weigh it. Three hundred pounds of $20 bills is $3.6 million; twenty pounds of $100 bills is about $1 million.

Colombian cocaine and marijuana cartels evolved rapidly from a 1960s cottage industry that supplied drugs to North American distribution networks into vertically integrated multinational corporations that control their product from harvest to street dealers. Cartels run a sophisticated business with lawyers, accountants, bankers, and investment and transportation experts. They provide a commodity strictly regulated by the law of supply and demand. Cartels are subject to strict operational principles: expertise, efficiency, solvency, discipline, security, and violence—not your usual list of business skills.

They must have expertise in cocaine smuggling and distribution or they'd get fried by the cops and the competition. They have to be efficient in getting the drugs to the street or they'd lose their customers to other dealers. They must remain solvent because drug dealing is a business that requires a substantial cash flow—a lot of money has to be paid out now, never tomorrow. Discipline is enforced with death. A member must be disciplined enough to do jail time rather than rat on the group, knowing the cartel will support his family while he is imprisoned. Security means always being on the lookout for the heat and knowing how the cops operate.

And finally, the last and most important operating principle, violence. Violence is used during ripoffs, in battles over turf (such as the Cocaine Cowboy wars in Florida), as a means of revenge (the old eye for an eye), as retribution for services not rendered (they can't really complain to the Better Business Bureau), to knock off competitors on the organizational ladder (self-promotion in its extreme form), to eliminate informants who threaten the cartel's security, and to get rid of witnesses who could compromise a good business deal. Even family members who don't hold up their end of the deal are killed like perfect strangers. Soldiers found a working hangman's gallows during a raid on El Mexicano's estate. Life has little worth in Colombia.

Although the Medellin and Cali drug-trafficking cartels have become household names, hundreds of smaller cocaine-trafficking organizations operate on the same principles. To be successful and to survive, the operators of a cartel have to insulate themselves from prosecution and must shield their organization from attempts by the cops to dismantle the business through arrests. Both goals can be accomplished by running the business like a terrorist organization or an intelligence network. The leaders farm out specialized work to contractors who do their job and know nothing else about the operation. Native farmers in Bolivia and Peru strip land and plant coca. Coca merchants buy or make coca paste in pits. Transporters fly the paste to clandestine laboratories. Chemists process the paste into cocaine hydrochloride. Smugglers transport the cocaine into the United States in their own planes or boats, or with those provided by transporters. Electronics experts scan radio frequencies and monitor law-enforcement actions, jam radars, and plot smuggling routes. Brokers link up sellers and buyers. Forgers provide false passports, visas, and other documents; craftsmen provide false suitcases with secret compartments, boats with fake fuel tanks or hollowed-out hulls — anything that can conceal drugs; lawyers bail out and defend arrested workers with cash provided by money men; and launderers cleanse illegal profits. Drug-trafficking cartels are equal-opportunity employers. If you can do the job, they'll pay you good money for it. If you blow it, you're dead.

At the bottom of this organization are tens of thousands of independent pushers who get the drugs to 45 million marijuana-smoking and 7 million cocaine-using North Americans.

Cartels are careful when hiring specialists, preferring to take into the organization only family members or people known to them. Specialists have no loyalty except to their pocketbooks. They work for the highest bidder. A suitcase maker, for example, will be paid $5,000 to craft a name-brand suitcase able to conceal a kilogram of cocaine.

One cartel member is more important than the others.

"There is only one person, in my estimation, that knows the entire operation end to end and what is going on anywhere in the world at any given time, and that is the comptroller of the organization," Mermelstein said. "That gentleman's nickname is 'Jota,' which stands for, it is the letter J. He works directly for the cartel. He is not only controlling the brothers' money and merchandise, he is controlling Escobar's, El Mexicano's. He's got the books, the master books, if you will, over the entire operation."

Cocaine cartels are like multinational corporations with subsidiaries. They bid for coca paste like commodity brokers, they transport it like shippers, they refine it like chemical companies. They get it into the United States like import-export agents, they sell it like marketers through distribution chains, and like financial wizards they move their money around to pay their organization's debts and to protect it from being seized.

There are several ways to do this. Drug traffickers often deal in cash because it leaves no paper trail. However, it certainly leaves a bulge in the local economy. When the Colombians expanded their smuggling operations into Florida in the late 1970s, for example, Miami banks sent surpluses of $3.9 billion to the Federal Reserve when banks across the country were reporting currency shortages. The same phenomenon is happening in California and Texas today as Colombians shift their operations to the less-policed west coast.

When cash is deemed too bulky for traveling, it is often converted into cashiers' checks, money orders, or travelers' checks. Teodoro Ariza-Ibarra, a Colombian arrested in Puerto Rico, had ten cashiers' checks in his right shoe, each for $500,000. Money can also be moved by electronic transfer to foreign banks, or by buying commodities such as gold, or by investment in equities.

People from all walks of life help the cartel launder dirty money. An easy buck is like an easy woman: everyone wants a piece of the action, but no one wants to get caught with it or take it home.

"Legitimate business in Colombia basically exists because of—excuse the expression—narco-dollars in the United States," Mermelstein said. "Colombian law restricts the amount of money that can be sent out of the country for foreign purchases. I am talking about large industrials—the sugar industry, the cement industry, the textile mills all need equipment and raw materials from the United States. This has to be purchased, so they need dollars available in the United States. They can't get too much of those dollars out of Colombia, or not enough of what they need. But yet the drug dealers have all of this excess money in the United States and want the pesos in Colombia. It is a symbiotic relationship. We supply the dollars in the United States, you return it to us in pesos in Colombia.

"A cement mill or a sugar mill needs $15 to $18 million worth of new equipment to be purchased in the United States. They need that money in the United States and they can't get it out of Colombia. So they are contacted by a drug dealer who has that money in the United States, turns that money over to a legitimate business in the United States, and a legitimate business in Colombia pays the bill in the local currency. We shipped a lot of [money] directly into Colombia also."

The Medellin cartel does not like investing its profits in the United States, where they can easily be seized. Drug dealers prefer to spend it in Colombia and elsewhere in South America. They also have investments in Holland and France, as well as large bank accounts in Luxembourg and Switzerland, and sizeable holdings in the Israeli diamond market.

Sometimes cartels mix the business of laundering with pleasure. One of their greatest pleasures is soccer. The *narco-traficantes'* wealth has allowed them to buy a controlling stake in Colombia's national soccer team and the official franchise to develop the government-controlled emerald-mining business.

The South American Football Confederation banned international competition in Colombia in September 1990 after hoods in Medellin

threatened David Cardellino, the Uruguayan referee, with death if he
didn't favor Medellin's Atletico Nacional in a match against the Brazilian
champion, Vasco da Gama. Cardellino was offered *plata o plomo*—
money or lead.

The threat made soccer officials wonder if the ownership of Colombian soccer teams by drug traffickers had anything to do with Colombia's national team reaching the World Cup finals for the first time in
twenty-eight years in 1989. Ten of Colombia's fifteen best soccer teams
are funded with drug money. Justice Minister Rodrigo Lara Bonilla
sounded the alarm in 1983 when he said cartels owned Colombian
soccer. He was assassinated by the cartels in 1984.

Gonzalo Rodriguez Gacha owned the Millionarios soccer club before
he was killed in a shoot-out with police in December 1989. Rodriguez
Orejuela owned the Cali soccer club, America. Edgar Garcia Montilla,
an American shareholder, was charged in Switzerland with trying to
launder drug money by buying contracts of European and Latin American soccer players.

The ability to buy the best players is not the reason that trafficker-
owned teams have won games. The competition among drug traffickers
is so intense that they kidnap referees and threaten to kill them if their
team doesn't win. Referee Alvaro Ortega was gunned down in
November 1989 after teams from Medellin and Cali—the strongholds of
two cartels—tied. Drug traffickers are a sporting lot.

"I am sure that at least Escobar and one or two of the Ochoas went to
the Olympic games in Seoul," Mermelstein said. "They travel to the
bullfights in Mexico City and in Spain. Fabio Ochoa, Jr., is a bullfight
aficionado and considers himself a first-class bullfighter. They do a lot of
traveling, depending upon their own hobbies—world-class soccer
games will take them out of their country into whatever country is
holding the World Cup matches."

Medellin cartel leaders have shown better business sense, acumen, and
judgment than businessmen in legitimate enterprises. They don't fear
getting their hands dirty and can be found on muddy jungle runways
loading kilos of cocaine onto planes. It is only one way they ensure the
success of their business. They take a personal interest in the people who
work for them, ensuring they are content and have all the equipment they
need to carry out operations. Much of the day-to-day running of the
operation, such as hiring pilots, security, and money laundering, is done
by subordinates.

The Medellin cartel not only smuggles the cocaine into North America, but has installed its own people on the continent to distribute the
drug to dealer networks.

"During the time that I was bringing it into Miami—in late 1983, 1984, and part of 1985—I was taking care of some of their distribution. But they did always maintain their own distribution network in the United States, which had one supervisor who controlled Miami, Houston, New York, and California. Each individual distribution network had its own head in place in various areas. All of these people were handpicked in Colombia and sent up from Colombia. The man that runs the United States was picked by the cartel. The men in charge of the individual regions were picked by the cartel. And basically from that point on, the people are on their own."

Supervisors are responsible for the actions of the people they pick. Cardona was responsible for Mermelstein. When Mermelstein became an informant, Cardona was killed.

The cartel buys counterfeit passports and visas for its employees. Cardona had two or three Colombian passports with American visas; several Venezuelan passports with American visas; a Mexican passport with an American visa; and an American passport—all bought from clever forgers in the underworld paperwork industry. Cartel leaders travel on their own planes, from turboprops to jets. When they fly public, they don't worry about being nabbed in airports.

"As far as Immigration and Customs in South America and Central America, they have no worries or problems at all," Mermelstein said. "As an example, in Cardona's office in Colombia, he opened up his safe one day and had a complete set of immigration stamps from Panama, Costa Rica, and Colombia. He used to stamp his own passports. As far as passing through the airport, a $100 bill inside your passport, they don't open anything or ask any questions. You just walk right through."

Colombian traffickers are careful about whom they deal with. The Medellin cartel does not deal with traditional organized crime.

"We were told to stay away from them. They do not trust them, nor will they do business on a direct basis with them. They specialize basically in ripping off a shipment. If you are out to make a delivery to a Mafia representative, chances are he is going to steal it and blow you away without paying for it. They have had that happen on several occasions and they just stopped all business completely. So if they want any of the cocaine coming out of Colombia, I would assume that they are dealing with a middleman or two, three steps down the road."

Cartel leaders build churches, schools, housing projects, sports stadiums, sanitation facilities, and roads and, most importantly, provide jobs to win the support of the communities around their bases. The Ochoas, Pablo Escobar, and Gonzalo Rodriguez Gacha in Colombia and

Roberto Suarez in Bolivia have become heroes—Robin Hoods—for the masses with their narco-welfare programs. Drug barons have argued that their business creates jobs the government can't in an otherwise cash-strapped economy. "It it were not for these hot dollars," Carlos Lehder said, "Colombia would be in worse shape than Argentina." Escobar, who controls the newspaper *Medellin Civico*, said that drug money has forestalled in Colombia "a grave crisis similar to that of other Latin American societies."

"I used to ship a lot of sporting equipment from the United States for the poor towns in Colombia for distribution down there," Mermelstein said. "[The drug barons] are very much involved. On Cardona's ranch, there are three small towns within the ranch property itself. On Vera Cruz, Jorge's property, there are five or six small towns. These towns owe their livelihood and subsistence to these people. Escobar has put low-income housing through the slums of Medellin and outlying areas for the poor people at no charge. They take the Robin Hood approach in Colombia, if you will. The poor people are their basic protection. It is their basic work force also."

The Barrio Pablo Escobar low-income housing project on a hilltop in eastern Medellin shelters more than 400 families whose previous homes had been huts in the city's dump. Escobar, ruthless in his cocaine dealing, has sent gifts to project children every Christmas and to every mother on Mother's Day since the complex was built in 1984. Someone tore down a sign at the project's entrance in 1988 that described it as part of Escobar's plan to eradicate Medellin slums. Would any of the residents—given the opportunity—claim the Colombian government's $250,000 reward for information leading to Escobar's arrest? You've got to be kidding.

Escobar and the Ochoas had little to do with the Bahamas because they took their cocaine directly into Florida. Another member of the cartel used the Bahamas extensively, exposing the sun-drenched islands to acts of piracy and terrorism not seen for hundreds of years. Carlos Enrique Lehder Rivas, a cocaine multi-billionaire now twiddling his thumbs in an American jail, was described by prosecutor Robert Merkle: "He pursued a singular dream . . . to be the king of cocaine. He was to cocaine transportation what Henry Ford was to cars." Lehder's plastic-wrapped kilos of cocaine were easily distinguished—they bore Nazi swastikas, the trademark and birthright of a man who personified the term narco-terrorist.

Carlos Lehder decided in 1978 to take over an island in the Bahamas to serve as a refueling and transfer point for the boats and planes that transported his tons of cocaine and marijuana from Colombia to the US.

He chose Norman's Cay, a strip of sand six miles long and two miles wide that is part of a chain of islands called the Exuma Cays. Norman's Cay is thirty-five miles southeast of Nassau, east of Andros Island and west of Eleuthera Island. Lehder began buying property there in mid-1978 under the guise of an investor because Norman's Cay had what he needed: a harbor and a 3,300-foot long airstrip that he would lengthen. He was well received by the cay's inhabitants, who preferred him to two other potential investors: Howard Hughes and the fugitive US financier, Robert Vesco. Vesco taught Lehder the art of money laundering and introduced him to Fidel Castro, under whose protection he lives in Cuba.

Lehder was born in Colombia, the son of a German engineer father and a Colombian schoolteacher mother. He spent his teenage years in the Bronx, where he began his apprenticeship in the trade that was to become his lifelong pursuit. He was arrested for possession of 200 pounds of marijuana and spent two years in federal prison in Danbury, Connecticut, where he predicted in 1974 that cocaine would become the new drug craze in the United States. He returned to Colombia even more determined to become the world's most successful drug smuggler.

By 1979, he was already a multi-billionaire. But he wanted more. By the end of the year, he owned half of Norman's Cay, the Norman's Cay Yacht Club with a ten-room hotel, restaurant, and bar, the landing strip, and beachfront property on Smuggler's Cove. He paid cash for everything, including private homes he bought. When owners refused to sell, Lehder's goons machine-gunned their houses. As soon as he had all the property he wanted, Lehder chased everyone off the island, including yachtsmen who stopped in—even Walter Cronkite. Visitors to the island were shot at, swamped by speedboats, towed out to sea, and buzzed by helicopters.

Lehder brought in eighty security guards, mostly Colombians, but some Germans, to protect his fleet of jets, helicopters, propeller-driven planes, speedboats and sailboats, the hangars, generators, radar and radio equipment he installed on Norman's Cay behind barbed-wire fences, guard towers, and machine-gun turrets.

"We were an armed camp," Stephen Yakovac, a Lehder employee who rode shotgun on drug shipments to the US, told the jury at his boss's trial. "We had M-16s, .357-magnums, .30 and .40-calibers.... The flow of money went from a couple of suitcases to boxcar loads. It was absolutely mind-boggling. ... Counting it got to be such a chore."

Lehder's planes quickly dumped their cocaine at rural airstrips on busy Saturday afternoons before flying to an airport to clear customs. "We would go through the customs shack on Saturday afternoon,"

Yakovac said. "We never had trouble. The customs officials had a television and always had one eye on 'Wide World of Sports'."

Flights of cocaine came and went undisturbed, although there were a few unfortunate incidents. Lehder's first marijuana flight out of Norman's Cay went bust when someone forgot to open a fuel valve on the C-46. The plane hit the water after takeoff and remains there to be seen by anyone flying over Norman's Cay or boating off its shore.

Norman's Cay became invulnerable even to the Bahamas Defence Forces, which raided the island three times, coming away with little to show for their efforts. Lehder was never taken into custody and a Bahamian Commission of Inquiry found in 1984 that to ensure his freedom, Lehder had bribed police and government officials, including one official who tipped him off about raids. Although five Bahamian Government Cabinet ministers had to resign in the wake of the inquiry, the findings did little to support or squelch pervasive rumors that Prime Minister Lynden Pindling was himself on the payroll of drug smugglers. The inquiry concluded:

> It is apparent that the Prime Minister's expenditure over the years from 1977 has far exceeded his income. However, none of the known sources of funds made available to him appear to have been drug related. As to the unidentified deposits, the sources of which are still unknown, all that can be said is that there is no evidence before the commission upon which we can form a conclusion as to whether or not these unidentified funds were drug related.

Lehder ran his operation out of Norman's Cay from 1979 to early 1983. During that time, he paid an official in the Cuban Ministry of Tourism $10,000 to ensure he could hide out in Cuba if he had to. He moved his smuggling operation to Andros Island until 1984, when he returned to Medellin to live a lifestyle fit for the rich and heinous.

Cocaine as a Commodity

Studying cocaine as a commodity reveals how little law-enforcement and other experts know about the drug and its market. The price of cocaine, like all commodities from corn to pork bellies, is a slave to the law of supply and demand. If supply is high and demand low, prices drop. If supply is low and demand high, prices rise. Until late 1989, US officials estimated that 100 tons of cocaine were imported into the country every year. If this figure were correct, large seizures of the drug would curb supply in these times of high demand and drive up prices. In September

1989, DEA agents snapped a six-dollar padlock on the door of a suburban Los Angeles warehouse and found 21.4 tons of cocaine and $10 million cash in 1,100 cardboard boxes—the largest seizure in American history. In early November 1989, 5.5 tons of cocaine were found in ten-gallon drums of sodium hydroxide in a Queens, New York, warehouse. In all, about eighty-five tons of cocaine were seized that year.

If the estimate that 100 tons of the drug enter the US every year were correct, prices should have gone into the stratosphere. They didn't. Cocaine prices have dropped steadily since 1985—from $55,000 a kilo to $11,000 a kilo in Florida, with a rebound to about $20,000. Obviously, there's a lot more cocaine coming into North America than anyone ever imagined.

There is a rule of thumb among law-enforcement personnel that few will publicly admit to: they estimate they seize less than 5 percent of what enters the country. It's not likely that 10,000 tons of cocaine finds its way into North America every year, but 1,000 tons is a more likely figure than 100 tons. All this cocaine is not destined for the North American market. The Colombian *narco-traficantes* have started warehousing their cocaine in the US and Canada for transshipment to Europe and Japan, which are notorious for fanatically imitating American trends. The North American record for ingesting an estimated 75 percent of the world's cocaine could quickly be shattered if Nipponese nostrils developed a flair for the powder.

Fighting the Cartels

The United States is attacking drug smuggling on different fronts. It tries to stop the drug at source through eradication programs; it tries to intercept drugs before they get into the US; and it is now going after cartel leaders. The first two operations have dented, but not stopped, smuggling. The prospect of extradition to the US, however, has had a severe impact on cartel traffickers.

Eradication of crops and destruction of labs "can't work because we have a very bad habit: we announce what we are going to do before we do it," Mermelstein said. "What we do is stated in the press; what area is going to be hit, during what program, at what particular time. Plus the fact we are dealing with the local police and the local governments in South America, and that's a direct line to the cartel.

"[The cartel owns South American governments] either through bribes or through fear. They take the money or they die. And they have proven what they can do." Only high-ranking military officials in Colombia can't be bought or scared by the cartels. "The cartel is so afraid of these people. We're basically talking about the old feudal class system, the military class, the generals who have been generations of military people, people whose integrity cannot be bought and people who have the troops to back up their own protection."

Right-wing cocaine baron Roberto Suarez Gomez and the Bolivian military support each other. Bolivia's military regimes—starting with General Hugo Suarez in 1971—financed the neophyte cocaine industry in the 1970s with bank loans that were supposed to pay for the development of cotton farms and other legitimate agricultural pursuits. Instead, the money was used to build laboratories and airstrips and to acquire the precursor chemicals needed to convert cocaine base into cocaine hydrochloride. In return, cocaine traffickers financed General Luis Garcia Meza's cocaine coup in 1980 and worked hand-in-hand with his regime until democracy returned to Bolivia in 1982. The general and his underlings were fond of Nazis and brought Klaus Barbie to Bolivia to set up death squads to intimidate peasants and protect their fleet of smuggling planes. He also repaid Roberto Suarez by giving control of the ministry of the interior to his nephew.

The Bahamian government dealt directly with the Medellin cartel.

"I was personally offered by a representative of the Bahamian Government in late 1984 a deal where I would be allowed to purchase all of the cocaine confiscated in the Bahamas for shipment to the United States," Mermelstein said. "They wanted it set up on a partnership deal. It would cost $2,000 per kilo to pay off the people who were guarding it, plus the various low-level ministers. Brought to the United States—my people would be responsible for bringing it to the United States—sold in the United States and then split profits 50-50: 50 percent Bahamian government, 50 percent cartel. We were setting it up, but I was arrested at the time. . . . A good deal of US officials [agents] are on payrolls. We never had any on ours, but we knew who did and what they were doing."

Interdiction has failed to stop the flow of cocaine for several reasons, one being that the US Coast Guard and Customs agents flying intercept missions use published radio frequencies. Though they scramble their communications to foil eavesdroppers, activity on the frequencies alerts smugglers that the bears are in the air.

"We had people that were assigned nothing but radio duty," Mermelstein said. "They would sit in front of an HF radio—a high-frequency radio—twenty-four hours a day, listening to see if they could pick up the frequencies that the government was using, and when the government changed frequencies, picking up the new frequencies. If we didn't have the current government frequencies, we just would not fly."

Interdiction is also hampered by American law-enforcement agencies stumbling over each other.

"You've got a tremendous lack of cooperation between your agencies—I mean a tremendous lack of cooperation," Mermelstein said. "The FBI won't tell the DEA what they are doing; the DEA won't tell the FBI what they are doing; nobody wants to talk to Customs. Everybody has their own specialties; everybody wants the headlines, and everybody wants the budget appropriations, so everybody is out to make their own record and nobody wants to help anybody else.

"In my personal estimation, right now there is somewhere between 30 and 40 percent overlap in what the DEA, FBI, and Customs are doing. By that, I mean they are investigating the same people at the same time and not sharing the information. This is an overlap in manpower and funds, so we can cut that out. Basic coordination between the agencies— let each agency do what they are specialized in doing.

"In my own estimation, as far as controlling the street, it is the DEA, the best street people in the world. Support for the DEA should be done through the FBI, who are the best detail men in the world, but who are terrible in a street operation. And anything up to the borders of the United States should be handled by Customs. That is where their big strong point is.

"I can give you a perfect example. I was pulled out for a debriefing session eight, ten months ago by the DEA. They wanted to corroborate a report that they had received from an FBI debriefing session, something that they thought I would know something about. Now, for me to be transported to a debriefing session is a complicated and expensive proposition for the government, plus a dangerous situation for myself and my family.

"OK. The debriefing session is set up and I am moved to point X. I sit down with the DEA agents and they start going through the questions that they have for me and I start answering the questions. And this agent gets a very strange look on his face and asks me if I have ever been debriefed by the FBI on this particular subject. I stated that yes, I had. And I was asked if I was assigned a code name by the FBI—the FBI likes using code names instead of C.I. [confidential informant] numbers—and I said yes, I was. I was asked if I knew it, and I told them that I did. I told them what that code name was, and the papers flew up in the air. They were debriefing me and using me to corroborate my own statements. When these papers were given to the DEA, the DEA agent asked specifically who code name such-and-such is and was given false information."

US undercover operations against smuggling networks are too timid to cause much harm. The fuzz end up with toe jam while the bad guys get away.

"It's just the fact that the government wasn't establishing any penetrations," Mermelstein said. "The ones they could pick up—they could pick up a boat captain or the street people or things like that—but getting into the higher levels where they have to get to stop them, they're not allowed to do it. In order to set up a proper penetration the way a penetration should be set up, you are going to have to establish a man's credibility within the organization. The only way to establish a man's credibility within the organization is to allow kilos to hit the street. To allow cocaine to hit the street. The DEA is not prepared to do this. I think they are precluded from doing it, although the FBI is notorious for doing it.

"You know, it's just a matter of judgment. My personal opinion is [that it's] the only way it can be done. I'd rather have 200 kilos hit the street occasionally than allow 15,000 a month to come through on a month-to-month basis. If you want to go after it, you go after the top. Taking the street people off the streets, all that's going to do is fill up the jails because there are more street people than you can jail."

How would Mermelstein stop drug smuggling?

"The first place of vulnerability would be the crop. I'd spray. I'd use a herbicide especially directed to an alkaloid, which the coca plant is, to destroy only alkaloid, and just spray Bolivia, Peru, and Colombia. If you eliminate the crop, you eliminate the rest of the problem. We'd have to step on a few toes, but we're dealing with generations of American lives. I've been told it takes approximately 200 kilos of coca leaves to produce 1 kilo of cocaine hydrochloride. And that's a lot of leaves. We're talking plantations of coca plants."

Another way to hinder cartel operations is to make it more difficult for members of the organization to communicate with each other.

"The first thing is make one slight change in telephone company procedure and totally foul up their communications with the United States. The only thing we have to do there is, on the pay phones, make sure there are outgoing calls only and that they cannot receive an incoming call, and you completely eliminate their beepers and communications system in the United States.

"The entire operation is predicated on the communication and getting in contact with the people that the cocaine is going to be given to and who the money is going to be received from. None of this communication is handled through somebody's home phone. They are afraid of using a home phone because of interception of the line. They use pay phones, and they are constantly changing pay phones. And the way it is set up is through the beeper systems. Everybody walks around with a beeper. They are called from a pay phone and they return the call from a pay phone."

Threatening the government of Colombia with economic sanctions to make it act against the cartels is futile. The cartels threaten government officials with death—a threat that carries more weight than the withholding of money from the country.

The cartels use corruption, blackmail, and violence to influence their enemies: the government, the courts, law-enforcement and public anti-drug movements. Their often-achieved goal is to stifle policies that could jeopardize the drug business, paralyze the judicial process that could put them behind bars, nullify law-enforcement efforts against drug traffickers by cultivating informants within police ranks, and win over the public's sympathy and support to weaken political resolve to fight drugs. What politician will back an issue that won't win votes?

Many politicians' campaigns are underwritten with drug money. They know to whom they owe favors, especially if they want to be re-elected. Between 1981 and 1984, more than 200 Colombian policemen were fired and 100 members of the country's air force were discharged for connections with drug traffickers. In 1985, Colombia's attorney general was investigating 400 judges with alleged links to traffickers. The Colombian army seized documents from the ministries of justice and foreign affairs during raids on cartel houses in Medellin in 1987. The head of intelligence for the army's fourth brigade was discharged in 1988 for links with drug traffickers. Colombia's institutions have been corrupted and co-opted.

Drug traffickers give judges trying their cases the same choice they offer soccer referees: *plomo o plata*—lead or silver; a bullet for a conviction, money to drop the charges. Between 1988 and 1990, four major cartel members were freed by the courts: Jorge Luis Ochoa, Gilberto Rodriguez Orejuela, Evaristo Porras, and José Santacruz Londono. Anti-drug crusaders are gunned down by hit teams picked in the slums and trained at a special cartel-financed school for hit men, who are called *sicarios*.

Colombia is one of the most violent countries in the world. Murder is the primary cause of death for men aged fifteen to forty-four, and the second cause of death for all age groups. There were 22,468 murders in Colombia in 1990—365 of them police officers killed by the drug cartels. By comparison, 23,300 Americans were murdered that year.

Four hundred people are murdered every month in Medellin, Colombia's second-largest city after Bogotá, and the murder capital of the world—that's more than thirteen murders a day. Medellin has an estimated 2,500 *sicarios* who kill for the drug cartels. When the Medellin cocaine cartel temporarily stopped its terrorist attacks on June 27, 1990, 230 *sicarios* signed up under a government amnesty program to rehabilitate drug criminals. It was the only way to make money while unemployed.

Captain Marshall Frank was commander of the homicide unit of the Dade County Public Safety Department in Miami in 1980 at the height of the cocaine wars; he expressed his frustration at trying to catch Colombian drug traffickers, many of whom move every three to six months, or whenever police get too close to them.

"Attorneys are on retainer at all times and seem to virtually remain on call," Frank said. "If found with large amounts of cash, they will generally disclaim it, regardless of the quantity. Immigration authorities are nearly powerless in their role of enforcing laws. The illegal Colombians involved in the organized crime networks are apprised of every trick in the book in order to avert prosecution or deportation and remain at large with impunity.

"It appears to us on the surface without being an intelligence unit that their financial resources are infinite. We had information at one point that one of these smaller Colombian organized crime groups was working with an extraneous budget of about $1 million just for their day-to-day expenses, not to have anything to do with narcotics. We have had occasions to find people with large amounts of cash in their possession and discarded it and say the cash was not theirs. One classic example was a fellow who inadvertently got into an automobile accident and left the scene. He wasn't injured too badly and the vehicle was identified to him and we went to his house later and asked him if the $300,000 in cash in his trunk was his. He said he never saw it or heard of it. Didn't know anything about it.

"We have had other occasions where we would approach Colombian people and they just throw an envelope—brown envelope—under the car, in the trash and then we will retrieve it and it will contain $25,000 or $35,000 which they will not acknowledge possession of or knowledge of. They move—when I referred to them as nomadic in nature—they move from house to house at times on a moment's notice, they will rent houses in the most exclusive neighborhoods for $2,000 a month or more, putting up six months' in advance, and they will buy the most expensive equipment, Betamaxes, various furniture that goes into the house. When things get a little hot, they will disappear overnight and leave everything behind.

"To say that law-enforcement efforts are frustrating is an understatement. We operate within a fishbowl. Every tactic and every move that an officer makes is, or will be, under the closest of scrutiny, either by the media, the courts, special-interest groups, the department administration, and even other law-enforcement agencies. We are expected to perform every function picture perfect. If not, criminals go free and the police are publicly criticized.

"To solve these crimes and obtain convictions there must exist one or more of three essential elements: a confession, a reliable and voluntary witness, or undisputable physical evidence. In these times, it appears that we must totally rely on the availability of evidence which is in itself a rare commodity.

"These criminals never confess, and voluntary witness testimony is rapidly becoming obsolete. Not only are we faced with a witness's fear of reprisals from the underworld, but the public exposure they experience through the Freedom of Information Act has had a chilling effect on investigations, inhibiting even further our capabilities in bringing criminals to justice. In short, the few remaining tools law enforcement has left are gradually being chipped away."

On top of that, corruption makes it easier for drug traffickers to operate.

"A kilo of cocaine base which is purchased from Peru at a cost of $3,500 will be refined and sold 90 percent pure in the United States for $50,000. After that kilo is cut and distributed, it will yield up to $250,000 on the streets. Kilos of pure cocaine are being smuggled into this country by the hundreds every month. The profits are astronomical.

"People from all walks of life use it. It is not a ghetto drug. It would be pure ignorance to believe that police and public officials are uncorruptible in light of the tremendous cash flow drugs produce. Ideologically, we would like to think corruption can be averted. However, those small percentages of rotten apples in every barrel, so inclined, will succumb to the overwhelming temptations of drug money."

Extradition

What do cartel members fear the most?

"American justice . . . because it is something that they cannot control. It is something they cannot buy," Mermelstein said.

Cartel members would rather rot in a Colombian jail than be extradited to the United States to face drug charges. The cartel has argued vigorously, with some success, that the on-again, off-again 1979 extradition treaty with the United States is an infringement of Colombian rights.

The *narco-traficantes* have tried desperately to have their trade legalized to gain acceptance into Colombian society. They are the country's largest landowners and despite the weak peso, continue to repatriate billions of dollars yearly that they pump into the economy—not as much a display of nationalistic fervor as a flaunting of their machismo. They want their countrymen to see how successful they are as businessmen. They have even offered twice to pay off partially, if not fully, Colombia's foreign debt.

Still, the *narco-traficantes* are not welcome in the country's social clubs. The exclusive Club Colombia in Cali refused to admit José Santacruz Londono, a leader of the Cali cartel. In retaliation, Santacruz built a duplicate of the club in a Cali suburb with a clay tennis court, a swimming pool, and a 100-foot satellite dish. The criminal stigma implied by American indictments against cartel members keeps them on the fringes of the society whose recognition and approval they so desperately want. The extradition treaty is the most salient reminder of that rejection.

"From any point of view, the extradition of nationals has no reason for existing, and even less reason exists for making a pact with a country which does not even have borders with the United States and where customs have not one iota of affinity to ours," Carlos Lehder wrote in the Medellin newspaper *El Colombiano* in 1982.

The Colombian Supreme Court overturned the extradition treaty in June 1987, preventing the extradition of Jorge Ochoa, who was arrested in November that year. However, the government revived the treaty by emergency decree after the cartel assassinated Luis Carlos Galan, the leading Liberal Party candidate for president, on August 18, 1989.

The degree to which cartel members fear extradition is reflected in their secret meetings with Colombian government officials in Panama in May 1984. The result was a signed memorandum. Cartel members fled Colombia to avoid a public-supported government crackdown on drug traffickers following the assassination of justice minister Rodrigo Lara Bonilla by cartel hit men on April 30, 1984. The hit came seven weeks after a raid on the cartel's Tranquilandia laboratory in which police seized nearly fourteen tons of cocaine. Police and soldiers arrested suspected drug traffickers and seized their assets. A military tribunal was struck to try the cases and the government said it would extradite traffickers to the United States.

It was in a climate of fear that Pablo Escobar, Jorge Ochoa, Luis Angel, Gonzalo Rodriguez Gacha, and other cartel leaders claiming to represent the top 100 cartel members met separately with Alfredo Lopez Michelsen, former president of Colombia, and Carlos Jimenez Gomez, then the country's attorney general. The Colombian government and the cartel were both seeking a working agreement. Understandably, the cartel representatives underlined that they did not represent their most dangerous member, Carlos Lehder.

The cartel members wanted amnesty for their crimes so they could return to Colombian society—a deal similar to that offered to Communist guerrillas. They also wanted the extradition treaty scrapped so they could be judged in Colombia. They argued they were loyal Colombian citizens and denied they were trying to undermine the country's institutions. They offered to get out of the cocaine business, dismantle the cartel that produced 80 percent of the country's cocaine, and turn over their planes, runways, and laboratories to the government. On top of that, cartel leaders offered to bring into Colombia the many billions of dollars in profits they had stashed in banks and real estate around the world. And if that wasn't enough, the cartel offered to combat the drug problem in Colombia and to find substitute crops for the coca and marijuana plants they had induced farmers to grow. Lastly, they promised to stay out of politics.

A nice deal, eh? They spend up to twenty years wheeling and dealing cocaine and marijuana, kill thousands of people, make billions of dollars, and live luxuriously. Now they want to be forgiven, allowed to keep their ill-gotten wealth, and shielded from the wrath of the fearsome Yanquis.

Colombian president Belisario Betancur, who had given his blessing to the secret talks, buckled under the public furor caused by the revelation his government had been negotiating with criminals and quickly ended the proposed deal. On July 19, 1984, in a communiqué, he said, "There has not been, there is not now, nor will there ever be any kind of understanding between the government and the signers of the memorandum."

Similar talks were held in June 1983 between Rafael Otazo Vargas, head of Bolivian president Siles Zuaro's Advisory Commission on Narcotics, and Roberto Suarez Gomez, that country's most notorious cocaine baron. Suarez was bolder than the Medellin cartel members. He wanted the Bolivian government to legalize his cocaine operation in return for $2 billion in four installments to help pay off the country's foreign debt. Although the proposal wasn't accepted, it wasn't without precedent. Bolivian drug traffickers underwrote the year-end bonus to government employees in 1985.

Colombian drug traffickers know the government can't afford to prosecute them. When the Colombian government declared war on the cocaine cartels after the assassination of Rodrigo Lara Bonilla in 1984, Fabio Ochoa surrendered himself to police. "I have nothing to fear," he said. He was released on bail after six weeks when the most serious charge that could be laid against him involved illegal possession of firearms.

Fabio Ochoa once again was first to surrender himself on December 19, 1990, taking up Colombian President Cesar Gaviria on his promise to waive extradition to the United States and to reduce jail terms by up to half for drug traffickers who surrender and confess. The thirty-three-year-old leader of the Medellin cartel is wanted on charges in New

Orleans that he smuggled more than $1 billion of cocaine into the United States and plotted the 1986 murder of US Drug Enforcement Administration informant Barry Seal. Ochoa gave himself up at a church near Medellin and was locked up in cell No. One of Block One at an ultra-secure prison in Itagui. The prison is guarded by police and soldiers at the request of drug traffickers who mistrust police. Ochoa was obviously testing President Gaviria's promise and his older brothers, Jorge Luis, forty-one, and Juan David, forty-two, watched along with other traffickers.

Jorge Luis Ochoa, the number two man in the Medellin cartel, also surrendered, on January 15, 1991, in exchange for the Colombian government's promise not to extradite him to the US where he is wanted on drug charges. Pablo Escobar Gaviria, the cartel's leader, finally surrendered on June 19, 1991, hours after Colombia's constitutional assembly tentatively approved a ban on extradition to the United States. Escobar gave videotapes of his life to reporters before being flown by helicopter to a jail custom-built to his specifications in his home town of Envigado, near Medellin. The jail has a soccer field, television and games room, private baths, and gardens. Escobar, who fears reprisals from family, friends, and business partners of the hundreds of people whose deaths he allegedly ordered over the years, hand-picked the forty guards who will protect him in prison. Colombian officials estimate Escobar's campaign of terror against the state in 1989 and 1990, including more than 300 bombings, killed more than 1,000 people. Escobar's deal with the Colombian government appears to have ended at forty-six the number of accused Colombian drug traffickers extradited, tried, and jailed in the United States. The Colombian government has promised lenient sentences for drug traffickers who surrender. Escobar, who is worth between $2 billion and $5 billion, may be jailed for as little as five years. Traffickers who have surrendered have not been asked and have not promised to stop their drug operations, which they can easily control from their jail cells. *Le plus ça change . . .*

7

More than a Matter of Honor:
Violence as a business tool in the drug underworld

"You can go a lot further with a kind word and a gun than you can with a kind word alone."
—AL CAPONE.

Violence and corruption are the two pillars on which organized crime is built. Gangsters are ruthless killers who know that an ounce of fear is worth a pound of lead. Fear and money are the grease that keeps the machinery of organized crime running smoothly. Gangsters use violence to scare competitors and victims. It also keeps partners in line. Murder, assault, blackmail, intimidation, coercion, arson, bombings . . . are all business tools in the gangster's arsenal.

Gangsters use violence most often when they establish a new business, such as drug trafficking, take over another gang's turf, or defend their own territory. The younger the organization, the more likely it is to use violence. Los Angeles street gangs, Colombian distributors, Cuban traffickers, and California marijuana farmers are far more trigger-happy than outlaw bikers or members of La Cosa Nostra. A mobster will seek counsel before killing someone. A biker might think twice before pulling the trigger. But younger gangsters will shoot anything that moves, including the family dog and the caged budgie.

Violence is also an excellent way to rid oneself of pesky informants and witnesses who threaten the gangster's or the organization's ability to make money. It is extremely useful when taking over a business to show a recalcitrant owner what his tibia looks like—with the help of a crowbar.

Gangsters argue they are violent mostly with people in their own organizations or other members of the underworld, but it's no fluke that many killings take place in well-frequented restaurants, in the streets, in busy shopping malls, or that bodies often turn up in car trunks at airports. This public display of gangsters taking care of business is crafted to let the public know they are not to be messed with, especially when they are extorting money from you.

Drug trafficking is a $500-billion-a-year business worldwide, and violence is an integral part of the business. It keeps people's mouths shut and keeps other greedy gangsters at bay. In Chicago alone, there have been more than 1,100 gangland slayings since 1919. More than 300 people were killed in turf wars between the Outlaws and the Hell's Angels in Quebec between 1978 and 1985. It's more a matter of money than of honor.

It is estimated that 65 to 75 percent of murders are crimes of passion—"domestics" in police jargon. They are easy to solve because the victim was killed by someone he or she knew. Out of the 25 to 35 percent of murders that are not crimes of passion, nine out of ten are drug related. Someone stiffs a dealer for a $1,000 front. He doesn't want people to think he can't take care of business, so he hires talent for $500 to $1,500 to get rid of the problem. There are a lot of hitters out there who've blown away more than thirty people for $500 a pop. And they don't even count those they do for free as favors. The Bureau of Alcohol, Tobacco and Firearms has a file on more than 400 suspected professional hit men and arsonists who specialize in eliminating or intimidating gang members, competitors, informers, witnesses, businessmen, union officials, judges, jurors, police officers, prosecutors—anyone that anyone else wants to shut up. Intimidation works. About one of three drug-related murders gets solved. Fewer than 15 percent of the people charged in those cases get convicted. For some people, crime pays.

Some groups are more refined in their use of violence, some are more crass. But each achieves its objective. The mob, for instance, likes to think it offs people with class. It gives the contract to another mobster or an associate who studies the victim's habits until he can pick the best and surest time to kill. Every organized crime group has members who specialize in killing. Colombians, on the other hand, all seem able and willing to slaughter. Sometimes the victim, if he is a mobster, is killed as he walks into a meeting. Sometimes the body is left in the street, sometimes it disappears. Mobsters have been buried in the basements of social clubs and in the concrete foundations of buildings and highways. Some are supposedly buried in the New Jersey Turnpike. And who knows where Jimmy Hoffa lies? Theories range from the end zone on a football field to the space between two sesame seed buns. Some mobsters have been recycled through meat-packing plants and others have been shredded in wood-chipping machines. One mob hitter called Willie the Rat dumped stiffs in the sewers for rats to eat. Whichever way a mobster is killed, the mob is kind enough to visit his relatives and tell them not to set a place at the table for him any more. Family members understand they will never see him again.

FBI agent Jim Nelson gives an example of how gangsters expect and accept violence as a way of life:

"Back in 1975, we learned that a person by the name of Jerry Basciano, who is part of La Cosa Nostra in New York, was going to be killed. It is part of our policy and responsibility to notify that person that there is a contract on him and to notify the local police agency in the area. The day we learned Jerry Basciano was going to be killed, I went to see Jerry Basciano and told him I had information that he was going to be killed.

"Basciano, who is fifty-one years old, acknowledged that he was completely aware that there was a contract on his life. He discussed the situation in a convincing manner. He said he had chosen this life many years ago and was aware for many years that it is a horrible existence and the people involved are incredibly treacherous. He said that 'honor in this life' is something that only exists in the movies. However, he steadfastly declined offers of protection through relocation.

"Basciano flatly stated that he expects to be killed between today [November 25] and Christmas, and he named the people he thought were going to kill him. He said his only hope is that he can 'take some of them with me.' He said he will attend any meeting to which he is summoned by La Cosa Nostra and will not go into hiding or alter his routine.

"We made several other attempts to convince Mr. Basciano we would provide him protection, relocate him in return for testimony, and time and time again he said, 'Thank you, but I just hope to be able to take some of them with me.' He said, 'If you start tailing me, they are just going to delay it.' He was killed gangland fashion a few months later when he was in a coffee shop. Two men with a ski mask walked in and killed him."

Harold Morton was part of a Detroit drug gang that ran couriers from Europe to New York City. On November 17, 1977, Gloria Roe, Sandra Jones, and Morton were driven to the Detroit airport where the women bought tickets for New York City with money given them by Morton. The three of them arrived at John F. Kennedy Airport before noon. They took a taxi to Manhattan where Roe and Jones paid cash—Morton's, again—for round-trip tickets to Amsterdam. Morton then helped them obtain passports and the trio took a taxi back to JFK where they boarded a KLM flight to Amsterdam. They took two rooms at the Amsterdam Marriott Hotel and the women spent November 16 and 17 sightseeing and shopping. On November 18, Roe was called into Jones's room, given a package, and shown how to hide it in her crotch under her girdle. Jones had already tucked her parcel away. Then Morton asked

Roe to walk in front of him. "It looks fine," he said. They took a taxi to the airport and boarded a flight to New York City.

That same day, Morton, Roe, and Jones stood in different lines at JFK for customs searches. Jones and Roe were both detained and searched. Customs officers found half a pound of 29 percent pure heroin on each woman. Morton was detained, but released because he wasn't carrying drugs. Both women waived their rights and confessed to US Drug Enforcement Administration agents they were heroin mules for Morton. Jones offered to cooperate with the agents and testify against Morton. The women were arrested and taken to the Metropolitan Correctional Center.

On November 23, Morton was released on a $100,000 personal recognizance bond secured by property in Detroit. On December 5, Roe and Jones were represented in Federal Court by Gail S. Benson, an employee of S. Allan Early, Esq., of Detroit. Their bonds were reduced to $25,000 personal recognizance and they were released. Benson gave them airline tickets and the three returned to Detroit where Benson asked them to meet at her office the next day.

On December 6, Benson took the mules into a conference room and walked out. Morton walked in. He asked the women if they were willing to do time on the charges. Roe said she would if Morton took care of her family. Jones said she didn't want to go to jail. Morton told Roe to leave the room. Jones and Roe walked out of the conference room fifteen minutes later. Jones was upset and went to Roe's apartment. She told Roe she was scared and wanted to leave town immediately. Later that day, Jones called her sister in Montgomery, Alabama, and asked her to wire money for an airline ticket.

Later that evening, Morton and Hilda Singleton checked into the Michigan Inn in Southfield.

At 2:55 a.m. on December 7, Jones flew to Montgomery to see her sister and mother, who was attending a funeral. During the night of December 8 and morning of December 9, Jones and her mother flew to her home in San Diego.

On December 7, shortly after Jones landed in Montgomery, Morton called Thornell McKnight. They met in Morton's room at the Michigan Inn between 8 and 10 in the morning. Morton explained how he had been arrested with his two mules. He worried that "Miss S." had talked to the cops and would testify against him. He told McKnight he needed him for a "job." They discussed different ways of preventing Jones from testifying against Morton, including bribing her with money, having her go underground and leave the country, threatening her family, and killing her. Morton said he wanted to talk to Jones before deciding what to do. While Morton was in the washroom, McKnight asked Singleton if she could guarantee Morton would pay for the job. She promised he would.

McKnight drove Morton in his Checker Cab to Gloria Roe's house where Morton thought Jones was staying. Roe told McKnight that Jones had gone to visit her sister in Alabama earlier in the day. When Morton heard this, he went into the house and talked to Roe for ten minutes. He returned to the cab furious that Jones had run out on him and agreed to pay McKnight $3,500 to kill her. Morton then gave McKnight Jones's address and phone number in San Diego.

Later that night, Morton paid McKnight $1,500 at Ciro's Motel in Detroit. McKnight went to Detroit Office Equipment, Inc., and put $200 down on an $800 furniture order for his wife. Then he bought a .38-caliber snub-nosed revolver loaded with two bullets.

On December 10, one day after Sandra Jones arrived at her mother's house, McKnight left Detroit for San Diego. He checked into the Holiday Inn and called Jones. He said he was sent by the man and had money for her. He agreed to meet at her mother's house where he introduced himself to the family as T and asked to talk alone with Jones. They went to the bedroom where he said he had money from Morton. He also asked if she would cooperate with the cops and tried to dissuade her from doing so. McKnight then told Jones they had to pick up the money in Los Angeles. Jones said she'd drive up the next day and agreed to pick up McKnight at his hotel in the morning.

On December 11, Jones, her brother Collins, and her four-year-old son picked up McKnight in her 1969 Lincoln Continental. In Los Angeles, McKnight said his contact would refuse to hand over the money with anyone but McKnight present. Greed raised its furry little eyebrows and Jones left her son at the home of Collins's ex-wife. She left Collins at a motel. McKnight then directed Jones to an alley near the corner of Venice Boulevard and Cattaraugus Avenue. He asked her to stop the car, and while they talked, he shot her twice in the chest. She fell across the front seat.

McKnight jumped out of the car, ran down the alley, and dumped the gun into a trash bin. Then he ran along Venice Boulevard to the Venice Hotel where he asked the desk clerk to call a taxi, which took him to Los Angeles International Airport. He returned to Detroit that night.

On December 12, McKnight called Singleton to demand final payment for killing Jones. Singleton refused at first, saying she had no money. Then she agreed to give him $1,000. They drove to the IBM Federal Credit Union in Southfield where Singleton got a $1,000 cashier's check. She cashed it at a bank and paid him. Then they drove to the office furniture store where McKnight paid the balance on the furniture he had ordered for his wife. He dropped Singleton off at home and

deposited $540 in his checking account. That same day, without know-
ing that the only witness in the case had been killed, assistant US attorney
Rhonda Fields dismissed all charges against Morton.

On December 15, Morton and Singleton went to McKnight's house to
hear the details of the killing. Morton made sure McKnight didn't do or
say anything that would implicate him in the killing, then canceled a
$500 debt McKnight owed him.

Harvey Orville Dail was arrested in Belize for smuggling marijuana in
1978. While in jail in Belize City, he met an American who had been
serving a life sentence since 1973 for murder. Dail told Al Moore he
belonged to a large American smuggling organization. He also told him
another member of the gang was a fugitive from a 1976 drug case in
Reno. Dail offered to break Moore out of prison and offered him
$20,000 to kill the witness in the Reno case so the fugitive could return
to the United States. Dail was released in late July. Moore escaped on
August 11 and was driven to Guatemala by a native working for Dail.
Moore got immigration papers at the US embassy there.

On August 27, Moore flew to Houston, Texas, where he was met by
Dail. They flew to Tyler in Dail's private plane. On September 2, they
test-fired several handguns, then drove to Canton, where Dail bought a
Colt Python .357-magnum revolver under a false name.

On September 3, Dail gave Moore $1,850 for expenses as he was
about to board a plane to Los Angeles. He then told him his target was
Charles Hudson, also known as Charmin' Charlie, who lived on a golf
course in Saticoy, California. Dail flew the two handguns to Los Angeles
in his private plane on September 5.

Dail walked into Moore's room, number 31, at the Jacmar Hotel in
Los Angeles, at 9:23 in the evening.

Moore: "Well, we're going to find out in the morning . . . if I ever get
my damn old boots on. Hey, did you . . . check the ammunition out on
that son of a bitch? Did ya fire some rounds through it?"

Dail: "I run six through it."

Moore: "OK. You brought the .357 and the .38 both?"

Dail: "Yeah."

Moore: "OK."

Dail: "Now I bought, I brought . . . what was left of that old ammunition we had there and I bought some hollow points."

Moore: "What, .357s?"

Dail: "Smith and Wesson hollow points. . . . I run six, seven through
it."

Dail and Moore went to a bar, then bought beer at a liquor store on the
way back to the hotel. Dail took a briefcase containing a Colt Python

.357-magnum revolver and a .38-caliber handgun and ammunition from the trunk of his car and left it in Moore's room before returning to his room at the Holiday Inn in Van Nuys where he had registered as Mr. Ellis. Dail called Moore one minute after midnight on September 6:

Moore: "I took the .357 out and popped one cap on it."

Dail: "No, no problems."

Moore: "No problems, brother, it's beautiful."

Dail: "OK . . . it's got the kick you want."

Moore: "It's got it just like I want it."

Dail: "OK. Good."

Moore called Dail later in the day on September 6:

Moore: "Now, ahhh . . . I don't think we're going to carry either one of these guns back with us, Harvey."

Dail: "OK. No sweat."

Moore: "All right, I'm going . . . I'm going to dump both of them."

Dail: "No sweat."

Over the telephone on September 7:

Moore: "He's dead."

Dail: "Well . . ."

Moore: "I'm fixing to drop him and both the guns, too. . . . Now, I'm going to have to clean up the back of the car."

Dail: "Well."

Moore: "Like I said, don't tell me how to do this and I won't tell you how to fly your plane."

Dail: "I won't."

The two men flew out of Van Nuys airport back to Texas in Dail's private plane. Moore showed Dail the bloody clothing and papers he had taken from Hudson. On September 8, Dail paid Moore $16,000 in a cardboard box in Tyler. On October 30, Moore was arrested for extradition to Belize, but was released after forty-five days when formal documents for extradition failed to arrive. Dail paid a lawyer a $10,000 retainer to handle Moore's case. He then asked Moore to kill two other people. One was a witness in a drug case in Colorado. On December 15, Dail gave Moore a handgun and the front-door key to the second target's house. He told Moore he'd get $50,000 for killing the man.

That's when the game ended for Harvey Dail. Shortly after getting his immigration papers, Moore tipped off DEA agents in Guatemala City that Dail had hired him to kill a witness in a drug case. DEA agents ran the operation from that point, alerting Hudson and supplying Moore with Hudson's bloody clothes and papers to convince Dail he had carried out the hit. The DEA said that Leland René Quinn, the fugitive who cannot return while Hudson is alive to testify, is involved in smuggling in Mexico and South America.

No other battle for drug turf brings to mind the machine-gun gangster shoot-outs of the Roaring Twenties more than the Cocaine Cowboy wars in southern Florida in the late 1970s and early 1980s. Shootings were so numerous that Uzi became a verb. Americans Uzied Cubans, Cubans Uzied Colombians, Colombians Uzied anyone, including themselves. There were 101 drug murders in Miami alone in 1981. Here are examples of those drug shootings:

Someone didn't want to pay Alberto Estevez the $10,000 he was owed, so they put a contract on his life. Hunters found his body on March 3, 1978. He had been shot in the head.

A maintenance man investigating a foul odor coming from an apartment found the badly decomposed bodies of Guadalupe Paul Gonvalez and his girlfriend, Geraldine Schafer, on May 31, 1978. They had been shot. Gonvalez was a major drug importer and manufacturer of counterfeit Quaaludes.

The bodies of Nelson Lopez and Jackie Bain were found on July 12, 1978, in their spiffy Biscayne Bay condominium surrounded by twenty pounds of marijuana scattered on the floor. Bain was shot in the ear while she slept.

Two black men went to the house of Julio Chavez to buy thirteen ounces of cocaine on July 18, 1978. They forced Chavez and his girlfriend to undress and lie on the bed while they ransacked the house and stole their jewelry. Chavez was shot in the back. His girlfriend was raped.

Christine and Ronald Wright thought they could rip off some "gorillas" for their weed with a suitcase of counterfeit money. They were wrong. Their bullet-riddled bodies were found next to the suitcase in the trunk of a car in a wooded area on July 18, 1978.

Jésus Rivera was an unemployed Puerto Rican pilot working for two Cuban brothers importing large quantities of marijuana into Florida. On October 29, 1978, his body was found floating in the Atlantic Ocean one mile southeast of Soldier Key. His hands and feet were handcuffed and his body was placed inside a zippered sleeping bag weighted down with five weightlifting plates.

On December 1, 1978, the body of an unidentified white man who had been shot in the head was found floating in a canal. The body had been in the water four or five days, during which an alligator had ripped off the left arm. Only the thumb and index fingers were left on the right hand.

On December 27, 1978, two fishermen found the remnants of an unidentified white man lying on a canal bank. He had been shot twice behind the right ear four or five days earlier. His legs were cut off at the knees and both arms were sliced off at the shoulders. The butcher failed in his attempt to cut off the head. The legs and one arm were found on Grassy and Duck Keys.

Raphael Sosa had a parking lot dispute over drugs with the piano player from a fashionable restaurant-lounge on January 27, 1979. He pulled a shotgun and blew the piano player away. On February 22, two men walked into a Latin nightclub, ordered patrons to stand back, and gunned Sosa down.

Barbie Hall knew quite a bit about fire bombings and drug deals. Too much, one couple thought. They shot her and dumped the body in a field where it was found on February 16, 1979.

Ruben Echeverria and Julio Gaona were two illegal Colombians heavily involved in the drug trade. Someone popped them with a .32-caliber silencer-equipped gun, put their bodies inside a large television box, and dumped them in a field. They were found on January 18, 1979, two or three days later.

Rudolph Billings was a high-rolling black dude who had just put down some heavy cash for 100 pounds of marijuana on March 21, 1979. As he got behind the steering wheel of his car to drive away, another black dude reached in and shot Billings in the chest so he could rip off the marijuana.

On April 3, 1979, Daniel Quintana went to the washroom of a bar where drug dealers met. He was found with a bullet hole in the ear.

Esther Ramirez Rios, also known as Estrella Ollos, was a Colombian who worked for several of her countrymen smuggling large quantities of cocaine into the United States. On April 17, 1979, she was found lying in a rural field, her feet tied, her wrists handcuffed, a rope tied around her neck, tape across her mouth, and three stab wounds in her chest. She had suffocated. The man who killed her was found similarly bound in the trunk of a car involved in a machine-gun shoot-out on the Florida Turnpike.

On May 20, 1979, the body of Oscar Penagos-Rios was found on the roadside in Miami Springs. He had been shot twice in the back of the head. He had a lot of American and Colombian money in his pockets — proving the hitter was no thief.

Gerardo Arraque was shot in the head in the apartment of a Colombian woman who ran a large cocaine-smuggling operation. His body was found on May 27, 1979, on the roadside in the residential area of Coral Gables.

On June 15, 1979, Enrique Gato parked his car across the street from a sidewalk café in Little Havana. Contract killers spotted him and chased him down a side street, guns blazing. Gato collapsed in a driveway and while curious neighbors watched, one of the killers stood over him and shot him once more.

In the spring of 1979, Jésus Bellver's dead stepson was dumped from a Cadillac onto the steps of Baptist Hospital. He had ripped off drug dealers for $200,000. On August 24, 1979, someone dressed as a mailman walked into Bellver's house and terrorized his fifteen-year-old daughter with a knife while searching for drugs and the stolen money. When Bellver got home, he was shot in front of his daughter and eight-year-old son.

On September 15, 1979, a thirty-foot boat was seen running in circles offshore at Haulover Beach. On board, Marine Patrol officers found Robert Mahoney dead with a bullet in the head and Roy LeDoyen about to die from bullets in the head and chest. They pulled Luis Marzan's body from the water. A lot of marijuana-smuggling operations end on the high seas.

Edward Forcer was a black kingpin in the white powder business in Dade County. He dealt in cocaine and heroin. His dealing days ended when someone cuffed his hands behind his back and shot him in the head and leg with a .22-caliber silencer-equipped pistol on September 30, 1979.

By 1981 the body count was so high in Miami that the morgue literally overflowed. The Dade County medical examiner rented a refrigerated hamburger van to keep the stiffs from rotting.

The carnage wrought by Colombia's drug traffickers in their country since they assassinated the leading presidential candidate, Senator Luis Carlos Galan, on August 18, 1989, best exemplifies their use of violence as a tool in the drug business. The *narco-traficantes* have intimidated the Colombian government into once again reneging on its extradition treaty with the United States and striking a deal with *Los Extraditables* that allows them minimum punishment for surrendering in Colombia instead of being shipped to the United States to face drug charges.

Galan was gunned down by drug cartel hit men in front of thousands of supporters and television cameras at a political rally. He continually criticized politicians whose campaigns were funded with dirty narco-dollars. His assassination convinced the government to declare war on drug traffickers. During the following week, 11,000 people were picked up by police, and the government promised to extradite all traffickers wanted in the US. Soldiers raided the palatial estates of drug lords and seized millions of dollars in assets. The estate of one small trafficker had eighteen staff members, fifty thoroughbred horses, and a small lake with 100 swans. The El Aguila, one of Pablo Escobar's estates forty-five miles north of Medellin, had a huge altar in the lobby near a life-sized crucifix of Christ on a thick crystal base.

Los Extraditables, as the drug traffickers wanted in the US are known, counterattacked on Thursday, August 24, 1989, with a declaration of war on the state and a flurry of bombings. They objected to attempts to extradite Eduardo Martinez Romero, a thirty-five-year-old economist and alleged money manager for the Medellin cartel. He was wanted in Atlanta, Georgia, on charges of laundering $1.2 billion in cocaine money.

Jorge Ochoa Restrepo, father of three sons who started the Medellin cartel, wrote an open letter to Colombian President Virgilio Barco: "Let there be dialogue, let there be peace."

Pablo Escobar, the multi-billionaire cartel leader known as Don Pablo or The Godfather, threatened a campaign of death if the government didn't accept the traffickers' peace offer. "There will be some deaths, always more deaths. I will give orders. Some journalists and some magistrates—they will pay."

Death threats forced Justice Minister Monica de Greiff to flee to the United States to hold a press conference in which she stated she would not bow to pressure to resign. She left her husband and son in the US to return to Colombia. Within weeks, she resigned and returned to the States.

Raids on traffickers' estates intensified by the end of August, as did the retaliatory bombings. A gallows was found in the yard of Gonzalo Rodriguez Gacha, El Mexicano, in the town of Pacho fifty miles north of Bogotá. True to the man's schizophrenic nature, 500 wrapped dolls to be given as gifts at Christmas were found inside the house. El Mexicano was both revered and feared in Pacho, where he handed out thousands of dollars or a death sentence on a whim. When his seventeen-year-old-son Freddy walked into a bar, the doors were locked to everyone else until he left. He had amassed more than $7 billion by age forty.

"He is barely forty-one or forty-two but he was Pacho's master and he demanded respect for his status," said Colonel Jaime Uscategui Ramirez, who led the army raid on El Mexicano's Pacho estate. "If a car got in his way and the driver did not apologize, he was a dead man. Nobody here had the right to protest without putting his own life at stake."

Drug traffickers evaded capture, thanks to corrupt police and army officials. However, they couldn't buy off a police general and sociologist, Miguel Maza Marquez, director of the Administrative Security Department (DAS), a special police unit. DAS investigated links between drug traffickers, right-wing landowners, and paramilitary self-defence groups in an attempt to understand the violence that gripped Colombia. There are more than 140 identified *autodefensas*, which were sanctioned in 1965 under a law aimed at left-wing guerrillas who threatened to take over the government.

Deserters from paramilitary groups told DAS that El Mexicano had hired British and Israeli mercenaries to train drug cartel hit men and paramilitary groups that protected drug traffickers' estates in martial arts, explosives, and first aid. Some of the mercenaries had trained contra guerrillas trying to topple Nicaragua's Sandinista government.

The revelation that Israeli mercenaries were training goons for drug traffickers embarrassed Israel. Israeli Defence Minister Yitzhak Rabin said that one or two companies may have been operating in Colombia, but he tried to water down allegations that former Israeli army officers were training hit men for the Medellin drug cartel. Israel feared the issue could harm its lucrative arms exports to Colombia.

One Israeli company alleged by Colombian officials to have trained cartel employees was Hod Hahanit (Spearhead), a security and arms-trading firm. Company head Yair Klein, an Israeli reserve lieutenant colonel, was told by an Israeli official in that country to leave Colombia to avoid arrest. Klein denied the allegations. He said he thought his clients were honest ranchers who feared Communist guerillas.

The drug traffickers also started a right-wing political organization called National Restoration Movement (MORENA) to destabilize the country's politics. The movement is backed by the traffickers' private armies, which have slaughtered countless people whose political leanings displease cartel leaders.

Colombian Supreme Court Judge Hernando Baquero Borda was given the onerous task of buttressing Colombia's extradition treaty with the United States in 1986. He worked hard at the job, traveling to West Germany to research extradition laws. He started receiving letters with Medellin postmarks.

"Hi, Miserable. The war has just begun. We're not afraid of anything. Absolutely nothing. . . . We know you are anti-nationalist, pro-gringo, defender of the policy of the CIA. If the treaty doesn't fall, you and your family will." It was signed, "The Extraditables."

Judge Baquero and his bodyguard were shot dead early in the morning of July 31, 1986. The killings were no longer preceded by written threats after August 24, 1989. They had had an effect.

On Monday, September 25, 1989, a Medellin judge, citing lack of evidence, dropped charges against the two leaders of that city's drug cartel accused in the assassination of Colombia's attorney general. Pablo Emilio Escobar Gaviria and José Gonzalo Rodriguez Gacha had been charged with planning the January 25, 1989, killing of attorney general Carlos Hoyos. They also had been charged with complicity in the 1988 kidnapping of Andres Pastrana, a Bogotá mayoral candidate. He was freed during an army raid and won the election.

On Tuesday, September 26, 1989, the M-19 leftist guerrilla group published a full-page ad in *El Tiempo*, Colombia's largest newspaper, urging the government to pardon drug traffickers and to stop extraditing them to the US. The same day, a bomb exploded at the Cartegena Hilton, killing two doctors.

Drug cartel *sicarios* on motorcycles gunned down two employees of the newspaper *El Espectador* in Medellin on October 10. The murders followed thirteen bombings in three Colombian cities overnight. The following day, Pablo Escobar asked the media to mediate a truce between The Extraditables and the government.

"Colombian peace is more important than the considerations and conceptions of the other governments of the world. . . . In the same way that war decrees can be issued so can peace decrees be issued," Escobar said in a letter. He asked the director of Bogotá's *La Prensa* to ask the government on behalf of the cartel to end its all-out war on drug traffickers.

More than 1,000 newspapers across North and South America simultaneously published an editorial on Thursday, October 11, condemning the terrorism unleashed against Colombians by drug traffickers. Members of the InterAmerican Press Association ran the editorial in support of *El Espectador*. Escobar and his thugs threatened massive attacks on the Bogotá daily newspaper if it didn't stop distributing in Medellin. The 102-year-old newspaper criticized the drug barons for waging war against the government. Drug barons dealt with media opposition by killing more than fifty Colombian journalists in the 1980s.

"What is at stake in Medellin at this moment is not just freedom of the press. It is freedom itself," said the editorial written by Augusto Nunez, managing editor of *O Estado de São Paulo*, a Brazilian daily. "Not even the bloodiest civil war provides a precedent for one of the combatant groups blowing up an entire city. . . . The latest development in the dirty war waged by drug traffickers in Colombia against the institutions of that country confirm that the audacity of criminals knows no bounds.

"It suggests, too, that drug merchants will not hesitate to extend the range of their victims—up to now limited to authorities and journalists who dare combat them in their efforts to bring the Colombian government to its knees and oblige it to stop enforcing the law."

In reference to the killing of two *El Espectador* employees: "The bodies of the victims were still lying in the streets when the drug traffickers delivered their threat literally to blow up Medellin. . . . The terror claimed by the drug cartels on the Colombian free press has no parallel in the history of the continent. Not even the most freedom-hating governments have tried to institutionalize the systematic extermination of journalists who defend laws and institutions as the Colombian criminals are trying to do."

The immunity that traffickers have from arrest and prosecution, the editorial continued, "can only be explained by the fact that their circle of friends includes men in strategic positions of power in the government, police and even the armed forces."

In the midst of the violence wrought by the drug traffickers, the M-19 guerrilla group signed a peace accord with the Colombian government in November. It announced on November 17 it would surrender its weapons to the Socialist International in Santo Domingo, the rebel headquarters southwest of Bogotá.

Even more stunning was the revelation in military intelligence reports leaked at the end of November that twenty-nine Catholic priests were active members of the National Liberation Army, one of largest and most ruthless of Colombia's six leftist guerrilla groups. Colombian bishops tried to avert a slaughter of priests by stating that "two or three" of the priests on the list were guerrillas and the rest were just helping poor peasants.

"Certainly there are some," said Archbishop Mario Revollo Bravo. "But a list that large needs further study."

The doctrine of liberation theology was drafted at a bishops' conference in Medellin in 1968 with the blessing of the Vatican. It was an attempt to define the role of priests in a region of the world beset by political and religious activism. It gives priests the option to side with groups against the state. There have been several incidents of priests and nuns being slaughtered by both right-wing and leftist guerrillas in Latin American countries.

Churches have responded to the killings and stirred up public sympathy and ire by stating the victims were neutral workers helping the poor. It's easy to say and believe thousands of miles away. For those in the field, it's often obvious that the religious orders are no more neutral and peaceful than the people they help.

If the church advocates guerrilla action and social activism among its members, it must accept their deaths as an occupational hazard. The church no longer has a claim to neutrality and immunity in Latin America. It has taken sides and must pay the price.

But none of this is new. Missionaries have always sided with the people they found easiest to convert and helped them fight their enemies — be it in Africa, South America, or colonial Canada, where priests were tortured, burned at the stake, eviscerated, and had their hearts eaten by Indian captors.

The Extraditables stepped up their campaign of terror on November 27, 1989, by bombing a Colombian Boeing 727 that exploded over Bogotá, killing all 107 people on board. The bomb was planted to kill five informants who gave police information that led them to Pablo Escobar's hideout. Escobar reportedly escaped wearing only his underwear.

On Tuesday, December 5, Judge Bernardo Jaramillo Uribe, who was investigating drug traffickers, was assassinated while strolling through Medellin. He was the fourth judge to be killed in fifteen weeks.

At 7:30 on the morning of December 6, a 1,000-pound dynamite bomb inside a truck was exploded outside the Bogotá headquarters of the Department of Administrative Security, Colombia's federal intelligence and security agency, killing fifty-two people and injuring 600. Buildings in a two-mile radius were damaged by the blast, which destroyed sixty cars and left a crater fifteen feet deep and thirty feet wide in the road. DAS director General Miguel Maza Marquez, an avowed enemy of the Medellin drug cartel, was not injured. The cartel tried to kill him on May 30, 1989, with a car bomb that killed seven people and injured fifty.

On December 7, US Attorney General Dick Thornburgh announced that $61.8 million in cash and high-yield certificates belonging to José Gonzalo Rodriguez Gacha had been frozen in banks in Luxembourg, Switzerland, Austria, Britain, and the United States. El Mexicano had transferred $20 million to Panama before his assets were frozen.

El Mexicano never got a chance to spend the money. He was killed in a shoot-out with police on Friday, December 15. His seventeen-year-old son, Freddy, and fifteen others died in the battle near the Caribbean port of Covenas in northern Colombia. The pig farmer who became a billionaire trafficking cocaine and rose to the number two position in the Medellin cartel had lived for two months with a $600,000 bounty on his head. The Colombian government offered the same reward for Pablo Escobar, who had begun his criminal career as a pickpocket and car thief.

El Mexicano was buried with his son and five bodyguards in a common grave in Sincelejo on Saturday, December 16, by authorities who used $700 in public funds to pay for the burial. The family had the bodies of El Mexicano and Freddy exhumed on Sunday, December 17, and flown by private plane to Bogotá. They were then driven to Pacho for burial in luxurious coffins. El Mexicano's body was claimed by two brothers. Freddy's was claimed by his mother, one of El Mexicano's mistresses.

On February 17, 1990, the Colombian army displayed $35.5 million in cash and 352 pounds of gold bars and jewelry seized from five of El Mexicano's ranches. The army's 1989 budget was $27 million.

On Monday, December 18, intelligence reports said Colombian drug lords had taken out a $30-million contract on the life of US President George Bush.

One month later, on Wednesday, January 17, 1990, the Medellin cocaine cartel issued a communiqué that admitted the Colombian government had won the war on drugs. The drug traffickers said they would stop their campaign of violence in return for a pardon.

An Israeli businessman linked to mercenaries who trained the Medellin cartel's hit men and paramilitary security forces was killed sometime in January 1990. The body of Arik Afek was found on January 25 in the trunk of a car parked at Miami International Airport. Afek had lived outside Miami. He allegedly helped Israeli Army Lieutenant Colonel Yair Klein escape Colombia after he was identified as a trainer for drug traffickers' guards.

On February 12, three days before the anti-drug summit in Cartagena, Colombian investigators found ten French-made anti-aircraft Stinger missiles in a drug trafficker's stash.

Two days later DAS director General Miguel Maza Marquez accused Lieutenant Colonel Klein of training the men who bombed the Avianca Boeing 727 on November 27, 1989. "This is the person who has done the most damage to Colombia" and who is responsible under Colombian law for the deaths, General Maza said. Lieutenant Colonel Klein had returned to Israel, which does not have an extradition treaty with Colombia. General Maza also revealed that an investigation by Colombian police and Interpol found evidence that two Basque separatists belonging to the Basque terrorist organization ETA had carried out acts of terrorism in Colombia.

In a press statement issued on March 31, The Extraditables threatened to explode an 11,000-pound bomb in Bogotá for every drug trafficker extradited to the United States. In addition to the 200 people already killed since the Medellin cartel declared war on Colombia's government on August 24, 1989, the traffickers said they would execute judges, politicians, and members of the Cano family, which owns the *El Espectador* newspaper. The Colombian army distributed hundreds of thousands of pamphlets on April 17 offering $500,000 for information leading to the arrest of Pablo Escobar.

On April 26, a suicide hit man opened fire with a submachine gun in a jetliner to kill Carlos Pizarro, former leader of the M-19 guerrilla organization and who was running for president. He was the third presidential candidate assassinated by drug traffickers in eight months, the fourth in less than three years.

The hit man, twenty-five-year-old Alvaro Rodriguez, picked up the submachine gun in the airplane washroom where it had been hidden by an accomplice before takeoff. He took a seat two rows behind Pizarro. A few minutes later he stood up, pulled the gun from underneath his black leather jacket, leaned over a row of passengers, and fired thirteen bullets, most of them into Pizarro's head. Bodyguards in turn killed the assassin. Pizarro, thirty-eight, was flying from Bogotá to Barranquilla to campaign. Police arrested two men armed with submachine guns at the Barranquilla airport; they had orders to kill Pizarro if he walked off the plane.

Two Colombian men linked to the Medellin cartel were arrested in May 1990 for trying to buy Stinger missiles in Tampa, Florida. The FBI said the men offered to pay a $1-million down payment in cocaine money for 120 Stingers and fifty automatic rifles to be flown to Colombia. They offered to pay $5 million for a plane and the weapons and $1 million to those who stole them. Drug traffickers planned to use the weapons against the Colombian government. Shoulder-fired Stinger missiles use a homing device to aim themselves at the heat generated by an aircraft's engine. They cost $14,000 each on the legitimate arms market.

While the two prospective weapons buyers appeared in court on May 8, Israeli officials were trying to find out how 200 of their assault rifles had ended up in the hands of Colombia's Medellin cartel. Israel had shipped 400 Galil and 100 Uzi submachine guns and ammunition worth $250,000 to the Caribbean island of Antigua's 700-member security force in March 1989. Two hundred of the Galils were found on El Mexicano's ranch after his death. Suspicions quickly focused on two former Israeli army officers, Yair Klein and Maurice Sarfati.

Documents show Sarfati arranged the arms purchase for Antigua with a May 16, 1985, letter from Antigua cabinet secretary Lionel Stevens, naming Sarfati as a special envoy. Israel authorized the deal after receiving two letters dated November 9, 1988, from Vere Bird, Jr., security adviser for his father, Prime Minister Vere Bird. The letters confirmed Sarfati's role as special envoy to deal in arms and promised the guns would not be sold to third parties.

US Customs agents were investigating allegations in November 1990 that an Israeli network based in Miami provided weapons and training for Colombian drug traffickers. They were also looking into allegations the network helped ship automatic guns to Medellin cartel leader Gonzalo Rodriguez Gacha through Antigua. Investigators in Antigua had concluded the deal had been arranged by Israelis. Klein was convicted in Jerusalem on November 29, 1990, of the unauthorized export of military equipment.

On May 11, 1990, Carlos Guerro Rodriguez, the city of Medellin's security chief, was assassinated by gunmen who shot into his jeep when it stopped at a traffic light. Seven police officers were killed throughout Medellin in seventy-two hours. Three car bombs killed 26 people and wounded 178 in Bogotá and Cali on Saturday, May 12.

During the week from Monday, May 7, to midnight Sunday, May 13,

503 people were murdered in Colombia, a country of 30 million. Canada, with a population of 26 million, has about 650 murders a year. More than 140,000 people were murdered in Colombia in the 1980s.

The Colombian justice system doesn't deter crime. Only 3 percent of those who committed crimes in Colombia in 1989 were punished.

On Wednesday, June 13, Colombian police stormed an apartment in an exclusive Medellin suburb looking for Juan Jairo Arias Tascon, leader of the Medellin cartel's network of hit men and the man responsible for coordinating the cartel's terrorism campaign against the government. Police shot Arias dead when he resisted.

After ten months of living on the run and waging war, Pablo Escobar managed to evade capture, but was so scared of betrayal that he regularly killed his aides to purge his organization of potential traitors.

On July 7, the Colombian attorney general's office, which had been investigating the corruption of government officials by drug traffickers, asked President Virgilio Barco to strip the former head of the national police of his retirement benefits because he was allegedly on the payroll of drug traffickers. José Guillermo Medina Sanchez could not explain how his police salary payed for two luxurious houses and two apartments in Bogotá, an apartment in Cartagena, a farm, a Mercedes-Benz, eight show horses, and numerous certificates of deposit and bank accounts. He lost his job in January 1989 after being linked to cocaine traffickers.

On Saturday, August 8, the Colombian police Elite Corps shot and killed Gustave Gaviria, the forty-one-year-old cousin of Pablo Escobar. Gaviria ran the Medellin cartel's drug operation while Escobar was on the run. He was wanted on murder charges in Colombia. The US wanted him extradited on drug charges.

On August 22, Colombian police in Medellin arrested Humberto de Jésus Parra Salinas, who assumed control of the Medellin cartel's 100 teams of hit men after the shooting of Juan Jario Arias Tascon. Parra, who used the name Alfredo Vasquez and went by the nickname "the baker," was ranked among the top ten cartel leaders before so many were killed.

By the end of the 1990, the *narco-traficantes'* use of violence had persuaded the Colombian government to renege once more on its extradition treaty with the United States. The government promised traffickers they would not be extradited if they surrendered and confessed their crimes. The Extraditables were guaranteed reasonable prison terms. Violence had again succeeded as a tool in the criminal underworld.

8

Narco-terrorism:
Drugs as a political weapon

"We follow Fidel's orders to penetrate and addict US youths with drugs to prevent them from thinking, to prevent them from having opinions, to prevent them from speaking, and to keep the population asleep. As Lenin said of religion, that religion is the opium of the people, and so we are giving them real opium."
—A LIEUTENANT COLONEL IN THE CUBAN NAVY EXPLAINS WHY CUBA PROTECTS AND ESCORTS SHIPS AND PLANES SMUGGLING MARIJUANA AND COCAINE FROM COLOMBIA TO THE UNITED STATES.

"[The Cuban government] are convinced that by undermining the ability of North American youngsters to resist drugs, they can destroy the enemy without firing a shot. The strength of an army is in its youngsters, and whoever is able to destroy these youngsters morally will be able to destroy the army."
—MAJOR JUAN RODRIGUEZ MENIER, FORMER CUBAN INTELLIGENCE AGENT WHO DEFECTED TO THE UNITED STATES IN 1987.

Cuba straddles the most heavily traveled drug-trafficking routes in the world. US Customs and Coast Guard officials say Cuba has become their biggest obstacle to interdicting drug smugglers, who seek safety in its skies and waters, which American pursuers are forbidden to enter. They have seen Cuban patrol boats protect mother ships offloading cocaine and marijuana to feeder boats in Cuban waters. Smugglers' planes intercepted on their way into Florida have veered back into Cuban airspace and dropped their loads where US agents can't pick them up.

Cuban President Fidel Castro has for decades denied helping drug traffickers. He claimed to have no knowledge that his officials were involved with drug smugglers. He told the world he was against drugs.

Fidel Castro lied. He seeks out drug ventures not only for the money they bring his cash-strapped Communist regime, or for the weapons drug money buys for the revolutions Cuba supports around the world, but because Fidel Castro considers drugs the doomsday weapon against capitalist Yanquis. Castro has not only plotted to destroy North America with drugs—he's doing it. His partners in crime are Yanqui-hating Colombian drug traffickers.

Castro used the 1980 Mariel boat lift from Cuba to Florida to plant thousands of Cuban agents in North America to operate his drug network. Mario Estevez Gonzalez, a former Cuban intelligence agent, said he was assigned to sell drugs to promote violent crime, addiction, and corruption in North America. Estevez sold cocaine, methaqualone tablets, and marijuana in New York, northern New Jersey, and Florida. He earned about $3 million for Castro in fifteen months.

Castro encouraged revolutionary governments and rebel movements in Central and South America to get involved in drug trafficking. Raul Castro and Humberto Ortega, brother of Sandinista leader Daniel Ortega, met in September 1981. Nicaragua later became a safe transshipment point for Colombian drug traffickers, according to Antonio Farach, a Nicaraguan diplomat who defected to the United States.

"The drugs were used as a political weapon because in that way we were delivering a blow to our principal enemy," Farach said. "The drug trafficking produced a very good economic benefit which we needed for our revolution. We wanted to provided food to our people with the suffering and death of the youth in the United States."

Politics and economics attracted Castro to drug trafficking—the politics of death and the economics of necessity.

Communism has failed as a political system in the Soviet Union and eastern Europe. The Soviet Union can no longer afford to support Communist regimes around the world. Neither can Castro.

Cuba is in serious debt because of the money it spends underwriting guerrilla and liberation movements around the world. Cuba has spent more than 1 billion pesos a year in Angola—more than the revenue from its cash crop, sugar. The Soviet Union spends $4 billion a year on Cuba. That's $12 million a day. The Kremlin has demanded that Cuba become self-sufficient. No more sharing the wealth, comrade. Neither country has an internationally accepted currency and both need hard cash to buy goods outside their borders. Castro gets his hard cash from drugs.

Drugs are not a major problem in the USSR compared to the chemical plague in the United States because the ruble can't be spent outside the Soviet Union. Drug traffickers don't want funny money. The Soviets will quickly share the American drug nightmare if their currency gains international acceptance.

Who are narco-terrorists? They are insurgent groups who seek to overthrow governments, such as the M-19 or 19th of April Movement and the Revolutionary Armed Forces (FARC) in Colombia, the Sendero Luminoso in Peru, the Sikhs in India, the Tamils in Sri Lanka, the Shan United Army in Myanmar (Burma), the mujeheddin in Afghanistan, and the contras in Nicaragua, to name a few. They are governments who seek to overthrow other governments through drug-funded revolutions, such as Cuba's attempts to destroy the US with drugs and its funding of guerrilla groups such as the M-19 movement in Colombia, and the United States' attempt to overthrow the Sandinistas in Nicaragua with drug-funded contra rebels. They are international drug traffickers such as Pablo Escobar and Carlos Lehder, who use drug profits to support their nationalistic and anti-American schemes.

The largest and most worrisome narco-terrorist threat to North America comes from Cuban and Colombian drug traffickers. Cuba's involvement in drug trafficking has been mentioned in courts only twice. But enough defecting Cuban intelligence agents substantiate the threat.

Four Cuban officials were indicted in Miami in 1982 for drug trafficking. They refused to appear in a Miami court and stayed in Cuba where Fidel Castro sheltered them and denounced the charges although non-Cubans in the case were convicted. Two indictments handed down in 1988 and 1989 also allege that Cuba was used as a transshipment point for drugs from Colombia with the aid of Cuban officials. This case appears to have spurred Castro into action, since one of the Cuban officials named by the leader of the smuggling ring was later tried and shot in Cuba. Although allegations of Cuban involvement in the drug trade have been made since 1963, only these two investigations by the US Drug Enforcement Administration have documented the claims.

In the first case, Jaime Guillot-Lara, four high-ranking Cuban officials, and nine others were indicted in Miami in November 1982 on drug-smuggling charges. Guillot-Lara was accused of conspiring with Cuban officials to use Cuba as a safe transshipment point for cargoes of marijuana, cocaine, and methaqualone. Guillot-Lara, a Colombian, fled before he could be arrested. The four Cubans — including two members of the Communist Party Central Committee — were Vice-Admiral Aldo Santamaria Cuadrado; Fernando Rabelo Renedo, former Cuban ambassador to Colombia and later ambassador to Nicaragua; René Rodriguez Cruz, president of the Cuban Institute for Friendship with People; and Gonzalo Bassols Suarez, former minister-counselor to Colombia.

Guillot-Lara was a power-hungry Colombian *narco-traficante* who dreamed of becoming president of his country by arming the Cuban-supported leftist M-19 guerrilla movement in Colombia with weapons paid for with drug money. The M-19 is one of the USSR's favorite terrorist groups in South America. Jaime Bateman, military leader of the M-19, was trained in Moscow. From 1977 to 1981, Guillot-Lara shipped 2.5 million tons of marijuana, eighty pounds of cocaine, and 25 million methaqualone tablets from Colombia to the US. Colombian trafficker Johnny Crump introduced Guillot-Lara to Cuban officials at the Cuban

Colombian cartel employees load mother ships with marijuana at a Guajira peninsula port. The Colombian government suspended all flights in the area for three days. A navy gunboat protected the operation. (PHOTOS: US CUSTOMS)

"We fly low to keep America's heads high," is the airborne smugglers' motto. Two planes drop bales of drugs near the Bahamas while a third is stripped of its booty by boaters after crashing. (PHOTOS: US CUSTOMS)

(right) Big Ed epitomizes the drug warrior on US Customs air interdiction teams that hunt smugglers along the Florida coast. (PHOTO: YVES LAVIGNE)

(bottom) Bert Sousa, an ex-marine helicopter pilot and now a Sacramento police officer, stands beside marijuana grown by outlaw bikers in Butte County, California. (PHOTO: PRIVATE COLLECTION)

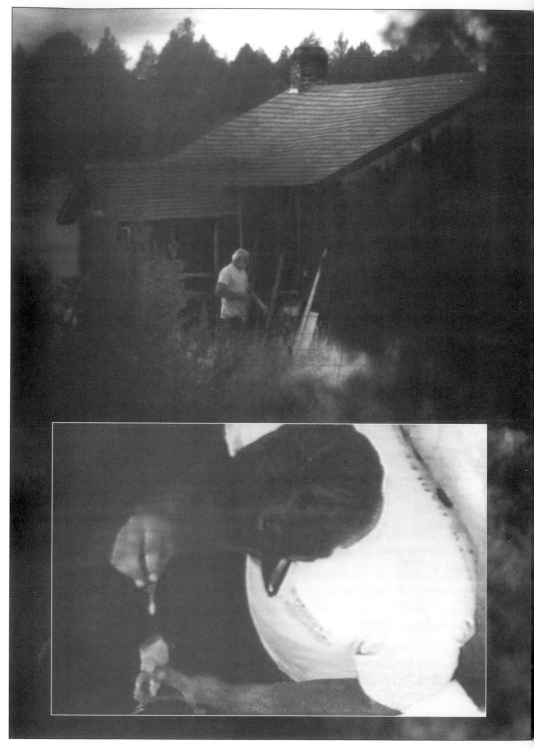

Hell's Angel Odis (Buck) Garrett smokes outside a California building in which police found a methamphetamine laboratory and a large quantity of speed. (PHOTO: US DRUG ENFORCEMENT ADMINISTRATION)
(inset) A Hell's Angels associate shovels a spoon of crank up his nose at a motorcycle event attended by the gang. (PHOTO: UNDERCOVER NARC)

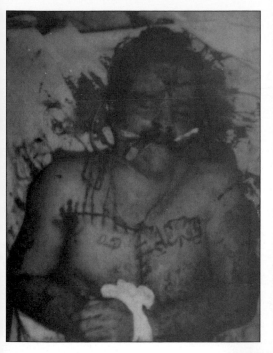

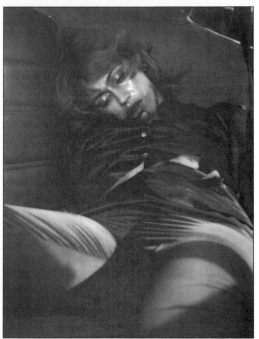

(top left) Dennis Murphy angered the Aryan Brotherhood by not supplying the prison gang with drugs while free between stints at Folsom Prison. (PHOTO: FOLSOM PRISON STAFF)

(top right) A Colombian victim of Florida's Cocaine Cowboy wars in the late 1970s and early 1980s. (PHOTO: METRO DADE POLICE DEPARTMENT)

(bottom) Hell's Angels chemist Brutus Geoffrion and other members of the gang's North Chapter were executed for ripping off the gang. (PHOTO: SURETE DU QUEBEC)

(top left) Metro Toronto Police detective Heinz Kuck arrests a 15-year-old for possession of hash in the city's notorious Parkdale area. (PHOTO: YVES LAVIGNE)

(top right) A handful of crack seized from a dealer. (PHOTO: YVES LAVIGNE)

(bottom) Five-and-a-half kilos of crack cocaine worth $500,000 found in the apartment of a kingpin of the Oak Park Bloods in Sacramento, California. (PHOTO: US BUREAU OF ALCOHOL TOBACCO AND FIREARMS)

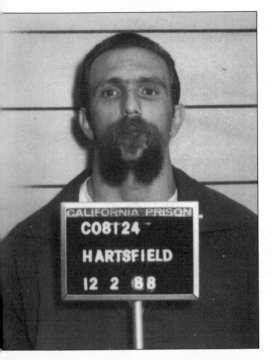

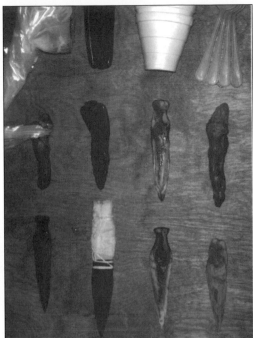

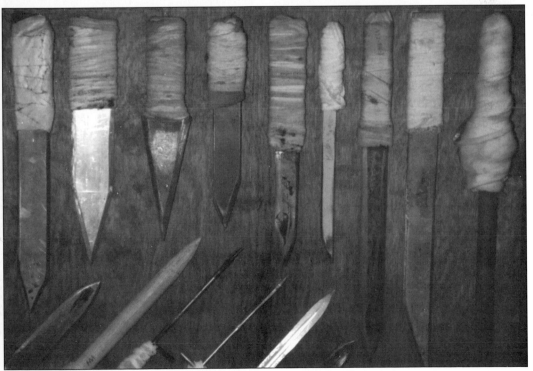

(top left) Robert Sydney (Toilet) Hartsfield has spent all but two years behind bars since his arrest for burglary at age 12. (PHOTO: FOLSOM PRISON STAFF)

(top right) Inmates in California's Folsom Prison melt plastic spoons, styrofoam cups, combs and bags into slabs they shape into knives. (PHOTO: YVES LAVIGNE)

(bottom) Inmates grind any piece of metal into a shiv. Drug users make their own hypodermic needles and pipes. (PHOTO: YVES LAVIGNE)

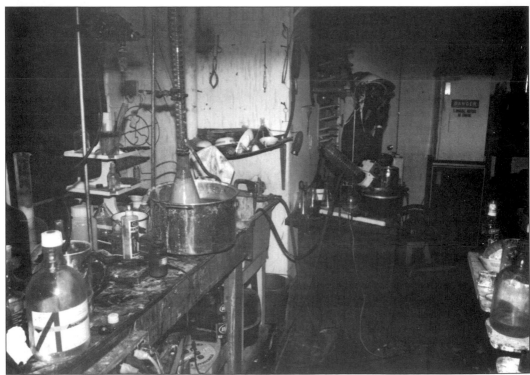

(top) Former Kung Lok leader Danny Mo, Chinese pop star Anita Mui and the author. The photograph was taken on April 26, 1991, by a business partner of Mo and Asau Tran, the most powerful Vietnamese gangster in Canada. Tran, the photographer and a woman were assassinated as they left the Pot of Gold restaurant in Toronto's Chinatown on August 16,1991.

(bottom) A downtown Toronto methamphetamine laboratory operated by a chemist working for the Satan's Choice motorcycle gang. (PHOTO: METRO TORONTO POLICE)

embassy in Bogotá in 1979 and acted as the link between Guillot-Lara and Cuban ambassador Fernando Ravelo in subsequent smuggling operations during which the Cubans agreed to protect drug shipments in Cuban territory. In 1980, Guillot-Lara paid Cuban officials $10 a pound for marijuana shipped through Cuba. Mother ships anchored in Cuban waters where they offloaded to feeder boats from Florida and the Bahamas.

Guillot-Lara was an efficient businessman who didn't waste time or money. During one boat run in 1981, he met a ship off the Panamanian coast and picked up fifty-five boxes, each containing ten Belgian FAL rifles, and ninety boxes of 1,000 rounds of 7.62mm cartridges. Then he picked up a load of marijuana off the coast of Guajira Peninsula. The guns, ammo, and marijuana were transferred to a truck at the port of Dibulla and taken to a clandestine airstrip. Five M-19 guerrillas guarded the shipment until an Aerospeca cargo plane hijacked by their comrades arrived to pick up the guns and ammunition and flew them to a base on the Orteguaza River. The marijuana had already been picked up by the US pilot of a small private plane and flown to Florida.

Guillot-Lara was arrested on false documentation charges in Mexico on November 25, 1981. Both the US and Colombian governments failed to have him extradited. He was freed on September 30, 1982, and fled to Spain.

Lieutenant Colonel Antonio de la Guardia was a powerful man in Fidel Castro's government. He was head of the secret MC department in the Ministry of the Interior. His job was to circumvent the American trade embargo and smuggle American high technology and medical supplies into Cuba. He did his job well. Lieutenant Colonel de la Guardia operated a worldwide network of intelligence agents who worked as export merchants in front companies established through holding companies to acquire the goods Cuba needed. He also ran a shipping operation that included Panamanian-registered freighters and speedboats that traveled between Panama, Florida, and the US, as well as around the world.

Captain Miguel Ruiz Pao was one of Lieutenant Colonel de la Guardia's agents. Pao is the crafty devil who hatched a drug-smuggling scheme that could make a lot of people rich. His cousin, Reinaldo Ruiz, lived in California and supplied small smuggling planes to the Medellin cartel. Pao asked his cousin Reinaldo and his son Ruben to fly to Cuba in January 1987. He introduced them to Lieutenant Colonel de la Guardia and outlined his deal: for a cut of the action, Cuban officials would let Ruben Ruiz land and refuel his drug-laden planes on Cuban soil. They would also help him transfer drugs to speedboats that would take them to

Florida. This was the greatest opportunity the Ruiz boys had had since they moved to the land of opportunity.

On April 10, 1987, Ruben and Reinaldo refueled in Panama on a flight between southern Florida and Colombia. The next day, they flew their first load—240 kilograms of cocaine—from Colombia to Cuba. They landed at the Varadero military base where soldiers transferred the contraband to a ship called the *Flerida*, which a military patrol boat escorted out of Cuban waters.

On May 9, 1987, a MIG flown by a Cuban air force pilot escorted Ruben Ruiz and his planeload of 1,000 pounds of cocaine to the Varadero airfield. The smugglers varied their techniques. Sometimes the cocaine was loaded onto speedboats that made the final ninety-mile dash to the Florida coast. Other times, bundles of cocaine with fluorescent lights were dropped to speedboats in the safe harbor of Cuban waters. Lieutenant Colonel de la Guardia and other Cuban officials were paid $3.4 million for helping the Ruiz family and their pilots ship six tons of cocaine through Cuba to the United States during fifteen runs.

Then Reinaldo and Ruben Ruiz ran into some bad luck. It seems that one of the pilots they hired to fly one of the smuggling missions was an infiltrator for the Drug Enforcement Administration—Hu Chang.

Reinaldo and Ruben were tricked into talking about their links to Cuba in a room equipped with a hidden video camera.

"The money went in Fidel's drawer," Reinaldo Ruiz, who by then headed a seventeen-member cocaine operation, said of the $3.4 million paid to Cuban officials. In March 1989, Reinaldo and Ruben Ruiz pleaded guilty in Miami to charges of smuggling cocaine through Cuba with the help of Cuban officials. Although Reinaldo Ruiz did not name the officials in court, he offered their names during plea bargaining before sentencing. He identified Tony de la Guardia, Amado Padron, and Miguel Ruiz Pao.

Lieutenant Colonel de la Guardia and his aide, Major Amado Padron, were undeterred by the arrest of Reinaldo and Ruben Ruiz. They started moving cocaine through Cuba on their own.

Their luck also ran out. And Fidel Castro used their bad luck to clean up several problems on the home front as well as his international image. Castro had watched Panamanian strongman and good friend Manuel Noriega get indicted in Florida for drug trafficking. The February 1988 charges against Noriega related to events that occurred between 1981 and 1986. Noriega was accused of accepting $4.6 million in bribes from the Medellin cartel to protect cocaine shipments, drug runners, and money-laundering operations in Panama; of sheltering drug smugglers; of allowing the Medellin cartel and its leaders to move their operations to Panama in 1984 following a government crackdown on traffickers after the assassination of Colombian Justice Minister Rodrigo Lara Bonilla; of arranging the shipment of cocaine-processing chemicals to Panama for the cartel; of trying to smuggle 1.4 million pounds of marijuana into the US; of accepting a $1-million bribe from traffickers who shipped their drugs through Panama and laundered their money there. Castro was well aware of Noriega's dealings with the Medellin cartel. A frightened Noriega flew to Havana in 1984 to ask Castro to save his ass from the wrath of Medellin drug barons. The traffickers had paid Noriega to protect their labs, yet Panamanian Defence Forces raided one of them. Noriega was in big trouble and begged Castro to mediate the dispute before he got killed. Castro intervened in what Noriega's former aide José Blandon called a $5-million "misunderstanding."

Castro also watched as Carlos Lehder, an infamous leader of the Medellin cartel, become the first Colombian to be extradited to the United States to face drug-trafficking charges. Lehder, an avowed Nazi, boasted he would destroy America with drugs. He was convicted in May 1988 of smuggling 3.3 tons of cocaine into the US in 1979 and 1980, only two years of his lengthy smuggling career. He was sentenced to life in prison and has apparently started singing.

Castro knew the finger would soon point his way. He ordered an investigation of Lieutenant Colonel de la Guardia and others. Investigators found 156 kilograms of cocaine and $1.1 million in cash in iceboxes and under fresh concrete sidewalks at the houses of six officials.

Investigators also turned up evidence that promised to solve an embarrassing political problem that had plagued Fidel Castro for months. General Arnaldo Ochoa Sanchez, one of the most respected military officers in Cuba because of his good treatment of soldiers, had been talking against Cuban involvement in Angola—a war in which Castro had spent most of Cuba's much-needed money. Castro could not let General Ochoa run off at the mouth, but he also couldn't clamp down on him because of the general's popularity. An unfounded, brazen attack on General Ochoa would have prompted a military coup against Castro.

So the dictator was pleased when investigators looking into drug trafficking came up with three charges against Ochoa: using army resources for black-market profiteering while serving in Angola in 1988; stealing $161,000 from Nicaragua's Sandinista army in a fraudulent 1987 arms deal; and plotting to ship Colombian cocaine into the US in 1988.

Several witnesses supported the charge of black-market trading, which was also brought against Lieutenant Colonel de la Guardia—an enterprising Communist, that one. The ripoff of Sandinista money happened in March 1987. General Ochoa, who was head of Cuba's military advisors to Nicaragua from 1982 to 1985, told Sandinista chief of staff General Joaquin Cuadra he could get him American weapons for $161,000. General Ochoa then ordered his aide, Captain José Martinez, to deposit $115,000 of that money into Captain Martinez's personal account in Panama. The rest of the money was paid to a Panamanian middleman who didn't buy guns and didn't return the money. The Sandinistas did receive some East Bloc weapons in 1988, but nothing worth the money they had paid General Ochoa. If the general thought he had made easy money, he was wrong. Sandinista General Cuadra sent a confidential report on the incident to Fidel Castro.

The charge of plotting to set up a drug-smuggling ring against General Ochoa arose out of a scheme he hatched with Lieutenant Colonel de la Guardia, whose brother he had served with in Angola. Lieutenant Colonel de la Guardia was already involved with the Reinaldo Ruiz smuggling operation when he suggested to General Ochoa early in 1988 that he send Captain Martinez to Colombia to make arrangements with the Medellin cartel to help them ship cocaine through Panama and Mexico for a fee. Lieutenant Colonel de la Guardia, who had the power to demand paperwork without anyone questioning him, got a Colombian visa for Captain Martinez.

Major Amado Padron, Lieutenant Colonel de la Guardia's aide, and Captain Martinez met with cartel representatives in Havana in May 1988, to lay the groundwork to the trip. No deal was worked out because Pablo Escobar, who was already entrenched in Panama and Mexico, wanted surface-to-air missiles instead to shoot down drug-enforcement helicopters that were raiding his cocaine-processing laboratories. He also wanted to set up labs in Cuba and Angola. And he wanted assurances he could hide in Cuba if things got too hot elsewhere.

The scheme's failure probably disappointed General Ochoa, who had dreamed, in his own words, of a "really big business, not just a business of kilos." He had planned to have profits laundered by a Panamanian friend who would invest the money in Cuban tourism.

Cuban investigators arrested fourteen Cuban officials on June 12, 1989, three days before Cuba admitted for the first time ever that government and military officials had helped Colombian drug smugglers since 1987 with air drops to boats, by refueling smugglers' planes on military airstrips, and by unloading cocaine from planes.

The fourteen officials were tried quickly and found guilty by a tribunal of forty-nine military officers—one of them was Vice-Admiral Aldo Santamaria, one of the four Cuban officials indicted with Guillot-Lara in 1982. All the indicted officials testified they had committed the acts they were charged with. General Arnaldo Ochoa Sanchez and

Lieutenant Colonel Antonio de la Guardia, and their aides, Captain José Martinez and Major Amado Padron, were executed by firing squad on July 13.

Castro used the trial to rid himself of General Ochoa, whom the military could hardly support, given his confessions to the military tribunal. Castro said he was shocked and horrified that trusted, high-ranking members of his government became involved in drug trafficking.

"While our party was declaring that it had nothing to do with drug trafficking, I was involved in it," General Ochoa said. "I want to tell my comrades-at-arms," he later said before sentencing, "that I believed I betrayed my country and I say, in all honesty, one pays for treason with one's life."

Castro tried to soften his image during the trial by asking the United States to discuss publicly with Cuba ways to prevent drug traffickers from using Cuban airspace, airstrips, and waters to get their drugs to the US.

Two of Castro's former intelligence agents say the Cuban president is lying when he denies knowledge of drugs shipped through Cuba.

Manuel de Beunza is a former major in the Cuban Counter Intelligence Service who risks being assassinated by the Fifth Directorate of State Security in Cuba—which executes officials abroad—for defecting in Canada. De Beunza's first CIS assignment after being recruited in 1965 was in the penetration and infiltration division of the department of state security.

Two years later, he was transferred to the DEM—Special Department of the Ministry of Interior—where he headed a counterintelligence group for a sector. He later graduated from the Mariel Navy Academy as a jet pilot trained in survival and counter-guerrilla warfare.

He worked counterintelligence in Asia, Europe, and Central America and sent coded messages back to Cuba from the ships on which he traveled. Among other assignments, he was ordered to penetrate the intelligence service of Chile and the Israeli Mossad in Denmark, where six Cuban ships were being built.

He fought in Vietnam in 1972. In November 1975, he fought in Angola as a member of the First Battalion of Special Troops. He returned in 1978 to fight in Huambo Luango.

He is a much-decorated soldier of the cold war and real wars. He worked in Section 4-2 of the counterintelligence service and worked in Fidel Castro's support group to operate and establish private companies abroad to by-pass the US trade blockade against Cuba. His rank gave him access to classified information. He said Cuba has been involved in drug trafficking since 1978.

De Beunza was sent to Canada in 1982 to start up and operate a company called Columbus Enterprises for a Panamanian holding company, Elhan Financial Corporation. He was company president from 1982 until June 14, 1987, when he defected.

"I had to report personally to Fidel Castro, once per year, on every activity that we conducted in Canada," he said.

He testified at length before a Senate committee about Cuba's intricate international espionage and drug-smuggling operations.

"The company known as Happy Line was created under the explicit orders of Fidel Castro. Orders were given to Osmany Cienfuegos to file it in Panama to evade the US embargo against Cuba and cooperate with drug-smuggling operations. This shipping line was made up of several ships flying the Panamanian flag, with home base in Cuba at the military port of Mariel, docking at Barlovento in Havana. What better proof can I give you than one of the ships was called *El Delphin, The Dolphin*, bearing the Panamanian flag and Cuban crew and with false Panamanian passports, under Captain Antonio Redondo San Martin.

"These ships brought in things that were otherwise banned under the blockade: computers, software, high technology, and other stuff. Besides, these ships had a role in drug trafficking by meeting at a point in Quitasueno, which is located between Cuba and Panama. There, ships coming from Colombia met, taking the drugs to Cuban ports where it would be turned over for transshipment to Florida. This company . . . has 50 percent of its check holders who belong to Cuba, these are endorsed on the back and are kept in a vault at the Cuban National Bank, and 50 percent belongs to Manuel Antonio Noriega and Carlos Duque of Panama.

"All these events began in 1980-1981, and it all began with this firm. More. This firm was not really a bogus organization as was said during the trial [of Colonel Antonio de la Guardia]. Instead, this firm had professional accountants working for it who were graduates of Cuba's Economics College, and who meticulously kept track of all expenses incurred by the firm.

"I came across this information because I used to take part in so many meetings that took place in Havana relative to several enterprises that belonged to the MC and were managed by Colonel Antonio de la Guardia . . . companies that had been created through holding [companies] and were managed by Cuban personnel—all of them counterintelligence officers. And the objective, I repeat, was to evade the embargo, with the proceeds not being used for the benefit of Cubans. Instead, these monies went to a bank that Cuba has in London, the

Havana International Bank. These funds were used by Castro himself to finance activities such as subversion in Central America, weapons purchases in Europe, help to guerrillas, help to subversives."

De Buenza visited the Soviet submarine base in Riga, USSR, in July 1978:

"In Riga, I met Vice Admiral Pedro Perez Betancourt, who is [now] the chief of the Cuban navy, and who was then the leader of the Cuban mission in Riga, who were at that time learning about the submarines that were about to be handed over to Cuba at that time. I remember that one night, in one of those houses that Russians call *dachas* that Betancourt had available to him, he drank more than his fill and then confided in me that he was feeling bad about the weakness of Aldo Santamaria, who was then the Cuban navy chief." A little political backstabbing here.

"The latter's problem was that he carried out orders given him by Raul Castro in a resentful manner. When we requested to know what kind of activities it was that the Cuban naval chief objected to, we found out that Cuban naval forces work in drug trafficking, providing escort and transshipment for drugs in Cuban waters. It was a big surprise for us to know that by 1978, Cuba was involved in drug trafficking and that it was ordered by Raul Castro.

"I later found out that Colonel Generoso Escudero, chief of the Cienfuegos naval district, a man who had won many decorations, was dismissed and sent to prison due to the fact that during maneuvers carried out by units under his command, some marijuana had been lost, only to wind up in a garbage dump, where some people took it for their personal use. Raul Castro, during the trial against Escudero, dismissed and dishonored this man, who was apparently doing a good job in all orders assigned to him. Even the Cienfuegos Unit was punished. The name Guards' Unit was removed.

"Personnel from Fidel's security also took part in drug trafficking, as you will see in the story I am going to tell you now. Colonel Noel Comesamas, chief, naval section, of Fidel's national security, as he was going in his car, received an emergency call from the Personal Security Unit about something or other in Caleta, or El Caleton, on the southern tip of Cuba, near Cienfuegos. We all went in his car to this unit and the problem was that a small plane had a forced landing and it was loaded with marijuana. The help required was to help the small plane make emergency repairs and keep going in a way that no one knew about it, not even air traffic controllers. When I saw all of this, I asked Colonel Noel Comesamas, and later Lieutenant Colonel Rivero Rivero, second in command at the naval station, who was my classmate at the Mariel Naval Academy, why this type of activity was being sponsored by the Cuban government.

"Their answer was that: 'We follow Fidel's orders to penetrate and addict US youths with drugs to prevent them from thinking, to prevent them from having opinions, to prevent them from speaking, and to keep the population asleep. As Lenin said of religion, that religion is the opium of the people, and so we are giving them real opium.' . . .

"I also met Rodriguez Peralta, who had been a prisoner in Portugal for his part in helping African guerrillas and who, after returning to Cuba, was appointed to the Central Committee and was appointed Chief of Border Patrol for the Interior Ministry. He was also dismissed by Raul Castro for refusing to take part in drug trafficking. Today, Rodriguez Peralta, a former hero of Cuba, is ignored and is out of work and he goes around the streets asking for cigarettes.

"I can also report having personally seen [US fugitive financier] Robert Vesco, who lives in a house in Havana that Fidel gave him, in a place called Barlovento, also called Marina Hemingway. I have also seen Robert Vesco go out fishing with Fidel, using Fidel's own personal yacht, the *Yaguaramas*, and, yes, he lives in Cuba and enjoys all the privileges, as he is one of Fidel's protegées hiding under Fidel's magnanimous protection. . . .

"I was in Saigon. I know that on the day when Saigon's name was changed to Ho Chi Min City, there were Cuban merchant vessels traveling to and from the old American base at Danang to pick up weapons left there by US troops. Those weapons are loaded and on top, they place a load of rice. Those ships did not go through the Panama Canal. Instead, they travel around the tip of Africa to avoid being detected by US. They arrive at Santiago and Mariel, the cargo is handed over to the Americas Committee, headed by Manuel Pineiro.

"Those weapons are later sent by barges to all those guerrillas in Central America. They are ready, if detected, to dump their entire cargo to the bottom of the ocean, later to declare that they were lost at sea as defined by international maritime law. They could claim that they came near the coastline to pick up their route to be able to continue. They do this in Cuba all the time to prevent being caught transporting Soviet rifles and weapons.

"Fidel trains many soldiers to go join guerrillas in Central America. The main training area is in Guanabo, also known as the zero point. All this training in survival and terrorism, including indiscriminate killing, is taken by Raul and Fidel nonchalantly. . . .

"Those of us who know Fidel intimately, who carried out so many missions, know that Fidel is knowledgeable of all the evil that is carried out—the terrorism that he has exported to Latin America, drug trafficking—and all of that because of greed for money.

"The firm he had in Canada was ordered to obtain all the items he had a liking for. And this firm had several bank accounts for that purpose. And that is the money used for all his personal tastes. That is how, when Brezhnev died, I received a call in the early hours of the morning from Cuba and I was ordered to purchase the coat, gloves, and hat for Fidel to wear at Brezhnev's funeral in Moscow. And not only for Fidel, but also for fifty other high-ranking officials in Cuba. I asked how soon they needed all those items and they told me everything had to be in Cuba in forty-eight hours because Brezhnev's funeral was not going to wait for coats. I left home for the Cuban consulate hoping that they would have sent me all the needed measurements for all those coats. All that could be done was to make a factory stop all other work and work on this order. And that was how it was eventually done.

"The coats did not leave on a regular Cubana Airlines flight. Instead, they sent Fidel's executive airplane, which came for no other purpose. That is how Fidel spent some $100,000. That is not unusual. When Fidel wants to eat fried rice, he sends for cans of Chinese bean sprouts to be sent to Cuba on the next flight of Cubana Airlines.

"On weekends, when Fidel was going fishing and his hooks broke or had no camera to take pictures of himself on the boat, I was called regardless of the hour in the night to go and buy the things and to send them on the next flight of Cubana de Aviacion. One time he was going hunting. I was ordered to buy refrigerators for Fidel Castro. His bill for dog shampoo and dog medicine was $5,000 per month.... Fidel's favorite [drink] is Royal Salute, which is twenty-one-year-old Chivas Regal. In private conversations, Fidel would boast that he did not drink Chivas Regal twelve years as long as he can get the older one.

"Aside, Fidel has accused Ochoa of trafficking in diamonds. But in reality, Fidel himself has created a corporation through Osmany Cienfuegos. That company ... operating in Angola, was managed by [a Cuban Army] captain and it looted Angola. Using diplomatic pouches, diamonds and precious stones leave, bound for London. This loot is received in London by [many] firms. . . . Angolan coffee was brought to Cuba. It was repacked and later resold as Cuban coffee.

"Fidel has created . . . [a] firm which is based in Los Angeles, California, and in Panama. US-made movies are transferred onto video cassettes, dubbed, and then sold freely for foreign exchange. One of his firms . . . based in Mexico City—used to send US-made movies to Cuba. Copies are made and then distributed among the Cuban elite. These movies are shown in seven viewing rooms run by the Cuban Institute of Film—ICAIC—with headquarters on 23rd and 12th. Fidel has a private screening room.

"Once again the blockade is evaded.

"It is impossible that Fidel did not know what Antonio de la Guardia and other Panama operatives were doing. The same is true of his Mexico operatives, and again true of his operatives in other places. Let us remember that he has a firm in Japan . . . that does smuggling of all kinds, such as counterfeiting and blank passports to enable terrorists and spies to be deployed to different places. I remember that the chief of Economic Police used to travel to Mexico, to deal in gold and precious stones. All kinds of changes are made in Panama. They have stores in the Free Trade Zone. They engage in all sorts of transportation of goods done through their personnel in USA and in Florida—all working to evade the embargo.

"[General] Efigenio Amejeiras was also among the forty-nine generals who would sit in judgment of Ochoa. What embarrassment. Ochoa must have felt pretty bad when he learned that Efigenio Amejeiras was one of his judges, because Amejeiras had been censured by Castro during the sixties. . . . Also sitting in judgment was Vice-Admiral Aldo Santamaria, who refused to involve naval units in drug trafficking and who had a suicide attempt over this issue and who is sought by US justice for drug trafficking.

"Cuban intelligence has Section K. Its business is checking and double checking. This section is charged with keeping track of enemy agents and also to check on the Cuban military. It routinely investigates all high-ranking officers in the Armed Forces and Ministry of the Interior to see if anyone spends beyond their official salaries, what opinion they have of Fidel's speeches, what opinion they have concerning the USSR, international issues. They routinely check the license plates of automobiles visiting their houses, the correspondence they receive, and so many other things. The purpose is to know all there is to know about the loyalty of officials.

"Fidel is lying when he says he was not aware of what de la Guardia was doing in Panama. . . . How is it possible that intelligence didn't know and didn't detect conversations with speedboats that talk to Cuba radio, that talk to the planes that could bomb places in Cuba? How is it that planes could fly undetected over Cuba without all the sophisticated radar systems not registering their path? . . . Counterintelligence in Cuba works systematically to know of every move—to follow about not just officers of the Ministry of the Interior, but civilians as well. Anyone handling a lot of money, doing business abroad, going in and out of the country with contracts and contacts in foreign countries, is consistently under surveillance.

"It is important to note that all information regarding Cuban high officials reaches the Castro brothers every morning, as is everything that is summarized in press bulletins, as well. There are also political bulletins that never reach any newspapers, prepared by the Ministry of the Interior. This covers people who have been killed, criminal activities, rapes, robberies, etc. . . . it even includes jokes against the regime and Fidel. . . .

"There is great dissatisfaction within the Ministry of the Interior and within the Armed Forces because everyone is aware of the corruption inside and the style of life that the higher officials can attain. There are state secrets such as Fidel's being married and Raul having been divorced from Vilma Espin and married to a Bulgarian. There is the sheer fact that they preach communism and socialism and live like bourgeois. . . . The true drug traffickers, no matter how much they want to cover it up, are Fidel and Raul Castro Ruz."

Oscar Valdez, a Cuban who defected in Canada in May 1986, worked twenty-five years for the Cuban government in England, Canada, Czechoslovakia, and in Africa. He traveled extensively though South America, the Middle East, and Africa on clandestine missions monitoring military operations.

His brother is Ramiro Valdez, Cuba's former Minister of the Interior, one of the most powerful men in Castro's government. The link gave him access to information and highly placed friends in government and the military. He defected while president of a company in Canada that Castro had set up to evade the US trade embargo against Cuba. He explained to a Senate committee Cuba's involvement in drug trafficking.

"We have heard and we have read the accusations that Castro has made against Arnaldo Ochoa implicating him in drug trafficking. Fidel Castro says that drug trafficking began in Cuba in 1987. . . . These actions that Fidel Castro says that began in 1987 actually began in the five years between 1975 and 1980. In those years I made several missions to Latin America and on one of those I saw Ambassador [Fernando] Ravelo, who was then ambassador of Cuba to Colombia, make contact with drug traffickers in Colombia. Amongst those traffickers was Pablo Escobar Gaviria. . . . Also, in Cuba I personally saw drug traffickers that I had seen previously in Colombia. One of the venues that is most used by the drug traffickers is a place where cockfighting takes place and this is owned by a man by the name of Guillermos Frias.

"I was also president of a company called Mercuriu—Mercury—in Cuba. The principal of this firm, its president, was a man by the name of Ramon Cuenca Montoto and he was located in Panama. This company is owned 50 percent by Castro and 50 percent by Manuel Noriega. The

front in Panama for this company, for the company called Mercuriu, is
Carlos Duque and Carlos Wilkinson.

"This man Duque was the contact between Fidel Castro and Manuel
Pineiro, who was the man in charge of Central America. He was chief of
the Central American Department. He is still chief today of the Central
Committee. Mr. Pineiro is Fernando Ravelo's boss. Fernando Ravelo is
the ambassador of Nicaragua [in July 1989]. He is also Ramon Cuencau's
boss, as well as the boss of Jésus Albesu, who is presently in the embassy
here in the United States.

"We have been watching Fidel Castro trying to implicate General
Arnaldo Ochoa, Tony de la Guardia, Martinez, and Amado Padron in
international drug trafficking—placing all the responsibility upon these
members of the Armed Forces and of MININ [Ministry of the Interior]
who, according to Fidel Castro, are the drug traffickers who utilize
Cuba, Cuba's airports, Cuban navy warships, border patrols, and all
necessary means belonging to Cuba in order to pursue their lust for
profits, their lust for riches, accusing these men of being corrupt and
immoral.

"Those of us who understand perfectly how entities such as the State
Security System function, who know what surveillance and control
methods are used by MINFAR [Ministry of the Armed Forces] and
MININ, can state that it is impossible for any narcotics trafficking to go
on without the explicit consent and knowledge of Fidel and Raul Castro.
For those who know what life is like in Cuba, for those who know that
people there live under a Communist regime, of the Fidel and Raul brand
of Communism, in a country where you cannot make one move either at
work nor at home, not even in your own private life without the state
entities knowing about it. That is why the so-called Committees for the
Defence of the Revolution are constantly in surveillance. That is why at
the workplace there are Surveillance Committees, all of which make up a
structured system in which the slightest movement on your part has to be
reported to your superiors, and subsequently in the chain of reporting, it
ends up on Fidel and Raul's desk. . . .

"I'd like to mention what I know and personally saw, at the onset of
the beginning of the narcotics traffic operations between Cuba and
Colombia. In the years between 1975 and 1980, the Colombian Ambassador was a Mr. Fernando Ravelo. I was present in the embassy of
Colombia in Cuba when a group of drug traffickers began to establish
relations with Ambassador Ravelo. The embassy headquarters in Cuba
was the center for contacts for Fernando Ravelo. He followed instructions from Fidel Castro to begin to set up a drug-trafficking network.

"I have personal knowledge of this because I was in the Colombian embassy with the then commercial attaché, Orlando Guillen. He pointed out some of the drug traffickers that were there, amongst whom was Pablo Escobar Gaviria. . . . Fidel Castro had established contacts to initiate drug contraband operations using Cuba as the intermediary point in order to introduce drugs into the United States.

"As you know, the government of the United States has indicted three Cuban officials for drug trafficking. They are Fernando Ravelo, Aldo Santamaria, and René Cruz. Throughout this entire trial [of General Ochoa], in which Fidel Castro tried to clean up his image and tried to implicate other people in the drug smuggling, at no time did he mention that these three were the three men who began drug trafficking in Cuba.

"Subsequent to these contacts that I observed being made together with Mr. Fernando Ravelo and the drug traffickers in Colombia, I myself saw some of these drug traffickers again. I saw Mr. Gaviria and his cousin called Escobar in Cuba several times involved in the purchase of livestock, according to take them to Colombia. I also saw them in Cuba at cockfights in a special arena . . . in a city called Managua.

"This place is custom built with all luxuries imaginable, featuring precious woods, stained glass, air conditioning, with all the comforts, luxuries, and amenities found in a place built for cockfights. Escobar's cousin was a frequent visitor to Cuba with the excuse of buying livestock and fighting cocks to take to Colombia.

"The Cuban officials that worked at that time in the embassy, as well as the commercial office, have knowledge of the activities that were going on at that time in Colombia. The American Department of Central Committee of the Party, which is under the direction of Mr. Manuel Pineiro, also known as Red Beard, was well aware of the activities of drug trafficking initiated by Fidel Castro. . . .

"Fidel had to eliminate Arnaldo Ochoa—he was a political danger to Fidel Castro because Arnaldo Ochoa was a leader to many because of his concern for the men under his command. Arnaldo Ochoa had the courage to say to Raul Castro that they were wrong about the war in Angola, that they were wrong about the wars they were fighting in other African countries, that they were wrong about the guerrillas that Fidel Castro's Cuban revolution was subsidizing in Central and South America. That is why in the first speech that Raul Castro refers to this matter he states that if Arnaldo Ochoa had shown more cooperation none of this would have happened. And indeed, a more cooperative attitude would have been shown on the part of Arnaldo Ochoa if he had continued to serve Fidel and Raul Castro in their thirst for power and their conceited pretenses of intervention in world affairs.

"If there had been no political problem and if it had only [been] a drug problem, then truly, it would not have been necessary to shoot Arnaldo

Ochoa, Tony de la Guardia, Martinez, and Amado Padron. No one is going to be shot for involvement in drug trafficking, least of all in Cuba. The Cuban Penal Code stipulates fifteen-year jail terms for offenders. Fidel could not afford to send Ochoa to jail because Ochoa had become a living idol, as well as Fidel's greatest political competitor.

"We are not saying that Arnaldo Ochoa was not involved in drug trafficking. . . . We are simply not able to believe that Raul and Fidel Castro did not know about those activities because we personally saw how contact with drug traffickers began. . . .

"It is simply impossible for the brothers Castro not to know that airplanes were dropping their loads of drugs into Cuban waters. . . . And we know that Fidel's obsession is to prevent an attack, be it by air or sea. Besides the high sophistication of Cuba's radar systems, Cuba has highly proficient personnel manning those systems—personnel specially trained in the USSR. . . .

"Those firms in Panama were created by Fidel Castro and Tony de la Guardia with the cover-up that we have explained [through holding companies and shields to do an end run around the US embargo]. Fidel saw in those firms the cover-up he needed to organize his drug-trafficking networks because those companies were able to go around with impunity and were able to ship any merchandise to Cuba without anybody objecting. That is where Fidel saw an opportunity to introduce drug trafficking. . . .

"The same firms are also able to cover up Fidel's links to Noriega. Because when Noriega had problems with the Medellin cartel, where did he get help? Noriega went to see Fidel Castro. Why? Because Fidel is a business partner in the drug trade. Both were doing business with the Medellin cartel and no one was in a better position to help than his business partner, especially one who knew the Medellin cartel so well."

Narco-Traficante/Narco-Terrorist

The *narco-traficantes* in Colombia, Bolivia, and Peru have established an alternative economy without national or ideological boundaries. Communist guerrilla groups in all countries have set aside their anti-capitalist beliefs to reap the monetary benefits of dealing with *narco-traficantes* by acting as bodyguards or by protecting their cocaine-processing laboratories. They also exact heavy duties from coca farmers, processors, and anyone in the narcotics business who crosses their path under the guise of equitably distributing the wealth. They claim to use the money to advance their Communist ideals—terrorist dreams built on healthy capitalist narco-dollars.

Colombia is the best example of why gun controls don't work. It is one of the most difficult countries in the world in which to obtain a permit to own guns. Yet every criminal from Barranquilla to Bogotá—including thousands of pre-teen hit men—has access to submachine guns, or high-powered semi-automatic pistols, which are illegal in Colombia. Gun controls are made to keep firearms out of the hands of innocent bystanders, victims. Criminals don't care if the law says you can't own a gun. They understand only one thing: bullets. So they strive to make sure they have more fire power than the next guy.

Drug traffickers in Colombia go to great lengths to obtain weapons, their favorite being compact assault pistols, high-powered handguns, and assault rifles. The guns of choice among narco-assassins—the *sicarios*—are American-made MAC-10s or MAC-11s. The three Colombian presidential candidates assassinated during the 1989 election campaign were gunned down with RPB MAC-10s or MAC-11s. The motorcycle hit teams also prefer these guns to mow down judges, journalists, and government officials. The favorite assault rifle among drug traffickers is the Colt AR-15, although guerrillas seem to be getting their hands on Chinese-made AK-47s and American-made Ruger Mini-14s, all of which are chambered for .223-caliber cartridges.

Colombia's violent, blood-splattered history belies the tendency to blame the last decade of violence on drugs. Drugs were a contributing factor in the ungodly 22,468 murders in 1990, but Colombians are merely continuing a long tradition of bloodletting. Where else in the world can you find "violentologists"—students of violence?

The violence in Colombia today has its roots in a horrible era called *la violencia*—the years between 1949 and 1958 when the liberal and conservative parties declared war on each other. Colombia traditionally has been a two-party state, with political issues being black or white. Only with the recent recognition of a Communist party have Colombians started to look at the grays in between. Colombians take their politics seriously. More than 135,000 people were killed during *la violencia*. Colombians who chose not to fight for either side were still involved in the battle. They formed self-defense paramilitary groups called *autodefensas* to protect themselves from the warring political factions. More than 100 *autodefensas* exist today.

During the ten years of fighting, the Colombian government had no control over the country, its people, or the economy. The military justifiably seized power in 1953 and ran the country while forcing the liberals and conservatives to hammer out their differences. The military handed the reins of power over to a provisional government founded on compromise in 1957. To this day, that government has been unable to fully take control of Colombia. The government exercises its power only in the cities. The rest of the country belongs to roving bands of

Communist guerrillas, paramilitary groups such as the *autodefensas*, and *narco-traficantes* and their private armies. Colombian courts have little power. Fear of death prevents judges from acting against the *narco-traficantes*. The army can't wander too far off the beaten path because Communist guerrillas and paramilitary groups control the countryside.

Today, the bombings and assassinations of judges, politicians, government officials, journalists, and rival drug traffickers in Colombia make the prohibition-era gangster wars in Chicago look like child's play.

Until 1981, Colombia's *narco-traficantes* had indulged in vigilante attacks by setting loose their motorcycle hit men and right-wing goons, but had not considered more widespread and organized terror campaigns. They were content to sit back and enjoy their illegal and rapidly growing wealth. That changed with the kidnapping on November 12, 1981, of Fabio Ochoa Restrepo's twenty-six-year-old daughter, Marta, by the leftist Colombian Movimiento 19 de Abril—the April 19th Movement, more popularly known as M-19. The Marxist guerrilla group, formed in 1973, has about 2,000 violent members with links to Cuba, Nicaragua, and Libya. The M-19 kidnappers demanded $12 million from the cocaine-rich Ochoas for Marta's return.

Until that day, wealthy traffickers had silently paid ransoms to guerrilla groups who financed their operations by kidnapping and extorting payments from cocaine farmers and traffickers. The kidnapping prompted 223 major *narco-traficantes* in the Medellin area, who really were the new landed gentry trying to protect their properties, to meet with their military allies and create a formidable death squad that has executed hundreds, if not thousands, of left-leaning Colombians. The meeting also gave birth to the Medellin cartel.

The cartel called its army MAS—Muerte a Secuestradores, Death to Kidnappers—and announced through leaflets dropped from a plane into a Cali soccer stadium three weeks later that MAS would start slaughtering Communist guerrillas who leeched their money from hardworking Colombians "like us, who have brought progress and jobs to Colombia."

MAS squads were so well-organized that they captured M-19 guerrillas within days. The shaken leftist group quickly released Ochoa's daughter. That didn't appease the power-hungry cartel leaders. They viewed all leftists, whether socialist or Communist, as a threat to their existence. The military members of the MAS death squads—fifty-nine army officers were suspected of belonging to the group initially—were more than happy to be turned loose to slaughter those who made the drug barons uncomfortable. They shot lawyers, university professors, union and peasant leaders.

Then Gonzalo Rodriguez Gacha and Pablo Escobar Gaviria enlisted the support of MAS to clear out Communists from an area where they were buying land—the Middle Magdalena valley in the Magdalena River basin in north-central Colombia. The group they wanted expelled from the region was called FARC—the Colombian Armed Revolutionary Group, the oldest Communist guerrilla group in South America, formed in 1966 when rebel peasants joined the Communist Party. FARC's estimated 7,000 members are violent and connected to Cuba, Nicaragua, and Libya. The Colombian army gradually defeated FARC guerrillas, forcing the movement's thirty-nine fronts to settle in sparsely inhabited parts of the country. In the north, the guerrillas extorted money from wealthy ranchers and farmers.

Escobar, Rodriguez Gacha, and other cartel leaders bought land in the Middle Magdalena valley that had been abandoned by the fearful ranchers. (*Narco-traficantes* have bought an estimated 2.5 million acres of agricultural land in Colombia and revived the country's farming industry.) At the same time, Lieutenant Colonel Alvaro Hernan Velandia led counterinsurgency troops though the area to wipe out FARC. Velandia was also a member of MAS. It didn't take long for the ranchers' anger, the military's blood lust and MAS's streak of violence, all underwritten by the cocaine wealth of the cartel leaders, to drive FARC out of the valley.

FARC settled in Colombia's Amazon Valley in the southeast. When Bolivian and Peruvian coca farmers failed to meet growing demands as cocaine became the North American drug of choice in the late 1970s, peasant farmers moved into the area to grow less potent, but just as desirable, coca plants. These operations were underwritten by the cartel, which hired workers to clear swaths in the jungle, which they turned into coca farms. They also supplied plantation owners with the chemicals to make coca paste. It didn't take long for the old egalitarian commies to sense a potential cause—and a source of money. FARC guerrillas moved in and fixed salaries for plantation and coca pit workers. They took their cut from the plantation owners, as they did for all crops in their area. They also exacted a 10 percent tax from cartel workers shipping drugs through FARC territory.

FARC allegedly stopped its terrorist activities in 1984 when it signed a peace agreement with the government of Belisario Betancur. The deal allowed FARC to form a leftist political party called U.P.—Union Patriotica. More than 600 of its members have been killed by cartel *sicarios* since 1984.

The cartel war against the U.P. is being waged for financial reasons. The cartel leaders can't tolerate paying taxes and high salaries for plantation workers in southeast Colombia, knowing the money is funding FARC and U.P., whose political stances are anathema to the outright capitalist posture assumed by drug traffickers. They are funding their worst political enemies. On top of that, the drastic drop in price of a kilo of cocaine, from $55,000 in 1983 to $11,000 in 1990 in Florida, prompted the cartels to cut the expense of dealing with FARC.

Once again, the cartels and the army joined forces to clear the commies out of the coca patch. They killed eight U.P. members. In retaliation, FARC killed six members of the cocaine-dealing Plata family, which had contracted with Gonzalo Rodriguez Gacha. Government prosecutors allege that Rodriguez Gacha paid $120,000 for the murder of Jaime Pardo Leal, head of U.P., in October 1987. Ironically, Carlos Lehder's right-wing Latin Nationalist Movement (MLN) had supported the Communist Leal in the May 1986 presidential election because he opposed the extradition treaty with the United States.

Carlos Enrique Lehder Rivas, the most radical of the Medellin cartel's leaders, is the *narco-traficante* most closely associated with the term narco-terrorist. The US Drug Enforcement Administration calls Lehder the Gadhafi of international cocaine traffickers.

"Coca has been transformed into a revolutionary weapon for the struggle against American imperialism. The Achilles heel of imperialism are the *estimulantes* of Colombia. . . . The Third World's atomic bomb" is how Lehder described cocaine.

"He hoped that by flooding [the US] with cocaine, it would disrupt the political system," said a former Lehder acquaintance, George Jung.

Lehder embodied his nationalistic, Nazi-worshipping, cross-bred ideals in a political party that espoused the extreme elements of both the right and left ends of the political spectrum: the Latin Nationalist Movement (MLN). Lehder, who said Hitler was "the greatest warrior of all time," attracted thousands of supporters who believe in the superiority of the Latin race. His politics appeal to the anti-imperialist Communist extremists, the nationalistic right wing of the military, and the racist in all. He pleased the military with talk of a 500,000-man army to keep Americans out of Colombia and away from the source of their strength—cocaine. He also suggested a military alliance among South American countries—a southern hemisphere counterpart to the North Atlantic Treaty Organization.

Lehder, the consummate pragmatist, even flirted with leaders of the leftist M-19 movement, whose guerrillas he used as bodyguards, even though the MLN political platform opposed Communism, as well as imperialism, neocolonialism, and Zionism. It was expedient for the facist MLN to support Communist candidate Jaime Pardo Leal's election bid. Lehder had good reason to fear the extradition treaty. Shortly before the Colombian Supreme Court overturned it in June 1987, he became the first *narco-traficante* extradited to the United States to face drug charges.

Lehder, like Fidel Castro, supported the M-19 movement and strove to corrupt America with drugs. When US pressure forced his smuggling operation off Norman's Cay, then Andros Island in the Bahamas in 1983 and 1984, and as political pressure against traffickers mounted in Colombia after the Medellin cartel-ordered assassination of the country's minister of justice in 1984, Fidel Castro allowed him to set up cocaine-processing labs on a military base in Cuba.

Pablo Escobar, the most powerful leader of the Medellin cartel, also curried favor with Castro by financially supporting the M-19 movement and the Sandinistas in Nicaragua. His operation on Cayo Piedra, a tiny island north of Cuba, was protected by the Cuban navy. The Cuban air force flew him to Nicaragua. Escobar was easy with his easy money. He sent the M-19 movement 1,000 Czech pistols for Christmas in 1984.

Other cartel leaders were quick to publicly dissociate themselves from Lehder's views, even though they supported them privately. Threats to overthrow the existing system were not the best way to endear themselves to the government and army. Pablo Escobar said in the newspaper *Medellin Civico*: "I share with them [FARC] a desire for a Colombia with more social equality for all, but I do not agree with their plans to obtain power by means of weapons, because to achieve power there exists a democratic system, faithfully watched over by our army, guardian of the constitution, and of the laws of the Republic."

Of course he'd say that. The cartel controls the existing government, army, court, and police systems through corruption and intimidation. Why change a good thing for the sake of change?

In secret meetings in Panama with two Colombian representatives in 1984, Medellin cartel leaders—including Pablo Escobar and Gonzalo Rodriguez Gacha, who spoke for the top 100 cocaine traffickers in their group—made it clear that unlike Carlos Lehder, they had no affinity with guerrilla organizations. "We have no connection, nor do we accept any such connection, with armed guerrillas. Our activities have never been intended to replace the democratic and republican form of government," the traffickers said in a communiqué. An outright lie.

The following year, the Medellin cartel hired M-19 guerrillas for $4 million to storm the palace of justice in Bogotá and destroy all files on 200 cartel members. The guerrillas took 300 hostages when police trapped them in the building. It took Colombian soldiers and police twenty-eight hours in a siege that started on November 7, 1985, to re-

take the government building. During the fighting, forty M-19 guerrillas, eleven Supreme Court justices, thirty-nine other hostages, and
seventeen soldiers and security guards were killed.

Unlike Colombia and Bolivia, the drug trade in Peru is not controlled by
cartels or even local *narco-traficantes*. Bolivia, the Andean country most
dependent on coca production, produces one-third of the world's coca
leaves, mostly in the Chapare Valley. The business pumps $300 million
into the country's economy every year and employs 250,000 people.
     Peru is a breadbasket for the Colombian cartels whose middlemen buy
the coca paste made by peasants in the Upper Huallaga Valley—200
miles long and 30 to 40 miles wide on the eastern foothills of the Andes.
More than one-half of the world's coca leaves are produced in the valley,
bringing $500 million to $700 million in foreign exchange into the
country every year. Much as in Colombia, rebels have learned to fund
their revolutionary movement by exacting a percentage from the 60,000
peasant families growing coca and producing paste, and by collecting a
tax from the buyers of coca paste. In return, the rebels protect the
farmers from US-sponsored coca-eradication teams and cartel armies.
     The Maoist Sendero Luminoso (Shining Path) rebels moved into the
Upper Huallaga Valley in 1984 after carefully studying the Communist
takeover of Vietnam. The valley, much like the Vietnamese terrain,
offers them a forest canopy under which they can roam unobserved on
their systematic raids against local and state government institutions. In a
sense, they are like the Khmer Rouge in Cambodia. They use whatever
weapon is at hand to fight for their cause—in this case, cocaine—but
warn peasants that once the war is won, they must abandon the dirty task
of producing drugs. The Sendero Luminoso, formed in 1969 as an
offshoot of the Communist party of Peru by professors at Huamanga
University in Ayacucho, has about 7,000 members who aren't aligned
with rebels in other countries. Their goal is to agitate the peasants into
overthrowing the government.

Shooty-Shooty, Bang-Bang

Though arms-smuggling rings exist, most guns that reach Colombia do
so on a piecemeal basis. Many Colombian visitors to the United States
pay for their trip by buying a gun and selling it for a huge profit on their
return home. More organized gun traffickers use straw purchasers—
Americans who can legally buy guns—to buy dozens, sometimes hundreds, of guns at different stores. The gun used to kill the Union
Patriotica candidate for the Colombian presidency, Bernardo Jaramillo,
on March 22, 1990, was legally bought by a man in southern Florida.

Traffickers find ways to get the guns to Colombia. Sometimes they use established smuggling routes that funnel everything from watches to refrigerators to heavy equipment. Sometimes they hide the guns in appliances, electronic equipment, or scuba tanks.

Traffickers also steal guns from shipments intended for the Colombian military or police. French-made missiles destined for the Colombian Air Force were found during the raid on a *narco-traficante*'s estate in February 1990.

Most of the Colombian *narco-traficante* guns used to kill presidential candidates, judges, government officials, police officers, and journalists are bought in southern Florida. Firearms traffickers fly to Miami from South America on a morning flight. They rent a car at the airport using a Florida driver's license obtained during a previous trip or stop at the driver's license bureau to get one. Then they drive to a gun shop, falsify a federal firearms form, and return in seventy-two hours to pick up their guns. They leave town quickly, before the gun shop informs the Bureau of Alcohol, Tobacco and Firearms about their huge purchase. You can stand in front of any gun shop in Miami and watch Colombians in rental cars pull up all day long.

The easiest way for traffickers to get the guns out of the United States, believe it or not, is to stuff them into checked luggage at the airport. Most airlines don't X-ray checked luggage. However, the problems in Colombia have prompted Avianca Airlines to X-ray checked luggage. Other arms smugglers hide their contraband in cargo. A Venezuelan man tried to smuggle handguns out of Miami in scuba tanks. A Colombian hid guns in a crate labeled "auto parts." Though many freight companies don't ship guns, they don't X-ray cargo and depend on the honesty of the shipper. Every day, hundreds of shipping containers are put aboard ships headed for South America at the Miami Seaport, Port Everglades in Fort Lauderdale, and the seaport in West Palm Beach. A former police officer from the Virgin Islands hid twenty-five small-caliber pistols in a car he shipped home from Florida.

Guns used by Communist insurgents come from a wide variety of sources. As a gesture of goodwill, the Communist M-19 guerrillas surrendered guns to the Colombian government. Among them were twenty-five M-16 machine guns lost in Vietnam, three M-16 machine guns lost from US bases in the United States, and one M-16 machine gun sold to the government of Nicaragua.

There is no limit to the ways *narco-traficantes* and Communist guerrillas get guns, ammunition, and other weapons.

A few days before President George Bush met with Andean country leaders at the drug summit in Cartagena, Colombia, in February 1990, Colombian Ramiro Suarez Gomez was arrested by agents of the Miami

ATF, the US Secret Service, and the FBI. They had chased Suarez since 1987. During that time, he bought more than 300 semi-automatic rifles in gun shops from Miami to Daytona to Tampa using false names, addresses, and places of birth. He shipped the guns in air freight from Miami to Cartagena to fictitious names. He then returned to Cartagena, assumed the fictitious names, and picked up the guns. When finally arrested in Miami, he had nine assault rifles broken down and packaged, $30,000 cash, a tool to erase the serial numbers on the guns, and ledgers detailing his gun purchases and expenses. The guns had all been bought by Colombian drug traffickers.

A Colombian citizen and his two Colombian-American brothers were arrested in Houston, Texas, trying to ship thirty M-1 carbine receivers and two handguns to Colombia on a domestic airline. The cargo was hidden in radios, television sets, and stereos.

A Colombian and two Latinos used a woman four months pregnant to falsify documents to buy and receive ten Uzi rifles and ten AR-15 rifles to ship to Colombia.

A Colombian and an Italian bought more than 100 AR-15s and grenades in Los Angeles for the Cali cartel and shipped them on Avianca Airlines to Colombia hidden in stuffed animals and toys.

A Guatemalan bought twenty-seven AR-15 rifles in Los Angeles and illegally exported them to Colombia. Five rifles were seized in a jungle cocaine lab by the Colombian National Police. Another was surrendered by an M-19 guerrilla.

Although there has been much speculation, there is little fact to support the theory that the Soviet Union is behind the drugging of America. Colombian entrepreneurs started drug trafficking on their own. They didn't shelter their operations in Cuban and Nicaraguan territory until interdiction pressure by the US forced them to. To extend their smuggling networks through these countries before it was necessary would have cost them needlessly in payoffs to officials. Castro and other anti-American governments used traffickers only after they had established their business ties to North America and needed safe harbors near the US to continue their operations.

Cuba was a conduit for narcotics into the United States long before Castro deposed the Batista regime. Charles (Lucky) Luciano and other mobsters funneled their southeast Asian heroin into Florida through Cuba, which was the mob's playground. They used Cuba for the same reasons the Colombians do—it is only ninety miles from the American border.

General Jan Sejna was secretary of the Czechoslovakia Defense Council and chief of staff in the Ministry of Defense in that country before Soviet tanks rolled through the streets of Prague in the spring of 1968. Sejna fled and sought political asylum in the United States. He said he attended a meeting of Warsaw Pact leaders chaired by Soviet Premier Nikita Khrushchev in 1962. Krushchev said Warsaw Pact countries should sell drugs to western nations to fill their coffers and destabilize western societies.

Many people would like to believe this statement. The only problem is that drugs were not a major problem in North America at the time. Although there were heroin addicts, no one foresaw the mass epidemic of drug use that began in the mid to late 1960s among North American youth. No one foresaw the marijuana boom or the cocaine boom. No one dreamed of crack cocaine or ice. And in 1962, Soviet satellite countries such as Bulgaria and Hungary were not on everyone's smuggling route.

The defection of Bulgarian KDS Colonel Stefan Sverdlev in 1971 added a bit more weight to the argument that the Soviet Union was behind a plot to drug the west. The KDS is the Bulgarian Committee for State Security. Sverdlev said a KDS directive dated July 16, 1970, was drafted in 1967 after the heads of Warsaw Pact security services met in Moscow. The directive discussed various ways to destabilize western countries. One of those methods was drugs. The only documented evidence that a Soviet Bloc country has been involved in drug smuggling involves Kintex, the Bulgarian state trading organization. Kintex has been exposed as a smuggler of both drugs and weapons.

Western intelligence services have spent billion of dollars and countless manpower years gathering information on the Soviet Union and its allied countries. They have been quick to sound the alarm whenever they perceive a threat to the west.

Not one intelligence agency can provide a shred of evidence that the Soviet Union is involved in a plot to drug North America. Many experts are quick to claim they must be. There is no need for such "experts" in the world of intelligence. Fact, not fiction, must rule.

Part III

I SPY . . .

9

Good Guy, Bad Guy:
The fine gray line

This is the story of a chubby good old boy who done good by doing bad with more balls than brains; it is also the story of a plane and the changing shadows it cast on the Central American landscape; but most of all, it is a sad tale of political opportunism that gnaws away at the judicial system and prevents law enforcement from putting the grab on bad guys.

Good guy, bad guy. The distinction between them is sometimes a fine gray line and those who tread it are the most treacherous of all.

Adler Berriman (Barry) Seal, a former Green Beret and commercial pilot bored out of his shady southern tree, took to flying dope into the United States for a kick and some easy millions somewhere near the end of the disco decade. He had quite a business going, and more than a few airplane companies in the backwater of Mena, Arkansas, paid their bills retrofitting his planes with such necessities of long-range flight as rubber bladders to hold extra fuel. Mind you, the hippies that preceded Seal in the business used waterbeds laid on the bottom of the plane and weighed down with bales of marijuana to force fuel to the engines. But Seal was a modern-day smuggler accustomed to the finer things in life— like $500,000 and up for every trip he made. In the two years before this story really starts, Barry Seal made at least fifty trips from Colombia to the United States during which he smuggled more than 10,000 kilograms of cocaine for Jorge Ochoa, Pablo Escobar, Carlos Slater, Gonzalo Rodriguez Gacha, and other Medellin cartel members.

One day, Seal started having problems with his luck. On April 26, 1983, Drug Enforcement Administration agents in Fort Lauderdale arrested him on cocaine charges in Operation Screamer. In the hiatus between this traumatic event in his life and the next stroke of bad luck, fate started shifting around all the little gizmos that figured in the following two years of Seal's life.

On June 17, 1983, Roy Stafford of Jacksonville, Florida, bought a Fairchild C-123K, tail number N4410F, from the United States Air Force. On July 12, 1983, Stafford registered the C-123K with the Federal Aviation Administration. On August 16, 1983, he sold the C-123K to Doan Helicopter, Inc., of Daytona Beach, Florida. On the same day, Harry Doan registered the C-123K with the FAA for Doan Helicopter, Inc.

Then, another stroke of bad luck for Seal. In February 1984, he was convicted by jury trial in Fort Lauderdale on a methaqualone charge. Seal knew he'd do time so he devised a scheme to postpone the inevitable. On March 9, 1984, he registered a Lockheed Lodestar (N513V) with the FAA. The twin-engine plane can carry 6,000 to 7,000 pounds.

The plane hadn't been registered for twenty-four hours when once again, fate shoved means and opportunities in Seal's direction. On March 10, Colombian police, following signals from electronic beepers the DEA had hidden in drums of ether bought by the Medellin cartel in the US, raided the Tranquilandia (land of tranquility) complex of nineteen cocaine-processing laboratories, serviced by three airstrips, that the cartel believed invulnerable in the deep jungle of the Coquita Province 400 miles southeast of Bogotá. The complex had a dormitory for eighty workers equipped with a dishwasher, refrigerator, orange and white flush toilets made of Italian marble, a microwave oven, a Betamax video recorder, and a library of pornographic magazines for horny hombres. Chickens and pigs were flown in daily to feed the workers. As many as 1,000 people worked on the complex, which could produce 300 tons of cocaine a year. Police seized 27,500 pounds of cocaine—two Roseanne Barrs short of fourteen tons—in Tranquilandia's thirty-five-mile radius. They dumped about $1.2 billion of cocaine into the Yari River. What it did to the fish is anybody's guess.

Two days later, on March 12, the first of many work orders was written on N513V at Rich Mountain Aviation in Mena, Arkansas. Meanwhile, Seal decided to make a deal to lessen his expected jail term. But he was unable to make headway with federal prosecutors and his DEA case agent because it seems Seal and the agent had a personality conflict. The agent wouldn't even let Seal explain what he had to offer. Did he miss out on the opportunity of a lifetime! Seal called and then traveled to Washington and made his pitch to Customs agent Jim Howell, who was assigned to the Vice President's Task Force. Howell was a bit more tuned in than the first agent, and he took him to the DEA where he met with agent Kenneth R. Kennedy. Kennedy referred Seal to

DEA agents Robert Joura and Ernst Jacobsen in group six of the DEA's Miami field division. They started to debrief him on March 27.

(Coincidentally, Jacobsen assisted in Seal's first arrest in 1972 for trying to fly ammunition and explosives to Mexico from New Orleans and Louisiana to arm anti-Castro Cubans. Those charges were dropped eighteen months later.)

"Mr. Seal said that he could deliver approximately 3,000 kilos of cocaine and pick it up from the Ochoa organization of Bogotá, Colombia," Jacobsen told a Congressional Subcommittee on the Enforcement of Narcotics, Firearms, and Money Laundering Laws. "Within the next three to four weeks, we began to actively look into the thing and we found out that Mr. Seal was, in fact, stating the truth. . . . Mr. Seal had been out of the cocaine business for approximately four months during the time that he was at the trial. He had the phone numbers and the connections to get back into it at any time. Once I debriefed him, Mr. Seal re-established contact with the cocaine cartel."

On March 28, Seal had a busy day. He was debriefed by DEA in Miami, pleaded guilty to two additional charges, and was authorized as a confidential informant by assistant United States attorney Steve Leclair in Fort Lauderdale. The debriefing continued on March 29.

"Mr. Seal contacted a guy by the name of Carlos Bustamante and Felix Dixon Bates, who represented the Jorge Ochoa organization," Jacobsen said. "Felix Dixon Bates is the pilot who formerly had flown with Fabio Ochoa, Jorge Ochoa's father. He had been a pilot that flew a lot of animals into the exotic farm that the Ochoas have in Colombia. He flew the father all around Colombia for years. After a certain time, Bates asked Seal to come to Miami to assist in their operations."

At that time, Bustamante had been chief American distributor of the Ochoa family's cocaine for eight to ten months. He was paid $300 for every kilogram he received. Then he farmed them out to smaller distributors across the country.

It didn't take long for Seal to get back into action. On April 7, Seal and Bates ferried a Titan 404 (N2685U) from Miami to Medellin for the cartel. On April 8, Seal and Bates met with Jorge Ochoa in Colombia. Bates acted as interpreter for Seal, who spoke little Spanish. They discussed landing strips in Colombia and arranged to get all the cocaine to one of them. Seal mentioned he was flying small twin-engine planes that required a 300- to 350-gallon rubber fuel tank in the passenger compartment. He wanted to find refueling stops so he could dump the bladder and pack more cocaine into the plane. Ochoa said he knew of a 6,000-foot airstrip in Nicaragua that would solve the problem.

Jacobsen mentioned the Nicaraguan airstrip in his report to DEA superiors, copies of which went to Washington. The CIA was at his door several weeks later.

"I was called down to the front office, taken into one of the assistant agents in charge office where I met with some CIA officials. They were interested in the strip in Nicaragua and they wanted any and all information that we might have on its location and anything that we had on it. . . . They wanted any and all information that they could get on Nicaragua and the drug trafficking. They called me probably daily just to get an update on what information that we were getting from Mr. Seal."

Seal took a slow route home, passing through Panama on April 10, entering Guatemala the same day, and leaving on the eleventh. On April 17, Seal met with Bustamante and other members of the Ochoa organization in Miami. On the eighteenth, Seal, Emille Camp, Bates, and three Colombians flew to Mena, Arkansas, from Miami to check out the plane (N513V) Seal wanted to use to smuggle the cartel's cocaine.

On April 19, Jacobsen debriefed Seal in Miami. The next day, the Colombian government, through the DEA in Bogotá, gave approval for a confidential informant to enter and leave the country with a load of cocaine. This is called creating a safe window for the plane—a route on which it will not be bothered. Later that day, Seal flew to Nassau for the weekend. On April 22, Seal, Bates, and Emille Camp flew to Panama from Nassau. On April 24, Seal met with Jorge Ochoa, Pablo Escobar, and Luis Angel in Panama. Seal negotiated a deal with Luis Angel to trade his boat, the *Lauren Lee*, and a Hughes 500 helicopter (N2834X) for a Merlin 3B airplane (N1012T) owned by the cartel.

"They went down there to discuss the trip, plus Luis Angel was looking for a boat that he could load with 3,000 kilos, 3,000 to 4,000 kilos of cocaine to smuggle into the west, off the San Diego coast," Jacobsen said. "Mr. Seal negotiated with him for the *Lauren Lee*. . . . The *Lauren Lee* was about a 90- or 95-foot converted fishing boat. It had a heli pad on the back. It had bladder tanks for fuel in the front running all the way through it. Mr. Seal was going to utilize it to run cocaine from Colombia, put it in the middle of the Gulf and bring his helicopters in, land them on the *Lauren Lee*, refuel them, bring them into south Louisiana through the oil rigs and he was going to trade that boat. . . . Well, at that time, he had the Howard 350 he couldn't utilize. He had a King Air he had been using before that was repossessed. So he needed an aircraft to travel around. So he traded the *Lauren Lee* for a Merlin-type aircraft so he could travel between Baton Rouge and Miami and Miami and Colombia."

On April 25, another safe window was created for Seal to fly into Colombia.

Seal flew out of Panama to the Bahamas on April 25. On April 26,

Joura and Jacobsen debriefed him in Miami. Then Seal and Jacobsen, posing as Seal's crony, met with Bustamante, who gave them the keys to a motor home to be used to transfer the cocaine Seal was going to fly into Miami. On April 28, an engine burned out on Seal's Lockheed Lodestar (N513V) during a test flight in Mena, Arkansas, and the trip to Colombia was delayed.

Then, once again, fate started moving the players around the game board to create more opportunities. On April 30, Colombian justice minister Rodrigo Lara Bonilla was assassinated in his white Mercedes-Benz on a Bogotá street in retaliation for the raid on the Tranquilandia lab. A machine-pistol-toting cartel hit man on a red Yamaha motorcycle pumped seven bullets into the thirty-eight-year-old politician. The Colombian president, Belisario Betancur Cuartas, declared "war without quarter" on drug traffickers, and cartel members fled the country. Jorge Ochoa's father was jailed to harass the traffickers. This exile, though it lasted only thirty days, changed the fate of many powerful men in the United States.

On May 8, DEA supervisor Joura reported in a memo that Seal had learned the Ochoa organization was moving much of its operations to Nicaragua. An assistant special agent in charge reported this to the CIA, which expressed "considerable interest."

On May 14, Bates and Peter Everson, an aviation mechanic, ferried Seal's helicopter to Panama to exchange it for the Merlin plane. Bates planned to meet Seal in Panama. On May 18, Seal flew from Miami to Panama for the meeting. On May 19, they met with Jorge Ochoa, Pablo Escobar, Luis Angel, Fabio Ochoa, Gonzalo Rodriguez Gacha, and Frederico Vaughn in Panama City. These cartel members planned to stay in Panama until things cooled off in Colombia. They wanted the Hughes 500 helicopter to fly acetone, ether, and other supplies from the coast to cocaine laboratories they were setting up in Panama.

On May 21, Vaughn, Seal, and Bates flew from Panama City to Managua on Copa Airlines. Vaughn showed Seal a 3,000-foot military airstrip (Los Brasiles) five miles northwest of Managua to be used for refueling and transshipment. Vaughn was introduced to Seal as a representative of the Nicaraguan government in drug smuggling, a lieutenant working in a civilian capacity for either the minister of the interior or the minister of defense. Seal also visited Vaughn's house in Managua to set up a radio room in a storage shed. Then Vaughn gave Seal all the radio codes for entering and leaving Nicaragua.

Seal returned to the United States where the CIA helped identify the military strip. On May 23, Seal was sentenced to ten years in Fort Lauderdale and was remanded. On May 25, he was released from custody on an appeal bond and continued his undercover work.

On May 28, Seal and Emille Camp left Mena, Arkansas, for Colombia at 2:30 a.m. in the Lodestar (N513V). Camp accompanied Seal as co-pilot on this mission because Bates had developed cocaine and marital problems. At 1:00 p.m. Seal radioed he would be landing in Colombia in thirty minutes on a jungle dirt strip. The plane was greeted by Carlos Lehder, who ordered Indians to load 1,500 to 3,000 kilograms of cocaine into it. The added weight made it impossible for the aircraft to take off from the muddy strip. The plane crashed on takeoff after its right wheel sank in the mud.

Seal and Camp weren't bothered by the accident. They stood on the fuselage of the overturned plane and smiled for Lehder's camera. The cocaine was unloaded and stored. The Indians burned the plane, cut it up, and buried it.

Then Lehder took Seal and Camp on a three-day jaunt through the jungle and showed them three or four stash houses containing 3,000 to 4,000 kilograms of cocaine each. Then they returned to Medellin where Jorge Ochoa gave them a Titan 404 loaded with 660 kilograms of cocaine at another clandestine airstrip. Although the tail number on the plane was N700FL, Seal believed it was the same plane he had ferried to Colombia with Bates on April 7. Escobar suggested that Seal try the new trafficking route through Managua where he could refuel at the Los Brasiles airport before continuing to the United States.

On May 30, Seal called Jacobsen from Medellin and explained the situation.

"So Mr. Seal left Colombia [on June 3], flew to Nicaraguan airspace, gave the prearranged codes to the Managua International Airport," Jacobsen said. "Managua International Airport directed Mr. Seal to what I call FAA people, military officials at this other strip [Los Brasiles]. Mr. Seal gave them the code names. They directed Mr. Seal in. After Mr. Seal landed, they refueled the aircraft, but one detail they had forgot . . . is that in Nicaragua, private aircraft can't fly past 6:00 p.m. They finished the refueling at approximately 6:30 or 7 o'clock and it was approaching dark. Mr. Seal departed with Mr. Camp. They departed the airstrip, left Mr. Vaughn, Pablo Escobar at the strip.

"As they were proceeding out of Managua over the mountains, Sand-inista anti-aircraft fire began shooting at them. They shot at Mr. Seal's left engine. So Mr. Seal got back on the radio and couldn't contact anybody at the clandestine military strip, so he had to fly into Managua International Airport with an engine gone. When he landed, the military surrounded the aircraft and arrested Mr. Seal and Mr. Camp. . . . At that time Mr. Seal told them that Frederico Vaughn would take care of it.

"They were not to touch the cocaine but just secure it. The military then took Mr. Seal to the Somosa bunker where they detained him overnight. This is a bunker where it is just a real primitive jail.

"In the morning, Frederico Vaughn came and got Mr. Seal and Mr. Camp out of jail, apologized to them, and told them the cocaine was stored [by Nicaraguan military personnel] and everything was all right. Then they took Mr. Seal to a mansion in Managua that was being utilized by Pablo Escobar and the cocaine cartel. The cocaine cartel was establishing cocaine laboratories, processing laboratories in Managua at that time and Pablo Escobar was there, Gonzalo Rodriguez Gacha was there and all of their laboratory operators were staying in this mansion.

"Mr. Seal took pictures of the mansion from the outside and from the inside, which we did have. He stayed there for approximately three days, meeting with cartel members and discussing their operations. After approximately three days, Pablo Escobar gave Mr. Seal and Emille Camp a ride back from Nicaragua [on June 6] to Nassau, Bahamas, in a private aircraft [a Cessna Cheyenne III, tail number HK 2772P] and Mr. Seal returned to the United States the next day on commercial airlines."

On June 10, Seal stumbled. He bought the C-123K former military transport plane with a ramp at the back to allow vehicles to drive into the hold. He dubbed his new plane *The Fat Lady*. On June 18, he traded the Merlin 3B, N1012T, that he got from Luis Angel to Harry Doan for the C-123K. Then, with the help of his new well-connected friends in government, the C-123K was flown to a military base in Ohio where structural and engine repairs were done on a priority basis over ten days. Thirty to forty people worked on the plane twenty-four hours a day. On June 23, the C-123K was flown to Homestead Air Force Base in southern Florida where the CIA outfitted it with cameras. The DEA innocently believed the cameras were installed for their benefit, to help them identify the airstrip and build their case against cartel members.

"They put one camera in the nose and they put one camera . . . in a box inside, shooting down the ramp toward the back of the aircraft," Jacobsen said. "Mr. Seal was given a remote control button to put in his pocket."

Jacobsen and Joura, posing as Seal's henchmen, picked up $454,000 from Paul Etzel, a representative of Carlos Bustamante, who gave them the money in plastic bags taken from the trunk of his Toyota in a restaurant parking lot. It was payoff money for the Sandinistas in Managua.

On June 24, Seal, co-pilot Emille Camp, and mechanic Peter Everson flew the C-123K from Homestead Air Force Base via Key West to Los Brasiles. Besides the payoff money, the plane carried $200,000 of sophisticated electronic equipment: high-frequency radios, scanners, and hand-held radios to allow the cartel to talk around the world.

The C-123K landed at Los Brasiles airport at 10:00 a.m. on June 25. It was met by Frederico Vaughn, Pablo Escobar, Gonzalo Rodriguez Gacha, and others. They loaded about 666 kilos of cocaine onto the plane as Seal worked the hidden camera with the button in his pocket. The resulting photos show him, Rodriguez Gacha, Escobar, Vaughn, and others carrying burlap bags full of cocaine into the plane. Because the hose on the strip's pressurized fuel pump wasn't long enough to reach the interior tank, a fuel truck was backed up inside the plane; it took nine hours to pour 5,000 gallons of aviation fuel into the tank by bucket. The plane took off at about 8 p.m. and returned to Homestead Air Force Base at 4:50 a.m. on June 26.

The CIA immediately took the film from the cameras and flew it to Washington. The DEA took custody of the cocaine.

On June 27, the CIA informed Jacobsen that the nose camera in the plane had malfunctioned. The rear camera, however, produced some extremely incriminating photographs showing not only the cartel members but Sandinista military personnel out of uniform helping to load cocaine onto the plane. Then, they stunned Jacobsen.

"They said they wanted to release the pictures," Jacobsen said. "CIA wanted to release it to the press. To show that the Sandinistas were dealing in cocaine. They told me the CIA in Langley wanted to—that the pictures were being taken over to the White House and that they wanted to release them to the press.

"We were in the middle of probably the most significant cocaine investigation of my career, and I know that probably one of the most significant investigations in DEA history. We had a chance to probably get together and arrest all the cartel members. . . .

"We said absolutely not. We went to the bosses in Miami DEA and told them what the CIA was trying to do and requested that they call Washington and stop it. Which was done."

The DEA continued with its sting operation, loading the cocaine into a $40,000 mobile home for which Bustamante had given them the keys. Then they faked an accident by arranging for someone to ram the mobile home with one of the agency's surplus cars. At 10:05 p.m. on June 27, a Florida Highway Patrol officer investigating the accident found the cocaine, which was conveniently seized, since the DEA is prohibited from allowing drugs to hit the streets, even during undercover operations.

The cartel got suspicious after the accident and hired a lawyer for $70,000 to look into Seal's background. They barely knew Seal, who they called El Gordo (the fat man), although they had just paid him $500,000 to bring a shipment of cocaine into the US. Even though the DEA had Seal's court records sealed, the lawyer found out about his arrest and conviction on the methaqualone charge and that he was awaiting sentencing. He passed the information to Bustamante.

Even so, greed easily overrode suspicion. The cartel decided to take advantage of Seal's large cargo plane and arranged for him to fly cocaine base from South America into Managua. They wanted him to fly 18,000 kilograms of base to the processing labs in Managua every two weeks. The cocaine was to be flown to Mexico, then the US. They agreed to pay Seal $1 million for every shipment he got into the United States. They also asked him to fly to Managua to pick up 900 kilograms of cocaine. But they didn't want him to come down with an empty plane. They gave him money to buy toys for Sandinista officials—bicycles, outboard motors, rubber rafts. Bustamante also gave him $1.5 million of cocaine profits in two suitcases and two cardboard boxes to deliver to the cartel in Managua.

On June 29, a US attorney and the DEA administrator decided that Seal should find an excuse not to bring the 900 kilograms of cocaine into the United States because they would have to seize it again and blow the undercover operation.

The same day, a curious incident hinted that something was amiss in shadowland. General Paul Gorman, head of Southern Command and head of all American forces in Central and South America, made a speech to the American Chamber of Commerce in El Salvador in which he mentioned Nicaraguan involvement in drug smuggling. He had received his information during a White House briefing. Shortly afterward, someone called the DEA office in Washington and said the story of the C-123K picking up cocaine in Nicaragua and flying it into the US had been leaked to the *Washington Times*. The DEA convinced the *Times* to sit on the story for one week.

Despite these warnings that someone was leaking information about the undercover operation, Seal, Camp, and Everson flew the C-123K from Key West to Los Brasiles and delivered $1.5 million in cash and toys to Frederico Vaughn and Pablo Escobar on July 7. A CIA operative in Managua had radio contact with Seal during the flight to Nicaragua. The cartel had 700 to 800 kilos of cocaine at the airstrip ready to load onto the plane. Seal told Escobar he had received a warning red light from his US ground crew and didn't want to risk losing the cocaine. Escobar thanked him for saving him a loss. The C-123K refueled and took off. It landed at New Smyrna Beach, Florida, at 4:50 a.m. on July 8.

On July 17, a *Washington Times* story by Edmond Jacoby alleged Nicaraguan involvement in cocaine and detailed some of the operation involving Seal. The next day, the DEA scrambled to obtain search and arrest warrants before the suspects could go into hiding. The damage was done.

"Mr. Seal was so entrenched in the cartel that they were going to show him all of their assets in the United States, all their strips, all their storage areas in Georgia, Florida," Jacobsen said. "They were going to show him a 40,000-acre ranch in the Yucatan that they owned, that they wanted to take [use] when they took the drugs from Managua to Mexico. . . . From Mexico they would fly into the United States in small aircrafts, 400 and 500 kilos at a time. They were going to show him their whole operation.

"The second thing was that Mr. Seal had agreed to try to get together all the cartel members in one place where they could be arrested. We were in the process of doing that when the story broke." The continuing investigation would also have allowed the DEA to chart the cartel's trafficking routes from Bolivia and Peru. The only cartel people arrested and convicted were Bustamante, Etzel, and three others in Miami. The press leak ruined an investigation that could have put a significant number of cartel leaders behind bars.

On August 7, Senator Paula Hawkins held a press conference on the Sandinista involvement in drugs. She released to the press four photos taken during Seal's July 25, 1984, trip to Los Brasiles. She showed, but didn't release, a high altitude photo of Los Brasiles airport taken by a U-2 spy plane.

Seal, meanwhile, was up to his armpits in charges. On December 20, he was indicted in Louisiana. The next day, he was arraigned and released on a $250,000 personal bond. On January 1, 1985, FBI special agent Dale Hahn debriefed him in Louisiana. On January 8, Seal pleaded guilty to the Louisiana charges.

On February 20, Emille Camp died in a plane crash near Mena, Arkansas. On July 16, Seal sold the C-123K, which had been sitting idle at Rich Mountain Aviation in Mena, Arkansas, since June 1984, to Harry Doan for $250,000.

On October 28, 1985, Seal was sentenced to six months in a halfway house run by the Salvation Army in Baton Rouge, Louisiana. He worked as an aviation consultant, a job he drove to every day. He refused to safeguard his life in the witness protection program, which would have given him a new identity. On February 19, 1986, three Colombian nationals with machine guns murdered the best informant the DEA had ever had. Seal was worth $28 million when he died in a Baton Rouge street.

"[Max Mermelstein, a former Medellin cartel employee turned government informant,] did tell us there was a contract on Barry Seal's life," said Richard Gregorie, former chief assistant US attorney in Miami. "We informed Barry Seal of this. He was very much aware of it when he was killed. . . . Mermelstein said, 'I think I know who did it. He tested the weapon in my basement, and he fired it through a water-filled wastebasket and a telephone book. And if you go to that house and dig out the basement wall, you'll find the bullets, and if you match them, you'll see they are the same ones that killed Barry Seal.' Mr. Mermelstein was in jail when Seal was killed, so we knew he wasn't present at the scene. We sent ATF agents over to the house—it was then owned by somebody else, who gladly let us go to the basement. We tore up the wall, found some bullets in it, sent them to ballistics, and compared them, and sure enough, they were exact matches."

On March 16, 1986, US President Ronald Reagan used a photo of Frederico Vaughn taken during Seal's June 25, 1984, flight to Nicaragua in a nationwide television appearance seeking support for a contra aid package from Congress.

On March 28, Harry Doan sold the C-123K for $475,000 to persons represented by Ed Garay. Payment was made by a check drawn on the account of Southern Air Transport, a company with a long history of links to the CIA. On October 5, the Sandinista defense forces shot down the C-123K over Nicaragua. Eugene Hasenfus was the only crew member to parachute to safety, only to be captured and made to confess on international television that he was on a mission for Lieutenant Colonel Oliver North and retired Air Force Major General Richard Secord to airdrop military supplies to the contras.

In July 1990, Hasenfus and the family of a pilot who died in the C-123K crash, William Sawyer, went to trial in a lawsuit against Secord and Southern Air Transport demanding death benefits for Sawyer and reimbursements for Hasenfus' wife for money spent getting him out of prison. Felix Rodriguez, a former CIA agent who helped coordinate the supply pipeline to the contra rebels, testified the planes were so poorly equipped they used over-the-counter fuzz busters from Radio Shack to detect enemy radar, the same devices used by lead-footed drivers to warn of police radar speed traps.

Rodriguez said he quit the operation in June 1986. He testified he delivered a letter to Oliver North from crew members who complained their navigational equipment was inadequate for the low-level flying they were doing to avoid Sandinista anti-aircraft guns and radar.

"They hit a tree in Costa Rica because they were off course," Rodriguez said.

Lawyers for Hasenfus introduced a letter from Richard Gadd, who had helped set up the contra supply operation. Gadd alleged in his disposition that Secord decided how money was to be spent and made policy decisions, Gadd said. Corporate Air Services, he added, was used as a front to hide the involvement of Southern Air, which was at one time owned by the CIA and still did contract work for the US government. After five days of deliberations, the jurors ruled against the plaintiffs and said Southern Air and Secord couldn't be enforced to pay either the death benefit or the money to Hasenfus' wife.

Something was definitely amiss in shadowland. While the good guys chased the bad guys, some of them were also treading that fine gray line that divides them. While the DEA and Seal tried to set up the Medellin cartel for a bust, others working parallel to them pursued a different agenda.

First of all, who was Frederico Vaughn? According to US Senator William Hughes, chairman of the so-called Contra Hearings, he may have been more than a Sandinista official.

"Our staff recently called the number in Managua, that same number [where Seal called Vaughn at home]," Hughes said. "In fact, we have had investigators call it a number of times. We were successful in placing a call and talked to somebody at that number and we were told by a domestic employee who answered the phone that we had reached the residence of the member of the United States embassy in Managua. A check with the embassy confirmed that the individual was a member of the United States embassy staff at that number. He was one of the persons expelled from Nicaragua [in the fall of 1988].

"We have done some checking on the telephone number since then. Our embassy says that the house in question and the phone number in question was taken over by the embassy in 1985. We were not able to ascertain who the number was assigned to in June and July of '84, but we are advised by the husband of the owner that the residence in question has been continuously rented by the United States embassy or other foreign missions since 1981."

Was Frederico Vaughn, who has disappeared, a CIA operative within the Sandinista government?

And how does the CIA fit into the story? Well, the CIA kept track of the DEA undercover investigation daily. After Seal returned from Managua with a load of cocaine and the incriminating photographs, DEA officials in Washington met twice with the CIA at the White House—on June 27 and June 29.

Ron Caffrey, chief of the DEA's cocaine desk in 1984, told a congressional subcommittee of his involvement in the June 29 meeting.

"I recall that I gave a [one-hour] briefing after his return with the drugs and prior to his return with the money," Caffrey said. "I gave that briefing . . . to Oliver North of the National Security Council, a CIA person by the name of Dewey—his first name is Dewey—and another person. [Duane (Dewey) Claridge is the CIA agent who ran then-CIA director William Casey's Nicaraguan project].

"I displayed the photographs that we had and pointed out some of the defendants who were in the picture. It was my sense of it that they were familiar with the investigation. They were very well aware of the significance of [the investigation]. . . . In fact, the CIA representative, in pointing out Frederico Vaughn in the photographs—I knew that Frederico Vaughn was a defendant in the case, but frankly I didn't know [who] he was—and the CIA representative told me that he was an associate of a government official, a Nicaraguan government official, which was news to me at the time.

"Colonel North asked me hypothetically if we were going to return with the aircraft and the money, why we couldn't land the plane somewhere outside of Nicaragua, outside the airport in Managua, and maybe turn the money over to the contras. . . .

"[North] did ask me when this investigation could go public, when the information could be released. And I said certainly at some point in time it would, but we had a lot of things to finish off the investigation prior to that. [North] did indicate to me there was a vote coming up [in Congress] at some point in time on an appropriations bill to fund the contras.

"I told him that public disclosures would probably be made by the US Attorney's office at the proper time, but that we had a number of things that we still had to do in the investigation, namely, we had arrests to make.

"We didn't discuss putting the photographs out in the press. What he asked is could the story be told in the press, that is, the story about flying into Nicaragua and the government being involved."

The meeting with North marked the first time in Caffrey's twenty-four years at the DEA that the National Security Council had shown any interest in a law-enforcement operation.

Dave Westrate was assistant administrator for the DEA in 1984. He attended both the June 27 and June 29 meetings.

"On June 27 there was myself, Colonel North, Mr. Dewey Claridge of the CIA, Kennedy Grafanrid, who was, I understood, assistant to the president and Gregg Johnstone of the Office of Indian Affairs at the State Department," Westrate said.

"The meeting opened with a presentation of the photographs by Mr. Claridge. The photos were passed around the room and discussed. The second thing that we discussed was whether or not to release—the release of the facts in this case would in any way influence the pending vote in Congress. And interestingly enough the conclusion of the group was that it probably, in the end, would not.

"I think it was quite clear . . . that the people at the White House felt that having derogatory information on members of the Sandinista Government would be helpful in this vote.

"We also discussed at some length the rules about press releases in cases, most of which I led, because I wanted to make certain that everybody understood that there was within the criminal justice system a very strict protocol on media coverage of investigations, and we were quite concerned that—I wanted to be certain nothing happened in this case that would be different from any other case, because clearly we expected to be prosecuting some of the most major cocaine traffickers in the world and didn't want to prejudice the prosecution. . . .

"At that meeting [June 29], Mr. Caffrey was present," Westrate said. "He and I went there, according to my notes, Mr. Claridge, Mr. North, and again, Mr. Johnstone. The purpose of this meeting was to just keep everybody up to date and also to report the fact that the cocaine had actually now been delivered and the seizure played in Miami. Again to reiterate the fact that we had future plans and we were going to proceed with our future plans."

From the DEA's perspective, Westrate does not consider the operation a success.

"No, not in terms of its potential. I don't believe it really was. . . . We got basically your bucket-issue Miami distribution organization. We got the highest Colombian recipient in Miami, the people associated with that person, a nice cocaine seizure, and I think we probably got a very small percentage of the potential intelligence that we could have gotten had we been able to pursue this with a clear field."

In the end, the Medellin cartel never set up its laboratories in Nicaragua. Cartel members fled Colombia because of political heat in the wake of Lara Bonilla's assassination and uncertainty caused by the raid of the Tranquilandia lab. The revelation and premature end of the DEA's undercover investigation caused by the press leak frightened the traffickers out of Nicaragua and back to their more familiar grounds in Colombia.

Frank Monastero, assistant administrator for the DEA in 1984, pointed out another tragic result of the press leak.

"If whoever did leak it would have waited just a little bit longer, they would have had more incriminating information about what involvement the Sandinista government, in fact, may have had in that case," Monastero said. The Seal case was the first and only time the Sandinista government has been linked to drugs.

Senator William Hughes, chairman of the contra investigation, blamed the CIA and Oliver North for blowing the investigation by leaking information to the press.

"There were some who were willing to compromise, for political purposes, a major drug-enforcement initiative, which had the realistic possibility of apprehending and bringing to American justice one or more of the four most infamous leaders of the so-called Medellin cartel in Colombia. That this DEA operation was compromised is, to me, clear. Less clear, but even more disturbing if it is true, is the possibility that the facts of the case are not as they appear; that significant facts which bear on the case may have been suppressed, including from the law-enforcement personnel carrying out the operation; that events may have been not only managed but manipulated and manufactured for the purpose of exposing those supposed facts for political purposes.

"[The Barry Seal case is] an example of a case that was jerked around by the intelligence community, in my judgment, to serve purely political ends, and blew probably one of the most important cases that perhaps the DEA has worked on.

"DEA certainly would have no reason to leak an operation they considered to be a major operation. . . . The only agencies that really had some reason to leak was—and suggested it—was the National Security Council, Oliver North, and the CIA. . . . The CIA wanted to get it out. . . . There is no question it was Oliver North trying to get the photographs out.

"It was either the CIA or North, Colonel North, or both. I mean, the CIA, from the very beginning, wanted to expose the case because of the contraband coming in from Nicaragua, and Colonel North went to great lengths to persuade the DEA. . . . And I have no doubt that that's an instance where, in fact, there was a political objective, and that is to attempt to provide some embarrassment to the Sandinista government before a vote in the Congress.

"My greater concern goes to the degree to which the course of criminal justice in our country is altered in such cases because of interests which are extraneous to our justice system, and often hostile to the interest of justice.

"[The criminal justice system is] a system of justice which exists to promote justice and to apprehend and punish criminals, rather than one which is seen as just another resource to be exploited to promote other agendas, including purely political agendas."

Carlos Lehder added fuel to the fire during a May 1990 interview with ABC TV in the federal prison in Marion, Illinois, where he was serving a life sentence plus 135 years for cocaine smuggling and operating a continuing criminal enterprise. Comments by the forty-year-old Lehder indicated that, like Lieutenant Colonel North and other White House officials who supported the contras, Colombian drug traffickers also backed the right-wing guerrillas in their attempt to overthrow Nicaragua's Sandinista government.

"We did give a great deal of money to the contra cause," Lehder said. "I gave. We put up the first time about $10 million to the contras. [In all] around $20 million in cash went to help the contras."

Adolfo Calero, a former director of the Nicaraguan Resistance, a contra umbrella group, denied receiving money from drug traffickers.

Lehder also said ousted Panamanian dictator Manuel Noriega took money from anyone who offered it.

"Noriega was always on the payroll of American intelligence, but he was always also on the payroll of the Soviet intelligence, the Cuban intelligence, and the Israeli intelligence. At the same time, he was on the payroll of some Colombian traffickers."

The problems caused by political interference in this case didn't end with the intervention of the CIA and Oliver North. Richard Gregorie, former chief assistant US attorney in Miami, prosecuted the Seal undercover case. He described to a Senate subcommittee the difficulties in trying to nab one of the cartel leaders.

"We indicted a large number of cartel leaders, including Pablo Escobar and Gonzalo Rodriguez Gacha, also known as The Mexican, and Jorge Ochoa," Gregorie said. "Interestingly enough, although they weren't in the United States when we indicted them, Jorge Ochoa and another cartel leader, this one from the Cali cartel, a gentleman by the name of Orejuala—Gilberto Rodriguez Orejuala—went to Madrid, Spain, to open the market in Spain. When they got there, the Spanish police found them, arrested them, threw them in jail on the United States provisional arrest warrants, and were ready to extradite them back to the United States.

"I twice went to Spain to see if we could get the Spanish government to send them back to the United States. After we had had these provisional arrest warrants for close to a month, the Colombians submitted their own extradition process in competition with ours. What did our State Department do? Nothing. They said, well, that's just the process.

"The first Colombian extradition request was for bullfighting bulls, that they were improperly imported. Well, the Spanish court said that's not serious enough. So the Colombians by then had copies of our extradition papers, which were translated into Spanish, so they merely copied our charges and charged that they wanted Ochoa back in Colombia.

"Approximately a year later, Mr. Ochoa and Mr. Gilbert Rodriguez Orejuala were sent home to Colombia, three weeks later to be back on the streets. The only people in the State Department [in the United States embassy in Spain] that I talked to that had any knowledge about this extradition were an elderly gentleman who was in charge of those affairs—he was going to retire in a month or so and did not really want to do anything that was going to rock the boat—and an elderly secretary who seemed to be the most knowledgeable person in the embassy about what was going on and certainly supplied very little encouragement about getting Mr. Ochoa out.

"But that was not the end of it. The Colombians actually caught Mr. Ochoa again in 1987. He was driving a Honduran general's car. What he was doing with the Honduran general's car is not clear, but an honest Colombian policeman arrested him, put him in jail. The DEA immediately flew a plane to Colombia. 'Put him on the plane, send him back to us, we'll try him.' A week passed, two weeks passed. I send brand new extradition papers down to Colombia, because by that time Barry Seal had been murdered by the Colombians and Max Mermelstein had provided us new information, so we redid the extradition papers, sent them to Colombia. Unfortunately, three weeks later, Mr. Ochoa was back on the street.

"[In October 1988] I received information that Mr. Ochoa was visiting Venezuela on a regular basis, that he was going to a place in Venezuela to rest and recreate, that he had been there several times. US Customs had an informant, a citizen of South America . . . who says, 'Hey, he's there, you could get him.' We made plans to do it. During the course of the plans, the minister of justice from Venezuela was coming to Miami—actually, he was coming through Miami to go someplace else. He said, 'I'd like to stop and see Mr. Gregorie to talk about this proposal.' Sure enough he came to my office, I talked with him. He says, 'Look, the guy is an undesirable alien. We don't want him in Venezuela. If you'll go with the Venezuelan police, we'll catch him, we'll put him on a plane and send him back.'

"The Marshal's Service, US Customs, said, 'We'll get a plane there, we'll send him back.' This was sometime in October [1988]. Sure enough, we were ready to go, and a week later, apparently the minister of justice had gone back and mentioned this plan either in our embassy or to somebody in the Venezuelan government. I started getting calls in Washington that the Venezuelan ambassador [US ambassador in Venezuela] was furious that some assistant United States attorney in Miami had the audacity to deal with the minister of justice of a foreign country and was going to take it upon himself to arrest some individual in Venezuela without cooperating with the State Department. Everything was put on hold.

"He put the clamps on it. He stopped it, insisted that there be meetings. I got word back—and this is not direct—the word that I got back was: 'No assistant United States attorney is going to be responsible for burning down my embassy.' Now, that may be a reference to the fact that when Mata Ballesteros, a very high-level cocaine dealer, was arrested in Honduras, there was a riot, and fire was set to the embassy.

"The informant in this matter called me a few weeks ago, and I had a personal conversation through an interpreter with him. What he said was that he had been called in because the cartel had done their own investigation, having either read in the newspaper or figured out from some other source that this plan had been arranged, and they had done their own investigation of where the leak was, who it was that was setting Ochoa up, and that they had played a tape for the informant of a tape-recorded conversation coming out of the embassy of the United States to some other official, which indicates to me that the cartel actually has the ability to intercept our communications.

"So in my career I indicted the biggest cocaine dealers in the world twice, had at least one of them in jail twice and was unable to get him to the United States, and had a very viable plan a third time to get him to the United States and try him, and the State Department killed it."

Sherman M. Funk, Inspector General for the US State Department, after a program audit of the department's Bureau of International Narcotics Matters, said in January 1990 that the State Department had failed to assign high priority to narcotics matters either within the department or with foreign countries.

In testimony before a Senate committee on international narcotics matters on February 20, 1990, Funk said, "Clearly, one of the major deficiencies in the government's past anti-narcotics efforts has been its fitful, off again, on again aspect and its reliance on publicity about big seizures and major convictions.

"The national drug strategy calls on us to dig in for the long haul, and this means a reliance instead on much effort that will be both undramatic and difficult and that will demand, particularly overseas, a degree of interagency coordination and cooperation which is anathema to turf-conscious bureaucrats."

This is one more example of the US government's apparent lack of commitment to combat drugs. The president of Venezuela told Dr. Norman A. Bailey, former National Security Council senior staff member, that the United States does not seem interested in Venezuela's help fighting drugs or even Libyan terrorists.

"He indicated that the Venezuelan government was extremely concerned that they were not going to be immune to drug activities much longer," Dr. Bailey said. "They were surrounded by islands and countries where drug activities were extremely important, and they felt they were going to be the next target, particularly for transshipment to Europe, which at that time was being opened up as a major market for the cocaine dealers, and people were going through Venezuela, into Spain and so forth, and back and forth in this effort, using Venezuela and Spain as transshipment points.

"He simply brought up the question—I didn't ask him, he volunteered it. He said, 'One thing I don't understand is why your government does

not seem to be interested in working with us to prevent this.' Then, as
we were discussing that—and of course, he brought up the Panamanian
situation, and he claimed—and I have no independent knowledge of
this—that the Venezuelan government had been providing the American
government with information about Noriega and the PDF [Panamanian
Defense Forces] for years without any visible effect—and then he
simply mentioned as another example, or something else that puzzled
him, that at the time the United States was retaliating for the bombing of
the nightclub in Berlin, the Venezuelan government had identified two
or three Libyan agents who had come through Venezuela and so on, and
had notified the United States, and nothing had happened. They weren't
asked to do anything about it."

10

Stemming the Drug Flow:
The great white fart, bogeys in Bogey land, and ten frothing nymphomaniacs

"We fly low to keep America's heads high."

—MOTTO OF NARCOTICS AIR SMUGGLERS.

One minute out of Homestead Air Force Base, headed toward Bimini, I drank in the splendor of hues of blue and green on rippled water where an Atlantic wind scratched its way toward Florida. The sky and sea blended at no discernible point. Hot sun poured through the Citation's scratched plastic window to toast my chest. The bumpety-bump-bump of the plane thudding through disturbed air massaged my spine. Then a memory crawled out from under the stacks of my voracious childhood reading and sent a chilled shudder through my upper back and neck. We were flying into the northwest corner of the Bermuda Triangle, an apparently tranquil ocean that has sucked more than 1,000 souls into nothingness. Extending from Florida to Bermuda to Puerto Rico to Florida, the Triangle is one of the great mysteries of our time. No one who has disappeared here in 115 years has been found.

"The Bermuda Triangle," I yelled to an air interdiction officer at the back of the plane.

"What?"

"We're flying into the Bermuda Triangle."

"Yeah. We do it every day."

"Don't you ever worry?"

"What?"

Every day. But that day I was on board. Just my luck.

The *Cyclops*, a 600-foot US Navy ship, disappeared here with 309 crewmen after sailing from Barbados in 1919. The US Navy lost an entire formation of five Avenger torpedo bombers on a navigational training mission over the Bermuda Triangle on December 5, 1945. Flight 19's fourteen fliers were never seen again. A search plane with thirteen crew went looking for Flight 19 and vanished. A US C-54 plane disappeared 100 miles from Bermuda in 1947. Twenty-nine crew members disappeared with the freighter *Ithaca Island* in 1968. The *Milton Iatrides* and thirty crew vanished in 1971. Later that year, a US Air Force Phantom II jet fighter blipped off the screen with its pilot and instrument officer eighty-five miles southeast of Miami. Jets that scrambled to the plane's last coordinates found nothing on a sunny day in water no deeper than twenty feet. None of the planes or ships that disappeared made distress calls. None had the time.

The disappearances have been blamed on a myriad of possible causes, ranging from mechanical failure to UFOs. Some people refuse to believe anything is amiss and label the Bermuda Triangle a fanciful contrivance of the press. A reasonable explanation does exist, but has been ignored by many who fear its scientific basis will dampen the mystery. It certainly doesn't assuage the fear.

Donald Davidson was a chemist working for the National Research Council in Ottawa, Canada, in 1984 when he published his amazing theory explaining the disappearance of planes and ships in the Bermuda Triangle. Davidson's theory is so simple and based on such hard fact that it seems inconceivable that the scientific community would ignore it in favor of groundless speculation.

Davidson described how water molecules under extreme pressure or cold bind with large amounts of methane molecules to form solid ice-like masses called gas hydrates. One liter of water can hold 171 liters of methane. Gas hydrates have a higher melting temperature than ice and can exist while water flows around them. They are formed under oceans all over the world. In areas where conditions don't fluctuate, such as under the polar ice cap, they become mountainous in size. Methane is produced by rotting plants and animals. Marsh gas, which most people see as spastic bubbles darting to the surface of the water, is methane. Farts are methane. Methane occurs anywhere where something rots, even at the bottom of the ocean.

Davidson outlined two possible scenarios for the Bermuda Triangle. His first explanation involves immense masses of gas hydrates sitting on, and floating over, the ocean floor. The fluctuating Gulf Stream brushes over them and the warm water melts them, releasing massive amounts of pressurized methane. For every liter of water warmed up, 171 liters of methane are released. Vast throbbing clouds of methane bubble upward. The gas expands into humongous bubbles as pressure decreases near the surface to create a stinky, frothy ocean surface. A ship caught in this froth would sink through the bubbles because it is no longer supported by water. The engines of a plane flying over the rising cloud of gas would stall for lack of oxygen. A plane's engines could also ignite the highly flammable methane and be blown out of the sky. Both ship and plane would sink instantly to the bottom of the frothy ocean. The methane dissipates and a mystery is created.

Hydrates have been found in the Gulf of Mexico where ships' captains reported sighting frothy, aerated water at the turn of the century. They were smart enough not to investigate, knowing the ocean would not support their ships. Ships have mysteriously disappeared off the north-west coast of Australia much as they do in the Bermuda Triangle. Planes often hit air pockets and drop hundreds of feet until they fall through the pocket. Imagine a methane pocket that goes to the bottom of the ocean.

Davidson's second disaster scenario involving hydrates has pockets of methane gas trapped under a layer of hydrates beneath the sea floor. The methane escapes through fissures in the seabed caused by earthquakes or volcanic action and rises to the surface to wreak havoc.

Though hydrates are found on ocean floors around the world, the Bermuda Triangle is unique because the edge of the warm Gulf Stream drifts into its boundaries. The Triangle is also one of the most highly traveled parts of the world, with several hundred commercial and private planes and boats traversing its boundaries every week. The odds of a ship or plane passing over a discharge of methane gas are greater in the Bermuda Triangle than anywhere else in the world. Not that it hasn't happened anywhere else. How many disappearances of planes and ships can be blamed on melting hydrates? Just when you thought it was safe to go back into the water, the great white fart gurgles to the surface. The Bermuda Triangle does not distinguish between good guy and bad guy. Both must traverse its boundaries daily to do business.

Mangled metal spots Bimini's jungle where pilots succumbed to nocturnal illusions while trying to land tons of cocaine and marijuana on the unlit runway that is the last safe stop in the 1,100-mile run from Colombia to Florida. The pilot of the US Customs Service interceptor jet points out a boneyard of rusting fuselages heaped by a bulldozer beside the short runway. The shallow, turquoise ocean washes over other planes that ran out of fuel hundreds of yards from shore or whose pilots misread their altimeters. A large cargo plane sits like a mirage in a foot of water on a sand bar.

The Cessna Citation II C-550 banks sharply for another look from 100 feet up at the island that marks the last leg of the world's most sophisticated smuggling operations.

Bimini is fifty miles from the southern tip of Florida, where an estimated 75 percent of cocaine and marijuana used in the United States, and 90 percent of Canadian coke and weed, enters North America. Pirates and smugglers — *contrabandistas* — have plied the seas that wash over the Cay Sal Banks and through the Old Bahama Channel and the Straits of Florida since there was booty to be plundered and contraband to be smuggled. The British smuggled guns to the Confederacy from Bimini during the American Civil War. Rumrunners kept America wet with shipments from its harbors during Prohibition. Smugglers have boated and flown their marijuana and cocaine across the waters from Colombia and Jamaica since the mid-1960s, shielding their operations behind a myriad of islands and along jagged coastlines.

Florida has 8,246 miles of shoreline, 250,000 privately registered boats, more than 10,000 privately registered planes, and more than 250 registered airports, including landing strips on farms. Florida is the American state closest to South America — Miami is 1,100 miles from Barranquilla, Colombia, an easy flight or boat ride. Miami International Airport handles more import-export cargo than any other US airport. The ports of Miami, Fort Lauderdale, Tampa, and Jacksonville receive millions of tons of import and export goods for and from Colombia. This volume of business gives smugglers a means of getting drugs into the country and also a way of returning to South America goods bought with the profits of drug sales. South Florida is also an international banking center whose Spanish-speaking employees make it convenient for South American drug traffickers to wire their profits out of the country in their own language.

Smugglers from all walks of life, in all makes of planes and boats, make their final mad dash from Bimini, hoping to sneak chemical fortunes through the invisible web of radar that protects the American shoreline. The most daring pilots on both sides of the law confront each other daily in the skies around the island in what may be one of the last great non-military modern-day adventures.

"The flying is as good as it gets outside of actual combat," said Roger (Mad Dog) Garland, acting chief of the US Customs Service Air Branch in southern Florida. Garland, an EC-47 pilot in Vietnam, was awarded the Distinguished Flying Cross. His nickname reflects his tenacity in pursuing smugglers. In the course of his career, he has landed on roads and chased them through swamps.

"We have arrested every profession you can imagine except a nun: judges, lawyers, airline pilots, even a priest. You would think that these people would understand the risk involved," said Bill, a Customs pilot. Most of the agents quoted are identified by first name only to protect them from vengeful Colombian smugglers. ("We don't want our men to be found dead in the bathtub.")

Customs agents call them dopers and bad guys. Greed makes the smugglers fly without lights one to 100 feet above the Caribbean Sea, around or over Cuba, over the Straits of Florida toward the glimmering necklace of lights that links the fabled keys stretching along the only live reef in North America. They try to land undetected on legitimate landing strips, roads, sod farms, even drainage canals. Some planes land at Bimini to refuel before continuing. Others dump fifty-pound bales of marijuana or cocaine under cover of darkness to go-fast speedboats that circle in the waters off Bimini like sharks. The speedboats, some of which can reach speeds of 100 miles an hour, then try to outrace the Customs speedboats that patrol the cuts running from the Atlantic Ocean to the intercoastal waterway that extends the length of Florida. More adventurous smugglers ignore Bimini and fly 2,000 miles straight up the seventy-second parallel, 460 miles offshore, to the eastern seaboard. Customs agents call the run the New York Express. Planes fly it 500 to 2,000 feet above the waves. By comparison, the average commercial airliner flies at an altitude of 30,000 feet.

Many smugglers load their planes and boats in Colombia. Sometimes mother ships, usually rusty tankers loaded with fifty-pound bales of marijuana, meet speedboats and fishing boats in open water at night to transfer their cargo. The Colombian government canceled overflight privileges for three days in 1982. Mad Dog was curious. He flew a Cessna Citation II to the Colombia coast and cruised the shoreline until he had confirmed his suspicions. He returned with color photographs that now hang on the walls of the Customs office at Homestead Air Force Base. The photographs show freighters being loaded with truckloads of marijuana. They also show Colombians sitting on top of open trucks carrying hundreds of the bales along dirt roads leading to the loading area. Mad Dog beat a hasty retreat when a heavily armed Colombian government gunboat protecting the operation rounded a bend. He got a photograph of that, too.

Mad Dog and other Customs officials estimate that 90 percent of the smugglers fly just over the surface of the ocean at night to avoid being detected by radar.

"We've chased them where you see the wake of the prop stirring the water, leaving two white trails," said Jack, the co-pilot. "Most of these guys fly on a wing and a prayer. They run without lights at night with no reference point. On a dark night, when you have few stars in the sky and a few boats with lights on the ocean, you don't know which end is up. It all looks the same. You have to go by your gauges."

Most crashes are caused by improperly set altimeters. Smugglers need precise altimeter readings because they fly so close to the surface of the ocean. Air pressure changes dramatically between Colombia and Florida. Pilots won't risk revealing their positions by radioing an airport control tower for a correct reading. They prefer to fly with improperly calibrated instruments.

Between 1975 and 1985 there were 1,494 narcotics-related air crashes and 661 deaths in the United States. One infrared videotape shows a twin-engine plane on a black background of water. White trails suddenly appear as the propellers skim the surface. The pilot tries to gain altitude. The plane tilts slightly and a wing tip dips into the ocean. The plane shatters and sinks.

Faster planes sometimes piggyback their way into the United States by tucking themselves under legitimate planes so that both aircraft appear as one blip on the radar screen. Since the upper planes have filed flight plans, they aren't questioned by the agents monitoring radar screens at C3I, the Customs command, control, communications, and intelligence center in Miami. A similar center is located at March Air Force Base in California. Their crews receive and coordinate surveillance and intelligence information. They track suspect planes and boats and launch interceptors to visually identify and track the target. Then a Black Hawk helicopter with a bust crew is called in to make the arrest.

Some planes that make it to the mainland undetected drop their bales of contraband to waiting accomplices rather than land. Their aim is not always accurate. "Marijuana can be dangerous to your health," said co-pilot Jack. "You get hit by a fifty-pound bale from 1,000 feet, it can do some damage. A cow was killed by a bale in a north Florida pasture. One man got up to go to the bathroom in Fort Lauderdale in 1979 and heard a crash in his bedroom. A bale of marijuana fell through the roof onto the bed."

The US Customs air interdiction program in southern Florida was a covert operation until March 1987, when officials decided that the big-time smugglers had figured out how it works. Publicity, agents figured, might deter less committed dopers.

I was the first writer allowed to fly on Customs missions to interdict drug smugglers. In 1987, I flew four missions, three of them in Cessna Citation II jets equipped with the APG-66 search radar used on the US Air Force F-16 Falcon fighter. The radar locks in on a target and determines how far away it is, its altitude, air speed, and how fast it's closing in. The planes also have Forward Looking Infrared (FLIR) scopes that allow night vision and the videotaping of pursuits and the transfer of drugs from planes to boats. I spent another four days at Homestead in February 1990.

Customs aircraft are equipped with five radios, including VHF, VHF-

FM, long-range HF, and the military UHF. Radios are fitted with scramblers to prevent interception of communications. As a precautionary measure, the radios are encrypted and the frequencies are changed frequently during conversations so that a question asked on one channel is answered on another. Customs planes are also fitted with several navigational systems: an inertial system that gauges the plane's movement and where it is anywhere in the world; the Omega navigational system, good offshore anywhere in the world; and the LORAN C system used along the American coast and in the Gulf of Mexico to pinpoint the plane's location through a computer-based receiver that displays the plane's latitude and longitude coordinates.

The use of aircraft to patrol the US border began in 1919 when a section of the Army Air Service was assigned to hound Pancho Villa and other Mexican *bandidos* who crossed into the States to escape Federales. The air interdiction program in Florida began in the 1970s when it was understood that Colombians were pouring over the border with tons of marijuana, cocaine, and counterfeit Quaaludes. The Customs Service got four Grumman S-2 Trackers and four Grumman OV-1 Mohawks from the Department of Defense. Their success in interdicting smugglers forced the bad guys to use more sophisticated planes and equipment. The one-upmanship has continued to this day.

Surveillance of smugglers is done by Lockheed P-3B Orion, Grumman E-2C Hawkeye, and US Air Force E-3 Sentry AWACS planes with radar domes that cruise large ovals in the southern skies. The P-3 AEW (Airborne Early Warning) plane scans the air and surface for 196,250 square miles in one sweep of its General Electric APS-125 radar. It can stay airborne for fourteen hours at an altitude of 28,000 feet and can cruise 4,600 miles at 380 miles per hour. The E-2C Hawkeye can patrol in any weather at an altitude of 30,000 feet. Its APS-12 radar can detect targets within 260 miles. It automatically tracks targets and its high-speed processing computers allow it to track 600 targets and control forty airborne intercepts simultaneously. The US Air Force Sentry E-3 AWACS (Airborne Warning And Control System) is a nearly indestructible high-capacity radar station and command and control center that can operate at any altitude in any weather.

Interception and tracking is done by Cessna Citation jets, Piper Cheyenne twin-engine turboprop CHETS (Customs High Endurance Trackers) that can stay aloft for six hours and land on a 3,500-foot runway, Beechcraft King Airs, Cessna 206s, and Cessna 404s. Interception helicopters include Hughes 500, Bell 206 Jet Rangers, and Bell UH-1 Hueys.

Busts are made by the crews of Sikorsky UH-60A Black Hawk military helicopters. These workhorses replaced the sporty Bell AH-1G

Cobras in 1983. The Cobras could seat only two people to the Black Hawk's seven. The Black Hawk is designed to seat more people, but the rear of the craft has been converted into a massive gas tank to increase its range. A Black Hawk was one of six aircraft tracking a single-engine Cessna containing 744 pounds of marijuana from the Caribbean to Leesburg, Virginia, in December 1986. The Black Hawk swooped down on the fleeing pilot as he bolted for a pickup truck near the runway at Leesburg Municipal Airport. The helicopter had flown for eleven hours, 500 feet off the surface of the Atlantic Ocean, 500 miles offshore during the pursuit. The helicopter also has a public address system mounted on its fuselage and a 30-million candlepower night-sun search light. The night-light, along with the standard searchlight and landing light, has an infrared mode that allows the bust crew to use their ANVIS-6 night vision goggles when they fly blacked out.

The air interdiction program is coordinated from two C3I centers — one at March Air Force Base in Riverside, California, and one in Miami. The centers house a multitude of computers and large screens on which radar technicians monitor Federal Aviation Administration radars, the Joint Surveillance System radars, and military radars, including those of the North American Air Defense Command.

They also maintain radio contact with technicians in radar planes such as the E-2Cs and P-3 Orions that fly large ovals in the southern skies. The C3I centers also monitor radar information from five tethered $15-million aerostats that gather information from an altitude of 10,000 feet. These Fat Alberts look down on planes coming up from the Guajira Peninsula of northern Colombia and from Jamaica, something the ground radars can't do until the planes are so close to the coast they can zip on in. Fat Alberts can also pick out a plane flying at wave height against sea clutter with their Doppler radar.

Airliners show up on the screen as a squawk and flight number. Other planes on flight plans show up as squawks and are watched to ensure they go to their destination. Small planes with little squawks or no transponder are watched carefully. Nearly 150,000 private planes enter the United States every year, 7,500 of them carrying drugs. Technicians can check flight plans on FAA computers. When radar technicians detect a suspicious plane or an informant tips Customs agents about a shipment of drugs, C3I launches a Customs interceptor to track the target and read its N number so C3I can check its registration.

"We circle the plane and get behind it," Mike the pilot said as the Customs jet closed in on a target plane. "We lock it in on the radar. The radar will tell us when someone is looking at us with radar. Otherwise, you can't see a plane approaching from behind. We usually intercept from below. If you come in from above, he might pull up and crash into you. We sit on his tail, get right behind within twenty feet to get the tail number for identification." He said this as he pulled so close to the target plane you could pee on its tail if you weren't pissing into the wind.

C3I calls up maps and charts on its screens during a chase to guide interceptor planes and bust crews to potential landing sites.

Sixty-two pilots, more than half of them Vietnam veterans, and thirty-nine air interdiction officers who operate the radar and infrared scope, work out of a hangar at the end of an old runway on Homestead Air Force base. They are the modern-day Untouchables, working, as did Eliot Ness, for the Department of the Treasury. Ness bagged rumrunners. These guys nail dopers. They use jets and turboprop and piston-prop planes to track and chase smugglers' planes and boats. Pilots bend propeller tips for extra power during pursuits. Once the tracking plane determines where the smugglers will land, one of two Customs Sikorsky UH 60A Black Hawk helicopters carrying a heavily armed assault team is dispatched to cut the plane off as it lands. The helicopters, nicknamed Coke Buster, have followed fine military tradition for every smuggling operation they busted: green marijuana leaves and white cocaine leaves are stenciled on their fuselages for every successful bust.

Flying with a bust crew in a Black Hawk requires a tight sphincter and cojones the size of coconuts. Hesitate fastening your seat belt and kiss your ass goodbye. These suckers often fly with their doors open and you're sitting right on the edge of nothing on a slick seat with the helicopter rising 3,000 feet a minute. If the eleven-foot tail rotor doesn't get you, the sudden stop will. Never walk toward the back of a helicopter when disembarking. You can't see a spinning rotor. And unless you're a midget, duck when walking away from it. The main rotor spins four and a half feet off the ground in a fifty-three-foot diameter. The pilot and co-pilot are first in the helicopter during a scramble and start the two T700-GE-700 turboshaft engines that develop 1,560 horsepower each right overhead. The first priority is to put on a headset to block out the noise and hear the commands so you know what is going on. Then put on a life jacket and buckle the seat belt. If the helicopter crashes in the ocean, hang on to your seat or the handle on the fuselage as a reference point until it flips upside down. They always do.

Then leave through the gunner windows if the doors are shut. Evacuation is done by order of who is closest to the windows. There are seven people to evacuate: two gunners, two Bahamian soldiers, the pilot, co-pilot, and me. The person dragging out the life raft shouldn't pull the handle to inflate it until it is completely out the window.

There's little to worry about when flying with the best pilots in the world. But bureaucracy doesn't tempt fate. A US Customs Service Black Hawk helicopter out of Homestead crashed into the ocean forty miles north of Cuba while chasing a smuggler on the night of November 2, 1989. Five of the six crew members were rescued. Co-pilot George Saenz was not found. I signed a disclaimer three months later in case the unexpected happened while flying over the Bermuda Triangle.

These are the credentials of some of the Customs pilots flying out of Homestead in February 1990: two were from a US Air Force academy; one was an F-16 pilot; two flew F-4s; a Marine Corps pilot flew both fixed-wing and helicopters; army helicopter pilots; highway patrol pilots; a jet pilot for the Puerto Rican National Guard; a navy pilot with 1,600 hours of flying off aircraft carriers; a pilot who earned the Distinguished Service Cross in Vietnam.

"We hire pilots first and teach them law enforcement," said Larry Karson, a Customs pilot, air branch supervisor, and former Army paratrooper. "With the kind of flying we do, we can't afford to do it otherwise."

Customs pilots must be able to scramble any aircraft. Before they are considered for a job, they must have 1,500 hours of flying time, 250 pilot-in-command hours, 500 multi-engine hours, and 500 hours flying by instruments and at night. Once they're hired, they go through eight weeks of criminal investigation school and eight weeks of Customs basic investigators' school in Glyncoe, Georgia. Then they take a three-week aviation enforcement course in Arizona and a two-week sensor training course in Corpus Christi, Texas. That's followed by a grueling but clean two days being tested in an altitude chamber and practicing escaping from a cockpit under water after a crash. Back at Homestead, the new pilots go through a two-week sensor course and weapons training. Their shooting abilities are tested every three months. They must pass to keep the job. Air interdiction officers also take ten hours of ground pilot school in case the pilot of their plane dies or becomes ill.

Air interdiction officers are also criminal investigators. They run the radar and Forward Looking Infrared sensor systems on Customs aircraft. They are part of the bust crew in Black Hawk helicopters and jump out to arrest smugglers. They are often used as observers during tracking flights and go undercover during follow-up investigations to gather evidence for trial.

Bust crews aboard the copters are armed with Heckler and Koch .223-caliber machine guns, Steyr Aug .223-caliber machine assault rifles, AR-15 semi-automatic rifles, pump-action shotguns with spare shells taped to the stock, and handguns in hip or ankle holsters. They also wear bullet-proof vests and night-vision goggles worth $8,000 a pair. Royal

Bahamian Police officers stationed in the BAT cave at Homestead Air Force Base participate in arrests in the Bahamas to give Customs agents the right to land there as part of Operation OPBAT — Operation Bahamas, Turks, and Caicos. The police officers prefer to wear camouflage military fatigues rather than the jeans and T-shirts preferred by the Vietnam veterans who fly Customs jets. They also strap combat knives to their ankles and wield M-16 machine guns and antiquated but highly effective Sten guns. The favored weapon among smugglers is the MAC-10 submachine gun. "The smugglers aren't armed for us," said Jack, a pilot. "It's for the Colombians. They'd get more time for shooting at us than for smuggling."

The Bahamian police officers, called Bandits by everyone, are a smuggler's nightmare. Although Customs agents can't shoot unless their lives are threatened, Bandits shoot anything that moves. They play by the rules of war. The good guys made a bust during a dope drop in March 1988. One speedboat raced away with the Black Hawk in pursuit. A Bandit fired his Sten gun across the boat's bow. No reaction. He fired into the bow, hitting the driver in the knees with ricochets and dropping him. The boat continued. He emptied a magazine into the outboard motors. Dead stop.

Tracking a suspected smuggler in daylight over the Bahamas produces interesting reactions from islanders. "People in the Bahamas see this all day, every day," said Jack the co-pilot. "They come out and wave and yell to the smugglers, 'Throw your load to us.' "

Many islanders are unfriendly toward US Customs agents. Some Bahamian Customs agents don't like their American counterparts, either. Bill the co-pilot described how he watched a plane dump bales of marijuana to waiting speedboats. He landed behind the smuggler in Bimini and asked the Bahamian Customs agent whether he was going to inspect the plane.

"No plane land here, mon," the official replied.

On Monday, April 20, 1987, about 100 party-goers on the beach near Freeport attacked two Bahamian soldiers, two US Customs agents, and two US Drug Enforcement Administration agents with rocks, bricks, and bottles as they landed behind a Piper Aztec they had watched dumping twelve bales of marijuana into the ocean forty miles south of Bimini. Shots were fired at the helicopter that airlifted the men out. A bullet that failed to penetrate the windshield would have hit the pilot in the head. "I think they might have wanted the drugs that were aboard the airplane," Mad Dog observed.

On April 8, 1989, the US Drug Enforcement Administration hired two American pilots to work undercover to pick up a suspected drug smuggler and 300 kilograms of marijuana in Jamaica and return to

Gainsville, Florida. The plane ran low on fuel and made an emergency landing in the Bahamas on the return trip. The DEA alerted Bahamian police that the pilots were undercover agents. The police arrested them anyway and locked them up in Foxhill Prison near Nassau. The Bahamian government was playing hardball because US officials had complained the country was doing little to fight drug smuggling. The Bahamians delighted in making the Americans crawl. They ignored explanations and pleas from the US Ambassador to the Bahamas and the Assistant Deputy Secretary of State.

In fact, Bahamian National Security Minister Loftus Roker had the nerve to announce the arrests at a political rally in Nassau:

"[The DEA] tell me we're not fighting hard enough, we're not doing enough to stop drug trafficking," Roker said. "A couple of days ago, we caught a plane loaded with marijuana with two American DEA agents aboard. What about that?"

Smugglers will do anything to avoid capture. "We've had them drop toilet paper out to foil the [turbine] engines," said Jack the co-pilot. "We've had them shoot flares at us. They'll throw out documents and papers that will incriminate them."

"We've had them ditch their airplane in the intercoastal waterway near Palm Beach," Mike the pilot said. "They ditch in the water and wade to shore. We notify the police. One time, these guys were on a street corner trying to hail a cab soaking wet when they were picked up."

"Bad guys even sink their planes in deep water or burn them to prevent seizure," Mad Dog said.

Sometimes bad guys crash their planes in the most embarrassing places. With the entire ocean to crash into, one doper put his plane down nose first beside Suzanne Pleschette's yacht.

Mad Dog has had a number of unnerving experiences chasing smugglers. "We picked up this Cessna 210 at Tampa one night. All of a sudden he brakes off at landing and climbs to 10,000 feet and levels off heading toward the Gulf. We followed him, then pulled up beside the plane. The doors were wired up and the cockpit was empty. He jumped out at 10,000 feet when we were at 11,000. We had an unmanned missile over the Gulf. The copter was at 3,000 feet. As he fell, he heard the pounding of the blades. He landed blocks from his house."

The pilot was later arrested and his plane was last seen flying over the Gulf of Mexico, where it would run out of fuel and crash before nearing land. The pilot's chin was severely scraped. It was his first parachute jump and he pulled the rip cord at 5,000 feet. He was upside down at the time and a cord snagged under his chin and snapped him right-side up when the chute opened.

Another time, Mad Dog and his crew chased a single-engine plane over Florida. "I see three big explosions and call in to say he's throwing hand grenades at us," he said. "Then he lands on the Florida turnpike. I followed right behind him. One guy jumped out with a flashlight to stop traffic because the other plane was out of control. The bad guys took off through the swamp, but left their passports behind. We finally figured out he wasn't throwing grenades at us. He was about to land in a canal they thought was a road. They put the plane on full throttle to gain altitude and flew through seven Fort Pierce power lines. They closed the city down for four hours. Those wires are one inch in diameter. They also cut twelve inches off their propeller. That plane must have been shaking like crazy."

The Black Hawk helicopter once chased two smugglers who fled their plane. The copter hovered two feet off the ground over tiny shrubs so members of the assault team could jump out. A 270-pound agent jumped first. The man behind him momentarily froze as he watched the hefty man disappear into the darkness. The dark dots underneath the helicopter were not shrubs. They were fruit trees in an orchard. The first man had jumped from twenty feet. The second man followed for fear of being called a coward. The two smugglers, watching the jump, surrendered immediately.

"We see guys getting killed," Mad Dog said. "They disintegrate when they hit the water and we can't find the bodies. The Citation was tailing a plane once when it slowed over Bimini. The Citation had to veer around it. It startled the pilot, who stalled and crashed. A Bahamian deputy minister's son died in that crash. The guys [smugglers] on the ground said that Customs had shot the plane down. All allegations were dropped when bales of marijuana started bobbing up around the wreck. Two years ago, we were chasing a DC-6 [with a cargo of marijuana]. He got into a thunderstorm which we flew around and he never came through. We found five bodies the next day. They had been eaten by sharks."

Customs agents at the air branch were monitoring the UHF radio frequency one day when they heard a suspicious transmission to someone on the ground. The pilot asked that the hangar doors be open so he could taxi in. The agents figured he was going to Tamiami airport and called the Dade Police Department. Police searched two hangars and found a tape recorder inside a Beechcraft Baron. It contained a recruiting tape for smugglers detailing the pilot's entire trip: "That's so-and-so. He made $400,000 in the last few months. He's an Eastern pilot." The pilot had Indians at a Colombian airstrip talk to someone on tape. He interviewed the crew of an Aerostar that crashed on takeoff. They were waiting for a plane with space to take them back to the United States. The crew said they took the data plate off the crashed plane because it would not be recovered and they were going to steal an Aerostar in the States and put the plate on it. The pilot's tape was so detailed he even mentioned when he was having a shit. The man was eventually caught landing in Orlando with a load of cocaine.

Bill, a pilot, followed a twin-engine Lockhead Lodestar at 100 feet for seven hours to northern Georgia on a black, moonless night. "His ground crew turned off the runway lights when they heard us behind him. He crashed into the trees and burned. They recovered 4,000 pounds of unburned marijuana." Denis, another pilot, recalled how a US Navy Phantom F-4 fighter was scrambled to intercept a smuggler's plane. "He overshot the plane from behind and sliced it in half. He sliced four people in half at the shoulder."

A Broward County detective remembered an incident involving another US Navy F-4 in the mid-1970s. "One guy who had a Lear jet made one trip a week from Colombia to North America. He made so much money he had the plane repainted every week and changed its registration number. One day they had an AWAC [a US Navy observation plane] out of Homestead watching him. They scrambled two F-4s. They came alongside him and used international signals to ask him to follow them in. He tried to turn into the F-4s. Then he tried to ram them over the Everglades. They got permission to fire off his nose. The next thing you know, one of the pilots says over the radio, 'Oh, my God. I just hit him.' A commercial flight was landing in Miami at the time. The Eastern [Airlines] pilot told Miami tower he saw a fireball over the Everglades. Miami tower advised the pilot it was swamp gas."

Another time, two men — one of them a Canadian — being chased by a Customs plane flew 400 feet over Disneyland, landed the plane on a dirt runway, shoved the throttle wide open, and jumped out after aiming the plane at the hangar. The plane got stuck in sand and Customs officials had to smash its windows to reach in and turn the engine off. Meanwhile the two men escaped in a car that another agent pursued in a two-man Cobra combat helicopter. He landed in a parking lot and arrested the men running through a shopping center while changing their clothes.

Because they can hire the best lawyers, smugglers are brazen in their dealings with Customs officials. "Two go-boats were being chased," said Denis the pilot. "Three men threw open the throttle on one and jumped out. When we caught six men in the second boat, three of them were wet. They said, 'Hey man, why are you picking on us? Haven't you ever been fishing?' The officer's reply was, 'Yeah, with a fishing rod. I've never jumped in and chased them.' "

Frustrated Customs agents sometimes play as dirty as smugglers do.

"We tailed this guy for a long time and couldn't nail him," said Red Denmat, Customs director of aviation operations for the eastern US and a legend among interdiction agents. "We hot-wired his tail lights so that when he turned them off to evade us, the tail lights went on. We caught him."

Customs agents are most often frustrated by smugglers who seek haven in the Bahamas, where American agents can't make arrests unless they have Bahamian officials on board their plane or boat. Denis the pilot tells how one helicopter pilot vented his frustration on a smuggler who got away with a speedboat full of marijuana. "The go-boat ran to Bimini and tweeked his nose at the Coast Guard pursuer. The Black Hawk pilot dumped 200 gallons of aircraft fuel from his tank into the go-boat."

In the early 1980s, a Cessna 206 carrying 600 pounds of marijuana was spotted coming over Bimini. The Citation II and a King Air with a bust crew were launched after it. The Citation landed in Charlotte, North Carolina, to refuel. The control tower informed the Customs agents on a discreet frequency that the Cessna was also planning to land in Charlotte. Ground control guided the Citation to the end of runway 31. The Cessna landed. The King Air landed behind him. The controller told the Cessna to taxi to the end of the runway and turn right. When he did, the Citation turned on its lights to reveal four Customs agents with shotguns aimed at the Cessna. The pilot was a student at New York State University.

Radar picked up a northbound Piper Apache near Marco Island on Florida's west coast early one evening in 1988. A Black Hawk helicopter was vectored to the northwest to cross its flight path. A Citation pulled up beside the plane and could see the pilot and two passengers. The Citation followed the plane to an airport in Delray Beach and guided the Black Hawk to the site using the FLIR. The helicopter landed and the bust crew rushed the pilot as he walked away from the hangar after closing the doors. They put him on the ground and one agent walked into the hangar. His adrenaline started pumping when he noticed the two passengers in the back of the plane. After a while they hadn't moved and the agent moved in. He thought the faces looked familiar. Prince Charles and Lady Di sat nonchalantly, apparently oblivious to what was happening. The agent climbed into the plane and pulled the rubber masks off the head-and-shoulder mannequins that sat on 300 kilos of cocaine.

"All pilots do something in surveillance or during a chase they wish they hadn't done," said Bill, an experienced Customs pilot. "Mine was in River Oaks, a development north of Okeechobee. We were following a Piper Aztec. He detected us at the south end of Lake Okeechobee and threw his dope out. He landed at the north end at River Oaks. The Black Hawk was thirty-five minutes away. I'm trying to land on a grass strip at night. I'm trying to have the Citation, which is above me, line me up with the runway with its infrared. I almost landed in a canal until I noticed the poles going by me, so I pulled up. After the third try, I landed on the runway. I forgot it was the fall and there was dew on the grass. I hit the brakes and slid. The smugglers had left their plane in the middle of the runway. There was a one-foot-deep drainage ditch on the side of the runway. I put my left wheel in the ditch to get the right wing tip high enough to go over the smugglers' plane. Then I turned around. They got away."

Many of the pilots who fly planes of dope into the United States are aces. They fly under extreme conditions without instruments. Most of the landing strips where they pick up the drugs are makeshift mud swaths in jungles. Some of them are carved into hillsides, where only a high-winged plane can land without clipping the bushes on either side of the strip. The plane lands going uphill to slow down quickly and takes off going downhill so Mother Nature can help it gain speed with its heavy load. The average load is 500 kilos.

The first sizeable cocaine bust by the Customs air branch in Florida came in 1980 when officials opened the trunk of a car. Bill the pilot had chased a Cessna 310 in his King Air. The plane got away after landing on a sod farm west of Fort Lauderdale. One hour later, Bill returned to the site in a helicopter and found a car near the landing strip that had run into a tree after missing a left turn. He found 356 pounds of cocaine in the trunk. Each spherical kilo was stamped with a swastika, the mark of Carlos Lehder, the Nazi-worshipping leader of the Medellin cartel.

The following day, the Citation was cruising between two thunderstorms at night when Customs agents noticed a Cessna 404 with no lights. They followed it to Tampa International Airport and seized 386 pounds of cocaine marked with swastikas and bearing the names of the people it was destined for.

"After that, it was one after another," Bill the pilot said. "At that time it took a while for them to figure out how to beat us. They saturated the shore. They could afford to lose. We must have hurt them. They got larger planes. I arrested one guy in Tennessee who was ready to go to Denver from Colombia. We're seeing more long-distance smuggling now to avoid south Florida." Smugglers are now using turboprop planes and flying at higher altitudes to land in Nova Scotia.

"We went from total saturation by smugglers to the point where they put spotters on the ground," said Bill. "Smugglers would fly over spotters who would listen for tailing planes. If spotters warned hot, they would turn to the Bahamas and drop their loads. The law didn't allow us to charge them then. The laws have now changed so we can charge them if we retrieve the contraband. They'd land and unload in the Bahamas before we got Bahamians on our crews and boat the stuff over. Then came the age of the airdrop. We're still in it. Many of them drop their cargoes over Cuban airspace where we can't go. The go-fasts pick them up in Cuban waters."

In the early 1980s, Customs planes weren't equipped and didn't have plans to follow long-distance flights like the New York Expresses.

On a dark, overcast night in 1984, Customs agents in a Citation II watched a DC-6 from Colombia dump bales of marijuana off a conveyor belt to speedboats in the ocean near Andros Island. The bales, marked with fluorescent lights, looked like fireflies in the water. An army helicopter arrived with a bust crew. The helicopter hovered in front of a boat to stop it from getting away. A blade hit the water and cracked. The copter sank in five feet of water 200 yards from shore. The FLIR screen in the Citation overhead showed spray and steam, with the speedboat squirting out of the picture. Thirty seconds later, the copter radioed that the crew was OK. The speedboat beached one-quarter mile away in a bay. The Citation crew watched the smugglers on infrared, fearing they would shoot at the copter. The speedboat left when the helicopter arrived to airlift the downed crew out. The next day, Customs agents flying over the wreck noticed something they could not have seen at night — hundreds of sharks swimming around the helicopter.

Customs agents know many of the smugglers they don't manage to catch. They keep tabs on them, though. Two Canadian smugglers loaded their plane with cocaine in Colombia. The plane developed engine problems on takeoff. They unloaded, fixed the plane, and reloaded. By then someone had tipped off the police and the smugglers barely got away. The co-pilot later took six bullets in Bolivia. The pilot was arrested in Florida for falsely registering a plane.

In October 1986, Customs radar picked up a Cessna 320 near Bimini. A retired Dominicana airlines Boeing 727 pilot and his son, a private pilot, were arrested for having an illegal fuel system in the plane. The seized plane was returned after the pilots paid a fine. Customs agents believed they were testing the system to see if they'd get caught on the way back into the States. In 1988, the son was arrested in North Carolina after being wiretapped while he negotiated to fly a load from Colombia to North Carolina.

Florida isn't the only border smugglers violate. One night the power went out in San Diego. A smuggler following Interstate 805 in a Cessna 206 hit a power line and a bridge overpass. Eight hundred pounds of marijuana and body parts were strewn all over the highway. The plane's engine soared over the bridge, over two roads, and into the back end of a Volkswagen.

Bill was flying a Customs jet to Houston in December 1985 when he got a call to intercept a Cessna flying across southwest Texas. Air controllers in Austin vectored the plane to the target while blocking off airspace five miles around Bill's plane. A helicopter joined the chase and hovered beside the Cessna as it landed south of Waco and turned on its night sun, lighting up the scene like something out of *Close Encounters*. The Cessna took off into the clouds and landed at a small airport in Marlin. The plane didn't roll far. When the Cessna was scared off at Waco, the pilot forgot to retract his landing gear. When he landed in Marlin, he retracked the wheels, thinking he was letting them down. The pilot ran away from the crashed plane. A sheriff's bloodhound found the doper and chewed his butt off.

While the folks in the Bahamas hate dope-busting Customs agents, the good guys have supporters in the western states as well. Farmers along the borders out west shoot at Customs patrol planes they think are the goddam dopers.

It might sound adventurous to follow a boat with a plane, but it's as boring as hell after the first thirty minutes. This is the hardest part of being a Customs agent. We flew a large oval pattern five miles behind a fishing boat suspected of being en route to a rendezvous with a mother ship. A US Coast Guard helicopter was on its way to help us watch the fishing boat. The sun set before it arrived. I broke out the M&Ms and started munching.

We heard over the radio that a US Navy Pegasus-class hydrofoil, which can cruise at 100 knots, had stopped a go-fast. In the meantime, the fishing boat sought refuge in Cuban waters, knowing we could not fly into the Cuban Air Defense Identification Zone (ADIZ). We broke surveillance and buzzed off toward Key Largo, seventy miles north, eyes peeled for the hydrofoil. It can stop a smugglers' speedboat by pulling up alongside and cutting its engines. The wake of the jet-propelled boat plopping into the water makes handling a speedboat impossible.

The world around us was a black void. The horizon had gobbled up the sun and the odd boat on the ocean looked like a star. I put a chocolate M&M on the intrument panel. It didn't slide. We were flying right-side up and level after all. The lights of Key Largo appeared in the darkness and nostalgia creeped through the night. It was Saturday night down there in Bogey land. Up where we were — another bogey land — there was no time. Everything was measured by the gas tank.

We walked into the Customs radio room at Homestead Air Force

Base at 8 p.m. after a four-hour surveillance mission. I ate my dinner of M&Ms and a Coke. M&Ms and orange juice are my usual breakfast fare. They give me the energy to get going in the morning.

Denis the pilot had practiced several abrupt landings when we returned to Homestead. Customs police have to drop their planes at full speed behind a smuggling aircraft and stop yards from its tail while a Black Hawk helicopter lands in front to prevent bad guys from running away. To do this, pilots approach the bad guy's plane at a 90-degree angle, veer sharply to get behind it, slam on the air brakes, drop the landing gear to scrub more speed, and shove the sucker into reverse when they hit the tarmac. It's the next best thing to being mobbed by ten frothing naked nymphomaniacs. And a lot safter.

One of two red phones in the radio room rang at 9:21 p.m. The Operations Duty Officer answered. Two US Navy F-16 fighters on coastal patrol spotted a plane flying low and dark from Colombia to Florida at 140 knots. The primary target was forty miles northeast off Key West. The Command Duty Officer pressed a button and the scramble horn blared across the airfield. A Customs interceptor jet must be airborne and heading toward its target in eight minutes. The pilot, co-pilot, air interdiction officer, and I strapped ourselves in. Ground crew unplugged the Auxiliary Power Unit and pulled the chocks from under the wheels. Double thumbs up from the ground crew. A call by the ODO to the Homestead Air Force Base control tower on the second red phone, a direct hotline, got immediate clearance for the Citation. The C3I center in Miami plotted an intercept course and radioed the coordinates to the co-pilot, who broke out the maps and started plotting. All this before we got off the ground.

We lifted off and veered 180 degrees to get on course. Conversations between C3I, the Customs jet, the F-16s, and the Navy control center crackled over five radio frequencies that were constantly changed by computer. A Navy pilot alerted the center that the single-engine high-wing plane was northbound at 6,000 feet. He asked if he could pull up behind the plane to read its identification number. He was told not to get closer than 500 feet.

"Will maintain surveillance on the bogey until the Customs interceptor has contact on the bogey," the pilot answered in a southern drawl.

"It appears the target is in a gradual descent. He's 5,000 feet now."

The planes are still too far away to show up above the sea of clouds on the Forward Looking Infrared monitor. The air interdiction officer jots notes by flashlight.

"The bogey seems to be tracking a 040 heading."

"Copy."

The radar in the Customs plane picked up the target plane and the two F-16s thirty miles away.

"We have you in sight."

"I had three blips out there. I took the first one," the air interdiction officer said as he locked his radar on the target plane.

"I'm gonna have the fighters break on the left," the pilot said.

The first F-16 was one mile behind the target. The second fighter was two miles behind the first fighter. The Customs jet was now seven miles behind the target, four miles behind the F-16s. The fighters were too fast to maintain constant surveillance behind the target plane and kept breaking off in long loops before getting back on track several miles behind the plane. They repeated the process every time they got too close.

"I got the visual on the target 5 degrees to the left of the nose," the Customs pilot said.

"I just locked in," said the air interdiction officer.

The F-16s broke off left on the FLIR screen. All we could see out the window was the fire of their engines and their running lights. The target plane was still running without lights. The co-pilot juggled maps trying to plot possible landing sites for the other plane.

First he appeared to be headed toward an airfield in Naples. Then it looked like he might land in Fort Myers. The Customs jet closed in and the plane was clearly visible in the dark Florida sky on the infrared monitor. The white plane on dark background was flying at 2,000 feet. The Customs jet tracked it at 3,000 feet. The Black Hawk helicopter was vectoring across the state to join in the chase. The target plane veered slowly to the right. The Customs pilot decided to go into a tight 360-degree turn to get down behind the target plane to read its tail number. One minute and forty seconds later, the jet completed the turn, dropped 1,000 feet, and the target plane was nowhere in sight.

The Customs jet and Black Hawk helicopter searched the area for twenty minutes. The smuggler lucked out. He had dropped quickly to a landing strip while the jet was circling down behind him. Except for a brief conversation between the pilot and co-pilot to determine how to prevent losing a target this way again, little was said on the return flight to the base.

You Too Can Identify Smugglers

More than 80 percent of the cocaine smuggled into North America arrives by plane. More than 80 percent of the world's cocaine comes from Colombia. Only 46 of every 1,000 planes suspected of smuggling drugs into North America is stopped. The Untouchables at Homestead admit they may stop 1 percent of the cocaine shipped north from South America.

Smugglers and their planes behave differently from non-smugglers and these characteristics make them stand out.

In flight:
— The planes fly at low altitudes and climb suddenly near airports.
— Their pilots don't respond to radio queries and they flee from law-enforcement planes.
— The planes have missing passenger seats for no legitimate reason.
— The plane windows are covered with curtains or are taped over.
— The planes contain foreign charts.
— The planes contain numerous boxes, duffel bags, and containers.
— When intercepted, their pilots jettison objects to vehicles over open ground or to boats over water.
— The planes fly without lights at night.

On landing:
— Large vehicles equipped with radios to talk with the pilot wait near the landing area.
— The planes land at remote runways lit by headlights or fires.
— The planes meet vehicles and leave quickly.
— The planes refuel from 55-gallon drums or from the back of pickup trucks.

On the ground:
— The planes have chipped paint, muddy wheels; lack wheel pants; are dirty or dusty; and the propellers are beat up — evidence of landings on dirt strips.
— The interiors smell of strong perfumes or other odors used to cover the smell of marijuana.
— The air shocks are overinflated and tires oversized to operate on dirt strips.
— The planes have new paint, added doors, extra fuel tanks, false or altered registration numbers.
— The planes are parked far from the line shack.
— The pilots won't leave the plane unattended during ground servicing.
— The pilots pay for fuel and services with cash.

From 1980 to 1988, 1,250 planes worth $130 million were stolen in the United States, more than half of them in Florida, California, and Texas. Many of these were custom-ordered by drug smugglers in South America. Colombian cartels hire teams to seek out, steal, and deliver to Colombia expensive turboprop planes. The teams case airports, such as in resort areas like Hilton Head, South Carolina, where wealthy individuals and corporations use turboprop planes. The thieves chat up owners in bars and find out how long they are staying. Then they call the airport and have the plane prepared to leave. They pay cash or bill the company.

Fleets of stolen turboprops — King Air 200s and 300s, Piper Cheyennes, and Aerocommanders — operate out of drug bases near Medellin, Colombia, and Guadalajara, Mexico. They have also been spotted in Haiti and on other Caribbean islands. Colombia cartels have more than twenty Commander 900s, 980s, and 1000s flying between Colombia and southern Mexico. Many plane thieves fly loads of electronic equipment such as televisions, video recorders, radios, and toasters into Mexico and return with loads of drugs.

Smugglers also pirate boats on the high seas. This fact was brought to light most dramatically in 1980 when Illinois State Representative Harry Yourell and his son Peter stopped their twenty-five-foot cabin cruiser beside the *Kalia III* anchored at Pipe Cay in the Bahamas. They found a bloated body in a dinghy astern of the boat, which was peppered with shotgun pellets and smeared with blood. The boat appeared to have been ransacked. The glasses and bikini bra of sixty-four-year-old Patti Kamerer were lying on the deck. She had left Fort Myers with her fifty-five-year-old husband William on April 28 for a six-month cruise of the Bahamas. Her last log entry on July 25 was "Moored at Pipe Cay."

Yourell called the Bahamian cops, who flew over the boat. The body had disappeared by the time a police boat arrived the next day. The Bahamian government, ever conscious of harming tourism with bad press, denied there had been a body in the dinghy — until Yourell made public a photograph he had taken of it. Then the government changed its tune and admitted that a police constable aboard the plane had seen the body. Government officials denied there were shotgun holes and pellets in the boat, although they had been seen by three people.

Pipe Cay is just south of Norman Cay, which the Medellin Cartel leader, Carlos Lehder, took over in the late 1970s as a refueling stop for his cocaine-laden planes from Colombia en route to the United States. His goons were notorious for shooting at yachtsmen, including Walter Cronkite, who tried to anchor off Norman Cay. Patti Kamerer was probably taken to Lehder's stronghold. The body in the dinghy was probably her husband. The Bahamian government owes it to Kamerer's family to solve her killing or at least find her body, if it hasn't been dumped in the ocean. As the Bahamian tourist bureau says, "It's better in the Bahamas."

The light reading of a boater in the Bahamas probably saved the lives of everyone on the forty-seven-foot cruiser *Rig-n-Tom* in 1979. Pat Vaughan was reading Peter Benchley's novel *The Island*, about modern Bahamian piracy and misleading distress calls, when an SOS call crackled across the radio. Skipper Thomas Loberg and his wife Rignor were about to reply to the caller's request that they give their position — he did not volunteer his — when Vaughan intervened and demanded Loberg ask the caller for *his* position. The radio went silent. A high-powered fishing boat showed up five minutes later and chased the *Rig-n-Tom*, which sought shelter near a sailboat.

Blue Lightning: The US Customs Service Marine Interdiction Program

The sun had set. I turned the helm of the US Customs speedboat over to the agent next to me after blasting underneath a low bridge south of Don Johnson's waterfront house on Miami's intercoastal waterway. The night air chilled and we started thinking coffee. The agents conferred over the best spot to pick up a java and cracked open the throttle halfway to get there — fifty miles an hour on a pitch-black waterway about 300 yards wide cluttered with sand bars. We had got stuck on one already that night. Tears streamed out of my eyes to the side of my head and into my ears as I tried to read the depth gauge and infrared scanner and marine radar that outlined the shore. Ten feet, eight feet, two feet. I'm gator bait if this sucker hits a sand bar.

Then we spotted a bunch of friendly faces on a concrete wharf lit by yellow lamps on two utility poles. The boat chugged in beside another Customs boat. There are many waterfront restaurants on the waterway, but stopping there for coffee is asking for trouble. A lot of dopers would welcome the opportunity to flatten a narc. So we moored several hundred yards from a cut to the ocean. If a bad guy zoomed in with a load of dope, we had seconds to get on his ass or he'd be gone.

There was no coffee on the wharf, no heat, but the stories were fascinating. Tales of CIA boats full of nasties — maniacs in Zodiacs — bombing up and down the waterway en route to mysterious assignments, Spanish swear words slashing through the night as some Cuban refugee's elbow slipped and his arm slid into the water that he believed was full of beasties waiting to eat him.

What . . .? Thunder roared by and a white wall of water hissed toward shore as darkness swallowed the thunder.

The chase was on. Nothing but Toby's asshole ahead of us and we were going full throttle up the tailpipe. All of a sudden it didn't matter if we hit anything. Even so, I strained my eyes with the hope I'd get a fraction of a second to jump into the air before the boat smeared itself against a sea wall. It doesn't work, but it keeps the mind off other disturbing thoughts.

The radar showed something in the water dead ahead. A boat. A boat with a hole in its hull. And there was the buoy that made the hole. I was thankful the bad guys had hit it first. So the boat got a free tow back to a Customs house. As the parade chug-chugged along near a bridge, two go-fasts streaked out of nowhere into nowhere. Forget the holey boat. Someone slashed the line and a power U-turn sent us back up Toby's asshole. One of the go-fasts disappeared. One was pulled over. It turned out to be the radar boat.

The radar boat runs ahead of the load boat and tells him through a single sideboard radio when he can come through. Many of these are faster than Customs boats, churning the waves with four or five outboard motors. Load boats also use spotter planes and land-based spotters to check for Customs boats. The go-fasts get their loads of marijuana and cocaine from planes that drop bales into the ocean near Bimini or in Cuban waters after flying up from Colombia or Jamaica. The speedboats have to zip over fifty to ninety miles of Atlantic Ocean and into one of thousands of sheltered inlets or up the intercoastal waterway before calling it a night. They run dark and usually deke into the intercoastal waterway through the southernmost cuts: Cape Florida, Bear, Government, Haulover, or Port Everglades cuts.

"The dopers outrun us frequently," said a Customs officer with the Miami Marine Patrol, who operated the boat. "It's hard to chase boats at night. If they turn off their lights, you have to follow the ripples of the wake. It's like being in the closet with the lights off. Sometimes when we chase them, they run back out to the ocean. A lot of boats run their mufflers underwater. We turn off our engines during a chase if we lose them so we can hear them. It's nothing for dopers to abandon a $200,000 go-fast. It's a business expense.

"They have night-vision goggles, police frequency scanners, single sideboard radios to communicate between boats; they run counter surveillance on us; they know the number of boats we have and where. They have aircraft to watch us and they run decoys. We'll stop it and they'll run a load boat past us. They mold their boats around the drugs. We cut them open with Skill Saws. There are companies that specifically equip boats for smuggling. They build what you want. On one boat we lifted the back stairs, pulled out the fuel tank, and found a drug compartment that ran the length of the boat."

There's really no such thing as a go-fast. It's a generic term for Cigarette boats, Apaches, Midnight Expresses, or other ocean-racing speedboats.

"The most powerful boat I've seen," said the Customs officer as the already dark night got darker, "was a thirty-five footer with two 625-horsepower engines. It was built and designed like a Cigarette boat. He outran everybody we had. We caught him, though. He had dumped 100 bales during a chase and nobody picked them up. We just went after him."

Smuggling dope by boat and chasing dopers has changed over time. "Years ago they stacked bales in the open," a Customs officer said. "The better we get, the more the bad guys try to find better ways to get it in." So Customs officers keep their eyes open for raised waterlines, listing boats, the smell of fresh fiberglass, new matting, and try to figure out what's taking up the area in a boat — legit space or secret compartments. Customs agents now use fiber optics to explore the dark recesses in boats rather than hacking through with Skill Saws. Sometimes they make a bust on a cold hit. Most of the time they work with intelligence. There's always someone out there willing to rat out to get even.

The majority of the smugglers they catch are Latinos. Although they are armed, they don't often shoot at Customs agents. That would get them a longer jail term than smuggling. Dopers would rather lose their booty and run to chance smuggling another day. They carry guns to protect themselves from their friends.

Many dopers and their boats disappear in the Bermuda Triangle. There's no great mystery to their deaths, though. More often than not they die because of greed or negligence. Go-fasts blow up because smugglers pile bales of marijuana around the engines. It ignites explosively and burns quickly and fiercely. Many potheads have gone up in smoke this way. Sometimes fuel lines leak and poor ventilation caused by stacked bales of marijuana allows fumes to build up until a spark sends shark bait flying in all directions.

Successful air interdiction and radar monitoring has forced an increase in airdrops to go-fasts since 1988, especially in the Cay Sal Banks, as smugglers were driven away from the Bahamas and areas covered by aerostat had ground-based radars. There were at least three major smuggling operations a week in and around Cuban waters, including the Cay Sal Banks and the Old Bahama Channel in 1989. More ships were observed cutting through Cuban territorial waters on their way to Florida. They also sought shelter in Cuban waters to avoid pursuers. At the same time, smuggling planes were observed flying through VFR (visual flight rules) corridors over Cuba to airdrop and land drugs in Bahamas and Florida.

The Cuban route makes interdiction extremely difficult, since planes use Cuba as a shadow to avoid radar detection. This route puts them safely within ninety miles of Key West before they can be picked up by

US radar. From that point, they slingshot right into the US or make their drops to go-fasts. By the time the planes are that close, assuming they are spotted as they leave Cuban airspace among dozens of other planes in the area, interdiction teams often can't be mobilized fast enough to stop them.

Traffickers have also started looking for new routes — through Mexico and across the border to Texas and California. They use cargo containers and ship waterproof cocaine base on the bottom of ships. Many smugglers also leave from countries other than Colombia for their final run into the United States. They fly out of Panama or Belize and up the western side of the Gulf of Mexico, where interdiction is weak at best. Smugglers have stash houses and private airstrips carved out with air-lifted bulldozers on many of the 750 desolate islands between Florida and Cuba. They also stash bales of cocaine and marijuana in the Keys. Customs helicopters hover low over the ground to flatten the grass when looking for hidden dope.

The major cities that cocaine is smuggled into have one common characteristic — a large Spanish-speaking population.

"Most of the cocaine traffic is Hispanic-controlled," said a senior Customs official in Miami. "They want a good banking center, good air travel, and a big Hispanic community to hide in. We're talking a limited number of smuggling groups. It's well controlled. When you're talking tons, amateurs ain't a threat. It's like the personal computer field — the people who are good stayed in the business."

The boat we were sitting in was no lagoon-churning Cuisinart. It was a deep-V hull Chris-Craft Stinger with twin 440-horsepower engines that propelled it from crest to crest of ten-foot Atlantic swells at seventy miles per hour. That sucker banged the water harder than a New Orleans whore trying to set an attendance record at a Latin Quarter cat house. These Customs officers love their boat so much they gave my brass-rivetted motorcycle boots dirty looks as I stood on the concrete wharf in the late afternoon waiting for the OK to board.

I donned my sneakers and hopped in, checking the cabin for the AR-15s in case some seagull shit on me. The boat took it nice and easy down the Miami River while I checked for doper spies all round. Then we churned through Biscayne Bay. It's a scary body of water, especially when the troughs of swells expose a suck-muck bottom. Pelicans stared at us from stumps. I stared back while the Customs officers checked out a boat they stopped, hands on their holstered guns.

Then the guys told me Biscayne Bay was a great place to fish for dolphin.

"Dolphin?"

"Yeah, it's great eating. You can get it in any restaurant around here."

"Dolphin? Like. Like . . ."

"No, not like Flipper. Dolphin is a kind of fish."

"Why do they call it dolphin? Goddam tree huggers are going to go nuts over this one."

The Customs boat got out into the Atlantic and the swells heaved us around like the rebound on a frameless waterbed. We pulled up beside a humongous cruiser and it was like looking up the side of a six-story building. I couldn't even reach the ladder.

We were at our stakeout on the intercoastal waterway. We sat on the calm water with the engines turned off, listening for the hardrock throb of a gut-busting engine. I hugged myself because a fiberglass boat gets damn cold when dew forms on the seat. There must have been a breeze in the dark because the boat rocked slowly. Then a thud at the back. I look down but couldn't see anything. Then another thud. What the . . .? I looked up to see a goddam snake as thick as my arm standing straight up against the side of the boat next to my head, inching its way upward. Then it plopped into the boat across my lap. Thud. Holy fuck. The boat was crawling with snakes I couldn't even see.

I stood up and shuddered hard. The Customs officers nearly jumped out of their seats. I guess they had been dozing too.

The Customs officers were telling stories again so I wouldn't scare the shit out of them by hopping out of another nightmare.

"I was lying in the boat at night," one Customs officer said. "It was pitch black. The mosquitoes were biting. Then a porpoise blows beside the boat. It scared the shit out of me. The porpoise plays with the boat and tries to figure out who you are."

Great, I thought, they've been eating those floating bales of marijuana.

"One evening I was coming in five miles offshore," said the other officer. "The water changed five times. Everything was like glass in a square where it rained. Outside that square, the water was choppy. I know people who went out and never came back."

"We had a whale out there early one morning," the first officer said. "We though it was a boat. He was way out of the water. We kept going and going, then we saw a water spout. He let us get within thirty feet and he dove. We turned that Cigarette right around and opened it up. There are loggerhead turtles out there as big as a desk, but they dive if they hear you."

The Blue Lightning Strike Force is the nemesis of drug-hauling speed-boaters. The strike force was formed in 1985 to coordinate US Customs and Coast Guard and state and local law-enforcement attempts to nail high-speed boats that hauled tons of coke and pot into Florida. The

strike force was named after the two-week Operation Blue Lightning in
April 1985, in which twenty-five American and Bahamian law-enforcement agencies used 85 boats, 30 planes, and 775 people to crack down on
drug smuggling between the Bahamas and southern Florida. Agents
conducted spot raids along 700 miles of the Bahamian archipelago to
drive smugglers into a net covered by radar, planes, and boats along 150
miles of Florida coastline. They seized 6,533 pounds of cocaine, 33,872
pounds of marijuana, and arrested fifty-eight suspected smugglers.

The force is coordinated by the Blue Lightning Operations Command
Center, a Star Wars-like control room with technology equal to that of
military command centers. The operations center monitors the same
radars — including aerostats — that feed information to the air interdiction C3I center. The Blue Lightning Operations Center concerns itself
only with boats though. And it is so effective that heavy-duty security
measures have been taken to protect it. The BLOC Center on the tenth
floor at 51 SW 1st Street in Miami is so secure that a hungover employee
probably couldn't remember the codes to punch into electronic locks to
gain access.

The dark glassed-in room that houses the computers and technicians
is alive with pinpricks of colored light. This is not a job for the color
blind. Computers convert radar data into graphics on five-by-seven-foot
screens. A red line indicates the twelve-mile limit for US coastal water.
Technicians try to spot targets outside the limit to reduce the unneces-
sary stopping of local boats. Blue asterisks indicate targets. A computer
numbers each and gives its heading and speed. Green spots are designated landmarks used to plot intercepts. Radars can even spot wooden
sailboats by the reflection off their masts. One of the most difficult boats
to detect with rooftop radar is the fiberglass Midnight Express, which
rides two-and-a-half feet off the water. The aerostat radars pick it up
with no problem. Blue Lightning boats are equipped with transponders
that show their position on the screen, allowing the center to coordinate
the interception of bad guys. But even high-tech is not perfect.

"We sent a plane after a thunderstorm," said Patrick, a highly placed
Customs agent. "Occasionally the radar sees weather."

The US Customs Marine Interdiction Program alone has 220 boats
cruising the waterways for dopers. Blue-water boats are used for long-
range surveillance missions; utility boats are used to support busts;
interceptor boats are used in high-speed chases of doper speedboats.

Don Aronow was the most famous powerboat racer and designer in
the world. The world-champion racer designed the Donzi and the
Cigarette boats that are loved by racers and smugglers alike. Sometimes
the job descriptions are interchangeable. Aronow's Miami-based
Aronow Power Boats, which supplied his USA Racing Team, designed,

built, and signed a special speedboat for the US Customs Service Marine Interdiction Program in 1984. The twin-hull catamaran is thirty-nine feet long and twelve feet wide and is powered to speeds of seventy miles an hour on a cushion of air by twin Mer-Cruiser 575-horsepower engines with custom-header exhaust. The boat can keep up a chase for 300 miles between refills of its three aluminum gas tanks that hold 288 gallons of fuel. The patrol boat was christened *Blue Thunder* and started chasing bad guys hauling loads of marijuana and cocaine on Valentine's Day, 1985. Its catamaran hull allows it to maintain high speeds in choppy water and skim over waves that would destroy conventional powerboats. It can turn full speed in a radius of forty-five feet compared to a fifty-foot radius at reduced speeds for regular speedboats. Aronow's innovative design gave Customs agents an advantage over the bad guys who also used his boats.

A car pulled up beside Aronow's car in Miami early in 1987. The occupants of both cars rolled down their windows. Someone pumped half a dozen bullets into the designer.

In the late evening of October 18, 1984, Customs patrol officers stationed on Marco Island in Florida started monitoring suspicious radio transmissions from a sixty-two-foot fishing boat called *Partnership*. The boat appeared to be broadcasting its course and location in code. Customs cracked the code within an hour and vectored a patrol boat to the *Partnership*. Customs agents boarded it south of Everglades City at 11 p.m. and found forty pounds of marijuana residue in its fishing wells. Residue. Imagine how much that boat was carrying.

The shipment of marijuana had been moved ashore in smaller boats and hidden somewhere in the dangling tentacle roots of mangrove-covered islands and inlets that scorpions, water moccasins, rattlesnakes, alligators, and cloud-like swarms of mosquitoes call home. Cops set up a roadblock on US 41 to prevent the bad guys from driving the stuff out. Then Customs agents, sheriff's deputies, and forest rangers hopped into their boats and scoured the waterways near the seized *Partnership*, looking for broken branches or scuffed mangrove roots. At 11 a.m. on October 19, two agents and an Everglades Park forest ranger slowly made their way up Secret Creek, where they found five small boats pulled up on shore and 785 bales of marijuana — 45,000 pounds of pot. Someone sweated and gave a lot of blood to the mosquitoes while unloading that stuff.

Customs agents have a nifty gizmo to detect speedboats. It's called a Hydracoustic Boat Detection System. A hydrophone suspended in the water senses engine and propeller sounds, which are processed in a sensor and transmitted to a base station. The sounds are given numbers and their locations are identified, allowing boats to be deployed to investigate them. Dolphins should have a great time with this one.

On February 22, 1986, the Blue Lightning Operations Command Center vectored a Customs boat from Marco Island to two fishing boats: the *Nice & Easy* and the *Aiakatsi*. Both had been tracked since meeting with a mother ship sixty miles west of Marco Island. Customs agents found 500 bales of marijuana on the boats.

On April 7, 1986, Customs and Florida Marine Patrol officers followed two boats into Bluewater Trailer Park and found 2,000 pounds of marijuana on one of them.

On August 6, 1986, the Command Center spotted a boat on radar nine miles east of Baker's Haulover cut, but didn't have any boats in the area to intercept it. A Customs agent on land watched the boat approach shore and capsize while trying to maneuver through an inlet one-quarter mile from the cut. The Coast Guard found eighty-four bales of marijuana weighing 5,000 pounds aboard.

On August 9, 1986, the Monroe County Sheriff's Office was tipped off that a boat was offloading marijuana behind a house under construction on Loeb Street on Key Largo. They found twenty-five bales of marijuana weighing 1,832 pounds. The boat that had carried the weed was found abandoned up the canal where the bales were found.

On August 16, 1986, Key Largo Marine Enforcement officers on routine patrol tried to stop a boat four miles off the Upper Florida Keys Reef Line. The boat tried to ram the Customs boat three times during a high-speed chase. The officers shot a hole in the boat's starboard fuel tank and found twenty-four bales of marijuana weighing 1,000 pounds.

On September 3, 1986, Customs officers watched four men take a boat out of the water at the Phil Foster Boat Ramp in Riviera Beach. When they approached, two men ran away. They found 665 pounds of marijuana and one gallon of hash oil below deck in false compartments.

On August 26, 1986, Customs agents and Florida Marine Patrol officers boarded a boat and figured out it was going to be used to smuggle drugs. They put the boat on lookout. On September 3, the Coast Guard spotted it 108 miles southwest of Loggerhead Key. The boat tried to flee. Coast Guard officers found 20,000 pounds of marijuana bales below deck.

On August 22, 1986, Customs officers boarded the *White Marlin* and figured she was going for a load after finding supplies associated with secret compartments. The Coast Guard stopped the boat on September 7 because it had been put on a tag list. They didn't find any secret compartments and let the boat continue to Fort Lauderdale. Blue Lightning Operations Command Center advised Customs marine units who searched the boat in Fort Lauderdale with Coast Guard officers. They found the secret compartment in the hull below the salon. Inside were 1,300 pounds of cocaine.

On September 8, 1986, Customs radar picked up a speedy go-fast flying across the Florida Straits toward Islamorada. A Customs boat chased the go-fast and watched as nine duffel bags with 500 pounds of cocaine were tossed overboard. The boat crashed into a sea wall. Four more bags with 400 pounds of cocaine were found in the wreckage.

On September 9, 1986, the Coast Guard boarded the *Ocean Safari* twenty miles northwest of Cuba and found 9,000 pounds of marijuana in the fish hold, which had been converted into a secret compartment.

On November 6, 1986, Customs officers heard voices in the mangroves off Card Sound Road in upper Key Largo. They approached on foot and saw three men carrying bales of marijuana into the mangroves from the water's edge where 1,800 pounds of weed had been dropped off.

On November 6, 1986, Customs agents and Boca Raton cops staked out a house as a possible offload site used by the Orta-Gonzalez smuggling ring because of heavy vehicle and boat traffic. At 4:30 a.m., they saw men unload bales of marijuana from a boat docked behind the house. They found 5,300 pounds of marijuana.

On November 9, 1986, Customs agents watched a 1981 GMC pickup towing a ski boat from a ramp in Key Largo. They noticed a bale of marijuana on the boat's deck.

On November 17, 1986, Customs officers watched a boat run without lights one and one-half miles off Key Largo. They found 6,000 pounds of marijuana and night-vision goggles on board.

On July 13, 1989, at 7 a.m., US Coast Guard officers on the cutter *Seahawk* boarded and seized a thirty-two-foot fishing boat, *Mohigan Too*, in the Old Bahama Channel thirty miles north of Cuba. They found 1,089 pounds of cocaine that had been airdropped by a plane that flew near, but not inside, Cuban airspace.

During one close chase, a doper's go-fast jumped a sea wall in Miami's Golden Beach and flew twenty-seven feet before landing in someone's front lawn. Customs agents found three kilos of cocaine on the escaping boaters. But they made the mistake of leaving the boat unattended overnight. The next day, they found that someone had removed 184 kilos of cocaine from two hidden compartments in front of the boat's engine. Agents chopped the boat apart and found another 184 kilos.

One of the oddest sights in the waters south of Florida has to be bobbing bales of marijuana and cocaine. Either someone forgets to pick it up after an airdrop or they just can't find it. Whatever the reason, a lot of people are finding a lot of dope on the edge of the Gulf Stream. If the king-sized worms that eat garbage in the stream ever get into the dope, they're gonna get mighty mean come cold turkey time. And what about sharks? Those suckers eat anything. I won't even get into whales and squids.

These findings of dope on the water were selected at random from one year — 1986:

On April 26, Customs officers found fifty-three bales of marijuana floating near Marker 27 in Hawks Channel.

On August 6, some guy out in his boat told the US Coast Guard he saw duffel bags floating off Elliot and Boca Chita Keys. The good guys found fifteen duffel bags and two packages containing 1,592 pounds of cocaine. The next day, Blue Lightning Command Center was told a load of bales was bobbing in the waves near Elliot Key. They found sixty-seven bales of marijuana weighing 6,700 pounds and 200 pounds of cocaine.

On August 23, a boater told the Coast Guard he saw bales of marijuana floating eight miles from Pacific Light. They found eighty bales of weed in the water.

On September 16, the Coast Guard found ten bales of marijuana weighing 943 pounds floating off Cape Florida.

On November 6, the Coast Guard found 464 pounds of cocaine in nylon bags floating between seventeen and twenty-seven miles northwest of Bethel Shoal Lights.

On November 10, a security officer for the Kennedy Space Center found a duffel bag with forty-four pounds of cocaine washed ashore at Playa Linda Beach at Cape Canaveral. On November 13, NASA security officers found two more green duffel bags with eighty-eight pounds of cocaine on the north shore of Cape Canaveral.

On March 10, 1982, three Customs inspectors in Miami went through every box of cargo that arrived on a Tampa Colombia Airlines flight from Medellin, Colombia. Although airline employees tried to foil the search by mingling a pallet of cargo with previously searched cargo, the inspectors found 3,906 pounds of cocaine in the last pallet they checked. It was the largest cocaine seizure in US history and an eye-opening indication that Colombian cartels were using commercial shipments to smuggle tons of cocaine into the United States. Officials shuddered to think how long this had been going on. Contraband Enforcement Teams, which had operated on an ad hoc basis since 1979, received the official stamp of approval in November 1982.

Until 1979, drug smugglers who used commercial cargo planes and ships to transport their goods did not hide their contraband. They just added an extra box to a legitimate shipment for an accomplice to pick up at the other end. No one expected Customs agents to check all boxes. In

1979 Customs agents suspected there might be drugs in cargo shipments and surprised themselves when checks proved them right. Commercial shipments were rife with dope. The seizures were easy because the drugs weren't hidden. By 1980, smugglers realized they just couldn't ship drugs any more. They had to smuggle them in commercial goods, relying on the sheer volume of cargo to hide their contraband. More than 7 million containers enter the US every year. Customs agents just can't check everything that enters the country.

The Miami Contraband Enforcement Team, working twenty-four hours a day, like the air branch interdiction team and the Blue Lightning marine interdiction team, started finding 150-pound shipments of cocaine in pallets of cut flowers that arrive daily from Colombia. The scent of the flowers masks the smell of cocaine and prevents trained dogs from sniffing out the drug. Also, there is intense pressure on agents to clear perishable items quickly to get them to market. The Colombian cartels know that and know it is physically impossible to open the 10,000 to 15,000 flower boxes that arrive in Miami between 2 and 5 a.m. every day. Avianca ships twenty-three pallets of flowers on each plane. Customs agents started poking long screwdrivers into flower boxes, watching for powder on the blade. Then an ingenious agent devised a three-and-one-half-foot rod that resembled a metal tube cut lengthwise. He poked the rod into boxes and any cocaine that was in the cavity filled the rod. In 1984, they made 188 seizures of 9,145 pounds of cocaine and 34,082 pounds of marijuana this way.

Late at night on February 13, 1985, Sidney Reyes, district director of Customs for Washington, D.C., plunged the long metal probe into a box of cut flowers on an Avianca Airlines Boeing 747 cargo jet from Bogotá. Reyes was not a regular at this job. He was on a training course to learn new drug-detection techniques. When he pulled out the probe, white powder spilled to the ground and convinced him that the metal rod was one hell of a detector. He had punctured one of thirty-two flower boxes filled with 2,478 pounds of cocaine. The shipment was destined for a Canadian consignee. Evidence indicates that Avianca employees knew the plane was carrying cocaine. Customs seized the $199-million plane two days later after completing their investigation and triggered a meeting that involved the Colombian ambassador to the United States. Avianca gave Customs cash and a letter of credit for $1,982,400 to cover a possible $50-a-pound fine for carrying the cocaine. Customs had found 5,576 pounds of cocaine in thirty-four seizures on Avianca planes from 1980 to 1985. The company promised to clean up its act. The plane was still flying between Colombia and Miami in 1987.

Colombian smugglers are inventive. While cut flowers are a good cover to smuggle cocaine, many more ingenious methods have been used. It has been hidden in counterfeit Dial soap and in the pistons of spare aircraft engines. Smugglers liquify cocaine, put tropical fish in a clear bag of water, and put that bag inside a bag of liquified cocaine. You can't tell there are two bags and no one would suspect a fish to act normally if it were swimming in a cocaine solution. Some smugglers saturate various materials with cocaine solutions to get the drug across the border.

Twenty of 100 drums of concentrated pineapple juice taken off an Avianca flight in January 1986 contained 3,227 pounds of cocaine. A probe pushed into a paper-wrapped yam in a forty-foot container came out white. The cocaine-filled yams were made out of plaster rolled in dirt while wet. The false wall of a cargo container contained 6,900 pounds of cocaine. Often commercial cargo and personal luggage get the sniff treatment from Louie, the dope-sniffing dog. He's a determined little devil, sticking his snout into everything that looks like it might contain cocaine — all for a reward from his master.

The latest scheme to smuggle drugs into the United States comes right out of a James Bond movie. Smugglers attach nets full of drugs — usually water-impervious cocaine base — to the underside of cargo ships with powerful magnets and suction cups. Scuba divers slash the net off when the shop docks and swim away with the drugs.

"It's the hottest technique around," said Robert Randolph, vice-president of south Florida operations for Crowley Caribbean Transport. "They throw it into a speedboat and they're gonzo."

Crowley and another shipping company have hired scuba divers to check the underside of their ships as they arrive in Port Everglades. They have found empty nets attached to the hulls.

Weapons are hidden inside radios and television sets. Customs agents look for marks on the screws. Money is also a big-ticket smuggling item. The cartels want cash sent back to Colombia to pay their business expenses. Anyone taking more than $10,000 out of the United States must declare the money. Wads of bills have been found in the false bottoms of cargo boxes and vacuum cleaners; in foot powder containers; $50,000 was found in a scuba tank that was too heavy and proved to contain no air when the valve was opened. One shipment of pork rinds contained $1.8 million.

Customs agents called rovers cruise airport terminals looking for potential smugglers, mentally checking off 200 possible tipoffs that someone is carrying drugs. When they suspect someone, they approach and talk casually. They look for signs of nervousness. Then they take the person aside and check his or her baggage.

The stomach carry continues to be a favorite way to smuggle drugs. Avianca flight 52 ran out of fuel during its second attempt to land at New

York's Kennedy International Airport on January 25, 1990. The Boeing 707 crashed fifteen miles from the runway, killing seventy-three passengers. One survivor had twenty-nine 1.25-inch long cocaine packets in the twenty-seven feet of his intestines. Another passenger had twenty-four two-inch long bags of cocaine in his digestive tract.

Not all mules survive the experience. One man with 120 packets of cocaine in his gut died in a 1970 flight from Venezuela to New York because the coke leaked through the natural skin condoms it was packed in. The guy should have used latex condoms. They're also cheaper than natural skin.

Although detection of hidden contraband requires legwork and brainwork to pick out targets, high-tech gizmos reach in where noses, fingers, and eyeballs can't. Vapor detection systems that sniff chemical vapors from cocaine and marijuana in mail, in luggage, and on passengers have been in the works for years. So has a neutron backscatter device that can detect narcotics hidden in vehicles and cargo containers by directing a neutron beam at the target and analyzing the returning neutrons. Narcotics are detected because the hydrogen they contain reflects neutrons with less energy than do other elements. The portable neutron backscatter device can detect narcotics behind metal walls and in vapor-tight compartments. This is the same device that detects even minute amounts of explosives at airports. Customs agents use all sizes of X-ray machines to look into parcels. The most interesting is a tire X-ray machine that finds drugs inside tires without taking the rubber off the wheels. Dielectric discontinuity machines allow the measuring of large quantities of letters for electrical characteristics that are then compared to the signatures of narcotics and explosives.

Why is some of the contraband found on planes coming from Colombia not discovered before the plane takes off?

"Bogotá Customs has a multi-million-dollar X-ray machine," said Rudy, a Contraband Enforcement Team officer. "The bad guys say whoever runs the machine dies. So the machine is not used. An employee of Avianca Airlines found sixty pounds of cocaine one time and reported it to Customs. He was shot by a hit man on a motorcycle as he left work the next day."

Colombian cartels have a standing $300,000 reward for anyone killing any North American law-enforcement agent who affects their drug operations. US anti-drug czar William Bennett quit his job in November 1990 after a growing number of threats to his family. Bennett lasted only eighteen months as the first American director of drug control policy. In a speech in September 1990, he said that "the drug problem — in general, nationwide — is no longer getting worse, and in some very significant aspects it is now getting better. Not victory, but success."

In fact, the drug problem *is* getting worse. And there's no sign it will improve. President Bush should select better candidates for such high-profile jobs. The war against drugs can't be run by quitters. What kind of an example did Bennett set by quitting? He can't take the heat yet thousands of law-enforcement agents do their jobs every day under threat of death. Thousands of Colombians are slaughtered by the drug barons every year, yet the US government wants Colombians to fight harder against drugs.

How do Customs agents size up the smuggling situation today?

"When you start enforcement," said Mike the pilot, "the people you lock up first are those who are not very good at it. Over time, those left have adapted and found ways to circumvent law enforcement."

"There is no drug war," said Big Ed, the Drug Warrior. "If it was a war, we would wipe out producers in Colombia, Bolivia, and Peru. But we don't, for political and economic reasons. Coke has been a legitimate part of the native culture for hundreds of years. It is also a native source of income. We can't just go in and spray chemicals. That would harm more innocent people than bad guys.

"If we had shot down planes ten years ago, we would have deterred smuggling. Today too many groups object to chasing planes. The pilots' association is against chases because they say innocent pilots could be chased."

The pilots' association wouldn't be supporting members who make a lot of money moonlighting, would they?

Law-enforcement agencies are often at odds with each other as they compete like children for public attention and money. They are quick to dump on each other and grossly inflate their own worth. Worst of all, they often mess up each other's investigations. One Customs official assesses the differences between agencies.

"Each agency has a different philosophy on how to stop drugs and therefore have disagreements on how to do it. Each agency also wants to look good and get a bigger chunk of the money pie. The Coast Guard policy is that if they can turn a load south, they call it a soft kill. Our position — if you accept the premise that one in ten loads is caught [they actually catch about one in 100] — if you turn him back, that's your one in ten. If you turn him back once, the odds are he'll make it the second time he tries. If you don't catch the guy, you haven't succeeded. It's a problem of attitude. We stand away from an aircraft and follow. The Coast Guard gets close and lets the smuggler see them.

"The DEA would like to roll people so they can arrest a bigger person. If you just busted your ass arresting someone, you don't want to see the

DEA let them walk. The DEA says they see the bigger picture. They are the lead agency in drug enforcement. They want to turn over one pilot and get a guy like Noriega or Escobar.

"It's not so much that agencies are in a turf war rather than a difference of philosophy. Customs works borders. The DEA works both sides — domestic and international narcotics. Customs is responsible for smuggling. The State Department is supposed to handle international affairs, but State puts the worst people in narcotics because it is a career-limiting position.

"The FBI is also involved in narcotics. Like the DEA, they don't do the street; they do smuggling groups. We have taken down FBI agents. An unlit plane flew into Pompano. We launched an interdiction team. We played it cool. We suspected they were FBs (FBI agents). We stopped an FBI plane coming over the Mexican border. They started drawing their guns. A cop on our team recognized them as cops.

"Now we have an arrangement with them. They wanted an arrangement to breach border and not to clear Customs — but we would know who it is breaking Customs. My own airplanes clear Customs. Even the US president clears Customs. The astronauts cleared Customs when they brought rocks back from the moon."

Part IV

KITCHEN MAGICIANS

11

Green Acres:
Hothead potheads and reefer madness in the Emerald Triangle

"You're not going to get my pot, assholes."
—MARIJUANA GROWER FIRES THREE SHOTS AND THREATENS A CAMPAIGN
AGAINST MARIJUANA PLANTING TEAM RAIDING POT PATCHES HIDDEN IN
NORTHERN CALIFORNIA FORESTS.

"You can run, but you can't hide."
—UNOFFICIAL MOTTO OF CALIFORNIA'S CAMP RAID TEAMS.

A fiction writer could not have plotted the events that conspired to make marijuana the number one cash crop in Calfornia — worth about $2.5 billion a year, according to the National Organization for Reform of Marijuana Laws — and the number two cash crop in the United States after corn, valued at $15 to $20 billion.

During the late 1960s and early 1970s, North American hippies cured their brains and lungs with tons of Mexican marijuana smuggled across the border by soon-to-be-wealthy entrepreneurs. Pot use was so wide-spread, and the movement to legalize it so vocal, that major tobacco companies sensed mega-dollars wafting from the pungent smoke and climbed over each other in a rush to register brand names for the new weed they hoped to sell to an eager market. After all, you had to smoke pot to be cool, and no one dared ruin the trip with dire warnings of lung cancer. So names like Acapulco Gold quickly found their way into official Washington drawers, waiting for marching orders.

The US government was well aware that the country was going to pot and that 95 percent of it came from Mexico. In a naive attempt to curb the problem, the United States gave Mexico six planes, six helicopters, and an unlimited supply of the herbicide Paraquat in 1975 to spray marijuana crops. The plan was to whack the weed before it could be harvested. Not bad as plans go. But any diplomat worth the odor eaters in his underwear knows you can't trust Mexicans. And if you can, you're paying them too much.

The Mexicans, armed with planes and copters, sprayed only the crops of farmers not paying *mordida*. And to this day, when snoopy reporters come around to photograph the spraying, two helicopters are dispatched: one loaded with Paraquat, the other with water.

Not to be outdone by the hastily conceived plans of faraway gringos, Mexican farmers quickly harvested tainted crops before the herbicide killed and discolored the marijuana. They molded bales in trash compacters and shipped the stuff to the States. Needless to say, much of the marijuana seized in California in the late 1960s and early 1970s was heavily contaminated with Paraquat. Not that anyone knew, though, because no one was talking. But users noticed a difference in their weed and newspapers began accusing the American government of poisoning its citizens.

The G.D. Searle drug company in Chicago tested marijuana for a local youth agency in 1978. The agency asked kids to drop off samples of their marijuana at offices across the city. In one batch of forty samples tested, thirty-nine showed traces of Paraquat. The tests did not measure the herbicide's concentration.

While the US and Mexico put a damper on Tijuana marijuana, the Bahamian government booted American spiny-lobster boats out of its waters. More than 250 lobster catchers — many of them Cuban refugees — were left without any way of earning money with their boats. Colombian marijuana growers were quick to respond to the cry for marijuana in the US as Mexico's pot fields dried up. They didn't have to look far to find boats to smuggle it. By 1978, Colombians supplied 70 percent of the weed smoked in the United States. More and more cocaine found its way into those shipments as North American noses started panting for the stuff. By 1980, the Colombians, whose marijuana was of poorer quality, started concentrating on cocaine. It was easier to smuggle and more profitable.

While urban hippies were getting paranoid about the contents of the baggies in their coat pockets, luck befell those who participated in the mass exodus from cities to transplant the drug subculture in rural areas of northern California. They began to grow their own marijuana. And thanks to two discoveries, their harvests packed one hell of a wallop.

The first was the discovery that preventing the pollination of female marijuana plants produced an awesome high-potency bud at the tip of the plant. This type of marijuana, called sinsemilla, occurs only when male plants are segregated from the females. With no other interests, the females sublimate their desires and send 70 percent of their energy to the tops. This increases the concentration of tetrahydrocannabinol (THC) from an average of 3 percent in Mexian marijuana to 12 percent in sinsemilla. The THC content of some sinsemilla has been found as high as 20 percent. Since Mexican, Colombian, and Thai marijuana had only a

3 percent potency, California weed became the drug of choice among traffickers.

The second event that sped up the development of California's home-grown marijuana industry was the discovery by growers of vast tracts of empty federal lands in the northern part of the state, particularly in the adjacent counties of Humboldt, Mendocino, and Trinity. These counties were beseiged by growers looking for out-of-the-way plots to grow their illegal crops. Forested lands once used only by hunters, fishermen, and hikers quickly became the home to fields of sinsemilla, earning the three counties the unifying name of Emerald Triangle. The area is now known as the sinsemilla capital of the world.

The appellation Emerald Triangle is derived from two sources: the bright green sparkle of the marijuana plants caused by cannabis resin in the leaves and buds makes them stand out brilliantly against the dull green background of surrounding trees. Triangle is appropriated from the Golden Triangle of Myanmar (Burma), Laos, and Thailand, which produces much of the world's opium.

Although many of the hippies who set out for the countryside may have had peaceful intentions, the marijuana growers were the Charles Mansons of the movement. They quickly appropriated the land around their crops, blocked off roads, and shot at anyone who approached the property. The growers were not the freeze-dried hippies legend would have us believe; they were bad-ass dudes who came from all walks of life, from Catholic priests to Vietnam veterans. Even the Ku Klux Klan grew marijuana for funds to promote its political aspirations.

By 1978, the sheriffs in the Emerald Triangle complained to Congress that their small police departments could not protect their counties from being taken over by the marijuana growers. Towns that seemed sleepy to outsiders were hotbeds of criminal conspiracy. Hardware stores stocked the paraphernalia of marijuana growing: miles of pcv pipe, grow bags and buckets, fertilizers, deer repellent, 1,000-foot plastic hoses, automatic timers and regulators for water systems; the list was endless. Congress passed the buck to the US Drug Enforcement Administration, which gave two pilots the task of finding out what the hell was happening in northern California. One of them was arguably the best flyer in the country, Charlie Stowell.

"We found one and a half million acres of federal land occupied by marijuana growers," Stowell said in his Sacramento office. "We couldn't get in without getting into a firefight." Stowell is not one to back down from a fight. He has become to marijuana growers what Eliot Ness was to bootlegging gangsters during Prohibition.

"We surveyed the area from airplanes," Stowell said. "We saw thousands of marijuana gardens planted in the northern part of our state.

This happened in four years, from 1974 to 1978, and we didn't even know it was going on. They had a four-year head start on us.

"The reason they got ahead of us and no one talked about it is that at the same time marijuana growing was taking root up there, the northern part of our state was going through two economic hardships: the fishing industry and the timber industry had been whittled down to practically nothing. The marijuana growers were seen as an economic boon to the counties. The growers promised at town meetings to build schools [shades of the Colombia drug cartel barons] and get them involved in growing marijuana and make them millions of dollars. That's why for four years the growers prospered without being noticed.

"By 1978 there was no economic boom. Money moved out of state to offshore banks. There were big power struggles between locals growing marijuana and out-of-towners. By 1978, the situation was out of control."

Stowell recommended that the DEA help the three counties fight the infestation of cannabinoids. They got $10,000, and Operation Sinsemilla, the first battle of the war against marijuana in the Emerald Triangle, was launched with machetes and weed eaters. The years from 1978 to 1983 were laced with violence as marijuana growers killed anything they felt threatened their crop. They booby-trapped their plots against two- and four-legged intruders, with some success.

By 1983, someone realized that $10,000 wasn't making a dent in the marijuana fields. Twelve murders linked to marijuana cultivation were reported in these counties between 1980 and 1983. There were hundreds of nasty run-ins between marijuana growers and hikers, ranchers, campers, horse riders, and hunters. Landowners were warned at gunpoint to keep off parts of their property where marijuana gardens had been planted and US Forest Service and Bureau of Land Management workers were run out of the woods by angry growers.

BLM biologist Mary Coburn unwittingly parked her truck, with a US Forest Service emblem on the door, near a marijuana patch in August 1983. She had parked near a stream to survey it. She hadn't walked fifty feet when a bullet pinged off a rock five feet from her. She ran to the truck as bullets whizzed around her. Two hollow-point bullets slammed through the door before she could get the truck into gear and get away.

The growers also buried quite a few patch pirates, ripoff artists who snatched buds. But they weren't the only thieves marijuana growers had to watch out for. Growers ripped each other off for equipment, money, and plants. One person having rock salt taken out of his behind in a Eureka hospital admitted he had been pirating a pot patch when the grower shot him. Most growers carry guns during the summer and all of them are armed at harvest time. Marijuana growers really don't have much to do once their pot is planted, except tend to it once in a while. So they drift through the woods looking for threats to their livelihood.

The violence linked to marijuana cultivation in California's fourteen major marijuana-growing counties and the inability of local police departments to deal with the problem finally led to the formation of a multi-agency task force called Campaign Against Marijuana Planting (CAMP) in 1983. CAMP was made up of twenty-seven federal, state, and local law-enforcement agencies to eradicate marijuana gardens in the counties of Humboldt, Trinity, Mendocino, Del Norte, Siskiyou, Sonoma, Lake, Butte, Yuba, Sierra, Santa Cruz, Santa Clara, San Mateo, and Monterey. It was the most sophisticated, and has become the most successful, anti-drug program in the United States.

CAMP team members started out armed with pistols. Some carried AR-15 .223-caliber semi-automatic rifles. After a few run-ins with the bad guys like Mary Coburn had, they armed themselves for jungle combat. Besides an assortment of semi-automatic pistols, they pack .357-magnum revolvers, fully automatic CAR-15 rifles, and semi-automatic 12-gauge shotguns. They use high-tech equipment such as star-light scopes and long-range listening devices to locate pot patches and potentially dangerous growers. They approach every garden as if it were an armed Viet Cong camp, sending in camouflaged reconnaissance teams to scout the area for booby traps and ambushes. They swoop into growers' camps aboard helicopters, jumping out to secure the area and make arrests while the chopper provides a throbbing whump, whump, whump, whump fighting rhythm. But the battles are not all high-tech. Most CAMP work is foot-slogging through the bush in search of tiny pot patches in millions of acres of forest.

CAMP runs its own training schools every spring. The Drug Enforcement Administration has a special pot-spotter school in Georgia where it grows hidden marijuana gardens laced with booby traps. The DEA teaches pot raiders how to spot gardens from the air and how to survive while ripping them out.

Every US president declares a war on drugs and tries to make it look as if he invented the idea. Nearly every administration since the turn of the century has taken on dope fiends in one form or another. The last major assault on marijuana prior to CAMP — which is being imitated on a national level across the US by the DEA — was President Richard Nixon's Operation Intercept in 1969, which attempted to stem the flow of marijuana from Mexico, with some success. So-called experts have blamed the shortage of marijuana in 1969 for the mass experimentation by kids with drugs such as LSD, MDA, and other mind-altering drugs. This is bone-headed reasoning.

The first major CAMP raid was prompted by a supposedly fictitious article in a biker magazine that told how Butte Creek in Butte County was controlled by outlaw bikers who posted guards along the roads and had closed off a bridge to limit access to prime marijuana-growing areas. The article mocked law enforcement's alleged inability to shut down the hard-nosed bikers who had taken over the area.

"The article was a slap in the face to every police officer in the state," said Bert Sousa, a Sacramento police officer and helicopter pilot who learned his trade in the Marines and still flies Cobra gunships in the reserves. "Law enforcement reclaimed Butte Creek in 1983," said Sousa, who flew armed crews into the area in a UH-1 (Huey) helicopter. "When we left, it was like a burning village in Vietnam.

"At one point, we spotted a garden on the bank of the Feather River. I couldn't land because of the dense brush, so team members had to drop from the skids and walk out to be picked up."

That day the team also discovered a drip-irrigated garden with a plastic water line that was buried for half a mile. It tapped into a power station's hillside water pipe.

CAMP team members hacked down marijuana plants, arrested suspected growers, collected evidence, removed cultivation equipment such as irrigation pipes, fertilizer bags, pumps, generators, even all-terrain vehicles. Growers were well served by a counterculture literature that covered everything from coddling seeds to protecting the patch. The plants and evidence were loaded into nets that were hooked to steel cables dangling from Sousa's Huey helicopter. He hauled the load to a landing zone where the week's take was counted and torched.

CAMP created an air force of spotting planes and helicopters to pinpoint targets for raid teams. At times, the operation had three choppers in every county. Pothead supporters tracked the flight paths of helicopters and warned garden owners that the spies were in the sky. A Redway radio station in Humboldt County ran bulletins warning growers where choppers had been spotted.

Marijuana plots flash fluorescent green when the sun hits them at a certain angle. Nevada County Sheriff's deputies were flying over manzanita-covered ground near North Colombia one day when a deputy spotted a green flash. They turned the plane around and flew over the manzanita again. Flashes of green all around. They mapped the site from the air — just above Cherokee Diggins near Tyler Foote Crossing Road. A few days later they staked out the 150-plant garden and arrested a twenty-eight-year-old southern California man after he turned on a well pump that fed an intricate irrigation system.

Marijuana growers are an adaptable lot, and once they figured out why planes were spotting their patches, many bent their plants over and tied them down to expose the dark underside of the leaves. That's not the best way to grow pot, however.

Growers also went to court in an attempt to ground CAMP reconnaissance planes and helicopters. On September 2, 1983, three northern California residents, the National Organization for the Reform of Marijuana Laws (NORMAL), and the Civil Liberties Monitoring Project filed a federal class-action lawsuit alleging that CAMP ground and air operations, especially helicopters, violated civil rights. The lawsuit was amended in November 1983, and the number of plaintiffs was increased to twenty-two. They sought $20 million in damages among other claims. After years of legal wrangling, CAMP and the potheads signed a Consent Decree in December 1987. These are the major provisions of that agreement:

"1. CAMP is prohibited from operating helicopters closer than 500 feet from any structure, person or vehicle, unless the helicopter is landing or taking off, or unless safety otherwise requires. Helicopters will also take the most direct flight path passing over the fewest possible residences. In general, helicopters conducting surveillance must comply with FAA regulations . . . which regulate altitude operations. Ground operations involving homes or curtilage, absent exigent circumstances, will require a search warrant. Pre-raid briefings and planning, and documentation reflecting those briefings and any deviations from them, will be required to minimize risk of violating the terms of the Consent Decree."

So CAMP teams must return to base and obtain a search warrant after spotting a marijuana garden. The mandatory pre-raid briefings are also time-consuming. And what do you think happens during this time? Some pothead growers could harvest their crops and split.

"2. Former Napa County Superior Court Judge Thomas Konsgaard will act as a hearing officer. His role will be that of a finder of fact on any alleged Consent Decree violation. These factual findings will be conclusive as to plaintiffs, but not as to defendants, who will be entitled to de novo review by the federal district court. The plaintiff's burden of proving any alleged violation of the Consent Decree shall be by clear and convincing evidence. The reasonable costs and expenses of the hearing officer will be borne by defendants."

So the potheads must provide evidence to prove the deal was violated. At least there's some semblance of justice here. But the state pays for the whole show. The potheads, not CAMP (i.e., John Q. Public), should pay the bill.

"3. The Consent Decree will expire after three years [in 1990] unless the plaintiffs prove a knowing violation of the Consent Decree by clear and convincing evidence. If the plaintiffs prove such a violation, the Consent Decree will terminate only after two consecutive years in which no proven violation has occurred.

"4. Plaintiffs will dismiss their class certification motion for damage claims. None of the damage claims, whether by named or unnamed plaintiffs are included in this settlement, which affects only injunctive relief sought in the complaint."

The damage claims were bopped around court schedules for a while. In 1988, lawyers for the potheads dropped claims of twenty of the twenty-two plaintiffs. Then a trial date was set for late 1989, but an out-of-court settlement was reached first. The two plaintiffs did not receive any money, but their lawyers' fees were paid by CAMP as set out in the Consent Decree. So far, no violations of the Consent Decree have been proven. The Redway radio station that broadcast the location of CAMP helicopters also aired daily broadcasts of alleged civil rights violations by CAMP — all in the name of public service.

The pothead civil-liberties argument against CAMP reconnaissance flights was dealt a severe blow by the California Supreme Court when it ruled in 1987 that random aerial surveillance flights are constitutional. However, the court also ruled that the state legislature should establish standards to "balance the needs of law enforcement against the legitimate privacy expectations of affected citizens."

Although the same court outlawed aerial inspection of individual, enclosed back yards in another case, the 1987 decision rejected a claim by Allan Mayoff of Humboldt county that the flights that led to his arrest constituted an arbitrary violation of his privacy. Mayoff was arrested in August 1980, after police raided his property and seized 144 marijuana plants spotted by a plane.

"The realities of air travel force a modern householder to assume that his yard and anything in it are in plain view from the air," the court ruled. "Aerial surveillance conducted at a reasonable height and in a non-intrusive manner cannot be deemed unreasonable."

The court found that CAMP reconnaissance flights were not carried out to observe "the details of human activity" and that Mayoff's marijuana garden was viewed from an altitude "at which the possibility of intrusion on private activities below is remote."

The economic prosperity promised by marijuana growers never materialized, though the residents of the Emerald Triangle kept hoping. The dream was shattered for many of them in 1983 when violence by growers forced them to face reality: they had been had. The promise of easy money was a scam to align them with money-grubbing criminals who cared nothing for the Emerald Triangle other than its isolation for growing a cash crop.

Supporters of the growers say the profits stay in their communities. Though some dope money is spent on land, gardening equipment, vehicles, and supplies, much of it is taken out of the area. About 60 to 70 percent of the marijuana profits in Humboldt County leave the county. The rest may be used to buy land. Since growers pay three to four times what a plot of land is worth to ensure they get the best land available, land prices are driven up to levels that more legitimate buyers can't afford and won't pay.

Most marijuana growers in the Emerald Triangle are from other parts of California or from other states; few are locals supplementing their income. The Humboldt County post office is swamped by change-of-address requests at the end of the growing season. Another indicator that growers come from outside the county is the dearth of U-Haul type trailers during the marijuana harvest. All the trailers in the Emerald Triangle are rented one-way only as growers haul their crops home. Monterey County, where marijuana gardens are smaller than those in other counties, may be the only north-coast county where marijuana is grown for sale locally.

Many organized criminal groups finance marijuana cultivation, from co-ops to outlaw motorcycle gangs. Investors in southern California pool their cash and reap their profits when the harvested crop is sold. That money never finds its way back to the local communities that have had to endure the violence, pollution, slaughter of wildlife, and destruction of the environment while growers tend their crops.

Two years into the CAMP program, organizers had this to say about the public attitude toward growers in the Emerald Triangle.

"There seems to be little public sentiment for the commercial marijuana grower. In past years, growers have tried to build a 'flower child' image whose activities have done no harm to anyone and, in fact, have brought prosperity to economically depressed communities. The facts are that because of the violence associated with marijuana cultivation and the type of people that basically make up the growers' subculture, the quality of life has diminished where growers have taken foothold in the community. The proceeds from their illegal activities really have very little if anything at all to do with stimulating local economics.

"For several years, in some parts of California, marijuana cultivators have engaged in nothing more than a low-risk high-profit criminal enterprise. CAMP has raised the risk considerably. Growers who have been involved in the business for five to ten years or more find it hard to accept the fact that what they do is or should be illegal. Some openly preach civil disobedience to support their cause. Henry David Thoreau was an advocate of civil disobedience against what an individual might perceive to be an unjust law. Thoreau said, however, that one must be prepared to and accept the consequences of their acts of civil disobedience. Most growers don't feel strongly enough about their cause to accept the consequences of their acts."

1984

The year 1984 was the most violent in marijuana country, with eight murders and seventeen booby-trapped sites. Much of the violence stemmed from growers trying to protect their sinsemilla buds from patch pirates. Hunters, hikers, and ranchers were also attacked by growers. A real estate woman tripped two traps while showing a property to clients in Butte County. Little of the violence was aimed at law enforcement. The year saw some of the last large gardens before growers started planting smaller patches that are more difficult to spot from the air. A garden with 5,100 plants was found on private property in the Blocksburg area of Humboldt County. A garden with 8,000 plants was found on US Forest Service land in Tuolumne County.

Marijuana growers also had to be wary of pot mercs — Vietnam veterans disguised as hunters, but armed with machine guns and stun grenades, who excelled in ripping off growers at harvest time. These mercenaries have offered their services to CAMP and have been turned down.

The violence that plagued the New Rivers Drainage Area of Trinity County was finally curbed in 1984 after marijuana growers had given the area a nasty reputation that kept hikers away. They even torched a USFS ranger station. That year the sheriff's department and the US Forest Service formed a task force to patrol the 640,000-acre wilderness area. The patrols also curbed marijuana growing. More than 12,000 plants were ripped out on public lands in 1983 compared to 600 in 1984, when campers and hikers began to return to the area.

On July 19, a grower standing in his marijuana patch shot at a CAMP helicopter on a reconnaissance mission in southern Humboldt County.

On July 29, a sniper shot and killed a Kettempom man working on his deck. The man had a marijuana garden on his Trinity County property.

On August 9, feuding growers set a 200-acre fire that threatened fifty homes.

On September 10, one of two men walking through Helltown Canyon in Butte County on his way to a swimming hole was seriously injured when he tripped a pipe bomb.

On September 11, a CAMP team ripping out a garden in the Sprowl Creek area of Humboldt County surprised a machete-wielding grower who thought he was being ripped off. He dropped his weapon and ran when he realized he was confronting a CAMP crew. He left his wife behind to be arrested.

On September 12, three dudes from Sunnyvale in Mendocino County were driving through the backwoods of Willits when they stopped to have a leak. One of the guys was shot in the leg while he stood in the bush. His leg had to be amputated.

On September 14, armed patch pirates were ripping out plants from a 160-plant garden in Humboldt County when the owner started shooting at them. They shot back. One pirate fled and rolled his car. Police do not know if he died from the crash or from the bullet in his body.

On September 17, a woman armed with a rifle forced two US Forest Service workers in Tahoe National Forest in Nevada County to leave the area. She shot over their heads as they walked away. She also challenged forest service and sheriff's officers who came by later in the day to investigate. She claimed she hadn't shot at anyone, she just cleared her gun. She was arrested and forty marijuana plants were destroyed.

On September 22, one of two men riding horses on private property next to public land in Mendocino County was attacked by two growers. The second rider chased them off. Police found a twenty-two-plant garden beside the trail.

On September 23, a deer hunter was found shot to death in a marijuana garden in Mendocino County.

On September 23, two deer hunters who wandered into a marijuana garden in the Yolla Bola area of Shasta Trinity National Forest, Trinity County, were stopped by three men armed with a shotgun, an AR-15, and an Ingram carbine. They were escorted out of the area and told not to come back or to tell anyone about the eight- to sixteen-foot tall plants.

On September 24, someone shot at a man who wandered into a marijuana garden in the Forest Ranch area of Butte County. He got the hell out as fast as he could, his car being hit three times.

On October 1, a grower in Mendocino County's Redwood Valley area shot at three teenage patch pirates stealing his buds. He hit one of them and reported the attempted theft to the sheriff!

On October 2, sheriff's deputies investigating automatic gun fire in the Salmon Creek area of Humboldt County heard a shotgun blast. They found two armed men holding two other men prisoners at gunpoint. The armed men were charged with kidnapping and false imprisonment.

On October 2, a bunch of patch pirates was looting a marijuana greenhouse in Marin County when the grower shot and killed one of them. The rest ran.

On November 24, Humboldt County sheriff's deputies searching for two missing men thirteen miles southwest of Weitchpec on State Route 169 found their rotting bodies in a secluded campsite. Both had been shot. The campsite was used by the growers of a nearby marijuana patch.

1985

Unlike violence in the previous year, violence in 1985 was aimed at law enforcement, with not one instance of aggression directed at citizens. Booby traps were found in only five of the 684 marijuana gardens raided by CAMP. These ranged from punji boards to rat-trap shotgun shell traps to fishhook traps.

On July 19, two armed growers threatened a Bureau of Land Management employee they thought was a CAMP worker.

On July 25, someone took three shots at a CAMP team and their helicopter on a landing site in the Hoopa Indian Reservation in Humboldt County. The hillside shooter misjudged the distance and the bullets hit the ground near the helicopter.

On August 7, someone shot up a CAMP helicopter parked overnight on the Willow Creek property of a Humboldt County deputy sheriff, causing $100,000 in damage and rendering it inoperable.

On August 12, someone shot at another CAMP helicopter after it had inserted a raid team in the Hoopa Indian Reservation. The shooter called CAMP's Garberville headquarters two hours later and threatened that there would be more shooting if CAMP didn't stop raiding marijuana gardens on the reservation. Someone shot at the helicopter again the next day.

On August 14, two men drove up to two CAMP workers filling up at a gas station and asked, "How many people did you kill today? Fucking murderers." Earlier that day, a grower was killed during a stakeout of his Butte County garden by another police agency.

On August 22, a shooter took three shots at a CAMP helicopter in Mendocino County.

On September 9, a bullet went through a CAMP helicopter flying at 2,000 feet over Shasta County.

On September 11, someone shot at a CAMP team ripping out a marijuana garden on Skyview Road in Mendocino County. The weed was planted in rows interspersed with corn and flowers.

On September 12, two Humboldt County sheriff's deputies were watching a grower sleep in his Willow Creek marijuana garden. He woke up and fired twelve shots at them before running off.

On September 23, a CAMP team ripping out a booby-trapped garden in Southfork Mountain in Trinity County was shot at.

On September 23, a driver pulled his car up beside a CAMP fuel truck on a Mendocino County highway and threatened the CAMP worker with an Uzi submachine gun. The truck driver braked. The armed man got out of his car and said, "You fuckers got my plants. You're a CAMP raider and you should die. Get out of here." The gunman then drove off, lost control of his car further down the highway, and rolled over.

1986

There were no murders in 1986, but gardens were certainly booby-trapped and a CAMP helicopter was shot at. This kind of activity was toned down compared to the two previous years. Growers had begun to realize murder was giving them bad press. It also created the kind of enemies who don't forget, serious enemies with the law on their side. One man who supported the growers started tipping off cops about pot patches after he was shot at simply for being in the wrong place at the wrong time: "Being shot at changes your mind about some things."

It was a sad year for CAMP raiders, who not only sought the gardens before harvest but the drying sheds and distributors afterwards. Pilot Noah Stinnett, Jr., and CAMP raiders Dale Rossetto and Larry Breceda, Siskiyou County sheriff's deputies, died when their reconnaissance plane crashed on July 31 in Oregon, just over the county line. The plane may have been shot down.

CAMP's success at curbing marijuana cultivation was demonstrated by the dramatic increase in prices for sinsemilla marijuana in California. A plant that had sold for $2,000 in 1985 could command $4,000 in 1986. An ounce of sinsemilla marijuana that sold for $160 rose to $300 and $400. Dopers all over the state complained that their pushers couldn't keep them supplied. Pushers had to divvy up their supplies to ensure that all their customers got at least half an ounce. And California residents being what they are, you can bet they were screaming their lungs out in protest.

By this time, constant airplane and helicopter surveillance had made 4,000-plant gardens a thing of the past. They were just too easy to spot from the air. CAMP drove growers further into the bush and made it more difficult for them to grow pot.

Growers resorted to planting smaller thirty- to forty-plant gardens on hillsides and in remote areas. They camouflaged their plants with plastic and overhanging branches. They even adapted their irrigation systems to water the plants on steep hills, installing gravity-flow irrigation controlled by electric timers. One grower in Monterey County hand-painted his plants with orange, yellow, and brown watercolors to hide them from spotter planes. Another intertwined his plants with pine trees.

On April 22, 1986, a man hiking on US Forest Service land in Nevada County became entangled in a fishhook booby trap near an old marijuana garden. A US Forest Service agent investigating the site tripped one of many rat-trap shotgun shell booby traps, which struck the shell primer but didn't discharge.

On April 23, a grower approached a man cutting firewood in the Jackson State Forest, put a shotgun muzzle behind his ear, and ordered him to leave. Later, fifty marijuana plants were found nearby.

On May 20, a watchdog bit a Shasta County deputy sheriff while he ripped out a marijuana garden.

On August 5, a Fresno County deputy sheriff shot and killed a pit bull that attacked him while he ripped out a garden.

On August 15, El Dorado sheriff's deputies and US Forest Service agents found a sophisticated pipe-bomb booby trap in a garden on Forest Service land. They found another pipe bomb that had not been positioned and ten fishhook booby traps.

The same day, someone left a message on the CAMP headquarters' answering machine threatening to shoot down any planes and helicopters and start forest fires.

On August 19, a Humboldt County deputy sheriff broke his leg while chasing a grower in a marijuana garden.

On August 25, the Monterey County Sheriff's Office received a phone call from a man threatening to kill ten deputies for every pound of marijuana seized during raids in the county.

On August 27, threatening notes addressed to landowners were found in two gardens adjacent to each other:

Mr. and Mrs. S:

"Please don't do anything rash about these plants. Talk to your friends first and you will be compensated and/or at last resort they can be moved. Phone call would be counter-productive and dangerous to all concerned."

On September 7, a Fresno County sheriff's deputy shot and killed another pit bull that attacked him in a marijuana garden.

On September 14, 11,860 acres of US Forest Service land were burned in Fresno County. The fire started 1.5 feet from a trail leading to a marijuana garden and 200 feet from the growers' camp.

On September 15, four pipe-shotgun booby traps were found in a Mendocino County marijuana garden.

On September 18, a Humboldt County deputy sheriff ripping out a marijuana garden tripped a rat-trap shotgun shell booby trap. The pellets had been removed from the shell and only the wadding hit him. Seven more traps were also found there.

On September 22, the fuselage of a CAMP helicopter was creased by a bullet during a mission.

On September 23, a dynamite booby trap activated by a blasting cap was found in a marijuana garden on US Forest Service Land in Siskiyou County.

On October 5, ten CAMP vehicles were sabotaged in Humboldt County while they were parked overnight. Thirty-six tires were punctured and sugar was poured into two gas tanks.

On October 11, four hikers in Humboldt County were chased out of a garden by growers who shot at them. One hiker was caught and searched and told he would be killed if he had any marijuana buds on him.

On October 12, seven tires on two CAMP vehicles were punctured in Humboldt County.

1987

Pot growers surprised CAMP raiders with a new idea in 1987: portable gardens. They grew their plants in bags or buckets that they continually moved around. If the gardens were spotted from the air, growers moved them before the CAMP team arrived. Some such gardens were found suspended in the forks of trees twenty feet off the ground.

CAMP raids are usually scheduled from July to October, when the marijuana plants are big enough to be visible from the sky. Local law-enforcement agencies get their hands on 600 plants before CAMP swings into action. In 1987, however, 20,000 plants were destroyed before CAMP even got its camouflage gear on. Three reasons were given for this: an early spring allowed the growers to plant early; the growers wanted to grow and pick their plants before CAMP started; and the media predicted a bumper pot crop that year.

That bumper crop never had a chance. The largest forest fires in twenty years destroyed 1 million acres of heavily forested lands that summer. Firefighters stumbled over a lot of pot patches and growers. No one knows just how much marijuana was burned.

There were eighteen incidents of violence and one murder in northern California pot patches in 1987. CAMP eradication teams raided 740 gardens, ten of which had booby traps: fishhooks strung at eye level, hypodermic needles, shotgun-shell rat traps, and a punji board. A ⅜-inch steel wire was strung across a CAMP helicopter loading zone to down a copter. Another garden was protected by a sophisticated electronic warning system, dogs with remote-controlled probe collars, and weapons, including an Uzi with a laser scope. Dynamite and pipe bombs were found near two other gardens. CAMP raiders had to kill two animals that attacked them in gardens: a pit bull terrier and a wild boar.

On July 29, 1987, a wild boar charged a CAMP team member ripping out a garden in the Rock Pile area of Sonoma County. He shot the boar three times without killing it. Another team member fired the fatal shot.

On August 3, a CAMP team member found a punji booby trap in a hole in a garden in the Laytonville area of Mendocino County.

On August 4, CAMP team members found thirty booby traps in a Sonoma County garden. The large rat traps with three large nails hammered through them were set and hung by wires at face height in trees around the garden. Some of them were set at the base of plants where a person's feet would be when ripping out the pot.

On August 11, a pilot trying to land a CAMP helicopter in a landing zone near a marijuana garden in the Eel Rock area of Humboldt County spotted a ⅜-inch wire strung between two trees in his path. He backed off and flew around the trap.

On August 19, a Humboldt County sheriff's deputy serving a search warrant near Ettersburg was attacked by a pit bull terrier, which he shot.

The same day, CAMP team members ripping out a 337-plant garden in Humboldt County found a loaded shotgun set to fire when a monofilament line was tripped. The gun was aimed at a bag of dog food.

On August 24, a Sonoma County sheriff's deputy serving a search warrant on a grower found a quarter pound of dynamite and blasting caps.

The same day, a CAMP team member found two rat-trap shotgun shell booby traps in a marijuana garden near 8 Mile Ridge in Humboldt County.

On September 3, a raid team found an armed grower in an underground guard shack while they moved into a garden in Feather Falls, Butte County.

On September 10, a trigger-happy grower in Humboldt County shot at what he thought was an animal trying to eat his plants. He shot his friend in both thighs, severing a major artery. A CAMP crew flew in by helicopter to save the man's life.

On September 24, a Mendocino County sheriff's deputy stepped on a punji stake booby trap that drove one nail into his boot. The trap was made of two boards with nails driven through them and a leather thong holding the boards together. The boards were in an open pit covered with branches. When an invader steps on the thong and drives it into the pit, the two boards clamp around his foot and ankle.

On September 22, an eradication team ran into a grower armed with a .38-caliber pistol and a shotgun who was responding to an electronic alarm set off by the raiders. He surrendered. The team found an Uzi with a laser sight, a Helo Nova stun gun, a flare gun, a sawed-off carbine, two shotguns, and five watchdogs with remote-control-activated electronic probe collars. The growers used walky-talkies to communicate with one another.

On September 28, a team found razor blades and hypodermic needles attached to the bottoms of plants.

On October 12, growers ambushed five patch pirates trying to steal their sinsemilla buds in Lake County. Three pirates were shot during the shoot-out. A California Highway Patrol helicopter was called in to fly out a grower who had a heart attack.

On October 13, patch pirates in Mendocino County shot and killed a grower while he slept in his trailer and wounded a man in another trailer before loading up a truck with marijuana plants plucked from a garden.

1988

More and more discoveries of marijuana gardens in parts of southern California seemed to indicate that CAMP was forcing growers out of the state's fourteen northern counties. Large gardens were found in San Diego, Riverside, and San Bernardino. One group had established a network of gardens with 18,000 plants in the Cleveland National Forest, San Diego County.

On July 19, 1988, US Forest Service special agents staked out a 534-plant garden on public lands near Trinity Lake in Trinity County. They videotaped two men tending the garden. The two ran away when the agents tried to arrest them. Special Agent Frank Packwood caught up with the least fleet-footed of the two. They wrestled. The man bit Packwood's left index finger, then smashed his head with a rock. The grower then grabbed Packwood's gun from the stream bed where it had fallen during the struggle, pointed it at the agent, and threatened to shoot him if he moved. Then he ran off and ditched the gun as he went. He had been arrested in 1985 for growing marijuana on his own property. That experience had taught him to grow his weed on public lands.

On September 11, 1988, all hell broke loose in a hippy commune in the Rail Road Flat area of Calaveras County where four men lived with two women. That day, three members figured out that the other three were pirating sinsemilla buds from their co-op garden. One of the furious potheads whipped out a .30-30-calibre rifle and shot another man in the arm, leaving it dangling at the elbow. He shot again and the man fell. Then he put the gun to his fallen colleague's temple and blew off part of his head.

The other man and woman accused of stealing buds hoofed it to a truck and tried to get away. The armed pothead wasted both of them, blowing off part of the woman's head in front of five of the communal children, aged seven to fourteen. The three bodies were loaded into the truck and driven 200 yards where they were dumped in manzanita and covered with tarp and brush. The killers planned to dismember the bodies and dissolve them in an acid bath later. They drove the truck to Amador County near Ione and torched it. That afternoon, one of the kids called the cops, who arrested the three adults and ripped out a 110-plant garden. Peace and love forever.

On September 27, two patch pirates hit a garden near Ukiah, in Humboldt County. The growers ambushed them. One pirate split. The second was caught and beaten before he was released.

On July 19, a CAMP team member ripping out a garden in the Little River Airport area of Mendocino County found two holes, each two feet deep and eight inches wide, on a trail leading to the garden. The holes were covered with leaves.

On August 3, eradication team members ripping out a 734-plant garden in the Iron Peak area of Mendocino County found three punji booby traps.

On August 10, someone slashed a tire on a US Forest Service van used by CAMP and smashed eggs on it outside a Garberville motel.

On August 22, eradication team members found a punji and monofilament line strung at eye level while ripping out a 169-plant garden in the Gopherville area of Mendocino County.

On August 29, a team member found a set steel animal trap in a 104-plant garden.

On August 31, a team in the Davidson Plain area of Mendocino County found ankle-level trip wires tied to two cowbells in a 152-plant garden and a two-by-four-foot nailboard.

On September 14, team members found a nailboard and blasting caps in a 68-plant garden in the Bear Creek area, Humboldt County.

1989

The CAMP program caused marijuana cultivation to drop by 66 percent from 1983 to 1989 and doubled the price of prized sinsemilla marijuana.

CAMP had honed its operations since 1983 to become extremely efficient in finding and destroying pot patches. In 1983, CAMP destroyed less than one-third of the gardens it spotted. In 1989, 99 percent of the plants spotted were destroyed. By 1989, growers had shrunk and tried to camouflage their plants from reconnaissance planes and helicopters. As a result, helicopters were increasingly necessary for CAMP workers to spot their quarry. Other trends that developed under CAMP pressure: smaller, more heavily budded plants and portable gardens in grow bags and buckets.

The higher percentage of plants destroyed doesn't mean that CAMP is wiping out all marijuana gardens, just that it has improved its ability to get at the gardens spotted from the air.

From 1983 to 1989, CAMP teams ripped out 906,044 marijuana plants weighing 3,485,028 pounds and worth $2.36 billion on the street. They arrested 1,261 suspects in 4,111 raids. They found eighty-two booby-trapped sites and seized 1,572 guns, 198 vehicles, $209,711 in cash, and $19.7 million in land.

Three murders linked to marijuana cultivation were committed in 1989; five gardens raided by CAMP teams were booby-trapped, and three teams were shot at. CAMP officers have not shot at anyone since the program began in 1983.

At 3 a.m. on July 31, 1989, someone threw a Molotov cocktail at a CAMP equipment truck in the parking lot of the Garberville Hotel. The gasoline-filled Coors beer bottle with cloth rope tied around its neck flared briefly and then went out.

Later that day in Humbolt County, a CAMP worker following a water line found a rat trap with a spent shotgun shell fixed to it mounted to a tree at ankle level in a 700-plant garden.

On August 14, a raid team and Sonoma County deputies arrested a man with four handguns, four rifles, and four shotguns at a fifty-plant garden protected by three nailboard booby traps and five watchdogs.

On August 15, automatic weapons were fired across a canyon at a raid team hacking a 390-plant garden. A second team was flown in to secure the area while the first finished its job of ripping out the weeds.

On August 16, three shots were fired at CAMP members being inserted by helicopter in the Chemise Creek area of Humboldt County after someone yelled at them, "You're not going to get my pot, assholes!"

On August 26, someone punctured the tires on seven CAMP vehicles parked at the North Coast Inn in Arcata.

In early September 1989, three people were shot — two killed and one wounded — during an argument over cultivation in a garden of 350 recently transplanted sinsemilla plants.

On September 11, someone fired six shots at raid team members being dropped off into a 363-plant garden in the Redway area, Humboldt County. No one was hit although the shots were fired within 200 feet.

On September 14, six to twelve shots were fired 300 to 500 yards from a ninety-three plant garden being ripped out by CAMP members and deputies in Trinity County's Danger Point area. Two growers said they were target practicing with a .30-06-caliber rifle.

On September 18, CAMP raid team members found six rat-trap shotgun shell booby traps nailed to trees in an already harvested garden on the Van Dyke Ranch in Mendocino County.

On September 21, a CAMP worker tripped a monofilament line connected to a rat-trap shotgun shell booby trap, discharging a 20-gauge shotgun shell. No one was hurt. Five similar traps were found in the 353-plant garden in the Blocksburg area of Humboldt County.

On September 23, three hunters stumbled across a garden in the Piercy area of Mendocino County. One man stayed behind to rip off some plants after his buddies left. His body was found several weeks later buried in a shallow grave near the harvested garden. He had been shot.

On September 27, CAMP raid team members found a monofilament-line fishhook booby trap while ripping out a ninety-one plant garden in the Willits area of Mendocino County.

Later that day, agents from the Bureau of Land Management raided a 175-plant garden in the Whale Gulch area of Mendocino County and arrested a man. Darkness forced them to set up camp. Another grower hiding in the bushes screamed threats at them throughout the night. A CAMP team was flown in the following morning to help them wipe out the garden.

Year	Plants Spotted	Plants Destroyed	% of Plants Destroyed
1983	891,438	303,089	34.0
1984	345,397	256,976	74.4
1985	333,694	309,001	92.6
1986	242,976	223,529	87.0
1987	323,064	289,833	85.0
1988	373,670	330,297	88.0
1989	329,042	328,901	99.9

Not all marijuana gardens are spotted from the air. Michigan-Cal Lumber Co. workers stumbled across a pot patch of seventy 24-inch plants in the Eldorado National Forest near Sacramento in June 1988.

They reported their find to the sheriff's office and deputies kept a close eye on it. By July 18, the plants were seven feet tall. On August 9, deputies videotaped John Charles Deierling, a forty-three-year-old Sacramento lawyer, spraying the remaining forty plants in the patch. They arrested him and found a .357-magnum revolver in a holster in his backpack. Superior Court Judge Terrence Finney sentenced Deierling, who said he was growing the pot for personal use, to six months in jail. "He's a professional with the opportunity to see what happens with this kind of conduct. . . . He's got to pay the piper," Judge Finney said.

In a moment of compassion, the judge also put him on three years' probation that would end if the lawyer stayed sober for eighteen months. In that case, he recommended that Deierling's license to practice be reinstated. The judge told Deierling that he could apply for a work furlough program in Sacramento after he served sixty days, or one-third of his sentence. As required by state law, he fined him $200, ordered him to pay the $50 lab fee to analyze the marijuana, forbade him to take illegal drugs, drink alcohol or frequent bars while on probation, and ordered him to submit to tests to see whether he was complying with the court order. He also ordered the lawyer to submit himself, his vehicles, and his houses to police searches any time they requested. He also had to register as a narcotics offender, pay the cost of administering his probation, and complete an alcohol-counselling program.

El Dorado County Supervisor Michael Visman was a rising political star who pushed for more law enforcement and championed anti-crime causes. His establishment family had grown apples and pears on Apple Hill for three generations. After two years as supervisor, the forty-one-year-old's clout was being felt. He was talking about running for the state assembly. He regularly had breakfast with his rural constituents. He fought vigorously for a local water project.

On October 12, 1988, Visman was appointed to the board of directors of the El Dorado County Citizens Against Crime Alert Program. The next day, a US Forest Service officer flew his helicopter over the Camino area looking for pot patches. He spotted sixty plants in a blackberry thicket 100 yards from a house on Hassler Road, part of a thirty-seven-acre ranch.

On October 14, the pilot and drug officers knocked on the door to arrest the owner. Michael Visman answered. The police found a water line running from the house to the pot patch. They also found evidence of an indoor marijuana garden in the basement — three types of growing lights, hoses, timers, fans, and a thermostat. Besides the drug charges, Visman was accused of stealing electricity for over three years from the Pacific Gas and Electric Co. by by-passing a meter.

Visman told police he let his brother Mark grow pot in the basement. At trial, his lawyer argued Visman's wife grew flowers and vegetables in the basement for a dying brother-in-law. Investigation showed the plant buds had been repeatedly harvested as new buds sprouted to replace those that had been picked — a growing technique that produces premium pot, since the top, or bud, is the most potent part of the plant.

Visman said he was a victim of US Forest Service agents seeking revenge for his attack on the foresting practices of their friends. They had found a way to get back at him by exposing marijuana that could have been planted by Mexican farm laborers who worked in the orchard, the politician claimed. Yet, on the day he was arrested, Visman said to police, "I've ruined my life. What will happen to me?"

A jury convicted Visman of conspiring to grow marijuana, aiding and abetting the cultivation of marijuana, and providing a place for growing marijuana. Only after the conviction did he admit to a probation officer that he allowed his brother to grow marijuana on the ranch for half the profits.

US District Judge Edward J. Garcia said that Visman "tested the system with his lies and lost." He sentenced him to two and a half years in jail. The felony conviction means he can never again hold political office.

One of the major successes of the CAMP program was turning public attitude against the marijuana growers in the Emerald Triangle, although growers in those countries retain pockets of support. Many locals consider them folk heroes and argue that marijuana should be grown to make paper to prevent redwood harvesting. The pro-marijuana group seems embedded in Garberville, a town perpetually caught in a time warp.

Garberville, in southern Humboldt County, is probably the only community in North America that opposes the law-enforcement crackdown on drugs. Residents get downright ornery when someone attacks their marijuana, a plant to which they have a deep emotional and financial attachment. The Garberville library has the most comprehensive selection of books on pot in the world.

Ironically, while the back-to-the-earth movement initiated the now-commercial growing of marijuana in the wilds, it is their environmental awareness that is rebelling against the excesses of careless, greedy growers.

California Department of Fish and Game officers started to assess the environmental impact of marijuana growers in 1983. They found that growers killed off any animals they considered a threat to their plants: mice, birds, rabbits, deer, anything. They protected their gardens with fences, animal traps, poison, snares, booby traps, and guns. Wildlife officers estimated that growers killed 1,600 deer in 1984 — equal to the number legally killed by 17,000 hunters during hunting season. In fact, 50 to 60 percent of marijuana gardens raided contained evidence that deer or other animals had been killed. The remains of twenty-five deer were found in two gardens.

Some growers stalked animals. Others set traps. Deer were found with their fore or hind quarters blown off by rat-trap shotgun shell booby traps set along trails. Growers hung fresh strips of bear hide from plants and trees around marijuana gardens in the misguided hope the scent would keep marijuana-munching deer away. Bear rarely eat deer; they're too difficult to catch. Growers caught bears with heavy cable snares placed around piles of rotting fish. Deep bloody ruts in the ground show how the animals tried desperately to break free until they were killed or starved to death.

Growers also set out poisoned food. Game wardens found deer too emaciated from warfarin poisoning to run away. They let themselves be picked up. Growers also used the poison Havoc, which is 186 times more toxic than warfarin. Half an ounce of Havoc burns out a deer's digestive tract, causing it intense pain until it starves to death. These poisons in deer can also harm any humans who eat the deer meat.

Growers also used as much as 300 pounds of rodenticides an acre, wiping out not only rodents but all the wildlife in the area. All these poisons, along with nitrogen fertilizers, found their way into streams, threatening salmon and trout breeding.

Careless marijuana growers started more than twelve accidental fires between 1980 and 1983. Feuding growers started a 200-acre fire in El Dorado County in 1984. They clear-cut land to allow sunlight to reach their precious weed patch. The barren ground also allowed water to erode the soil and muddied streams. Lakes and streams were polluted by chemical and organic fertilizers that growers spread abundantly, and by concentrated high-nitrogen fertilizers that leached into ground water and upset the chemical balance of streams, killing invertebrates.

Growers in Trinity County used urea-type fertilizer made of turkey or chicken shit because marijuana-growing magazines describe it as more organic. But these fertilizers also polluted streams and affected fish reproduction. Growers who used bat guano (Spanish for shit) from New Mexico caves also endangered their lives because the shit stimulates microbes that congest the lungs.

Growers also left behind all kinds of trash after harvesting their marijuana: irrigation hoses, plastic swimming pools, bags of fertilizer, plastic bags and pails, wire fencing, booby traps, garbage, shit, tools, cabins, tents, among hundreds of items.

The California Department of Fish and Game participated in the CAMP program in 1985 and produced a report that shocked many environmentalists who had supported the growers and held them up as examples of successful back-to-the-earth do-gooders. The Department of Fish and Game report says:

> In spite of not getting to see everything, our suspicions of the magnitude of wildlife violations by marijuana cultivators were confirmed.
>
> While we leaned more heavily on the physical evidence of deer being shot, and took a cautious stand on the poison issue last year, it seems the reverse may now be true. We are still unable to cite numbers or measurable impact by the use of rodenticides and other poisons, but the presence of these chemicals is now undeniable.
>
> As mentioned in an earlier report, many of the growers have become sensitized by the media attention. In a marijuana cultivation journal called "Sinsemilla Tips" the editor commented on the hypocrisy of demonstrating against the spraying of paraquat, while placing rodenticides or otherwise killing animals to protect a crop. Elaborate measures had been taken, in many instances, to physically protect plants from deer. Garden plots were almost always fenced.
>
> Physical evidence indicates that the number of deer shot by growers is commensurate with any other group living on the land in these rural areas. Poaching is a serious problem on the northcoast, and many of the people who live in these rural areas consider wild harvest to be acceptable. Marijuana growers seem to be no greater threat, except that, because of marijuana cultivation, there are now far more people out there living off the land than ever before.
>
> Of greater concern to us is the amount of poison we found. Over 80 percent of the gardens had evidence of rodenticides, and chemicals of some king (fertilizer, insecticide, herbicide, or rodenticide) were evident in all gardens. While the nature of rodenticides makes the discovery of victims nearly impossible, the manner of application was shocking in most cases. Chemicals that are for commercial application under controlled conditions were broadcast indiscriminately. We did not record a single instance where rodenticides were placed in a manner to avoid consumption by non-target species. It should also be noted that these chemicals are compounded with grains, nuts, or other desirable foodstuffs to make them attractive for consumption. Nearly every species, except for carnivores and reptiles, would be attracted.
>
> Another condition that we had previously overlooked was the impact on water sources by cultivators. Springs, water holes, and streams are common sources for the water needed to produce marijuana. Our investigations revealed that a significant number of these sources had been utilized in a manner that would negatively

impact wildlife. Spring boxes, which prevent evaporation and water
loss by absorbtion into the soil, also prevent animals from drinking
there. Water holes were converted to polycarbonate tanks which
store water more effectively, but completely exclude wildlife. In
others pumping mechanisms or human interference had caused
animals to water elsewhere. A significant impact was noted in one
high-tech garden where the grower had built a dam on a stream to
impound the total flow. A gasoline powered pump was capable of
pushing 90 p.s.i. of pressure in a 1.5-inch plastic pipe ½ mile uphill.
At the top of the hill, the water was held in nine 1,000-gallon
containers, and then disbursed through an elaborate irrigation system, including fertilizer injection. The bad news is that we discovered young steelhead trout in the impoundment, and upstream.
The fate of those below the dam was certain.

Seven cases are in various phases of preparation, or moving
through the judicial system. Two recent cases illusrate the value of
game wardens in marijuana investigations.

The first resulted from anonymous information about a local
rancher killing mountain lions, and culminated in the arrest of the
rancher for illegal possession of two mountain lion and 80 bobcat
pelts, and freshly killed deer and processed marijuana. It was reported that the rancher was a major supplier to the Las Vegas area.
At the time of the search we found $65,000 in cash, 1,000 ounces of
pure silver, and records that delighted the Internal Revenue Service.

In the second case, one of our people was on a CAMP raid when
some growers were encountered. Our officer asked what they were
doing, and they responded: "Hunting." Whereupon they were
asked to produce hunting licenses, and submit their weapons for
inspection. The hunters didn't have licenses, and their shotguns
were illegal for hunting. The subsequent search produced explod-
ing ammunition, fully-automatic weapons, silencers, and an array of
other illegal firearms and implements.

"People in rural counties have always been pro-environmental,"
Stowell said. "When we found growers poisoning fish streams with
fertilizer and killing deer who ate marijuana, we portrayed them in the
media as large business concerns destroying the environment. Once they
found out these idiots were harming the environment, the locals helped
us. By 1986 they'd let us land our helicopters on their land."

Criminals are hardy and resilient, especially when there's money to be
made. Growers responded to CAMP pressure by moving to other parts
of California, elsewhere in the United States and then, finally, indoors
where they are more difficult to find. (The irony being that economic
hardships created by CAMP caused them to move their gardens to

Kentucky and Oklahoma: a reversal of the 1930s drought-and-Depression-fueled migration that brought the Okies to California ... the drought and depression are now in the marijuana gardens of California.)

"We've created a monster," Stowell said. "We've driven them from outdoors to indoors. We've displaced them from the hills to Santa Barbara and San Diego where the emphasis is on year-round growing. The two record gardens found in 1989 were in San Diego. Now they look for targets of opportunity and grow for one or two years and move on." CAMP's unofficial motto, is "You can run, but you can't hide."

If advertisements in a pothead magazine are any indication, the indoor pot-growing business is booming. In 1985, *High Times* magazine carried ads from nine companies selling indoor gardening equipment such as sun lamps, timers, watering devices, soil, fans, and containers. By 1991, eighty-one companies were flogging their wares in the pothead version of *Home and Garden*. Of course, the firms doing the advertising claim they don't know their equipment is being used to grow dope. Who the hell reads ads in a doper magazine besides potheads and narcs?

Actually, a lot of people do. Mobsters realized two decades ago that marijuana entrepreneurs were making a lot of money. That gave rise to a new Cosa Nostra enterprise: dealing for dollars. Mobsters have kidnapped associates in large-scale marijuana operations and demanded exorbitant ransoms for their return. In some cases, the money was paid. In others, the kidnap victim was considered expendable. Whatever the outcome, no one was in a position to call in the cops.

Indoor growing is not as newfangled as some people make it out to be. Hippies of old started their plants indoors and transplanted the seedlings outdoors for the growing season. It was an expensive way to grow pot. Growers have now found that indoor growing may be the best way to make a fortune from marijuana cultivation. Although it requires a heavy outlay of cash for the specialized equipment, indoor growing allows year-round cultivation of four crops instead of the one or two crops that can be grown outdoors in optimum conditions.

The largest indoor marijuana-growing operation ever busted in California would shame most legitimate hothouse operators. The Placer County Investigations Unit, the sheriff's Marijuana Eradication Team, and the officers from the Roseville and Lincoln police stormed a Loomis barn in 1989 and found 8,049 female plants worth $25 million growing in the most sophisticated indoor garden investigators had ever seen. Police estimated the operation reaped two harvests a year worth a total of $50 million.

Metal halide lamps bathed mature plants, while sensitive seedlings were lit with softer light. An oxygenator filled the room with fresh air, which numerous fans kept circulating to cool the plants. Ceiling exhaust fans sucked out warm air. All of this was powered by electricity allegedly diverted from the Pacific Gas and Electric Co. by by-passing a meter. Police arrested two people who lived in a trailer next to the barn and seized $10,000 cash from a nearby house.

Indoor marijuana gardens are as hard as hell to find. Pot cops who have seen action in Vietnam know of an expensive piece of machinery that can help them pinpoint the bad guys from the sky. Forward Looking Infrared (FLIR) cameras sense the surface heat from objects and provide video screen images of what they scan. Although the images resemble negatives, they are so sharp a viewer can see someone throw a lit cigarette at 500 feet. US Customs interdiction planes in Florida use a more expensive version of these FLIR cameras — the same one used in F-16 fighter planes — to track blacked-out drug-trafficking planes at night. The Gro-Lites and other lamps used to light indoor pot gardens generate tremendous amounts of heat that FLIR sensors can also pick up.

US Drug Enforcement Agency agents first used the FLIR in April 1989 to spot an indoor marijuana garden in Los Angeles. They seized 644 plants, $553,000 in cash, four private planes, three vehicles, and a $3-million mansion.

The FLIR had to be shelved, however, pending the outcome of a federal court case in which the defendants argued that use of FLIR to detect drugs was illegal and Orwellian. They argued the cops were acting like Big Brother, roaming the skies with their heat-sensing spies to nab indoor pot growers. The court ruled in August 1989 that the DEA had used the FLIR to confirm a tip and had not used the FLIR during a fishing expedition to find pot gardens. The ruling allowed drug agents to take to the skies in their search for bad guys.

The second use of the FLIR later in 1989 by the DEA and the Placer County sheriff's office proved a bit embarrassing. A helicopter equipped with the FLIR pinpointed two buildings suspected of housing marijuana gardens. The cops raided the first building and found only plant scraps. It appears the occupants had heard the helicopter and made off with thirty quickly harvested plants.

The raiding party then struck out for the second location. Blush, blush, blush. The heat the FLIR had detected there was generated by a pile of decaying horse shit and hay. Which leads one to question the validity of the information that allowed the cops to check out the building with the FLIR in the first place. (Maybe they incorrectly interpreted someone claiming that Farmer so-and-so had some mean shit in his barn.) Anyway, the owner wasn't home to laugh at the $115,000 high-tech gizmo that led a pack of cops to his pile of shit. So they left a copy of the search warrant at his house to explain the footprints.

The cops got their act together by the end of May 1990 and used the FLIR to find a 100-plant indoor garden worth $300,000 in Lemon Cove in Tulare County. Police arrested a man and wife, both sixty-six, their son, and another man.

Another indoor garden in two rooms of a south Sacramento house contained sixty-five marijuana plants worth $200,000 along with growing equipment also worth $200,000 — carbon dioxide injectors, lava rocks to grow the weed hydroponically (sure beats lugging all that dirt around), a variety of growing lights, temperature-monitoring equipment, and plastic buckets. The operation was so sophisticated that the sinsemilla plants were not grown from seed, but cloned from leaves using a special cloning fluid. Justin Wolfe, a forty-seven-year-old child-care ombudsman for the California Department of Social Services, was charged with illegally cultivating marijuana.

Pot Facts

— Cannabis is an annual weed that can survive temperatures of 25 degrees Fahrenheit.
— More than half of the cannabis plant is moisture (50 to 60 percent).
— The taproot on a cannabis plant is only one foot long. Most of the roots grow laterally.
— Cannabis seeds germinate in six or seven days.
— One hundred cannabis seeds weigh 1 gram.
— One plant can produce 100,000 seeds.
— Cannabis plants mature in twenty to twenty-two weeks at a height of ten to twelve feet.
— Five thousand cannabis plants grown three feet apart will cover one acre.
— Only 13 percent of a dried plant is smokeable leaves.
— One plant will bear three-quarters of a pound of dried leaves. The plant can yield three to four pounds of dried leaves if leaves are picked throughout the growing season.
— A sinsemilla plant will yield one pound of dried leaves.
— One acre can produce 500 to 600 kilograms of dried leaves.
— Only 4 to 15 percent of a plant's weight in leaves can be made into hashish.
— Twenty to 28 percent of a plant's weight in leaves can be made into hashish oil.
— One pound of dried sinsemilla buds or shakes (leaves) yields 908 1-gram joints.
— One joint will keep a person stoned for two hours, though the chemical stays in the body longer.

— A 1,000-watt metal halite lamp covers fifty square feet of an indoor garden.

For people who claim their ten- to thirty-plant marijuana gardens were grown for personal use, not for purposes of trafficking, Charlie Stowell has this to say:

"A ten-plant garden equals ten pounds of useable material or 4,540 grams or 9,080 marijuana cigarettes. Again using the average intoxication period of two hours per cigarette, a ten-plant garden would provide 18, 160 hours of intoxication.

"There are 8,760 hours in one year. Therefore, if one individual grew ten plants for personal use, processed the marijuana, and began smoking the material at a rate of one joint every two hours, twenty-four hours a day, 365 days year round, he would finish his personal use in 756 days or 2.1 years. Twenty plants would be consumed in 4.2 years, thirty plants in 6.3 years.

"Now considering the fact that dried and processed marijuana loses approximately 3 to 6 percent of Delta 9 THC every year and is practically nil after the second year no matter how it is preserved or stored, the ten-plant garden for personal use immediately becomes a myth as there is no way humanly possible to consume that amount before the product is rendered useless."

Homegrown sinsemilla marijuana has made great inroads in the international pot market. In 1984, Colombia supplied 42 percent of the marijuana smoked in the United States. Mexico supplied 20 percent; 14 percent came from Jamaica; 12 percent was grown in the US; and 12 percent came from other sources. In 1988, Colombia supplied 37.2 percent; 25.6 percent came from Mexico; 25 percent from the United States; 6.1 percent from southeast Asia; 4 percent from Latin America; 1.8 percent from Jamaica; .3 percent from Belize.

Pot growers are sprouting like weeds themselves across the United States. In 1989, 5,605,460 marijuana plants weighing 2,548 metric tons were destroyed in the US. The DEA estimates this represents half the US crop, which was 5,096 metric tons. That crop made the US the second leading producer of marijuana in the world after Mexico. Colombia dropped out of the picture with a 1989 crop of 2,810 metric tons compared to 6,665 metric tons in 1988. The Colombian government seized 884 of those tons.

The figures for the American marijuana crop don't include the 124 million low-potency marijuana plants called ditchweed that were destroyed in 1989. Nebraska alone destroyed 73 million ditchweed plants.

Although California is the sinsemilla capital of the world, other states produce more marijuana. Here the top ten marijuana-producing states in

1989 in terms of number of plants seized: Missouri — 1,212,737 plants; Hawaii — 1,144,835; Kentucky — 596,512; Tennessee — 547,353; Oklahoma — 401,797; California — 328,824; Alabama — 163,395; Michigan — 127,882; North Carolina — 100,649; Georgia — 99,620.

In 1989, 5,767 people were arrested for growing marijuana in the United States; 1,021 of them were caught in California. And $29,545,033 in assets were seized.

A group of thirty marijuana growers from Albuquerque and Santa Fe, New Mexico, called themselves The Company and franchised three indoor pot gardens in 1989, two in New Mexico and one in Colorado. They ran the largest marijuana operation ever busted in the US — 9,526 plants and 550 pounds of processed marijuana were seized.

The northernmost bust went down in North Pole, Alaska, where police seized 459 plants in an indoor garden that provided starter plants for other gardens across the state.

Police made the largest marijuana seizure in Illinois history in 1989 when they found 58,012 pot plants interspersed with corn in White County. The weed was grown by the Marion County Marijuana Cooperative, which operates in fourteen states.

The largest seizure in Colorado history was made in 1989 when police seized 1,260 marijuana plants weighing 5,500 pounds in an indoor garden in Elbert County.

Those narcs don't miss a thing. When they busted Frank William Festag for growing marijuana indoors in Eureka, California, they found copies of a *High Times* editorial contract for a magazine article written by Festag under the pen name "Frank William Holliday." Festag was paid $300 for an article titled "I Smoked Pot With Bigfoot."

A raid on an indoor garden in Humboldt County netted 689 marijuana plants, $180,000 cash, and some former cops. Police charged a retired Humboldt County sheriff's lieutenant and a former California Highway Patrol officer.

How much do potheads like sinsemilla? Well, compare the prices they are willing to pay for their pot of choice. In 1989, commercial grade marijuana from Colombia, Mexico, or the US sold on the street for $700 to $1,200 a pound. Sinsemilla sold for $1,200 to $4,000 a pound on the street.

Marijuana cultivation is not only a California problem, though mass cultivation of the plant started there. In 1988, for example, 1,998,502 plants worth $2 billion on the street were destroyed in the five westernmost states: 5,191 plants in Alaska; 373,670 plants in California; 1,522,235 plants in Hawaii; 61,560 plants in Oregon; and 35,846 plants in Washington.

Oregon

Many Oregon pot growers moved their operations indoors in 1988 to avoid getting caught by high-flying cops. A barn in Yamhill County housed 281 marijuana plants in three rooms equipped with automatic timers to water, fertilize, and light the plants. A cooperative ran five separate indoor gardens in Yamhill, Multnomah, Washington, and Clackamas counties. The cooperative sold its dope, most of which was sealed in cans and exported to other states, for $2,000 a pound.

In Portland, 2,384 marijuana plants were found in the home of the general manager for Hyrotech Company of Portland, which supplies grow lights and equipment to indoor gardeners. Elsewhere in Portland, 258 plants were found in an underground bunker linked by tunnel to a nearby house. An indoor garden near Deadwood turned out a crop of marijuana every forty-five days. An underground garden in Eugene hidden under the floor of a building produced thirty pounds of weed every three months. Police found many of these buildings with hidden marijuana gardens under a concrete floor and suspect they are commercially manufactured for growers.

An enterprising grower in Harney County grew 488 marijuana plants in a large metal building in which he installed a 100-kw diesel generator to power sixty 1,000-watt grow bulbs. He bought a 2,700-gallon fuel truck to service the generator, which gobbled up so much fuel that the grower had to drive 100 miles from Burns to Ontario every two months to refill the truck. The seized generator now powers the Harney County 911 dispatch center during power outages.

Hawaii

Though Hawaii ranks forty-seventh in population in the US, it is ranked second in marijuana arrests. Cops there destroyed 28 percent of all plants eradicated in the United States in 1988. Increased enforcement, increased forfeitures of land and homes, and a change in the public's taste for drugs have led to a decline of marijuana cultivation on the islands. Crystal meth (ice) and cocaine have now become the preferred drugs of sale, since they produce a better return on investment.

Alaska

Here indoor gardens are in. Until November 1990, possession of four ounces of pot at home for personal use was legal in Alaska. Now it can fetch a ninety-day jail term and $1,000 fine. Not much, is it? Cops also admit no money is budgeted to crack down on pot so charges will be laid only if pot is found in the course of other investigations. Some war on drugs.

Washington

Indoor gardens were in vogue in Washington State too, where one was found in the basement of a day-care center. Growers were heavily armed in 1988. Four growers of an indoor garden in Cowlitz County had bears, wolves, and cougars prowling the area around their grow building. They also had four framed membership certificates in witchcraft and black magic groups.

Many indoor gardens have caught fire because of faulty wiring in buildings where growers by-passed electric meters and installed heavy-duty lights and generators. Firemen and narcs were called to one such emergency by the grower himself who ran out to greet them yelling that he too was on fire. There was no fire. The man had snorted a quarter ounce of cocaine in forty-eight hours. A twenty-acre property that contained a marijuana garden was surrounded by a seven-strand electric fence and patrolled by an armed grower and his dog.

Outdoor growing techniques in Washington State were modified to avoid detection. Marijuana plants were tied down and made to run under brush like vines. Plants were mixed with rows of corn. Crops were planted in cleared-out spaces in heavy underbrush through which an access tunnel had been cut. Groups of four and five plants have been grown on and inside massive stumps in heavy undergrowth. Indoor growers also showed ingenuity in the design of their gardens. One garden was equipped with battery-operated water valves, a drip system and pressure regulator connected to a spring that fills a watering barrel. One garden was hidden inside a cargo container buried under a metal building that housed another garden. A 15,000-square-foot warehouse was divided into ten rooms each equipped with ten halide reflectors and timed automatic irrigation and lighting. A computer was programmed to inject carbon dioxide into plants in one garden. One Washington real estate agent sold homes with growing facilities already installed. Marijuana growers in Washington, like those elsewhere, preferred small, high-yield plants fourteen to twenty-four inches high, which produce buds eight to twelve inches long. Indoor growing techniques allow cannabinoids to grow as much marijuana in a twenty-by-twenty-foot room as they would on half an acre outdoors.

The best excuse for growing marijuana was given to police by an indoor grower who said she had four children by four different fathers who had all left her. "If you had that to face, wouldn't you smoke dope too?" she asked them.

In a hundred-year-old Dutch country mansion called Cannabis Castle, a former heroin addict turned professional breeder has invented better marijuana, and dopers are beating a path to his door. Nevil Schoenmakers took a flying leap at a loophole in the Netherlands' law books in 1984 and formed a company called the Seed Bank — sort of a eugenic sperm bank for gifted plants. He trips around the world — the United States, Thailand, Hungary, Afghanistan — looking for potent strains of marijuana. The thirty-four-year-old knows good weed when he whiffs it. He sorts the seeds by hand using screens and sells them for $5 each. Five bucks for a seed that goes to pot? You bet. And the Seed Bank has all kinds of seeds to choose from. Its catalog is advertised in *High Times*, the second most successful 1960s publication since *Rolling Stone* magazine. Unlike *Rolling Stone*, *High Times* has not sold out its editorial policy of giving potheads what potheads want — a gentle shove toward a good stone. A lot of people must like being shoved around, because the American magazine sells 85,000 copies per issue.

Schoenmakers's best customers are American. They buy 90 percent of his stock. Most of his mail orders — cash in advance; no fronting, man; and the cash has to be wrapped in carbon paper to prevent postal snoops from seeing it — are from California, Florida, Michigan, and New York. And although it's illegal, the seeds are mailed from within the United States in clear plastic bags inside unmarked packages with no return address. For the serious customer, Schoenmakers has a hotline, direct to his castle, over which he doles out pot-growing information. The druggie-turned-entrepreneur is a perfect product of the peace generation that preached free love, free this, free that. Like the rest of the long-haired, tie-dyed freaks, he has sold out those beliefs. He makes $1 million a year selling pot seeds. In God we trust.

Nevil Schoenmakers, the Sultan of Seeds, isn't the only entrepreneur in the wacky weed business to make a fortune through advertising. Michael Cesar, who calls himself the Pope of Pot, ran a toll-free hotline out of New York City that dispatched marijuana-bearing couriers from a Greenwich Village comic shop to Manhattan customers, police said. Cesar was arrested in November 1990, when police put a lid on his 1-800-WANT-POT hotline that allegedly raked in $30,000 a day. The alleged drug operation used five bicycle messengers who peddled one-eighth of an ounce of marijuana in packages that sold for $50 to customers.

"These people got marijuana delivered like most people send out for coffee," prosecutor Sterling Johnson said.

The operation's five telephone lines "were always ringing off the hook," said Thomas Fahey, narcotics squad captain. "This guy does very well selling pot."

Police seized ten pounds of marijuana and $3,000 in cash during a raid on the hotline offices. Police said Cesar, forty-eight, ran a similar hotline called DIAL-A-JOINT in the past and was convicted of drug dealing in 1980, 1983, and 1988, for which he served two prison sentences. Cesar happens also to be high priest of the Church of the Realized Fantasy, which preaches against money and for easy sex and drugs. The more things change, the more they stay the same. Today, as in the sixties, the best way to get laid is to start a church.

12

Hell's Angels:
Taking care of business

"Any indicia of membership in the HAMC is indicative of a readiness, willingness and ability to engage in illegal activity."
— KEVIN P. BONNER, FBI AGENT.

"This is the best crank in the world. We make it ourselves."
— GARY KAUTZMAN, PRESIDENT OF THE SAN FRANCISCO CHAPTER, DROPS A SHOEBOX OF METHAMPHETAMINE ON A TABLE IN HIS OFFICE ON MAY 1, 1982.

Outlaw motorcycle gangs, by their own account, exist to live outside the law. There are more than 800 outlaw biker gangs in North America. Most of them are involved in the drug trade. The Hell's Angels Motorcycle Club is the most sophisticated and powerful of these gangs. They were the first such gang to get into drugs and they have set the pace and example for others to follow.

The distinction must be made between Hell's Angels the club and Hell's Angels the business. The club is about motorcycles. The business is about crime. Their most profitable crime is drugs. How did a bunch of dirtbags with little more than gas money in their jeans in the 1960s become a multinational drug ring? Sheer balls, enterprise, and opportunism.

The Hell's Angels were founded on March 17, 1948, during the kick-ass dawn of the outlaw biker movement in southern California. They remained a relatively anonymous bunch of greasy brawlers little known outside California until their Labor Day run in Monterey on September 6, 1964. Two teenaged girls claimed they were raped by the gang and accordingly four Hell's Angels were arrested. Newspapers reported how the bikers allegedly dragged the girls away from their dates on the beach and had sex with them in the dunes. The story spread along the coast like a dose in a fern bar and set in motion the wheels that made them media heroes and celebrities for their homespun violence in an era that rebelled against authority.

The Hell's Angels did anything for kicks in the early 1960s. Little white pills stretched their lives into the desperate crash of dawn. But the

Angels, like all greaseballs, preferred booze to drugs. They dealt a little weed and speed, but only to skim a bit for themselves.

The girls had not been raped. Ironically, the false charges forced the Hell's Angels into the rank underworld of large-scale speed manufacturing and drug trafficking. They were financially unstable in the 1960s. The guys who worked had menial jobs to pay for rent, gas, oil, and booze. Legal costs incurred to fight the Monterey rape charges left them hard up for cash. They were on the brink of extermination. A hefty push by the cops could have toppled them. They needed money to survive. Some members decided to sell speed to recoup their losses, a one-shot deal. An Angel contacted a chemist and got the formula to manufacture methamphetamine. Thus they got hooked on easy money and a bid to top up club coffers turned into an international and ongoing enterprise.

In early 1965, the Hell's Angels boasted four chapters and a group of homeless nomads in California, and one chapter in Auckland, New Zealand. That soon changed as national media coverage of a hyped attorney general's report on the gang made them a cultural curiosity. The Hell's Angels had become the official American nightmare.

The Angels had built their reputation for violence by emulating Marlon Brando in the 1954 movie *The Wild One*. They built their drug business by imitating Brando in *The Godfather*. The club grew quickly. Although many original members were Second World War veterans, the new generation consisted of disgruntled Vietnam War vets who brought to outlaw motorcycle gangs much-needed skills in explosives and weapons and military contacts to arm them.

The next step on the Angels' trek into the drug world was helped by a good writer who is now a famous writer. The Hell's Angels were bound to link up with the hippies sooner or later in the turbulent California streets in the 1960s. Hunter S. Thompson made the connection sooner. He hung out with the Angels three days a week in mid-to-late 1965 to research a book on the gang. He liked the action and the women. The Angels weren't into drugs at the time, but by the time Thompson finished his book he had an inkling that bad things were on the horizon.

The writer was slugging back beer with Oregon wildman Ken Kesey in a San Francisco bar one summer day. Kesey's novel *Sometimes a Great Notion* had been published the previous year and remains his generation's best tribute to individualism. Kesey was a pioneer in drugs and mind expansion in the 1960s. He tripped around with his Merry Pranksters, bodies decked out in Day-Glo, minds stretched out on LSD. The legendary Neal Cassady, stud extraordinaire, buddy and inspiration to Jack Kerouac, who made him literature's muscleman manic, chauffeured the weirdos around in a hippy-colored bus with a destination sign that read "Further." Cassady was a natural speed-freak who blasted through life on a timetable that ended sometime during a cold Mexican night three years later. He passed out and died of exposure while counting railway ties on a desolate stretch between two towns on February 4, 1968. The Holy Goof succumbed to goofballs.

Thompson took Kesey to the Box Shop garage after they finished their beer and he introduced him to some Angels. In turn, Kesey invited the club to his place in La Honda for a bash on Saturday, August 7. Forty Hell's Angels led by Sonny Barger were greeted by a sign that read "The Merry Pranksters Welcome the Hell's Angels." The Angels met the New Left intelligentsia—including poet Allen Ginsberg and acid guru Richard Alpert—who helped them gain acceptance among the hippies. The freaked-out pranksters plied the Angels with LSD and thus ushered them into the world's largest mass consumer market for illicit drugs, the Haight-Ashbury community.

Shortly after the Angels connected with the hippies, the motorcycle club incorporated in California in 1966 to curb imitators spawned by eighteen years of kicking ass. The articles of incorporation describe the Angels as a club dedicated to the promotion and advancement of motorcycle driving, motorcycle clubs, motorcycle highway safety, and all phases of motorcycling and motorcycle driving.

Some of the California chapter rules demonstrate what concerns the Hell's Angels most:

(1) No dope burns.
(2) On California runs, weapons will be shot only between 0600 and 1600. Penalty for violation: patch pulled.
(3) No spiking the club's booze with dope.
(4) No throwing live ammunition into bonfires on runs.
(5) No messing with another member's wife.
(6) You can't pull the patch of another chapter's member.
(7) No snuffing a member with his patch on. (You can only snuff a member of your own chapter.)
(8) No using dope during a meeting.

That sure takes the fun out of partying.

During the first half of the club's life, the Angels beat and pissed on people in a pathetic grab for recognition. They spent the second half of their existence trying to dismantle the anti-social image and cultivating an inconspicuous conspicuousness. It's a tricky balancing act the Angels call "taking care of business." It means the Hell's Angels are just as bad as ever, but you'd never know unless you're part of the underworld they crawl around in.

The transformation began around San Francisco Bay in 1967; the alchemist's stone was lysergic acid diethylamide. The Hell's Angels were everything the flower children were not in the mid-1960s; they spelled peace with an *ie* and the only beads they had were on gun barrels. The spoiled generation rebelled: gave away free love, spurned all-American red meat for veggies, and fried its brains with the most unnatural chemicals. It also latched onto—hoping the rebellious image would rub off—the only true counterculture around: the Hell's Angels. The bikers didn't understand why the flower children took to them. They stank, they were crude, and they hated wimpy, long-haired faggots. But the love generation spread its legs and the Angels fucked the flakes in more ways than one.

The hippies dubbed the Hell's Angels the "People's Police" and turned them on to a wider variety of drugs than they had known. It was a symbiotic relationship. The Angels wasted no time becoming parasites. They quickly grasped that a handful of pushers made a fortune selling acid to the psychedelic fur brains. The smell of money brought out the shark in several ambitious Angels, including George (Baby Huey) Wethern, vice-president of the Oakland chapter. Wethern tracked down the acid king, the legendary underground chemist, Augustus Owsley Stanley III. Wethern tapped the source and cornered the LSD market in California. He twisted arms and enlarged nostrils with the cold barrel of a .45-caliber handgun to drive out competition. He owned the club's biggest gun collection.

Owsley was a twenty-five-year-old job hopper when he signed up at the University of California at Berkeley in 1963. He added "dropout" to his résumé within one semester. All he got out of university was a twenty-four-year-old chemistry major girlfriend called Melissa who knew how to make acid. Sexual chemistry led to his famous Purple Owsley LSD and other highly marketable pieces of chalk soaked with the stuff of dreams. Owsley reportedly made $1 million selling his shit before acid was outlawed in April 1966. Ken Kesey and psychologist Timothy ("turn on, tune in, drop out") Leary were among his best promoters as they garnered followings of snug-assed tighties with talk of multi-colored mind- and snatch-expanding experiences.

Just as the late 1960s gave North Americans a chance to re-assess their values—and then quickly forget they doubted them—so the era gave the Hell's Angels and other outlaw motorcycle gangs a drug subculture that fattened their coffers. Americans now spend more than $80 billion a year on illegal drugs. Canadians spend $10 billion, a frighteningly high figure when you consider the American population is ten times that of Canada.

Wealth made the club tone down its hell-raising and work toward a better public image to fend off police attention, which hurts profits. Men once reconciled to a brawling working-class life unexpectedly found themselves in mortgage-free homes with three cars. They had traded the chips on their shoulders for bucks in the pockets. The Hell's Angels could disappear forever into suburbia if not for the rivalry for drug-trafficking territory.

Many a greedy doper chases the American dream with a nose full of white powder and an M-60 machine gun tucked under his arm. The Hell's Angels' flirtation with anonymity is at best sporadic. Sidewalk assassinations and car bombings have replaced the parking-lot rumbles. Profit replaced pussy as the Angels' reason for being in a netherworld where the existential question is answered with a dry bed and a wet snatch.

The transformation of the Hell's Angels from a motorcycle gang into an international drug-trafficking network was a masterpiece of business ingenuity greased with sweat and blood. The Angels decided early to concentrate their efforts on LSD, PCP, and methamphetamine. They make the drugs in clandestine laboratories and control the distribution network from wholesalers to street-level pushers. It's a secure system, tough for any cop to crack. The self-contained network also eliminates competition. More importantly, complete control allows gang leaders to maximize profits—they cut pure speed with baby laxative, Vitamin B, or PCP before it goes to the next rung on the distribution ladder. The drug is diluted at every level, earning the seller a larger profit.

Now the transformation is complete. As an FBI agent, Kevin P. Bonner, said about the Hell's Angels following a twenty-six-month undercover investigation that ended on May 2, 1985, "The HAMC is an organization which lives for or lives on drugs."

The Hell's Angels Motorcycle Club is well suited to operate as a criminal organization, whether it's selling crank or corpses. Angels are committed to live outside the law. They are a closely knit group sworn to secrecy. The club's seventy-five chapters in thirteen countries on four continents form a reliable international pipeline for contraband and a dependable communication network. Chapters hide fugitive Angels and provide them with false identification and a cover. Members have disappeared for years in this counterfeit underground. The Hell's Angels maintain safe houses in northern New York State for Canadian members on the lam.

Many of the Angels who commit crimes can depend on the support of non-members — men and women. In turn, these non-members have their own networks of friends.

The Hell's Angels Motorcycle Club is organized to insulate its leadership from prosecution. The club is hierarchically structured and well disciplined so it can function even after the arrest of members. It has a code of silence that its members sometimes enforce with death and camouflages orders through layers of bosses who protect themselves through graft and corruption.

The Hell's Angels' organization chart resembles that of traditional organized crime, with which the club slowly aligned itself during the 1970s and 1980s. The club's East Coast and West Coast officers carry out the same duties as does traditional organized crime's Commission when they regulate and oversee club business such as the creation of new chapters. The chapter president is equivalent to the family boss. The secretary-treasurer is sometimes the most logical member and offers advice like a *consigliere*; a lawyer who is a club associate also may act in this capacity. The vice-president is like a Mafia underboss. The sergeant-at-arms and road captain are like *caporegima*, or lieutenants. And the members are soldiers.

The Hell's Angels and traditional organized crime operate the same way. They control the area where they commit crimes. They corrupt police and public officials to insulate themselves from prosecution. They use associates and fronts to manipulate and influence people.

While drug trafficking is the Hell's Angels' main source of income, the club is involved in countless other crimes. Angels are opportunistic and flexible. If a new member shows safe-cracking talents, a chapter suddenly finds itself involved in a new enterprise. Angels fiddle with these crimes in their spare time: arson, assault, blackmail, bombing, burglary, corruption, extortion, forgery of government documents, gambling, gun running, insurance fraud, international white slavery, kidnapping, truck hijacking, loansharking, motorcycle and automobile theft, murder, pornography, prostitution, rape, robbery, and weapons thefts from military bases. Traditional organized crime families commit the same crimes.

The Angels learned the merit of keeping a low profile when they worked for the mob. Angels set the trend in outlaw motorcycle gang fashions and cultivated the grub look for more than two decades to instill fear. The mob taught them that conspicuousness is a weakness in the drug business. Angels today are more likely to wear suits than colors. They still value the grinning death's head, but keep it for funerals, runs, initiations, and laying heavies. Angels, like the undercover policemen who tail them, prefer street clothes to blend in with their surroundings. They've replaced their Harleys with Corvettes, Lincolns, and Cadillacs. The new mob shows class.

The Hell's Angels promise their crank is the world's best. It's true. But they don't say anything about its purity. The only Angel regulation about diluted drugs is that you don't sell them to a fellow Angel. It's also club law that you don't sell shit to anyone. Burns hurt business.

"Selling somethin' bad would be putting my patch on the line. That's against the rules," said James (Gorilla) Harwood, former vice-president of the Hell's Angels, Troy, New York, chapter and security officer for the club's East Coast chapters. Harwood explained what happened to an Angel who sold bad dope.

"The guy lost his patch for a year. Plus, he had to pay back all the money that he made off it. The Hell's Angels, we're in the business to make money. But it gets around when we're scum, scumbags like that."

The Hell's Angels strive for quality control, but not all crank cookers are equal.

"I'm a dope dealer. I know my business," said Ronald (Big Cheese) Cheeseman, former president of the Hell's Angels, Binghamton, New York, chapter and head of the club's Mid-State chapter on July 14, 1983.

Cheeseman was one of the club's biggest methamphetamine producers on the east coast. He had a moveable lab he alternated between Binghamton and a house on a dirt road in Montrose, Pennsylvania, where he kept tanks of ether in the chicken coop and $15,000 of glassware in the kitchen. He also dealt in cocaine smuggled into Florida in a Dominican Republic diplomatic pouch. He shipped his speed across to Canada in cookie boxes.

Cheeseman's crank was not as good as that made in California.

"The methamphetamine that came from Binghamton was brown and smelled like perfume and it had a real violent taste," Harwood said. "Plus it wouldn't get you high. It was sort of like a club joke."

The Oakland Angels got lucky in the early 1970s. They recruited a Richmond, California, oil-company chemist to cook methamphetamine for them full-time. He taught members in many chapters how to make the drug. The Hell's Angels became the country's top crank producers and control 75 percent of the California market. Four Angels made $6 million selling crank at the wholesale level between 1976 and 1979. The Angels send technicians to chapters around the world to teach them how to produce the crank. According to a former Hell's Angel who testified before a U.S. Senate Committee, a New York college chemist taught four Manhattan chapter Angels how to make base drugs to produce methamphetamine.

Through the control of chemists, the Hell's Angels cornered the methamphetamine market. According to law-enforcement agencies in both countries, the club owns or controls most speed labs in California and British Columbia. Associates run the labs to distance the Angels from prosecution. Former Hell's Angels hit man James (Brett) Eaton said the club takes over methamphetamine laboratories two ways: "They find someone already making speed and say, 'OK, now you make it for us.' "

Sometimes they are subtler in their approach. They pay a chemist $25,000 for five pounds of crank and front him $25,000 for the next shipment. "Now the guy owes the club."

One Hell's Angels' lab in central Ohio can produce $14 million of speed a month. It supplies druggies from Ohio to California and in West Virginia, New York, and New Jersey. The lab in North Carolina was staffed by a New York-trained chemist in the late 1970s and produced most of the speed sold by the southern and Omaha, Nebraska, chapters.

The Hell's Angels buy and steal the chemicals they need to make methamphetamine. Sergey (Sir Gay) Walton, president of the Oakland chapter in January 1977, stole enough laboratory glassware and chemicals during a break-in at a chemical company to set up several labs. He was helped by Angel Kenny Owen, president of the Vallejo chapter, and drug dealer Henry Crabtree. Owen used the name of D & H Speed Engineering to order forty pounds of chemicals needed to make speed from a Portland firm.

Crabtree wasn't around to see the club's drug business expand. He found it too monolithic in 1978 and broke off his dealings with the Angels one year later to work for himself.

"I got kind of tired of all the killings. The game of hustling is fun when you're down in the small rackets. When you get in the big rackets, it ain't fun. The hustling part of it I enjoyed. I still would. The killing part, no."

One Angel paid the white supremacist Aryan Brotherhood to ice Crabtree. They missed.

The drug business made killers of the Hell's Angels. They leaned on debtors for a while, then cut their losses. Carl Billam, twenty-four, was a drug-dealing associate of the club from Summerville, South Carolina. Four men jumped him outside the can at the Nashville East Club in Charleston at 2:30 a.m. on October 12, 1979. He died five days later from a knife wound to the gut. Police issued a warrant for the arrest of a Hell's Angel and former Green Beret, Artie Ray Cherry. Federal police raided Cherry's home on unrelated weapons charges on October 18. He avoided arrest when he produced a driver's license that identified him as Vincent Mark Guinta. He disappeared before local police arrived to serve the murder warrant.

Jerry David Guy, an associate of the Hell's Angels in Durham and Winston-Salem, North Carolina, owed the club money in late 1980. The thirty-seven-year-old man and Pamela Merrell Boaz, twenty-two, were found in an abandoned tobacco shed on November 6—stiffed.

Hell's Angels in eastern Canada decided in 1985 to eliminate their unruly

North chapter because it attracted too much police attention. Most North chapter Angels were cocaine addicts, unpredictably violent and undependable in business. They stole $98,000 from the newly chartered Halifax chapter, failed to share with other chapters profits from two secret speed laboratories, and killed anyone they didn't like. They were known by Hell's Angels around the world as the club's sex, drugs, and rock-and-roll chapter. It wasn't good for business.

The North chapter, based in Laval, Quebec, was eliminated at a meeting of eastern Canada Hell's Angels on Sunday, March 24, 1985. Five North chapter Angels were gunned down as the meeting started. Their bodies were wrapped in sleeping bags, weighed down with concrete blocks, weightlifting plates and chains, and dumped in the St. Lawrence Seaway. They weren't taking care of business, so the club took care of them.

Traditional organized crime and outlaw motorcycle gangs argue they commit victimless crimes—that they cater to society's vices, and customers come to them willingly. Angel cocaine dealer Gorilla Harwood rejected that argument when he walked into his house and found his daughter imitating her father and his friends.

"My daughter was taking a straw and a mirror and putting it up the noses of her stuffed animals."

Speed kills. Cocaine slaughters. Montreal Hell's Angel Noel Mailloux was a former Wild One from Hamilton, Ontario. He joined the Angels in Quebec with Walter Stadnick, and both men spent a lot of time in their home town, which is controlled by enemy Outlaws and Satan's Choice. Mailloux was a heavy cocaine user. He dusted his nostrils with $21,000 of the white powder from December 25, 1982, to February 18, 1983. At the best of times, he was paranoid. He saw Outlaws behind every stare and death in every glare. He carried a knife and a .357-magnum revolver. He checked his car for bombs.

Mailloux, like other Hell's Angels, had an affinity for strippers. The thirty-year-old biker spent the first two weeks of February 1983 at the house of his girlfriend, Connie Augustin, where he snorted coke and talked about an Outlaw who might kill him. The twenty-four-year-old stripper worked local clubs to support her four-year-old son, Stewart Hawley.

Mailloux started a coke binge on Valentine's Day. He got the coke from a bouncer at a downtown Hamilton hotel Mailloux talked with the bouncer over the telephone later in the day. He hung up convinced the bouncer's coke was bad. He also suspected he was an Outlaw associate.

Mailloux lived paranoia to its grisly end. Another stripper, Cindy Lee Thompson, eighteen years old, visited Augustin's house. Mailloux convinced them that the bouncer set them up for an Outlaw hit. They turned off the lights and waited in the dark. Mailloux sat on the boy's stool with his loaded revolver.

Augustin decided after midnight that Mailloux was getting too weird. She got her son and Thompson in the front seat of her car and tried to escape. Mailloux jumped into the back seat, put the gun to Augustin's head, and ordered her to drive. She leaped out at the first red light. She hoped Mailloux would chase her and give Thompson and her son a chance to escape. The Angel pulled the trigger as she opened the door. A bullet tore through her arm and right breast. She kept running. He shot the baby and the other stripper in the head and took off after Augustin.

"He's going to kill me!" Augustin screamed as she tore down the Hamilton Mountain suburban street. She ran up to John Perrins's car and grabbed the door handle. The twenty-five-year-old steelworker watched Mailloux fire two shots at her and he sped away.

"I thought maybe they were out partying and decided to make a scene and acted out this little scene."

Perrins stopped and watched Augustin run to the car of his twenty-six-year-old workmate, Kevin Pomeroy. Mailloux caught her before she could get into the car and shot the driver in the arm and chin.

"I felt a burning sensation in my chin. He didn't say anything. He looked like he had something on his mind and he didn't care whether he shot me or not."

Pomeroy drove away and Mailloux turned to Augustin.

"I looked up and he was looking at me. . . .He pulled the trigger, but there was no bullets left in the gun."

Augustin dashed off. Another driver stopped for her. Mailloux disappeared into the darkness. Hamilton-Wentworth Regional Police Sergeant Charles Bamlett spotted the Angel in a nearby field and approached cautiously. Mailloux crouched and held the gun in both hands. Bamlett was 100 feet away.

"He was squeezing the trigger. I could hear it going click, click, click, and he was saying 'Bang, bang, bang.' "

Hell's Angels informants told authorities in the 1980s that on each coast representatives of various chapters had formed an unofficial meth-amphetamine board of directors to ensure that chapters didn't tread on each other's territory. The board also issued customer lists. Angels can't sell to anyone outside of its list. The rule is good for business and security.

Every chapter holds at least one monthly business meeting called "church." Club matters are discussed openly. However, if members wish to negotiate drug deals they do so on paper, with sign language, or on a blackboard during innocuous conversation. Some members are so worried about police bugs that they discuss deals only outside the clubhouse.

Angels who deal drugs give part of their drug profits to the chapter in weekly dues — usually $20. The chapter then pays into the club's national treasury. The Hell's Angels also keep a multi-million-dollar defense fund to which members and chapters are occasionally asked to contribute, especially after a major bust. Some of the dues money is used to support the families and businesses of jailed members. The club also has a TCB (taking care of business) fund for security/intelligence officers and hit men. Sandy Alexander thanked two potential drug buyers on December 29, 1983, for what they are doing for the Hell's Angels, as a large part of money the members make through dealing goes to the club.

All Hell's Angels were assessed a $250 fee at the 1981 U.S.A. run to help defray the legal cost of the Omaha chapter's RICO trial.

"In the Barger trial [1979-1980]," Clarence (Addie or Butch) Crouch, former vice-president of the Cleveland chapter, testified in front of a Senate Committee, "each person was assessed I think it was $100 the first time. But then once they got to selling the T-shirts and the bumper stickers and all that, it was a full-page ad taken out in a motorcycle magazine called *Easyrider* [*sic*] did not cost us anything, and all the moneys from that went into that fund there, which caused a lot of trouble in the club, because they wanted a counting of how much money it was, but Oakland would not tell them, which I assume, from what I have gathered from a lot of hearsay and talk and everything, that it was quite a lot of money. They were taking bags each day from the post office to Oakland."

T-shirts and posters sold through ads in *Easyriders* are now com-nonplace. Those on sale to raise money for four Montreal chapter Angels on trial for the liquidation of the North chapter on March 24, 1985, read, "Free East Coast Canada," and show a pair of hands breaking manacles.

Chapters and members are leery of flaunting their wealth for fear they will be leaned on by less successful Angels.

"They do not let each other know in case something comes up," Addie Crouch said.

"One charter is not assessed more than another charter, so everybody kind of plays it poor . . . every member places a low profile on money, because money always puts everybody out on front street."

Some Hell's Angels are millionaires. Crouch named one in New York, one in Cleveland, and one in Oakland.

"They are there to back any play that is really heavy, any kind of really heavy trials that come down or anything. They always feel that they can fall back on them.

"They made most of their money from drugs. They have got fronts. [One] owns [a] restaurant out in Oakland. And [one] owns a little bar there in Cleveland, a couple of bars. And [one] just — he stays way back — New York don't flaunt their money at all."

Angels register property in the names of parents or girlfriends to hide their wealth. One member of the Manhattan chapter spends $400,000 a year on good times. He rents a yacht in New Jersey for a week to party. He periodically stays in the penthouse suite at the Plaza Hotel with one of his many sweeties and fucks his brains out for three days. He rents cars, as do many Angels, and when hungry doesn't hesitate to walk into the poshest restaurant and order the most expensive items on the menu. Angels know life is short. They enjoy it while they can.

Several Angels in Quebec and British Columbia are also millionaires. Michel (Sky) Langlois, former president of the Hell's Angels in Canada, owned a 1981 Harley, a car, and an airplane. He received $400 a week from 112628 Canada Inc., the Montreal chapter's registered name, in 1985.

Rick Ciarniello, Hell's Angels' president in British Columbia and owner of a blue Lincoln with vanity plates that read "ANGELS," denied in 1985 that members are wealthy.

"What a fairy tale. You're gonna have one helluva time finding any millionaire bikers. There's no such thing. The truth is, we are a group of people who like motorcycles. It's so simple that anybody can grasp it."

Ciarniello also denied in a radio interview with the author that the British Columbia Hell's Angels have a black member; the club constitution says that members must be white. The black Angel was a respected member of the Satan's Angels Motorcycle Club before that club's members became Hell's Angels. The original members kept the black member in the club despite death threats from the Angels' Oakland and Cleveland chapters.

The lower British Columbia mainland has a rapidly expanding drug market within easy reach of the California drug network. BC Angels make most of their money selling cocaine. The four Angel chapters in BC control all outlaws motorcycle gang activity in the province as well as forty registered companies.

The BC Angels own a campground called Angel Acres in Nanaimo. The heavily wooded property has a large in-ground swimming pool, trailers, and a bandshell. Angels and prospects guard the chained-off roadway into the property, part of which is off limits to anyone but Angels. The BC Hell's Angels hosted more than 3,000 bikers from across North America at their anniversary party on August 2 to 4, 1986.

The Para-Dice Riders from Toronto made the event a mandatory one-month run for the club's thirty-nine members during the gang's twenty-fifth year. It is unusual for any Toronto gang to show such support for either the Angels or Outlaws.

The Hell's Angels Motorcycle Club imposes strict accountability on drug dealers. Even Angels who brag about being high-school dropouts keep books to record customers, drug deals, debts, and profits. Many chapters, such as the Lynn-Salem, Massachusetts, and the Sorel, Quebec, chapters, keep their records on computer floppy disks, which are easily hidden and transported. Computers also allow the transmission of information between chapters over telephone lines using modems. Volumes of information can be transmitted in minutes and none of it can be easily listened to by prying ears.

The club treats the business seriously. James (Gorilla) Harwood had a brush with discipline in 1982. The Manhattan chapter tried to collect $100,000 it had fronted Harwood in methamphetamine. He didn't deny receiving the drugs, but had not kept records. New York had. Troy, New York, Angels dug Harwood's grave and dusted it with lime. Murders within the club don't have to be sanctioned by East or West Coast presidents, but these officers are sometimes consulted for their greater grasp of the implications of the killing. Troy Angels paid a courtesy call on Sandy Alexander to inform him they planned to do in Harwood. They asked for his opinion, not his sanction. They wanted him to assess the repercussions. Alexander told them not to kill. Instead, the Angels pulled Harwood's patch for ten months so they could get the money back.

Like thousands of businessmen, the Angels use courier services to get drugs to customers overnight. Gary Kautzman, president of the San Francisco chapter, shipped drugs east through United Parcel Service in May 1982. He paid a UPS employee for seven years to ensure the shipments weren't ripped off. Manhattan vice-president Howard Weisbrod sent drugs via air-freight services such as Federal Express and Emery in 1984.

The Angels also ship their crank from California to New York by train, usually in a suitcase carried by a prospect. No one bothers train passengers or their luggage. Harwood sent drugs to Canadian chapters by rail in the late 1970s and 1980s and once transported cocaine in his daughter's luggage. An Angel planned to haul crank from Oakland to Alaska in toolboxes in early March 1985. He bought so much he used a trunk instead.

Angels who carry drugs in their cars continually worry they'll be caught. Phillip Utley, vice-president of the Durham, North Carolina, chapter, and prospect Ronnie Broadwell delivered drugs to Baltimore, Maryland, in February 1985. They hid the drugs in the car's emission-control system. Harwood delivered drugs from Staten Island, New York, to Baltimore on March 22, 1985. He hid them in the car's door panel. A Quebec Angel flew drugs to an airstrip near Salem, Massachusetts. Canadian Angels exchange speed with American members for LSD, heroin, and cocaine.

The earth-bound Hell's Angels are also taking to the water with an ever-expanding fleet of smuggling boats. But being an expert motorcyclist doesn't qualify one to sail. Richard Snyder, a member of the Monterey chapter, scrambled to safety as his boat sank off Hawaii in March 1985 with fifteen tons of marijuana in the hull.

The Angels are continually on guard for narcs and use the latest technology to check their clubhouses for bugs. They also use less sophisticated techniques to foil electronic eavesdroppers. They crank up radios, televisions, or record players to drown out conversations when they conduct drug deals at home. They also unplug telephones to foil equipment that can eavesdrop on conversations held in a room with a phone in it. Angels refuse to talk business in cars for fear they are bugged.

Angels use complex codes when they deal over the telephone. But they hop a plane to discuss transactions in person when business is too important to trust even their phone codes. Angels use their telephones so often that many of them have speed dialers that allow them to ring their regular contacts with one touch of a button. Sandy Alexander, president of the Manhattan chapter in 1985, had one. So did chapter vice-president Howard Weisbrod and Harwood. Gorilla screamed into the telephone one day just in case he was being bugged, "Any cops raid this house, I'm shooting the first that comes through the door!"

Technology alleviates some of the fear of using telephones. Mobile cellular phones are a boon to bikers and mobsters. Few police forces have the technical ability to tap the radio frequencies on the ninety-nine channels that cellular phones operate on. A person who travels through a large city could be automatically switched through fifteen channels in ten minutes. Police don't have the technology to follow such rapid switches. The equipment to track a cellular telephone call costs $100,000. And you need one of these for every caller you chase. Police need complete conversations to build solid cases against drug dealers. The problem was compounded in 1987 by the introduction of call incrypters that transform cellular telephone conversations into gibberish for any third parties who listen in.

Angels consistently operate on the premise that they are being followed and continually try to thwart surveillance, real or imagined. James (Oats) Oldfield, president of the Charleston, South Carolina, chapter in April 1985, drove past a motel where he was supposed to meet someone and doubled back through parking lots. He took a circuitous route on the way home and sat in a parking lot for half an hour before continuing.

Angels rarely carry drugs when they deal. They bury them and tell buyers where to pick them up. Business is so brisk that bikers wear pagers on their belts that alert them with an inaudible buzz when a customer calls. The pagers also display the incoming number digitally.

Oats Oldfield wrote to club members in jail in January 1991, informing them of a letter from Sonny Barger that noted the club is losing members faster than it recruits them. Oldfield also mentioned that Mitch, a Hell's Angel from Rochester, New York, suggested that members write to US servicemen in the Persian Gulf to interest them in the club. Oldfield thought it would be a good idea to recruit from the military since the Hell's Angels Motorcycle Club was formed by veterans of the Second World War. He asked Angels to find a list of soldiers participating in Operation Desert Storm and share it with the club.

The club is a professional, sophisticated organization run on business-school principles. Few chapters blow their profits on parties, drugs, and booze any more. The price paid by the North chapter in Quebec in March 1985 was a lesson to all Angels.

Chapters invest part of their money in legitimate businesses as fronts to launder illegal earnings. The club sent a member to an Ohio college to learn accounting in the early 1980s. Today Angels own amusement arcades, auto salvage and wrecking yards, bars and clubs, entertainment companies, food-producing and catering companies, massage parlors, motorcycle shops, real estate, restaurants, construction firms, antique stores, firearm shops, vending machine companies, tattoo parlors, billiard parlors and trailer parks, private security firms, auto and truck paint shops, investment firms, apartment buildings, resort hotels, trucking firms, ice-cream shops, tow-truck companies, and many luxurious homes.

Sergey Walton, former president of the Hell's Angels Oakland chapter, told investigators for the President's Commission on Organized Crime that the club had a "buy out, burn out, bomb out" program to launder profits from its methamphetamine business while he was a member in the sixties and seventies. Front men bought failing businesses to legitimize the cash. Companies that didn't sell were burned or bombed. The club also laundered money through real estate, he said.

"You try to sidestep the IRS, you get yourself money managers," said one former Hell's Angels hit man, James (Brett) Eaton. "Money is power. It buys policemen, judges."

Legitimate club businesses also provide jobs for Angels who need a job unrelated to crime in order to be released from jail on parole.

Douglas Chester (Dutch) Schultz, the thirty-two-year-old president of the Hell's Angels' San Diego chapter, owned the Rich Man Poor Man Limousine Service in 1985. He had fourteen cars and a bus in the lot and a .45-caliber assault rifle in the office. At times he also had more than fifty pounds of methamphetamine under car seats. He sold the stuff out of his office at 4252 40th Street. The limousine service was profitable. Schultz owned a 1964 Bentley, a 1970 Mercedes-Benz, a Rolls-Royce, a thirty-foot limousine, four Lincolns, and a Cadillac.

Not all Hell's Angels are rapists, drug traffickers, or murderers. Many join for motorcycling and club camaraderie. Some club members run legitimate businesses. Charlie Magoo Productions is a thriving Oakland, California, company that stages country music concerts. The company was formed by James (Fu) Griffin with his wife Corrie. The couple met in the anthropology library at the University of California in Berkeley in 1976. She was Griffin's Spanish tutor. He was out on parole after he had spent eight years in jail on a narcotics conviction.

Given their business operations today, the new breed of Hell's Angels is very conscious of publicity and image. They use lawsuits to intimidate people from writing about them.

The Hell's Angels Montreal Inc. sued the Hamilton *Spectator* for libel when the southern Ontario newspaper published a story about Noel Mailloux two years after he murdered Cindy Lee Thompson and four-year-old Stewart Hawley in a haze of paranoia and coke.

"The plaintiff states and the fact is, that Noel Mailloux was not a member of the Hell's Angels at the time of the publication of the article, nor at any time thereafter. By reason of the foregoing, the plaintiff has suffered serious injury to its character, credit and reputation."

The fact is that Mailloux was a Hell's Angel when he murdered. The lawsuit went nowhere. It's just another example of how the Hell's Angels use money as muscle in an attempt to shut people up.

The Hell's Angels have denied repeatedly the club is a criminal organization. US Marshal Budd Johnson, a drug investigator in San Diego, said this after a 1984 bust of the club:

"The Hell's Angels today are the new Mafia. The Angels are twenty-five years ahead of other gangs. They went from a loose-knit bunch of guys to an organized crime family."

Flexibility and adaptability are among the Angels' most formidable assets. They converted their most psychotic members into hit men when the battle for drug-trafficking turf got violent in the early 1970s. Some Angels knocked off the competition for a thrill. Others killed brother Angels when financial success bred paranoia and fear of rats in the pack.

A biker's colors scare off most of the competition. But there's always some asshole who thinks he can screw the club. Harwood sports the Filthy Few tattoo. He was just as mean before he joined the Angels. The drug dealer was a member of the Breed in 1974 when he laid a heavy on a band promoter who sold drugs on his turf in Albany, New York. He met the man at a junkyard. The dealer wanted to show Harwood something in the trunk of his car. He pulled a shotgun on the biker. Harwood — 300 pounds of tattoos — broke it in half and and beat the dealer. He also liked to shred rival bikers' chests with the nails of his leather wristband. He helped murder four members and two old ladies of the rival Invaders on January 7, 1981, in a fight for the methamphetamine market in Richmond, Virginia. The victims, including club president Steve Smith, were shot between the eyes.

Harwood, like his brother Angels, knows that subtlety is the thinking man's muscle. He flexed it when necessary. He paid a judge to put in a few good words for some buddies at a hearing.

"It wasn't bribing him," Harwood said. "We paid him. That wasn't a bribe."

Harwood, with thirty-three convictions that include rape and sodomy, is so well versed in the law that he lectured Baltimore bikers on how to beat Title 18, United States Code, Section 1962, the Racketeer-Influenced and Corrupt Organizations (RICO) statute.

The Angels don't always beat the rap. Jail is sometimes a worse fate than death on the job. Many Angels, despite precautions, get nailed for selling drugs, pussy, and fear. They also get caught when they rape. And Hell's Angels rack up quite a few sodomy convictions.

Angels don't like jail cells. The club has bondsmen and lawyers on call twenty-four hours a day to ensure members don't spend too much time behind bars. The club once posted $3-million bail for eleven California members who were picked up in a chauffeur-driven limousine.

Imprisoned Angels don't rely on the club's mystique for protection. They ally themselves quickly with other outlaw bikers or white-power groups. The most notable of these in the southwest and western United States is the Aryan Brotherhood. The Angels use the racists for an occasional hit.

The club ensures jailed members don't feel forgotten. They write, visit, and deliver all the necessary drugs to them. Angels rented a plane on Sonny Barger's birthday in 1974 and dropped leaflets on Folsom Prison wishing him happy birthday. Tom (The Bomb) Alexanian worried in his jail cell where he served a sentence for the murder of Angel Digger Hansen. His wife had told him some guy was on her case. Alexanian wrote to inform Gorilla Harwood of the situation. Harwood convinced the dork to stop bugging the lady.

Most people are suckers for stars. The Hell's Angels are no exception. The courts are lenient with celebrities and the public accepts their flaws as necessary artistic idiosyncracies, even if their art is violence. The Hell's Angels have a genuine interest in partying with other stars, many of whom are big drug consumers. The Angels also understand that cavorting with North America's only royalty and society's court jesters helps legitimize the grinning skulls on their backs. Hollywood's wackos bring out the best and the worst in the Hell's Angels.

James Harwood tensed as he watched a crouched figure pounce from car to car to sneak up on the Troy clubhouse. Harwood had pulled guard duty that night and wondered at an enemy bold enough to tackle the club alone. Before he could squeeze off a shot, Harwood recognized the man. It was John Belushi re-enacting a scene from his hit movie, *Animal House*. Belushi, who died in a Hollywood bungalow at the age of thirty-three on March 5, 1982, of a speedball overdose, was just goofing around on his way to visit Harwood.

Belushi was also one of the most embarrassing stars attracted to the Hell's Angels. Once John (Pirate) Miller found the rotund, drug-addicted comedian whining for methamphetamine outside the clubhouse. The Angels let him into their drug supply to shut him up.

Humor marks a fine line between life and death among Angels. Normal people shrug off a lapse in taste. In the company of Angels, the teller of a bad joke risks having his asshole torn out through his ears. Robin Williams couldn't nanoo-nanoo his way out of a joke that offended Sandy Alexander, president of the Hell's Angels Manhattan chapter in the late 1970s. Williams had joked on "Saturday Night Live" that something was as much fun as being gang raped by a bunch of Hell's Angels. Pirate Miller and sergeant-at-arms Vincent (Big Vinnie) Girolamo visited the set of "Saturday Night Live" on a day when Williams was hosting the show. They pulled a knife on him in a backstage elevator and threatened to make sliced pork of Mork's dork if he didn't apologize for his earlier crack on national television. Williams is a saner man than he lets on. He complied after he changed his wet pants.

A New York City radio mega-star had a run-in with the Hell's Angels on the NBC set of "Goodnight America." Alcohol and pills loosened his mind and tongue.

"You guys don't look so tough," he challenged.

An NBC security guard saved his ass. The man realized while he sweated in a locked room that he must apologize or die. The Angels didn't want to talk with him. A telephone caller warned he'd get stiffed. He apologized several times during his morning radio show. Big Vinnie walked into the studio and nodded OK through the window.

"I'm so afraid of them I'll contribute to their defense fund if they ask me to," he said.

While drug dealing has made the Hell's Angels wealthy and powerful, it has also undermined the principles on which the club is founded. Money has replaced brotherhood as the bond between Angels. Colors, an Angel's most sacred possession, are occasionally sold for services or narcotics connections, not for loyalty to the club. Chapter leaders are often the richest Angels. Much of their wealth comes from members who watch their money get sucked to the top of the pyramid. Jealousy sneaks into the brotherhood. Members are loyal to the man who will make them rich. Competition for the best drugs, the best deals, the best customers, the best turf gnaws at the club. Angels see enemies in friends. They kill. Those who fear they are next will rat when arrested. More busts. More paranoia. Like traditional organized crime, the Hell's Angels Motorcycle Club has become an organization from which you don't retire. Greed has succeeded where years of police work failed.

For this reason, William (Wild Bill) Medeiros left the club: "The more you get into the business part, the more you're going to screw your brother. When we got into big business, we cut each other's throats. Years ago, we'd know a guy before he joined. People now ask what will the guy do for the club? What will he bring in? Before, if a guy was down and out, we'd give him money."

John (The Baptist) LoFranco was a pro boxer who started his career as a Hell's Angels with the Manhattan chapter. He moved to the Mid-State chapter, then to the floating Nomads chapter in 1984. He ended up behind bars one year later when an Angel fingered him as the operator of a movable drug lab with Big Cheese Cheeseman. A reflective LoFranco wrote this letter, which was read at the 1985 annual Sturgis, South Dakota, classic motorcycle run:

"It's time for our true colors to come out. Please don't let others be able to say, 'They're just like the Breed, Pagans or Outlaws — when the going gets tough, they rat on one another or they don't help each other.'

It's time to show others and ourselves there is a difference between Hell's Angels and all the others.

"I remember when I first came around. Hell's Angels didn't talk to hang-arounds or prospects about drugs. If anything, Hell's Angels would check you out to see what you had. Somehow we stopped communicating. How else could this happen? We have forgotten our basics.

"We must go back to basics, so we can see just how much a person or persons want what we have. I don't mean drugs or money, either. I mean what a Hell's Angel has when everything else is gone. His pride."

LoFranco's letter stirred the Angels. When the FBI busted more than 100 Angels and associates on May 2, 1985, the rest of the club was grateful. "Thanks for cleaning out our deadwood," they said. And the Hell's Angels rebuilt. Forty years of police arrests seem to have strengthened, not weakened the club. It's almost as if regular busts were part of the natural selection process to weed out the weak in the outlaw motorcycle world.

In testimony before a Senate Committee on Organized Crime, Crouch summed up his fourteen years as an Angels in Cleveland, Ohio:

"I joined because of a brotherhood, and I thought it was a good idea. There are always a lot of theories. Everyone had different theories about it. It was all the same thing — we were all one family, one big brotherhood, we would all stay together. Our kids would be Hell's Angels and this and that.

"There are some members that are sixty-something years old and their kids are Hell's Angels now. You know, it was something that we would all grow old and be proud of — and our brotherhood — but after we got into the war [with the Outlaws] and then after the senseless killing of women and children, numerous times, women getting killed and everything, it just kind of tore at the whole, and then people got into drugs really heavy and the dealing of drugs. They accumulated big money.

"They had different ideas. After *The Godfather* movie and everything, it kind of evolved all into just on big organization for profit. They got away from the brotherhood, the whole thing of it, and now it is nothing to kill somebody. There is no fist fighting any more. If you are in a bar, or something like that, and some drunk jumps on you, or something like that, or you get mad at somebody, they do not like, they used to just fist fight with him. They will just wait — push him off or something — and then wait and shoot him.

"It is killing now. It is not fist fighting. All the honor, all the dignity has gone out of it, and everyone knows, but everyone just keeps holding on hoping for a better day, which the better day just keeps getting worse and worse and worse."

13

Gazing Upon Medusa:
Clandestine drug laboratories and the lure of easy money

"I look back upon nine years that I was involved in the methamphetamine business as a very negative nine years of my life. I went from being a very successful businessman in the truck-repair business to not being able to look myself in the mirror and like myself. I have a blood disorder from oxygen-poor blood. My respiratory system, I fried it with very strong acid fumes. My eyesight is very bad. My hearing is impaired. All my teeth fell out. So I basically ate up my body. I wonder why I'm still alive."

—A FORMER DRUG COOKER.

Drug manufacturing has gotten more men into the kitchen than TV dinners. North Americans with little education have developed an intense interest in chemistry and set up clandestine drug laboratories anywhere they can cook—from plastic-bucket PCP labs in closets to mobile crank labs in motor homes to fortified underground bunkers that churn out thousands of pounds of illicit chemicals for fun and profit. You too can make thousands of dollars in your spare time without leaving home.

A formula and $1,000 will start anyone in the drug-cooking business. Some apartment labs produce an ounce a week. Others produce hundreds of pounds. An Oklahoma apartment lab was rigged to vent odors down the kitchen drain so neighbors wouldn't complain. The cooker produced five pounds, or 2,270 grams, of crank for $3,000 in equipment and chemicals. At the time, crank was selling for $100 a gram in Oklahoma, netting $227,000 and grossing $224,000. You can't make that kind of money selling Rice Krispies squares. For those with a flair for cuisine art, it's easy money.

The most common and profitable clandestine labs produce methamphetamine, its precursor P2P or phenyl-2-propanone, or ice; cocaine or crack; PCP (phencyclidine); and a variety of designer drugs. Only designer drugs require sophisticated chemistry expertise to manufacture. While their name sounds cute and trendy, designer drugs are the deadliest chemical on the streets. They are to drug users what rat poison is to rats.

Because of the hazardous chemicals they use, clandestine labs are not only health hazards for the people who work in them, but major threats to anyone within breathing distance. Lab cookers often don't know how dangerous the chemicals they play with are. Those who know are often too fried from exposure to the fumes to be careful. Generally, meth-amphibian cookers are not the smartest lot. Whatever brains they start out with soon go down the condenser tubes. One bright light cooked crank in the underground garage of an apartment complex. He was extremely lucky. He smoked while he worked and could have leveled the building had the cigarette ignited chemicals. Ether, which is needed to manufacture crank, is so volatile that poor ventilation and careless handling will make it explode. A quart of ether will blow up a railway car. Clandestine labs use gallons of it, which they purchase in fifty-five-gallon drums.

Sacramento firemen were called to the house of an elderly couple who were having difficulty breathing on their front porch. They were given oxygen and first aid. The fire captain smelled ether in the air and snooped around until he found the fumes coming from an open window next door. Some fool was cooking crank and venting deadly fumes toward his neighbors.

A couple in New Castle, New York, a suburb of the Big Apple, rented out their house for two years while they lived in Japan. The family that moved in paid the rent and all bills. They mowed the lawn and weeded the flowerbeds. In the summer of 1989, they disappeared. The owners returned in the fall to find their well and septic tank contaminated with the toxic chemicals tetrachloroethene, dichloroethene, acetone, and toluene. Samples from the well and septic system in March 1990 contained 4,000 parts per billion of tetrachloroethene and 14,000 parts per billion of dichloroethene, all used in cocaine-processing. Anything above five parts per billion is a health hazard.

Colombian smugglers circumvent drug interdiction teams by shipping cocaine base to the US in nets strung to the underside of cargo ships since it is impervious to water. Instead of transforming the base into cocaine hydrochloride in jungle laboratories, they are now doing it in North America. Enterprising little devils.

Clandestine lab operators are a major environmental hazard. They dump tons of toxic chemicals down sewers, on farmland, in suburban back yards, and along roadsides. Sometimes they leave drums of wastes in garages, barns, houses, and apartments where they cooked. The chemicals range from deadly to deadlier, from cancer-causing to highly explosive.

Mobile PCP and crank labs wend their way through the intricate backroads of scenic north-coast California. Bureau of Land Management officers and US Forest Service agents regularly stumble across illegal chemical dump sites. A thirty-gallon drum of thionyl chloride—which ignites on contact with air, explodes on contact with water, and kills if inhaled or absorbed through the skin—was found in one dump. The cost of cleaning up the dump: $15,000. Five fifty-five-gallon chemical drums were found along the Sacramento River.

The proliferation of clandestine laboratories across the United States has prompted the creation of special task forces to track and shut them down. The Sacramento Clandestine Laboratory Task Force was formed in 1986 to combat the exponential growth of drug laboratories on the west coast. About half the labs busted in the States are taken down in California—more than 400 in 1989, 105 of them by Sacramento raiders. The cops work harder to nail methamphibians.

"We're maybe getting 5 to 10 percent of what's out there," said Bert Bruce, coordinator of the multi-agency Sacramento Clandestine Laboratory Task Force. Lab operators are mobile. They're paranoid and edgy. They pack up and shift their operations within hours. Some labs are built into mobile trailers so nosy neighbors never get a chance to investigate the smell of dirty laundry coming from the house next door. The lure of easy money has created so many labs that it's impossible to find them all, let alone bust them.

"One of the problems is rogue chemical houses," said Bruce. "So many chemical companies have sprung up and 99 percent of their trade is to clandestine lab operators. Before 1989, we didn't have a law controlling the sale of precursor chemicals. Now there are reporting requirements to the DEA if certain amounts of chemicals are sold."

The chemical company lobby was so powerful that politicians didn't feel pressure to control chemical sales to illegal cookers until 1989. Every American president since 1962 has declared a war on drugs and yet no one has thought of pulling the rug out from underneath the guys who make them. Chemical companies objected to requirements to report chemical sales because of the paperwork it would create. They didn't worry that the chemicals they sold ended up making illicit drugs that corroded the country's moral and social fiber.

A veterinarian in Washington State was approached by the owner of a Seattle chemical company with a deal: for $1.6 million he would provide the vet with a formula and enough chemicals and equipment to manufacture 1,000 pounds of methamphetamine a month. The vet had been suspected, but never convicted, of smuggling cocaine from South America by surgically implanting it in the uteruses of race horses. The vet found an isolated farm in east Washington, set up a crank lab in the barn, and produced his first 1,000 pounds of meth. He packed it in suitcases and took most of it to Atlanta on domestic airlines to sell to an Italian organized crime family.

"They'd do the hotel switch," said Bruce. "He put the bag in the hotel room and leave the key at the desk. The key was picked up, the dope removed, and money left in its place. We arrested them and seized their lab when they were going into production again. The first run was P2P. [Phenyl-2-propanone is the agent used in the traditional way of making methamphetamine. The Hell's Angels prefer this method.] For the second run they were going to use the ephedrine method. [This is a more volatile but easier way of manufacturing the same stuff.] We seized 157 pounds of meth. There was so much I didn't think it was meth. I thought it was ephedrine. We also seized one ton of ephedrine."

Until the law controlling the sale of precursor chemicals came into effect in California in August 1989, lab raiders had to use their wits alone to catch cookers. Raiders noticed quite a few bad guys walking out of the Grau-Hall Scientific supply store with glassware and chemicals. Raiders approached the company in 1988 and told them they were tired of seeing cookers buy their supplies there. The company allowed narcs to work in the store and videotape people buying chemicals and equipment. They also noted license plate numbers and watched buyers' houses, setting up several busts.

The Clandestine Lab Task Force in San Diego set up a similar operation in the suburb of El Cajon. Raiders helped Charles Hill set up a chemical supply company called Triple Neck Scientific after the flask crank cookers use. He did a thriving business in ephedrine, red phosphorous, and all the chemicals one needs to make illicit drugs. Customers talked with Hill about formulas and problems cooking crank.

"In my three years of doing business, I would say I had no more than three legitimate customers," said Hill. The customers were "some of the lowest scum I've ever seen. I've seen 'em send their kids in to do business. I've seen 'em send their mothers in."

Tape recorders and video cameras recorded all the conversations and sales to nearly 500 suspected cookers. On March 19, 1989, eighty-five people were charged with methamphetamine production and trafficking. Raiders seized 860 pounds of ephedrine and 450 pounds of crank.

Busting clandestine labs is dangerous not only because of the explosive chemicals involved, but also because of the volatile nature of cookers fried by their own chemicals.

"Once we went to a trailer," said Jeff Alaways, deputy sheriff in Nevada County, California. "The smell of ether was really intense. As we approached the door we noticed there were two subjects inside. As we opened the door, one of the subjects threw an object at my feet. That ignited. I also noticed that he was pushing other glassware onto the floor which was also igniting. He grabbed another object in his hand and began to throw it. At that time I shot him. And at the same time, the trailer ignited, blew up. I was knocked out of the trailer approximately ten feet with my clothes on fire."

A cooker in Vian, Oklahoma, was so determined police wouldn't seize his lab that he rigged a bomb made of ether-soaked rags inside a plastic bag. He inserted an electrical wire inside the bag, ran it from the lab to a nearby metal building, and from there to the mobile home he lived in. As police walked up to his mobile home, the cooker plugged the wire into a power outlet and detonated the bomb in his lab, causing a flash fire. Toxic fumes kept police and firemen away from the burning building. The chemicals used to cook crank and other drugs such as PCP can cause cancer and severe heart, lung, liver, and blood damage. Fumes can burn skin and eyes. Many of the chemicals are stored in body fat and destroy cells over time.

Methamphibian cookers use a range of booby traps to protect their labs and warn them against raids by police or ripoff artists. Primitive to sophisticated, all have one thing in common—they are deadly. Some labs have punji boards embedded with nails buried around the building. Other cookers cut the rattles off rattlesnakes' tails and let the reptiles roam the lab at night. During the day, they hide them in cupboards to spring out at raiders. Sometimes a monofilament line is strung across pathways leading to the lab and connected to explosives, alarms, or even chemical traps. The simplest chemical trap has a glass of hydrochloric acid leaning against a door next to a plate of cyanide crystals. The glass is knocked over when the door is opened, mixing the acid with the crystals and creating hydrogen cyanide gas—a homemade gas chamber.

Investigators have learned not to touch light switches, which may also be rigged to explosives. They are careful about switching on their own flashlights, too, since the smallest spark can ignite chemical fumes. Cookers fill one-gallon plastic bottles with explosives such as Tobex and wire the bomb to the light socket in the fridge. Open the door and your midnight snacking days are over. An electronic blasting cap wired to a timer is placed in a bottle of ether that contains a vial of gasoline.

Another favorite: methamphibians, like many drug dealers, stuff a quarter pound of C-4 plastic explosive in a VHS videotape with an electronic blasting cap that detonates when inserted into the tape player. This booby trap was devised with the knowledge that cops like to look at porno flicks they find during raids. That kind of blow job no one needs.

A Texas lab was rigged with a bomb made of twelve oilfield per-
forators wired to a detonator. The front door of an Oregon lab was
wired with a 10,000-volt charge. Cookers always anticipate being
busted. A fully silenced MAC-11 semi-automatic pistol was found on a
rafter in one lab so the cooker could grab it when the cops told him to put
his hands up.

Members of the Clandestine Lab Task Force in Sacramento, California,
don't think much of methamphetamine lab operators. The following
profile is prominently posted in the staff lunch-conference room next to
photographs of really ugly people usually found in Rio Linda. Methamphibians are a distinctive bunch.

CLANDESTINE METHAMPHIBIAN 6 TOED MUTANT PROFILE:

> Including but not limited that:
> (if you notice a pattern of other attributes, simply add them to the
> profile)
> 1. Huminoids resembling the poor white trash-okie syndrome, ie
> . . . looks similar to a mixture of Larry, Darryl and Darryl with a
> dash of wannabe biker thrown in;
> 2. Mutant huminoids possessing 6 or more toes or other mutated
> appendages or abnormalities;
> 3. Long dirty greasy hair sideburns and/or mustache and beard;
> 4. Wearing dark or black clothing or hats with Harley Davidson
> emblems and eagles;
> 5. Speaks with a Rio Linden accent, ie., talks funny, southern drawl
> and has trouble pronouncing big words—can't spell;
> 6. Is related to everybody in the area through "incest is best"
> mentality and interbreeding;
> 7. Smells bad or has chemical odors about their person, very dirty:
> 8. Under the influence of crank and/or Budweiser beer and is very
> paranoid, ie., looks in rear view mirror a lot;
> 9. Has numerous cult related tatoos about their mutated person;
> 10. Worships guns, crossbows, knives, and explosives;
> 11. Has a dislike for the police, narcs, snitches, and Rush
> Limbaugh;
> 12. Drives a shitty car or motorcycle (only American—no japs);
> 13. Drives a Harley Davidson motorcycle and keeps it in their
> house;
> 14. Lives in a dumpy, dirty, cluttered, smelly house surrounded by
> yardcars in a Rio Linda type town, usually there are 6 month old
> dirty dishes throughout the kitchen, hypodermic needle-syringes
> all over the house;

15. Has guard dogs such as pitbulls, dobermans, etc., and other exotic laboratory animals—may even practice bestiality;
16. Wears biker sunglasses after dark;
17. Usually has naked pictures of his or her ugly mutated cohabitant;
18. When shopping for chemicals or laboratory apparatus, the humunoid has a shopping list of misspelled chemicals, pays cash and often doesn't have enough money;
19. Often keeps methamphetamine oil in freezer alongside of steaks and two year old ice cream;
20. On Welfare and or states that he/she/it is self employed as a pig, chicken or worm farmer or auto body-fender repair business etc.
21. Thinks they know how to cook!

The sun started to heat the early morning Sacramento air as our convoy of police cars and trucks sped through a confusing maze of streets on July 19, 1990. We had been briefed an hour earlier in the offices of the Clandestine Laboratory Task Force and shown a map of the target. Everyone was heavily armed except me and the chemist who had come up from San Francisco for the raid. She rode in my car at the end of the procession. A tipster had ratted to the feds that there was a boxed laboratory in the garage of a house inhabited by an alleged hit man for the Hell's Angels with four or five kills to his credit.

We pulled around the last corner to see the team surround the house, identify themselves, and give the occupants time to respond before kicking in the door and storming the place. As houses go, the digs were small. The occupant was humping a juicy little tart in the bedroom when the guns came through the door. The raid team secured the house, back yard, and garage within a minute and we trotted in.

I immediately headed for the garage. All that was left of a laboratory, if there was one, was a large scale. Indentations in the carpet indicated that large square objects had been recently moved. A brand new car in the garage turned out to be one of six recently stolen from a nearby dealership. A technician had the thing dusted from end to end for fingerprints within minutes.

Someone lifted the mattress in the bedroom and a kilo of white powder sat next to a .357-magnum revolver and a large knife. The bed was surrounded by radio-monitoring equipment.

A television monitor sat on a table next to the bed. Someone turned it on. Hey, the back door to the house. I ran out and found the camera hidden under the eave of the garage. Another channel showed a view of the front yard. It took a couple of narcs a few minutes to spot the camera lens where the rear side reflector should have been on a rundown Ford

Econoline van parked in the drive next to the house. A crafty little wizard had rigged a video camera inside the van to monitor the front yard and door. These cameras can be indicators of paranoia, a curiosity about the world, a hang-up about dogs shitting on the lawn, or a fear of nasty visitors.

Back in the house, the male occupant said the kilo of powder was cornstarch he kept in case of a ripoff. He planned to give it to thieves so he wouldn't be killed. An on-the-spot test by the San Francisco chemist showed the man was telling the truth. But why would an honest man fear being ripped off by thugs looking for large quantities of drugs? And the car in the garage? Well, a friend asked if he could keep his wheels in there out of the sun. And what about the smaller scale in the kitchen with a piece of paper taped to it indicating the various weights in which drugs are sold? So the guy had a fascination with weight.

Crank

Crank is a west coast phenomenon that grew in popularity across the United States as the Hell's Angels Motorcycle Club expanded. The Angels are believed to control 75 percent of the crank market in California, an enterprise they pioneered and want to monopolize. Outlaw bikers—there are more than 800 gangs in the US and Canada—control 75 percent of the North American crank market. Crank is a biker drug.

The best case the Sacramento Clandestine Laboratory Task Force had going in 1990 was the bust of Odis "Buck" Garrett, one of the longest standing members of the Hell's Angels Motorcycle Club. He was arrested with three other people in November 1989 after lab raiders searched a cabin on the 1,400-acre Yankee Jim Ranch in the northeast corner of California near the Modoc National Forest. The raiders say they found the makings of a large speed lab and enough chemicals to make $600,000 worth of methamphetamine. Carl H. Dulinsky of Vallejo and D.L. Braddock and Harris B. Shimel of Oroville were indicted with Garrett on methamphetamine charges.

The Yankee Jim Ranch, valued at $302,000 in 1990, is registered under the name of Karen N. Johnson, Garrett's secretary. The US attorney's office in Sacramento moved to seize the northern part of the ranch in February 1990 under criminal forfeiture laws. The southern part of the ranch is owned by people not connected to Garrett. The federal Bureau of Land Management had long ago slated the ranch as a desirable property to buy and preserve for public hunting and fishing. The bureau also wants to control a creek that runs across the property. In a dry state like California, watershed control is a major consideration. US Attorney Edward L. Knapp said it would cost about $25,000 to clean up chemical-contaminated soil in a drainage ditch near the cabin that housed the clandestine lab.

Buck Garrett was further charged in August 17, 1990, with organizing and operating a large-scale methamphetamine distribution ring with clandestine laboratories in San Bernardino, Butte, and Modoc counties. The thirty-six-count indictment seeks forfeiture of more than $2 million in property from the forty-seven-year-old Garrett, including ranches in Ione, Oroville, and Alturas, a house in Shingle Springs, a Rockwell Aero Commando airplane, forty-three head of cattle, a cutting horse called Bucky Badger O'Lena, two GMC pickup trucks, a Case 580 DX backhoe tractor, a Case 1150 bulldozer/crawler, and a ten-horse trailer — all alleged to have been bought with drug money. Garrett allegedly supervised five people who manufactured and distributed more than thirty kilograms of speed from 1985 to 1989 at the Gold Valley Ranch near Essex in San Bernardino County, at the Crystal Clear Ranch in Oroville in Butte County, and at the Yankee Jim Ranch near Alturas in Modoc County. He allegedly used $848,151 from the sale of that speed to buy a seventy-seven-acre ranch in Ione and $119,245 to buy the Yankee Jim Ranch.

An investigation by the US Drug Enforcement Administration, the Bureau of Alcohol, Tobacco and Firearms, and the Internal Revenue Service resulted in methamphetamine, money laundering, and weapons charges being brought against Garrett. He is also charged with leading a continuing criminal enterprise. This charge carries a mandatory life sentence and a maximum fine of $2 million.

Carl H. Dulinsky of Vallejo, D.L. Braddock and Harris B. Shimel of Oroville, William Sanders of Shingle Springs, Eldon McCann of Citrus Heights, and Wayne Havens of Ione were indicted on related charges. Garrett is alleged to have laundered $85,000 through Havens to buy the LB Ranch in Ione in 1987. Havens was charged with arranging money transactions so they wouldn't have to be reported.

One of the best-hidden labs in California was found in the mid-1980s on a property owned by Rat Miller, former member of the Oakland chapter of the Hell's Angels. The house and lab were in Calavaras County near the Cowbell Mine. A team missed the lab when they first raided the place. When they returned, they found a concrete bunker sixty feet beneath a warehouse. Police claim the lab had sliding glass doors and the chemist was sealed in to cook or die. Fumes were vented on a hillside far from the house. Unfortunately for the team, most of the lab had been moved by the time they raided the property a second time. Rat Miller was well-connected. He had all of Crosby, Stills, Nash, and Young's gold records in his house. David Crosby's number was in his phone book.

A lab run by a suspected Hell's Angels associate in Butte County in 1988 was installed inside a twenty-eight-foot long, seven-foot diameter culvert pipe buried ten feet underground. A four-foot culvert pipe ran to the lab from a horse stall in the barn, where the entrance was covered with a cement slab and hay. The lab was equipped with electricity and a venting system to flush out fumes and bring in fresh air.

Bikers either set up their own labs, take over other people's labs, or force chemists to work for them.

Gerald Lukaniuk was struggling to get his special-effects business off the ground in Toronto—Hollywood North—in the spring of 1985. He needed money for materials and a large studio. A friend said he could get the money for him and a businessman lent Lukaniuk $10,000. The entrepreneur rented the second floor of an industrial building on Jefferson Avenue in downtown Toronto.

Then his nightmare began. The interest rates on his loan were suddenly inflated and he was told he now owed $30,000. He was told he had to make enormous weekly payments or else. Lukaniuk didn't understand how this could be. The businessman said he got the money from friends and arranged for Lukaniuk to meet them at the nearby Wheat Sheaf Tavern.

Three tough-looking men met Lukaniuk at the tavern. They didn't say who they were. They just said they had no problem accepting the fact Lukaniuk couldn't pay his first installment on the loan. They told him they knew he was a trained chemist and handed him a whiskey bottle containing phenyl-2-propanone, used to make speed. Lukaniuk realized he was being squeezed. He returned to his Jefferson Avenue studio and ordered the chemicals and equipment he needed to cook methamphetamine. He played hardball and screwed up the first two batches just short of the finished product.

The three businessmen summoned him to another meeting at the Wheat Sheaf. They told him they were members of the Satan's Choice Motorcycle Club and knew where to find his wife and children. They warned him not to fuck up again. The Choice are one of Ontario's oldest outlaw motorcycle gangs with a long history of involvement with drugs and violence. Three Choice chapters in Ontario and one in Quebec were taken over by the Outlaws Motorcycle Club from the United States in the spring of 1977.

The takeover of four of the Choice's twelve chapters dates back to the police raid on August 6, 1975, of a clandestine PCP laboratory on a remote island on Oba Lake, 150 miles north of Sault Ste. Marie in northwestern Ontario. Police seized nine pounds of PCP and 236 pounds of chemical stew one step from completion, worth $60 million

Canadian when the beaver buck was worth more than the American dollar. Two Choice members were jailed, including Bernie Guindon, founder and national president of the Satan's Choice. He entrusted the club's presidency to Garnet (Mother) McEwen, of the St. Catharines chapter, who convinced four chapters to break away and join the Outlaws.

On December 5, 1979, the Hell's Angels took over the Popeyes in Montreal and started a war with the Outlaws over drug turf. Today, the Satan's Choice are in the dubious position of being able to provide the Hell's Angels with their first foothold in the province of Ontario, where the club has been unable to open a chapter. Hell's Angels from Montreal have been negotiating with Choice officers near Toronto since 1988 to have Choice chapters become Hell's Angels. The Angels were dangling the prospect of huge drug profits as bait. But some craftier Choice members realize the Hell's Angels will eliminate more than two-thirds of the Choice members when they take over. Even bikers like to die old.

Lukaniuk knew the Choice by reputation and didn't want to die. He returned to the lab and started cooking. Motorcycle gangs being what they are, one loose-lipped member tipped off the cops, who started watching Lukaniuk on March 27, 1985. Bikers have a strange sense of loyalty. They'll rat on fellow gang members and continue their own criminal activities hoping the cops will give them a break for turning in others. Lukaniuk cooked late at night when the nearby Molson's brewery opened its vats. The sweet smell of hops and barley masked the stench of speed. Lukaniuk finished his cooking at 3 a.m. and the cops sneaked into the lab with a chemist to take samples of his product. They sneaked in six times until they found on May 10 he had made five pounds of pure speed worth $3.4 million (Cdn.) when diluted to 10 percent purity on the street.

Lukaniuk cooked the speed using the simplest method. He mixed P2P with methylamine in isopropyl alcohol in a flask fitted with a condenser. He reduced the mixture with aluminium foil and/or aluminium powder, which yielded a mix of methamphetamine, leftover chemicals from the reaction, and gray-white aluminium and aluminium salts. Then he filtered the material to remove solids and let the goop evaporate to produce an oily methamphetamine. This is normally mixed with hydrochloric acid to create the white powder known as speed that is sold on the street.

Police also seized ten grams of PMA (4-Methoxyamphetamine) from Lukaniuk, which could have been made in his lab. The hallucinogenic drug has often been passed off as the love drug MDA, though it is ten times more powerful and has killed many of its users. PMA disappeared from Ontario streets in 1973 after it killed nine people in a six-week period in Toronto, Mississauga, Hamilton, and Kitchener—cities with a strong Choice presence. Outlaw bikers have always controlled the chemical drug market in Canada and the US. Three PMA users died in Toronto in 1985. The drug, which can be inhaled or injected, causes acute respiratory depression, which leads to heart attacks.

Lukaniuk pleaded guilty to drug charges so there wouldn't be any testimony in court and the bikers were not mentioned. He kept his mouth shut and did the time.

Crank

Methamphetamine, or crank, is the poor man's cocaine. The crank subculture is mainly white, working class, and poor. White trash to some. It is the product of the white biker subculture, which has grown rich keeping poor white folk paranoid in the fast lane. Crank keeps users up for days. It makes them speed along, eyes darting all over looking for narcs. Paranoia strikes deep.

Crank also makes people violent. Crank murders are easy to identify. The victim is stabbed eighty-five times, he head cut off, and his arms twisted out of their sockets. Cranksters don't stop killing until they're exhausted.

Methamphetamine, like other drugs, pushes body and mind beyond their limits and gives users a terrifying glimpse of human circuitry gone awry. Meth kicks the central nervous system into action as adrenaline does. That's why it's called uppers, speed, and crank. The yellowish-white powder can be snorted or mixed with water and injected. It sends blood pressure through the ceiling, decreases appetite, increases alertness and energy, and keeps the sandman at bay. Users are generally speedy and aggressive. Heavy amphetamine users get run down from lack of sleep and food. They suffer amphetamine psychosis, which is similar to paranoid schizophrenia, and become violent. They usually need barbiturates, alcohol, and opiates to calm down. As a last resort, they kill themselves.

Strippers and topless and bottomless dancers like crank because it gives them the energy to dance five hours a day and keeps them nice and slim. A twenty-two-year-old stripper or hooker has a hard time competing with flat-bellied eighteen-year-olds, so crank becomes boopsie's little helper and extends her life—until she dies or burns out at twenty-six.

Outlaw bikers gained their reputation for violence from their behavior on crank. The drug keeps them up for days and the more paranoid they get, the more violent they become. Speed kills in many ways. It is the bikers' drug. They popularized it. They make it. They sell it.

While some gangs such as the Hell's Angels can afford legitimate chemists to make crank, sending experts to visit chapters around the world to teach members how to make Angel crank, most gangs resort to cookers. Chemists follow formulas. Cookers follow instructions. Since there are more cookers than chemists, there is a lot of impure crank on the market snapping brain cells at the root.

It might be cool to have a buzz, but that sound you hear is brain cells going off like firecrackers. Pretty soon you're operating on the most primitive part of the brain, the same mass of cells that drives a salamander to eat worms and slugs. You're jerking your arms and legs, hopping around like a huge cock being whacked off, and continually looking over your shoulder for whoever it is that's burning that hole in the back of your head.

Man, it's so macho to snort and shoot crank.

San Diego is the crank capital of the world. Blame the nice weather, the abundance of outlaw motorcycle gangs, and one of the largest groupings of sailors in the world. San Diego is a cooker's dream and law-enforcement officials have a nightmare that crank will follow in the footsteps of crack and head east where a huge market is always on the lookout for new kicks. If crank can break through its white trash barrier into college campuses and society's upper echelons, biker labs might as well be printing money. If you think crack addicts are scary, wait till you see streets full of cranksters wired up for violence day after day.

It's difficult to comprehend how a beautiful city like San Diego can be home to so many cranksters. There are more meth lab busts, speedster arrests, hospitalized freakout cases, and meth-heads in treatment programs in San Diego than anywhere else in the world. In 1988, 32 percent of the adults arrested for felony crimes in San Diego tested positive for methamphetamine compared to 1 percent of the adults arrested in New York City. Makes you wonder why the west coast gets a reputation for being laid-back while New Yorkers are always portrayed as wired. The crank in San Diego at any given moment could probably fuel the fighter jets at Top Gun for a year. The US Drug Enforcement Administration estimates more than five tons of meth is cooked in San Diego every year. One of four clandestine labs busted in the US is done in San Diego. Violence? Raiders found 269 weapons in one lab.

Meth is the easiest drug to cook and sell because unlike cocaine, which goes through five or six steps before reaching the user's nostrils, crank is a mom-and-pop operation. Coke has to be grown, picked, processed, smuggled, distributed, and sold. Crank can be made with store-bought chemicals over the weekend and sold on the street Monday morning.

There are two ways to cook crank: one involves phenyl-2-propanone and methylamine; the other involves mixing ephedrine with red phosphorous and hydriotic acid. It takes about twenty hours to cook phenyl-2-propanone, an hour to distill the stuff, and about five hours for the final reaction to produce speed. That's a fast cook. A good cooker can probably produce a finished product in twenty-four to thirty hours.

Ice

American cookers turned to Canadian chemical companies after passage of US legislation in 1989 requiring chemical supply companies to record sales of chemicals that can be used to manufacture illicit drugs. Meth cookers in Montana crossed the border into Saskatchewan, Alberta, and British Columbia to buy their chemicals. For some weird reason, Montana is a major center for ice, a crystallized form of methamphetamine that can be smoked like crack cocaine, and meth cookers are scrambling to meet the demand. Ice is cheaper than cocaine, packs a hell of a wallop, and is highly addictive—all the ingredients a pusher wants in a drug. Since ice is methamphetamine, it gives users the same burst of energy and mean streak that crank does, but faster.

Meth hasn't changed much since it was first made by a Japanese chemist in 1919. Like most drugs dopers play with, it was first taken orally, then injected, then snorted. The 1980s was the decade when people discovered they could smoke drugs they had never thought of putting into a pipe.

Chemists fiddled with cocaine, heroin, and crank to make them smokeable for two reasons: dopers wanted more bang for their buck and bought the drugs that gave it; sales dropped as the fear of AIDS spread through intravenous drug use. Dopers are an irrational lot and will use any old dirty needle when they need a fix. Shooting galleries are a sure place to get AIDS as bloody needles are passed from vein to vein. Even crack heads smoking up in parking garages know enough to use a condom when balling a chick who offers pussy for smoke.

I've walked through dozens of crack houses and smoking spots across North America. Besides the mandatory pop cans and matchbooks used to smoke the shit, there were always condom wrappers on the floor. There weren't too many used condoms, though. Maybe someone swallowed the evidence.

In the 1960s, you knew a square trying to be hip was lying when he talked about smoking speed and cranking up grass. What sounded crazy then is the in-thing today. It is only fitting that the ice craze started in the hottest of the United States—Hawaii. Ice appeared on the islands in 1985 under the names of rock candy and Hawaiian salt. The translucent ice crystals were 98 to 100 percent pure speed and one gram smoked in a glass pipe gave ten to fifteen hits. So far, two forms of ice have been found: a translucent or clear rock crystal that is water based, burns quickly, and leaves a milky white residue in the pipe bowl; yellow meth is oil based, burns more slowly, lasts longer, and leaves a brownish or black residue in the pipe.

Ice keeps users physically and psychologically up from four to fourteen hours, though large doses can be pissed out seventy-two hours after smoking. Although it keeps users awake and hyper, ice gnaws away at the body's energy reserves and prevents their replenishment through sleep. It pushes the body to its limits and eats it up. Use it long enough and you lose weight. Lack of sleep and psychological dependence cause fatigue, depression, anxiety, insomnia, and a psychotic state. Toxic psychosis sets in and the whole world is after you. You see and hear things. Your heart rate goes beserk. Your circulation system collapses. You fall into a coma. You die.

There's nothing wrong with methamphibians doing themselves in as long as they don't impose their problems on others. But a 1990 survey of pregnant mothers in a Queens, New York, hospital showed traces of ice in the babies. The hospital handled an average of six meth overdoses a day in 1990 compared to one a day in 1989.

It's so hard to be cool these days. How is a straight person supposed to keep up with these rapidly changing drug trends and the names they engender?

Hawaiians call their glass smoking pipes "bongs." The difference between a crack pipe and an ice pipe is in the construction.

Crack (coke) burns hotter than ice (crank). A crack pipe is made of two sections: one holds the cocaine, the other holds a liquid coolant. A screen between the sections keeps the crack from falling into the coolant. The crack is lit with a flame in the top half of the pipe and the fumes are sucked through the coolant chamber on the way to the mouth and lungs.

An ice pipe has only a bowl in which the ice is heated with a flame placed under it. While the ice turns to gas, fingers are placed over the hole at the top of the bowl and a vent hole in the stem. The user then sucks in the gas. Ice heads usually have burn marks on the finger that seals the hole in the bowl. Nose-picking helps it heal more quickly.

Crack

Crack starts out as cocaine hydrochloride, the powdered cocaine people shove up their noses. Making it requires a mixture of one-third cocaine hydrochloride, two-thirds baking soda, and a bit of water. Mix the cocaine and baking soda. Add water and stir to make a paste. Put the paste in a baby-food jar and put the jar in a pot of boiling water to cook. The heat dissipates the hydrochloric acid in the cocaine and leaves cocaine base. The soda acts as a catalyst and binds with the base. After cooking for about ten minutes, break the jar and take out the milky hockey puck. Use a razor blade or X-acto knife to cut rocks off the hard chunk of crack.

This recipe is not as accurate as it looks and anyone out there who uses it to make crack will lose his investment. Crack can be made only with pure cocaine. Dominicans and blacks, North American-born or Jamaican, cut their cocaine with dextrose, baking soda, lidocaine, strychnine, anything to maximize their profits. Their coke is rarely more than 50 percent pure. Colombians, Bolivians, and Peruvians, on the other hand, sell cocaine that is 95 to 100 percent pure. If the cooking process starts with impure cocaine, or if too much baking soda or water is added, all you get is useless mush.

An eight-ball of powder cocaine (⅛ of an ounce) bought for between $170 and $200 (prices vary) can be cooked into three grams of crack to be cut into thirty $40 rocks that sell for $1,200. That's a $1,000 profit for ten minutes of cooking and three hours of selling.

Crack is a black phenomenon. It started in California and migrated to New York City in 1985. Cookers from New York, Buffalo, Chicago, and Detroit taught black kids in Toronto housing projects how to cook it in late 1986. Different American gangs, especially Jamaican posses, are muscling into virgin Canadian territory. Toronto is rife with publicly funded housing projects for black immigrants. The posses set up a paramilitary network they keep supplied with cocaine and reap the benefits.

Jamaican gangsters might sound stupid on the phone, but they are discussing the elements of capitalism: production—from South America; distribution—mules, runners, territories to break into and protect; exchange—stash houses, safe houses; sales—crack houses, drive-through spots; communications—twelve-year-old lookouts with two-way radios on bicycles, blacked-out windows for spotters with night scopes, police frequency scanners. Through the patois, dude, you'll hear them discussing business techniques taught in ivy-league schools. You don't need a college education to be a businessman. The street is also a good place to learn.

Crack: a piece, a rock, a stone, a lick. The dealer takes it out of a plastic film canister or a plastic bag that contains a few rocks. Most of his night's dope is stashed in case he gets ripped off or arrested. If the cops show, he flicks it. Rocks vary in size: $20, $30, $40, $60, $80, and $100. A $40 rock lasts three or four smokes. Addicts are very intelligent and resourceful when it comes to smoking crack. Many cities have bylaws against owning and selling smoking pipes in head shops. Most of those pipes are useless for crack anyway. They have small air chambers that are all right to burn hash, which requires little heat, but crack needs a lot of heat to melt. And superheated vapor can destroy lungs quickly. Crack smokers need a pipe with a large air chamber to cool the smoke before they inhale it.

The best, most popular, and readily accessible crack pipe on the market is the aluminum pop can. Addicts prefer Coke cans because they are thinnest and easiest and fastest to work with. The addict will suck the smoke through the can's drinking hole. The surface of the can furthest from the drinking hole is flattened and a dozen tiny holes are punched through it. A blaster slot is cut in the side of the can. A thin layer of cigarette ash is tapped down over the holes to prevent the melting crack from seeping into the can before it evaporates. It also creates a bed for the cocaine rock.

A lighter is useless to heat the crack because it gets too hot to hold over the rock. Crack smokers rip the cover off a match book and separate the two sheets of match sticks. Then they rip two matches off a sheet and use the base to hold them. They use two paper matches because crack needs a lot of heat to melt. The addict then keeps a thumb over the blaster and inhales the vapor as the rock melts. As the rock disappears, the addict slips the thumb off the blaster and inhales all the vapor from the chamber. A rock should melt in the time it takes for the matches to burn.

Picking through the litter of pop cans in an underground parking garage tells you what kind of drugs are being used there. Junkies cut up pop cans in which they boil heroin over a flame. They pour the liquid into a vial, then suck it into a needle through cotton.

Addicts who smoke at home often use another method that is kinder to the throat and lungs. They fill a cup one-third full with water and cover it with aluminum foil, which they secure with an elastic band or string. They make little holes in the foil and an incision for a mouthpiece on the other side of the cup. They melt the rock the same way they do when smoking with a can, but the water cools the vapor.

A commercial glass crack pipe that gets sooty with use is called a devil's dick. Smoking crack is the quickest way to get cocaine into the body. It takes three to five seconds to get a high that lasts ten to twelve minutes. Then comes the crash and the need for more.

Just as the most profitable sector of the automobile industry is the parts business, so drug paraphernalia is a multi-billion dollar enterprise. Drug-related items such as pipes can be legally made in the US, but can't be imported, exported, or sold across state lines. As with much of the drug industry, organized crime controls most of the paraphernalia business, where a three-cent pipe sells for $8.

According to the US Customs Service, one of the largest manufacturers of such equipment in North America is Huan "Danny" Teng, a thirty-nine-year-old who is an alleged member of the Fook Ching gang of Chinese heroin smugglers. American officials had trouble finding the Taiwanese entrepreneur in 1990 after discovering a crack vial factory that produced $73 million in vials a year. Customs agents looking for him found the factory on April 23, 1990, in the Greenpoint section of Brooklyn, New York. Chinese workers ran a twenty-four-hour assembly line that made 2 million crack vials a day with plastic injection, cooling, and grinding machines.

The discovery came two months after police raided New York City warehouses containing $28 million in drug paraphernalia such as 178 million polyethylene heroin bags, 107 million vials, and 1.9 million crack pipes. It took twenty-five Customs agents three days to conduct an inventory and load the paraphernalia into eleven forty-five-foot tractor trailers. Remember when hippies used to make the stuff and sell it in head shops run by East Indians? The times they are a-changing.

Cocaine

Cocaine is still the nostril cleaner of choice among athletes, movie stars, uptown cuties, honky-tonk angels, juke-joint johnnies, hookers, yuppies, and whatever groovin' Americans of African descent call themselves these days. Coke is mostly snorted, but can be injected alone or with heroin to form speedballs.

What kind of a blast does a speedball give? Ask John Belushi. The more adventurous, those whose nostril linings are burnt out, sprinkle coke on their gums, swirl it around their assholes, or smear it on their snatches. Cocaine is like a desperate one o'clock Romeo; any hole will do. The white crystal powder makes you feel like WOW, everything is so clear, I'm so strong, I'm so smart, let's boogie. At the same time, it can dissolve membranes, cause hallucinations, stop breathing, fry the brain, inhibit pissing, and prevent hard-ons.

The smiling Peruvian and Bolivian Indians in *National Geographic* photographs who showed tits without uproar decades before *Playboy* magazine was born chewed the leaves of the Erythroxylon bush. Inca high priests and nobles drank a coke concoction—the original original taste—to seek religious truth. Today, starving peasants chew the leaves to stave off fatigue and hunger.

Sigmund Freud, whose sexual hang-ups society has willingly imposed on itself for a hundred years, boasted in papers published in the 1880s that cocaine cured depression, alcoholism, and morphine addiction. The man who brought us sublimation didn't recognize substitution. The Coca-Cola Company subliminally seduced taste buds through the brain when it laced its original-taste Coke with coke in 1902, a practice stopped in 1903.

While much of the cocaine used in North America is cooked in South American jungle labs, cocaine-processing labs have been sprouting in the States since the mid-1980s. Coca base is shipped to the US, often in large nets fastened to the underside of cargo ships where it is nearly impossible to detect. It is then processed into cocaine hydrochloride in the labs.

Colombian drug barons set up their North American labs after the company's President Belisario Betancur passed legislation in January 1983, which required special permits to possess ether, acetone, and other chemicals used in cocaine production. No permits were issued in 1984 and the chemicals became much sought after. Smugglers couldn't supply demand. The price of a fifty-five-gallon drum of ether jumped from $1,400 in 1983 to $7,400 in 1984.

The Colombians set up labs in Florida to compensate. Labs busted in Florida in 1984 and 1985 had 10 to 500 gallons each. These are not jungle labs. They are near populated areas. Ether is a dangerous chemical. It cannot be stored long before it forms other chemicals that are extremely shock sensitive and highly flammable. Ten to fifteen drums of ether will flatten two city blocks. Highly explosive peroxide deposits form on the inside of previously opened ether containers.

To give cookers their due, they're pretty inventive at times. They use popcorn machines to dry and process coca base.

LSD

LSD is another drug bikers are fond of. Lysergic acid diethylamide starts life as a fungus called ergot that rots rye and other grains. LSD is made from the alkaloid lysergic acid that is squished out of ergot. The white, odorless drug is sold as little colored pills or as drips on blotter paper. Enterprising packagers print groovy messages such as "LOVE" on their product. Others stamp Donald Duck or Mickey Mouse faces on the tabs. Acid makes you see things that aren't there. It disintegrates the boundaries between objects and turns the world into an ambulatory Dali painting. It makes you tingle and leaves a weird taste in the back of your brain.

Timothy Leary and old hippies say it expands the mind. Right. The same way MDA expands the snatch.

PCP

PCP, or phencyclidine, was developed by Parke-Davis Labs as an intravenous anesthetic called Sernyl for humans undergoing surgery, but bombed out in 1965 when it caused convulsions during surgery, delirium, and hallucinations. Shrinks considered using it to treat flakes but backed off. Veterinarians used PCP as an animal analgesic called Sernylan until the critters starting acting as weird as human users.

PCP hit the streets illegally as the peace pill, peace, and hog in the 1960s. The crystal white powder is also called angel dust, lovely, love boat, and horse tranquilizer. Some people call PCP "naked" because users strip to cool off from the hot flashes it causes. Others call it Hinckley after Ronald Reagan's would-be assassin.

PCP is snorted, injected, or eaten, but is most often smoked with marijuana or parsley—a mixture called killerweed. Many people have smoked PCP without knowing it. Pushers often spray PCP on parsley or low-potency marijuana to produce killerweed. It gives users hallucinations and they keep buying the stuff thinking they're getting super weed. Some ripoff artists spray the weed with roach killer or formaldehyde to give it the chemical smell users associate with PCP.

PCP short-circuits the body's electrical system in the name of fun. It fucks up a person's ability to handle information from the brain and the outside world. It distorts time, space, hearing, and sight. It zaps memory and logic. Panic and violence take over. Sometimes a dusty old door creaks open and a nasty mental problem squirts out—artificial schizophrenia at its best.

PCP is made with two chemicals in a five-step process. One of them is bromobenzene, a motor-oil additive more commonly used to make plastics. PCP is as dangerous to make as it is to ingest. The cooking produces hydrogen cyanide gas, which is used in gas chambers, and it explodes if it comes into contact with water, another by-product of the process.

The stuff is so easy to make it can be cooked in plastic buckets. All a cooker needs is precursor chemicals, the materials that become the finished product; reagents, which react with the precursors but don't become part of the final product; and a solvent, which dissolves precursors, dilutes mixtures, and separates or purifies chemicals.

Piperidine is the crucial precursor to make PCP. Cookers steal the stuff from legitimate laboratories if they can't get it from chemical companies without being reported to the government. The James

Holcomb organization, a thirty-five-member gang that produced and distributed PCP across the United States from its base in Maryland, had contacts inside the Eastman Kodak Co. who stole the necessary precursor chemicals for them, including piperidine. Some cookers can synthesize piperidine from a kilogram of black pepper. Canada is a great source of this chemical and other PCP precursors for American labs.

PCP has to be cooked in remote labs because of the strong smells it produces. The ether and acetone are also volatile. The Pagans Motorcycle Club had a PCP lab in an apartment in Cheverly, a Washington suburb in Prince George's County, Maryland. The cookers used ether as a solvent. One day the ether ignited and blew both cookers to motorcycle heaven and left ten families without a home.

One undercover narc was scared shitless after taking a job driving a mobile home around as a cooker produced PCP in the back. The Maryland State Police finally decided to bust the lab halfway through the cooking process rather than risk the man's life. Some labs have been set up in transport trucks that roared along highways where no one could smell the fumes. Raiding a lab during intermediate cooking stages is most dangerous to one's health because that's when the cyanide gas is produced.

"I was involved in an investigation of members of the Pagans Motorcycle Club," Corporal Terry Katz of the Maryland State Police testified before a Congressional subcommittee. "In the investigation, we used an informant who has now been relocated under the witness security program. The lab operation he was involved in produced PCC, the intermediate stage of PCP. That PCC went from Maryland, where it was produced in a residential area, to North Carolina by way of Virginia and then back to Virginia.

"During the investigation we seized a van which I was asked to drive with the PCC back to the FBI office. I left all the windows of the van open. I had the air vents on full blast. The drive took about half an hour. When I got to the FBI office and parked the van, the evidence was removed and locked away.

"As I got out of the van, I noticed that I had a severe headache. It was so severe in fact that it felt like somebody had taken their thumbs and pressed them against the side of my eyes. In fact, I noticed and became quite alarmed that I could open my eyes wider but I couldn't close them. Now, I know what the physiological effects of PCP are, so I became very concerned about a reaction. It took about half an hour for that involuntary muscle reaction to go away and I still had a severe headache that lasted several hours."

According to testimony before a 1983 Senate Subcommittee on

Organized Crime, the Pagans make and distribute most of the methamphetamine and PCP in the northeastern United States—worth about
$15 to $20 million a year. They intimidate competing dealers to corner
the market. They have their own chemists and laboratories, which
supply dealers in Virginia, Maryland, Connecticut, New York, New
Jersey, Pennsylvania, and Ohio. They also deal in cocaine, marijuana,
and killerweed. The Pagans are unsophisticated and lack business ethics,
though they are highly organized. Unlike the Hell's Angels, they don't
care about the quality of the methamphetamine they sell. The mother
club controls distribution and everyone else down the line wants part of
the action. The drug is cut every time it moves from one level to the next.
It's a ripoff by the time it hits the street.

The drug network is extensive and intricate.

"I had one person that I took, dressed him up in a three-piece suit, I
put him on an airplane," former Pagan high-roller Edward Jackson (a
pseudonym) testified before the Senate subcommittee. "He stopped
with PCP and traded even up for speed from a club called the Para-Dice
Riders from [Toronto] Canada. He would stop in Pittsburgh. The next
stop would be the Outlaws." He would continue on to Wisconsin,
Michigan, Iowa, the West Coast, and come back around the bottom of
the country through Arizona, Texas, with the Bandidos, who were our
brother club. End up with the Outlaws down in Florida, and then stop
back in Virginia and the mother club would have a stash of drugs and
$25,000 in cash. That went on once a week. He would start out with just
killerweed. He would deal even up for speed, have different speed and
killerweed, get hallucinogenic from the west coast, downers from Texas
and Arizona."

A common interest in methamphetamine production and trafficking
strengthened the Pagan link with traditional organized crime. From
1977 to 1981, Ronald Raiton, of Dresher, Pennsylvania, was one of the
big east coast suppliers of the chemicals needed to make methamphetamine. He supplied P2P to Ronald Kownacki, a New Jersey
businessman aligned with the Pagans, and to Iganazio Raymond Anthony (Long John) Martorano, a member of the Bruno organized crime
family. Chemists who worked in houses, apartments, and trailers in
public campgrounds turned the P2P into methamphetamine.

Kownacki was the Pagans' major methamphetamine supplier. He sold
the drug to a south New Jersey Pagan called Buckets, who distributed it
to Pagan mother club members in New Jersey, Delaware, and Philadelphia. Kownacki paid the Pagan president $500 a week for protection
and bought a bar for gang members to hang out in.

Kownacki's business ran something like this: he paid Raiton $4,500
for one gallon of P2P and forked over an additional $10,000 to the Bruno

crime family for every gallon; he then sold every pound of meth-amphetamine to Buckets for $9,000; Buckets diluted each pound 50 percent and sold each new pound for $10,000 to mother club members. They further diluted it and sold it to other Pagans for $900 an ounce. The Pagans learned to manufacture their own P2P after Kownacki was jailed in 1981.

William Terrance (Lance) Costello, a former Marine reservist and machinist who joined the Pagans in 1970 to drink beer and fight, learned quickly that bikers are unforgiving businessmen.

"Dealing drugs in the Pagan organization is quite different from the activities of an individual dealer on the street," Costello said. "The very nature and structure of the Pagan organization breeds an element of fear among its members which characterizes Pagan drug dealing and other illegal activities. When you deal drugs for the Pagans, you know without any question that, should you perform less than expected the people above you would cut you off from drugs or kill you."

Many members launder their drug and prostitution money through legitimate businesses, such as motorcycle repair shops, which they also use to fence stolen parts. The club owns a trucking company in the northeastern US. Pagans consistently obtain sophisticated weapons, which they use or sell to radical groups and other motorcycle gangs. They have automatic weapons, plastic explosives, dynamite, hand grenades, and blast simulators for the cruise missile that they distribute through the club network.

It's surprising their network works—Pagans are stoned more often than not.

"During meetings it would almost come to a contest," said Pagan Edward Jackson. "In fact, one mother club meeting where I was at, we actually chose up teams and we put so many lines of speed down, so many Tuinals, so much coke, and we just did three Tuinals, two of speed, two of killerweed; it became a contest.

"Everybody used drugs all the time. During the six years I was a Pagan, I was fearless, ruthless, and always under the influence of narcotics. My personality drastically changed because of my narcotics habits. On a given day I would awake, take speed to wake up, do cocaine, take some downers, and smoke killerweed. It's not difficult to have Pagan members carry out illegal and often ruthless acts because they are generally extremely high from some sort of drug use. In fact, most Pagan members simply follow instructions from mother club members and chapter presidents. They really have no concept of the overall operations."

But even the drugged-up Pagans have standards. They measure a man's impairedness by his ability to handle a motorcycle.

"It was my understanding as sergeant-at-arms and Pagan enforcer inside the club that if you could start your motorcycle and ride it, then you could ride it," Jackson said. "During funerals, when there was more than one chapter, the national sergeant-at-arms would carry a bat with him and would ride up alongside of the pack and anybody who wasn't riding properly would get swatted in the back. That is why we always had trucks following the pack. They would pick up the people that were discarded to the side of the road."

Lance Costello considers himself a victim of Pagan overindulgence.

During testimony to a Senate subcommittee he said: "I feel I have lost some of my intelligence. I have lost my memory. During the times I was using these drugs, my thoughts weren't coherent. A friend of mine was stabbed — one of the members — and if I could have loaded my gun at that time, I would have killed the person. But I couldn't get the bullets into my gun because I was so messed up. . . . When I worked in the liquor store for Mark Fox [then Pagan national treasurer], I could add up about fifteen different items in my head without using a cash register. I am lucky to do two or three now without some paper."

Costello let prodigious drug profits slip away as easily as his thoughts.

"I bought a van. I always spent it on parties. A day wouldn't go by that I spent less than $200 a day. Most of the people in my chapter were idiots. They had been using drugs for longer than I had. Most of them came from a disadvantaged background, where it wouldn't be as true in some of the other chapters. But providing these people with drugs, they owed me, when I left, large amounts of money. And I, for a long time, supported them.

"At one time I rented a house for about $400 — five-bedroom house where I had four or five of them living with me because, even though I would give them drugs, they still couldn't support themselves. They would sell the drugs, they would spend the money, they would party on the drugs. Some people after a period of time aren't capable of looking after themselves."

Most police forces have horror stories of five or six police officers having trouble arresting someone on PCP because of his tremendous strength. People on PCP have thrown people off their backs, broken apart handcuffs, and continued to attack after being shot five times. Cops dread arresting PCP users, who tend to be violent and out of touch with reality.

"These people believe that they're fighting the devil, a tiger, or a gorilla," Corporal Katz said. "So, now you're faced with subduing a person that, on one hand, has superhuman strength and then doesn't feel pain. Because of this PCP reaction, there have been deaths and injuries to

PCP users who have not been able to be restrained and to police officers called upon to restrain the people.

"Five physically fit police officers from [a Maryland State Police narcotics unit] went out to arrest one person that was on PCP. The reason for the large number of people was that he was a known PCP abuser. The suspect weighed about 135 pounds and was approximately five feet six inches tall. It took all five members to get that one suspect handcuffed. But before he could be placed in custody, a lengthy struggle ensued in which, as they later reported, the officers thought they were going to lose. Imagine one man against five, and he almost wins; an amazing drug when one considers how violent and tragic it would have been had just one officer attempted the arrest, as he or she could have lost their life."

Paranoia is almost too mild a term for PCP users. A longtime PCP user walked uneasily around his house in Randallstown, Maryland, on Christmas Day 1983. He believed that his fourteen-month-old son was the devil. He decapitated the boy—well nearly, the head dangled from spinal nerves.

Police shot and killed a twenty-eight-year-old railroad porter stoned on PCP after he slashed his mother with a broken bottle and was about to kill her. A teenager who smoked PCP ran over his dog and then shot himself. A PCP user in Los Angeles tore out his own eyeballs. Another one in Washington tore the skin off her face. She thought she was covered with insects.

In April 1984, James Megenhardt, Jr., was four months old and enjoying his first spring in Glen Burnie, Maryland. His next-door neighbor wasn't having as great a day. He was stone on PCP and was convinced the baby was full of demons. He scalded and stabbed the child to death.

Eight Washington, D.C., men stoned on PCP desperately wanted money. They jumped forty-seven-year-old Catherine Fuller and dragged her into an alley. They beat her, pinned her to the ground, and ripped off her clothes. Then they cheered as one punk shoved a bicycle handlebar up her ass. She died.

One of three people admitted to the emergency ward of St. Elizabeth's mental hospital in Washington is fighting demons in the wonderful world of PCP psychosis. Users don't call the drug the Key to St. E's for nothing. Three of four emergency mental cases handled at Washington's Crisis Resolution Unit are PCP freaks. Children as young as two months are showing up in Washington hospitals in comas, drooling, hallucinating, or slurring their speech after breathing secondhand PCP fumes in a room where adults have smoked killerweed.

Being burned out on PCP doesn't mean being tired. It means brain cells have literally been destroyed and words just don't make it from the brain to the tongue when needed.

The PCP monopoly of white cookers associated with outlaw motor-cycle gangs weakened in the late 1980s as blacks and Hispanics got into the business to provide their poor clients with a heavy drug they could afford. Blacks and Hispanics now control much of the PCP business in the Baltimore-Washington area. Dusters, as PCP abusers are known in some parts, are so common in Harlem now that the area is called the dust bowl. One naked duster ran down a street in the Bushwich section of Brooklyn, grabbed a baby from a father's arms, and smashed it on the sidewalk.

Designer Drugs

Designer drugs. Now there's a sign of the times. Drugs designed just for you: the Me Generation. The ultimate clandestine lab Frankenstein creation—a pill that turns you into someone else.

Dealers around San Jose, California, in 1982 introduced junkies to what they described as a synthetic heroin called China White after the much sought-after southeast Asian heroin. The new stuff was designed by a chemist trying to synthesize meperidine (Demerol). He was trying to create the analog MPPP. He screwed up the cooking and the batch he produced contained the neurotoxin MPTP. More than 500 junkies used it, many of them only once. They quickly displayed symptoms of Parkinson's Disease. Twenty people in their twenties immediately froze. They became instant statues. They could not move. They had dared to look at Medusa and lost.

One man used heroin every day for five years. His pusher turned him on to synthetic heroin. It fried his brain cells. His upper body went rigid. He drooled. He shook. He shuffled like an octogenarian. Like the other junkies, he couldn't stand up by himself. He had to be told to move his left foot forward, then the right. One man used drugs regularly for fourteen years. He injected three doses of synthetic heroin and became a trembling vegetable. These lives were instantly rushed from twenty-five to seventy-five, stripped of fifty years by a quick fix.

The symptoms of Parkinson's Disease did not hit them gradually. Two people were driving along the freeway when they froze. They literally lost all ability to move. One man got out to fix his car and became paralyzed. One man plopped into his porridge one morning—immobile. Three hundred of these people showed up at the Santa Clara County Hospital in the mid-1980s. They need round-the-clock medical atten-tion to live.

These junkies were victims of MPTP, a drug that never should have hit the streets. But no one monitors underground cookers and the cookers don't test their stuff before they sell it. Junkies are their guinea pigs. Synthetic drugs claim many victims. Because they are undetectable, they are a perfect drug for parolees. One chemist working an entire weekend can produce enough fentanyl to supply the entire United States for six months—and store the stuff in a closet.

Designer drugs were given their name by Dr. Gary Henderson at the University of California in Davis. The term referred to the ability of underground chemists to create drugs for clients. The drugs weren't new, but were variations on old standbys such as heroin. The drugs were really designed to evade laws—chemical warfare waged by phantom chemists. Drug laws must specify the chemical structure of the drug being controlled. Cookers of illicit drugs change the formula slightly to produce a drug that no longer falls under the legal definition; it may have an extra fluoride or carbon molecule. It usually takes several years for law enforcement to catch on that there's a new drug out there and make it illegal. New drugs are impossible to detect with drug tests because no one looks for them.

There is no way of knowing how many designer analogs are on the street. Labs can't detect them unless they know their exact chemical structures. Addicts can't detect them. All they're looking for is a rush. Coroners are confused by young people with needle marks in their arms dying of heart attacks, brain seizures, lung failures, or collapsed circulatory systems with no trace of detectable drugs in their systems. It's a filthy little game in which everyone tries to stay one step ahead of the law and one back of the grave. Unfortunately, in many cases, one step ahead of the law is the grave.

Fentanyl, which is used in hospitals as an anesthetic, is 100 times stronger than morphine and twenty to forty times more powerful than heroin. Its analog—3-methyl fentanyl—is 3,000 to 4,000 times more powerful than heroin.

A drop of 3-methyl fentanyl on the head of a pin will KILL fifty people. The drug has killed dozens, if not hundreds, of unsuspecting addicts who overdosed on the improperly cut synthetic. Junkies have been found dead and labs haven't been able to determine what killed them because they don't know what they're looking for. Only Dr. Henderson's lab and a Drug Enforcement Administration lab can identify some of the designer drugs.

A debate rages about an analog of both methamphetamine and LSD, if you can imagine the combination. The analog is MDMA—Ecstasy to some, Extasy to others. It first showed up legally in magazine ads for homosexuals. Queers used to sniff the stuff in bath houses and pork themselves silly, running from cubicle to cubicle, slapping a glop of Crisco shortening on their asses from a bucket near the front door and slipping their rods up the nearest back door. AIDS is taking care of that.

Until Ecstasy was temporarily banned in 1985 pending studies of its potential dangers, the analog was touted as the LSD of the eighties. Psychologists boasted it opened people's minds and made them drag out garbage they couldn't face while undergoing conventional therapy. People all of a sudden remembered acts of sexual abuse from way back. For this reason, psychologists want the drug legalized. This is part of a growing movement among psychologists to gain the right to prescribe drugs. Remember, psychologists are not medical doctors. A proper understanding requires knowledge of the physical, not the psychological.

These nutbars want drugs like MDMA legalized because it saves them work. They're looking for shortcuts. There is a disturbing undercurrent in society to seek salvation from our failure by owning up to sexual inadequacies and abuses that in most cases don't exist. Sex has become a scapegoat. Once again society is heading into a repressive sexual age. The more we repress sex the more fucked up society becomes.

The fentanyl series of drugs was first synthesized by the Janssen Pharmaceutical Company in Belgium. Fentanyl is used during surgery in hospitals as an analgesic-anesthetic called Sublimaze, which was introduced in the United States in 1968. Different versions of fentanyl have been synthesized by underground chemists, the most successful being 3-methyl fentanyl, which hit the California streets in the fall of 1983 and killed seventy-seven people by 1985.

Fentanyls are cut with sucrose or lactose so that less than 1 percent of what the junkie buys is an active drug. Though color means nothing, it allows dealers to give their products exotic names that attract junkies. Pure white fentanyl has been sold as Persian White heroin; light tan fentanyl has been called China White or Synthetic Heroin; light brown fentanyl has been called Mexican Brown. They are difficult to tell from organic heroin and a lot of people have been sold the synthetic under guise of the real thing. One black drug-trafficking organization shipped a load of fentanyl to New York from California beside a corpse in a casket in 1980. An ideal box for the stuff.

Though fentanyls produce the same effects as heroin, they have additional surprises. They can stop breathing, they slow down the heart, and they tighten chest muscles—leading to what is called wooden chest. Fentanyl's only illicit use until people started killing themselves with it was to make race horses run faster. If you want to know which drugs will be popular on the streets in the next decade, check your local paddock.

Fentanyls and other synthetics are going to kill a lot of people over the next ten years. They're cheap to produce. They're legal until discovered and declared illegal. Crack has shown that there's an unlimited market for cheap, highly potent drugs. Greedy chemists will flood the market with cheap, untested synthetics. Some will have no side effects except to instantly create addicts. Others, like MPTP, will cripple and kill. The lucky will die fast. Some of the junkies who survived MPTP in the early 1980s have to be medicated every three hours to function. This first designer drug disaster, not unlike the thalidomide fiasco, will not be the last. Hundreds of clandestine cookers scheme to line their wallets with people's lives.

Part V

KILLING FLOOR

14

Prison Gangs:
Gangsters in blue denim suits

"Violence is an act of intelligence."
      – PHILOSOPHY OF THE BLACK GUERRILLA FAMILY PRISON GANG.

There's more than a grain of truth in the adage that prisons are schools where criminals learn new ways to make money illegally. An industrious drug dealer can make a fortune behind bars despite the supposed restrictions imposed by walls, bars, fences, guards, and repeated body and cell searches. Since demand is high and supply is controlled, prisoners have little choice but to pay what dealers demand, which is usually four times the going rate on the street.

The scent of drug money behind bars elicits a blood lust that makes the business deadly even for the toughest dealers. Drug dealing in North American prisons has created a new class of gangsters whose tentacles spread into the communities that banished them. These new gangsters are members of once-benign prison gangs now responsible for killing more people on the street than in prison.

Prison gangs control drug dealing behind bars, either by smuggling and selling, or by exacting a percentage from independent dealers. As with all organized crime groups, drug profits and the liberal use of violence have allowed prison gangs to create nearly indestructible criminal empires. We'll never get drugs off the streets if we can't keep them out of prisons.

The first prison gangs were formed to protect members, who tend to be from the same ethnic background, from attacks by other prisoners. They reflect a dramatic increase in violence in our world. Until about thirty years ago, even prisons were safe from the senseless violence that is now commonplace in North American cities. As the outside world got tougher, so did life behind bars. And the first prison gangs saw the light.

It didn't take long for the violent career criminals to turn the organizations into criminal enterprises specializing in drug trafficking, robbery, extortion, and murder. They weren't free to prey on free society, so they preyed on a captive population.

For twenty years, prison gangs operated behind bars only. By 1980, they were using prisons as an operations base to recruit and train new members and to plan and direct criminal activities on the outside by paroled gang members. Prison gangs scout street gangs for runners and lookouts for their drug deals and robberies. They use the punks to extort money. Reward is membership in the prison gang once the street gang member gets busted and sent to jail.

Most crimes committed by prison gangs, especially murders, are now committed on the streets. In a good year, four out of five killings by prison gangs take place in any prison community. Since 1975, there have been more than 700 prison gang murders in California, 96 of which were committed in 1977. Gang members kill and maim to intimidate rival gangs, extortion victims, and competing drug dealers. Gangs also use murder to maintain internal security and discipline, bully witnesses, and eliminate threats to the organization. Under threat of death, gang members are expected to carry out hits assigned to them. Since the murders are intended to instill fear, they are particularly gruesome. One man was stabbed in the chest and bludgeoned. He was crushed by a pickup truck and dragged several blocks before the driver got out and shot him in the head.

Seven prison gangs operate behind bars and on North American streets: the Mexican Mafia, the Nuestra Family, the Black Guerrilla Family, the white supremacist Aryan Brotherhood, the Texas Syndicate, the Consolidated Crip Organization, and the Red Rags. The gangs are best organized and most dangerous in the California prisons, where they originated.

The Mexican Mafia, also known as "La EME," was formed by members of different street gangs from east Los Angeles in the Deuel Vocational Institution in Tracy, California, in 1957. Its 250 to 300 members are nearly all first- or second-generation Mexican-Americans who control drug trafficking in most prisons, especially San Quentin, Folsom, and the California Institute for Men in Chino. While other prison gangs deal heroin and cocaine by the ounce, the Mexican Mafia deals in pounds. Members associate with traditional organized crime mobsters and, on the outside, indulge in robbery, prostitution, loan-sharking, and bookmaking.

The Nuestra Family (La Nuestra Familia) was formed by Mexican-Americans from central and northern California as a defense against the Mexican Mafia, now its major rival in the struggle to control drug trafficking in prisons. The Nuestra Family first appeared in 1965 at the Correctional Training Facility in Soledad, California. Members are prone to violence and are vindictive, which makes it difficult to establish a truce between the gangs. Even their drug business sometimes suffers because they are more concerned with their hit lists and killing rivals. The family was led by General Robert (Babo) Sosa, a Puerto Rican from Santa Barbara, until his impeachment in 1980 for allegedly ordering needless murders. The General's autocratic rule was replaced with a more democratic council called La Mesa. Nuestra Family members cannot leave the organization unless dead—blood in, blood out. La Mesa sends coded messages to its members on the street, including orders for contract hits, in *Teen Angel* and *Low Rider* magazines.

The Black Guerrilla Family was formed at San Quentin prison in 1966 by George Jackson, a member of the Black Panther Party who felt the organization was not doing enough to help its brothers behind bars. The gang is divided into a revolutionary faction that has links to other extremist groups, and a criminal faction that specializes in drug trafficking. Several plots by the BGF to assassinate California public officials have been uncovered over the years. The gang was first formed as the Vanguards, a name that was changed after Jackson was killed trying to escape from San Quentin on August 21, 1971. The BGF philosophy: "Violence is an act of intelligence."

The BGF oath:

> If I should break my stride and falter at my comrade's side, This Oath Will Kill Me.
> If ever my word should prove untrue, should I betray this chosen few, This Oath Will Kill Me.
> Should I submit to greed or lust, should I misuse the people's trust, This Oath Will Kill Me.
> Should I be slow to take a stand, should I show my fear to any man, This Oath Will Kill Me.
> Should I grow lax in discipline, in time of strife refuse my hand, This Oath Will Kill.

The Aryan Brotherhood is a white supremacist gang that started in San Quentin in the early 1960s. Its members align themselves with the Mexican Mafia, especially to initiate racial confrontations. Although at one time some of its members were bikers, ABs don't tolerate what they call "booger eaters."

The Texas Syndicate was formed in Folsom Prison in 1974 by inmates from the Lone Star State to protect their behinds behind bars. Although the gang has about twenty-five members, it is feared in California prisons for its policy of swift retribution. Like the other gangs, it deals drugs and extorts.

The Consolidated Crip Organization, the newest prison gang, is an extension of the notorious black Crips street gang from Los Angeles. So many Crips ended up behind bars in the early 1980s that they decided to remain Crips instead of joining other prison gangs. They have taken to wearing their blue bandannas in prison.

Corrections officials fear this new gang could easily overrun older prison gangs and take over all criminal enterprises within the prison system. While the older prison gangs have hundreds of members, with perhaps 2,000 in all, there are about 13,500 Crip gangsters in California.

Members of the Red Rags prison gang belong to the Bloods street gangs from Los Angeles. Blood members behind bars, like the rival Crips, wear their colors: red bandannas. There are about 4,500 Bloods in southern California.

The Aryan Brotherhood was founded in California's San Quentin Prison in the early 1960s as a self-protection group of whites, mostly from Richmond. In 1971, General Jack Malone, who was murdered five years later, and Theodore (T.D.) Bingham steered the AB into crime: narcotics, extortion, prostitution, and murder. Despite their macho image, the AB held male prostitutes in high esteem because of the money they brought in. The AB quickly gained control of San Quentin and Folsom prisons as membership grew and the gang gained a stranglehold on the narcotics trade.

By the early 1980s, the AB usurped the Mexican Mafia as the most powerful prison gang, thanks to its ruthless pursuit of narcotics profits. They now employ associates to do their business for them, insulating themselves from arrests and longer jail terms. They even demand that any white prisoner smuggling drugs into prison give one-third of his stash to the AB. But the AB got sloppy. When the gang first got into the drug business, members sold dope but didn't use it. Over time, AB members started using drugs themselves. That was their downfall.

"They got so violent when they didn't get dope that a lot of people got stabbed," said Ken Kukrall, a corrections officer at Folsom Prison. "One AB had a man killed for $5 marijuana debt."

Today the Aryan Brotherhood has allied itself with the Mexican Mafia for protection and to control drug trafficking in prisons. The two gangs also help each other carry out contract hits on members of the rival Nuestra Family and the Black Guerrilla Family. Despite their hatred of blacks, the AB tried to form an alliance with the BGF in 1987 to assault and kill correctional officers. The fact that white supremacists would

consider dealing with blacks indicates how deeply rooted their homi-
cidal tendencies are.

Some AB members have also struck a loose alliance with the followers
of Charles Manson. Manson's devoted sluts have sent letters and nude
photographs to AB members to entice them to support Manson. Manson
followers have tried to help AB members break out of jail and some of
Charlie's psychotic followers call themselves Aryan Sisters.

The shamrock, called the rock or the brand, is the symbol of the Aryan
Brotherhood. Members have it tattooed on their skin so there is no doubt
where their allegiance lies. Some gang members even have the shamrock
and the initials AB tattooed on their faces or hundreds of times from head
to foot. The shamrock is etched onto weapons used in hits to ensure
everyone knows the ABs are taking care of business. Gang members
must swear to and live up to the Aryan Brotherhood oath, copied here
from a painting by a prisoner in Folsom Prison:

> An Aryan brother is without a care,
> He walks where the weak and heartless won't dare,
> And if by chance he should stumble and lose control,
> His brothers will be there, to help reach his goal,
> For a worthy brother, no need is too great,
> He need not but ask, fulfillments his fate,
>
> For an Aryan brother death holds no fear,
> Vengeance will be his, thru his brothers still here,
> For the brotherhood means just what it implies,
> A brother's a brother, till that brother dies,
> And if he is loyal, and never lost faith,
> In each brother's heart, will always be a place,
>
> So a brother am I, and always will be,
> Even after my life is taken from me,
> I'll lie down content, knowing I stood,
> Head held high, walking proud in the brotherhood.

AB

There are many ways to get drugs into prisons, most of which involve a
woman visitor hiding the stuff in her vagina and giving it to the inmate
during a visit. He stuffs it up his ass. And although everyone knows it's
done this way, few inmates are ever caught bringing it in, even when
guards notice that a prisoner's ass is smeared with Vaseline to ease
insertion into his rectum.

"It's called the keister stash and it's a good one," said Dan Elledge, a corrections officer at Folsom. "You can't find it with an X-ray. We make them bend over and look up their ass, but can't find it if it's well hidden.

"Wendall (Blue) Norris, an AB, was one of the three members of The Committee, which ruled the gang. He stretched his asshole with two Driad roll-on deodorant bottles to insert contraband," Elledge said. "He smuggled a .22-caliber derringer and a Buck knife up his ass."

Some smugglers by-pass the vagina-to-bum method and the woman, during a prolonged kiss, slips the drugs into the prisoner's mouth for him to swallow. He later pukes it up or sifts through his shit.

One dealer in Folsom Prison went to the gym washrooms or the toilets in the yard after his wife passed him drugs in the visitors' room and pulled them out of his ass to distribute to inmates who had already paid for them.

You can laugh at the kind of guy who ends up behind bars, but you can't put him down for lack of creativity and ingenuity. Prisoners constantly devise new ways to hide their dope and accessories. Some hollow out felt pens to hide hypodermic needles and drugs. Others pry the bottom off shaving cream cans to create a stash.

Cons are just as ingenious at making weapons for hits. They melt plastic spoons together into a chunk of plastic they shape into a blade. They do the same with combs, Styrofoam cups, and even the fiberglass in cigarette filters. These pieces of prison handiwork, if not seized, always end up in someone's heart.

Because prisoners can't keep cash outside their trust account in the joint, they use a technique called mail outs to buy and sell drugs. A buyer gets someone on the outside to deliver payment for the drugs to the seller's outside contact. Sometimes the seller has the buyer instruct a friend on the outside to wire money through Western Union to the seller's outside contact. The drugs are released—often shipped by Federal Express—to be smuggled into prison once the money is received and a visitor is designated to carry them in for the buyer. As a last resort, sellers sometimes have buyers wire money from their trust accounts to the seller's outside contact. This is a slow method of payment, since it can take one month for the money to be transferred. It is also a risky way of doing business because prison security and investigation units monitor trust withdrawals.

The basic drug-trafficking organization behind bars consists of a distributor, who arranges the financing, purchase, and smuggling of drugs from the street into prison, then the distribution and sale to inmates; mules, usually wives or girlfriends of inmates, smuggle the drugs into prison; traffickers hold and cut the drugs for distribution and sale; enforcers ensure the drug debts are paid.

Why do drug dealers go to such extremes to sell their wares behind bars? They've got a guaranteed market and complete control over the prices. This is a price list compiled in February 1990, comparing drug prices charged by prison gangs in California prisons to street prices:

	Approximate Street Value	Approximate Institution Value
marijuana	ounce: $200 gram: $15-20 joint: $5	ounce: $350-$400 gram: $25-$40 joint: $10-$15 bindle: $20 cap: $25-$40
heroin	ounce: $2,500 gram: $90-$120 hit: $30	ounce: $5,000 gram: $250 hit: $50 paper: $80
cocaine	ounce: $1,000 gram: $80 line/hit: $5-$10	ounce: $2,000-$2,500 gram: $150-$200 line/hit: $20
speed	ounce: $800 gram: $50 paper: $20 hit: $10	ounce: $1,500 gram: $175 paper: $50 hit: $25

If a distributor buys a gram of speed for $50 on the street and breaks it down to ten papers, he makes a profit of $450. If a $100 gram of heroin yields twenty hits, that's a $1,900 profit. Break the grams down to even smaller units and the profits are so great that some dealers don't want to leave prison.

Those who choose to stay behind bars must contend with and survive the violence. The Aryan Brotherhood's reputation for bloodletting cannot be exaggerated.

In June 1977, members of the Aryan Brotherhood, two associates of the Charles Manson family, and a member of the Symbionese Liberation Army in Old Folsom Prison planned to take over a cell block and execute inmates they considered enemies. Key to this plan was a Walther P-38 9mm pistol and twenty-seven rounds of Speer hollowpoint bullets that had been smuggled into prison and hidden in a cell in Program Housing Unit 1. The scheme called for the quick killing of the two gunmen and three correctional officers on the unit so the inmates could strip them of their weapons, slaughter their enemies, and escape. The plan was thwarted when the Walther was found during a routine search.

On May 27, 1981, Wendall (Blue) Norris, leader of the Aryan Brotherhood, pulled a loaded North American Arms Corp .22-caliber revolver on Solano County sheriff's deputies while being escorted to court. He pulled it out while sitting in the back seat of the car in which he was being driven to court and told the deputies to keep driving in the fast lane or they would die. They bailed out and Norris was captured.

On October 7, 1985, two cylinders wrapped in tape were found during a search of the maintenance shop in the license plate factory at Old Folsom Prison. One container held a detonating cap. The other was filled with powder found in C-4 military explosives, a wristwatch converted into a timing device and two flashlight bulbs wrapped in tape with wires soldered to them. The cylinders were hidden in the temperature control unit for the license plate baking oven. The Brotherhood had planted the bomb to destroy the factory in revenge for what they believed was unfair treatment by the prison administration.

On February 22, 1986, a suspected AB member slipped his handcuffs with a shim made from a Copenhagen chewing tobacco can and stabbed three correctional officers with a knife made of metal cut from his cell door. This was in retaliation for the near shooting by a correctional officer in the prison yard of an AB member trying to stab a Red Rag gang member to death.

At 1:40 p.m. on November 26, 1986, an AB associate threw a spear through the tray slot of his cell at a passing correctional officer. It bounced off the man's body armor. The hit had been ordered by the Aryan Brotherhood out of anger for losing their contact visits, through which they obtained contraband.

On June 22, 1987, a correctional officer shot and wounded an AB member during a stabbing in the prison yard. Two days later, the officer began to receive threatening phone calls at his mother's house. He was also harassed while driving to and from work by a white man who pretended to be shooting at him. On June 26, neighbors watched a black man take two photographs of the officer's house. On July 3, Wendall Norris said, "I can get to a computer on the streets and get anyone's address. I can get any of your [correctional officers'] addresses and have someone on the streets go up to them with a gun and blow their head off."

On July 8, the correctional officer was driving home southbound on Enterprise Boulevard in West Sacramento when a black man leaned out of an oncoming car and discharged a shotgun into the windshield of the officer's car.

On November 2, an AB member boasted that Judy Box, another AB's fiancée, worked for the California Franchise Tax Board in Sacramento and had access to a computer system that contained personal information on correctional officers. By monitoring phone calls from inmates, officers discovered that Box was instrumental in the Aryan Brotherhood conspiracy to murder prison officials.

On November 19, an AB member released on parole prepared to carry out his mission of assassinating correctional officers with the help of personal information obtained by the gang. On November 20, a search of Box's house and office revealed letters and photographs of Brotherhood members and a list of eight Folsom Prison officers, beginning with the warden. She got four years in jail for her part in the conspiracy.

On December 12, 1981, a correctional officer searching the cell of an AB associate found a homemade, double-barreled derringer tucked in the inmate's waistband. The gun was cocked and loaded with .38-caliber bullets. He had been ordered to shoot a member of the Black Guerrilla Family who was in trouble with his gang. The hit on the BGF member was ordered as a gesture of good faith to create a bond between the Aryan Brotherhood and the BGF.

When they're not killing behind bars, AB members kill on the streets.

On February 19, 1983, AB member Curtis Price drove to Humboldt County in northern California and murdered Richard Barnes, father of Steven Barnes, an AB dropout who had testified against the gang. He also killed Elizabeth Ann Hickey, who found out Barnes had stolen the murder weapon from her father's house. Price is now on death row in San Quentin. The AB have warned they will kill corrections staff if a band member is executed.

Two brothers, one an AB and the other a gang associate, arranged for another AB to buy drugs from the Hell's Angels. The Angels refused to sell. An AB leader instructed the foiled buyer to return to the Angel house and kill Colleen Williams, the girlfriend of a man in the house. The leader said he ordered the shooting because Williams had bad-mouthed the Aryan Brotherhood and praised the Hell's Angels in the visiting room at Old Folsom Prison. He complained that Williams had said AB leader Blinky Griffin "wasn't shit." He ordered that she be shot in the mouth. Williams was shot seven times and another man in the house three times. Both survived.

The shooting upset Barry Mills, leader of the federal prison system ABs. The leader who ordered the shooting sent Mills a newspaper article that said Williams was with two black men when she was shot. Mills no longer had any problem with the shooting.

Tony Bilicic, a suspected AB member, insulted a member of the Mexican Mafia in December 1982. The EME member put out the word that Bilicic was ratting on drug smugglers at Folsom. He was stabbed to death three days after Christmas. Richard (Bear) Clemence dropped out of the AB in November 1982. Two suspected AB members dropped him out of life with a knife. The AB ordered the stabbing death of Daniel (Gypsy) Free at the weight pile in Old Folsom Prison on May 12, 1983, because he dropped out of the Satan's Few motorcycle club.

As part of an attempted truce between the Aryan Brotherhood and the Black Guerrilla Family, the ABs asked the BGF to kill one of their own members. Edward (Hodari) Brooks was stabbed to death in the exercise yard at Old Folsom Prison on March 24, 1984. In a further attempt to avoid war between the AB and the BGF, Michael Gehman, a suspected AB member, was stabbed to death in the main kitchen at Old Folsom as a sacrifice to the BGF.

The AB ordered the hit of Robert Clemendin, who was stabbed to death on January 2, 1985, because he kept assaulting his cell mate. The cell mate had paid the AB for protection. Gordi Gaskill thought he could sell drugs in Folsom Prison without giving a cut to the Brotherhood. A knife put an end to that disrespect on August 29, 1986. Gregory (Bandit) Guerra was stabbed to death in an exercise yard at Old Folsom Prison for failing to carry out a hit ordered by the AB. John Hodges, an AB middleman in drug deals, was killed by the gang because he cut and stepped too hard on drugs—a ripoff. He used the drugs he siphoned off.

An AB leader said that while on parole during the 1970s he accepted a contract from the Hell's Angels to kill a rat. He subcontracted the hit to AB members Richard Gardner and Dennis Murphy. They went to a house where the rat was supposed to be. He wasn't there.

However, they discovered the house was a Hell's Angels' crank house. Murphy stole five pounds of crank and $40,000. Murphy also told the Hell's Angel cook he would now be working for the Aryan Brotherhood. The cook refused and Murphy shot him in the hands.

This started a war between the Hell's Angels and the Aryan Brotherhood in which Gardner was killed. The AB leader who had accepted the contract in the first place ran into the Hell's Angel who had given it to him in San Francisco Jail. The AB leader apologized for the shooting of the cook and the theft. They worked out a truce on condition that the AB leader be told who killed Gardner so the ABs could retaliate. The Hell's Angel told him and agreed the killer could be murdered without retaliation by the motorcycle gang.

On May 25, 1987, Dennis (Irish) Murphy, an AB member of ten years, looked up from his bunk to see his cell mate drag his mattress to the doorway and block the exit. The tier tender walked in and stabbed Murphy to death. An AB leader allowed the hit because Murphy was not taking care of business for the gang while he was in prison or on the street. The killer had approached the leader for a knife to kill Murphy. A short time later, he was approached by Murphy himself, who said he feared he was going to be hit. The leader, out of a sense of fair play, gave Murphy a piece of metal cut from his cell so he could make a knife to defend himself.

Lest the impression be given that the AB is responsible for all prison violence, here's some handiwork of other prison gangs.

In 1979, Dr. Donald Claude Bulpitt, thirty-six, offered the Mexican Mafia $15,000 to kill Charles Snodgrass, an informant working for the California Bureau of Narcotics Enforcement. The contract was assigned to Salvador Guttierrez Buenrostro, who lived in a halfway house after being released from federal prison. On September 11, Buenrostro shot Snodgrass in the head as he walked to his car two blocks from Pasadena Police Department headquarters.

In March 1985, an associate of the Aryan Brotherhood, Frank Carl Harshner, was shot dead for an unpaid drug debt at the Pomona, California, home of a Mexican Mafia member. That same month, a Black Guerrilla Family member and an associate stabbed and bludgeoned Mary Hampton to death after a drug deal. In April 1985, paroled members of the Mexican Mafia in San Diego tied up four people and shot them for unpaid drug debts. One of the victims lived. In June 1985, three Black Guerrilla Family members killed correctional sergeant Hal Burchfield in San Quentin Prison with a spear made from a prison bed frame. The killing was in retaliation for the killing of a Crip gang member the previous year.

Robert Sydney Hartsfield, thirty-six years old, has spent all but two years behind bars since his first arrest for burglary at age twelve. Prison is the only life he knows. "I've been pretty much state-raised." His few forays into the outside world seemed more like crime sprees in Disneyland to him, leaving him with pleasant memories to fill the voids between drug deals in Folsom Prison. Syd, or Toilet as his more intimate friends call him, was busted twice more for drugs and is fed up reviewing his short reel of memories in the hole—the solitary confinement cell which is prison for people who commit crimes in jail. He is quite happy to kill time telling an outsider in July 1990 how his life went askew after he left his hometown of Comox, British Columbia, at age eleven to live with his stepbrother in Las Vegas.

"I didn't know what drugs were in B.C.," said Toilet. "I come down here and found myself in the pit of the devil. My stepbrother was a dealer in cannabinol, THC. He was doing underground 8mm movies. I'd get drugs from him. I did drugs because it was the in thing [in the mid-1960s]. My role model was my stepbrother who was covered with jewelry and drove big cars. He supplied me with purple double dome [acid], four-finger lid [four joints in a baggie], orange 25 [acid], and fender benders [reds].

"I was not a poor little kid," Toilet said to emphasize that everything he did, he did by choice. "At first I'd do little burglaries just to do them, for something to do. I did the heroin trip once or twice, then left the scene. At Elko, Nevada, I had my first run-ins with the law, at twelve, for burglaries. I was locked into a prison for kids for an indeterminate amount of time, which was one to one and a half years.

"Because I went in at that age, I was impressed by older kids. It became a springboard for me to increase my knowledge in burglary procedures. I returned to that prison five times in ten years, the last time when I was seventeen. I got out just before I turned eighteen and went to adult prison for burglary.

"In those days there were no drugs in prisons," said Toilet. "Sometimes I'd take Dramamine, a motion-sickness drug that spins your wheels. Sometimes I sniffed gas from the lawnmowers in the auto shop. The Dramamine we got when we went to town with the counsellor on day passes. He went shopping for his kids and we went to the pharmaceutical area and stole drugs. We stole Vicks inhalers, which you chew like gum or put in coffee. I wasn't desperate. It was something to do.

"Another drug we used was Darvon, a pain relaxer. One was shaped like a bullet and one was blunt. The blunt one had a small codeine pill in it. You open the capsule, dump the buffer, take the sugar coating off the pill, and crush three pills to get high. With Talwin, we'd get a hypodermic outfit and take out the plunger. You put in the pill and water, put the plunger back in, cold shake, and inject. We'd get Valium from the medical staff who'd believe any excuse we gave them. Then the inmates would sell it."

Toilet started dealing narcotics during a short release from the Carson City Prison in 1975. That year he also began his career as a crankster.

"When I got out of prison I started dealing heroin. Heroin was the big thing back then. I would get on front an eighth or a sixteenth and guarantee the money. I was able to trade my heroin for crank. It wasn't no big trade. I paid $200 for eighteen bags of heroin and made $150 profit. It was for my own bones. The profit wasn't so much monetary, it was for my use. A couple of terms when I was on the street I was doing it to get my little shot."

Toilet has been a regular at California's Folsom Prison since 1979.

He's done ten stints there with little time on the streets. But to hear him tell it, "the short times I was out there I made up for the time I wasn't." Asked if he wouldn't prefer to live the outside life full-time instead of considering it a holiday, he pondered and replied, "It's kind of sad, now that you bring it to my attention." But he couldn't be deterred from boasting about his hell-raising on the outside.

"I've had short spurts out there on the street. I've had new cars and stuff, but only for thirty days at a time. I don't even have a driver's license. But I do have six social security numbers and twenty-three aliases, whatever suited my fancy. I had a Robert tattoo so I had to put ten names with Robert something. I was doing credit cards. I had my own credit card press and had 500 credit cards and 200 names."

Toilet came by his nickname quite honestly, so to speak. "It was one of those handles you acquire. It has two meanings. I had someone's quantity of drugs. I used them up and told him the man [prison guard] had come in and I had to flush them. Another time I had a mini .22 five-shot [revolver] without a hammer keistered in the toilet. The man came around testing the shitter and flushed it.

"The .22 was brought into the visitors' area by a woman in her vagina. She gave it to her boyfriend and he stuffed it into his rectum. I just happened to come across it. I was holding it for someone else. The gun situation was that we were going to take the cell block over with guards as hostages and kill people there. But that one gun got flushed. The other gun, well, a person went to court and he pulled it on the escort officers. The officers jumped out of the wagon."

Toilet has been strongly associated with the white supremacist Aryan Brotherhood in Folsom Prison which shares one motto with other gangs: "In with blood, out with blood." It means you kill to get in and leave dead.

"My in blood, yeah. Well, when I was being sponsored I was in 4A where there was no one to kill. It was just white dudes. You can't very well kill your own. So there was nothing for me to induce myself with.

"I got married in prison," he said. "I got my wife from another dude. I was getting drugs and giving him crank to pay off debts he wasn't. The Mexicans stabbed him up. I called his wife to tell her he was out in the box. I made my speech. She became my bank." (She collected payments on the outside for drugs sold to inmates on the inside.)

"My wife would bring it to me. She carried it in her hand. She just hands it to me. Up to an ounce. I would sell thirteen to fourteen grams for $500 and keep the rest for myself. Normally I wouldn't cut it. I'd like to be known as selling good stuff. They'd pay me with cash, or had a wife or relative on the outside send money to the box or designated address within ten days."

Money is nearly useless behind bars, where drugs are the most sought-after currency. That's why dealers need someone reliable on the outside to handle the cash and smuggle in the drugs. Toilet's wife wasn't too reliable.

"She would fuck up a couple of times, would spend it or leave me. I wanted to knock off the box and kill the family. I thought it was time to impress these people I thought were God's gift to the prison population [the Aryan Brotherhood].

"Then I was paroled and decided I didn't want to kill her. That put me in a bad spot with the ABs. That was my ticket. I had to explain to them when I got back in. I was put on the back burner for four years. My sponsor was still here. He protected me."

Toilet also bought meth cooked by the Misfits motorcycle gang in Sacramento. He dealt with them only because they had drugs. Most hard-core prisoners don't think much of bikers.

"I ain't no biker," Toilet said. "They're booger eaters. When the Hell's Angels were in Folsom, Sonny Barger was here, they were OK. They had their own thing and weren't a political force. Behind bars they had to deal with me. I had the bag. Outside, they had the bag."

How profitable is drug dealing behind bars?

"I own a house where the wife lives. I bought five cars and two bikes [motorcycles], a lot of jewelry, and a lot more drugs. All with money made this term [the past two years]. Right now I'm not doing any drugs because I'm in the hole. I was busted with five grams of crank and fifteen caps of weed. I had a bad week—busted two times. It was just one of those things."

15

The Quest for Prince Valium:
Sex, crime, and the abuse of prescription drugs

Prescription drug abuse may be more rampant, costly, and deadly than the abuse of illicit drugs in North America, though you could never tell from the macho drug-war rhetoric politicians spout. There's glamour in mounting the guard against foreign drugs. Cocaine and marijuana, like it or not, are sexy subjects. No one wants to hear about everyday people frying their brains on Valium.

Most doctors will tell you momma needs a little helper once in a while. It's easier to pop pills into her mouth than figure out what's ailing her. So licit drugs, obtained illegally, have slipped through the back door into subconscious acceptance in North America. There are no high-profile bad guy traffickers to covertly admire for their free-marketing genius while damning their success. The users are so low key it's difficult to sell them as a menace to society. No reefer madness here. Nope. All is safe on the western front.

Sixty-three percent of persons admitted to hospital emergency wards in North America for drug overdose have taken too many prescription drugs. Drugs dealers who claim their business has no victims because everyone involved makes money — except for the addict who gets high — are wrong. Prescription drugs probably exact a higher toll on North American society than cocaine, marijuana, heroin, and hallucinogens combined.

Ever wonder why Canadians appear so docile in situations where Americans would fly off the handle? Canadians are the biggest users of prescription drugs in the world, according to a government study in the late 1980s. They are also the world's biggest abusers of prescription drugs. Beneath its seemingly normal exterior of wool-tuqued, beer-guzzling, back-bacon-munching hockey fans, the Great White North harbors a stunned, grinning populace with Demerol-soaked brains.

Although law-enforcement officials venture to estimate the value of the illicit drug market worldwide at $500 billion—a figure based on crop estimates, drug seizures, and subsequent fluctuations in prices—they have no idea what the illegal prescription drug market is worth. The cost to society of the addicts' quest for these drugs cannot be tallied. Except for thefts and robberies of drugstores, the illicit trade in prescription drugs is so intangible, and its practitioners so elusive, that police and health officials cannot weigh its worth or count the bad guys.

Police say they are aware of only 2 to 10 percent of the addicts and the crimes they commit to get prescription drugs. In Ontario alone, between $2.6 million and $3.4 million in prescription drugs are stolen yearly from drugstores, each of which has a 50-50 chance of being broken into. Multiply the take by a factor of about 1,000 to get the street value of the drugs and you're looking at big money.

The average bank robbery in Canada nets the criminal about $2,500. Knock over a ma-and-pa drugstore at 7 p.m. and if you get one bottle of Dilaudid tablets, a heroin substitute, you get four times as much as the bank robber. And the tablets don't have serial numbers.

Theft is only one way addicts and the dealers who feed them get their supply. They also forge prescriptions and fake ailments to defraud the health care systems of countless more millions. The business is worth more than $1 billion a year in California alone.

The most graphic indicator of the degradation wreaked by prescription drug addiction is the ease with which women addicts sell their bodies for drugs and the willingness of doctors to trade pills for pussy and head. Addiction rots the moral fiber and the self.

"They'd sell their grandmother to get the drug if they had to," said Dr. John Carlisle, associate registrar in charge of investigations for the College of Physicians and Surgeons of Ontario. "They know no limits. Ordinary morality means nothing to the drug addict. All that's important is the drug."

The addicts' quest for uppers and downers is too often aided by unscrupulous doctors and pharmacists who line their pockets and their beds by selling prescriptions and drugs. More often, though, they are themselves the victims of manipulative addicts. Doctors and pharmacists are vulnerable to the addicts' ploys because they are trained to trust and help people. Drug abusers look for a doctor who is gullible or criminal. They have a grapevine along which they pass the names of doctors who give them drugs. They hit the suckers fast. Doctors often don't become suspicious until they look into their waiting rooms one day and see them filled with addicts.

Crooked doctors and pharmacists can triple their income prescribing and selling to addicts. They charge from $50 to $100 a prescription. Of course they also take the chance of being caught. Addicts have loose tongues. Sometimes they scare doctors into giving them drugs. The easiest way for a doctor to get rid of a person threatening to break into his office or rob a drugstore is to write a prescription. Lists of doctors who are easy sources of drugs are sold on the street. Their practices are soon overrun with addicts. Addicts buy and sell blank prescription pads stolen from negligent doctors' desks for $10 to $15 a sheet.

Prescription mills, or script mills, are opened under the guise of weight-loss or medical clinics as fronts to illegally distribute prescriptions for Dilaudid, Talwin, and Percodan, which are sought by addicts. These prescriptions are written by doctors who have no qualms taking money for scripts that they know will be sold on the streets.

A New York City pharmacist received and distributed 1,300,300 doses of prescription drugs stolen from air-freight shipments at John F. Kennedy Airport. For this he got two years in prison and was fined $20,000. In 1979, thirty to thirty-five doctors in the Detroit area alone were convicted for writing such prescriptions. They received from $20 to $30 a script for signing their names to 1,000 prescriptions.

Laura Norberg had a badly infected tooth. Doctors couldn't figure out the cause of her headaches and prescribed a narcotic painkiller, Fiorinal. Norberg soon became addicted to the drug and sought it out. She started going to different British Columbia doctors with the same fraudulent complaint and was prescribed Fiorinal each time to deal with the symptoms. She also traded sexual favors with the elderly Dr. Morris Wynrib in return for the drugs.

She was charged with double-doctoring in 1985. She mentioned in a pre-sentence report after she pleaded guilty that she had traded her body for Dr. Wynrib's prescriptions. She was given an absolute discharge. Wynrib was charged with trafficking. The charges were dismissed on humanitarian grounds after the court was told he was dying of cancer.

Norberg then sued Wynrib for sexual assault and negligence for accepting her sexual favors in return for Fiorinal prescriptions. She lost and appealed the decision. The British Columbia Court of Appeal ruled she couldn't sue the doctor because her own conduct had been "illegal or immoral" in sexually exploiting the elderly doctor. The ruling was based on the legal principle of ex turpi causa—persons involved in illegal or immoral acts can't sue each other for the consequences of those acts.

"She went voluntarily [to have sex about twelve times with the doctor in his apartment] in order to get drugs with a clear understanding of the sordid arrangements to which she had agreed," Chief Justice Allen McEachern wrote.

Feminist groups reacted predictably. They argued that Norberg was a victim and the court didn't understand how women can be easily and gently coerced into having sex. They pressed to have the case appealed to the Supreme Court of Canada.

Just how little does law enforcement know about the scope of prescription drug abuse? First of all, although millions of dollars' worth of drugs are stolen from pharmacies each year, more drugs are obtained through scams such as forged prescriptions. While the Royal Canadian Mounted Police estimate the value of licit and illicit chemical drug sales every year in Canada in their National Drug Estimate, the police force says that a breakdown of this figure for prescription drugs alone "does not exist." Which makes you wonder what figures their total estimate is based on.

A little arithmetic with a few of the many prescription drugs that were stolen or disappeared in one year helps define the street value of prescription narcotics and controlled drugs. These figures do not include drugs obtained through forged prescriptions or other scams.

In 1984, 522,671 tablets of the painkiller codeine were stolen across Canada. At $1.50 each, they are worth $784,006 on the street; 1,035,292 milliliters of Novahistine DH, a painkiller containing hydrocodone, were stolen. At $120 for 250 milliliters on the street, it is worth $496,940; 11,935 Dilaudid tablets, a painkiller containing hydromorphone, were stolen. The pills sell for up to $50 apiece, a haul worth $596,750; 182,468 tablets of the painkiller Percodan, containing oxycodone, were stolen. At $5 a tablet on the street, the stolen drugs are worth $912,340; 127,134 tablets of Talwin, an analgesic containing pentazocine, were stolen. At $12 a pill, these tablets were worth $1,525,608; among controlled drugs, 17,628 tablets of the tranquilizer Mandrax, which contains methaqualone, were stolen. At $5 each, they are worth $88,140 on the street; 65,656 tablets of the stimulant Ritalin containing methylphenidate were stolen. At $8 a pill, they are worth $525,248. So far, that's $4,929,032 and you can keep counting for days.

Two cases from south-central Los Angeles illustrate the extent of the problem and the violence associated with this part of the drug trade.

Ralph Brothers Market and Pharmacy was a small drugstore in south-central Los Angeles that Ralph Godoy bought in 1977 with a loan from the Small Business Administration. He listed his net worth at $159,275 when he applied for the loan in October 1976. In December 1978, he listed his net worth at $1,400,500 in an application to buy a Las Vegas casino. He presented the seller with $102,000 cash from a briefcase to open an escrow account on the casino and had to be persuaded to buy a cashier's check instead. Not bad for a pharmacist whose salary was fixed at $25,000 a year by the terms of his loan with the Small Business Administration.

Ralph Godoy was a pharmacist who had decided to supplement his earnings. He bought 1.2 million methaqualone tablets, better known as Quaaludes or ludes, from legitimate wholesalers who fill pharmacy orders. His drugstore dispensed more than 300,000 ludes in 1978. By contrast, 120 Thrifty Drug Store pharmacies dispensed a total of 50,000 during the same period. Another 600,000 ludes somehow found their way out of the dispensary and into the streets through forged prescriptions, inventory shortages, and improper counter sales.

It seems Godoy was one of the more enterprising applicants to the Small Business Administration program. He hired three people to work for him—a pharmacy assistant and two pushers to distribute the drugs and collect money. The assistant worked as manager of the pharmacy and helped package the ludes and count the money. He was also the straw owner of the Whisky Creek nightclub, bought with lude money. Godoy wasn't selling the ludes one at a time; he sold them by the bottle. He charged $1,000 for a 500-tablet bottle of ludes. One buyer bought forty-two at one time.

Business boomed for about a year and a half until William (Fat Tom) Futrell and David Matsumoto, the distributors, were caught selling 24,000 ludes to undercover police officers on December 18, 1978. A few days earlier, Godoy and his assistant Michael Frost had traveled to Las Vegas to buy a casino. Godoy figured he could make enough money selling ludes for five years to set himself up for life. So it came as a great surprise that his two distributors had been arrested. When the shock wore off, Godoy muttered that if he were jailed, he'd hang on to enough money to have the rat who sent him up killed.

About one week after the arrest of Futrell and Matsumoto, Godoy offered Richard Jeffrey $12,000 in cash or ludes to kill the two runners for fear they would talk to the cops and blow his operation. Jeffrey argued with Godoy and finally convinced him not to kill Matsumoto. Godoy told Jeffrey that Frost would point out Futrell's home. Godoy eventually hired another hitter to kill Futrell. When this man told him the runner was dead, Godoy replied, "He deserved to die."

But Godoy was not a trusting man. He told Jeffrey on January 30, 1979, about hiring the other killer and asked him to check if Futrell was dead. When the law caught up with Godoy in August 1979, Godoy offered Jeffrey $20,000 to kill the man who supposedly had killed Futrell. He then listed several bars in the San Fernando Valley where he could find him. Godoy got twelve years in jail.

About the time Ralph Godoy was setting up his pharmacy in 1977, the only doctor in the town of Caruthers, southwest of Fresno, died. With no one in town to write prescriptions, David Wheaton Hall's pharmacy, which had served the small farming community since 1966, went out of business. Hall opened another pharmacy in nearby Clovis only to declare bankruptcy in 1980. Then his nineteen-year marriage fell apart. Uprooted, Hall floated around for two years, prospecting for gold, scuba diving, flying, selling Amway products, and manufacturing costume jewelry. But he was a pharmacist at heart and wanted to get back into the business.

One Sunday morning in October 1982, as Hall sat in the Clovis library reading the *Los Angeles Times*, he noticed an ad for a pharmacist. It had been placed by Josephine Brown, who needed a qualified pharmacist behind the counter of her Slauson Avenue Pharmacy in south-central Los Angeles to get a state pharmacy license. Hall said he'd take the job if he thought he could make a go of it.

He rented a room in a nearby motel and drove around the neighborhood in his Toyota pickup truck assessing the area's business potential. The area was black, poor, and drug-infested. It was sandwiched between the San Diego and Harbor freeways, which funneled dopers to the streets around the pharmacy to buy drugs from street-corner pushers. On the positive side, Hall noticed there were no competing pharmacies for six blocks, there were many doctors' clinics within one mile of the pharmacy, and many elderly people who would need his services lived in the neighborhood. He took the job and embarked on an adventure that occurs once in a lifetime. If you're lucky.

First, Hall went through the sales records left by the previous pharmacist and found that drugs were being sold in quantities and at prices that didn't make sense. In four weeks, for example, the pharmacy had filled 2,400 prescriptions, many for Preludin and much-abused codeine-based medicines, at $85 to $125 a pop—two to four times the usual price. Then he began to receive phone calls from people asking, "Can I get a script busted?"—meaning "Will you fill a fake prescription?" The owner of the café across the street told Hall he suspected the former pharmacist was selling drugs to addicts. He had seen line-ups at the back door at night.

Hall had never dealt with drug addicts and crooked doctors in the small town of Caruthers, although he was well aware of the vast market for illegal prescription drugs. He decided to report his findings to the

California Board of Pharmacy, which regulates pharmacists. He got nowhere with them.

Hall was pissed off, to say the least. He called the federal Drug Enforcement Administration and spoke with John Uncapher, an agent who specialized in prescription drug abuse. The next evening, Hall met with DEA agents in a car parked at a McDonald's restaurant near the pharmacy. He gave them the sales receipts and other paperwork that pricked his curiosity. The agents asked him to become a "pen pal." They asked him to write down everything he saw or heard, including license plate numbers and conversations. The DEA realized they had a rare opportunity to shut down a major prescription drug operation. They asked Hall to take a lie detector test and then they officially made him a confidential informant, code number 0012, in an investigation they labeled Operation Rx. It wasn't long before Hall was dubbed Rex. He wasn't paid to work undercover, since paid informers have little credibility in court. However, he still had his drugstore salary of $1,000 a week.

DEA agents knew there was a problem with prescription drug abuse in south-central Los Angeles because of a reporting system for commonly abused drugs that exists in many states and in the Canadian province of Alberta. Doctors must prescribe those drugs on a triplicate form that gets filed in a central registry. This allows the monitoring of unusual numbers of prescriptions and unusually busy doctors. Although the DEA could pinpoint certain suspect doctors, they knew that arresting a few doctors wouldn't solve the problem. They had to sweep an entire operation off the streets. Hall the pharmacist offered them that opportunity. If an illicit prescription drug network operated out of that pharmacy in the past, it would return when the pharmacy re-opened.

The DEA arranged to postpone issuance of the Slauson Avenue pharmacy license until a proper surveillance operation was set up and Hall was trained to work undercover. Most importantly, he learned how to work miniature tape recorders strapped to his ankles or hidden in his briefcase. He also learned to manoeuver suspects in rooms with two-way mirrors so they would face a camera.

The agency even rigged an apartment in Burbank to help Hall sting the doctors who wrote phony prescriptions. It was equipped with a two-way mirror and a video camera with monitors in the next apartment, which was occupied by narcs. They even invented a druggie airline attendant girlfriend who was never there because she was off working. But they did leave airline cookie packages in a bowl on a table. One of those narcs was Dale Ferranto of the California Bureau of Narcotics Enforcement. Besides being an expert on prescription drug abuse, he is one of

California's two court-recognized steroid experts and a pioneer in the crackdown on steroid manufacturing and smuggling.

Hall went into business on January 13, 1983, dressed in a T-shirt, jeans, and sneakers. He looked like the people who wanted his drugs. Within hours, word spread that scripts were being filled on Slauson Avenue. The store had been registered in the name of Floyd Brown during the previous druggist's tenure and transferred to that of his wife, Josephine, before Hall was hired. The couple had given Hall a list of fairly steep prices to charge for drugs. This confirmed Hall's suspicions that his customers were dopers; none of them ever complained about prices. Within days, greed took over and Floyd Brown was upping the prices. Sixty tablets of Preludin, which had sold for $72 when the store opened, now sold for $100. And then, "He told me to tell the Preludin customers that we were out of Preludin and that our order hadn't come in yet. Then, when the customers really wanted it bad, we could charge $120."

It wasn't long before the phone calls from phony clinics started. When they did, the phone rang every twenty minutes. They sent streams of patients over with prescriptions to be filled. The "patients" were actually runners for a large-scale drug operation run by high-level dealers called transporters who bought the clinics and the doctors as fronts to get the prescriptions. The transporters then had their pushers sell the prescription drugs to addicts. For example, a tablet of Dilaudid, a heroin substitute, could be bought at the pharmacy for about fifty cents. A pusher could sell it to a junkie for $55. The junkie crushed the tablet, cooked it in a spoon of water over a flame, and injected the solution. Doctors got rich filling prescriptions at $20 and $100 a pop—more than $1,000 a day—with names they picked from phone books; dealers got filthy rich; runners, who were often old people, made enough money to eat and pay their rent; pharmacists made their cut; and junkies got high.

Hall kept track of the doctors and clinics who called him. He always called them back—over a bugged telephone—to confirm they had written the prescription and to maintain that personal touch. Floyd Brown even took Hall on a tour of the area clinics to let them know the pharmacy welcomed their business.

That was the curious thing about Floyd. Even though he wasn't a pharmacist, he dispensed drugs. And the doctors always dealt with him. In fact, Floyd would sell drugs from the dispensary then buy prescriptions from doctors to cover them. After all, the state keeps track of drug sales and each tablet sold must be accounted for by a prescription.

But not all doctors dealt with Floyd Brown. With time, more of them started to deal with the easy-going pharmacist who invited them back to his Burbank apartment to talk shop. In the shady business of prescription drug trafficking, the doctors welcomed the opportunity to deal with a pharmacist who was up front with his crookedness. Hall let them know he was selling drugs out the back door, much as Brown was doing, and needed scripts to account for them. The doctors were only too willing to oblige—for cash. In all, Hall lured twenty-one people before the video camera that caught them in the act of breaking the law. One of those doctors was Dr. John Berrel Barnes, Jr., twenty-nine years old, a Yale Medical School postgraduate after obtaining an undergraduate degree at Princeton. He was the son of a dentist to boot. Barnes signed a lot of scripts for the Mar-Vel clinic run by Velveteen Jackson, a smooth-talking operator who sweet-talked doctors into the underworld.

"She said you let the doctor do the wrong, you never suggest it to him," Hall said.

Barnes's scripts were always written out to former patients so he couldn't be nailed for giving drugs to people who did not exist or whom he had never seen in his office. Barnes was on drugs the first night he visited Hall's apartment. Over a drink, he admitted, "I haven't been doing this . . . long, and when I came out of medical school, I just wanted to practice medicine." Then he added that he was just starting to understand how much the "dirty" stuff was worth.

"I'm learning too," said Hall.

"We got our license on the line," Barnes said. "Anyway, what you want to do?"

"I'd like to get about, uh, you can tell me what's fair, OK?" Hall said.

"All right," Barnes replied.

"I'd like to get, uh, say four Quaaludes, scripts for Quaaludes, and, uh, three, say for Preludins," Hall said.

With the video camera running, Barnes wrote out five prescriptions for Preludin and five for Quaaludes and charged Hall $100 for each. Hall gave Barnes $1,000 in marked $20 bills.

Hall came close to blowing his cover several times, but quick thinking saved him. Once, the bugged pharmacy phone went on the blink and someone called for a Pacific Bell repairman who surely would have found the bug. As the repairman walked into the pharmacy, Hall yanked the phone cord from the wall and pointed out that someone had probably tripped over it. While the repairman went for parts, a DEA agent posing as a repairman quickly fixed the phone. Another time, a clinic owner wanted to talk business with Hall. As they walked into the owner's office, Hall pressed the switch that turned on the tape recorder hidden in his briefcase. The owner turned on him.

"You wouldn't be recording me, would you, man?"

"Me?" said Hall. "Of course not."

"Open your briefcase."

Hall opened the briefcase and when the owner tried to sift through the contents, he pulled it away.

"If you don't trust me, forget it," Hall said. "We don't need your business that bad."

"Be cool," the owner said. And they made their deal.

DEA brass called in Ferranto and the other agent running Hall in December 1983. They feared he might not be a straight shooter. Ferranto called their bluff and offered to hand in his badge if Hall was a bad guy.

DEA brass had two worries: they were being buried in the accumulating evidence and they had allowed the pharmacist to write 10,000 prescriptions for hundreds of thousands of tablets that could kill someone and lead to a lawsuit against the state. They wanted to pull Hall in and can the operation. They figured they had enough evidence to make a sizeable dent in the south-central Los Angeles prescription drug business. They did.

On January 13, 1984, exactly one year after he had started filling phony scripts, Hall had to sneak into the pharmacy with Ferranto and the other agent in the middle of the night to steal the records of his sales and remove the phone bug. The pharmacy lights were connected to a timer so the trio worked by candlelight. Ferranto got so frustrated when he couldn't get the bug out of the phone he ripped it from the wall. Hall locked the door while the agents drove away. Then he walked out to the street to meet them. But he had forgotten which car they were driving and tried to hop into the first one that slowed down. Wrong car. He finally got into the right one and was spirited out of Los Angeles on a plane that night.

The next day, Hall's bloodstained Toyota pickup truck was found at Angeleno Avenue and 1st Street in Burbank. There was a bullet hole in the passenger window. The body was nowhere to be found. The store owners were quizzed by police about their pharmacist, who appeared to have been dealing with the wrong kind of people the previous night. The scuzbags in the prescription drug underworld figured Hall's luck had run out. Sixteen months later, after the evidence was reviewed and a case constructed, an indictment would be brought down that would send sixteen of them to jail and cause licensing authorities to revoke the licenses of nearly thirty doctors, nurses, and clinic owners.

When the case made headlines in May 1985, record keepers in the central registry noted a 14 percent drop in triplicate prescription forms. Doctors were reading the newspapers. As for Hall, he has a new name, a new face, a new drugstore in a new town, but he still drives the Toyota pickup.

Prescription drug addicts are a varied and imaginative lot. A housewife illegally quadruples her weekly Valium prescription by changing the doctor's 10 to 40 with two strokes of a pen. A poolhall punk pays $50 for a small bottle of codeine-based cough syrup to numb his senses. A nurse slips an ampule of pain-killing Demerol from the hospital dispensary into her pocket and later injects it into her upper arm. Prescription drug addicts, responsible for a multi-billion-dollar crime wave, come from all walks of life—housewives, doctors, pharmacists, nurses, students, cab drivers, welfare recipients, even old-age pensioners.

No one knows how many of these addicts there are. You can bet, though, that they're paying a terrible price to feed their chemical hunger. Many of them spend their entire day trying to get a drug and waiting for it to take effect. Attendance in drug treatment programs is an important measure of the problem's growth. When the drug therapy program started at the Addiction Research Foundation in Toronto in 1970, 95 percent of patients were heroin addicts. Today, half the patients are hooked on prescription narcotics.

Canada has an advantage over the United States in being able to keep track of and regulate abuses of the health care system—Canada has a health care system whereas the United States doesn't. Officials curious about abusers of prescription drugs asked the Ontario Health Insurance Plan computer to add up the number of people who visited ten or more doctors during a six-month period: 2,500 people. The average person may see two doctors during that time span.

Most people who make multiple visits to various medical offices are probably addicts. They go from doctor to doctor and con them with fake symptoms to get prescription drugs. There are three types of addicts: the street person who usually abuses drugs such as heroin but turns to prescription drugs during shortages; the medical addict who first used the drug for medical problems and can't stop taking it; the professional addict who works in a job where the drug is available—a hospital, doctor's office, or pharmacy—and succumbs because of personal problems and easy access to it.

Addicts prefer prescription drugs because they're the clean products of government-inspected laboratories. Unlike street drugs, they are never cut with chemicals such as cleansing powder. Prescription drugs are more readily available than street drugs. The chance of a ripoff, a constant fear in the drug world, is minimal. And there's less of a chance they'll be arrested for having a bottle with a label on it if stopped by police.

Prescription drug addicts are not deterred from committing criminal acts to get their drugs because the punishment is minimal. They know they will get a small fine but no jail term. Addicts convicted of more than eighty double-doctoring charges in two years pay their fines and return to the street.

As with illegal drugs, desperation determines how these addicts get drugs. Some are con artists who don't break into pharmacies but spend most of the day going from doctor to doctor. People addicted to Dilaudid tend to resort to breaking and entering and armed robbery. They will do anything when their supply is cut off. The armed robbers of drugstores don't want money, just drugs.

Many addicts also traffic prescription drugs to juveniles who get sucked into the drug scene. There's a big market in narcotic cough syrups, which sell for $50 to $60 for a four-ounce bottle. The average addict of these is between eighteen and twenty-nine years old. There are fewer older addicts around because the drugs exact a heavy toll. Over time they build up in the body and run it down.

Doctors, nurses, pharmacists, and veterinarians are better served by therapy programs than most addicts. The colleges that govern these professions spend a lot of money caring for their afflicted members. In Ontario, for example, physicians can turn to Doctors on Chemicals; nurses are helped through Project Turnabout. The College of Physicians and Surgeons in Ontario even has a full-time psychiatrist to help addicted doctors.

Even so, "there probably aren't enough treatment programs to handle health professionals who become addicted to drugs," said James Dunsdon, a pharmacist and deputy registrar of the Ontario College of Pharmacists. "Drug addiction was traditionally handled through the cancellation of licenses to practice. The punitive approach drove the problem underground. Now the focus is on treating the problem. The public doesn't want doctors and nurses who are impaired on the job."

Despite advances made in treating drug addicts, the grip of the chemical on the body and mind is difficult to break. "The salvage figure for drug addicts is very low," said Dr. John Carlisle, associate registrar in charge of investigation for the College of Physicians and Surgeons in Ontario. "Some professional addicts recover because they have the motivation to do so. They have a good job to return to. A kid on the street with no job does not care to be rehabilitated."

Natalie, a nurse with nine years' experience at a large hospital in a major city, had been branded a thief, a forger, a fraud artist, and a drug addict at thirty. Her friends and colleagues knew her only as an exemplary nurse and single mother who worked hard to support a four-year-old boy. Natalie started using Tylenol 1, with codeine. "I bought it over the counter. That's how a lot of drug-addicted nurses get started."

Within weeks, the pills no longer soothed her. She turned to other drugs at work. Every nursing area in a hospital has a locked narcotics cupboard and a medication cart. Nurses who need drugs for patients sign them out on their own.

"I tried Demerol [a painkiller]," Natalie said. "There was some left at work from a patient dosage. I took it home. I injected it. It made me feel pretty good. One can take quite a bit of Demerol and not look impaired. In a matter of weeks, I was stealing four or five ampules at a time. . . . I started forging names on the pharmacy record. I would make up a patient name and forge a nurse's name. I just altered documents to get what I wanted. I stole Demerol and morphine for six months."

Natalie emphasized that she never used drugs while working, only at home.

"Every day I went to work I took some ampules. My first theft was a 50-milligram ampule. I injected that. In a month, I was in trouble. I mentally felt I needed something. When you take Demerol, it feels good. You have a sense of still being in control. I never slurred words or bumped into walls. It was never evident I was on drugs. When my supervisor found out, she would not believe it was me [stealing the drugs]."

Natalie took morphine about ten times but disliked the nausea it gave her. Demerol was her drug. It comes in 50-, 75-, and 100-milligram ampules. Patients are given about 75 milligrams before going into surgery. Natalie injected herself in the upper arm or leg with 200 to 900 milligrams of Demerol regularly for six months with syringes she also stole from the hospital.

"I don't think I was physically addicted."

Hospital officials became suspicious when one nurse spotted her own signature, a forgery, on the list of nurses taking out narcotics for patients.

"It wasn't difficult for them to trace it to me," Natalie said. "You get sloppy after a while, after doing it for months and months. It's like a cry for help. You know you're going to get caught. You make mistakes. Every time you sign out drugs you're nervous, but you do it."

One day, three plainclothes police officers arrested Natalie as she walked home from the hospital. She was charged with theft, fraud, and forgery. She was convicted, given a suspended sentence, put on probation for two years, and ordered to undergo mandatory drug treatment for one year.

"I was relieved I was caught. 'The nightmare is over,' I thought. . . . I would have allowed myself to go down the tube if I had not been arrested."

The hospital did not fire her. After a month's attendance at a treatment program for nurses, a project run by a major addiction clinic, she was given a desk job with the promise of being able to resume her nursing duties.

Natalie believes she has learned to deal with her personal problems by talking about them and she thinks she can leave her addiction behind. But the stigma of being a drug addict and criminal will stay with her for life.

"Having a criminal record has sent my job portability down the tubes," Natalie said. "I've been turned down at several places." And facing the nurses whose signatures she forged has also been difficult. "Some of my colleagues are supportive, some are not. They feel angry I would jeopardize them by using their names to obtain what I needed. I don't blame them for being angry."

No one knows how many nurses are dependent on drugs—not even nursing associations or the addiction specialists who run the clinic where Natalie was treated. About fifty nurses a year seek help through the program Natalie attended.

"The problem with nurses and drugs is just starting to surface," Natalie said. "The number of substance abusers will increase. I can't see myself doing it again, but most of the girls in my group have gone back to drugs. For the first time in my life I feel alive. I went a long time without smiling."

No one knows how many drug-addicted nurses steal prescription drugs from hospital—a crime police consider serious because of the large number of patients who could be harmed. Addicted doctors and pharmacists also steal drugs, but usually from their own offices or store stock, causing little harm to anyone but themselves. But nurses who steal drugs from patients can endanger several hundred lives a year and damage a hospital's reputation.

Addicted nurses use several scams to obtain codeine-based drugs, cocaine, and Demerol from hospital dispensaries and patients. In one case, a nurse noticed the patient was prohibited from receiving narcotics. Because the record showed the patient had received narcotics before, the drugs could have been given to him, with deadly consequences.

Nurses of all ages become addicted. Their job makes them susceptible to drug abuse—shift work and the stress of having people die in their arms take their toll on many nurses. The drugs are readily available and the nurses are confident they know them. The drugs help them live with pain, help them get through a long night. First the addiction is psychological, then physical.

Their own professional code of behavior compounds the pressure.

"We feel we have to submerge our problems, turn our attention to other people, and be compassionate and understanding," said Janet Gaskin, who started a treatment program in 1983 to help drug- or alcohol-addicted Ontario nurses. "Nurses think they have to be in control and on top of things at all times. The truth is that we aren't. We hit rocky places in life like everyone else. If we accept this, then everything's OK. But if we have to pretend we're in control, that's stressful. The drugs enable you to keep going. Drugs allow you to forget problems and block out the pain and the agony — for a while. Then they create their own problems."

Most nurses who seek help have drinking problems. Drug thieves are less likely to admit to a drug problem because they would be admitting to criminal acts as well. "It's much easier to admit you're drinking too much than to say you're stealing drugs," Gaskin said. "Nurses who steal from hospitals feel bad not only about being drug abusers, but also because they steal. These are two good reasons to avoid seeking help."

In most such cases, police have been called in by hospital officials after pilfering was noticed. That one incident can lead a persevering investigator on a paper trail that uncovers dozens of thefts in a six-month period. While it is easier for nurses to steal drugs from patients, many still take the greater risk of falsifying documents to get dispensary drugs.

The College of Nurses in Ontario, which regulates the province's 130,000 registered nurses and 5,000 registered nursing assistants, doesn't distinguish in its statistics between drug and alcohol abuse. Fewer than twenty nurses a year have come to the college's attention for substance abuse. That figure does not reflect those who voluntarily seek treatment.

Similar programs exist for doctors and pharmacists. About one in four of Ontario's 22,000 doctors becomes addicted to drugs or alcohol, according to the College of Physicians and Surgeons in Ontario. Ten to 15 percent of Ontario's 7,000 pharmacists become dependent on alcohol or drugs, according to the Ontario College of Pharmacists.

Prescription Drug Dealers

Prescription drug dealers set up a phony doctor's office in Toronto in 1985 and printed prescription pads bearing the name of a fictitious doctor and his telephone number. Pharmacists filling the prescriptions were assured when checking with the issuing doctor's office, as required by law, that they were legitimate. The dealers bought large quantities of Talwin and Ritalin through this scheme.

Talwin is an opiate with the generic name pentazocine. It is popular both on the street and in jail. Ritalin, a trade name for methylphenidate, is administered to calm down children who are overactive because of their body chemistry. It will send a normal person right through the ceiling.

From March to May, these dealers collected 10,000 pills through forged prescriptions. At $12 (Cdn.) a pill on the Toronto streets, their three-month take was $120,000. When police caught on to them and searched the doctor's office, all they found was an empty apartment and a telephone. The phone was forwarding calls to another number that police couldn't trace. The dealers were eventually caught, but only through the investigation of another group. Nine people were charged with thirty-five drug offenses for obtaining 65,000 Talwin and Ritalin pills worth $780,000 (Cdn.) from 1983 to 1986.

There is no end to the methods dealers and addicts will use to get drugs. Forging prescriptions and double or multiple doctoring are by far the safest and most common ways to get prescription drugs. Double-doctoring requires skill and moxie. It capitalizes on doctors' training to believe their patients and on their desire to heal.

"The scam is a one-on-one con between the patient and the doctor," said Corporal David Marinier, formerly on the prescription drug unit of the Royal Canadian Mounted Police drug squad in Toronto. The con is usually direct pressure put on the doctor for a problem that has only a drug solution—pressure that is difficult to deal with in a busy practice when pressed for time. "The patient is a drug seeker," Corporal Marinier said. "When he walks into the doctor's office, he knows what medication he wants. He will manipulate the doctor so he doesn't see he's a drug seeker. He'll say he's allergic to certain drugs to limit the choice of prescriptions. An addict who wants morphine will tell a dentist he's allergic to codeine or oxycodone."

Addicts prepare themselves well. They buy prescription drug compendiums that explain what pills contain the drugs they want and what symptoms they treat. The librarians at the Metro Toronto Reference Library can't keep the annual *Compendium of Pharmaceuticals and Specialties (CPS)* or the *Canadian Medical Directory*, with names, addresses, and phone numbers of all doctors in the country, on the shelf. They're stolen as soon as they're put out.

There's also a mimeographed sheet circulating in Toronto that shows how to write a prescription and what doctors' names to use. It also provides sample signatures of all staff members at a Toronto hospital, stolen from a hospital file.

An addict who wants an opiate or other painkiller fakes an illness for which these drugs would be prescribed. A fake patient complains of lower back pain, painful urination, and sometimes passing blood—the classic symptoms of kidney stones, which are treated with a painkiller.

The doctor asks for a urine sample. The patient urinates in the bottle and pricks his finger to add a drop of blood to the urine. The urinalysis and textbook symptoms persuade the doctor to prescribe painkillers to the patient.

One drug scam artist convicted for his offense visited thirty-one doctors and dentists in three months in early 1985 and got 665 tablets of hydromorphone—Dilaudid. The heroin substitute sells for about $1 a tablet at the pharmacy and up to $50 a pill on the street. One woman got prescriptions from 300 doctors in one year.

Some addicts travel a circuit. One group of drug dealers traveled across Ontario with crutches, canes, and tricks to fake symptoms to get drugs. Addicts put pepper in their noses and salt water in their lungs to fool doctors.

Even people passing forged prescriptions have a routine. A young woman walks into a busy pharmacy with a baby in arms. She may injure the baby to make it start squealing. The pharmacist's automatic reaction is to fill out the prescription and get the baby out of the store as quickly as possible.

A couple walks into a pharmacy. One person fakes a convulsion to draw people's attention. The accomplice goes to the pharmacy and steals pills. The guy on the floor then has a miraculous recovery. Once in Manitoba, a doctor called a pharmacy to say he'd written a prescription for 100 Demerol tablets for a man who would pick up the drugs. Still uneasy when the man showed up, the pharmacist called the doctor at the number listed in the telephone book. The doctor confirmed the prescription. Later that night, the still uneasy pharmacist called the doctor at home. The doctor said he had not been in the office all day. His office telephone had been call-forwarded to another number.

Addicts capitalize on everyone's trust. They use aliases, stolen identification, and false addresses. Because many doctors do not look at the patient's documents, addicts often read off a fake government health insurance number. The doctor does not find out he's been had until three months later when the health plan informs him the bill could not be processed.

The Friday Night Caper requires the moxie of sophisticated addicts. They break into doctors' offices in shopping centers, usually on Friday night or Saturday, and write ten to twelve prescriptions, which runners present to pharmacies. The script writers are versed in Latin terms, spelling, and dosages of drugs. And anyone can fake the garble that is a doctor's signature. A woman left in the doctor's office answers calls from pharmacists checking the validity of the prescription. Then she locks up the office without leaving any trace of a break-in. A variation on this scam has the telephone number of a phone booth printed on the fake prescription. An accomplice answers the phone pretending to be the doctor's receptionist.

A particularly brazen addict walked into a downtown Toronto pharmacy in the summer of 1989 and claimed to be an agent for all the residents of a nearby senior citizens' apartment building. He got 300 fake prescriptions filled in sixty days. A team of scam artists swarmed through Toronto in the summer of 1989 seeking Ritalin, which gives adult users an intense high when mixed with a prescription painkiller. They told doctors in medical clinics they suffered from narcolepsy, a sleeping disorder. They usually asked for 20-milligram tablets, which sell on the streets for $20 apiece.

The street dealers of prescription drugs often don't have to look far to find the chemicals. Dying cancer patients in Columbia, South Carolina, sold their prescription painkillers to a drug ring in 1990 to pad their wallets.

"It's a pitiful sight," said Sergeant Raymond Lee of the West Columbia Police Department. "They're so poor they're willing to take an Aspirin and put up with the pain."

The cancer patients at Veterans Administration Hospital were given Dilaudid free to ease their suffering in the months before they died. One patient made $2,500 a month selling his pills. Dealers who bought from patients befriended those who wouldn't sell and simply stole their pills. Relatives of patients also stole pills, which they sold to dealers for $25 apiece. The dealers sold the Dilaudid pills to heroin addicts for $40. Users crushed the pills into powder and injected them.

Dying patients in Winnipeg, Manitoba, hospitals also sold their painkillers in 1989. There is little surveillance of dying patients, who are given high doses of painkillers, because no one cares if they become addicted. Some of the patients sold their drugs to leave behind an inheritance.

Perhaps the most morbid scam is perpetrated by prescription drug addicts who read obituary notices to find out what diseases people died of. They know what drugs are used in most cases. If it's the drug they want, they'll knock on the door of someone who just died and pretend they're from the hospital, the doctor's office, or the Bureau of Dangerous Drugs. They say they're there to take the drugs off their hands. Cedomir Jovanovic, a thirty-one-year-old Toronto man, sold his dead mother's leftover liquid morphine in 1990. Unfortunately for him, he sold it and a quarter pound of grass to an undercover cop.

Besides continuing police efforts across Canada and the United States, only the province of Alberta and a handful of American states are directly engaged in combatting the burgeoning abuse of prescription drugs with their triple script programs that help identify drug abusers. Instead of filling out one copy of a prescription, doctors in Alberta and several states fill out three—one for the doctor's files, one that the patient gives the pharmacist, and one for the licensing association that regulates doctors.

The association uses a computer to detect patients who visit too many doctors for treatment of the same ailment. The association then alerts doctors to these patients. The computer also points out soft doctors—those who prescribe too often to the same people. This allows the association to investigate whether the doctor is being duped or is in league with an addict.

Law-enforcement agencies and health officials are responsible for curbing prescription drug abuse. Pharmacists in Canada are legally bound to report a loss of drugs within ten days to the Bureau of Dangerous Drugs. They must also record and report all sales. Every two months, the pharmacist sends a sales register to a screening service that gleans any irregularities in prescriptions or sales. Even this program is not foolproof. Four million prescriptions are written every year in Canada. They can't all be scrutinized. If an inquiry by the bureau suggests criminal activity, the Royal Canadian Mounted Police are called in.

Some local police forces have implemented their own programs to deal with prescription drug abuse. The Niagara Regional Police Force, which polices the area of Ontario across from Buffalo, New York, has an early warning system for the area's hundred drugstores. It is a pyramid-type alarm network. A pharmacist who becomes aware of an abuser calls two others, who each call two other pharmacists until all drugstores have been notified. Police and addiction experts address medical and pharmacy students about what drugs are in demand and who the abusers are.

When a narc like Dale Ferranto wraps up an intricate and extensive prescription drug abuse case like that involving David Hall's Slauson Avenue Pharmacy, you figure that's the apex of his career. How much more exciting does drug busting get?

Well, Ferranto gazed into his crystal ball and predicted that steroids would become a major drug problem with the Me Generation. Then he went back to school and wrote his Master's thesis on performance-enhancing drugs. His superiors gave him little support and recognition for his effort, perhaps because steroids, like prescription drugs, don't have the sex appeal of cocaine and speed.

Today, Ferranto is one of two law-enforcement steroid experts in California. His services are much sought after. In the wake of the Ben Johnson scandal at the 1988 Seoul Olympics, pressure is mounting to clean up athletics across North America. For Dale Ferranto, it's not a case of being in the right place at the right time. It's a case of being ready for what his instincts warned him were looming on the ever-expanding drug horizon.

16

Wackos Anonymous:
Tales from the edge

"Janis Joplin was a friend of mine. Jimi Hendrix was a friend of mine. John Belushi was at least an acquaintance of mine. Cass Elliot was one of my best friends. These people are all dead from drugs—and I went right ahead and did it."
– DAVID CROSBY WASTED TEN YEARS OF HIS LIFE WITH DRUGS AND DESTROYED A SUPERSTAR CAREER BUILT WITH THE SUPERBANDS THE BYRDS AND CROSBY, STILLS, AND NASH. HE HAS SINCE GONE STRAIGHT AND IS A VOCAL OPPONENT OF DRUG USE, ESPECIALLY COCAINE.

Welcome to the home of Vito (Beetle) Rodriguez, a heroin addict in Stockton, California, who, after showing off a bunch of neat guns and making threats to kill people, will take you into his tiny bathroom, cook some horse, and shoot up within inches of your face—while giving a running commentary, of course. If you still think dopers are normal people after spending time inside Beetle's head, donate your brain to a dog food factory.

Beetle and a weird friend I'll call Beardo are waving their rifles around proclaiming the creation of a new outlaw motorcycle gang called the Cherokee-Chocktaw Vikings. (No offense to the real gang, which exists somewhere in California.)

"In order to become a member of this organization, you have to execute a rat," Beardo said. Remember these words and who said them.

Off to the side a diapered baby no more than a year old cradled a baby pit bull terrier.

A clear plastic bag of heroin was dangled in front of the baby's nose. "This is like Dr. Scholl's foot powder," said a voice in the background.

Beardo sat on the bed with an M-1 carbine in his right hand and the baby in the other. "We're a brother club of the Hell's Angels Motorcycle Club of California, but I think we're tougher than the Hell's Angels," he said. I don't really want to hear this, considering my first book was an investigative history of that gang.

"This guy here was named after Sonny Barger, the originator of the

Hell's Angels," Beardo said, nodding at the kid. In fact, Sonny Barger joined the Hell's Angels in 1955, eight years after the club was formed. He did, however, become its most prominent member.

"You know how to drive a nigger crazy?" called a voice from the background. All kinds of people came and went as this conversation progressed. "Put him in a round room and tell him his chick's in the corner."

Beardo: "We will leave an imprint in society. We're definitely a strong organization. We don't like rats. We don't like police. My theory is kill them all. Let God sort them out."

Beetle brandished several rifles. "This is for the Puerto Rican revolution. The revolution against rats, Secret Service, FBI. We're ready for them this time. They've been screwing me around all my life. Anybody. We'll take the Angels on and send them to hell."

They walked around the kitchen smoking a joint and aiming their rifles at imagined enemies. "They'd love wearing this up their ass," someone said of an M-1.

Beetle, holding up an indictment, continued his tirade. "These papers here are what they call hanging papers. They want to hang a Puerto Rican."

Four armed Puerto Ricans stomped around the room. Beardo brandished a rifle and a sword. Someone pointed two rifles at the front door. "Do I get the first or second fed that comes in or both?"

Beetle and Sonny's mother proudly stood up their toddler, tucked a .25-caliber semi-automatic pistol into the front of his diaper, and taught him to draw the gun.

The next thing you know, Beetle was in the bathroom showing off his tattoos as he rolled up his sleeves. "This here is the ex-old lady's name. This is my son's name. This here my daughter's name."

Then he whipped out a bag. "This here is Puerto Rican medicine. Dr. cure-all specialty. This here is the real works to make your bones feel good." He took out the hypodermic needle, heroin, a grungy spoon, a knife and lighter, talking all the while.

"Put a little water on this little nail we got here. You ever seen yachts and Rolls-Royce all put together in one, uh? Check out these arms. See these little tracks here, there are plenty of yachts, mansions. Over the years I spent all kinds of mansions, you know what I mean? All kinds.

"Let's do a little medicine here. OK. I got a cold and this is going to make my cold feel better."

He unwrapped the plastic bag of heroin.

"It also makes my rod get hard. This is my cure-all for common colds. Guarantees you never get a cold. Use this every day you never get sick. Don't use it you get sick." He giggled.

He took the powder out of the bag with the knife blade and tapped it into the spoon by the sink. He squirted water from the needle twice into the spoon. Then he heated the spoon over the lighter.

"A little fire. Fire's a cure-all to germs and everything that's in the water. You don't want no germs. Come on, baby, light my fire. This stuff, man, I get a hard-on don't want to go down. It's stronger than penitentiary steel. And penitentiary steel is strong too."

He scraped the residue around the edge of the spoon into the solution. He added a clot of Kotex to the solution to filter out the grit as he sucked the liquid into the needle.

"Now we've got the situation under control. Put a little water on it to cool it down." He held the loaded needle under the tap next to a Blues Brothers tape. "There's about $1,200 there," he said, pointing to the bag of heroin.

"Now I got to find the right track I want to travel down." He searched his forearm in vain for veins. He slapped them. He cocked his right arm back. "Tracks are a little hard to come by. I like traveling. I like going all over. See this ring here," he said, indicating his left ring finger. "This ring given by a friend of mine. Fourteen-carat diamond." Bullshit.

He clenched his fist and had someone massage his forearm. "Got to make a vein pop up. Must make a vein pop up. Let's see if we can draw some blood into it. Angel's medicine. All right. I think we got a winner there." He tapped the needle into a vein on top of his left wrist. "Oh, yes." Blood flowed into the needle and filled it. He injected the bloody solution.

"I feel good. There. There it goes." His eyes glazed over and seemed to fade into the background of his pencil-thin mustache and the scraggly beard hanging from his chin.

"Adios, class is over. Now I feel good. I feel damn good now. I don't have a wrong in the world. This here makes me feel good every time and I'm horny."

Two weeks later, Beetle and the boys were busted. The first guy to roll over and rat? Beardo the rat killer.

Garry Murphy and Paul Cherrie sat in front of the tube in late July 1990, downing a few brews and flipping through the channels looking for an interesting show. Well, check this out—a documentary on toads, man. Cherrie was a reptile and amphibian freak. He collected them in his Toronto home. Murphy, legally blind, couldn't see what Cherrie was excited about, but he sure could hear it.

The brown South American cane toad—*bufus marinus*—produces a milky white liquid from its warts that can cause hallucinations.

Hot damn. Cherrie was beside himself. Hot damn. He had a genuine, eight-year-old, two-pound warty drugstore with hallucinogenic lumps right there in his collection.

"G'wawn."

"Yaaa."

Cherrie rushed out to get the little devil and brought him back with some cookies.

Cherrie ran his finger over the toad, gently squeezing the warts, and smeared the fluid on a cookie. He tasted it and gave the cookie to Murphy.

"He told me it was LSD, so I ate it," Murphy later said. Nothing happened for an hour. Murphy drank a few more beers.

WHAM!!! Holy jumpin' Jesus. Ontogeny recapitulated philogyny on the experiential plane and Murphy tripped back to a time before the brain's hemispheres were linked. He kept going, reaching farther back. Hell, farther back, when the brain was a critical cortical mass. He slid back into the slime—a quivering medulla oblongata thrashing in the ooze.

"Next thing I know I'm in the hospital."

Bufotenine may give great hallucination, but it is also toxic and causes seizures and vomiting. Murphy was treated with anti-convulsive and anti-inflammatory drugs to control seizures, blood pressure, and respiratory problems. Cherrie fared better. He was treated and released. Murphy's seizures continued.

His brother was incredulous. "You mean he sucked that toad?"

The toad was donated to the Metro Zoo and quarantined for thirty days.

After several days, Murphy checked himself out of hospital against doctor's orders. He had suffered fifteen convulsions and was still on medication.

"If a kid tried this, he'd be a goner," Murphy said. "Take it from a guy who tried it—it'll kill you. Don't lick toads."

A few days later, Murphy admitted himself to the psychiatric ward of Scarborough Grace Hospital because the toxin was still working him over. Somehow, Murphy's mind kept traveling back in time and he didn't like what he saw. He hanged himself on August 10 with the belt from his hospital gown.

Susan Barbier woke her thirteen-year-old daughter on May 8, 1988, and drove her through the Detroit streets to the apartment of Anthony Sawyer, a crack cocaine dealer she owed money to. The thirty-year-old mother of four paid her debt. She let Sawyer rape the girl. She traded her daughter's virginity for crack cocaine.

"[The girl] stands before the court today with a broken heart," Kelly

Ramsay, Assistant Wayne County prosecutor, said at Barbier's trial. "Mothers are supposed to protect their children against the hurt of society. Now this child can only dream of what a real mother should be."

The girl was too upset to read in court a statement in which she asked that Barbier be kept in jail long enough to prevent her from hurting the two youngest children, ages six and eight. Barbier got a life sentence. The drug dealer got forty to sixty years.

A twenty-three-year-old female crack addict met dealer Neville Douglas at a Toronto crack house in April 1988. She had no money. He offered her crack for a ride to another apartment. He put a knife to the woman's throat when they got to her car and made her drive to a park. He made her smoke crack and raped her. Then Douglas took the woman to an apartment where he made her suck his cock several times.

"I kept asking him to let me leave. He said I could leave when I learned how to do it right."

The woman escaped the following night, but the nightmare wasn't over—she was pregnant by her rapist, a man who had already fathered five children by three women. She had an abortion. Her fiancé and family disowned her.

"I have nothing. My father, his exact words to me were, he can't even stand to look at me, that looking at me makes him sick to his stomach."

Ricardo Aguilar walked the streets of Toronto late at night on September 8, 1990, stoned and horny. The twenty-five-year-old drifter was looking for a woman. He tried for two hours to break into six houses, forcing doors, looking for unlocked windows. He scaled a building wall near the University of Toronto and slipped into an apartment through an open window. There he hovered over a twenty-two-year-old woman he found in bed. He undressed, slid in beside her, and attacked. The noise woke her boyfriend in the next room and Aguilar fled. He was caught and sentenced to one year in jail.

Thirty-nine-year-old Christine Martin had an older lover, sixty-one-year-old Richard Alfredo. She surprised him after dinner in January 1990 with a green gelatin desert. Alfredo's heart rate and blood pressure went berserk after he ate it. Police say that Martin had laced it with copious amounts of LSD. Alfredo died of a heart attack. Martin was charged with murder.

A twenty-three-year-old crack addict walked into a Kansas City, Missouri, bar in late September 1989 and told a dealer she wanted a $20 piece of crack cocaine but had no money.

"I sure would like to have a baby boy," the woman dealer said.

They walked out to make the deal. The dealer walked back into the bar with the baby. A sharp-eyed woman who realized what had happened asked if she could hold the baby. Then she ran off with it and turned it over to the police.

William and Tracy Melton were arrested in a van parked in front of a Rockville, Maryland, Baptist church on March 31, 1980, by police answering a complaint about a screaming woman. The two were frisked and charged with possession of cocaine, marijuana, and LSD. William, twenty-seven, and his twenty-one-year-old wife were convicted. Friends expected them to be sentenced to a few months in a minimum security jail that rehabilitates drug offenders, though possession of cocaine can fetch twenty years in jail.

The courtroom was packed with parents and relatives the day of their sentencing. William put a white powder in his mouth and fell to the floor. While court officers attended to him, Tracy put a white powder in her mouth and keeled over. They had committed suicide with cyanide.

"They weren't even going to get a long sentence," circuit court clerk Howard Smith said. "You bet we're shocked. Nothing like this has ever happened in this courtroom before."

Dopers can sometimes be funny in court.

A Regina, Saskatchewan, judge had just finished speaking to a man who pleaded guilty to possessing marijuana about the danger of drugs. He asked the man if he had anything to say. The man flipped open a wallet taken from his back pocket and said, "Scotty, beam me up."

When the Ottawa city police found more than one pound of marijuana in Cindy Havens's house, they charged her with possession for the purpose of trafficking. No, no, Havens said. The marijuana is for the iguana. Then Havens pulled out Pogo, a two-foot long cannabis-cruncher. She swore she didn't know the stuff was marijuana. She just picked this green stuff in nearby Renfrew and the lizard loved it. Police identified the weed as Gatineau Gold, a local, low-potency pot not worth selling. Police argued in court, however, that Pogo wouldn't touch the stuff when Havens offered to show them it was all he ate.

"Was it the poor quality?" asked the judge, who let Havens off lightly with a $500 fine for possession.

Theron Morris and his wife Leila moved to Pompano Beach, Florida, after a long working life. They could have been anyone's grandparents. He was seventy-two. She was fifty-eight. He had been an engineer for Chrysler Corp. She had worked for United Airlines for twenty-three years. Three years later, their son Christopher was released from jail. He had been locked up on drug and assault charges. Theron and Leila accepted him into their home until they found him a place to live. They also bought him a car. Most of all, they tried to help him break his addiction to cocaine.

Police said they had a strange way of helping their son, who allegedly sold them $1,000 of fake cocaine they had planned to resell. Police also alleged that Chris and his former prison friend Martin Rector figured out an easy way to make money. They decided to kill Chris's former wife and her ten-year-old daughter to collect on a $35,000 insurance policy. They allegedly convinced Chris's parents to help them out.

Rector allegedly knocked on Sharon Morris's door posing as a flower delivery man. She wouldn't answer because he wasn't wearing a uniform. Then Rector and Chris's parents found out that the insurance policy on Sharon had lapsed. They allegedly decided to kill Chris. He was insured for $70,000.

One night at Theron Morris's house, Rector allegedly pulled a silencer-equipped .38-caliber revolver on Chris and made him lie on the floor. Theron allegedly tied Chris up with duct tape and helped load him into the car's back seat. Chris broke free. Rector allegedly shot him three times. Chris ran away. His father and friend chased him, told him they would take him to hospital, drove him to the town of Coconut Creek, and allegedly shot him three more times and left the body in the car. Then Rector allegedly conned John Woods, a drunken drifter, into confessing to the killing.

"I've been doing homicide for twelve years," said sheriff's deputy Lieutenant Tom Carney. "It's the strangest, most cold-blooded murder I've ever seen. It seems they were upstanding citizens, never had a brush with the law. They look just like any other grandparents you would find any place in the country."

David Aupont moved to Brooklyn from Haiti in late 1988. Eighteen months later, the twelve-year-old was taken to a neighborhood garage used by drug addicts and ordered to smoke crack cocaine. He refused and the thirteen-year-old boy who gave the order tied his hands behind his back, beat him with a baseball bat, doused him with a flammable liquid, and set him on fire. More than half his body was burned.

The Soviets and the Americans have a common problem along their respective shorelines on the Bering Sea—decapitated walruses are washing up by the hundreds. It seems that young Inuit (Eskimos) in Alaska have added another North American fad to their culture: drugs. Since Inuit in many communities have little use for the American dollar, or little chance to earn it, they've resorted to the time-honored barter system to get their fur-lined mitts on ganja fire sticks. Inuit dopers trade a walrus skull with two tusks for six joints of marijuana. Those ivory tusks, each the size of a man's leg, fetch $800 on the American black market. Sell it to the Arabs and you're filthy rich. The dopers skim their swift little skiffs across the Bering Sea—within sixty miles of comrade Boris at its narrowest—and plug hundreds of walruses with their .22-caliber rifles. They drag the carcasses onto ice floes and sever the heads with chain saws. Inuit are allowed to hunt without licenses and their artists are allowed to own ivory, which they carve. Black market ivory traders take advantage of this and shack up with female artists whose rights shield them from US Fish and Wildlife authorities who may find their huge stock of ivory.

Bob Heffernan was a soft-spoken English teacher who had suffered the taunts of students for twenty years at Troy Athens High School, in Troy, Michigan. Several students ambushed him in 1976 and cut off one side of a splendid handlebar mustache he had grown for the US bicentennial. Teachers described the pranks played on the forty-six-year-old man as cruel rather than humorous. "He is literally a persecuted man," said a fellow teacher.

He was in the habit of sipping coffee from a mug while teaching. After drinking his coffee during one class in the second week of December 1990, Heffernan fell to the floor convulsing and hallucinating. He thought he was having a fatal heart attack. Students had spiked his coffee with LSD.

A fourteen-year-old boy in Surrey, British Columbia, beat twelve-year-old Shawn Tirone to death with a rock in a wooded park on July 16, 1989, for cheating him on a drug deal. Although twenty youths knew about the murder, they said nothing and the body wasn't found until the following April 1. The killer bragged to friends he had killed a boy called Shawn. He told some kids the boy was bugging him all the time. He told others that Tirone kept $250 he had given him to buy drugs. Why did the other youths keep their mouths shut?

"I didn't want it to be true. I thought it was, but I didn't want it to be," said a sixteen-year-old youth.

"I wasn't sure what to believe," said a fifteen-year-old girl. "It just didn't seem like a fourteen-year-old would be able to kill someone." The maximum sentence for a youthful murderer in Canada is three years in jail.

Patricia Lelli and her husband Kelly McCarthy ran a crack house in their

Toronto apartment. For that they lost their two oldest children to the Children's Aid Society. Both were under three years of age. They gave up their youngest child, six-month-old Andrew, in late 1990 so he could be properly cared for.

"We're trying our best," Lelli said on December 6, 1990. "We're already saving money for them. We're trying to make a good life for them because we know we won't be around."

McCarthy, twenty-seven, became infected with the AIDS virus in 1984 while using a contaminated needle to inject heroin. He didn't know he had the virus until he developed severe headaches in June 1990. By then, he had infected his thirty-four-year-old wife through sexual intercourse. Lelli surprised a routine health board meeting discussing women and AIDS when she stepped forward and asked if she could speak.

"Anybody can catch it. What's so sad is it doesn't just affect one individual," she said. "The person has relationships, they have a family, it affects the whole family."

McCarthy didn't expect to live much longer. Lelli has been too afraid to return to the doctor since she tested positive for the virus. Their six-month-old son also tested positive, which is why they gave him up. Lelli and McCarthy knew they wouldn't be around to help their children through life. They wanted their children to know the horrendous costs of drug abuse.

"We are leaving a videotape for them which warns them to stay away from drugs and telling them about our situation," Lelli said. "We're trying to leave a lot behind for them—mainly warnings of not to do drugs and what can happen to them."

The dying couple asked Toronto mayor Art Eggleton to ensure that drug dealers are evicted from public housing projects like the one they lived in.

The traditional stereotype of the North American Indian as a bottle-clutching alcoholic on skid row is slowly changing to one in which the Indian clutches a hypodermic needle. A Canadian federal government report in December 1990 revealed a tragic increase of AIDS among native people that threatens to rival the devastating effect the disease has had in some African and Caribbean countries. Three factors explain the rapid spread of AIDS among native people; a high incidence of intravenous use of drugs such as cocaine, Talwin, and Ritalin—40 percent of 4,000 registered intravenous drug users in Vancouver are native; an incidence of sexually transmitted diseases four times the national average; and immune systems as weakened as those of people in the Third World through fighting a variety of illnesses.

The US Centers for Disease Control found that AIDS cases in US native Indians increased 91 percent from 1988 to 1990—more than any other racial group. What do these findings mean? AIDS is changing from a disease of white upper-middle-class gay men to a disease of the heterosexual under-class, thanks to intravenous drug use.

At least one Toronto doper a week catches the AIDS virus from a shared contaminated needle. AIDS prevention community groups want politicians to allow widespread needle exchange programs to ensure addicts have clean needles. Metro Toronto Police endorse needle-exchange programs run only by the city, not by community groups. The city program—The Works—has been distributing needles from a van since 1989. Perhaps the war against drugs would be better served by withholding clean needles and letting the fear of contracting AIDS from dirty needles deter drug use.

An inmate at Long Bay maximum security prison in Sydney, Australia, walked up behind a twenty-one-year-old prison guard, Geoffrey Pearce, in July 1990, jabbed a hypodermic needle into his ass and ran off yelling, "AIDS!"

"He stuck the needle in my backside and I knocked it out straight away, practically," Pearce said. "I ran straight into the supervisor's office, dropped my pants and one of the officers squeezed out the blood and washed it off with disinfectant."

Six weeks later, he tested positive for the human immunodeficiency virus (HIV) and has a 50-50 chance of developing AIDS in the next ten years.

"There's no use dwelling on what might have been or what happened or making yourself unhappy," he said. "Just because I am HIV positive doesn't mean I am going to die next week or whenever."

Twenty guards resigned and thousands went on strike when the incident was publicized. Six guards in Australian prisons have been stabbed with needles purported to contain the AIDS virus. Drug-using prisoners rioted when the guards started taking away their needles.

Brendan Rooney was the executive assistant to the vice-president of Ryerson Polytechnical Institute in Toronto. Higher learning was his career. So was getting high. He liked blotting out reality with opium and heroin, a costly pastime. Rooney embarked on a second career to pay for his habit—he robbed banks. He hit eight banks in twenty-one days for $17,000. His moonlighting ended when he ran into another careerist—a hold-up squad detective staking out a bank. Rooney embarked on a third career in 1990 when a judge sentenced him to six years behind bars.

Police in Hillside, New Jersey, had a cow in the summer of 1990 when they discovered that Bart Simpson stamps being circulated in the state were laced with LSD, which could be absorbed through the skin.

It's a rare year when LSD stamps bearing cartoon characters don't appear on the market. But try finding someone who has ever seen one. Where are they sold? Who makes them? Why would anyone give LSD away for free? Can you say "philatelist"?

Kids do the darnedest things. In August 1990 an eleven-month-old Toronto boy found some blotting paper among his father's belongings and played with it as any child would, scrunching and mashing it with his tiny little hands while his parents slept. Then the kid's world got bright and colorful and bizarre creatures came walking through the walls.

Well, they probably did, but the child couldn't really tell anyone about them because he couldn't talk. His parents took him to hospital for treatment of the LSD that soaked into his pores from the blotter. Daddy was charged with possession of LSD for trafficking.

Parents do the darnedest things, too. Police raided the house of a forty-one-year-old Toronto man in September 1990, looking for drugs. There was a little scuffle and a police officer dislocated his knee. The cops couldn't find any drugs—until one officer checked the lump in a one-year-old kid's diaper. He found 20 grams of cocaine and 3.5 grams of heroin snuggled up to the baby's bottom.

Timothy Rees told Toronto cops he killed his friend's ten-year-old daughter in March 1989 to get her "away from all the b.s." Rees was at a party given by Darla Thurcott's parents.

"I don't know what was in my head," Rees told police. "Everybody was sitting around partying and I got . . . up. I have a problem with cocaine and booze. I'm like Jekyll and Hyde. When I'm straight, I'm a nice person. . . . I went to her room, sat on her bed and strangled her. I choked her. She kind of went limp. She made a little squeak sound and then she went limp. Then I more or less sat there and told her no one would hurt her any more."

A pathologist said the girl had bruises around her anus and her corpse may have been sexually assaulted.

Giovanni Marinaro had an insatiable craving for crack cocaine on March 23, 1989. Marinaro was a tile-setter who spent most of his money on crack. He ran out of money while smoking in a Toronto crack house and begged and pleaded for a loan before being told to leave. The twenty-seven-year-old man was in tears that night as he walked into the apartment of his friend, Mario Cittadini, to borrow money. Cittadini refused and they started to fight. Cittadini pulled a knife. Marinaro wrested it from him and stabbed him eleven times. He stole a $50 bill and $10 in change from his buddy. Marinaro returned to the crack house with blood on his hands and face—and Cittadini's blood-stained watch.

Daniel Allain was a hyper, bouncy doper with needle marks in his arms and a hole in his wallet in July 1989. He visited a male friend who, along with a roommate, had a steady job. Allain drugged them, tied their hands behind their backs, and dragged them into the bathroom where he left one face down on the floor and the other in the bathtub. Then he tortured the men until they revealed their bank card numbers so he could withdraw thousands of dollars from their accounts. Then he ripped off their Toronto apartment. He untied his victims after a long weekend of horror. They were too frightened to call police.

In the meantime, Allain, accompanied by a Doberman pinscher, balanced a knife on the shoulder of another friend's mother and told her the dog would attack if she moved. He stole $120 in cash and $3,000 in jewelry from her. Allain pressed his luck when he returned to harass the two roommates; they finally called the police. Now Allain has a roommate of his own behind bars.

Daniel Brown started buying dope from street dealers in Corunna, Michigan, in the spring of 1990. He made more than 100 buys from fifty dealers. Well into September, Brown invited his new buddies to his wedding to the daughter of a big drug dealer. The music was to be provided by Spoc and guests were asked to check guns and knives at the door. After the band had played the song "I Fought the Law and the Law Won," the bride lifted her white gown and pulled a .38-caliber revolver from a leg holster. Police officers around the room were asked to identify themselves. All other guests were arrested in a sting that caught fifteen drug dealers. Police would have arrested more dealers, but Brown busted five of them the afternoon of the wedding and they warned others. Spoc is cops spelled backwards.

Some people just don't hold up under stress. A Volkswagen van stopped at a light in Miami Beach on August 4, 1990, rolled backwards as the driver shifted into gear, and bumped the car behind it. The car's driver flagged down a cop. The van's driver disappeared. The cop found 1,544 pounds of cocaine bricks worth $14 million in the van. Those hippies don't travel light. Personal use, man. Personal use.

A Bristol, Rhode Island, pizza shop's motto was "Nobody delivers better." A narc walked into the shop in January 1991 and ordered a pizza. He also asked for a bag of marijuana. "Sure, wait a minute," said an employee who got a bag from the manager. The narc took the pizza and the manager to go.

Earl Brown was on coke the night he heard voices telling him to take a two-year-old boy from a playground where he was playing with his sister and two brothers and take him home to his mother. The twenty-three-year-old Toronto schizophrenic grabbed the boy in September 1990 and walked away with him. The sister ran to neighbors who ran after Brown and rescued the toddler. Brown followed the neighbors to the kid's home and insisted the boy was his.

An eight-year-old Chicago girl didn't find mommy kissing Santa Claus under the Christmas tree in December 1990. She found a bloody butcher knife next to her mother's body. Inez Williams, thirty-seven, had a sock stuffed in her mouth, had had her throat slashed, and had been stabbed in the back and neck. A two-year-old girl Williams was babysitting cried from her stab wounds. Police searched the upstairs apartment and found bloody clothing hidden behind the fridge. They hit the streets and arrested a man trying to sell a Nintendo video game set and a clock radio stolen from underneath the Christmas tree. He was selling the presents for drug money.

Ramon Salcido put back quite a bit of booze and coke in his Redwood City, California, home one night in April 1989. The twenty-nine-year-old forklift operator started thinking that his twenty-four-year-old wife, Angela, was fucking around. He ended their argument about it by stabbing her to death. He drove to her parents' house and shot his mother-in-law and her two daughters. Then he slit his three daughters' throats. The youngest was one. The oldest was four. He dumped them in a landfill site. The two-year-old survived. Then he killed a co-worker at the winery who once tried to have him fired.

A fifteen-year-old Edmonton boy popped heart pills and mood depressants at a house party in November 1990. Afterwards he wandered the snowy streets in sub-zero weather for an hour, wearing only light clothing. He died of frostbite.

In October 1990, country singer Willie Nelson, a pot aficionado and

friend of the Hell's Angels, threw his support behind a Kentucky politician whose platform called for converting farmers from growing blue-
grass to smoking-type "grass." Democrat Gatewood Galbraith, a lawyer
running for governor, wants a "hemp-based economy" with heavy taxes
on legalized marijuana. The money would pay for hard drug programs.

"I don't think there's any big secret how I've felt about cannabis over
the years," Nelson said.

Carrie Fisher of *Star Wars* fame was far out in more ways than one. She
said in October 1990 that she took drugs while writing her book
Postcards from the Edge to add reality to the story about her recovery as a
drug-addicted actress.

"There's no way to do it well and not go through it somehow," she
said. "I had to go through a thing of starting and taking a little bit of
drugs, and more, and more. . . . My idea was pain reduction and mind
expansion, but I ended up with mind reduction and pain expansion."

Daniel Rakowitz talked about his feelings for his pet rooster and his
desire to be tried by a jury of his peers—marijuana smokers—during
mental competency hearings in New York in the summer of 1990. He
was found mentally fit to stand trial on charges of murdering his Swiss
girlfriend and boiling her body parts.

A section of the narcotics act in Canada prohibits literature that advocates drug use. The publisher of a London, Ontario, culinary magazine
was charged with a drug offense in January 1991, after he published a
recipe for marijuana-laced "hash brownies." A blurb said the 1960s
recipe "feeds both mind and body in a delightful way that will leave you
longing for more. . . . A word of caution, though, hash brownies alone
induce a buzz. If you wash them down with a few cold beers, let someone
else drive."

Carol Taylor's five-year-old daughter had a nasty pneumonia cough in
1990. The forty-three-year-old Providence, Rhode Island, heroin addict
gave the girl methadone to stop the cough. The child died.

From the report of a New York State Commission of Investigation into
corruption in the narcotics division of the New York City Police
Department:

> A study by the commission staff showed that during the 1970s,
> officers of the Undercover Unit of the Narcotics Division made
> 7,266 buys of narcotics, and made 4,007 arrests in connection

therewith. In all these city-wide arrests made in a year's time, a total of only 4.9 pounds of highly adulterated heroin were obtained, or about eight ounces of pure heroin. The cash used by police to make these purchases amounted to $91,197.50, over $11,000 an ounce. Surely, these [minor] arrests and seizures, at tremendous cost of manpower and actual cash outlay, have no impact upon the narcotics traffic in this city, and no impact upon organized crime.

Borders can be a problem, especially for a slicker from the Big Apple. Valeriano Montilla was a drug courier from New York City. The forty-three-year-old Bronx drug courier flew into Syracuse, New York, with cocaine and heroin in 1990. He thought he had landed in Buffalo and hired a taxi to search the city's west side for a bridge to Canada. He asked the taxi to take him to 1200 Niagara Street. The street only has seven blocks in Syracuse. And, of course, there was no bridge. He has plenty of time—twenty-seven months in jail—to learn to read a map.

Sometimes you have to wonder why dopers put so much trust in dope growers and smugglers. People who are paranoid about being followed by narcs, when there is about one narc for every 15,000 dopers, never question the potential health risks of the dope they buy. They're more worried about being burned with shit that won't get them off. Steubenville, Ohio, was hit by an outbreak of salmonella poisoning during the first two months of 1981 that felled thirty-seven people, most of them infants. It turned out the salmonella germs got into the area's supply of marijuana when the pot was dried on top of animal manure in a barn. Adult potheads had passed the germs to their children after handling the weed.

Ever wonder why old ladies smile so much? It was revealed in 1989 that an eighty-year-old British woman sniffed cocaine nearly every day for fifty-five years after it had first been prescribed for a nose irritation that bothered her while horseback riding. During that period, the woman snorted nearly thirteen pounds of cocaine, most of it obtained from doctors in France. Go granny, go granny, go granny, go.

Another diversion: Have you ever noticed that most American television commercials flog drugs to dull hemorrhoid pain, stop farting, and unplug clogged assholes? Americans have major rectal problems. They spend $1,369,863 on laxatives every day.

Both Lenny Bruce and Elvis Presley died of drug overdoses in the bathroom. Bruce, who pioneered dirty jokes and the freedom of speech movement, succumbed to heroin in 1966. Though theories abound about whether Presley died accidentally or committed suicide, he did keel over in the can in 1977 with more drugs in his body than a normal person could handle. He lived as long as his mother had—forty-two years.

Thirty-year-old Samy John Ianiri was stabbed during an argument over crack cocaine at 2:30 a.m. on January 30, 1991, in an apartment building parking lot in northwest Toronto. He ran off and was picked up by friends. They drove past a hospital. Ianiri got out of the car a few minutes later and fell dead on the sidewalk from knife wounds to the heart and lungs.

A fifty-eight-year-old Montreal woman used her seven-year-old grand-daughter as a go-between in drug deals in 1990. The girl negotiated with addicts and was found hiding in the bedroom with packets of heroin when police arrested her grandparents.

Twelve-year-old William Porter was kidnapped on December 5, 1989, by scumbags who wanted to extort $500,000 from his drug-dealing older brother. Richard Thomas Porter, twenty-five, who plied his trade in Harlem, refused to cooperate with the police investigation. The kidnappers cut off the boy's right index finger and left it with a taped message in a coffee cup in a restaurant.

"They cutted my finger off," the kid said on the tape. "Please help. I love you, Mommy."

On December 10, a woman gave a kid on the street a note to deliver to William Porter's aunt. That was the last time the kidnappers contacted the Porters. Richard Porter was shot to death in the Bronx on January 4, 1990. He is believed to have been looking for his brother. At the end of January William Porter was found in fourteen layers of black plastic garbage bags near a Bronx bicycle path. The kidnappers had bashed his head in.

Drugs have an amazing ability to numb pain and keep people alive when they should be dead. An Illinois heroin addict got into a shoot-out with police. He emptied his gun and tried to reload. He couldn't because the hail of bullets smacking into his chest and head kept him off balance. But he kept trying. The junkie took thirty-nine 9-mm bullets fired from semi-automatic pistols. One severed his optic nerve and blinded him. One shattered his wrist. Still he tried to reload his gun. He was finally felled by two 12-gauge shotgun slugs in the back.

A cocaine user hit by ten .38-caliber police bullets in the head and chest stopped only because he bled to death.

A Bronx crack addict stayed up after being hit by eighteen .38-caliber police bullets. He was stopped by a hollowpoint 12-gauge shotgun slug.

A New York City police officer was having a shoot-out with a drug dealer in an alleyway. He emptied his six-shot .38-caliber revolver and crouched behind garbage cans to reload. The dealer, who was armed with a high-capacity 9-mm pistol, sauntered up to the officer and shot him in the head.

Darrin Brown was a crack user and one of a gang of four thieves that ripped off a Whitby, Ontario, retirement home in 1990. He stayed in the car outside the building to act as a lookout while two of his buddies entered the home. He monitored police frequencies on a scanner and had a walky-talky to warn his buddies.

The fourth gang member, Janice Sinoski, worked in the retirement home and let the robbers in. They stole money from five rooms while residents slept and took a microwave, coffeemaker, video cassette recorder, and stereo. They gagged and bound Sinoski and punched her in the head to make her look like a victim.

Brown, the lookout, had five convictions for theft. And he is legally blind.

Atlanta dope dealers didn't like Buster, the drug-sniffing dog. They poisoned the five-year-old black Labrador retriever in April 1990. Buster got a full police funeral with honor guard and a seven-gun salute.

Good guys can play dirty, too. A former US narc worked the French Connection case in the early 1970s. He infiltrated the Marseilles underworld to find clandestine labs where morphine base was converted into heroin. He reported his finds to French police, but the labs always disappeared before they were raided. The narc knew he was dealing with crooked cops. He kept his mouth shut and left the country, only to reenter with a counterfeit passport and name. Then he tracked down two labs and blew them up.

A twenty-nine-year-old Calgary woman, wife of a soldier and mother of two children, entertained teenagers with drugs and booze in her Canadian Forces Base Calgary home and screwed a thirteen-year-old boy.

James Darby of Sebring, Florida, is believed to be the oldest crack dealer in the world. The eighty-one-year-old was arrested on cocaine charges for the fifth time in three years in May 1990. Cops charged him with possession of cocaine after they found a matchbox of cocaine residue on his bedroom floor.

"He's a good old guy, but he just can't seem to stop," Police Chief Robert Baker said. "He once told us he was just supplementing his Social Security income."

The retired citrus worker was first arrested outside a Sebring barber shop in 1987 with forty-one packets of crack cocaine in his pocket.

Walter and William Tucker are without doubt the world's most colorful crusaders for the legalization of marijuana. The long-bearded Ontarians, who would fit right into a ZZ Top video, managed to take their arguments to the Supreme Court of Canada without a lawyer. Their appearance before the country's highest court on Tuesday, January 22, 1980, marked the end of their long campaign through a series of courtrooms to have reversed a conviction for marijuana possession and a one-year suspended sentence.

The Tuckers had argued all along that the conviction violated their civil rights and religious freedom. They are missionaries for the Church of the Universe, in which marijuana use is a sacrament.

They appeared before the court in their blue denim overalls and looked up at Chief Justice Bora Laskin, whose textbook on constitutional law they quoted in every courtroom where they had fought — along with the Canadian Bill of Rights (now replaced by the Charter of Rights and Freedoms), the Bible, and the Magna Carta.

"If the Magna Carta has any basis in this court . . ." forty-six-year-old Walter began.

"It's marginal as far as narcotics is concerned," the Chief Justice said.

Walter started reading from a chapter on privacy from Chief Justice Laskin's textbook.

"If I may be permitted to interpret my own words, that section has absolutely no application here," he said.

Forty-two-year-old William stood and began to read from the Bible. "From the beginning of time . . ."

"That's going back too far for us," Mr. Justice Willard Estey said.

The Tuckers started but never completed their arguments.

"Well, I'll take it farther," Walter said. "I'll take it to the Bill of Rights."

"We are familiar with the Bill of Rights," Chief Justice Laskin said. "We are all of the opinion this is a case we ought not to hear. Leave to appeal is dismissed."

The Tuckers were in and out of the Supreme Court of Canada in twenty-four minutes.

Stripper Vivian Jerilynn McBain, known to Oshawa, Ontario, stripclub patrons as Stardust, took her twenty-one-month-old daughter Brandy to a restaurant on June 25, 1989. The baby ate spaghetti and toast. Stardust bought crack cocaine on the way home and smoked it with three men until 3 a.m. She bundled up the baby and took her to another house where she smoked more crack. Cranky little Brandy was given juice and milk.

Stardust took her baby home at noon on June 26. She said she didn't feed her from 7 o'clock that night until 11 a.m. on June 27 because the baby didn't ask for food. At noon she found Brandy in a coma. The child was clinically dead by the time she reached hospital, though doctors tried until July 1 to revive her. The twenty-seven-year-old mother said the cocaine made her sleep and she looked in on the child only two or three times. When she was convicted of criminal negligence causing death on Friday, February 8, 1991, Stardust was six months pregnant.

Ronald Lomas had washed down a few Valium with booze when he sold incense to Perry Szimedli in April 1989. Szimedli thought he was buying hash. The twenty-six-year-old confronted Lomas in the Dundas subway station to get his money back. The twenty-two-year-old Lomas pulled a blade and slashed Szimedli's neck, severing his spinal cord and jugular vein. Lomas split and left Szimedli lying on the ground bleeding.

"I could hear the blood coming out of my neck," Szimedli said. "I thought this must be a bad dream. I could hardly breathe. I was gasping for air."

Some asshole has developed a computer virus that leaves computer software stoned. He has infected a number of programs on floppy disks and more than forty companies across Canada, including the federal Employment and Immigration offices in Vancouver and the St. John's Institute of Fisheries, have suffered the effects of it. It eats up computer files and leaves the message "Your computer is stoned. Legalize marijuana."

Mary Kelly was a twenty-year-old pothead who refused to believe that smoking marijuana affected her ability to drive. She was bombing along in her new Pontiac Sunbird on November 18, 1989, with three buddies aged seventeen, nineteen, and twenty. They passed the joint around as Mary tore along County Road 12, between Highways 9 and 89 near Orangeville, Ontario. She lost control of her car on the desolate road and slammed into an oncoming car driven by sixty-five-year-old Glenn Ewing. Ewing and his sixty-nine-year-old wife, Vera, died. Kelly and her three friends also died. Their insides were ripped to shreds in the collision.

Analysts at the Centre for Forensic Sciences in Toronto, who test the blood of all drivers between the ages of sixteen and forty-five killed in accidents, found Kelly had the second highest level of tetrahydrocannabinol in her blood ever recorded. She had fifty nanograms of THC per 100 milliliters of blood. The average amount found in accident victims is two to three nanograms. Ten is considered high. A toxicologist who tested Kelly's blood figured she didn't even know she was driving a car.

So you think smoking a little grass won't hurt you? Ask Judge Douglas Ginsburg, President Ronald Reagan's nominee to the US Supreme Court in November 1987. Pot derailed his career as quickly as it did Mary Kelly's car.

Ginsburg admitted on Thursday, November 5, 1987, that he had smoked pot once in the 1960s and a few times in the 1970s. He made the admission after being asked by National Public Radio to comment on interviews that indicated he used marijuana while teaching at Harvard Law School and had once taken it to a party. Ginsburg said it was the only drug he had taken.

"It was a mistake," he said. "I regret it."

Both Reagan and Attorney-General Edwin Meese continued to support him for the Supreme Court appointment. Meese described Ginsburg's drug use as "a mistake ... during his younger days. ... It certainly does not affect his qualifications to sit on the Supreme Court, and he should be confirmed expeditiously."

White House spokesman Marlin Fitzwater said, "The president accepts his statement, doesn't feel that it influences his judicial qualifications, and the president stands by his nomination."

Fortunately, someone in the Republican Party showed some sense in the Ginsburg affair. Republican Senator Charles Grassley, a member of the Senate judiciary committee, said, "You like to think people who are appointed to the Supreme Court respect the law."

Ginsburg didn't get the job. Those few tokes took him over the line of what is acceptable for the highest judges in a land that is supposed to be waging a war against drugs.

Angelo Parisi and Perry Kent became folk heroes when they torched a crack house in their Detroit neighborhood in 1987. A jury acquitted them of arson charges. Parisi was arrested on June 2, 1990, for breaking into a parked car. He was placed on eighteen months' probation and ordered to undergo treatment for alcohol abuse.

Earl MacKeigan and his fifty-year-old mother, Mary Ann, were walking near their downtown Toronto home on July 6, 1990, when they were stopped by seven drug dealers. Mary Ann told them where to get off. They punched her in the face and knocked her down. She ran into her house to call police. The dopers beat her son and two of them stabbed him seven times, puncturing a lung.

Diana Rocco and her cousin Cristina Spataro, both four years old, found a syringe plunger in their Toronto day-care playground in August 1990. They took turns sucking on it and making popping sounds as they yanked it out of their mouths. A three-year-old girl digging in the sand near them pricked her finger on a syringe discarded by dopers.

The Miami-based Yahweh religious sect helped poor blacks with its message of hope and self-sufficiency and its anti-drug crusade. The sect's white-robed members opened supermarkets in poor black neighborhoods, renovated rundown housing projects, and hounded drug dealers off the streets. They aided development in black communities and owned real estate worth millions of dollars in the Miami area, including apartment buildings, grocery stores, a restaurant, and a motel.

Yahweh Ben Yahweh, the sect's charismatic leader, is better known as Hulon Mitchell, Jr., former pro football player for the St. Louis Cardinals and the Oakland Raiders. He claims to be the second coming of Christ and requires his disciples to surrender all their belongings to his Temple of Love.

Yahweh Ben Yahweh was arrested with twelve sect members on November 7, 1990, on arson, extortion, eighteen racketeering, fourteen murder, and two attempted murder charges. Yahweh allegedly ordered ritual killings in which body parts were cut off. An indictment says that sect members proved their loyalty to Yahweh with violence. Victims were allegedly taken into the Everglades and beheaded.

Sect members plotted "to murder at random individuals in the community as a rite of initiation into an ultra secret group within the Yahwehs called the Brotherhood," said US Attorney Dexter Lehtinen.

"One could only be admitted into the Brotherhood after killing a white devil and bringing a severed body part back to Mitchell as proof of a confirmed kill. Decapitation in the Everglades, the killing of individuals with parts of their bodies — often an ear — brought back to them to prove the murders were committed.

"Yahweh Ben Yahweh trusted no one. Yahweh Ben Yahweh made them bring back parts of the dead body to prove they had carried out the murders he directed."

The charges center on alleged attempts to murder disciples who didn't want Mitchell as leader and who disobeyed orders to kill.

No tale of drug users would be complete without a look at the man who turned more people onto drugs than did the CIA. Timothy Leary, the former Harvard psychology professor turned high priest of LSD, who took hallucinations out of asylums and onto the streets in the 1960s, is unrepentant. The man who first experimented with LSD and turned on the world, starting with hundreds of famous artists, writers, and high-fashion models; who flirted with the CIA, Weather Underground terrorists, Black Panthers, and John Lennon; who broke out of jail with the help of terrorists and escaped to Europe only to be kidnapped by the CIA in Afghanistan; this man still thinks LSD is a gas and, at age seventy, still drops acid.

LSD is a useful tool for intellectuals to expand their brainpower, he believes. If LSD has a bad image, blame the tight-assed establishment that uses it as a scapegoat, the cretins who indulge in excess and consequently freak out, and the inexperienced entrepreneurs of the sixties who gave buyers a product too potent for their minds to handle.

"Personal drugs, recreational drugs, are very much like personal computers and recreational computers," Leary said. "The difference in drug use between the sixties and the eighties is that today everyone is more sophisticated, more knowledgeable, and more realistic. Drugs, like computers, are ways for an intelligent person to activate new brain circuits. Ninety-five percent of the people who use illegal drugs, you never hear about them. They're silent, hardworking, intelligent people starting out to get control of their brain or their mind. It's the other five percent that causes the trouble.

"They are losers. If you want to self-destruct, you can use sex, booze, money, gambling. One way is drugs. But the problem is not drugs. The problem is recognizing, anticipating, and preventing drug abuse by this five percent."

Leary doesn't think that anti-drug programs and so-called wars on drugs help the losers.

"The . . . administration thinks that the only way to solve any problem is to war on it. The war on drugs is actually war on 60 million Americans who intelligently use illegal drugs. . . . There's not one shred of evidence connecting LSD or marijuana to chromosome damage. The American government has a war on drug usage. In war there is no truth, just information, propaganda, lies, confusion. That's the way you fight a war."

Even though he has spent forty-four months in jail for drug offenses, Leary still urges people to "turn on, tune in, and drop out."

He concedes, though, that times have changed.

"There's no drug culture any more because that's really a foolish and narrow view.

"To understand the explosion of drug use in the 1960s you must realize that Canadian and American society was moving from an industrial, mechanical civilization to what's called the information-communication age, in which brain power replaces smokestack-factory power.

"It's inevitable that the new generation coming up at that period is getting to be interested in activating and accessing and programming their brain just as they are now learning to process knowledge and information using the personal computer."

Leary said he's just a consumer of LSD and won't have anything to do with its production. He's happy, though, that it's not as potent as it was twenty-six years ago.

"The dosages that were used in the sixties were too strong. That's the terrible thing about prohibition—like alcohol prohibition in the twenties. When you push something underground, you invite carelessness, bootleg, bathtub, and gangster elements. One of the problems is that dosages were too high for unprepared people. In a new technology, it takes a generation to settle down and to work out the bugs. This is happening. Intelligent people are using drugs intelligently today.

"We were always doing our best to present the facts [in the sixties]. We didn't try to conceal the fact that we were on the frontier and that this was an uncharted realm and that we were explorers sending back signals. I regret that the climate became polluted by controversy and police action. But as we move from an industrial society to a brain society, everyone is frightened. It's one of those great transitional moments in history, like when we moved from the feudal to the industrial age and the Luddites tried to destroy the machines that were putting men out of work. Actually, if you were a farmer or a weaver, the machines threatened the essence of your identity. So I think that in a time like this we should be very gentle with each other. Let's not talk about wars against each other."

While he advocates intelligent drug use, Leary abhors abuse. When told that thirteen-year-olds take LSD and asked if their minds are ready for the drug, he said: "No, they're not and I totally disapprove of that. I encourage students and young people to keep their brains alive and sharp. They must be totally committed to intellectual excellence. I deplore young unprepared people using any kind of drug—alcohol, LSD, whatever. The problem is that in the context of war and propaganda that the government is doing, everything gets confused. Kids today are so disgusted and frightened by the doom and gloom that they blindly strike back in rebellion. . . . The real problem is alcoholism. In America there are 3 million teenage alcoholics."

Has dropping acid for more than twenty-five years affected Leary?

"I feel younger and happier and I'm more productive than I ever was. But I can't credit this to acid."

His chromosomes are still intact, the only flashback he has is his autobiography that bears that title, and if the drug really does cause one to space out, he wouldn't be able to hang on to his job as a consultant for personal computer firms.

"We're going to develop software for the personal computer that will do the same thing as LSD. It will accelerate and expand the brain."

17

Romancing the Stoned:
The debate to legalize drugs

"The only law that the narco-traffickers do not break is the law of supply and demand."
—COLOMBIAN PRESIDENT VIRGILIO BARCO.

"Market forces apply to drugs as they do to any other traded commodity. Hence, our endeavours will be frustrated if we fail to bring about a drastic and rapid reduction in demand for drugs."
—UNITED NATIONS SECRETARY-GENERAL JAVIER PEREZ DE CUELLAR TO A SPECIAL SESSION OF THE UN GENERAL ASSEMBLY ON FEBRUARY 20, 1990.

"I should like to make an earnest plea to drug consumers to realize that their habit is bringing our countries to the brink of disaster, that their addiction is fostering violence, crime, and corruption throughout the world."
—COLOMBIAN PRESIDENT VIRGILIO BARCO TO AN INTERNATIONAL DRUG CONFERENCE ON APRIL 9, 1990.

"It is up to you in the West to cut down demand. Otherwise your babies will be addicted."
—MYANMAR (BURMA) OPIUM WARLORD KHUN SA SAYS HE ONLY SUPPLIES DEMAND FOR HEROIN. ADDICTION IS NOT HIS PROBLEM.

"Anyone who talks in terms of legalizing drugs is willing to write the death warrants for people in the lower socioeconomic classes."
—JOHN LAWN, HEAD OF THE US DRUG ENFORCEMENT ADMINISTRATION.

Drugs can destroy North American society. Those who want to legalize drugs weaken the battle against this enemy within. When people under siege talk of barbarians at the gate, they mean on the outside. In the battle against drugs, some of the barbarians are on the inside. They cry out for the legalization of drugs. Money is their Trojan horse.

Like unthinking cancer, legalizers eat away at society's resolve and moral fiber. If successful, they will destroy the creature off which they feed and die with it, realizing too late they were wrong. Apologies are no substitute for reason.

The increasingly public debate on drug legalization is unprecedented in its support among community leaders, black and white. The mayors of Baltimore, Minneapolis, Washington, along with California congressmen, large newspapers, influential writers, and conservative thinkers have advocated that drugs be treated as a public health issue, not a criminal problem.

They say abolishing drug laws would reduce crime, free the overburdened justice system, and save billions of dollars now spent fighting the problem. It would allow governments to make money by taxing drugs. These are the meanderings of minds warped by greed. The drug legalization movement has nothing to offer addicts but more drugs. It has nothing for victims but more fear, sorrow, and death. It has nothing for society but carnage.

The love generation of the 1960s was a failed experiment. Responsibility, caring, and commitment have been discarded like used condoms. It seems these qualities prevented people from enjoying life, from feeling it.

Respectable and otherwise responsible people advocate legalization: Nobel laureate and economist Milton Friedman; neo-conservative apologist columnist and *National Review* editor William F. Buckley; *Harper's* editor Lewis H. Lapham; Baltimore mayor Kurt Schmoke; former Washington mayor Marion Barry, before he was nailed smoking crack in a hotel room.

Several aspiring politicians campaigned for legalization in 1990. Pouch-eyed Democrat Gatewood Galbraith made legalization of marijuana his gubernatorial platform in Kentucky, which was the top US marijuana producer before its ban in 1936. Back then it was used for rope and textiles. Galbraith's campaign slogan: "Get a head in government." He was photographed fondling a nine-foot high "wild" marijuana plant. Mark Creamer, a Kansas Democratic candidate for Congress, had to glad hand behind bars where he served a six-month sentence for lighting a reefer in a cop shop.

Though legalizers claim their ranks include every political stripe, they are mostly defeatist, money-grubbing neo-conservatives who put a price on morality and life; who would forsake those with a penchant for self-destructive drug addiction to a miserable existence.

They are the inhumane among us who would sell out values for a few bucks off their tax bill. They are power mongers who would relish creating a sub-class of drug-addicted human beings at the mercy of government for their daily fix. The strategy grotesquely resembles Hitler's final solution for Jews, homosexuals, and others he labeled deviants. First you identify them, then you herd them together, then you slaughter them.

As in Nazi Germany, one must always suspect those who offer degradation and humiliation to a group of people in the guise of making the world a better place. How long will it take for addiction treatment centers to become extermination camps? When will the so-called humanitarians decide to save even more money and do away with government-subsidized drug-maintenance programs? When will they realize that doing this will create a frenzied mob of dangerous junkies? When will they plot to kill them off secretly to prevent riots? How will they quell rumors of death camps? How will they explain the stench in boxcars used to take junkies on their last trips? They may get away with it by describing the slaughter as an environmentally friendly gesture.

The reasoning of conservative thinkers has always been discordant and expedient. In good times, they rail against government interference. When times get tough, they plead for government assistance. Legalizers want government to turn pusher. You have to wonder about conservatives who want to crush free enterprise, albeit criminal free enterprise, and hand its business over to government. These are the same people who say government has no business in the boardrooms of the nation. Do they secretly hope government will fail in the drug business and hand it over to the private sector? Wall Street, after all, knows a lot about cocaine from its experience as a consumer. It's a businessman's dream: a captive market conditioned and primed by government.

Those who would legalize drugs have not thought through the implications of embracing drug legalization. They have not learned from the body count that drugs kill. They have no sense of responsibility to the society in which they earn their wealth.

They say drug use is a matter of personal choice. But where does personal choice end and addiction take over? For crack cocaine, it happens in a matter of days, if not hours.

Ethan Nadelmann sparked the current debate to legalize drugs with magazine articles calling for the repeal of drug laws, the most influential in the September 1989 issue of *Science* magazine. Nadelmann, a media star who flogs his ideas on the talk show circuit, is a thirty-three-year-old Harvard lawyer and assistant professor of politics and public affairs at Princeton's Woodrow Wilson School of Public and International Affairs.

Nadelmann says the war against drugs can't be won; that despite costly interdiction programs there is more high-quality cocaine on the streets than ever; that there is so much potential farmland to grow the coca plant in South America that crop eradication programs are doomed to fail; that the $10 billion spent yearly in the US to fight drugs on the streets and in courts is wasted because the black market can't be beat; that the health problems caused by illegal drugs are minuscule compared to those caused by tobacco and alcohol; that legalization would drive crime out of the ghetto and the tax profits from selling drugs would pay for treatment programs for addicts and anti-drug education programs for children.

Nadelmann does not explain where the profit is in legalizing if the money made selling drugs is spent on treatment. He has no idea how legalization could be implemented, whether or not pregnant women, air traffic controllers, or surgeons would be allowed to use drugs. He does not suggest how these people could be prevented from using drugs if they are legally available to everyone.

"Selling drugs to children would, of course, continue to be criminalized," he says. If he believes his own argument that drug laws create criminals, he should recognize that banning drug sales to children would force organized crime to concentrate on the kiddie market.

Nadelmann is a board member of the Drug Policy Foundation, which was formed in 1987 in response to the Reagan administration's Zero Tolerance anti-drug policy. The foundation gets support from the ivory towers of academia and the rich who fear their tax dollars are not properly spent. Richard Dennis, former member of the Chicago Mercantile Exchange and president of the Chicago Resource Center, donated $2 million to the foundation for an annual "Drugpeace" prize given to people who advance the legalization cause. Unlike the National Organization for the Reform of Marijuana Laws, which was founded in 1970 to advocate the legalization of marijuana only, foundation members—doctors, lawyers, professors, and former judges—want all drugs legalized.

They argue that prohibition has failed and that a legalized, taxed, and regulated drug trade would save billions of dollars now spent on interdiction and law enforcement. They want to make money from drugs, not spend money fighting them. Nadelmann would exchange one pusher for another. The pusher he wants is the guy he pays his taxes to.

Nadelmann is a trained lawyer. He argues in favor of his client and ignores those facts that could incriminate him. He must believe his client to argue convincingly. In doing so, Nadelmann has fooled himself. In arguing for legalization, he advocates anarchy and genocide. How can a lawyer, in a society based on the rule of law, suggest abolishing laws essential to the integrity of its fabric? How can he advocate measures bound to create chaos and social upheaval, misery and death?

Nadelmann's is not the only voice that would lead us into the wilderness. In a *Newsweek* magazine essay in 1972 after President Richard Nixon declared war on drugs, Milton Friedman, the Nobel prize-winning free market economist, argued that heroin should be legalized. Ethically, he wrote, the government has no right to tell people not to use heroin, and economically, prohibition costs more to society than it's worth.

Friedman over the years:

• "I don't approve of drugs. I've never taken drugs or tried any. But I think they should be legalized because the harm being done by the prohibitionists is vastly greater than the harm being done by users."

• "The harm that is done by drugs is predominantly caused by the fact that they are illegal. You would not have had the crack epidemic if it was legal."

• "Prohibition is an attempted cure that makes matters worse—for both the addict and the rest of us. In drugs, as in other areas, persuasion and example are likely to be far more effective than the use of force to shape others in our image."

• "Legalizing drugs might increase the number of addicts, but it is not clear that it would. Forbidden fruit is attractive, particularly to the young."

Rape and murder are also forbidden. Do laws against these atrocities encourage people to rape and kill? Like all legalizers, Friedman assumes drug addicts are rational people who will listen to fatherly advice. He needs a dose of reality. No one holds economists responsible for erroneous forecasts. Economics is not a science, but an offshoot of numerology that tries its hand at fortune-telling with figures rather than cards or crystal balls. Economists don't deal with reality. They speculate. Friedman ought not to speculate with human lives.

US Federal District Court Judge Robert Sweet, a former deputy mayor of New York City and former federal prosecutor, believes drugs should be legalized because the present system isn't preventing the birth of 50,000 crack babies in the United States every year. He says people should be trusted with the responsibility of properly using narcotics, as they are entrusted with the right to use alcohol and tobacco. He does not explain how legalizing crack would reduce the number of crack babies.

The widespread use of tobacco and alcohol is the reason most often cited to legalize drugs. *Harper's* editor Lewis H. Lapham says cigarettes kill more people than do narcotics, so people should have legal access to drugs.

"In 1988, American hospitals counted 3,308 deaths attributed to cocaine, as opposed to 390,000 deaths in some way attributable to the use of tobacco and 100,000 deaths directly related to the excessive use of alcohol."

If anything, Lapham's statistics show that tobacco and alcohol should also be banned. Despite years of publicity about their detrimental health effects, people still smoke and drink. These figures are a good reason not to legalize drugs. We must learn from the folly of legalizing tobacco and alcohol that drugs kill.

"Among the strongest arguments in favor of legalization are the moral ones," Nadelmann states. "On the one hand, the standard refrain regarding the immorality of drug use crumbles in the face of most Americans' tolerance for alcohol and tobacco use. . . . Moral condemnation by the majority of Americans of some substances and not others is little more than a transient prejudice in favor of some drugs and against others.

"On the other hand, drug enforcement involves its own immoralities," he says. "Because drug law violations do not create victims with an interest in notifying the police, drug enforcement agents must rely heavily on undercover operations, electronic surveillance, and information provided by informants. . . . Indeed, enforcement of drug laws makes mockery of an essential principle of a free society, that those who do no harm to others should not be harmed by others, and particularly not by the state."

So Nadelmann believes saying NO to drugs is a prejudice the majority of North Americans will shed when they come around to his point of view. And he believes that investigating drug traffickers violates their rights. He says tobacco and alcohol are deadly, yet wants to add to the misery they create by legalizing more drugs.

James Q. Wilson was appointed chairman of the National Advisory Council for Drug Abuse Prevention in 1972. His job was to curb heroin addiction. He points out that at that time cocaine was considered a benign drug. Wilson best explained in the February 1990 issue of *Commentary* magazine why tobacco cannot be used as an argument to legalize drugs such as cocaine:

"We treat the two drugs differently, not simply because nicotine is so widely used as to be beyond the reach of effective prohibition, but because its use does not destroy the user's essential humanity. Tobacco shortens one's life, cocaine debases it. Nicotine alters one's habits, cocaine alters one's soul. The heavy use of crack, unlike the heavy use of tobacco, corrodes those natural sentiments of sympathy and duty that constitute our human nature and make possible our social life. To say, as does Nadelmann, that distinguishing morally between tobacco and cocaine is 'little more than a transient prejudice' is close to saying that morality itself is but a prejudice."

Legalizers say it is hypocritical to ban drugs while selling tobacco and alcohol. They're right. Let's ban tobacco and alcohol. Why should we compound our mistake and legalize drugs?

Legalization would undermine current programs to educate people about the dangers of tobacco and alcohol. Where is the logic in telling people that smoking is a health hazard when the same government sells deadlier drugs such as heroin, cocaine, crack, crank, and PCP?

There's a big difference between alcohol and hard drugs. About 10 percent of alcohol users become alcoholics. About 70 percent of hard drug users become addicts. Alcohol consumption soared 350 percent when Prohibition was repealed. Legalization of heroin in Britain caused a thirty-fold (3,000 percent) increase in addicts in the 1960s and 1970s.

There are 240 million Americans: 100 million use alcohol (15 million alcoholics); 56 million are tobacco addicts; 40 to 60 million have smoked marijuana (21 million are regular pot smokers); 6 million use cocaine (2.5 million are cocaine addicts); 5 million use heroin (500,000 are heroin addicts). These figures do not include PCP, methamphetamine, ice, the wide assortment of hallucinogens, prescription drugs, and whatever else turns dopers on. The numbers would swell if drugs were legalized.

Drugs are not a joyride. People use drugs to blow the lids off their gourds: cocaine means paranoia; PCP and crank mean paranoia and murderous tendencies; crack means paranoia, an uncontrollable craving for more drug, a willingness to do anything to get it; designer drugs create vegetables.

The cocaine user's life is an ongoing search-and-destroy mission—search for cocaine and destroy yourself with it. If drugs harm people and drug laws protect people, then legalizing drugs will harm people.

The crux of the legalization argument is *money*.

"You add it all up, and we're losing badly on the war on drugs. We'll never win that war. You have to legalize drugs to take the profit out of these drug czars that are making billions of dollars in cash," Donald Trump told Miami businessmen in April 1990.

Consider these excerpts from the September 7, 1989, lead editorial in the *Globe and Mail*, which bills itself as Canada's National Newspaper:

"It is time for radical thinking, and the most radical thought is this: Why not remove the principal cause of illegal drug activity by making the drugs legal? . . .

"Legalizing even hard drugs would enable governments to regulate the quality; some of the stuff out there is poisonous in more than the usual way. It would let governments tax the product, to raise money for the treatment of abusers and the education of children likely to become users. It would let governments label the product to tell users exactly what to expect from, say, cocaine—irreversible damage to the nose and heart, and a need to absorb increasingly more of the drug to realize the same effect. It would sap the traffickers and illicit networks of their power, and remove the incentive for neighborhood youths to tap into those networks. (Some would find other trouble to get into, but what else is new?)

"The arguments against legalization are several, and powerful. Legalization would probably attract new users and, whatever warnings the government attached, might be interpreted as society's stamp of approval on the drugs. While the plan would eradicate much of the crime associated with the drug trade, it would leave users open to the horrendous effects of the drugs. All the regulations in the world—restricting sales to those over 18, requiring users of some drugs to get prescriptions—would not relieve this route of its risks.

"What makes the route attractive is that it would drive a stake into the criminal world that feeds on the innocent and reduces cities—entire countries—to war zones. The world will always have drug abuse to contend with. By removing the cultivation and sale of those drugs from the underworld, and by placing the regulation of those drugs in government hands, countries would be able to deal with that abuse in the light. They could free up the resources they now use to chase the traffickers down blind alleys, ever hopeful and ever frustrated.

"A radical proposal. Shouldn't we consider it?"

The *Globe and Mail* is conservative politically and editorially. It thinks of itself as a businessman's newspaper, with much of its emphasis on business news. It is apparent the high cost of fighting drugs is the overriding reason the newspaper believes they should be legalized. Even after glossing over the harm caused to users, the editorial comes down on the side of the almighty dollar.

It is suspect for a newspaper that continually advocates that government privatize state-owned enterprises to suggest government take over the drug business.

The editorial shows no understanding of the drug business. The government can never control the cocaine business, let alone the entire drug industry. Coca plants grow only in certain areas, most of which are located in Bolivia, Peru, and Colombia. Even if governments in these countries could take over the growing and manufacturing of cocaine—which they couldn't because of all the armed groups involved in the trade—would they sell to North American governments at cut-rate prices?

Colombians have lobbied the US for years to legalize marijuana so they can stop fighting the problem at home and reap billions of dollars selling it to North America as a cash crop. They have made similar suggestions about cocaine. Governments of user countries would have to bid for cocaine on the commodities market. Money would bleed out of North America, turning banana republics into cocaine kingdoms. And much like the oil sheiks who forced North America to a standstill with an embargo in the mid-1970s, cocaine producers would have user countries under their thumbs.

Would we allow South American cocaine barons to advertise? Would Coca-Cola market the real thing? Would Buckley and Friedman invest in cocaine company stocks? Would they trust their grandchildren to hold off getting snowed until they turn eighteen? Would they explain to them their right to fry their brains and screw up their lives?

Legalize drugs and governments would get hooked on the money. Like the sin taxes of booze, tobacco, and gambling, drugs would provide a crutch for cash-strapped governments. The incentive would then be to create more addicts to generate more revenue. There has been no end to government lottery schemes since gambling was made legal. Governments feed on greed with multi-million-dollar weekly lotteries. Advertising hooks new players.

The financial argument for legalization is devoid of morality. It shows no care for addicts or society. Take this amoral attitude back to the last century and the American Civil War would not have been fought. If the almighty dollar were all that mattered, blacks would still be slaves today, providing cheap labor not only in the cotton fields, but in factories. It would save a lot of people a lot of money. But what would it do to humanity? Those who want drugs legalized don't care enough to look past their wallets.

Drugs are a problem because people buy and use them. The problem will disappear only when people stop buying and using drugs. Legalize drugs and you institutionalize the problem.

Legalizers say drug laws, not drugs, harm society. They argue that illegal drugs cause crime and legalization will reduce it.

US Justice Department figures show that 50 to 75 percent of men arrested for serious crimes test positive for recent drug use. A study of 254 crack addicts in Dade County, Florida, found they were responsible for 223,000 crimes in one year—an average of 877 crimes apiece.

Why would abusers of legalized drugs act any differently from abusers of the same illegal drugs? A dope fiend is a dope fiend—behavior does not change because society sanctions drug use. Alcohol is legal and responsible for more violence than any other drug. Legalizing alcohol has not stopped spouse beating or child abuse by those who use booze as a passkey for their warped drives. It certainly has not curbed drunk driving.

On the other hand, evidence shows that making drugs illegal reduces violence. Shortly after cocaine was outlawed in 1909, the chief of the division of drugs in the US Department of Agriculture noted that "in districts where druggists formerly dispensed cocaine, disorder has decreased so noticeably that it is commented upon by the neighbors and the police officers on the beats."

Legalizers argue that erasing drug laws will eliminate the criminal underworld that makes billions of dollars off narcotics. Really? Organized crime was centuries old when it came to North America, be it the Italians or the Chinese triads. Traditional organized crime fed off, but was not created by, Prohibition. It wasn't killed by the repeal of Prohibition. Hoods found other ways to make money illegally.

Legalized gambling has not forced organized crime out of the numbers racket. Organized crime now runs both legal and illegal gambling operations. It makes much more money than it did when gambling was outlawed and now launders its dirty money through its legal casinos. Let's not forget: crime came first; laws are a reaction to the problem.

Nadelmann says society is being destroyed because drug users who face criminal charges lose respect for laws. They had no respect for laws in the first place.

Other legalizers say drug laws destroy society by creating outlaws. Legalization would make these outlaws normal law-abiding people, they say. So legalizers would like to live in neighborhoods full of legal cocaine addicts? They would like to be passengers in planes piloted by cocaine addicts? They want their kids to be taught by cocaine addicts? They will entrust their precious money to bankers and investment consultants hooked on cocaine?

If prisons can be emptied by abolishing drug laws, why not erase all laws and turn prisons into homes for the homeless? No laws, no crime, no criminals. We could turn today's crimes into tomorrow's sporting events, sicking football teams on cheerleaders at half time.

A portion of society is criminal and always will be. Legalize some drugs and a black market will develop for those that remain illegal. Legalize all drugs, but limit access to them or tax them, then bootleg and cheaper untaxed drugs will appear. Give drugs away to adults and someone will peddle them to children.

Prescription drugs are legal, providing users have a good reason to want them. Yet a multi-billion-dollar black market exists for those who abuse prescription drugs. An entire underworld has developed to cater to, and profit from, the needs of prescription drug addicts. Many of the pushers are doctors and pharmacists. You can't legislate against greed.

Legalizers have facile answers. But they are not solutions. Treating the symptom rather than the cause does not solve the problem. Legalizers are akin to the doctors who praised morphine, then heroin, then cocaine as cures for addiction. Heroin was seen as a cure for morphine addiction. Cocaine was seen as a cure for alcoholism. One evil does not cure another.

Legalizers like Buckley claim violence will decrease with legalization. They assume all drug violence involves the criminal underworld. Most drug violence involves users who prey on the innocent, steal, and kill. Where do legalizers think dopers will get the money to support their habits?

Prohibition era violence may have been fueled by alcohol, but it was motivated by greed. The violence in society at large was quelled during Prohibition because of a lack of alcohol and increased with repeal. The temperance movement that preceded Prohibition was not an attack on the inherent evils of alcohol as much as a defense against wife-beating by drunken husbands. It was a desperate stand by abused women given little voice in society. It was a struggle by those courageous enough to leave the kitchen and take to the streets in an effort to confront the drunken violence against their sex to which society turned a blind eye.

The haunting parallel to the temperance movement can be found in cities across North America where frightened neighbors ban together to picket crack houses, harass drug buyers and dealers, and drive the unwanted scum from their neighborhoods. These people are not battling crack. They are fighting the fear and violence that come with it. They are struggling to regain freedom in their own yards.

While they argue that crime and violence will decrease with legalization, most legalizers concede drug use will increase with accessibility and the removal of the stigma of being an addict.

Nadelmann, however, does not think so. Here is his reasoning. The italicized comments in square brackets are mine.

"Perhaps the most reassuring reason for believing that repeal of drug prohibition laws will not lead to tremendous increases in drug abuse levels is the fact that we have learned something from our past experiences with alcohol and tobacco abuse. We now know, for instance, that consumption taxes are an effective method for limiting consumption rates and related costs especially among young people. [*Yet he also suggests that drugs be sold cheaply to undermine organized crime and the need for addicts to steal to pay for drugs.*]

"Substantial evidence also suggests that restrictions and bans on advertising, as well as promotion of negative advertising, can make a difference. [*Why legalize something so hazardous people must be warned of its dangers?*]

"The same may be true of other government measures, including restrictions on time and place of sale, bans on vending machines, prohibitions of consumption in public places, packaging requirements, mandated adjustments in insurance policies, crackdowns on driving while under the influence, and laws holding bartenders and hosts responsible for the drinking of customers and guests. [*It is curious for a man who calls drug laws an infringement on freedom by a meddlesome government to suggest a whole lot more government intervention that would require an expensive behemoth of a bureaucracy.*] . . .

"Legalization thus affords greater opportunities to control drug use and abuse than do current criminalization policies."

When cocaine prices dropped in the late 1980s to make the drug more available, hospital emergency ward admissions for cocaine-related problems tripled. When cocaine prices fell 80 percent in the Bahamas, cocaine-related admissions at Nassau's only psychiatric clinic went from zero in 1982 to 300 in 1984. Crack offers ghetto kids a cocaine high that was once affordable only to the rich. It is also dragging them into a hell of violence, insanity, and sickness.

Laboratory animals given unlimited access to cocaine choose it over food and sex until they die. Humans use cocaine in binges. Researchers have suggested that three out of four cocaine users might become heavily addicted if their appetite were not curbed by high prices and fear of getting caught. These restrictions now limit the rate of cocaine addiction to two out of ten users.

Legalizers who say drug use won't increase with legalization point to the fact that most American soldiers who used heroin in Vietnam stopped using it when they returned home. There were no laws to stop them from using it in Vietnam. They used drugs to ease physical and mental anguish, pain and fear of killing, and the horror of dying. They used drugs to numb their senses, relieve stress, and ease killing. They didn't have that need stateside. Laws also made it more difficult and dangerous to obtain heroin in the US.

Legalizers conveniently ignore the paranoia and violence bred by drugs. They turn a blind eye to the blood spilled by crazed dopers. They ignore the suicides among those whose reality is distorted by drugs. We are animals. Drugged animals are irrational and violent.

Advocates of legalization say legal drugs would lose their allure. Replace the word drug with murder, sodomy, blackmail, incest, bestiality, or rape in all arguments for legalization. Let's legalize rape. Would that reduce rape?

Addicts are not rational people who will live quiet, sheep-like lives when supplied with drugs. Addicts lie, cheat, and steal. They have no morals or values. They live for and on drugs.

Legalizing drugs will not dampen mental and physical destruction. It will not make an addict's home a nicer place to live. Children of addicts will grow up with losers for role models. Legalizers would encourage every generation to follow in the erratic and aimless footsteps of the previous generation of addicts. How can society teach children at school that drugs are bad and send them home to state-subsidized addicts?

These people want to legalize drugs to reap tax money to teach people not to use them. Legalization means go ahead, use it. It is the most powerful form of advertising. How can anyone realistically hope to convince people about the hazards of drugs and curb their use when society sells them?

Legalizers must be joking when they say packages of drugs would be labeled with warnings of their dangers. It hasn't worked for cigarettes and it won't work for anything else. Addicts don't reason, they crave.

Current needle exchange programs perpetuate the drug problem under the guise of protecting the health of addicts. Give addicts free clean needles and you remove the deterrence that dirty needles and death provide. Free clean needles ensure the addict lives to shoot up another day. These programs endorse drug addiction. They are also an admission and acceptance of the problem.

The argument that governments can make drugs safer by controlling them is irresponsible. Deaths caused by impure drugs are negligible compared to the damage pure drugs cause users. Purity is not an issue here. Drugs are the issue. Let's not lose track of that. Only insensitive, money-grubbing hypocrites advance the argument they care about addicts and wish them the purest of drugs. People who care don't want other human beings enslaved to drugs. They fight to shatter the chemical bonds that harness the addict's humanity. They wouldn't offer more drugs at cheaper prices.

Drugs are an attitude problem. We live in a society fueled by false values, motivated by insatiable greed, and captive to an overriding need for instant gratification. The attitude that drugs are OK must be changed. The drug-based lifestyle must be eliminated. As long as there is demand, there will be supply.

A survey of 710 1990 graduates of twelve top US business schools revealed a high acceptance of cocaine use and little willingness to report coking colleagues to management or the personnel office. The University of Pittsburgh study found that 59 percent of the business graduates would talk to the cocaine user; 36 percent would suggest counselling; 16 percent wouldn't do anything. By comparison, forty-four of one hundred corporate recruiters surveyed expect employees to report colleagues' drug use to management; 29 percent said they expect employees to report the problem to the personnel office; 13 percent expect employees to talk to the colleague.

Our society is built on the rule of law. Its dialectical opposite is anarchy. Laws controlling the sale and use of drugs are intended to safeguard both society as a whole and the individuals who make it up. Governments are supposed to protect their citizens from harm.

The drug problem has so far proven too tough for the feeble measures taken against it. The weapons used against drugs must equal or surpass them in power. Otherwise the fight is futile. So far the political will is lacking. The social will is stronger, but threatens to weaken under the onslaught of the legalization contingent. Some legalizers are self-centered dopers with hidden agendas; others are simply self-centered. They are the type who apologize when their misbegotten schemes fail. Apologies will not mend the irreparable harm caused by legalization.

We can no longer afford destructive social experiments like that of the 1960s' love generation that led to today's drug problem. The love generation was the largest consumer mass market for drugs in the history of the world. Society is not an experiment. Like the individual human, it is not a toy.

Rome died in decadence. A society that condones the drugging of mind and soul kills its reason for being. A government that promotes genocide has its citizens as accomplices. A citizenry that wants its government to practice genocide has a death wish. No animal other than humans threatens its social fabric with drugs. And humans pride themselves on being the only rational animal on the planet.

Legalization is not an option.

Epilogue

Gangsters can't sell drugs unless somebody buys them. Gangsters can't exist without people who take illegal shortcuts in life—shortcuts to pleasure, wealth, and power. The increasing number of gangsters across North America is a sad comment on the state of society. We live in a world that thrives on illusion: the illusion of pleasure, wealth, and power, however shortlived. People spend their lives escaping reality, through books, movies, soap operas. People are not happy with themselves. Everyone wants to be someone else. Few have the courage to live life and to do it their way. They all want to do it someone else's way. And the quickest way is through drugs.

The rate at which gangsters are taking over the streets is sad testimony to how spineless we have become. We live in an era of sheep. Though gangsters steal freedom, most people give it up.

While organized crime destroys North American society from within, drug lords and dictators intent on eliminating the North American way of life attack from abroad. Carlos Lehder has made cocaine his weapon against Yanqui imperialists. Cuban President Fidel Castro uses it to destroy North American capitalists. They want to disrupt North America with cocaine-induced criminal chaos, to weaken society by drugging its youth.

One of the most nefarious powers of money is its ability to corrupt. Greed has caused many people to sell their souls and turn a blind eye to the evil of drugs. Others—from police officers to judges to politicians—have compromised duties and trusts to more actively help the builders of criminal empires. California's marijuana-growing Emerald Triangle exemplifies the power of drug money to corrupt morals and values as entire towns conspire to shelter marijuana growers and their crops from eradication teams.

When they can't buy someone, narco-terrorists kill. In Colombia, they have assassinated more than 1,000 public officials, 12 Supreme Court justices, more than 200 judges and court officials, hundreds of policemen, and scores of journalists and anti-drug crusaders in the 1980s. They have their own armies and finance terrorist groups that protect their trade. Drug profits are so immense even in dinky countries like Peru that the Communist Sendero Luminoso rebels made more than half a billion dollars trafficking drugs in 1988.

Many financial institutions turn a blind eye to the filthy cash drug dealers bring them. Self-regulating banks do little to hinder the multi-billion dollar flow of drug money laundered through their accounts. Except for instances where aggressive law-enforcement tactics have exposed laundering operations, banks cannot be trusted to honestly join the fight against drugs. Banks and drug traffickers speak the same language: money. Bank officials smugly say their job is to safeguard money, not to question its origins. Only legislation and close scrutiny by law enforcement have forced banks to act where social responsibility and moral fiber should have guided their actions.

Drug money creates false economies that undermine legitimate business and erode the pillars of stable society. Those who praise organized crime as a manifestation of pure free market economy are seriously misguided. Organized crime doesn't compete; it eliminates competition. It manipulates stock prices, real estate prices, the price of consumer products. Organized crime is autocratic and fascist. It rules the market.

Despite attempts by criminals to endear themselves to the people around them with grand gestures, such as Colombian drug baron Pablo Escobar's construction of homes for the homeless, gangsters don't take from the rich and give to the poor. They victimize. They kill and grow rich on the soul-searing addictions of the weak.

It is often difficult to identify the bad guys in the world of drugs. Sometimes the "good guys" turn out to be the enemy.

The White House and administration of US President Ronald Reagan shielded the cocaine-smuggling networks of Colombia's Medellin cartel in the mid-1980s by impeding investigations that could have jailed the cartel's leaders. This was done to protect the Reagan administration's pet project: support of the contra rebel attempt to overthrow the Sandinista government in Nicaragua. The administration supported the contra rebels in defiance of Congress, which had serious doubts about doing so with public funds. This was a government that had pledged to fight drugs.

The CIA worries about spies infiltrating the United States. As it is, drug traffickers enter and leave at will, causing more damage than a thousand spies ever could.

Law enforcement made a terrible mistake in allowing traditional organized crime several decades to build itself a solid foundation. That error must not be repeated. Gangsters must not be allowed to set up impregnable empires. Once the leaders insulate themselves from arrest and prosecution, their organizations become self-perpetuating. Law enforcement must strike at the head, not the arms. If it can't get to the head, then all is lost.

Colombian drug cartels, prison gangs, triads, Chinese and Vietnamese street gangs, black street gangs like the Crips and Bloods, Jamaican posses, outlaw motorcycle gangs: all must be attacked and eliminated *now*. The Hell's Angels have already forged a nearly indestructible criminal empire that sells drugs, women, and death. Other gangs are not as well established. They are just starting to set down roots. Wipe them out now or there will be no tomorrow.

The best way to disarm criminal empires and put gangsters behind bars is to go after their money. Al Capone was not jailed for murder, prostitution, or drug trafficking, but for failing to pay his income taxes. But in the case of drug traffickers, a more extreme approach must be taken.

The billions of dollars spent on interdiction and enforcement without denting the drug market underline how widespread and entrenched drugs have become in North America society. The spending is an indicator, not a failure. It tells us that more drastic measures are needed to eradicate the problem.

If advocates of legalization don't mind anarchy in the streets and the wasting of human lives that would ensue if drug use were made lawful, they should not object if the misnamed drug war is stepped up to a higher level—where the high cost of investigation, interdiction, law enforcement, prosecution, and incarceration is eliminated by executing drug producers, smugglers, and dealers on sight: on street corners, in parks, in their homes. Blow their planes out of the sky. Torpedo their ships. It would be the ultimate solution. At this stage of the game, it's the only solution.

So far, drugs have been treated as a law-enforcement problem. They are more than that. Drugs threaten national security. Give the military a chance to wipe out the drug problem. Until this happens, war has not been declared on drugs. Police officers don't fight wars; soldiers do. It is hypocritical to call the actions against drugs taken so far a war. The battle to date has been an enforcement action. Only total war will stem the flow of drugs that threatens to corrode the fabric of society.

The bad guys have no qualms about killing. They know the harshest punishment they will get is a jail term—a mere business expense in their trade. Give them a taste of lead. Waste the scum.

Welcome to the 1990s. Have you sold your soul today?